A History of the Inquisition of Spain
Volume I
By Henry Charles Lea. LL.D.
Edited by Anthony Uyl

Woodstock, Ontario, 2017

A History of the Inquisition of Spain - Volume I
By Henry Charles Lea. LL.D.
Edited by Anthony Uyl

Originally Published by:
New York The MacMillan Company London: MacMillan & Co., Ltd. 1922; Copyright, 1906

The text of A History of the Inquisition of Spain - Volume I is all in the Public Domain. The layout is not in the Public Domain and is Copyright 2017© Devoted Publishing a division of 2165467 Ontario Inc.

Let us hear your philosophies and thoughts!

Contact us at: devotedpub@hotmail.com
Visit us on Facebook at: @DevotedPublishing
Visit our website for a full selection of print products: www.devotedpublishing.com

Published in Woodstock, Ontario, Canada 2017.

ISBN: 978-1-988297-79-8

Henry Charles Lea

Table of Contents

PREFACE 4
BOOK I - ORIGIN AND ESTABLISHMENT 5
   CHAPTER I - THE CASTILIAN MONARCHY 5
   CHAPTER II - THE JEWS AND THE MOORS 18
   CHAPTER III - THE JEWS AND THE CONVERSOS 35
   CHAPTER IV - ESTABLISHMENT OF THE INQUISITION 60
   CHAPTER V - THE KINGDOMS OF ARAGON 92
BOOK II - RELATIONS WITH THE STATE 116
   CHAPTER I - RELATIONS WITH THE CROWN 116
   CHAPTER II - SUPEREMINENCE 141
   CHAPTER III - PRIVILEGES AND EXEMPTIONS 151
   CHAPTER IV - CONFLICTING JURISDICTIONS 172
   CHAPTER V - POPULAR HOSTILITY 215
APPENDIX 221
   I - LIST OF TRIBUNALS 221
   II. - LIST OF INQUISITORS-GENERAL 226
   III - SPANISH COINAGE 228
DOCUMENTS 232
   I - LETTER OF KING FERDINAND TO THE INQUISITOR-GENERAL TORQUEMADA, July 22, 1486. 232
   II - EDICT OF MAY 30, 1492, REGULATING SETTLEMENTS WITH THE EXPELLED JEWS. 233
   III - TORQUEMADA'S INSTRUCTIONS TO INQUISITORS, Dec., 1484.[1339] 234
   IV - TORQUEMADA'S INSTRUCTIONS TO INQUISITORS, Jan., 1485.[1340] 236
   V - INSTRUCTIONS OF SEVILLE, 1500.[1341] 238
   VI - EXTRACTS FROM THE REGISTER OF THE RECEIVER OF CONFISCATIONS AT VALENCIA, 1485-1486. 239
   VII - BRIEF OF JULIUS II RESPECTING THE TROUBLES IN CORDOVA. 239
   VIII - PROPOSITION MADE IN OCTOBER, 1519, TO CHARLES V TO COMPOUND FOR THE CONFISCATIONS. 240
   IX - MEMORIAL FROM GRANADA TO CHARLES V IN 1526. 241
   X - BULL OF SIXTUS IV, APRIL 18 1482, TEMPORARILY REFORMING THE INQUISITION OF ARAGON. 242
   XI - KING FERDINAND TO POPE SIXTUS IV, MAY 13, 1482. 244
   XII - MEMORIA DE DIVERSOS AUTOS DE INQUISICION CELEBRADOS EN ÇARAGOÇA DESDE EL ANO 1484 ASTA EL DE 1502 EN QUE SE REFIEREN LAS PERSONAS CASTIGADAS EN ELLOS.[1344] 245
   XIII - LETTER OF CARLOS III TO THE POPE, DECEMBER 26, 1774, ASKING HIM TO CONCEDE THE FACULTIES OF INQUISITOR-GENERAL TO FELIPE BERTRAN, BISHOP OF SALAMANCA. 256
   XIV - RESIGNATION OF INQUISITOR-GENERAL SOTOMAYOR. 256
   XV - EXTRACTS FROM THE CONSULTA OF THE COUNCIL OF THE INQUISITION, MAY 5, 1646, ON THE INDEPENDENT SUPERIORITY OF INQUISITORIAL JURISDICTION OVER OFFICIALS. 257
   XVI - DECREE OF PHILIP IV CONCERNING DISOBEDIENCE, MARCH 26, 1633. 258
   XVII - PROCLAMATION ON THE ARRIVAL OF AN INQUISITOR. 259
   XVIII - MEMORIA DE LA REFORMA DE MINISTROS DEL SANTO OFICIO QUE HIZO HACER EL REY EN 1646. 260
   XIX - DECREE OF PHILIP III ON QUARRELS BETWEEN BISHOPS AND INQUISITORS. 260
FOOTNOTES 261

PREFACE

In the following pages I have sought to trace, from the original sources as far as possible, the character and career of an institution which exercised no small influence on the fate of Spain and even, one may say, indirectly on the civilized world. The material for this is preserved so superabundantly in the immense Spanish archives that no one writer can pretend to exhaust the subject. There can be no finality in a history resting on so vast a mass of inedited documents and I do not flatter myself that I have accomplished such a result, but I am not without hope that what I have drawn from them and from the labors of previous scholars has enabled me to present a fairly accurate survey of one of the most remarkable organizations recorded in human annals.

In this a somewhat minute analysis has seemed to be indispensable of its structure and methods of procedure, of its relations with the other bodies of the State and of its dealings with the various classes subject to its extensive jurisdiction. This has involved the accumulation of much detail in order to present the daily operation of a tribunal of which the real importance is to be sought, not so much in the awful solemnities of the auto de fe, or in the cases of a few celebrated victims, as in the silent influence exercised by its incessant and secret labors among the mass of the people and in the limitations which it placed on the Spanish intellect--in the resolute conservatism with which it held the nation in the medieval groove and unfitted it for the exercise of rational liberty when the nineteenth century brought in the inevitable Revolution.

The intimate relations between Spain and Portugal, especially during the union of the kingdoms from 1580 to 1640, has rendered necessary the inclusion, in the chapter devoted to the Jews, of a brief sketch of the Portuguese Inquisition, which earned a reputation even more sinister than its Spanish prototype.

I cannot conclude without expressing my thanks to the gentlemen whose aid has enabled me to collect the documents on which the work is largely based--Don Claudio Pérez Gredilla of the Archives of Simancas, Don Ramon Santa María of those of Alcalá de Henares prior to their removal to Madrid, Don Francisco de Bofarull y Sans of those of the Crown of Aragon, Don J. Figueroa Hernández, formerly American Vice-consul at Madrid, and to many others to whom I am indebted in a minor degree. I have also to tender my acknowledgements to the authorities of the Bodleian Library and of the Royal Libraries of Copenhagen, Munich, Berlin and the University of Halle, for favors warmly appreciated.

HENRY CHARLES LEA.
PHILADELPHIA, OCTOBER, 1905.

BOOK I - ORIGIN AND ESTABLISHMENT

CHAPTER I - THE CASTILIAN MONARCHY

It were difficult to exaggerate the disorder pervading the Castilian kingdoms, when the Spanish monarchy found its origin in the union of Isabella of Castile and Ferdinand of Aragon. Many causes had contributed to prolong and intensify the evils of the feudal system and to neutralize such advantages as it possessed. The struggles of the reconquest from the Saracen, continued at intervals through seven hundred years and varied by constant civil broils, had bred a race of fierce and turbulent nobles as eager to attack a neighbor or their sovereign as the Moor. The contemptuous manner in which the Cid is represented, in the earliest ballads, as treating his king, shows what was, in the twelfth century, the feeling of the chivalry of Castile toward its overlord, and a chronicler of the period seems rather to glory in the fact that it was always in rebellion against the royal power.[1] So fragile was the feudal bond that a ricohome or noble could at any moment renounce allegiance by a simple message sent to the king through a hidalgo.[2] The necessity of attracting population and organizing conquered frontiers, which subsequently became inland, led to granting improvidently liberal franchises to settlers, which weakened the powers of the crown,[3] without building up, as in France, a powerful Third Estate to serve as a counterpoise to the nobles and eventually to undermine feudalism. In Spain the business of the Castilian was war. The arts of peace were left with disdain to the Jews and the conquered Moslems, known as Mudéjares, who were allowed to remain on Christian soil and to form a distinct element in the population. No flourishing centres of industrious and independent burghers arose out of whom the kings could mould a body that should lend them efficient support in their struggles with their powerful vassals. The attempt, indeed, was made; the Córtes, whose co-operation was required in the enactment of laws, consisted of representatives from seventeen cities,[4] who while serving enjoyed personal inviolability, but so little did the cities prize this privilege that, under Henry IV, they complained of the expense of sending deputies. The crown, eager to find some new sources of influence, agreed to pay them and thus obtained an excuse for controlling their election, and although this came too late for Henry to benefit by it, it paved the way for the assumption of absolute domination by Ferdinand and Isabella, after which the revolt of the Comunidades proved fruitless. Meanwhile their influence diminished, their meetings were scantily attended and they became little more than an instrument which, in the interminable strife that cursed the land, was used alternately by any faction as opportunity offered.[5]

ABASEMENT OF THE CROWN

The crown itself had contributed greatly to its own abasement. When, in the thirteenth century, a ruler such as San Fernando III. made the laws respected and vigorously extended the boundaries of Christianity, Castile gave promise of development in power and culture which miserably failed in the performance. In 1282 the rebellion of Sancho el Bravo against his father Alfonso was the commencement of decadence. To purchase the allegiance of the nobles he granted them all that they asked, and to avert the discontent consequent on taxation he supplied his treasury by alienating the crown lands.[6] Notwithstanding the abilities of the regent, María de Molina, the successive minorities of her son and grandson, Fernando IV and Alfonso XI, stimulated the downward progress, although the vigor of the latter in his maturity restored in some degree the lustre of the crown and his stern justice re-established order, so that, as we are told, property could be left unguarded in the streets at night.[7] His son, Don Pedro, earned the epithet of the Cruel by his ruthless endeavor to reduce to obedience his turbulent nobles, whose disaffection invited the usurpation of his bastard brother, Henry of Trastamara. The throne which the latter won by fratricide and the aid of the foreigner, he could only hold by fresh concessions to his magnates which fatally reduced the royal power.[8] This heritage he left to his son, Juan I, who forcibly described, in the Córtes of Valladolid in 1385, how he wore mourning in his heart because of his powerlessness to administer justice and to govern as he ought, in consequence of the evil customs which he was unable to correct.[9] This depicts the condition of the monarchy during the century intervening between the murder of Pedro and the accession of Isabella--a dreary period of endless revolt and civil strife, during which the central authority was steadily growing less able to curb the lawless elements tending to eventual anarchy. The king was little more than a puppet of which rival factions sought to gain possession in order to cover their ambitions with a cloak of legality, and those which failed to secure his person treated his authority with contempt, or set up some rival in a son or brother as an excuse for rebellion. The work of the Reconquest which, for six hundred years, had been the leading object of national pride was virtually abandoned, save in some spasmodic enterprise, such as the capture of Antequera, and the little kingdom of Granada, apparently on the point of extinction under Alfonso XI, seemed destined to perpetuate for ever on Spanish soil the hateful presence of the crescent.

The long reign of the feeble Juan II, from 1406 to 1454, was followed by that of the feebler Henry IV, popularly known as El Impotente. In the Seguro de Tordesillas, in 1439, the disaffected nobles virtually dictated terms to Juan II.[10] In the Deposition of Ávila, in 1465, they treated Henry IV with the bitterest contempt. His effigy, clad in mourning and adorned with the royal insignia, was placed upon a throne and four articles of accusation were read. For the first he was pronounced unworthy of the kingly station, when Alonso Carrillo, Archbishop of Toledo, removed the crown; for the second he was deprived of the administration of justice, when Álvaro de Zuñiga, Count of Plasencia, took away the sword; for the third he was deprived of the government, when Rodrigo Pimentel, Count of Benavente, struck the sceptre away; for the fourth he was sentenced to lose the throne, when Diego López de Zuñiga tumbled the image from its seat with an indecent gibe. It was scarce more than a continuation of the mockery when they elected as his successor his brother Alfonso, a child eleven years of age.[11]

VIOLENCE AND TREACHERY

The lawless independence of the nobles and the effacement of the royal authority may be estimated from a single example. At Plasencia two powerful lords, Garcí Alvárez de Toledo, Señor of Oropesa, and Hernan Rodríguez de Monroy, kept the country in an uproar with their armed dissension. Juan II sent Ayala, Señor of Cebolla, with a royal commission to suppress the disorder. Monroy, in place of submitting, insulted Ayala, who as a "buen caballero" disdained to complain to the king and preferred to avenge himself. Juan on hearing of this summoned to his presence Monroy, who collected all his friends and retainers and set out with a formidable army. Ayala made a similar levy and set upon him as he passed near Cebolla. There was a desperate battle in which Ayala was worsted and forced to take refuge in Cebolla, while Monroy passed on to Toledo and, when he kissed the king's hands, Juan told him that he had sent for him to cut off his head, but as Ayala had preferred to right himself he gave Monroy a God-speed on his journey home and washed his hands of the whole affair.[12]

The ricosomes who thus were released from all the restraint of law had as little respect for those of honor and morality. The virtues which we are wont to ascribe to chivalry were represented by such follies as the celebrated Passo Honroso of Suero de Quiñones, when that knight and his nine comrades, in 1434, kept, in honor of their ladies, for thirty days against all comers, the pass of the Bridge of Orbigo, at the season of the feast of Santiago and sixty-nine challengers presented themselves in the lists.[13] With exceptions such as this, and a rare manifestation of magnanimity, as when the Duke of Medina Sidonia raised an army and hastened to the relief of his enemy, Rodrigo Ponce de Leon besieged in Alhama,[14] the record of the time is one of the foulest treachery, from which truth and honor are absent and human nature displays itself in its basest aspect. According to contemporary belief, Ferdinand was indebted for the crown of Aragon to the poisoning of his brother, the deeply mourned Carlos, Prince of Viana, while the crown of Castile fell to Isabella through the similar taking off of her brother Alfonso.[15]

A characteristic incident is one involving Doña Maria de Monroy, who married into the great house of Henríquez of Seville, and was left a widow with two boys. When the youths were respectively eighteen and nineteen years old they were close friends of two gentlemen of Seville named Mançano. The younger brother, dicing with them in their house, was involved in a quarrel with them, when they set upon him with their servants and slew him. Then, fearing the vengeance of the elder brother, they sent him a friendly message to come and play with them; when he came they led him along a dark corridor in which they suddenly turned upon him and stabbed him to death. When the disfigured corpses of her boys were brought to Doña María she shed no tears, but the fierceness of her eyes frightened all who looked upon her. The Mançanos promptly took horse and fled to Portugal, whither Doña María followed them in male attire with a band of twenty cavaliers. Her spies were speedily on the track of the fugitives; within a month of the murders she came at night to the house where they lay concealed; the doors were broken in and she entered with ten of her men while the rest kept guard outside. The Mançanos put themselves in defence and shouted for help, but before the neighbors could assemble she had both their heads in her left hand and was galloping off with her troop, never stopping till she reached Salamanca, where she went to the church and laid the bloody heads on the tomb of her boys. Thenceforth she was known as Doña María la Brava, and her exploit led to long and murderous feuds between the Monroyes and the Mançanos.[16]

Doña María was but a type of the unsexed women, mugeres varoniles, common at the time, who would take the field or maintain their place in factious intrigue with as much ferocity and pertinacity as men. Ferdinand could well look without surprise on the activity in court and camp of his queen Isabella, when he remembered the prowess of his mother, Juana Henríquez, who had secured for him the crown of Aragon. Doña Leonora Pimentel, Duchess of Arévalo, was one of these; of the Countess of Medellin it was said that no Roman captain could get the better of her in feats of arms, and the Countess of Haro was equally noted. The Countess of Medellin, indeed, kept her own son in prison for years while she enjoyed the revenues of his town of Medellin and, when Queen Isabella refused to confirm her possession of the place, she transferred her allegiance to the King of Portugal to whom she delivered the castle of Merida. At the same time the Moorish influence, which was so strong in Castile, occasionally led to the opposite extreme. The Duke of Najera kept his daughters in such absolute seclusion that no man, not even his sons, was permitted to enter the apartments reserved for the women, and the reason he alleged--that the heart does not covet what the eye does not see--was little flattering to either sex.[17]

VIRTUAL ANARCHY

The condition of the common people can readily be imagined in this perpetual strife between warlike, ambitious and unprincipled nobles, now uniting in factions which involved the whole realm in war, and now contenting themselves with assaults upon their neighbors. The land was desolated; the husbandman scarce could take heart to plant his seed, for the harvest was apt to be garnered with the sword and thrust into castles to provision them against siege. As a writer of the period tells us, there was neither law nor justice save that of arms.[18] In a letter describing the universal anarchy, written by Hernando del Pulgar from Madrid, in 1473, he says that for more than five years there has been no communication from Murcia, where the family of Fajardo reigned supreme--it is, he says, as foreign a land as Navarre.[19] That the roads were unsafe for trade or travel was a matter of course; every petty hidalgo converted his stronghold into a den of robbers, and what these left was swept away by bands of Free Companions.[20] Disorder reigned supreme and all-pervading. The crown was powerless and the royal treasury exhausted. Improvident grants of lands and revenues and jurisdictions, to bribe the treacherous fidelity of faithless nobles, or to gratify worthless favorites, were made, till there was nothing left to give, and then Henry IV bestowed licenses for private mints, until there were a hundred and fifty of them at work, flooding the land with base money, to the unutterable confusion of the coinage and the impoverishment of the people.[21] The Córtes of Madrid, in 1467, and of Ocaña in 1469, called on Henry to resume his improvident grants, and those of Madrigal, in 1476, repeated the urgency to Ferdinand and Isabella, who had been forced to follow his example. To this the sovereigns replied thanking the Córtes and postponing the matter. They did not feel themselves strong enough until 1480, when at the Córtes of Toledo, they resumed thirty million maravedís of revenue which had been alienated during the troubles, and this after an investigation which left untouched the gifts to loyal subjects and only withdrew such as had been extorted.[22] Respect for the crown had fallen as low as its revenues. A story told of the Count of Benavente shows how difficult it was, even after the accession of Isabella, for the nobles to recognize that they owed any obedience to the sovereign. He was walking with the queen when a woman came weeping and begging justice, saying that he had had her husband slain in spite of a royal safe-conduct. She showed the letter which her husband had carried in his breast, pierced by the blow which had ended his life, when the count jeeringly remarked "A cuirass would have been of more service." Piqued by this Isabella said "Count do you then not wish there was no king in Castile?" "Rather," said he, "I wish there were many." "And why?" "Because then I should be one of them."[23]

CHARACTER OF PRELATES

In such a chaos of lawless passion it is not to be supposed that the Church was better than the nobles who filled its high places with worthless scions of their stocks, or than the lower classes of the laity who sought in it provision for a life of idleness and licence. The primate of Castile was the Archbishop of Toledo, who was likewise ex officio chancellor of the realm and whose revenues were variously estimated at from eighty to a hundred thousand ducats, with patronage at his disposal amounting to a hundred thousand more.[24] The occupant of this exalted position, at the accession of Isabella, was Alonso Carrillo, a turbulent prelate, delighting in war, foremost in all the civil broils of the period, who, not content with the immense income of his see, lavished extravagant sums in alchemy. Hernando del Pulgar, in a letter of remonstrance, said to him, "The people look to you as their bishop and find in you their enemy; they groan and complain that you use your authority not for their benefit and reformation but for their destruction; not as an exemplar of kindness and peace but for corruption, scandal, and disturbance." When, in 1495, the puritan Ximenes was appointed to the archbishopric, one of his first acts is said to have been the removal, from near the altar of the Franciscan church of Toledo, of a magnificent tomb which Carrillo had erected to his bastard, Troilo Carrillo.[25]

His successor in the see of Toledo has a special interest for us in view of his labors to purify the faith which culminated in establishing the Inquisition. Pero González de Mendoza was one of the notable men of the day, whose influence with Ferdinand and Isabella won for him the name of "the third king." While yet a child he held the curacy of Hita; at twelve he had the archdeaconry of Guadalajara, one of the richest benefices in Spain, which he retained during the successive bishoprics of Calahorra and Sigüenza and the archbishopric of Seville; the see of Sigüenza he kept during the whole tenure successively of the archiepiscopates of Seville and Toledo, in addition to which he was a cardinal and titular Patriarch of Alexandria. With his kindred of the powerful house of Mendoza he adhered to Henry IV, until they effected the sale of the hapless Beltraneja, who was in their hands, to her father, Henry, for certain estates and the title of Duke del Infantado for Diego Hurtado, the head of the family, after which Pero González and his kinsmen promptly transferred their allegiance to Isabella. His admiring biographer assures us that he was more ready with his hands than with his tongue, that he was a gallant knight and that there was never a war in Spain during his time in which he did not personally take part or at least have his troops engaged. Though he had no leisure to attend to his spiritual duties, he found time to yield to the temptations of the flesh. When, in 1484, he led the army of invasion into Granada he took with him his bastard, Rodrigo de Mendoza, a youth of twenty, who was already Señor del Castillo del Cid, and who, in 1492, was created Marquis of Cenete on the occasion of his marriage, amid great rejoicings, in the presence of Ferdinand and Isabella, to Leonor de la Cerda, daughter and heiress of the Duke of Medina Celi and niece of Ferdinand himself. This was not the only evidence of his frailty of which he took no shame, for he had another son named Juan, by a lady of Valladolid, who was married to Doña Ana de Aragon, another niece of Ferdinand.[26]

CONDITION OF THE CHURCH

With such men at the head of the Church it is not to be expected that the lower orders of the clergy should be models of decency and morality, rendering Christianity attractive to Jew and Moslem. Alonso Carrillo, the archbishop of Toledo, can scarce be regarded as a strict disciplinarian, but even he felt obliged, when holding the council of Aranda in 1473, to endeavor to repress the more flagrant scandals of the clergy. As a corrective of their prevailing ignorance it was ordered that in future none should be ordained who could not speak Latin--the language of the ritual and the foundation of all instruction, theological and otherwise. They were forbidden to wear silk or gaily colored garments. As their licentiousness rendered them contemptible to the people, they were commanded to part with their concubines within two months. As their fondness for dicing led to perjuries, scandals and homicides, they were required thereafter to abstain from it, privately as well as publicly. As many priests disdained to celebrate mass, they were ordered to do so at least four times a year; bishops, moreover, were urged to celebrate at least thrice a year, under pain of severe penalties to be determined at the next council. The absurdities poured forth in their sermons by wandering priests and friars were to be repressed by requiring examinations prior to issuing licenses to preach, and the scandals of the pardon-sellers were to be diminished by subjecting them to the bishops. The bishops were also urged to make severe examples of offenders in the lower orders of the clergy, when delivered to them by the secular courts, and not to allow their enormities to enjoy continued immunity. The bishops, moreover, were commanded to make no charge for conferring ordinations; they were exhorted, and all other clerics were required, not to lead a dissolute military life or to enter the service of secular lords excepting the king and princes of the blood. As duels were forbidden, both laity and clergy were warned that if slain in such encounters they would be refused Christian burial.[27] That this effort at reform was, as might be expected, wholly abortive is evidenced from the description of the vices of the ecclesiastical body when Ferdinand and Isabella subsequently endeavored to correct its more flagrant scandals.[28] It was wholly secularized and only to be distinguished from the laity by the sacred functions which rendered its vices more abhorrent, by the immunities which fostered and stimulated those vices and by the intolerance which, blind to all aberrations of morals, proclaimed the stake to be the only fitting punishment for aberration in the faith. While powerless to reform itself it yet had influence enough to educate the people up to its standard of orthodoxy in the ruthless persecution of all whom it pleased to designate as enemies of Christ.

Yet in Spain the immunities and privileges of the Church were less than elsewhere throughout Christendom. The independence which the secular power in Castile had always manifested toward the Holy See and its disregard of the canon law are points which will occasionally manifest themselves hereafter and are worthy of a moment's consideration here. I have elsewhere shown that, alone among the Latin nations, Castile steadily refused to admit the medieval Inquisition and disregarded completely the prescriptions of the Church regarding heresy.[29] In the twelfth century the popular feeling toward the papacy is voiced in the ballads of the Cid. When a demand for tribute to the Emperor Henry IV is said to be made through the pope, Ruy Diaz advises King Fernando to send a defiance from both of them to the pope and all his party, which the monarch accordingly does. So when the Cid accompanies his master to a great council in Rome and kicks over the chair prepared for the King of France, the pope excommunicates him, whereupon he kneels before the holy father and asks for absolution, telling him it will be the worse for him if he does not grant it, which the pope promptly does on condition of his being more self-restrained during the remainder of his stay.[30] There is no trace of the veneration for the vicegerent of God which elsewhere was inculcated as an indispensable religious duty.

DISREGARD OF THE PAPACY

When such was the popular temper it is easy to understand that the prohibition to carry money out of the kingdom to the pope was even more emphatic than in England.[31] The claim to control the patronage of the Church, which was so prolific a source of revenue to the curia, met throughout Spain a resistance as sturdy as in England, though the troubled condition of the land interfered with its success. In Catalonia, the Córtes, in 1419, adopted a law in which, after alluding to the scandals and irreparable injuries arising from the intrusion of strangers, it was declared that none but natives should hold preferment of any kind and that all papal letters and bulls contravening this should be resisted in whatever way was necessary.[32] In Castile the Córtes of 1390 forcibly represented to Juan I the evils resulting from this foisting of strangers on the Spanish Church, but his speedy death prevented action. The remonstrance was renewed to the tutors of the young Henry III, who promptly placed an embargo on the revenues of foreign benefice-holders and forbade the admission of subsequent appointees. This led to a compromise, in 1393, by which the Avignonese curia secured the recognition of existing incumbents by promising that no more such nominations should be made.[33] The promise made by the Avignonese antipope was not binding on the Roman curia and the quarrel continued. Even if the recipient was a native there was little ceremony in dealing with papal grants of benefices when occasion prompted, as was shown in the affair which first revealed the unbending character of the future Cardinal Ximenes. During his youthful sojourn in Rome Ximenes procured papal "expectative letters" granting him the first preferment that should fall vacant in the diocese of Toledo. On his return he made use of these letters to take possession of the arciprestazgo of Uceda, but it happened that Archbishop Carrillo simultaneously gave it to one of his creatures and, as Ximenes refused to surrender his rights, he was thrown into a tower in Uceda--a tower he subsequently, when himself Archbishop of Toledo, used as a treasury. As he continued obstinate, Carrillo transferred him to the Pozo de Santorcas, a harsh dungeon used for clerical malefactors, where he lay for six years, resolutely refusing to abandon his claim, until released at the intercession of the wife of a nephew of Carrillo.[34] Evidently the Castilian prelates had slender respect for papal diplomas. About the same time, during the civil war between Henry IV and his brother Alfonso, when Hernando de Luxan, Bishop of Sigüenza, died, the dean, Diego López, obtained possession of the castles and the treasure of the see, joined the party of Alfonso, and, with the aid of Archbishop Carrillo, caused himself to be elected bishop. Meanwhile Paul II gave the see to Juan de Maella, Cardinal-bishop of Zamora, but Diego López refused to obey the bulls and appealed to the future council against the pope and all his censures. He disregarded an interdict launched against him and was supported by all his clergy. Maella died and Paul II gave the bishopric to the Bishop of Calahorra, requesting Henry IV to place him in possession. So secure did Diego López feel that he rejected a compromise offering him the see of Zamora in exchange, but the possession of Sigüenza happened to be of importance in the war; by bribery a troop of royalist soldiers obtained admittance to the castle and carried off López as a prisoner.[35]

It was the same even with so pious a monarch as Ferdinand the Catholic. When, in 1476, the archiepiscopal see of Saragossa became vacant by the death of Juan of Aragon, Ferdinand, with his father, Juan II, asked Sixtus IV to appoint his natural son, Alfonso, a child six years of age. The claim of the papacy to archiepiscopal appointments, based on the necessity of the pallium, was of ancient date and had become incontestable. In the thirteenth century Alfonso X had admitted it in the case of the archbishops, but when Isabella appointed Ximenes to the see of Toledo in 1495 the proceedings showed that the post was considered to be in the gift of the crown and the papal confirmation to be a matter of course.[36] So in the present case the request was a mere form, as was seen when Sixtus refused. The defect of birth could be dispensed for, but the youth of Alfonso was an insuperable objection, and Sixtus appointed Ansias Dezpuch, then Archbishop of Monreal, thinking that the services rendered by him and by his uncle, the Master of the Order of Montesa, would induce the king to assent. Dezpuch accepted, but Ferdinand at once sequestrated all the revenues of Monreal and the priory of Santa Cristina and ordered him to resign. On his hesitating, Ferdinand threatened to seize all the castles and revenues of the mastership of Montesa, which was effectual, and Sixtus compromised by making the boy perpetual administrator of Saragossa.[37]

ECCLESIASTICAL JURISDICTION LIMITED

Isabella, despite her piety, was as firm as her husband in defending the claim of the crown in these matters against the papacy. When, in 1482, the see of Cuenca became vacant and Sixtus IV appointed a Genoese cousin to the position, Ferdinand and his queen energetically represented that only Spaniards should have Spanish bishoprics and that the selection should be made by them. Sixtus retorted that all benefices were in the gift of the pope and that his power, derived from God, was unlimited, whereupon they ordered home all their subjects resident in the papal court and threatened to take steps for the convocation of a general council. These energetic proceedings brought Sixtus to terms and he sent to Spain a special nuncio, but Ferdinand and Isabella stood on their dignity and refused even to receive him. Then the Cardinal of Spain, Pero González de Mendoza, intervened and, on Sixtus withdrawing his pretensions, they allowed themselves to be reconciled.[38] They alleged that whatever might be the papal rights in other countries, in Spain the patronage of all benefices belonged to the crown because they and their predecessors had wrested the land from the infidel.[39] So jealous, indeed, were they of the papal encroachments that among the subjects which they submitted to the national synod assembled by them in Seville, June, 1478, was how to prevent the residence of papal legates and nuncios, who not only carried off much money from the kingdom, but threatened the royal pre-eminence, to which the synod replied that this rested with the sovereigns to do as their predecessors had done.[40] It is easy thus to understand why, in the organization of the Inquisition, they insisted that all appointments should be made by the throne.

In other ways the much-prized superiority of the canon over secular law was disregarded in Spain. The Córtes and the monarch had never hesitated to legislate on ecclesiastical affairs, and the jurisdiction of the ecclesiastical courts was limited with a jealousy which paid scant respect to canon and decretal. Nothing, for instance, was better settled than the spiritual cognizance of all matters respecting testaments, yet when, in 1270, the authorities of Badajoz complained of the interference of the bishop's court with secular judges in such affairs, proceeding to the excommunication of those who exercised jurisdiction over them, Alfonso X expressed surprise and gave explicit commands that such cases should be decided by the lay courts exclusively.[41] So little respect was felt for the immunity of ecclesiastics from secular law, in defence of which Thomas à Becket had laid down his life, that, as late as 1351, an ordenamiento of Pedro the Cruel concedes to them that they shall not be cited before secular judges except in accordance with law.[42] On the other hand, laymen were jealously protected from the ecclesiastical courts. The crown was declared to be the sole judge of its own jurisdiction, and no appeal from it was allowed. In the exercise of this supreme power laws were repeatedly enacted providing that a layman, who should cite another layman before a spiritual judge, not only lost his cause but incurred a heavy fine and disability for public office. The spiritual judge could not imprison a layman or levy execution on his property, and he who attempted it or any other invasion of the royal jurisdiction forfeited his benefices and became a stranger in the kingdom, thus rendering him incapable of preferment. The ecclesiastic who cited a layman before a spiritual judge lost any privileges or graces which he might hold of the crown. The layman who attempted to remove a cause from a lay court to a spiritual one was punished with confiscation of all his property, while any vassal who claimed benefit of clergy and declined the jurisdiction of a royal court forfeited his fief. In re-enacting these laws in the Córtes of Toledo, in 1480, Ferdinand and Isabella complained of their inobservance and ordered their strict enforcement.[43] No other nation in Christendom dared thus to infringe on the sacred limits of spiritual jurisdiction.

ECCLESIASTICAL IMMUNITY

Yet even this was not all, for the secular power asserted its right to intervene in matters within the Church itself. Elsewhere the ineradicable vice of priestly concubinage was left to be dealt with by bishops and archdeacons. The guilty priests themselves, even in Castile, were exempt from civil authority, but Ferdinand and Isabella had no hesitation in invading their domiciles and, by repeated edicts in 1480, 1491, 1502, and 1503, endeavored to cure the evil by fining, scourging, and banishing their partners in sin.[44] It is true, as we have seen above, that these laws were eluded, but there was at least a vigorous attempt to enforce them for, in 1490, the clergy of Guipuzcoa complained that the officers of justice visited their houses to see whether they kept concubines (which of course they denied) and carried off their women to prison, where they were forced to confess themselves concubines, to the great dishonor of the Church, whereupon the sovereigns repressed the excessive zeal of their officials and ordered them in future to interfere only when the concubinage was notorious.[45] A yet more significant extension of royal authority was exercised when, in 1490, the people of Lequeitio (Biscay) complained that, though there were twelve mass-priests in the parish church, they all celebrated together and at uncertain times, so that the pious were unable to be present. This was a matter belonging exclusively to the diocesan authority, yet the appeal was made to the crown, and the Royal Council felt no scruple in ordering the priests to celebrate in succession and at reasonable hours, under pain of banishment and forfeiture of temporalities, thus disregarding even the imprescriptible immunities of the priesthood.[46] So slender, indeed, was the respect paid to these immunities that the Council of Aranda, in 1473, complained that magistrates of cities and other temporal lords presumed to banish ecclesiastics holding benefices in cathedral churches, and it may well be doubted whether the interdict with which the council threatened to punish this infraction of the canons was effective in its suppression.[47]

One of the most deplorable abuses with which the Church afflicted society was the admission into the minor orders of crowds of laymen who, without abandoning worldly pursuits, adopted the tonsure in order to enjoy the irresponsibility afforded by the claim acquired to spiritual jurisdiction, whether as criminals or as traders. The Córtes of Tordesillas, in 1401, declared that the greater portion of the rufianes and malefactors of the kingdom wore the tonsure; when arrested by the secular officials the spiritual courts demanded them and enforced their claims with excommunication, after which they freely discharged the evil doers. This complaint was re-echoed by almost every subsequent Córtes, with an occasional allusion to the stimulus thus afforded to the evil propensities of those who were really clerics. The kings in responding to these representations could only say that they would apply to the Holy Father for relief, but the relief never came.[48] The spirit in which these claims of clerical immunity were advanced as a shield for criminals and the resolute firmness with which they were met by Ferdinand and Isabella are illustrated by an occurrence in 1486, in Truxillo, where a man committed a crime and was arrested by the corregidor. He claimed to wear the tonsure and, as the officials delayed in handing him over to the ecclesiastical court, some clerics who were his kinsmen paraded the streets with a cross and proclaimed that religion was being destroyed. They succeeded thus in arousing a tumult in which the culprit was liberated. The sovereigns were in Galicia, but they forthwith despatched troops to the scene of disturbance; severe punishment was inflicted on the participants in the riot, and the clerics who had provoked it were deprived of citizenship and were banished from Spain.[49] Less serious but still abundantly obnoxious were the advantages which these tonsured laymen possessed in civil suits by claiming the privilege of ecclesiastical jurisdiction. To meet this was largely the object of the laws in the Ordenanzas Reales described above, and these were supplemented, in 1519, by an edict of Charles V forbidding episcopal officials from cognizance of cases where such so-called clerics engaged in trade sought the spiritual courts as a defence against civil suits. A similar abuse, by which such clerics in public office evaded responsibility for wrong-doing by pleading their clergy, he remedied by reviving an old law of Juan I declaring them ineligible to office.[50] Thus the royal power in Spain asserted its authority over the Church after a fashion unknown elsewhere. We shall see that, so long as it declined to persecute Moors and Jews, Rome could not compel it to do so. When its policy changed under Isabella it was inevitable that the machinery of persecution should be under the control, not of the Church, but of the sovereign. We shall also see that, when the Inquisition inflicted similar wrongs by the immunities claimed for its own officials and familiars, the sovereigns customarily turned a deaf ear to the complaints of the people.

***

DISPUTED SUCCESSION

Such was the condition of Castile when the death of the miserable Henry IV, December 12, 1474, cast the responsibility of royalty on his sister Isabella and her husband, Ferdinand of Aragon. The power of the crown was eclipsed; the land was ravaged with interminable war between nobles who were practically independent; the sentiment of loyalty and patriotism seemed extinct: deceit and treachery, false oaths--whatever would serve cupidity and ambition--were universal; justice was bought and sold; private vengeance was exercised without restraint; there was no security for life and property. The fabric of society seemed about to fall in ruins.[51] To evolve order out of this chaos of passion and lawlessness was a task to test to the uttermost the nerve and capacity of the most resolute and sagacious. To add to the confusion there was a disputed succession, although, in 1468, the oath of fidelity had been taken to Isabella, with the assent of Henry IV, in the Contract of Perales, by which he, for the second time, acknowledged his reputed daughter Juana not to be his. He was popularly believed to be impotent, and when his wife Juana, sister of Affonso V of Portugal, bore him a daughter, whom he acknowledged and declared to be his heir, her paternity was maliciously ascribed to Beltran de la Cueva, and she was known by the opposite party as La Beltraneja. Though Henry had been forced by his nobles to set aside her claims in favor of his brother Alfonso in the Declaration of Cabezon, in 1464, and, after Alfonso's death, in favor of Isabella, in 1468, the latter's marriage, in 1469, with Ferdinand of Aragon so angered him that he betrothed Juana to Charles Duke of Guienne, brother of Louis XI of France, and made the nobles of his faction swear to acknowledge her. At his death he testified again to her legitimacy and declared her to be his successor in a will which long remained hidden and finally in 1504 fell under the control of Ferdinand, who ordered it burnt.[52] There was a powerful party pledged to support her rights, and they were aided on the one hand by Affonso of Portugal and on the other by Louis of France, each eager to profit by dismembering the unhappy land. Some years of war, more cruel and bloody than even the preceding aimless strife, were required to dispose of this formidable opposition--years which tried to the utmost the ability of the young sovereigns and proved to their subjects that at length they had rulers endowed with kingly qualities. The decisive victory of Toro, won by Ferdinand over the Portuguese, March 1, 1476, virtually settled the result, although the final treaty was not signed until 1479. The Beltraneja was given the alternative of marrying within six months Prince Juan, son of Ferdinand and Isabella, then but two years old, or of entering the Order of Santa Clara in a Portuguese house. She chose the latter, but she never ceased to sign herself Yo la Reina, and her pretensions were a frequent source of anxiety. She led a varied life, sometimes treated as queen, with a court around her, and sometimes as a nun in her convent, dying at last in 1531, at the age of seventy.[53]

Isabella was queen in fact as well as in name. Under the feudal system, the husband of an heiress was so completely lord of the fief that, in the Capitulations of Cervera, January 7, 1469, which preceded the marriage, the Castilians carefully guarded the autonomy of their kingdom and Ferdinand swore to observe the conditions.[54] Yet, on the death of Henry IV, he imagined that he could disregard the compact, alleging that the crown of Castile passed to the nearest male descendant, and that through his grandfather, Ferdinand of Antequera, brother of Henry III, he was the lawful heir. The position was, however, too doubtful and complicated for him to insist on this; a short struggle convinced his consummate prudence that it was wisdom to yield, and Isabella's wifely tact facilitated submission. It was agreed that their two names should appear on all papers, both their heads on all coins, and that there should be a single seal with the arms of Castile and Aragon. Thereafter they acted in concert which was rarely disturbed. The strong individuality which characterized both conduced to harmony, for neither of them allowed courtiers to gain undue influence. As Pulgar says "The favorite of the king is the queen, the favorite of the queen is the king."[55]

FERDINAND'S CHARACTER

Ferdinand, without being a truly great man, was unquestionably the greatest monarch of an age not prolific in greatness, the only contemporary whom he did not wholly eclipse being Henry VII of England. Constant in adversity, not unduly elated in prosperity, there was a stedfast equipoise in his character which more than compensated for any lack of brilliancy. Far-seeing and cautious, he took no decisive step that was not well prepared in advance but, when the time came, he could strike, promptly and hard. Not naturally cruel, he took no pleasure in human suffering, but he was pitiless when his policy demanded. Dissimulation and deceit are too invariable an ingredient of statecraft for us to censure him severely for the craftiness in which he surpassed his rivals or for the mendacity in which he was an adept. Cold and reserved, he preferred to inspire fear rather than to excite affection, but he was well served and his insight into character gave him the most useful faculty of a ruler, the ability to choose his instruments and to get from them the best work which they were capable of performing, while gratitude for past services never imposed on him any inconvenient obligations. He was popularly accused of avarice, but the empty treasury left at his death showed that acquisitiveness with him had been merely a means to an end.[56] His religious convictions were sincere and moreover he recognized wisely the invaluable aid which religion could lend to statesmanship at a time when Latin Christianity was dominant without a rival. This was especially the case in the ten years' war with Granada, his conduct of which would alone stamp him as a leader of men. The fool-hardy defiance of Abu-l-Hacan when, in 1478, he haughtily refused to resume payment of the tribute which for centuries had been imposed on Granada, and when, in 1481, he broke the existing truce by surprising Zahara, was a fortunate occurrence which Ferdinand improved to the utmost. The unruly Castilian nobles had been reduced to order, but they chafed under the unaccustomed restraint. By giving their warlike instincts legitimate employment in a holy cause, he was securing internal peace; by leading his armies personally, he was winning the respect of his Castilian subjects who hated him as an Aragonese, and he was training them to habits of obedience. By making conquests for the crown of Castile he became naturalized and was no longer a foreigner. It was more than a hundred years since a King of Castile had led his chivalry to victory over the infidel, and national pride and religious enthusiasm were enlisted in winning for him the personal authority necessary for a sovereign, which had been forfeited since the murder of Pedro the Cruel had established the bastard line upon the throne. It was by such means as this, and not by the Inquisition that he started the movement which converted feudal Spain into an absolute monarchy. His life's work was seen in the success with which, against heavy odds, he lifted Spain from her obscurity in Europe to the foremost rank of Christian powers.

Yet amid the numerous acts of cruelty and duplicity which tarnish the memory of Ferdinand as a statesman, examination of his correspondence with his officials of the Inquisition, especially with those employed in the odious business of confiscating the property of the unhappy victims, has revealed to me an unexpectedly favorable aspect of his character. While urging them to diligence and thoroughness, his instructions are invariably to decide all cases with rectitude and justice and to give no one cause of complaint. While insisting on the subordination of the people and the secular officials to the Holy Office, more than once we find him intervening to check arbitrary action and to correct abuses and, when cases of peculiar hardship arising from confiscations are brought to his notice, he frequently grants to widows and orphans a portion of the forfeited property. All this will come before us more fully hereafter and a single instance will suffice here to illustrate his kindly disposition to his subjects. In a letter of October 20, 1502, he recites that Domingo Muñoz of Calatayna has appealed to him for relief, representing that his little property was burdened with an annual censal or ground-rent of two sols eight dineros--part of a larger one confiscated in the estate of Juan de Buendia, condemned for heresy--and he orders Juan Royz, his receiver of confiscations at Saragossa, to release the ground-rent and let Muñoz have his property unincumbered, giving as a reason that the latter is old and poor.[57] It shows Ferdinand's reputation among his subjects that such an appeal should be ventured, and the very triviality of the matter renders it the more impressive that a monarch, whose ceaseless personal activity was devoted to the largest affairs of that tumultuous world, should turn from the complicated treachery of European politics to consider and grant so humble a prayer.

ISABELLA

In his successful career as a monarch he was well seconded by his queen. Without deserving the exaggerated encomiums which have idealized her, Isabella was a woman exactly adapted to her environment. As we have seen, the muger varonil was a not uncommon development of the period in Spain, and Isabella's youth, passed in the midst of civil broils, with her fate more than once suspended in the balance, had strengthened and hardened the masculine element in her character. Self-reliant and possessed of both moral and physical courage, she was prompt and decided, bearing with ease responsibilities that would have crushed a weaker nature and admirably fitted to cope with the fierce and turbulent nobles, who respected neither her station nor her sex and could be reduced to obedience only by a will superior to their own. She had the defects of her qualities. She could not have been the queen she was without sacrifice of womanly softness, and she earned the reputation of being hard and unforgiving.[58] She could not be merciful when her task was to reduce to order the wild turmoil and lawlessness which had so long reigned unchecked in Castile, but in this she shed no blood wantonly and she knew how to pardon when policy dictated mercy. How she won the affection of those in whom she confided can be readily understood from the feminine grace of her letters to her confessor, Hernando of Talavera.[59] A less praiseworthy attribute of her sex was her fondness for personal adornment, in which she indulged in spite of a chronically empty treasury and a people overwhelmed with taxation. We hear of her magnifying her self-abnegation in receiving the French ambassador twice in the same gown, while an attaché of the English envoy says that he never saw her twice in the same attire, and that a single toilet, with its jewels and appendages must have cost at least 200,000 crowns.[60] She was moreover rigidly tenacious of the royal dignity. Once when Ferdinand was playing cards with some grandees, the Admiral of Castile, whose sister was Ferdinand's mother, addressed him repeatedly as "nephew"; Isabella was undressed in an inner room and heard it; she hastily gathered a garment around her, put her head through the door and rebuked him--"Hold! my lord the king has no kindred or friends, he has servants and vassals."[61] She was deeply and sincerely religious, placing almost unbounded confidence in her spiritual directors, whom she selected, not among courtly casuists to soothe her conscience, but from among the most rigid and unbending churchmen within her reach, and to this may in part be attributed the fanaticism which led her to make such havoc among her people. She was scrupulously regular in all church observances; in addition to frequent prayers she daily recited the hours like a priest, and her biographer tells us that, in spite of the pressing cares of state, she seemed to lead a contemplative rather than an active life.[62] She was naturally just and upright, though, in the tortuous policy of the time, she had no hesitation in becoming the accomplice of Ferdinand's frequent duplicity and treachery. With all the crowded activity of her eventful life, she found time to stimulate the culture despised by the warlike chivalry around her, and she took a deep interest in an academy which, at her instance, was opened for the young nobles of her court by the learned Italian, Peter Martyr of Anghiera.[63]

ROYAL JURISDICTION

Isabella recognized that the surest way to curb the disorders which pervaded her kingdom was the vigorous enforcement of the law and, as soon as the favorable aspect of the war of the succession gave leisure for less pressing matters, she set earnestly to work to accomplish it. The victory of Toro was followed immediately by the Córtes of Madrigal, April 27, 1476, where far-reaching reforms were enacted, among which the administration of justice and the vindication of the royal prerogatives occupied a conspicuous place.[64] It was not long before she gave her people a practical illustration of her inflexible determination to enforce these reforms. In 1477 she visited Seville with her court and presided in public herself over the trial of malefactors. Complaints came in thick and fast of murders and robberies committed in the bad old times; the criminals were summarily dispatched, and a great fear fell upon the whole population, for there was scarce a family or even an individual who was not compromised. Multitudes fled and Seville bade fair to be depopulated when, at the supplication of a great crowd, headed by Enrique de Guzman, Duke of Medina Sidonia, she proclaimed an amnesty conditioned on the restitution of property, making, however, the significant exception of heresy.[65]

ADMINISTRATION OF JUSTICE

From Seville she went, accompanied by Ferdinand, to Córdova. There they executed malefactors, compelled restitution of property, took possession of the castles of robber hidalgos, and left the land pacified. As opportunity allowed, in the busy years which followed, Isabella visited other portions of her dominions, from Valencia to Biscay and Galicia, on the same errand and, when she could not appear in person, she sent judges around with full power to represent the crown, the influence of which was further extended when, in 1480, the royal officers known as corregidores were appointed in all towns and cities.[66] One notable case is recorded which impressed the whole nobility with salutary terror. In 1480 the widow of a scrivener appealed to her against Alvar Yáñez, a rich caballero of Lugo in Galicia, who, to obtain possession of a coveted property, caused the scrivener to forge a deed and then murdered him to insure secrecy. It was probably this which led Ferdinand and Isabella to send to Galicia Fernando de Acuña as governor with an armed force, and Garcí López de Chinchilla as corregidor. Yáñez was arrested and finally confessed and offered to purchase pardon with 40,000 ducats to be applied to the Moorish wars. Isabella's counsellors advised acceptance of the tempting sum for so holy a cause, but her inflexible sense of justice rejected it; she had the offender put to death, but to prove her disinterestedness she waived her claim to his forfeited estates and gave them to his children. Alvar Yáñez was but a type of the lawless nobles of Galicia who, for a century, had been accustomed to slay and spoil without accountability to any one. So desperate appeared the condition of the land that when, in 1480, the deputies of the towns assembled to receive Acuña and Chinchilla they told them that they would have to have powers from the King of Heaven as well as from the earthly king to punish the evil doers of the land.[67] The example made of Yáñez brought encouragement, but the work of restoring order was slow. Even in 1482 the representatives of the towns of Galicia appealed to the sovereigns, stating that there had long been neither law nor justice there and begging that a justizia mayor be appointed, armed with full powers to reduce the land to order. They especially asked for the destruction of the numerous castles of those who, having little land and few vassals to support them, lived by robbery and pillage, and with them they classed the fortified churches held by prelates. At the same time they represented that homicide had been so universal that, if all murderers were punished, the greater part of the land would be ruined, and they suggested that culprits be merely made to serve at their own expense in the war with Granada.[68] With the support of the well-disposed, however, the royal power gradually made itself felt; they lent efficient support to the royal representatives; forty-six robber castles were razed and fifteen hundred robbers and murderers fled from the province, which became comparatively peaceful and orderly--a change confirmed when, in 1486, Ferdinand and Isabella went thither personally to complete the work. Yet it was not simply by spasmodic effort that the protection of the laws was secured for the population. Constant vigilance was exercised to see that the judges were strict and impartial. In 1485, 1488 and 1490 we hear of searching investigations made into the action of all the corregidores of the kingdom to see that they administered justice without fear or favor. Juezes de Residencia, as they were called, armed with almost full royal authority, were dispatched to all parts of the kingdom, as a regular system, to investigate and report on the conduct of all royal officials, from governors down, with power to punish for injustice, oppression, or corruption, subject always to appeal in larger cases to the royal council, and the detailed instructions given to them show the minute care exercised over all details of administration. Bribery, also, which was almost universal in the courts, was summarily suppressed and all judges were forbidden to receive presents from suitors.[69] To maintain constant watchfulness over them a secret service was organized of trustworthy inspectors who circulated throughout the land in disguise and furnished reports as to their proceedings and reputation.[70] Attention, moreover, was paid to the confused jurisprudence of the period. Since the confirmation of the Siete Partidas of Alfonso X, in 1348, and the issue at the same time of the Ordenamiento de Alcalá, there had been countless laws and edicts published, some of them conflicting and many that had grown obsolete though still legally in force. The greatest jurist of the day, Alfonso Diaz de Montalvo, was employed to gather from these into a code all that were applicable to existing conditions and further to supplement their deficiencies, and this code, known as the Ordenanzas Reales, was accepted and confirmed by the

Córtes of Toledo in 1480.[71] This reconstruction of Castilian jurisprudence was completed for the time when, in 1491, Montalvo brought out an edition of the Siete Partidas, noting what provisions had become obsolete and adding what was necessary of the more modern laws. The result of all these strenuous labors is seen in the admiring exclamation of Peter Martyr, in 1492, "Thus we have peace and concord, hitherto unknown in Spain. Justice, which seems to have abandoned other lands, pervades these kingdoms."[72] The inestimable benefits resulting from this are probably due more especially to Isabella.

Yet I have been led to the conviction that her share in the administration of her kingdom has been exaggerated. The chroniclers of the period were for the most part Castilians who would naturally seek to subordinate the action of the Aragonese intruder, and subsequent writers, in their eagerness to magnify the reputation of Isabella, have followed the example. In the copious royal correspondence with the officials of the Inquisition the name of Isabella rarely appears. To those in Castile as in Aragon Ferdinand mostly writes in the first person singular, without even using the pluralis majestatis; the receiver of confiscations is mi receptor, the royal treasury is mi camera e fisco; the Council of the Inquisition is mi consejo. In spite of the agreement of 1474, the signature Yo la Reina rarely appears alongside of Yo el Rey, and still rarer are Ferdinand's allusions to la Serenissima Reina, mi muy cara e muy amada muger, while in the occasional letters issued by Isabella during her husband's absence, she is careful to adduce his authority as that of el Rey mi señor.[73] It is scarce likely that this preponderance of Ferdinand was confined to directing the affairs of the Holy Office.

There has been a tendency of late to regard the Inquisition as a political engine for the conversion of Spain from a medieval feudal monarchy to one of the modern absolute type, but this is an error. The change effected by Ferdinand and Isabella and confirmed by their grandson Charles V was almost wholly wrought, as it had been two centuries earlier in France, by the extension and enforcement of the royal jurisdiction, superseding that of the feudatories.[74] In Castile the latter had virtually ceased to be an instrument of good during the long period of turbulence which preceded the accession of Isabella; something evidently was needed to fill the gap; the zealous and efficient administration of justice, which I have described, not only restored order to the community but went far to exalt the royal power, and, while it abased the nobles, it reconciled the people to possible usurpations which were so beneficent. In the consolidation and maintenance of this no agency was so effective as the institution known as the Santa Hermandad.

LA SANTA HERMANDAD

Hermandades--brotherhoods or associations for the maintenance of public peace and private rights--were no new thing. In the troubles of 1282, caused by the rebellion of Sancho IV against his father, the first idea of his supporters seems to have been the formation of such organizations.[75] In these associations, however, the police functions were subordinated to the political object of supporting the pretensions of Sancho IV and, recognizing their danger, he dissolved them as soon as he felt the throne assured to him. After his death, his widow the regent Doña María de Molina, organized them anew for the protection of her child, Fernando IV, and again in 1315, when she was a second time regent in the minority of her grandson, Alfonso XI.[76]

The idea was a fruitful one and speedily came to be recognized as a potent instrumentality in the struggle with local disorder and violence. Perhaps the earliest Hermandad of a purely police character, similar to the later ones, was that entered into in 1302 between Toledo, Talavera and Villareal to repress the robberies and murders committed by the Golfines in the district of Xara. Fernando IV not only confirmed the association but ordered the inhabitants to render it due assistance, and subsequent royal letters of the same purport were issued in 1303, 1309, 1312 and 1315.[77] In 1386 Juan I framed a general law providing for the organization and functions of Hermandades, but if any were formed under it at the time they have left no traces of their activity. In 1418 this law was adopted as the constitution of one which organized itself in Santiago, but this accomplished little and, in 1421, the guilds and confraternities of the city united in another for mutual support and succor.[78] There was, in fact, at this time, at least nominally, a general Hermandad, probably organized under the statute of Juan I and possessing written charters and privileges and customs and revenues, with full jurisdiction to try and condemn offenders. It commanded little respect, however, for it complained, in 1418, to Juan II of interference with its revenues and work, in response to which Juan vigorously prohibited all royal and local judges and officials from impeding the Hermandades in any manner. The continuity, nominal at least, of this with subsequent organizations is shown by the confirmation of this utterance by Juan II in 1423, by Ferdinand and Isabella in 1485, by Juana la Loca in 1512 and 1518, by Philip II in 1561, by Philip III in 1601 and by Philip IV in 1621.[79] In the increasing disorder of the times, however, it was impossible, at that period, to maintain the efficiency of the body. In 1443 an attempt was made to reconstruct it, but as soon as it endeavored to repress the lawless nobles and laid siege to Pedro López de Ayala in Salvatierra its forces were cut to pieces and dispersed by Pedro Fernández de Velasco.[80]

Some twenty years later, in 1465, when the disorders under Henry IV were culminating, another effort was made. The suffering people organized and taxed themselves to raise a force of 1800 horsemen to render the roads safe, and they endeavored to bring the number up to 3000. It was a popular movement against the nobles and the king hailed it as the work of God who was lifting up the humble against the great. He empowered them to administer justice without appeal except to himself, he told them that they had well earned the name of Santa Hermandad and he urged them earnestly to go forward in the good work. The attempt had considerable success for a time, but it soon languished and was dissolved for lack of the means required to carry it on.[81] Again, in 1473, there was another endeavor to form a Hermandad, but the anarchical forces were too dominant for its successful organization.[82]

***

As soon as the victory of Toro, in March, 1476, gave promise of settled government, the idea of reviving the Hermandades occurred to Alfonso de Quintanilla, Contador Mayor, or Chief Auditor, of Ferdinand and Isabella. With their approval he broached the subject to leading citizens of the principal towns in Leon and Old Castile; deputies were sent to meet at Dueñas and the project was debated. So many obstacles presented themselves that it would have been abandoned but for an eloquent argument by Quintanilla. His plan was adopted, but so fearful were the deputies that the taxes necessary for its maintenance might become permanent that they limited its duration to three years. Under the impulse of the sovereigns it rapidly took shape and was organized with the Duke of Villahermosa, natural brother of Ferdinand, at its head.[83] No time was lost in extending it throughout the kingdoms, in spite of resistance on the part of those who regarded with well-founded apprehension not only its efficiency as a means of coercing malefactors but as a dangerous development of the royal power. Seville, for instance, recalcitrated and only yielded to a peremptory command from Isabella in June, 1477.[84] One of the reasons assigned, in 1507, by Ferdinand for assenting to the demoralizing arrangement under which the Archbishop of Compostella resigned his see in favor of his natural son, was that he had received the royal judges and the Hermandad throughout his province, in opposition to the will of the nobles and gentry.[85] When, in 1479, Alonso Carrillo and the Marquis of Villena made a final attempt to urge the King of Portugal to another invasion of Castile, one of the arguments advanced was the hatred entertained for Ferdinand and Isabella in consequence of the taxes levied to support the three thousand horsemen of the Hermandad.[86] In some provinces the resistance was obstinate. In 1479 we find Isabella writing to the authorities of Biscay, expressing surprise at the neglect of the royal orders and threatening condign punishment for further delay, notwithstanding which repeated commands were requisite, and it was not till 1488 that the stubborn Biscayans submitted, while soon afterward complaints came from Guipuzcoa that the local courts neutralized it by admitting appeals from its sentences.[87] It was in the same year that Ferdinand obtained from the Córtes of Saragossa assent to the introduction of the Hermandad in his kingdom of Aragon, but the Aragonese, always jealous of the royal power, chafed under it for, in December, 1493, Isabella, writing from Saragossa, expresses a fear that the Córtes may suppress it, though it is the only means of enforcing justice there, and in the Córtes of Monçon, in 1510, Ferdinand was obliged to approve a fuero abolishing it and forbidding for the future anything of the kind to be established.[88] In 1490 the independent kingdom of Navarre adopted the system and co-operated with its neighbors by allowing malefactors to be followed across the border and extraditing them when caught--even absconding debtors being thus tracked and surrendered.[89] The institution thus founded was watched with Isabella's customary care. In 1483 complaints arose of bribery and extortion, when she summoned a convention at Pinto of representatives from all the provinces, where the guilty were punished and abuses were reformed.[90]

The Santa Hermandad thus formed a mounted military police which covered the whole kingdom, under the Duke of Villahermosa, who appointed the captains and summoned the force to any point where trouble was threatened. Each centre of population elected two alcaldes, one a gentleman and the other a tax-payer or commoner, and levied a tax to defray the expense of the organization. The alcaldes selected the quadrilleros, or privates, and held courts which dispensed summary justice to delinquents, bound by no formalities and required to listen to no legal pleadings. Their decision was final, save an appeal to the throne; their jurisdiction extended over all crimes of violence and theft and they could inflict stripes, mutilation, or death by shooting with arrows. The quadrillero in pursuit of an offender was required to follow him for five leagues, raising the hue and cry as he went, and joined by those of the country through which he passed, who kept up the hunt until the fugitive was either caught or driven beyond the frontier.[91]

***

Great as were the services of the Hermandad in repressing the turbulence of the nobles and rendering the roads safe, its cost was a source of complaint to the communities which defrayed it. This was by no means small; in 1485 it was computed at 32,000,000 maravedís and subsequently it increased greatly; it was met by a tax of 18,000 maravedís on every hundred hearths and the money was not handled by the communities but was paid to the crown.[92] Nominally the organization was in their hands, but virtually it was controlled by the sovereigns, and when, in 1498, Ferdinand and Isabella, with an appearance of generosity, relieved the taxpayers and assumed to meet the expenses from the royal revenues, although they left the election of the alcaldes and quadrilleros in the hands of the local populations, yet the result was inevitable in subjecting it still more closely to the crown.[93] The institution became permanent, and its modern development is seen in the guarda civil. None of the reforms of Ferdinand and Isabella was so efficient in restoring order and none did more to centralize power. It was not only a rudimentary standing army which could be concentrated speedily to suppress disorder, but it carried the royal jurisdiction into every corner of the land and made the royal authority supreme everywhere. It was practically an alliance between the crown and the people against the centrifugal forces of feudalism, without which even the policy of Ferdinand and the iron firmness of Ximenes might have failed to win in the final struggle. When municipal independence likewise perished in the defeat of the Comunidades, the only power left standing in Spain was that of the throne, which thus became absolute and all-pervading. The new absolutism was embodied in the self-effacing declaration of the Córtes of Valladolid, in 1523, to Charles V, that the laws and customs were subject to the king, who could make and revoke them at his pleasure, for he was the living law.[94] How immense was the revolution and how speedily accomplished is seen in the contrast between the time when the Count of Benavente jeered at a royal safe-conduct and the people of Galicia scarce dared to receive a royal commissioner, and some sixty years later when, in the unruly Basque provinces, the people of San Sebastian, in 1536, appealed to the Emperor Charles V to relieve them from local nuisances, and royal letters were gravely issued forbidding the butchers of that town from erecting new stalls or skinning cattle in the streets and restricting the latter operation to places duly assigned for the purpose.[95] Thus the crown had become absolute and its interposition could be invoked for the minutest details of local government. He reads history to little purpose who imagines that this was the work of the Inquisition.

Another measure of no little importance in establishing the royal supremacy was the virtual incorporation in the crown of the masterships of the three great military Orders of Santiago, of Calatrava and of Alcántara. Under Henry IV a Master of Santiago had been able to keep the whole kingdom in confusion, and the wealth and power of the others, although not so great, were sufficient to render their chiefs the equals of the highest nobles. From Innocent VIII, in 1489, Ferdinand procured a brief granting him for life the administration of all three; and in her will Isabella bequeathed to him an annual income of ten millions of maravedís from their revenues.[96] As Ferdinand's death drew near, the Orders endeavored to be released from subjection, claiming that they could be governed only by their own members, but prudent care secured in time from Leo X the succession in the masterships to Charles V, who, after Leo's death, made haste to obtain from Adrian VI a bull which annexed them in perpetuity to the crown.[97]

***

It was impossible that a king so far-seeing and politic as Ferdinand and a queen so pious as Isabella, when reducing to order the chaos which they found in Castile, should neglect the interest of the faith on which, according to medieval belief, all social order was based. There were in fact burning religious questions which, to sensitive piety, might seem even more urgent than protection to life and property. To comprehend the intricacy of the situation will require a somewhat extended retrospect into the relations between the several races occupying the Peninsula.

CHAPTER II - THE JEWS AND THE MOORS

The influences under which human character can be modified, for good or for evil, are abundantly illustrated in the conversion of the Spaniards from the most tolerant to the most intolerant nation in Europe. Apologists may seek to attribute the hatred felt for Jews and Moors and heretics, in the Spain of the fifteenth and succeeding centuries, to an inborn peculiarity of the race--a cosa de España which must be accepted as a fact and requires no explanation,[98] but such facts have their explanation, and it is the business of the expositor of history to trace them to their causes.

***

The vicissitudes endured by the Jewish race, from the period when Christianity became dominant, may well be a subject of pride to the Hebrew and of shame to the Christian. The annals of mankind afford no more brilliant instance of steadfastness under adversity, of unconquerable strength through centuries of hopeless oppression, of inexhaustible elasticity in recuperating from apparent destruction, and of conscientious adherence to a faith whose only portion in this life was contempt and suffering. Nor does the long record of human perversity present a more damning illustration of the facility with which the evil passions of man can justify themselves with the pretext of duty, than the manner in which the Church, assuming to represent Him who died to redeem mankind, deliberately planted the seeds of intolerance and persecution and assiduously cultivated the harvest for nearly fifteen hundred years. It was in vain that Jesus on the cross had said "Father, forgive them, for they know not what they do"; it was in vain that St. Peter was recorded as urging, in excuse for the Crucifixion, "And now, brethren, I wot that through ignorance ye did it, as did also your rulers"; the Church taught that, short of murder, no punishment, no suffering, no obloquy was too severe for the descendants of those who had refused to recognize the Messiah, and had treated him as a rebel against human and divine authority. Under the canon law the Jew was a being who had scarce the right to existence and could only enjoy it under conditions of virtual slavery. As recently as 1581, Gregory XIII declared that the guilt of the race in rejecting and crucifying Christ only grows deeper with successive generations, entailing on its members perpetual servitude, and this authoritative assertion was embodied in an appendix to the Corpus Juris.[99] When Paramo, about the same period, sought to justify the expulsion of the Jews from Spain in 1492, he had no difficulty in citing canons to prove that Ferdinand and Isabella could righteously have seized all their property and have sold their bodies into slavery.[100] Man is ready enough to oppress and despoil his fellows and, when taught by his religious guides that justice and humanity are a sin against God, spoliation and oppression become the easiest of duties. It is not too much to say that for the infinite wrongs committed on the Jews during the Middle Ages, and for the prejudices that are even yet rife in many quarters, the Church is mainly if not wholly responsible. It is true that occasionally she lifted her voice in mild remonstrance when some massacre occurred more atrocious than usual, but these massacres were the direct outcome of the hatred and contempt which she so zealously inculcated, and she never took steps by punishment to prevent their repetition. Alonso de Espina merely repeats the currently received orthodox ethics of the subject when he tells us that to oppress the Jew is true kindness and piety, for when he finds that his impiety brings suffering he will be led to the fear of God and that he who makes another do right is greater in the sight of God than he who does right himself.[101]

DEVELOPMENT OF INTOLERANCE

In view of Spanish abhorrence of Jews and Saracens during the last five or six centuries it is a fact worthy of note that the Spanish nations of the medieval period were the latest to yield to this impulse of the Church. The explanation of this lies partly in the relations between the several races in the Peninsula and partly in the independent attitude which Spain maintained towards the Holy See and its indisposition to submit to the dictation of the Church. To appreciate fully the transformation which culminated in the establishment of the Inquisition, and to understand the causes leading to it, will require a brief review of the position occupied by the Jew and the Saracen towards the Church and the State.

***

PROGRESSIVE INTOLERANCE

In the primitive Church there would seem to have been a feeling of equality, if not of cordiality, between Christian and Jew. When it was deemed necessary, in the Apostolic canons, to forbid bishops and priests and deacons, as well as laymen, from fasting or celebrating feasts with Jews, or partaking of their unleavened bread, or giving oil to their synagogues, or lighting their lamps, this argues that kindly intercourse between them was only to be restricted in so far as it might lead to religious fellowship.[102] This kindly intercourse continued but, as the Church became mostly Gentile in its membership, the prejudices existing against the Jew in the Gentile world gathered strength until there becomes manifest a tendency to treat him as an outcast. Early in the fourth century the council of Elvira, held under the lead of the uncompromising Hosius of Córdova, forbade marriage between Christians and Jews, because there could be no society common to the faithful and the infidel; no farmer was to have his harvest blest by a Jew, nor was any one even to eat with him.[103] St. Augustin was not quite so rigid, for while he held it lawful to dissolve marriage between the Christian and the infidel, he argued that it was inexpedient.[104] [105] St. Ambrose was one of the earliest to teach proscription when he reproved Theodosius the Great for the favor shown by him to Jews, who slew Christ and who deny God in denying his Son, and St. John Chrysostom improved on this by publicly preaching that Christians should hold no intercourse with Jews, whose souls were the habitations of demons and whose synagogues were their playgrounds.[106] The antagonism thus stimulated found its natural expression, in 415, in the turbulent city of Alexandria, where quarrels arose resulting in the shedding of Christian blood, when St. Cyril took advantage of the excitement by leading a mob to the synagogues, of which he took possession, and then abandoned the property of the Jews to pillage and expelled them from the city, which they had inhabited since its foundation by Alexander.[107] That under such impulsion these excesses were common is shown by the frequent repetition of imperial edicts forbidding the maltreatment of Jews and the spoiling and burning of their synagogues; they were not allowed to erect new ones but were to be maintained in possession of those existing. At the same time the commencement of legal disabilities is manifested in the reiterated prohibitions of the holding of Christian slaves by Jews, while confiscation and perpetual exile or death were threatened against Jews who should convert or circumcise Christians or marry Christian wives.[108] The Church held it to be a burning disgrace that a Jew should occupy a position of authority over Christians; in 438 it procured from Theodosius II the enactment of this as a fixed principle, and we shall see how earnestly it labored to render this a part of the public law of Christendom.[109] This spirit received a check from the Arianism of the Gothic conquerors of the Western Empire. Theodoric ordered the privileges of the Jews to be strictly preserved, among which was the important one that all quarrels between themselves should be settled by their own judges, and he sternly repressed all persecution. When a mob in Rome burned a synagogue he commanded the punishment of the perpetrators in terms of severe displeasure; when attempts were made to invade the right of the Jews of Genoa he intervened effectually, and when in Milan the clergy endeavored to obtain possession of the synagogue he peremptorily forbade it.[110] So long as the Wisigoths remained Arian this spirit prevailed throughout their extensive dominions, although the orthodox were allowed to indulge their growing uncharitableness. When the council of Agde, in 506, forbade the faithful to banquet or even to eat with Jews it shows that social intercourse still existed but that it was condemned by those who ruled the Church.[111] In the East the same tendency had freer opportunity of expressing itself in legislation, as when, in 706, the council of Constantinople forbade Christians to live with Jews or to bathe with them, to eat their unleavened bread, to consult them as physicians or to take their medicines.[112]

Gregory the Great was too large-minded to approve of this growing spirit of intolerance and, when some zealots in Naples attempted to prevent the Jews from celebrating their feasts, he intervened with a peremptory prohibition of such interference, arguing that it would not conduce to their conversion and that they should be led by kindness and not by force to embrace the faith, all of which was embodied in the canon law to become conspicuous through its non-observance.[113] In fact, his repeated enunciation of the precept shows how little it was regarded even in his own time.[114] When, moreover, large numbers of Jews were compelled to submit to baptism in southern Gaul he wrote reprovingly to the Bishops Virgil of Arles and Theodore of Marseilles, but this did not prevent St. Avitus of Clermont, about the same time, from baptizing about five hundred, who thus saved their lives from the fanatic fury of the populace.[115]

These forced conversions in Gothia were the first fruits of the change of religion of the Wisigoths from Arianism to Catholicism. The Ostrogoths, Theodoric and Theodatus, had expressly declared that they could not interfere with the religion of their subjects, for no one can be forced unwillingly to believe.[116] The Wisigoths, who dominated southern Gaul and Spain, when adapting the Roman law to suit their needs, had contented themselves with punishing by confiscation the Christian who turned Jew, with liberating Christian slaves held by Jews, and with inflicting the death penalty on Jewish masters who should force Christian slaves to conversion, besides preserving the law of Theodosius II prohibiting Jews from holding office or building new synagogues.[117] This was by no means full toleration, but it was merciful in comparison with what followed the conversion of the Goths to Catholicism. The change commenced promptly, though it did not at once reach its full severity. The third council of Toledo, held in May, 589, to condemn the Arian heresy and to settle the details of the conversion, adopted canons which show how free had hitherto been the intercourse between the races. Jews were forbidden to have Christian wives or concubines or servants, and all children sprung from such unions were to be baptized; any Christian slave circumcised or polluted with Jewish rites was to be set free; no Jew was to hold an office in which he could inflict punishment on a Christian, and this action was followed by some further disabilities decreed by the council of Narbonne in December of the same year.[118] That freedom of discussion continued for some time is manifested by the audacity of a Jew named Froganis, not long afterwards, who, as we are told, in the presence of all the nobles of the court, exalted the synagogue and depreciated the Church; it was easier perhaps to close his mouth than to confute him, for Aurasius, Bishop of Toledo, excommunicated him and declared him anathematized by the Father, Son and Holy Ghost and by all the celestial hierarchy and cohorts.[119]

THE JEWS UNDER THE WISIGOTHS

The greatest churchman of the day, St. Isidor of Seville, whose career of forty years commenced with the Catholic revolution, did what in him lay to stimulate and justify persecution. His treatise against the Jews is not vituperative, as are so many later controversial writings, but he proves that they are condemned for their fathers' sins to dispersion and oppression until, at the end of the world, their eyes are to be opened and they are to believe.[120] That he should have felt called upon to compose such a work was an evil sign, and still more evil were the conclusions which he taught. They could not fail of deplorable results, as was seen when Sisebut ascended the throne in 612 and signalized the commencement of his reign by a forcible conversion of all the Jews of the kingdom. What means he adopted we are not told, but of course they were violent, which St. Isidor mildly reproves, seeing that conversion ought to be sincere, but which yet he holds to be strictly within the competence of the Church.[121] The Church in fact was thus brought face to face with the question whether the forcible propagation of the faith is lawful. This is so repugnant to the teachings of Christ that it could scarce be accepted, but, on the other hand, the sacrament of baptism is indelible, so the convenient doctrine was adopted and became the settled policy that, while Christianity was not to be spread by force, unwilling converts were nevertheless Christians; they were not to be permitted to apostatize and were subject to all the pains and penalties of heresy for any secret inclination to their own religion.[122] This fruitful conception led to infinite misery, as we shall see hereafter, and was the impelling motive which created the Spanish Inquisition.

Whatever may have been the extent and the success of Sisebut's measures, the Jews soon afterwards reappear, and they and the conversos became the subject of an unintermittent series of ecclesiastical and secular legislation which shows that the policy so unfortunately adopted could only have attained its end by virtual extermination. The anvil bade fair to wear out the hammer--the constancy of the persecuted exhausted the ingenuity of the persecutor. With the conversion to Catholicism ecclesiastics became dominant throughout the Wisigothic territories and to their influence is attributable the varied series of measures which occupied the attention of the successive councils of Toledo from 633 until the Saracenic invasion in 711. Every expedient was tried--the seizure of all Jewish children, to be shut up in monasteries or to be given to God-fearing Christians; the alternative of expulsion or conversion, to the enforcement of which all kings at their accession were to take a solemn oath; the gentle persuasives of shaving, scourging, confiscation and exile. That the people at large did not share in the intolerance of their rulers is seen in the prohibitions of social intercourse, mixed marriages, and the holding of office. The spectre of proselytism was evoked in justification of these measures as though the persecuted Jew would seek to incur its dangers even had not the Talmud declared that "a proselyte is as damaging to Israel as an ulcer to a healthy body." The enforced conversions thus obtained were regarded naturally with suspicion and the converts were the subjects of perpetual animadversion.[123]

Thus the Church had triumphed and the toleration of the Arian Goths had been converted into persecuting orthodoxy. History repeats itself and, eight hundred years later, we shall see the same process with the same results. Toleration was changed into persecution; conversions obtained by force, or by its equivalent, irresistible pressure, were recognized as fictitious, and the unfortunate converts were held guilty of the unpardonable crime of apostasy. Although the Goths did not invent the Inquisition, they came as near to it as the rudeness of the age and the looseness of their tottering political organization would permit, by endeavoring to create through the priesthood a network of supervision which should attain the same results. The Inquisition was prefigured and anticipated.

As apparently the Jews could not be exterminated or the Conversos be trained into willing Christians, the two classes naturally added an element of discontent to the already unquiet and motley population consisting of superimposed layers of Goths, Romans and Celtiberians. The Jews doubtless aided the Gallo-Roman rebellion of Flavius Paulus about 675, for St. Julian of Toledo, in describing its suppression by King Wamba, denounces Gaul in the bitterest terms, ending with the crowning reproach that it is a refuge for the blasphemy of the Jews, whom Wamba banished after his triumph.[124] In spite of the unremitting efforts for their destruction, they still remained a source of danger to the State. At the council of Toledo in 694, King Egiza appealed to his prelates to devise some means by which Judaism should be wiped out, or all Jews be subjected to the sword of justice and their property be appropriated, for all efforts to convert them had proved futile and there was danger that, in conjunction with their brethren in other lands, they would overthrow Christianity. In its response the council alludes to a conspiracy by which the Jews had endeavored to occupy the throne and bring about the ruin of the land, and it decrees that all Jews, with their wives, children and posterity, shall be reduced to perpetual servitude, while their property is declared confiscated to the king. They are to be transferred from their present abodes and be given to such persons as the king may designate, who shall hold them as slaves so long as they persevere in their faith, taking from them their children as they reach the age of seven and marrying them only to Christians. Such of their Christian slaves as the king may select shall receive a portion of the confiscated property and continue to pay the taxes hitherto levied on the Jews.[125]

Doubtless this inhuman measure led to indiscriminate plunder and infinite misery, but its object was not accomplished. The Jews remained, and when came the catastrophe of the Saracen conquest they were ready enough to welcome the Berber invaders. That they were still in Spain is attributed to Witiza, who reigned from 700 to 710 and who is said to have recalled them and favored them with privileges greater than those of the Church, but Witiza, though a favorite target for the abuse of later annalists, was an excellent prince and the best contemporary authority says nothing of his favoring the Jews.[126]

THE MOZÁRABES

If the Jews helped the Moslem, as we may readily believe, both from the probabilities of the case and the testimony of Spanish and Arab writers,[127] they did no more than a large portion of the Christians. To the mass of the population the Goths were merely barbarous masters, whose yoke they were ready to exchange for that of the Moors, nor were the Goths themselves united. At the decisive battle of Xeres de la Frontera, Don Roderic's right and left wings were commanded by Sisebert and Oppas, the dethroned sons of Witiza, who fled without striking a blow, for the purpose of causing his defeat. The land was occupied by the Moors with little resistance, and on terms easy to the conquered. It is true that, where resistance was made, the higher classes were reduced to slavery, the lands were divided among the soldiery and one-fifth was reserved to the State, on which peasants were settled subject to an impost of one-third of the product, but submission was general under capitulations which secured to the inhabitants the possession of their property, subject to the impost of a third, and allowed them the enjoyment of their laws and religion under native counts and bishops. In spite of this liberality, vast numbers embraced Mohammedanism, partly to avoid taxation and partly through conviction that the marvellous success of the Moslem cause was a proof of its righteousness.[128]

The hardy resolution of the few who preferred exile and independence, and who found refuge in the mountains of Galicia and Asturias preserved the Peninsula from total subjection to Islam. During the long struggle of the Reconquest, the social and religious condition of Spain was strangely anomalous, presenting a mixture of races and faiths whose relations, however antagonistic they might be in principle, were, for the most part, dominated by temporal interests exclusively. Mutual attrition, so far from inflaming prejudices, led to mutual toleration, so that fanaticism became reduced to a minimum precisely in that corner of Christendom where a priori reasoners have been tempted to regard it as especially violent.

The Saracens long maintained the policy adopted in the conquest and made no attempt to convert their Christian subjects, just as in the Levantine provinces the Christians, although oppressed, were allowed to retain their religion, and in Persia, after the fall of the Sassanids, Parsism continued to exist for centuries and only died out gradually.[129] In fact, the condition of the Mozárabes, or subject Christians, under the caliphs of Córdova was, for the most part, preferable to what it had been under the Gothic kings. Mozárabes were frequently in command of the Moslem armies; they formed the royal body-guard and were employed as secretaries in the highest offices of state. In time they so completely lost the Latin tongue that it became necessary to translate the scripture and the canons into Arabic.[130] The Church organization was maintained, with its hierarchy of prelates, who at times assembled in councils; there was sufficient intellectual activity for occasional heresies to spring up and be condemned, like those of Hostegesis and Migetio in the ninth century, while, half a century earlier, the bull of Adrian I, addressed to the orthodox bishops of Spain and denouncing the Adoptianism of Felix of Urgel, which was upheld by Elipandus, Archbishop of Toledo, shows the freedom of intercourse existing between the Mozárabes and the rest of Christendom.[131] We hear of S. Eulogio of Córdova, whose two brothers, Alvar and Isidor, had left Spain and taken service with the Emperor Louis le

Germanique; he set out in 850 to join them, but was stopped at Pampeluna by war and returned by way of Saragossa, bringing with him a number of books, including Virgil, Horace, Juvenal, Porphyry, the epigrams of Aldhelm and the fables of Avienus.[132] Mixed marriages seem not to have been uncommon and there were frequent instances of conversion from either faith, but Mozárabic zealots abused the Moslem tolerance by publicly decrying Islam and making proselytes, which was forbidden, and a sharp persecution arose under Abderrhaman II and Mahomet I, in which there were a number of victims, including San Eulogio, who was martyred in 859.[133]

This persecution gave rise to an incident which illustrates the friendly intercourse between Christian and Saracen. In 858, Hilduin, Abbot of S. Germain-des-Prés, under the auspices of Charles le Chauve, sent two monks to Spain to procure the relics of St. Vincent. On reaching Languedoc they learned that his body had been carried to Benevento, but they also heard of the persecution at Córdova and were delighted, knowing that there must be plenty of relics to be obtained. They therefore kept on to Barcelona, where Sunifred, the next in command to the count, commended them to Abdulivar, Prince of Saragossa, with whom he had intimate relations. From Saragossa they reached Córdova, where the Mozárabic Bishop Saul received them kindly and assisted them in obtaining the bodies of St. George and St. Aurelius, except that, as the head of the latter was lacking, that of St. Natalia was substituted. With these precious spoils they returned in safety to Paris, by way of Toledo, Alcalá, Saragossa and Barcelona, to the immense gratification, we are told, of King Charles.[134] The persecution was but temporary and, a century later, in 956, we hear of Abderrhaman III sending Recemund, Bishop of Elvira (Granada), as his ambassador to Otho the Great at Frankfort, where he persuaded Liutprand of Cremona to write one of his historical works.[135] When the Cid conquered Valencia, in 1096, one of the conditions of surrender was that the garrison should be composed of Mozárabes, and the capitulation was signed by the principal Christian as well as Moslem citizens.[136]

The number of the Mozárabes of course diminished rapidly in the progress of reconquest as the Christian territories expanded from Galicia to Leon and Castile. Early in the twelfth century Alfonso VI, in reducing to order his extensive acquisitions, experienced much trouble with them; they are described as being worse than Moors, and he settled the matter by the decisive expedient of deporting multitudes of them to Africa.[137] The rapid progress of his arms, however, had so alarmed the petty kings among whom Andalusia was divided that they had, about 1090, invited to their assistance the Berbers known as Almoravides, who drove back Alfonso on the bloody field of Zalaca. Their leader, Jusuf ibn Techufin, was not content to fight for the benefit of his allies; he speedily overthrew their feeble dynasties and established himself as supreme in Moslem Spain. The Almoravides were savage and fanatical; they could not endure the sight of Christians enjoying freedom of worship, and bitter persecution speedily followed, until, in 1125, the Mozárabes invited the aid of Alfonso el Batallador. They sent a roll of their best warriors, comprising twelve thousand names, and promised that these and many more would join him. He came and spent fifteen months on Moorish territory, but made no permanent conquests, and on his departure the wretched Christians begged him to let them accompany him to escape the wrath of the Almoravides. Ten thousand of them did so, while of those who remained large numbers were deported to Africa, where they mostly perished.[138] The miserable remnant had a breathing spell, for the atmosphere of Spain seemed unpropitious to fanaticism and the ferocity of the Berbers speedily softened. We soon find them fraternizing with Christians. King Ali of Córdova treated the latter well and even entrusted to a captive noble of Barcelona named Reverter the command of his armies. His son Techufin followed his example and was regarded as the especial friend of the Christians, who aided him in his African wars.[139] Yet this interval of rest was short. In 1146, another Berber horde, known as Almohades, overthrew the Almoravides and brought a fresh accession of savage ferocity from the African deserts. Their caliph, Abd-al-mumin, proclaimed that he would suffer none but true believers in his dominions; the alternatives offered were death, conversion or expatriation. Many underwent pretended conversion, others went into voluntary exile, and others were deported to Africa, after which the Mozárabes disappear from view.[140]

THE MULADÍES

Yet it was as impossible for the Almohades to retain their fanaticism as it had proved for their predecessors. When, in 1228, on the deposition of the Almohad Miramamolin Al-Abdel, his nephew Yahia was raised to the throne, his brother Al-Memon-Abo-l-Ola, who was in Spain, claimed the succession. To obtain the assistance of San Fernando III, who lent him twelve thousand Christian troops, he agreed to surrender ten frontier strongholds, to permit the erection of a Christian church in Morocco, where the Christians should celebrate publicly with ringing of bells, and to allow freedom of conversion from Islam to Christianity, with prohibition of the converse. This led to the foundation of an episcopate of Morocco, of which the first bishop was Fray Aguelo, succeeded by Fray Lope, both Franciscans.[141] Co-operation of this kind with the Christians meets us at every step in the annals of the Spanish Saracens. Aben-al-Ahmar, who founded the last dynasty of Granada, agreed to become a vassal of San Fernando III, to pay him a tribute of 150,000 doblas per annum, to furnish a certain number of troops whenever called upon, and to appear in the Córtes when summoned, like any other ricohome. He aided Fernando greatly in the capture of Seville, and, in the solemnities which followed the entry into the city, Fernando bestowed knighthood on him and granted him the bearing of the Castilian guidon--gules, a band or, with two serpents, and two crowned lions as supporters--a cognizance still to be seen in the Alhambra.[142]

***

The Muladíes, or Christian converts to Islam, formed another important portion of the Moorish community. At the conquest, as we have seen, large numbers of Christians apostatized, slaves to obtain freedom and freemen to escape taxation. They were looked upon, however, with suspicion by Arabs and Berbers and were subjected to disabilities which led to frequent rebellions and murderous reprisals. On the suppression of a rising in Córdova, in 814, fifteen thousand of them emigrated to Egypt, where they captured Alexandria and held it until 826, when they were forced to capitulate and transferred their arms to Candia, founding a dynasty which lasted for a century and a half. Eight thousand of them established themselves in Fez, where they held their own and even in the fourteenth century were distinguishable from the other Moslems. In Toledo, after several unsuccessful rebellions, the Muladíes became dominant in 853 and remained independent for eighty years. Together with the Mozárabes they almost succeeded in founding a kingdom of their own in the mountains of Ronda, under Omar ben Hafsun, who embraced Christianity. Indeed, the facility of conversion from one faith to another was a marked feature of the period and shows how little firmness of religious conviction existed. The renegade, Ibn Meruan, who founded an independent state in Merida, taught a mixed faith compounded of both the great religions. Everywhere the Muladíes were striving for freedom and establishing petty principalities--in Algarbe, in Priego, in Murcia, and especially in Aragon, where the Gothic family of the Beni-Cassi became supreme. After the reduction of Toledo by starvation, in 930, they become less prominent and gradually merge into the Moslem population.[143] This was assisted by the fact that they made common cause with their conquerors against the fanatic Almoravides and Almohades. The leader of the Andalusians against the latter was a man of Christian descent, Ibn-Mardanich, King of Valencia and Murcia. He wore Christian dress and arms, his language was Castilian and his troops were mostly Castilians, Navarrese and Catalans. To the Christians he was commonly known as the king Don Lope. Religious differences, in fact, were of much less importance than political aims, and everywhere, as we shall see, Christian and Moslem were intermingled in the interminable civil broils of that tumultuous time. In an attempt on Granada, in 1162, the principal captains of Ibn-Mardanich were two sons of the Count of Urgel and a grandson of Alvar Fañez, the favorite lieutenant of the Cid.[144]

***

THE JEWS UNDER THE SARACENS

In these alternations of religious indifference and fanaticism, the position of the Jews under Moslem domination was necessarily exposed to severe vicissitudes. Their skill as physicians and their unrivalled talent in administration rendered them a necessity to the conquerors, whose favor they had gained by the assistance rendered in the invasion, but ever and anon there would come a burst of intolerance which swept them into obscurity if not into massacre. When Mahomet I ascended the throne of Córdova, about 850, we are told that one of his first acts was the dismissal of all Jewish officials, including presumably R. Hasdai ben Ishak, who had been physician and vizier to his father, Abderrhaman II.[145] A century later their wealth was so great that when the Jew Peliag went to the country palace of Alhakem, the Caliph of Córdova, it is related that he was accompanied by a retinue of seven hundred retainers of his race, all richly clad and riding in carriages.[146] How insecure was their prosperity was proved, in 1066, when Samuel ha Levi and his son Joseph had been viziers and virtual rulers of Granada for fifty years. The latter chanced to exile Abu Ishac of Elvira, a noted theologian and poet, who took revenge in a bitter satire which had immense popular success. "The Jews reign in Granada; they have divided between them the city and the provinces, and everywhere one of this accursed race is in supreme power. They collect the taxes, they dress magnificently and fare sumptuously, while the true believers are in rags and wretchedness. The chief of these asses is a fatted ram. Slay him and his kindred and allies and seize their immense treasures. They have broken the compact between us and are subject to punishment as perjurers." We shall see hereafter how ready was the Christian mob to respond to such appeals; the Moslem was no better; a rising took place in which Joseph was assassinated in the royal palace, while four thousand Jews were massacred and their property pillaged.[147] Again they recuperated themselves, but they suffered with the Christians under the fierce fanaticism of the Almohades. Indeed, they were exposed to a fiercer outburst of wrath, for the robbery of the jewels of the Kaaba, which occurred about 1160, was attributed to Spanish Jews, and Abd-el-mumin was unsparing in enforcing his orders of conversion. Numbers were put to death and forty-eight synagogues were burnt. The Sephardim, or Spanish Jews, lost their most conspicuous doctor when, in this persecution, Maimonides fled to Egypt.[148] Still they continued to exist and to prosper, though exposed to destruction at any moment through the whims of the monarch or the passions of the people. Thus, in 1375, in Granada, two men obstructed a street in a violent altercation and were vainly adjured to cease in the name of Mahomet, when Isaac Amoni, the royal physician, who chanced to pass in his carriage, repeated the order and was obeyed. That a Jew should possess more influence than the name of the Prophet was unendurable; the people rose and a massacre ensued.[149]

***

SPANIARDS AND MOORS

While Saracen Spain was thus a confused medley of races and faiths, subject to no guiding principle and swayed by the policy or the prejudices of the moment, the Christian kingdoms were much the same, except that, during the early Middle Ages, outbursts of fanaticism were lacking. Brave warriors learned to respect each other, and, as usual, it was the non-combatants, Christian priests and Moslem faquis, who retained their virulence. In the fierce struggles of the Reconquest there is little trace of race or religious hatred. The early ballads show the Moors regarded as gallant antagonists, against whom there was no greater animosity than was aroused in the civil strife which filled the intervals of Moorish warfare.[150] When, in 1149, Ramon Berenger IV of Barcelona, after a laborious siege, captured the long-coveted town of Lérida, the terms of surrender assumed the form of a peaceful agreement by which the Moorish Alcaide Avifelet became the vassal of Ramon Berenger and they mutually pledged each other fidelity. Avifelet gave up all his castles, retained certain rights in the territory and Ramon Berenger promised him fiefs in Barcelona and Gerona.[151] More than this, the ceaseless civil wars on both sides of the boundary caused each to have constant recourse to those of hostile faith for aid or shelter, and the relations which grew up, although transitory and shifting, became so intricate that little difference between Christian and Moor could often be recognized by statesmen. Thus mutual toleration could not fail to establish itself, to the scandal of crusaders, who came to help the one side, and of the hordes of fresh fanatics who poured over from Africa to assist the other.

This constant intermingling of Spaniard and Moor meets us at every step in Spanish history. Perhaps it would be too much to say, with Dozy, that "a Spanish knight of the Middle Ages fought neither for his country nor for his religion; he fought, like the Cid, to get something to eat, whether under a Christian or a Mussulman prince" and "the Cid himself was rather a Mussulman than a Catholic,"[152] though Philip II endeavored to have him canonized--but there can be no question that religious zeal had little to do with the Reconquest. In the adventurous career of the Cid, Christians and Moslems are seen mingled in both contending armies, and it is for the most part impossible to detect in the struggle any interest either of race or religion.[153] This had long been customary. Towards the end of the ninth century, Bermudo, brother of Alfonso III, for seven years held Astorga with the aid of the Moors, to whom he fled for refuge when finally dislodged. About 940 we find a King Aboiahia, a vassal of Abderrhaman of Córdova, transferring allegiance to Ramiro II and then returning to his former lord, and some fifteen years later, when Sancho I was ejected by a conspiracy, he took refuge with Abderrhaman, by whose aid he regained his kingdom, the usurper Ordoño, in turn flying to Córdova, where he was hospitably received.[154] About 990 Bermudo II gave his sister to wife to the Moorish King of Toledo, resulting in an unexpected miracle. In the terrible invasion of Almanzor, in 997, which threatened destruction to the Christians, we are told that he was accompanied by numerous exiled Christian nobles. Alfonso VI of Castile, when overcome by his brother, Sancho II, sought asylum, until the death of the latter, in Toledo--a hospitality which he subsequently repaid by conquering the city and kingdom.[155] His court was semi-oriental; during his exile he had become familiar with Arabic; in his prosperity he gathered around him Saracen poets and sages, and among his numerous successive wives was Zaida, daughter of Al-Mutamid, King of Seville. His contemporary, Sancho I of Aragon, was equally given to Moslem culture and habitually signed his name with Arabic characters.[156]

ALLIANCES WITH MOORS

The co-operation of Christian and Moor continued to the last. In 1270, when Alfonso X had rendered himself unpopular by releasing Portugal from vassalage to Leon, his brother, the Infante Felipe and a number of the more powerful ricosomes conspired against him. Their first thought was to obtain an alliance with Abu Jusuf, King of Morocco, who gladly promised them assistance. The prelates of Castile fanned the flame, hoping in the confusion to gain enlarged privileges. Felipe and his confederates renounced allegiance to Alfonso, in accordance with the fuero, and betook themselves to Granada, committing frightful devastations by the way. Everything promised a disastrous war with the Moors of both sides of the straits, when, through the intervention of Queen Violante, concessions were made to the rebellious nobles and peace was restored.[157] So when, in 1282, Sancho IV revolted against his father and was supported by all the cities except Seville and by all the ricosomes save the Master of Calatrava, and was recognized by the Kings of Granada, Portugal, Aragon and Navarre, Alfonso X in his destitution sent his crown to Abu Jusuf and asked for a loan on it as a pledge. The chivalrous Moslem at once sent him 60,000 doblas and followed this by coming with a large force of horse and foot, whereupon Sancho entered into alliance with Granada and a war ensued with Christians and Moors on both sides, till the death of Alfonso settled the question of the succession.[158] In 1324, Don Juan Manuel was Adelantado de la Frontera; conceiving some cause of quarrel with his cousin, Alfonso XI, he at once entered into an alliance with Granada, then at war with Castile, and in 1333 his turbulence rendered Alfonso unable to prevent the capture of Gibraltar or to recover it when he made the attempt.[159] Pedro the Cruel, in 1366 and again in 1368, had Moorish troops to aid him in his struggles with Henry of Trastamara. In the latter year the King of Granada came to his aid with a force of 87,000 men, and, in the final battle at Montiel, Pedro had 1500 Moorish horsemen in his army.[160] One of the complaints formulated against Henry IV, in 1464, was that he was accompanied by a force of Moors who committed outrages upon Christians.[161]

It was the same in Aragon. No knight of the cross earned a more brilliant reputation for exploits against the infidel than Jaime I, who acquired by them his title of el Conquistador, yet when, in 1260, he gave his nobles permission to serve in a crusade under Alfonso X, he excepted the King of Tunis, and on Alfonso's remonstrating with him he explained that this was because of the love which the King of Tunis bore him and of the truce existing between them and of the number of his subjects who were in Tunis with much property, all of whom would be imperilled.[162] On the accession of Jaime II, in 1291, envoys came to him from the Kings of Granada and Tremecen to renew the treaties had with Alfonso III. To the latter Jaime replied, promising freedom of trade, demanding the annual tribute of 2000 doblas which had been customary and asking for the next summer a hundred light horse paid for three months, to aid him against his Christian enemies.[163] As late as 1405, the treaty between Martin of Aragon and his son Martin of Sicily on the one hand and Mahomet, King of Granada, on the other, not only guarantees free intercourse and safety to the subjects of each and open trade in all ports and towns of their respective dominions, but each party agrees, when called upon, to assist the other, except against allies-- Aragon and Sicily with four or five galleys well armed and manned and Granada with four or five hundred cavalry.[164]

All these alliances and treaties for freedom of trade and intercourse were in direct antagonism to the decrees of the Church, which in its councils ordered priests every Sunday to denounce as excommunicate, or even liable to be reduced to slavery, all who should sell to Moors iron, weapons, timber, fittings for ships, bread, wine, animals to eat, ride or till the ground, or who should serve in their ships as pilots or in their armies in war upon Christians.[165] It was in vain that Gregory XI, in 1372, ordered all fautors and receivers of Saracens to be prosecuted as heretics by the Inquisition, and equally vain was the deduction drawn by Eymerich from this, that any one who lent aid or counsel or favor to the Moors was a fautor of heresy, to be punished as such by the Holy Office.[166] In spite of the thunders of the Church the traders continued trading and the princes made offensive and defensive alliances with the infidel.

THE MUDÉJARES

Nor, with the illustrious example of the Cid before them, had Christian nobles the slightest hesitation to aid the Moors by taking service with them. When, in 1279, Alonso Pérez de Guzman, the founder of the great house of Medina Sidonia, was insulted in the court of Alfonso, he promptly renounced his allegiance, converted all his property into money, and raised a troop with which he entered the service of Abu Jusuf of Morocco. There he remained for eleven years, except a visit to Seville to marry Doña María Coronel, whom he carried back to Morocco. He was made captain of all the Christian troops in Abu Jusuf's employ and aided largely in the war which transferred the sovereignty of that portion of Africa from the Almohades to the Beni Marin. He accumulated immense wealth, which by a stratagem he transferred to Spain, where it purchased the estates on which the greatness of the house was based. The family historiographer, writing in 1541, feels obliged to explain this readiness to serve the infidel, so abhorrent to the convictions of the sixteenth century. He tells us that at that period the Moors, both of Granada and Africa, were unwarlike and were accustomed to rely upon Christian troops, and that princes, nobles and knights were constantly in their service. Henry, brother of Alfonso X, served the King of Tunis four years and amassed large wealth; Garcí Martínez de Gallegos was already in the service of Abu Jusuf when Guzman went there; Gonzalo de Aguilar became a vassal of the King of Granada and fought for him. In 1352, when Pedro the Cruel began to reduce his turbulent nobles to order, Don Juan de la Cerda, a prince of the blood, went to Morocco for assistance and, failing to obtain it, remained there and won great renown by his knightly deeds till he was reconciled to Pedro and returned to Castile. Examples might be multiplied, but these will suffice to indicate how few scruples of religion existed among the Spaniards of the Middle Ages. As Barrantes says, adventurous spirits in those days took service with the Moors as in his time they sought their fortunes in the Indies.[167]

***

It is thus easy to understand how, in the progress of the Reconquest, the Moors of the territory acquired were treated with even greater forbearance than the Christians had been when Spain was first overrun. When raids were made or cities were captured by force, there was no hesitation in putting the inhabitants to the sword or in carrying them off into slavery,[168] but when capitulations were made or provinces submitted, the people were allowed to remain, retaining their religion and property, and becoming known under name of Mudéjares.

The enslaved Moor was his master's property, like his cattle, but entitled to some safeguards of life and limb. Even baptism did not manumit him unless the owner were a Moor or a Jew.[169] That he was frequently a man of trained skill and education is seen in the provision that, if his master confided to him a shop or a ship, the former was bound to fulfill all contracts entered into by his slave.[170] Thus the free Castilian, whose business was war, had his trade and commerce to a considerable extent, as well as his agriculture, carried on by slaves, and the rest was mostly in the hands of the Jews and the free Moors or Mudéjares. Labor thus became the badge of races regarded as inferior; it was beneath the dignity of the freeman, and when, as we shall see hereafter, the industrious population was expelled by bigotry, the prosperity of Spain collapsed.

As for the Mudéjares, the practice of allowing them to remain in the reconquered territories began early. Even in Galicia they were to be found, and in Leon documents of the tenth century contain many Moorish names among those who confirm or witness them.[171] The Fuero of Leon, granted by Alfonso V in 1020, alludes to Moors holding slaves, and the Berber population there is still represented by the Maragatos, to the south-west of Astorga--a race perfectly distinct from the Spaniards, retaining much of their African costume and speaking Castilian imperfectly, although it is their only language.[172] Fernando I (1033-65), who rendered the Kings of Toledo and Seville tributary, and who was besieging Valencia when he died, alternated in his policy towards the inhabitants of his extensive conquests. In the early part of his reign he allowed them to remain; then he adopted depopulation, and finally he returned to his earlier methods.[173] Alfonso VI followed the more liberal system; when he occupied Toledo, in 1085, he granted a capitulation to the inhabitants which secured to them their property and religion, with self-government and the possession of their great mosque.[174] When, during his absence, the Frenchman, Bernard Abbot of Sahagun, newly elected to the archbishopric, in concert with his queen, Constance of Burgundy, suddenly entered the mosque, consecrated it and placed a bell on its highest minaret, Alfonso was greatly angered. He hastened to Toledo, threatening to burn both the queen and the archbishop, and only pardoned them at the intercession of the Moors, who dreaded possible reprisals after his death. His policy, in fact, was to render his rule more attractive to the Moslem population than that of his tributaries, the petty reyes de taifas, who were obliged to oppress their subjects in order to satisfy his exigencies. He even styled himself Emperador de los dos cultos. His tolerant wisdom justified itself, for, after the coming of the Almoravides, in spite of the disastrous defeats of Zalaca and Uclés, he was able to hold his own and even to extend his boundaries, for the native Moors preferred his domination to that of the savage Berbers.[175]

His successors followed his example, but it was not regarded with favor by the Church. During the centuries of mental torpor which preceded the dawn of modern civilization there was little fanaticism. With the opening of the twelfth century various causes awoke the dormant spirit. Crusading enthusiasm brought increased religious ardor and the labors of the schoolmen commenced the reconstruction of theology which was to render the Church dominant over both worlds. The intellectual and spiritual movement brought forth heresies which, by the commencement of the thirteenth century, aroused the Church to the necessity of summoning all its resources to preserve its supremacy. All this made itself felt, not only in Albigensian crusades and the establishment of the Inquisition, but in increased intolerance to Jew and Saracen, in a more fiery antagonism to all who were not included in the pale of Christianity. How this worked was seen, in 1212, when, after the brilliant victory of Las Navas de Tolosa, Alfonso IX advanced to Ubeda, where 70,000 men had collected, and they offered to become Mudéjares and to pay him a million of doblas. The terms were acceptable and he agreed to them, but the clerical chiefs of the crusade, the two archbishops, Rodrigo of Toledo and Arnaud of Narbonne, objected and forced him to withdraw his assent. He offered the besieged to let them depart on the payment of the sum, but they were unable to collect so large an amount on the spot, and they were put to the sword, except those reserved as slaves.[176] In the same spirit Innocent IV, in 1248, ordered Jaime I of Aragon to allow no Saracens to reside in his recently conquered Balearic Isles except as slaves.[177]

In spite of the opposition of the Church the policy of the mudéjalato was continued until the work of the Reconquest seemed on the point of completion under San Fernando III. The King of Granada was his vassal, like any other Castilian noble. He subdued the rest of the land, giving the local chiefs advantageous terms and allowing them to assume the title of kings. The Spanish Moors were thus reduced to submission and he was preparing to carry his arms into Africa at the time of his death, in 1252.[178] That Moorish rule, more or less independent, continued in the Peninsula for yet two centuries and a half, is attributable solely to the inveterate turbulence of the Castilian magnates aided by the disorderly ambition of members of the royal family. During this interval successive fragments were added to Christian territory, when internal convulsions allowed opportunities of conquest, and in these the system which had proved so advantageous was followed. Moor and Jew were citizens of the realm, regarded as a desirable class of the population, and entitled to the public peace and security for their property under the same sanctions as the Catholic.[179] They are enumerated with Christians in charters granting special exemptions and privileges to cities, safeguards for fairs and for general trade.[180] Numerous Fueros which have reached us place all races on the same level, and a charter of Alfonso X, in 1272, to the city of Murcia, in its regulations as to the cleansing of irrigating canals, shows that even in petty details such as these there was no distinction recognized between Christian and Moor.[181] The safeguards thrown around them are seen in the charter of 1101, granted to the Mozárabes of Toledo by Alfonso VI, permitting them the use of their ancestral Fuero Juzgo, but penalties under it are only to be one-fifth, as in the Fuero of Castile "except in cases of theft and of the murder of Jews and Moors," and in the Fuero of Calatayud, granted by Alfonso el Batallador, in 1131, the wergild for a Jew or a Moor is 300 sueldos, the same as for a Christian.[182] Yet the practice as to this was not strictly uniform, and the conquering race naturally sought to establish distinctions which should recognize its superiority. The Fuero of Madrid, in 1202, imposes various disabilities on the Moors.[183] A law of Alfonso X, who throughout his reign showed himself favorable to the subject races, emphatically says that, if a Jew strikes a Christian, he is not to be punished according to the privileges of the Jews, but as much more severely as a Christian is better than a Jew; so if a Christian slays a Jew or a Moor he is to be punished according to the Fuero of the place, and if there is no provision for the case, then he is to suffer death or banishment or other penalty as the king may see fit, but the Moor who slays a Christian is to suffer more severely than a Christian who slays a Moor or a Jew.[184]

In an age of class distinctions this was an inevitable tendency and it is creditable to Spanish tolerance and humanity that its progress was so slow. In the violence of the time there was doubtless much arbitrary oppression, but the Mudéjares knew their rights and had no hesitation in asserting them, nor does there seem to have been a disposition to deny them. Thus, in 1387, those of Bustiella complained to Juan I that the royal tax-collectors were endeavoring to collect from them the Moorish capitation tax, to which they were not subject, having in lieu thereof from ancient times paid to the Lords of Biscay twelve hundred maravedís per annum and being entitled to enjoy all the franchises and liberties of Biscay, whereupon the king issued an order to the assessors to demand from them only the agreed sum and no other taxes, and to guarantee to them all the franchises and liberties, uses and customs of the Lordship of Biscay.[185] Even more suggestive is a celebrated case occurring as late as the reign of Henry IV. In 1455 the chaplains of the Capella de la Cruz of Toledo complained to the king that the tax on all meat slaughtered in the town had been assigned to the chapel for its maintenance, but that the Moors had established their own slaughter-house and refused to pay the tax. Elsewhere than in Spain the matter would have been referred to an ecclesiastical court with a consequent decision in favor of the faith, but here it went to the civil court with the result that, after elaborate argument on both sides, in 1462 the great jurist Alfonso Díaz de Montalvan rendered a decision recognizing that the Moors could not eat meat slaughtered in the Christian fashion, that they were entitled to a slaughter-house of their own, free of tax, but that they must not sell meat to Christians and must pay the tax on all that they might thus have sold.[186] Trivial as is this case, it gives us a clear insight into the independence and self-assertion of the Moorish communities and the readiness of the courts to protect them in their rights.

EFFORTS AT CONVERSION

The Mudéjares were guaranteed the enjoyment of their own religion and laws. They had their mosques and schools and, in the earlier times, magistrates of their own race who decided all questions between themselves according to their own zunna or law, but suits between Christian and Moor were sometimes heard by a Christian judge and sometimes by a mixed bench of both faiths.[187] In the capitulations it was generally provided that they should be subject only to the taxes exacted by their previous sovereigns, though in time this was apt to be disregarded.[188] A privilege granted, in 1254, by Alfonso X to the inhabitants of Seville, authorizing them to purchase land of Moors throughout their district, shows that the paternal possessions of the latter had been undisturbed; they were free to buy and sell real estate, and although, when the reactionary period commenced, toward the close of the thirteenth century, Sancho IV granted the petition of the Córtes of Valladolid in 1293, forbidding Jews and Moors to purchase land of Christians, the restriction soon became obsolete.[189] Not only was there no prohibition of their bearing arms, but they were liable to military service. Exemption from this was a special privilege accorded, in 1115, at the capitulation of Tudela; in 1263 Jaime I of Aragon released the Moors of Masones from tribute and military service in consideration of an annual payment of 1500 sueldos jaquenses; in 1283 his son Pedro III, when preparing to resist the invasion of Philippe le Hardi, summoned his faithful Moors of Valencia to join his armies and, in the levies made in Murcia in 1385 for the war with Portugal, each aljama had its assigned quota.[190]

DENATIONALIZATION OF THE MUDÉJARES

A wise policy would have dictated the mingling of the races as much as possible, so as to encourage unification and facilitate the efforts at conversion which were never lost to sight. The converso or baptized Moor or Jew was the special favorite of the legislator. The Moorish law which disinherited an apostate was set aside and he was assured of his share in the paternal estate; the popular tendency to stigmatize him as a tornadizo or renegat was severely repressed. The Church insisted that a Moorish captive who sincerely sought baptism should be set free. Dominicans and Franciscans were empowered to enter all places where Jews and Moors dwelt, to assemble them to listen to sermons, while the royal officials were directed to compel the attendance of those who would not come voluntarily.[191] It is easy now to see that this policy, which resulted in winning over multitudes to the faith, would have been vastly more fruitful if the races had been compelled to associate together, and infinite subsequent misery and misfortune would have been averted, but this was a stretch of tolerant humanity virtually impossible at the time. The Church, as will be seen, exerted every effort to keep them apart, on the humiliating pretext that she would lose more souls than she would gain, and there was, moreover, sufficient mutual distrust to render separation desired on both sides. At a very early period of the Reconquest the policy was adopted of assigning a special quarter of a captured town to the Moors, and thus the habit was established of providing a Morería in the larger cities, to which the Mudéjares were confined. The process is well illustrated by what occurred at Murcia, when, in 1266, it was definitely reconquered for Alfonso X by Jaime I of Aragon. He gave half the houses to Aragonese and Catalans and restricted the Moors to the quarter of the Arrijaca. Alfonso confirmed the arrangement, dislodging the Christians from among the Moors and building a wall between them. His decree on the subject recites that this was done at the prayer of the Moors, who were despoiled and ill-treated by the Christians, and who desired the protection of a wall, to the construction of which he devoted one-half of the revenues levied for the repair of the city walls. It was the same with the Jews, who were not to dwell among the Christians, but to have their Judería set apart for them near the Orihuela gate.[192] Besides this segregation from the Christians in the cities there were smaller towns in which the population was purely Moorish, where Christians were not allowed to dwell. That this was regarded as a privilege we can readily imagine, and it is shown by the confirmation, in 1255, by Alfonso X of an agreement with the Mudéjares of Moron under which they are to sell their properties to Christians and remove to Silebar, where they are to build a castle and houses, to be free of all taxes for three years, their law is to be administered by their own alcadí and no Christian is to reside there except the almojarife, or tax-gatherer, and his men.[193] All this tended to perpetuate the separation between the Christian and the Moor, and a further potent cause is to be found in the horror with which miscegenation was regarded--at least when the male offender was a Moor. Intermarriage, of course, was impossible between those of different faiths and illicit connections were punished in the most savage manner.[194]

In spite of this natural but impolitic segregation, the Mudéjares gradually became denationalized and assimilated themselves in many ways to the population by which they were surrounded. In time they forgot their native language and it became necessary for their learned men to compile law-books in Castilian for the guidance of their alcadís. Quite a literature of this kind arose and, even after the final expulsion, as late as the middle of the seventeenth century, among the refugees in Tunis, a manual of religious observances was composed in Spanish, the author of which lamented that even the sacred characters in which the Korán was written were almost unknown and that the rites of worship were forgotten or mingled with usages and customs borrowed from the Christians.[195] The Mudéjares even sympathized with the patriotic aspirations of their Castilian neighbors, as against their independent brethren. When, in 1340, Alfonso XI returned in triumph to Seville, after the overwhelming victory of the Rio Salado, we are told how the Moors and their women united with the Jews in the rejoicings which greeted the conqueror.[196] Even more practical was the response to the appeal of the Infante Fernando, in 1410, when he was besieging Antequera, one of the bulwarks of Granada, and was in great straits for money. He wrote "muy afectuosamente" to Seville and Córdova, not only to the Christians but to the Moorish and Jewish aljamas and, as he was popular with them, they advanced him what sums they could.[197] The process of denationalization and fusion with the Christian community was necessarily slow, but its progress gave gratifying promise of a result, requiring only wise patience and sympathy, which would have averted incalculable misfortunes.

THE MUDÉJARES

In a financial and industrial point of view the Mudéjares formed a most valuable portion of the population. The revenues derived from them were among the most reliable resources of the State; assignments on them were frequently used as the safest and most convenient form of securing appanages and dowries and incomes for prelates and religious establishments.[198] To the nobles on whose lands they were settled they were almost indispensable, for they were skilful agriculturists and the results of their indefatigable labors brought returns which could be realized in no other way. That they should be relentlessly exploited was a matter of course. A fuero granted, in 1371, by the Almirante Ambrosio de Bocanegra to his Mudéjares of Palma del Rio, not only specifies their dues and taxes, but prescribes that they shall bake in the seigniorial oven and bathe in the seignorial bath and purchase their necessaries in the seignorial shops.[199] They were not only admirable husbandmen and artificers, but distinguished themselves in the higher regions of science and art. As physicians they ranked with the Jews, and when, in 1345, Ferrant Rodriguez, Prior of the Order of Santiago, built the Church of Our Lady of Uclés, he assembled "Moorish masters" and good Christian stone-masons, who constructed it of stone and mortar.[200] The industry of Spain was to a great extent in their hands. To them the land owed the introduction of the sugar-cane, cotton, silk, the fig, the orange and the almond. Their system of irrigation, still maintained to the present time, was elaborately perfect, and they had built highways and canals to facilitate intercourse and transportation. Valencia, which was densely populated by Mudéjares, was regarded as one of the richest provinces in Europe, producing largely of sugar, oil and wine. In manufacturing skill they were no less distinguished. Their fabrics of silk and cotton and linen and wool were exquisite; their potteries and porcelains were models for the workmen of the rest of Europe; their leather-work was unsurpassed; their manufactures of metals were eagerly sought in distant lands, while their architecture manifests their delicate skill and artistic taste. Marriages were arranged for girls at 11 and boys at 12; dowries were of little account, for a bed and a few coins were deemed sufficient where all were industrious and self-supporting, and their rapid increase, like evil weeds, was a subject of complaint to their Castilian detractors. Ingenious and laborious, sober and thrifty, a dense population found livelihood in innumerable trades, in which men, women and children all labored, producing wealth for themselves and prosperity for the land. In commerce they were equally successful; they were slaves to their word, their reputation for probity and honor was universal, and their standing as merchants was proverbial. There was no beggary among them and quarrels were rare, differences being for the most part amicably settled without recourse to their judges.[201]

It is not easy to set limits to the prosperity attainable by the Peninsula with its natural resources developed by a population combining the vigor of the Castilian with the industrial capacity of the Moor. All that was needed was Christian patience and good will to kindle and encourage kindly feeling between the conquering and the subject race; time would have done the rest. The infidel, won over to Christianity, would have become fused with the faithful, and a united people, blessed with the characteristics of both races, would have been ready to take the foremost place in the wonderful era of industrial civilization which was about to open. Unhappily for Spain this was not to be. To the conscientious churchman of the Middle Ages any compact with the infidel was a league with Satan; he could not be forcibly brought into the fold, but it was the plainest of duties to render his position outside so insupportable that he would take refuge in conversion.

DISTINCTIVE BADGES

The Church accordingly viewed with repugnance the policy of conciliation and toleration which had so greatly facilitated the work of the Reconquest, and it lost no opportunity of exciting popular distrust and contempt for the Mudéjares. We shall see how great was its success with respect to the Jews, whose position offered better opportunity for attack, but it was not without results as respects the Moors. It discouraged all intercourse between the races and endeavored to keep them separate. Even the indispensable freedom of ordinary commercial dealings, which was provided for by the secular rulers, was frowned upon, and in 1250 the Order of Santiago was obliged to represent to Innocent IV that it had Moorish vassals, and to supplicate him for license to buy and sell with them, which he graciously permitted.[202] The most efficacious means, however, of establishing and perpetuating the distinction between the races was that Jews and Moors should wear some peculiar garment or badge by which they should be recognized at sight. This was not only a mark of inferiority and a stigma, but it exposed the wearer to insults and outrages, rendering it both humiliating and dangerous, especially to those, such as muleteers or merchants, whose avocations rendered travel on the unsafe highways indispensable. When the Church was aroused from its torpor to combat infidelity in all its forms, this was one of the measures adopted by the great council of Lateran in 1216, in a regulation carried into the canon law, the reason alleged being that it was necessary to prevent miscegenation.[203] In 1217 Honorius III peremptorily ordered the enforcement of this decree in Castile, but, two years later, consented to suspend it, on the remonstrance of San Fernando III, backed by Rodrigo, Archbishop of Toledo. The king represented that many Jews would abandon his kingdom rather than wear badges, while the rest would be driven to plots and conspiracies, and, as the greater part of his revenues was derived from them, he would be unable to carry out his enterprises against the Saracens.[204] It was difficult to arouse intolerance and race hatred in Spain, and, when Gregory IX, about 1233, and Innocent IV, in 1250, ordered the Castilian prelates to enforce the Lateran canons, San Fernando quietly disregarded the injunction.[205] His son, Alfonso X, so far yielded obedience that, in the Partidas, he ordered, under a penalty of ten gold maravedís or ten lashes, all Jews, male and female, to wear a badge on the cap, alleging the same reason as the Lateran council, but he did not extend this to the Moors and, as his code was not confirmed by the Córtes for nearly a century, the regulation may be regarded as inoperative.[206] The council of Zamora, which did so much to stimulate intolerance, in January, 1313, ordered the badge to be worn, as it was in other lands, and later in the year the Córtes of Plasencia proposed to obey, but were told by the Infante Juan, who presided as guardian of Alfonso XI, that he would, after consultation, do what was for the advantage of the land.[207] In Aragon, the councils of Tarragona, in 1238 and 1282, vainly ordered the canon to be obeyed, and it was not until 1300 that the attempt was made with an ordinance requiring the Mudéjares to wear the hair cut in a peculiar fashion that should be distinctive.[208] In Castile, at length, Henry II, in pursuance of the request of the Córtes of Toro in 1371, ordered all Jews and Moors to wear the badge (a red circle on the left shoulder), but the injunction had to be frequently repeated and was slenderly obeyed. Even so, to it may be attributed the frequent murders which followed of Jews on the highways, the perpetrators of which were rarely identified.[209]

What was the spirit which the Church thus persistently endeavored to arouse in Spain may be gathered from a brief of Clement IV, in 1266, to Jaime I of Aragon, urging him to expel all Mudéjares from his dominions. He assures the king that his reputation will suffer greatly if, for temporal advantage, he longer permits such opprobrium of God, such an infection of Christendom, as proceeds indubitably from the horrible cohabitation of the Moors, with its detestable horrors and horrid foulness. By expelling them he will fulfil his vow to God, stop the mouths of his detractors and prove himself zealous for the faith.[210] The same temper was shown, in 1278, by Nicholas III, when he scolded Alfonso X for entering into truces with the Moors, and, by threatening to deprive him of the share granted to him of the church revenues, incited him to the disastrous siege of Algeciras, the failure of which led him to form an alliance with the King of Morocco.[211] Fortunately this papal zeal for the faith found no Ximenes in Spain to spread it among the people and to kindle the fires of intolerance. The Spanish Church of the period appears to have been wholly quiescent. The only action on record is the trivial one of Arnaldo de Peralta, Bishop of Valencia, from 1261 to 1273, who forbade, under pain of excommunication, his clergy from drinking wine in the house of a Jew, provided they should have heard of or should remember the prohibition; and he further vaguely threatened with his displeasure any cleric who should knowingly buy the wine of a Jew, except in case of necessity.[212]

INFLUENCE OF THE CHURCH

That, in the Confusion which followed the rebellion of Sancho IV against his father, there may have arisen a desire to limit somewhat the privileges of Jew and Moor is rendered probable by the legislation of the Córtes of Valladolid, in 1293, to which allusion has already been made (p. 63), but the decisive impulse which aroused the Spanish Church from its indolent indifference and set it earnestly to work in exciting popular hatred and intolerance, would seem traceable to the council of Vienne in 1311-12. Among the published canons of the council, the only one relating to Moors is a complaint that those dwelling in Christian lands have their priests, called Zabazala, who, from the minarets of their mosques, at certain hours invoke Mahomet and sound his praises in a loud voice, and also that they are accustomed to gather around the grave of one whom they worship as a saint. These practices are denounced as unendurable, and the princes are ordered to suppress them, with the alternative of gaining salvation or of enduring punishment which shall make them serve as a terrifying example.[213] This threat fell upon deaf ears. In 1329 the council of Tarragona complains of its inobservance and orders all temporal lords to enforce it within two months, under pain of interdict and excommunication,[214] and a hundred years later the council of Tortosa, in 1429, supplicated the King of Aragon and all prelates and nobles, by the bowels of divine mercy, to enforce the canon and all other conciliar decrees for the exaltation of the faith and the humiliation of Jews and Moors, and to cause their observance by their subjects if they wish to escape the vengeance of God and of the Holy See. This was equally ineffectual, and it was reserved for Ferdinand and Isabella, about 1482, to enforce the canon of Vienne with a vigor which brought a remonstrance from the Grand Turk.[215]

More serious was the effect upon the Jews of the spirit awakened at Vienne. That council, besides enacting very severe laws against usury, denounced the privilege accorded in Spain to Jews, whereby Jewish witnesses were requisite for the conviction of Jewish defendants. It did not presume to annul this privilege, but forbade all intercourse between the races wherever it was in force.[216] The Spanish prelates, in returning from the council in 1312, brought with them these canons and the spirit of intolerance that dictated them and made haste to give expression to it at the council of Zamora, in January, 1313, in a number of canons, the temper of which is so different from the previous utterances of the Spanish Church that it shows the revolution wrought in their mode of thinking by intercourse with their brethren from other lands. Henceforth, in this respect, the Spanish Church emerges from its isolation and distinguishes itself by even greater ferocity than that which disgraced the rest of Christendom. The fathers of Zamora invoked the curse of God and of St. Peter on all who should endeavor to enforce the existing laws requiring the evidence of Jews to convict Jews. They denounced the Jews as serpents, who were only to be endured by Christians because they were human beings, but were to be kept in strict subjection and servitude, and they sought to reduce this principle to practice by a series of canons restricting the Jews in every way and putting an end to all social intercourse between them and Christians.[217] The friendly mingling of the races, which shows how little the prejudices of the churchmen were shared by the people at this period, became a favorite subject of objurgation and required a long series of efforts to eradicate, but the Church triumphed at last, and the seeds of envy, hatred and all uncharitableness, which it so assiduously planted and cultivated, yielded in the end an abundant harvest of evil. What prepossessions of Christian kindness the prelates of Zamora felt that they had to overcome are indicated in the final command that these constitutions should be read publicly in all churches annually, and that the bishops should compel by excommunication all secular magistrates to enforce them.[218]

The Spanish Church, thus fairly started in this deplorable direction, pursued its course with characteristic energy. In 1322 the utterances of the council of Valladolid reveal how intimate were the customary relations between Christian and infidel, and how the Church, in place of taking advantage of this, labored to keep the races asunder. The council recites that scandals arise and churches are profaned by the prevailing custom of Moors and Jews attending divine service, wherefore they are to be expelled before the ceremonies of the mass begin, and all who endeavor to prevent it are to be excommunicated. The habit of nocturnal devotional vigils in churches is also said, probably with truth, to be the source of much evil, and all who bring Moors and Jews to take part with their voices and instruments are to be expelled. To preserve the faithful from pollution by Moorish and Jewish superstitions, they are commanded no more to frequent the weddings and funerals of the infidels. The absurd and irrational abuse whereby Jews and Moors are placed in office over Christians is to be extirpated, and all prelates shall punish it with excommunication. As the malice of Moors and Jews leads them craftily to put Christians to death, under pretext of curing them by medicine and surgery and, as the canons forbid Christians from employing them as physicians, and as these canons are not observed in consequence of the negligence of the prelates, the latter are ordered to enforce them strictly with the free use of excommunication.[219]

These last two clauses point to matters which had long been special grievances of the faithful and which demand a moment's attention. The superior administrative abilities of the Jews caused them to be constantly sought for executive positions, to the scandal of all good Christians. We have seen that under the Goths it was an abuse calling for constant animadversion. It was one of the leading complaints of Innocent III against Raymond VI of Toulouse, which he expiated so cruelly in the Albigensian crusades, and one of the decrees of the Lateran council was directed against its continuance.[220] In Spain the sovereigns could not do without them, and we shall have occasion to see that it became one of the main causes of popular dislike of the unfortunate race, for the Christian found it hard to bear with equanimity the domination of the Jew, especially in his ordinary character of almojarife, or tax-collector. As early as 1118, Alfonso VIII, in the fuero granted to Toledo, promised that no Jew or recent convert should be placed over the Christians; Alfonso X made the same concession in the fuero of Alicante, in 1252, except that he reserved the office of almojarife, and in the Partidas he endeavored to make the rule general.[221] The same necessity made itself felt with regard to the function of the physician, for which, during the dark ages, the learning of Jew and Saracen rendered them almost exclusively fitted. Zedechias, the Jewish physician of the Emperor Charles the Bald, was renowned, and tradition handed down his name as that of a skilful magician.[222] Prince and prelate alike sought comfort in their curative ministrations, and, as the Church looked askance on the practice of medicine and surgery by ecclesiastics, unless it were through prayer and exorcism, they had the field almost to themselves. This had always been regarded with disfavor by the Church. As early as 706 the council of Constantinople had ordered the faithful not to take medicine from a Jew, and this command had been incorporated in the canon law.[223] Another rule, adopted from the Lateran council of 1216, was that the first duty of a physician was to care for the soul of the patient rather than for his body, and to see that he was provided with a confessor--a duty which the infidel could scarce be expected to recognize.[224] It is therefore easy to understand why the general abhorrence of the Church for Moor and Jew should be sharpened with peculiar acerbity in regard to their functions as physicians; why the council of Valladolid should endeavor to alarm the people with the assertion that they utilized the position to slay the faithful, and the council of Salamanca, in 1335, should renew the sentence of excommunication on all who should employ them in sickness.[225] Nominally the Church carried its point, and in the prescriptive laws of 1412 there was embodied a provision imposing a fine of three hundred maravedís on any Moor or Jew who should visit a Christian in sickness or administer medicine to him,[226] but the prohibition was impossible of enforcement. About 1462, the Franciscan, Alonso de Espina, bitterly complains that there is not a noble or a prelate but keeps a Jewish devil as a physician, although the zeal of the Jews in studying medicine is simply to obtain an opportunity of exercising their malignity upon Christians; for one whom they cure they slay fifty, and when they are gathered together they boast as to which has caused the most deaths, for their law commands them to spoil and slay the faithful.[227] It was but a few years after this that Abiatar Aben Crescas, chief physician of Juan II of Aragon, the father of Ferdinand, vindicated Jewish science by successfully relieving his royal patient of a double cataract and restoring his sight. On September 11, 1469, pronouncing the aspect of the stars to be favorable, he operated on the right eye; the king, delighted with his recovered vision, ordered him to proceed with the left, but Abiatar refused, alleging that the stars had become unfavorable, and it was not until October 12 that he consented to complete the cure.[228] The friars themselves believed as little as royalty in the stories which they invented to frighten the people and create abhorrence of Jewish physicians. In spite of the fact that Ferdinand and Isabella, in the Ordenanzas of 1480, repeated the prohibition of their attending Christians, the Dominicans, in 1489, obtained from Innocent IV permission to employ them, notwithstanding all ecclesiastical censures, the reason alleged being that in Spain there were few others.[229]

REPRESSIVE LEGISLATION

The prescriptive spirit which dominated the councils of Zamora and Valladolid was not allowed to die out. That of Tarragona, in 1329, expressed its horror at the friendly companionship with which Christians were in the habit of attending the marriages, funerals and circumcisions of Jews and Moors and even of entering into the bonds of compaternity with the parents at the latter ceremony, all of which it strictly forbade for the future.[230] A few years later, in 1337, Arnaldo, Archbishop of Tarragona, addressed to Benedict XII a letter which is a significant expression of the objects and methods of the Church. In spite, he says, of the vow taken by Jaime I when about to conquer Valencia, that he would not permit any Moors to remain there, the Christians, led by blind cupidity, allow them to occupy the land, believing that thus they derive larger revenues--which is an error, as the Abbot of Poblet has recently demonstrated by expelling the Mudéjares from the possessions of the abbey. There are said to be forty or fifty thousand Moorish fighting men in Valencia, which is a source of the greatest danger, especially now when the Emperor of Morocco is preparing to aid the King of Granada. Besides, many enormous crimes are committed by Christians, in consequence of their damnable familiarity and intercourse with the Moors, who blaspheme the name of Christ and exalt that of Mahomet. "I have heard," he pursues, "the late Bishop of Valencia declare, in a public sermon, that in that province the mosques are more numerous than the churches and that half, or more than half, the people are ignorant of the Lord's prayer and speak only Moorish. I therefore pray your clemency to provide an appropriate remedy, which would seem impossible unless the Moors are wholly expelled and unless the King of Aragon lends his aid and favor. The nobles would be more readily brought to assent to this if they were allowed to seize and sell the persons and property of the Mudéjares as public enemies and infidels, and the money thus obtained would be of no small service in defending the kingdom." The Christian prelate, not content with directly asking the pope to adopt this inhuman proposition, sent a copy of his letter to Jean de Comminges, Cardinal of Porto, and begged him to urge the matter with Benedict, and in a second letter to the cardinal he explained that it would be necessary for the pope to order the king to expel the Moors; that he would willingly obey as to the crown lands, but that a papal command was indispensable as to the lands of others. It was only, he added, the avarice of the Christians which kept the Moors there.[231] We shall see how, two hundred and seventy years later, an Archbishop of Valencia aided in bringing about the final catastrophe, by a still greater display of saintly zeal, backed by precisely the same arguments.

This constant pressure on the part of their spiritual guides began to make an impression on the ruling classes, and repressive legislation becomes frequent in the Córtes. In those of Soria, in 1380, the obnoxious prayer against Christians was ordered to be removed from Jewish prayer-books and its recitation was forbidden under heavy penalties, while the rabbis were deprived of jurisdiction in criminal cases between their people. In those of Valladolid, in 1385, Christians were forbidden to live among Jews, Jews were prohibited to serve as tax-collectors, their judges were inhibited to act in civil cases between them and Christians and numerous regulations were adopted to restrain their oppression of debtors.[232] In 1387, at the Córtes of Briviesca, Juan I enacted that no Christian should keep in his house a Jew or Moor, except as a slave, nor converse with one beyond what the law allowed, under the heavy penalty of 6000 maravedís, and no Jew or Moor should keep Christians in his house under pain of confiscation of all property and corporal punishment at the king's pleasure.[233] It seemed impossible to enforce these laws, and the Church intervened by assuming jurisdiction over the matter. In 1388 the council of Valencia required the suspension of labor on Sundays and feast-days, and it deplored the injury to the bodies and souls of the faithful and the scandals arising from the habitual intercourse between them and the infidels. The dwellings of the latter were ordered to be strictly separated from those of the former; where special quarters had not been assigned to them, it was ordered to be done forthwith and, within two months, no Christian should be found dwelling with them nor they with Christians. If they had trades to work at or merchandise to sell they could come out during the day, or occupy booths or shops along the streets, but at night they must return to the place where they kept their wives and children.[234]

This segregation of the Jews and Moors and their strict confinement to the Morerías and Juderías were a practical method of separating the races which was difficult of enforcement. The massacres of 1391 showed that there were such quarters generally in the larger cities, but residence therein seems not to have been obligatory, and Jews and Moors who desired it lived among the Christians. In the restrictive laws of 1412, the first place is given to this matter. Morerías and Juderías are ordered to be established everywhere, surrounded with a wall having only one gate. Any one who shall not, in eight days after notice, have settled therein forfeits all his property and is liable to punishment at the king's pleasure, and severe penalties are provided for Christian women who enter them.[235] An effort was made to enforce these regulations, but it seemed impossible to keep the races apart. In 1480 Ferdinand and Isabella state that the law had not been observed and order its enforcement, allowing two years for the establishment of the ghettos, after which no Jew or Moor shall dwell outside of them, under the established penalties, and no Christian woman be found within them.[236] The time had passed for laws to be disregarded and this was carried into effect with the customary vigor of the sovereigns. In Segovia, for instance, on October 29, 1481, Rodrigo Alvárez Maldonado, commissioner for the purpose, summoned the representatives of the Jewish aljama, read to them the Ordenanza, and designated to them the limits of their Judería. All Christians resident therein were warned to vacate within the period designated by the law; all Jews of the district were required to make their abode there within the same time, and all doors and windows of houses contiguous to the boundaries, on either side, whether of Jews or Christians, were ordered to be walled up or rendered impassable. The segregation of the Jews was to be absolute.[237]

***

We shall see in the next chapter how successful were the efforts of the Church in arousing the greed and fanaticism of the people and in repressing the kindly fellowship which had so long existed. From this the Jews were the earliest and greatest sufferers, and it is necessary here to say only that in the cruel laws which marked the commencement of the fifteenth century both Moor and Jew were included in the restrictions designed to humiliate them to the utmost, to render their lives a burden, to deprive them of the means of livelihood and to diminish their usefulness to the State. These laws were too severe for strict and continuous enforcement, but they answered the purpose of inflicting an ineffaceable stigma upon their victims and of keeping up a wholesome feeling of antagonism on the part of the population at large. This was directed principally against the Jews, who were the chief objects of clerical malignity, and it will be our business to examine how this was skilfully developed, until it became the proximate cause of the introduction of the Inquisition and created for it, during its earliest and busiest years, almost the sole field of its activity. Meanwhile it may be observed that, in the closing triumph over Granada, the capitulations accorded by Ferdinand and Isabella were even more liberal to Jews and Moors than those granted from the eleventh to the thirteenth century, by such monarchs as Alfonso VI, Ferdinand III, Alfonso X, and Jaime I. Unless they were deliberately designed as perfidious traps, they show how little real conscientious conviction lay behind the elaborately stimulated fanaticism which destroyed the Jews and Mudéjares.[238]

CHAPTER III - THE JEWS AND THE CONVERSOS

To appreciate properly the position of the Jews in Spain, it is requisite first to understand the light in which they were regarded elsewhere throughout Christendom during the medieval period. It has already been seen that the Church held the Jew to be a being deprived, by the guilt of his ancestors, of all natural rights save that of existence. The privileges accorded to the Jews and the social equality to which they were admitted under the Carlovingians provoked the severest animadversions of the churchmen.[239] About 890, Stephen VI writes to the Archbishop of Narbonne that he has heard with mortal anxiety that these enemies of God are allowed to hold land and that Christians dealt with these dogs and even rendered service to them.[240] It is true that Alexander III maintained the ancient rule that they could repair their existing synagogues but not build new ones, and Clement III honored himself by one of the rare human utterances in their favor, prohibiting their forced conversion, their murder or wounding or spoliation, their deprivation of religious observances, the exaction of forced service unless such was customary, or the violation of their cemeteries in search of treasure, and, moreover, both of these decrees were embodied by Gregory IX in the canon law.[241] Yet these prohibitions only point out to us the manner in which popular zeal applied the principles enunciated by the Church and, when the council of Paris, in 1212, forbade, under pain of excommunication, Christian midwives to attend a Jewess in labor, it shows that they were authoritatively regarded as less entitled than beasts to human sympathy.[242]

How popular hostility was aroused and strengthened is illustrated in a letter addressed, in 1208, by Innocent III to the Count of Nevers. Although, he says, the Jews, against whom the blood of Jesus Christ cries aloud, are not to be slain, lest Christians should forget the divine law, yet are they to be scattered as wanderers over the earth, that their faces may be filled with ignominy and they may seek the name of Jesus Christ. Blasphemers of the Christian name are not to be cherished by princes, in oppression of the servants of the Lord, but are rather to be repressed with servitude, of which they rendered themselves worthy when they laid sacrilegious hands on Him, who had come to give them true freedom, and they cried that His blood should be upon them and their children. Yet when prelates and priests intervene to crush their malice, they laugh at excommunication and nobles are found who protect them. The Count of Nevers is said to be a defender of the Jews; if he does not dread the divine wrath, Innocent threatens to lay hands on him and punish his disobedience.[243] The Cistercian Cæsarius of Heisterbach, in his dialogues for the moral instruction of his fellow monks, tells several stories which illustrate the utter contempt felt for the feelings and rights of Jews, and in one of them there is an allusion to the curious popular belief that the Jews had a vile odor, which they lost in baptism--a belief prolonged, at least in Spain, until the seventeenth century was well advanced.[244] Even so enlightened a prelate as Cardinal Pierre d'Ailly, in 1416, reproves the sovereigns of Christendom for their liberality towards the Jews, which he can attribute only to the vile love of gain; if Jews are allowed to remain, it should be only as servants to Christians.[245] General prohibitions of maltreatment availed little when prelate and priest were busy in inflaming popular aversion and popes were found to threaten any prince hardy enough to interpose and protect the unfortunate race.

MEDIEVAL PERSECUTION

Of course under such impulsion there was scant ceremony in dealing with these outcasts in any way that religious ardor might suggest. When, in 1009, the Saracens captured Jerusalem and destroyed the church of the Holy Sepulchre, the rage and indignation of Europe assumed so threatening a form that multitudes of Jews took refuge in baptism.[246] When religious exaltation culminated in the Crusades, it seemed to those who assumed the cross a folly to redeem Palestine while leaving behind the impious race that had crucified the Lord, and everywhere, in 1096, the assembling of crusaders was the signal for Jewish massacre. It would be superfluous to recount in detail the dreary catalogue of wholesale slaughters which for centuries disgraced Europe, whenever fanaticism or the disappearance of a child gave rise to stories of the murder rite, or a blood-stained host suggested sacrilege committed on the sacrament, or some passing evil, such as an epidemic, aroused the populace to bloodshed and rapine. The medieval chronicles are full of such terrible scenes, in which cruelty and greed assumed the cloak of zeal to avenge God; and when, in rare instances, the authorities protected the defenceless, it was ascribed to unworthy motives, as in the case of Johann von Kraichbau, Bishop of Speyer, who, in 1096, not only saved some Jews but beheaded their assailants and was accused of being heavily bribed; nor did Frederic Barbarossa and Ludwig of Bavaria escape similar imputations.[247] It was safer and more profitable to combine piety and plunder as when, in April, 1182, Philip Augustus ordered all Jews to leave France by St. John's day, confiscating their landed property and allowing them to take their personal effects. His grandson, the saintly Louis, resorted without scruple to replenishing his treasury by ransoming the Jews and the latter's grandson, Philippe le Bel, was still more unscrupulous in 1306, when, by a concerted movement, he seized all the Jews in his dominions, stripped them of property, and banished them under pain of death. In England King John, in 1210, cast Jews into prison and tortured them for ransom, and his grandson, Edward I, followed the example of Philip Augustus so effectually that Jews were not allowed to return until the time of Cromwell.[248]

Spain remained so long isolated from the movements which agitated the rest of Christendom that the abhorrence for the Jew, taught by the Church and reduced to practice in so many ways by the people, was late in development. In the deluge of the Saracen conquest and in the fierce struggles of the early Reconquest, the antipathy so savagely expressed in the Gothic legislation seemed to pass away, possibly because there could have been but few Jews among the rude mountaineers of Galicia and Asturias. It is true that the Wisigothic laws, in the Romance version known as the Fuero Juzgo, remained nominally in force; it is also true that a law was interpolated in the Fuero, which seems to indicate a sudden recrudescence of fanaticism after a long interval of comparative toleration. It provides that if a Jew loyally embraces the faith of Christ, he shall have license to trade in all things with Christians, but if he subsequently relapses into Judaism his person and property are forfeit to the king; Jews persisting in their faith shall not consort with Christians, but may trade with each other and pay taxes to the king. Their houses and slaves and lands and orchards and vineyards, which they may have bought from Christians, even though the purchase be of old date, are declared confiscated to the king, who may bestow them on whom he pleases. If any Jew trades in violation of this law he shall become a slave of the king, with all his property. Christians shall not trade with Jews; if a noble does so, he shall forfeit three pounds of gold to the king; on transactions of more than two pounds, the excess is forfeit to the king, together with three doblas; if the offender is a commoner, he shall receive three hundred lashes.[249]

CONDITION OF SPANISH JEWS

The date of this law is uncertain, but it presupposes a considerable anterior period of toleration, during which Jews had multiplied and had become possessed of landed wealth. To what extent it may have been enforced we have no means of knowing, but its observance must only have been temporary, for such glimpses as we get of the condition of the Jews up to the fourteenth century are wholly incompatible with the fierce proscription of the Gothic laws. As the Spanish kingdoms organized themselves, the Fuero Juzgo for the most part was superseded by a crowd of local fueros, cartas-pueblas and customs defining the franchises of each community, and we have seen in the preceding chapter how in these both Moor and Jew were recognized as sharing in the common rights of citizenship and how fully the freedom of trade between all classes was permitted. In 1251 the Fuero Juzgo was formally abrogated in Aragon by Jaime I, who forbade it to be cited in the courts--a measure which infers that it had practically become obsolete.[250] In Castile it lingered somewhat longer and traces of its existence are to be found in some places until the end of the thirteenth century.[251] These, however, are not to be construed as referring to the provisions respecting Jews, which had long been superseded.

In fact, the Jews formed too large and important a portion of the population to be treated without consideration. The sovereigns, involved permanently in struggles with the Saracen and with mutinous nobles, found it necessary to utilize all the resources at their command, whether in money, intelligence, or military service. In the first two of these the Jews stood pre-eminent, nor were they remiss in the latter. On the disastrous field of Zalaca, in 1086, forty thousand Jews are said to have followed the banner of Alfonso VI, and the slaughter they endured proved their devotion, while, at the defeat of Ucles in 1108, they composed nearly the whole left wing of the Castilian host.[252] In 1285 we hear of Jews and Moors aiding the Aragonese in their assaults on the retreating forces of Philippe le Hardi.[253] As regards money, the traffic and finance of Spain were largely in their hands, and they furnished, with the Moors, the readiest source from which to derive revenue. Every male who had married, or who had reached the age of 20, paid an annual poll tax of three gold maravedís; there were also a number of imposts peculiar to them, and, in addition, they shared with the rest of the population in the complicated and ruinous system of taxation--the ordinary and extraordinary servicios, the pedidas and ayudas, the sacos and pastos and the alcavalas. Besides this they assisted in supporting the municipalities or the lordships and prelacies under which they lived, with the tallas, the pastos, the ninths or elevenths of merchandise and the peajes and barcajes, the pontazgos and portazgos, or tolls of various kinds which were heavier on them than on Christians, and, moreover, the Church received from them the customary tithes, oblations, and first-fruits.²⁵⁴ The revenues from the Jewish aljamas, or communities, were always regarded as among the surest resources of the crown.

The shrewd intelligence and practical ability of the Jews, moreover, rendered their services in public affairs almost indispensable. It was in vain that the council of Rome, in 1078, renewed the old prohibitions to confide to them functions which would place them in command over Christians and equally in vain that, in 1081, Gregory VII addressed to Alfonso VI a vehement remonstrance on the subject, assuring him that to do so was to oppress the Church of God and exalt the synagogue of Satan, and that in seeking to please the enemies of Christ he was contemning Christ himself.²⁵⁵ In fact, the most glorious centuries of the Reconquest were those in which the Jews enjoyed the greatest power in the courts of kings, prelates and nobles, in Castile and Aragon. The treasuries of the kingdoms were virtually in their hands, and it was their skill in organizing the supplies that rendered practicable the enterprises of such monarchs as Alfonso VI and VII, Fernando III and Jaime I.²⁵⁶ To treat them as the Goths had done, or as the Church prescribed, had become a manifest impossibility.

Under such circumstances it was natural that their numbers should increase until they formed a notable portion of the population. Of this an estimate can be made from a repartimiento, or assessment of taxes, in 1284, which shows that in Castile they paid a poll tax of 2,561,855 gold maravedís, which at three maravedís per head infers a total of 853,951 married or adult males.²⁵⁷ This large aggregate was thoroughly organized. Each aljama or community had its rabbis with a Rabb Mayor at its head. Then each district, comprising one or more Christian bishoprics, was presided over by a Rabb Mayor, and, above all, was the Gaon or Nassi, the prince, whose duty it was to see that the laws of the race, both civil and religious, were observed in their purity.²⁵⁸ As we have already seen, all questions between themselves were settled before their own judges under their own code, and even when a Jew was prosecuted criminally by the king, he was punishable in accordance with his own law.²⁵⁹ So complete was the respect paid to this that their Sabbaths and other feasts were held inviolate; on these days they could not be summoned to court or be interfered with except by arrest for crime. Even polygamy was allowed to them.²⁶⁰

While their religion and laws were thus respected, they were required to respect Christianity. They were not allowed to read or keep books contrary to their own law or to the Christian law. Proselytism from Christianity was punishable by death and confiscation, and any insults offered to God, the Virgin, or the saints, were visited with a fine of ten maravedís or a hundred lashes.²⁶¹ Yet, if we are to believe the indignant Lucas of Tuy, writing about 1230, these simple restraints were scarce enforced. The heretic Cathari of Leon, he tells us, were wont to circumcise themselves in order, under the guise of Jews, to propound heretical dogmas and dispute with Christians; what they dared not utter as heretics they could freely disseminate as Jews. The governors and judges of the cities listened approvingly to heresies put forth by Jews, who were their friends and familiars, and if any one, inflamed by pious zeal, angered these Jews, he was treated as if he had touched the apple of the eye of the ruler; they also taught other Jews to blaspheme Christ and thus the Catholic faith was perverted.²⁶²

This represents a laxity of toleration impossible in any other land at the period, yet the Spanish Jews were not wholly shielded from inroads of foreign fanaticism. Before the crusading spirit had been organized for the conquest of the Holy Land, ardent knights sometimes came to wage war with the Spanish Saracens, and their religious fervor was aggrieved by the freedom enjoyed by the Jews. About 1068, bands of these strangers treated them as they had been wont to do at home, slaying and plundering them without mercy. The Church of Spain was as yet uncontaminated by race hatred and the bishops interposed to save the victims. For this they were warmly praised by Alexander II, who denounced the crusaders as acting either from foolish ignorance or blind cupidity. Those whom they would slay, he said, were perhaps predestined by God to salvation; he cited Gregory I to the same effect and pointed out the difference between Jews and Saracens, the latter of whom make war on Christians and could justly be assailed.²⁶³ Had the chair of St. Peter always been so worthily filled, infinite misery might have been averted and the history of Christendom been spared some of its most repulsive pages.

When the crusading spirit extended to Spain, it sometimes aroused similar tendencies. In 1108, Archbishop Bernardo of Toledo took the cross and religious exaltation was ardent. The disastrous rout of Ucles came and was popularly ascribed to the Jews in the Castilian army, arousing indignation which manifested itself in a massacre at Toledo and in the burning of synagogues. Alfonso VI vainly endeavored to detect and punish those responsible and his death, in 1109, was followed by similar outrages which remained unavenged.²⁶⁴ This was a sporadic outburst which soon exhausted itself. A severer trial came from abroad, when, in 1210, the Legate Arnaud of Narbonne led his crusading hosts to the assistance of Alfonso IX. Although their zeal for the faith was exhausted by the capture of Calatrava and few of them remained to share in the crowning glories of Las Navas de Tolosa, their ardor was sufficient to prompt an onslaught on the unoffending Jews. The native nobles sought in vain to protect the victims, who were massacred without mercy, so that Abravanel declares this to have been one of the bloodiest persecutions that they had suffered and that more Jews fled from Spain than Moses led out of Egypt.²⁶⁵

This had no permanent influence on the condition of the Spanish Hebrews. During the long reigns of San Fernando III and Alfonso X of Castile and of Jaime I of Aragon, covering the greater part of the thirteenth century, the services which they rendered to the monarchs were repaid with increasing favor and protection. After Jaime had conquered Minorca he took, in 1247, all Jews settling there under the royal safeguard and threatened a fine of a thousand gold pieces for wrong inflicted on any of them and, in 1250, he required that Jewish as well as Christian testimony must be furnished in all actions, civil or criminal, brought by Christians against Jews. So, when in 1306 Philippe le Bel expelled the Jews from France and those of Majorca feared the same fate, Jaime II reassured them by pledging the royal faith that they should remain forever in the land, with full security for person and property, a pledge confirmed, in 1311, by his son and successor Sancho.[266] In Castile, when San Fernando conquered Seville, in 1244, he gave to the Jews a large space in the city, and, in defiance of the canons, he allotted to them four Moorish mosques to be converted into synagogues, thus founding the aljama of Seville, destined to a history so deplorable. Alfonso X, during his whole reign, patronized Jewish men of learning, whom he employed in translating works of value from Arabic and Hebrew; he built for them an observatory in Seville, where were made the records embodied in the Alfonsine Tables; he permitted those of Toledo to erect the magnificent synagogue now known as Santa María la Blanca, and Jews fondly relate that the Hebrew school, which he transferred from Córdova to Toledo, numbered twelve thousand students.[267] He was prompt to maintain their privileges, and, when the Jews of Burgos complained that in mixed suits the alcaldes would grant appeals to him when the Christian suitor was defeated, while refusing them to defeated Jews, he at once put an end to the discrimination, a decree which Sancho IV enforced with a penalty of a hundred maravedís when, in 1295, the complaint was repeated.[268] Yet Alfonso, in his systematic code known as the Partidas, which was not confirmed by the Córtes until 1348, allowed himself to be influenced by the teachings of the Church and the maxims of the imperial jurisprudence. He accepted the doctrine of the canons that the Jew was merely suffered to live in captivity among Christians; he was forbidden to speak ill of the Christian faith, and any attempt at proselytism was punished with death and confiscation. The murder rite was alluded to as a rumor, but in case it was practised it was a capital offence and the culprits were to be tried before the king himself. Jews were ineligible to any office in which they could oppress Christians; they were forbidden to have Christian servants, and the purchase of a Christian slave involved the death punishment. They were not to associate with Christians in eating, drinking, and bathing and the amour of a Jew with a Christian woman incurred death. While Jewish physicians might prescribe for Christian patients, the medicine must be compounded by a Christian, and the wearing of the hateful distinctive badge was ordered under penalty of ten gold maravedís or of ten lashes. At the same time Christians were strictly forbidden to commit any wrong on the person or property of Jews or to interfere in any way with their religious observances, and no coercion was to be used to induce them to baptism, for Christ wishes only willing service.[269]

ATTEMPTS AT CONVERSION

This was prophetic of evil days in the future and the reign of Alfonso proved to be the culminating point of Jewish prosperity. The capital and commerce of the land were to a great extent in their hands; they managed its finances and collected its revenues. King, noble and prelate entrusted their affairs to Jews, whose influence consequently was felt everywhere. To precipitate them from this position to the servitude prescribed by the canons required a prolonged struggle and may be said to have taken its remote origin in an attempt at their conversion. In 1263 the Dominican Fray Pablo Christiá, a converted Jew, challenged the greatest rabbi of the day, Moseh aben Najman, to a disputation which was presided over by Jaime I in his Barcelona palace. Each champion of course boasted of victory; the king dismissed Nachmanides not only with honor but with the handsome reward of three hundred pieces of gold, but he ordered certain Jewish books to be burnt and blasphemous passages in the Talmud to be expunged.[270] He further issued a decree ordering all his faithful Jews to assemble and listen reverently to Fray Pablo whenever he desired to dispute with them, to furnish him with what books he desired, and to defray his expenses, which they could deduct from their tribute.[271] Two years later Fray Pablo challenged another prominent Hebrew, the Rabbi Ben-Astruch, chief of the synagogue of Gerona, who refused until he had the pledge of King Jaime, and of the great Dominican St. Ramon de Peñafort, that he should not be held accountable for what he might utter in debate, but when, at the request of the Bishop of Gerona, Ben-Astruch wrote out his argument, the frailes Pablo and Ramon accused him of blasphemy, for it was manifestly impossible that a Jew could defend his strict monotheism and Messianic belief without a course of reasoning that would appear blasphemous to susceptible theologians. The rabbi alleged the royal pledge; Jaime proposed that he should be banished for two years and his book be burnt, but this did not satisfy the Dominican frailes and he dismissed the matter, forbidding the prosecution of the rabbi except before himself. Appeal seems to have been made to Clement IV, who addressed King Jaime in wrathful mood, blaming him for the favor shown to Jews and ordering him to deprive them of office and to depress and trample on them; Ben-Astruch especially, he said, should be made an example without, however, mutilating or slaying him.[272] This explosion of papal indignation fell harmless, but the zeal of the Dominicans had been inflamed and in laboring for the conversion of the Jews they not unnaturally aroused antagonism toward those who refused to abandon their faith. So long before as 1242, Jaime had issued an edict, confirmed by Innocent IV in 1245, empowering the Mendicant friars to have free access to Juderías and Morerías, to assemble the inhabitants and compel them to listen to sermons intended for their conversion.[273] The Dominicans now availed themselves of this with such vigor and excited such hostility to the Jews that Jaime was obliged to step forward for their protection. He assured the aljamas that they were not accountable for what was contained in their books, unless it was to the dishonor of Christ, the Virgin and the saints, and all accusations must be submitted to him in person; their freedom of trade was not to be curtailed; meat slaughtered by them could be freely exposed for sale in the Juderías, but not elsewhere; dealing in skins was not to be interfered with; their synagogues and cemeteries were to be subject to their exclusive control; their right to receive interest on loans was not to be impaired nor their power to collect debts; they were not to be compelled to listen to the friars outside of their Juderías, because otherwise they were liable to insult and dishonor, nor were the frailes when preaching in the synagogues to be accompanied by disorderly mobs, but at most by ten discreet Christians; finally, no novel limitations were to be imposed on them except by royal command after hearing them in opposition.[274]

These provisions indicate the direction in which Dominican zeal was striving to curtail the privileges so long enjoyed by the Jews and the royal intention to protect them against local legislation, which had doubtless been attempted under this impulsion. They were not remiss in gratitude, for when, in 1274, Jaime attended the council of Lyons, they contributed seventy-one thousand sueldos to enable him to appear with fitting magnificence.[275] The royal protection was speedily needed, for the tide of persecuting zeal was rising among the clergy and, shortly after his return from Lyons, on a Good Friday, the ecclesiastics of Gerona rang the bells, summoned the populace and attacked the Judería, which was one of the largest and most flourishing in Catalonia. They would have succeeded in destroying it but for the interposition of Jaime, who chanced to be in the city and who defended the Jews with force of arms.[276]

CONVERSION AND PERSECUTION

After the death of Jaime, in 1276, the ecclesiastics seem to have thought that they could safely obey the commands of Clement IV, especially as Nicholas IV, in 1278, instructed the Dominican general to depute pious brethren everywhere to convoke the Jews and labor for their conversion, with the significant addition that lists of those refusing baptism were to be made out and submitted to him, when he would determine what was to be done with them.[277] How the frailes interpreted the papal utterances is indicated in a letter of Pedro III to Pedro Bishop of Gerona, in April of this same year, 1278, reciting that he had already appealed repeatedly to him to put an end to the assaults of the clergy on the Jews, and now he learns that they have again attacked the Judería, stoning it from the tower of the cathedral and from their own houses and then assaulting it, laying waste the gardens and vineyards of the Jews and even destroying their graves and, when the royal herald stood up to forbid the work, drowning his voice with yells and derisions. Pedro accuses the bishop of stimulating the clergy to these outrages and orders him to put a stop to it and punish the offenders.[278] He was still more energetic when the French crusade under Philippe le Hardi was advancing to the siege of Gerona, in 1285, and his Moorish soldiers in the garrison undertook to sack the Call Juhich, or Judería, when he threw himself among them, mace in hand, struck down a number and finished by hanging several of them.[279] He offered no impediment, however, to the conversion of the Jews for, in 1279, he ordered his officials to compel them to listen to the Franciscans, who, in obedience to the commands of the pope, might wish to preach to them in their synagogues.[280] These intrusions of frailes into the Juderías inevitably led to trouble, for there is significance in a letter of Jaime II, April 4, 1305, to his representative in Palma, alluding to recent scandals, for the future prevention of which he orders that no priest shall enter the Judería to administer the sacraments without being accompanied by a secular official. This precaution was unavailing, for it doubtless was a continuance of such provocation that led to a disturbance, about 1315, affording to King Jaime an excuse for confiscating the whole property of the aljama of Palma and then commuting the penalty to a fine of 95,000 libras. The source of these troubles is suggested by a royal order of 1327 to the Governor of Majorca, forbidding the baptism of Jewish children under seven years of age or the forcible baptism of Jews of any age.[281]

During all this period there had been an Inquisition in Aragon which, of course, could not interfere with Jews as such, for they were beyond its jurisdiction, but which stood ready to punish more or less veritable efforts at propagandism or offences of fautorship. The crown had no objection to using it as a means of extortion, while preventing it from exterminating or crippling subjects so useful. A diploma of Jaime II, October 14, 1311, recites that the inquisitor, Fray Juan Llotger, had learned that the aljamas of

Barcelona, Tarragona, Monblanch and Vilafranca had harbored and fed certain Jewish converts, who had relapsed to Judaism, as well as others who had come from foreign parts. He had given Fray Juan the necessary support, enabling him to verify the accusations on the spot and had received his report to that effect. Now, therefore, he issues a free and full pardon to the offending aljamas, with assurance that they shall not be prosecuted either civilly or criminally, for which grace, on October 10th, they had paid him ten thousand sueldos. In this case there seems to have been no regular trial by the Inquisition, the king having superseded it by his action. In another more serious case he intervened after trial and sentence to commute the punishment. In 1326 the aljama of Calatayud subjected itself to the Inquisition by not only receiving back a woman who had been baptized but by circumcising two Christians. Tried by the inquisitor and the Bishop of Tarazona it had been found guilty and it had been sentenced to a fine of twenty thousand sueldos and its members to confiscation, but King Jaime, by a cédula of February 6, 1326, released them from the confiscation and all other penalties on payment of the fine.[282]

***

CURTAILMENT OF PRIVILEGES

Although Castile was slower than Aragon to receive impulses from abroad, in the early fourteenth century we begin to find traces of a similar movement of the Church against the Jews. In 1307 the aljama of Toledo complained to Fernando IV that the dean and chapter had obtained from Clement V bulls conferring on them jurisdiction over Jews, in virtue of which they were enforcing the canons against usury and stripping the Jewish community of its property. At this time there was no question in Spain, such as we shall see debated hereafter, of the royal prerogative to control obnoxious papal letters, and Fernando at once ordered the chapter to surrender the bulls; all action under them was pronounced void and restitution in double was threatened for all damage inflicted. The Jews, he said, were his Jews; they were not to be incapacitated from paying their taxes and the pope had no power to infringe on the rights of the crown. He instructed Ferran Nuñez de Pantoja to compel obedience and, after some offenders had been arrested, the frightened canons surrendered the bulls and abandoned their promising speculation, but the affair left behind it enmities which displayed themselves deplorably afterwards.[283]

In spite of the royal favor and protection, the legislation of the period commences to manifest a tendency to limit the privileges of the Jews, showing that popular sentiment was gradually turning against them. As early as 1286 Sancho IV agreed to deprive them of their special judges and, though the law was not generally enforced, it indicates the spirit that called for it and procured its repetition in the Córtes of Valladolid in 1307.[284] Complaints were loud and numerous of the Jewish tax-gatherers, and the young Fernando IV was obliged repeatedly to promise that the revenues should not be farmed out nor their collection be entrusted to caballeros, ecclesiastics or Jews. The turbulence which attended his minority and short reign and the minority of his son, Alfonso XI, afforded a favorable opportunity for the manifestation of hostility and the royal power was too weak to prevent the curtailment in various directions of the Jewish privileges.[285] We have seen, in the preceding chapter, the temper in which the Spanish prelates returned from the Council of Vienne in 1312 and the proscriptive legislation enacted by them in the Council of Zamora in 1313 and its successors. Everything favored the development of this spirit of intolerance, and at the Córtes of Burgos, in 1315, the regents of the young Alfonso XI conceded that the Clementine canon, abrogating all laws that permitted usury, should be enforced, that all mixed actions, civil and criminal, should be tried by the royal judges, that the evidence of a Jew should not be received against a Christian while that of a Christian was good against a Jew, that Jews were not to assume Christian names, Christian nurses were not to suckle Jews and sumptuary laws were directed against the luxury of Jewish vestments.[286]

This may be said to mark the commencement of the long struggle which, in spite of their wonderful powers of resistance, was to end in the destruction of the Spanish Jews. Throughout the varying phases of the conflict, the Church, in its efforts to arouse popular hatred, was powerfully aided by the odium which the Jews themselves excited through their ostentation, their usury and their functions as public officials.

A strong race is not apt to be an amiable one. The Jews were proud of their ancient lineage and the purity of their descent from the kings and heroes of the Old Testament. A man who could trace his ancestry to David would look with infinite scorn on the hidalgos who boasted of the blood of Lain Calvo and, if the favor of the monarch rendered safe the expression of his feelings, his haughtiness was not apt to win friends among those who repaid his contempt with interest. The Oriental fondness for display was a grievous offence among the people. The wealth of the kingdom was, to a great extent, in Jewish hands, affording ample opportunity of contrast between their magnificence and the poverty of the Christian multitude, and the lavish extravagance with which they adorned themselves, their women and their retainers, was well fitted to excite envy more potent for evil because more wide-spread than enmity arising from individual wrongs.[287] Shortly before the catastrophe, at the close of the fifteenth century, Affonso V of Portugal, who was well-affected towards them, asked the chief rabbi, Joseph-Ibn-Jachia, why he did not prevent his people from a display provocative of the assertion that their wealth was derived from robbery of the Christians, adding that he required no answer, for nothing save spoliation and massacre would cure them of it.[288]

CAUSES OF ENMITY

A more practical and far-reaching cause of enmity was the usury, through which a great portion of their wealth was acquired. The money-lender has everywhere been an unpopular character and, in the Middle Ages, he was especially so. When the Church pronounced any interest or any advantage, direct or indirect, derived from loans to be a sin for which the sinner could not be admitted to penance without making restitution; when the justification of taking interest was regarded as a heresy to be punished as such by the Inquisition, a stigma was placed on the money-lender, his gains were rendered hazardous, and his calling became one which an honorable Christian could not follow.[289] Mercantile Italy early outgrew these dogmas which retarded so greatly all material development and it managed to reconcile, per fas et nefas, the canons with the practical necessities of business, but elsewhere throughout Europe, wherever Jews were allowed to exist, the lending of money or goods on interest inevitably fell, for the most part, into their hands, for they were governed by their own moral code and were not subject to the Church. It exhausted all devices to coerce them through their rulers, but the object aimed at was too incompatible with the necessities of advancing civilization to have any influence save the indefinite postponement of relief to the borrower.[290]

The unsavoriness of the calling, its risks and the scarcity of coin during the Middle Ages, conspired to render the current rates of interest exorbitantly oppressive. In Aragon the Jews were allowed to charge 20 per cent. per annum, in Castile 33-1/3,[291] and the constant repetition of these limitations and the provisions against all manner of ingenious devices, by fictitious sales and other frauds, to obtain an illegal increase, show how little the laws were respected in the grasping avarice with which the Jews speculated on the necessities of their customers.[292] In 1326 the aljama of Cuenca, considering the legal rate of 33-1/3 per cent. too low, refused absolutely to lend either money or wheat for the sowing. This caused great distress and the town-council entered into negotiations, resulting in an agreement by which the Jews were authorized to charge 40 per cent.[293] In 1385 the Córtes of Valladolid describe one cause of the necessity of submitting to whatever exactions the Jews saw fit to impose, when it says that the new lords, to whom Henry of Trastamara had granted towns and villages, were accustomed to imprison their vassals and starve and torture them to force payment of what they had not got, obliging them to get money from Jews to whom they gave whatever bonds were demanded.[294] Monarchs as well as peasants were subject to these impositions. In Navarre, a law of Felipe III, in 1330, limited the rate of interest to 20 per cent. and we find this paid by his grandson, Carlos III, in 1399, for a loan of 1000 florins but, in 1401, he paid at the rate of 35 per cent. for a loan of 2000 florins, and in 1402 his queen, Doña Leonor, borrowed 70 florins from her Jewish physician Abraham at four florins a month, giving him silver plate as security; finding at the end of twenty-one months that the interest amounted to 84 florins, she begged a reduction and he contented himself with 30 florins.[295]

When money could be procured in no other way, when the burgher had to raise it to pay his taxes or the extortions of his lord and the husbandman had to procure seed-corn or starve, it is easy to see how all had to submit to the exactions of the money-lender; how, in spite of occasional plunder and scaling of debts, the Jews absorbed the floating capital of the community and how recklessly they aided the frailes in concentrating popular detestation on themselves. It was in vain that the Ordenamiento de Alcalá, in 1348, prohibited usury to Moors and Jews as well as to Christians; it was an inevitable necessity and it continued to flourish.[296]

Equally effective in arousing antipathy were the functions of the Jews as holders of office and especially as almojarifes and recabdores--farmers of the revenues and collectors of taxes, which brought them into the closest and most exasperating relations with the people. In that age of impoverished treasuries and rude financial expedients, the customary mode of raising funds was by farming out the revenues to the highest bidder of specific sums; as the profit of the speculation depended on the amount to be wrung from the people, the subordinate collectors would be merciless in exaction and indefatigable in tracing out delinquents, exciting odium which extended to all the race. It was in vain that the Church repeatedly prohibited the employment of Jews in public office. Their ability and skill rendered them indispensable to monarchs, nobles, and prelates, and the complaints which arose against them on all sides were useless. Thus in the quarrel between the chapter of Toledo and the great Archbishop Rodrigo, in which the former appealed to Gregory IX, in 1236, one of the grievances alleged is that he appointed Jews to be provosts of the common table of the chapter, thus enabling them to defraud the canons; they even passed through the church and often entered the chapter-house itself to the great scandal of all Christians; they collected the tithes and thirds and governed the vassals and possessions of the Church, greatly enriching themselves by plundering the patrimony of the Crucified, wherefore the pope was earnestly prayed to expel the Jews from these offices and compel them to make restitution.[297]

When prelates such as Archbishop Rodrigo paid so little heed to the commands of the Church, it is not to be supposed that monarchs were more obedient or were disposed to forego the advantages derivable from the services of these accomplished financiers. How these men assisted their masters while enriching themselves is exemplified by Don Çag de la Maleha, almojarife mayor to Alfonso X. When the king, in 1257, was raising an army to subdue Aben-Nothfot, King of Niebla, Don Çag undertook to defray all the expenses of the campaign in consideration of the assignment to him of certain taxes, some of which he was still enjoying in 1272.[298] It was useless for the people who groaned under the exactions of these efficient officials to protest against their employment and to extort from the monarchs repeated promises no longer to employ them. The promises were never kept and, until the reign of Ferdinand and Isabella, this source of irritation continued. There was, it is true, one exception, the result of which was not conducive to a continuance of the experiment. In 1385 the Córtes of Valladolid obtained from Juan I a decree prohibiting the employment of Jews as tax-collectors, not only by the king but also by prelates and nobles, in consequence of which ecclesiastics obtained the collection of the royal revenues, but when they were called upon to settle they excommunicated the alcaldes who sought to compel payment, leading to great confusion and bitterer complaints than ever.[299]

When the Jews thus gave grounds so ample for popular dislike, it says much for the kindly feeling between the races that the efforts of the Church to excite a spirit of intolerance made progress so slow. These took form, as a comprehensive and systematic movement at the Council of Zamora, in 1313, and its successors, described in the preceding chapter, but in spite of them Alfonso XI continued to protect his Jewish subjects and the labors of the good fathers awoke no popular response. In Aragon a canon of the Council of Lérida, in 1325, forbidding Christians to be present at Jewish weddings and circumcisions, shows how fruitless as yet had been the effort to produce mutual alienation.[300]

THE BLACK DEATH

Navarre had the earliest foretaste of the wrath to come. It was then under its French princes and, when Charles le Bel died, February 1, 1328, a zealous Franciscan, Fray Pedro Olligoyen, apparently taking advantage of the interregnum, stirred, with his eloquent preaching, the people to rise against the Jews, and led them to pillage and slaughter. The storm burst on the aljama of Estella, March 1st, and rapidly spread throughout the kingdom. Neither age nor sex was spared and the number of victims is variously estimated at from six to ten thousand. Queen Jeanne and her husband Philippe d'Evreux, who succeeded to the throne, caused Olligoyen to be prosecuted, but the result is not known. They further speculated on the terrible massacre by imposing heavy fines on Estella and Viana and by seizing the property of the dead and fugitive Jews, and they also levied on the ruined aljamas the sum of fifteen thousand livres to defray their coronation expenses. Thus fatally weakened, the Jews of Navarre were unable to endure the misfortunes of the long and disastrous reign of Charles le Mauvais (1350-1387). A general emigration resulted, to arrest which Charles prohibited the purchase of landed property from Jews without special royal license. A list of taxables, in 1366, shows only 453 Jewish families and 150 Moorish, not including Pampeluna, where both races were taxable by the bishop. Although Charles and his son Charles le Noble (1387-1425) had Jews for almojarifes, it was in vain that they endeavored to allure the fugitives back by privileges and exemptions. The aljamas continued to dwindle until the revenue from them was inconsiderable.[301]

In Castile and Aragon the Black Death caused massacres of Jews, as elsewhere throughout Europe, though not so wide-spread and terrible. In Catalonia the troubles commenced at Barcelona and spread to other places, in spite of the efforts of Pedro IV, both in prevention and punishment. They had little special religious significance, but were rather the result of the relaxation of social order in the fearful disorganization accompanying the pestilence and, after it had passed, the survivors, Christians, Jews and Mudéjares were for a moment knit more closely together in the bonds of a common humanity.[302] It is to the credit of Clement VI that he did what he could to arrest the fanaticism which, especially in Germany, offered to the Jews the alternative of death or baptism. Following, as he said, in the footsteps of Calixtus II, Eugenius III, Alexander III, Clement III, Coelestin III, Innocent III, Gregory IX, Nicholas III, Honorius IV and Nicholas IV, he pointed out the absurdity of attributing the plague to the Jews. They had offered to submit to judicial examination and sentence, besides which the pestilence raged in lands where there were no Jews. He therefore ordered all prelates to proclaim to the people assembled for worship that Jews were not to be beaten, wounded, or slain and that those who so treated them were subjected to the anathema of the Holy See. It was a timely warning and worthy of one who spoke in the name of Christ, but it availed little to overcome the influence of the assiduous teaching of intolerance through so many centuries.[303]

INCREASING HOSTILITY

When Pedro the Cruel ascended the throne of Castile, in 1350, the Jews might reasonably look forward to a prosperous future, but his reign in reality proved the turning-point in their fortunes. He surrounded himself with Jews and confided to them the protection of his person, while the rebellious faction, headed by Henry of Trastamara, his illegitimate brother, declared themselves the enemies of the race and used Pedro's favor for them as a political weapon. He was asserted to be a Jew, substituted for a girl born of Queen María whose husband, Alfonso XI, was said to have sworn that he would kill her if she did not give him a boy. It was also reported that he was no Christian but an adherent to the Law of Moses and that the government of Castile was wholly in the hands of Jews. It was not difficult therefore to arouse clerical hostility, as manifested by Urban V, who denounced him as a rebel to the Church, a fautor of Jews and Moors, a propagator of infidelity and a slayer of Christians.[304] Of this the insurgents took full advantage and demonstrated their piety in the most energetic manner. When, in 1355, Henry of Trastamara and his brother, the Master of Santiago, entered Toledo to liberate Queen Blanche, who was confined in the alcázar, they sacked the smaller Judería and slew its twelve hundred inmates without sparing sex or age. They also besieged the principal Judería, which was walled around and defended by Pedro's followers until his arrival with reinforcements drove off the assailants.[305] Five years later when, in 1360, Henry of Trastamara invaded Castile with the aid of Pedro IV of Aragon, on reaching Najara he ordered a massacre of the Jews and, as Ayala states that this was done to win popularity, it may be assumed that free license for pillage was granted. Apparently stimulated by this example the people of Miranda del Ebro, led by Pero Martínez, son of the precentor and by Pero Sánchez de Bañuelas, fell upon the Jews of their town, but King Pedro hastened thither and, as a deterrent example, boiled the one leader and roasted the other.[306] When at length, in 1366, Henry led into Spain Bertrand de Guesclin and his hordes of Free Companions, the slaughter of the Jews was terrible. Multitudes fled and the French chronicler deplores the number that sought refuge in Paris and preyed upon the people with their usuries. The aljama of Toledo purchased exemption with a million of maravedís, raised in ten days, to pay off the mercenaries but, as the whole land lay for a time at the mercy of the reckless bands, slaughter and pillage were general. Finally the fratricide at Montiel, in 1369, deprived the Jews of their protector and left Henry undisputed master of Castile.[307] What they had to expect from him was indicated by his levying, June 6, 1369, within three months of his brother's murder, twenty thousand doblas on the Judería of Toledo and authorizing the sale at auction, not only of the property of the inmates, but of their persons into slavery, or their imprisonment in chains with starvation or torture, until the amount should be raised. It was doubtless to earn popularity that about the same time he released all Christians and Moors from obligation to pay debts due to Jews, though he was subsequently persuaded to rescind this decree, which would have destroyed the ability of the Jews to pay their imposts.[308]

Yet the Jews were indispensable in the conduct of affairs and Henry was obliged to employ them, like his predecessors. His contador mayor was Yuçaf Pichon, a Jew of the highest consideration, who incurred the enmity of some of the leaders of his people. They accused him to the king, who demanded of him forty thousand doblas, which sum he paid within twenty days. With rancor unsatisfied, when Henry died, in 1379, and his son Juan I came to Burgos to be crowned, they obtained from him an order to his alguazil to put to death a mischief-making Jew whom they would designate. Armed with this they took the alguazil to Pichon's house in the early morning, called him on some pretext from his bed and pointed him out as the designated person to the alguazil, who killed him on the spot. Juan was greatly angered; the alguazil was punished with the loss of a hand, the judge of the Judería of Burgos was put to death and the Jews of Castile were deprived of jurisdiction over the lives of their fellows.[309]

We have already seen how the legislation of this period was rapidly taking a direction unfavorable to the Jews. The accession of the House of Trastamara had distinctly injured their position, the Church had freer scope to excite popular prejudice, while their retention as tax-collectors and their usurious practices afforded ample material for the stimulation of popular vindicativeness. The condition existed for a catastrophe, and the man to precipitate it was not lacking. Ferran Martínez, Archdeacon of Ecija and Official, or judicial representative of the Archbishop of Seville, Pedro Barroso, was a man of indomitable firmness and, though without much learning, was highly esteemed for his unusual devoutness, his solid virtue and his eminent charity--which latter quality he evinced in founding and supporting the hospital of Santa María in Seville.[310] Unfortunately he was a fanatic and the Jews were the object of his remorseless zeal, which his high official position gave him ample opportunity of gratifying. In his sermons he denounced them savagely and excited popular passion against them, keeping them in constant apprehension of an outbreak while, as ecclesiastical judge, he extended his jurisdiction illegally over them, to their frequent damage. In conjunction with other episcopal officials he issued letters to the magistrates of the towns ordering them to expel the Jews--letters which he sought to enforce by personal visitations. The aljama of Seville, the largest and richest in Castile, appealed to the king and, little as Henry of Trastamara loved the Jews, the threatened loss to his finances led him, in

August, 1378, to formally command Martínez to desist from his incendiary course, nor was this the first warning, as is shown by allusions to previous letters of the same import. To this Martínez paid no obedience and the aljama had recourse to Rome, where it procured bulls for its protection, which Martínez disregarded as contemptuously as he had the royal mandate. Complaint was again made to the throne and Juan I, in 1382, repeated his father's commands to no effect, for another royal letter of 1383 accuses Martínez of saying in his sermons that he knew the king would regard as a service any assault or slaying of the Jews and that impunity might be relied upon. For this he was threatened with punishment that would make an example of him, but it did not silence him and, in 1388, the frightened aljama summoned him before the alcaldes and had the three royal letters read, summoning him to obey them. He replied with insults and, a week later, put in a formal answer in which he said that he was but obeying Christ and the laws and that, if he were to execute the laws, he would tear down the twenty-three synagogues in Seville as they had all been illegally erected.[311]

THE MASSACRES OF 1391

The dean and chapter became alarmed and appealed to the king, but Juan, in place of enforcing his neglected commands, replied that he would look into the matter; the zeal of the archdeacon was holy, but it must not be allowed to breed disturbance for, although the Jews were wicked, they were under the royal protection. This vacillation encouraged Martínez who labored still more strenuously to inflame the people, newly prejudiced against the Jews by the murder of Yuçaf Pichon, who had been greatly beloved by all Seville.[312] No one dared to interfere in their defence, but Martínez furnished an opportunity of silencing him by calling in question in his sermons the powers of the pope in certain matters. He was summoned before an assembly of theologians and doctors, when he was as defiant of the episcopal authority as of the royal, rendering himself contumacious and suspect of heresy, wherefore on August 2, 1389, Archbishop Barroso suspended him both as to jurisdiction and preaching until his trial should be concluded.[313] This gave the Jews a breathing-space, but Barroso died, July 7, 1390, followed, October 9, by Juan I. The chapter must have secretly sympathized with Martínez, for it elected him one of the provisors of the diocese sede vacante, thus clothing him with increased power, and we hear nothing more of the trial for heresy.[314]

Juan had left as his successor Henry III, known as El Doliente, or the Invalid, a child of eleven, and quarrels threatening civil war at once arose over the question of the regency. Martínez now had nothing to fear and he lost no time in sending, December 8th, to the clergy of the towns in the diocese, commands under pain of excommunication to tear down within three hours the synagogues of the enemies of God calling themselves Jews; the building materials were to be used for the repair of the churches; if resistance was offered it was to be suppressed by force and an interdict be laid on the town until the good work was accomplished.[315] These orders were not universally obeyed but enough ruin was wrought to lead the frightened aljama of Seville to appeal to the regency, threatening to leave the land if they could not be protected from Martínez. The answer to this was prompt and decided. On December 22d a missive was addressed to the dean and chapter and was officially read to them, January 10, 1391. It held them responsible for his acts as they had elected him provisor and had not checked him; he must be at once removed from office, be forced to abstain from preaching and to rebuild the ruined synagogues, in default of which they must make good all damages and incur a fine of a thousand gold doblas each with other arbitrary punishments. Letters of similar import were addressed at the same time to Martínez himself. On January 15th the chapter again assembled and presented its official reply, which deprived Martínez of the provisorship, forbade him to preach against the Jews and required him within a year to rebuild all synagogues destroyed by his orders. Then Martínez arose and protested that neither king nor chapter had jurisdiction over him and their sentences were null and void. The synagogues had been destroyed by order of Archbishop Barroso--two of them in his lifetime--and they had been built illegally without licence. His defiant answer concluded with a declaration that he repented of nothing that he had done.[316]

The result justified the dauntless reliance of Martínez on the popular passion which he had been stimulating for so many years. What answer the regency made to this denial of its jurisdiction the documents fail to inform us, but no effective steps were taken to restrain him. His preaching continued as violent as ever and the Seville mob grew more and more restless in the prospect of gratifying at once its zeal for the faith and its thirst for pillage. In March the aspect of affairs was more alarming than ever; the rabble were feeling their way, with outrages and insults, and the Judería was in hourly danger of being sacked. Juan Alonso Guzman, Count of Niebla, the most powerful noble of Andalusia, was adelantado of the province and alcalde mayor of Seville and his kinsman, Alvar Pérez de Guzman, was alguazil mayor. On March 15th they seized some of the most turbulent of the crowd and proceeded to scourge two of them but, in place of awing the populace, this led to open sedition. The Guzmans were glad to escape with their lives and popular fury was directed against the Jews, resulting in considerable bloodshed and plunder, but at length the authorities, aided by the nobles, prevailed and order was apparently restored. By this time the agitation was spreading to Córdova, Toledo, Burgos and other places. Everywhere fanaticism and greed were aroused and the Council of Regency vainly sent pressing commands to all the large cities, in the hope of averting the catastrophe. Martínez continued his inflammatory harangues and sought to turn to the advantage of religion the storm which he had aroused, by procuring a general forcible conversion of the Jews. The excitement increased and, on June 9th the tempest broke in a general rising of the populace against the Judería. Few of its inhabitants escaped; the number of slain was estimated at four thousand and those of the survivors who did not succeed in flying only saved their lives by accepting baptism. Of the three synagogues two were converted into churches for the Christians who settled in the Jewish quarter and the third sufficed for the miserable remnant of Israel which slowly gathered together after the storm had passed.[317]

From Seville the flame spread through the kingdoms of Castile from shore to shore. In the paralysis of public authority, during the summer and early autumn of 1391, one city after another followed the example; the Juderías were sacked, the Jews who would not submit to baptism were slain and fanaticism and cupidity held their orgies unchecked. The Moors escaped, for though many wished to include them in the slaughter, they were restrained by a wholesome fear of reprisals on the Christian captives in Granada and Africa. The total number of victims was estimated at fifty thousand, but this is probably an exaggeration. For this wholesale butchery and its accompanying rapine there was complete immunity. In Castile there was no attempt made to punish the guilty. It is true that when Henry attained his majority, in 1395, and came to Seville, he caused Martínez to be arrested, but the penalty inflicted must have been trivial, for we are told that it did not affect the high estimation in which he was held and, on his death in 1404, he bequeathed valuable possessions to the Hospital of Santa María. The misfortunes of the aljama of Seville were rendered complete when, in January, 1396, Henry bestowed on two of his favorites all the houses and lands of the Jews there and in May he followed this by forbidding that any of those concerned in the murder and pillage should be harassed with punishment or fines.[318]

In Aragon there was a king more ready to meet the crisis and the warning given at Seville was not neglected. Popular excitement was manifesting itself by assaults, robberies and murders in many places. In the city of Valencia, which had a large Jewish population, the authorities exerted themselves to repress these excesses and King Juan I ordered gallows to be erected in the streets, while a guard made nightly rounds along the walls of the Judería. These precautions and the presence of the Infante Martin, who was recruiting for an expedition to Sicily, postponed the explosion, but it came at last. On Sunday, July 9, 1391, a crowd of boys, with crosses made of cane and a banner, marched to one of the gates of the Judería, crying death or baptism for the Jews. By the time the gate was closed a portion of the boys were inside and those excluded shouted that the Jews were killing their comrades. Hard by there was a recruiting station with its group of idle vagabonds, who rushed to the Judería and the report spread through the city that the Jews were slaying Christians. The magistrates and the Infante hastened to the gate, but the frightened Jews kept it closed and thus they were excluded, while the mob effected entrance from adjoining houses and by the old rampart below the bridge. The Judería was sacked and several hundred Jews were slain before the tumult could be suppressed. Demonstrations were also made on the Morería, but troops were brought up and the mob was driven back. Some seventy or eighty arrests were made and the next day a searching investigation as to the vast amount of plunder led to the recovery of much of it.[319]

This added to the agitation which went on increasing. With August 4th came the feast of St. Dominic, when the Dominicans were everywhere conspicuous and active. The next day, as though in concert, the tempest burst in Toledo and Barcelona--in the former city with fearful massacre and conflagration. In the latter, despite the warning at Valencia, the authorities were unprepared when the mob arose and rushed into the call or Jewry, slaying without mercy. A general demand for baptism went up and, when the civic forces arrived the slaughter was stopped, but the plunder continued. Some of the pillagers were arrested, and among them a few Castilians who, as safe victims, were condemned to death the next day. Under pretext that this was unjust the mob broke into the gaol and liberated the prisoners. Then the cry arose to finish with the Jews, who had taken refuge in the Castillo Nuevo, which was subjected to a regular siege. Ringing the bells brought in crowds of peasants eager for disorder and spoil. The Baylía was attacked and the registers of crown property destroyed, in the hope of evading taxes. On August 8th the Castillo Nuevo was entered and all Jews who would not accept baptism were put to the sword; the castle was sacked and the peasants departed laden with booty. The Judería of Barcelona must have been small, for the number of slain was estimated at only three hundred.[320]

At Palma, the capital of Majorca, some three hundred Jews were put to death and the rest escaped only by submitting to baptism. The riots continued for some time and spread to attacks on the public buildings, until the gentlemen of the city armed themselves and, after a stubborn conflict, suppressed the disturbance. The chief aljamas of the kingdom were the appanage of the queen consort and Queen Violante made good her losses by levying on the island a fine of 150,000 gold florins. The gentlemen of Palma remonstrated at the hardship of being punished after putting down the rioters; she reduced the fine to 120,000, swearing by the life of her unborn child that she would have justice. The fine was paid and soon afterwards she gave birth to a still-born infant.[321] Thus in one place after another--Gerona, Lérida, Saragossa--the subterranean flame burst forth, fed by the infernal passions of fanaticism, greed and hatred. It seems incredible that, with the royal power resolved to protect its unhappy subjects, these outrages should have continued throughout the summer into autumn for, when the local authorities were determined to suppress these uprisings, as at Murviedro and Castellon de la Plana, they were able to do so.[322]

If Juan I was unable to prevent the massacres he at least was determined not to let them pass unpunished; many executions followed and some commutations for money payments were granted.[323] The aljama of Barcelona had been a source of much profit to the crown and he strove to re-establish it in new quarters, offering various privileges and exemptions to attract newcomers. It was crushed however beyond resuscitation; but few of its members had escaped by hiding; nearly all had been slain or baptized and, great as were the franchises offered, the memory of the catastrophe seems to have outweighed them. In 1395 the new synagogue was converted into a church or monastery of Trinitarian monks and the wealthy aljama of Barcelona, with its memories of so many centuries, ceased to exist.[324] About the year 1400, the city obtained a privilege which prohibited the formation of a Judería or the residence of a Jew within its limits. Antipathy to Judaism, as we shall see, was rapidly increasing and when, in 1425, Alfonso VI confirmed this privilege he decreed that all Jews then in the city should depart within sixty days, under penalty of scourging, and thereafter a stay of fifteen days was the utmost limit allowed for temporary residence.[325]

***

EFFECTS OF THE MASSACRES

If I have dwelt in what may seem disproportionate length on this guerra sacra contra los Judios, as Villanueva terms these massacres,[326] it is because they form a turning-point in Spanish history. In the relations between the races of the Peninsula the old order of things was closed and the new order, which was to prove so benumbing to material and intellectual development, was about to open. The immediate results were not long in becoming apparent. Not only was the prosperity of Castile and Aragon diminished by the shock to the commerce and industry so largely in Jewish hands, but the revenues of the crown, the churches and the nobles, based upon the taxation of the Jews, suffered enormously. Pious foundations were ruined and bishops had to appeal to the king for assistance to maintain the services of their cathedrals. Of the Jews who had escaped, the major portion had only done so by submitting to baptism and these were no longer subject to the capitation tax and special imposts which had furnished the surest part of the income of cities, prelates, nobles and sovereigns.[327] Still the converted Jews, with their energy and intelligence remained, unfettered and unhampered in the pursuit of wealth and advancement, which was to benefit the community as well as themselves. It was reserved for a further progress in the path now entered to deprive Spain of the services of her most industrious children.

The most deplorable result of the massacres was that they rendered inevitable this further progress in the same direction. The Church had at last succeeded in opening the long-desired chasm between the races. It had looked on in silence while the Archdeacon of Ecija was bringing about the catastrophe and pope and prelate uttered no word to stay the long tragedy of murder and spoliation, which they regarded as an act of God to bring the stubborn Hebrew into the fold of Christ. Henceforth the old friendliness between Jew and Christian was, for the most part, a thing of the past. Fanaticism and intolerance were fairly aroused, to grow stronger with each generation as fresh wrongs and oppression widened the abyss between believer and unbeliever and as new preachers of discord arose to teach the masses that kindness to the Jew was sin against God. Thus gradually the Spanish character changed until it was prepared to accept the Inquisition, which, by a necessary reaction, stimulated the development of bigotry until Spain became what we shall see it in the sixteenth and seventeenth centuries.

That the Archdeacon of Ecija was in reality the remote founder of the Inquisition will become evident when we consider the fortunes of the new class created by the massacres of 1391--that of the converted Jews, known as New Christians, Marranos or Conversos. Conversion, as we have seen, was always favored by the laws and the convert was received with a heartiness of social equality which shows that as yet there was no antagonism of race but only of religion. The Jew who became a Christian was eligible to any position in Church or State or to any matrimonial alliance for which his abilities or character fitted him, but conversions had hitherto been too rare and the converts, for the most part, too humble, for them to play any distinctive part in the social organization. While the massacres, doubtless, were largely owing to the attractions of disorder and pillage, the religious element in them was indicated by the fact that everywhere the Jews were offered the alternative of baptism and that where willingness was shown to embrace Christianity, slaughter was at once suspended. The pressure was so fierce and overwhelming that whole communities were baptized, as we have seen at Barcelona and Palma. At

Valencia, an official report, made on July 14th, five days after the massacre, states that all the Jews, except a few who were in hiding, had already been baptized; they came forward demanding baptism in such droves that, in all the churches, the holy chrism was exhausted and the priests knew not where to get more, but each morning the crismera would be found miraculously filled, so that the supply held out, nor was this by any means the only sign that the whole terrible affair was the mysterious work of Providence to effect so holy an end. The chiefs of the synagogues were included among the converts and we can believe the statement, current at the time, that in Valencia alone the conversions amounted to eleven thousand. Moreover it was not only in the scenes of massacre that this good work went on. So startling and relentless was the slaughter that panic destroyed the unyielding fortitude so often manifested by the Jews under trial. In many places they did not wait for a rising of the Christians but, at the first menace, or even in mere anticipation of danger, they came eagerly forward and clamored to be admitted into the Church. In Aragon the total number of conversions was reckoned at a hundred thousand and in Castile as certainly not less and this is probably no great exaggeration.[328] Neophytes such as these could scarce be expected to prove steadfast in their new faith.

RISE OF THE CONVERSOS

In this tempest of proselytism the central figure was San Vicente Ferrer, to the fervor of whose preaching posterity attributed the popular excitement leading to the massacres.[329] This doubtless does him an injustice, but the fact that he was on hand in Valencia on the fatal 9th of July, may perhaps be an indication that the affair was prearranged. His eloquence was unrivalled; immense crowds assembled to drink in his words; no matter what was the native language of the listener, we are told that his Catalan was intelligible to Moor, Greek, German, Frenchman, Italian and Hungarian, while the virtue which flowed from him on these occasions healed the infirm and repeatedly restored the dead to life.[330] Such was the man who, during the prolonged massacres and subsequently, while the terror which they excited continued to dominate the unfortunate race, traversed Spain from end to end, with restless and indefatigable zeal, preaching, baptizing and numbering his converts by the thousand--on a single day in Toledo he is said to have converted no less than four thousand. It is to be hoped that, in some cases at least, he may have restrained the murderous mob, if only by hiding its victims in the baptismal font.

The Jews slowly recovered themselves from the terrible shock; they emerged from their concealment and endeavored, with characteristic dauntless energy, to rebuild their shattered fortunes. Now, however, with diminished numbers and exhausted wealth, they had to face new enemies. Not only was Christian fanaticism inflamed and growing even stronger, but the wholesale baptisms had created the new class of Conversos, who were thenceforward to become the deadliest opponents of their former brethren. Many chiefs of the synagogue, learned rabbis and leaders of their people, had cowered before the storm and had embraced Christianity. Whether their conversion was sincere or not, they had broken with the past and, with the keen intelligence of their race, they could see that a new career was open to them in which energy and capacity could gratify ambition, unfettered by the limitations surrounding them in Judaism. That they should hate, with an exceeding hatred, those who had proved true to the faith amid tribulation was inevitable. The renegade is apt to be bitterer against those whom he has abandoned than is the opponent by birthright and, in such a case as this, consciousness of the contempt felt by the steadfast children of Israel for the weaklings and worldlings who had apostatized from the faith of their fathers gave a keener edge to enmity. From early times the hardest blows endured by Judaism had always been dealt by its apostate children, whose training had taught them the weakest points to assail and whose necessity of self-justification led them to attack these mercilessly. In 1085, Rabbi Samuel of Morocco came from Fez and was baptized at Toledo, when he wrote a tract[331] to justify himself which had great currency throughout the middle ages. Rabbi Moses, one of the most learned Jews of his time, who was converted in 1106, wrote a dissertation to prove that the Jews had abandoned the laws of Moses while the Christians were fulfilling them.[332] It was Nicholas de Rupella, a converted Jew, who started the long crusade against the Talmud by pointing out, in 1236, to Gregory IX the blasphemies which it contains against the Savior.[333] We have seen the troubles excited in Aragon by the disputatious Converso, Fray Pablo Christía, and he was followed by another Dominican convert, Ramon Martin, in his celebrated Pugio Fidei. In this work, which remained an authority for centuries, he piled up endless quotations from Jewish writers to prove that the race was properly reduced to servitude and he stimulated the bitterness of hatred by arguing that Jews esteemed it meritorious to slay and cheat and despoil Christians.[334]

A History of the Inquisition of Spain: Volume I
OPPRESSION OF THE JEWS

The most prominent among the new Conversos was Selemoh Ha-Levi, a rabbi who had been the most intrepid defender of the faith and rights of his race. On the eve of the massacres, which perhaps he foresaw, and influenced by an opportune vision of the Virgin, in 1390, he professed conversion, taking the name of Pablo de Santa María, and was followed by his two brothers and five sons, founding a family of commanding influence. After a course in the University of Paris he entered the Church, rising to the see of Cartagena and then to that of Burgos, which he transmitted to his son Alfonso. At the Córtes of Toledo, in 1406, he so impressed Henry III that he was appointed tutor and governor of the Infante Juan II, Mayor of Castile and a member of the Royal Council. When, in the course of the same year, the king died he named Pablo among those who were to have the conduct and education of Juan during his minority; when the regent, Fernando of Antequera, left Castile to assume the crown of Aragon, he appointed Pablo to replace him, and the pope honored him with the position of legate a latere. In 1432, in his eighty-first year, he wrote his Scrutinium Scripturarum against his former co-religionists. It is more moderate than is customary in these controversial writings and seems to have been composed rather as a justification of his own course.[335]

Another prominent Converso was the Rabbi Jehoshua Ha-Lorqui, who took the name of Gerónimo de Santafé and founded a family almost as powerful as the Santa Marías. He too showed his zeal in the book named Hebræomastix, in which he exaggerated the errors of the Jews in the manner best adapted to excite the execration of Christians. Another leading Converso family was that of the Caballerías, of which eight brothers were baptized and one of them, Bonafos, who called himself Micer Pedro de la Caballería, wrote, in 1464, the Celo de Cristo contra los Judíos in which he treated them with customary obloquy as the synagogue of Satan and argues that the hope of Christianity lies in their ruin.[336] In thus stimulating the spirit of persecuting fanaticism we shall see how these men sowed the wind and reaped the whirlwind.

Meanwhile the position of the Jews grew constantly more deplorable. Decimated and impoverished, they were met by a steadily increasing temper of hatred and oppression. The massacres of 1391 had been followed by a constant stream of emigration to Granada and Portugal, which threatened to complete the depopulation of the aljamas and, with the view of arresting this, Henry III, in 1395, promised them the royal protection for the future. The worth of that promise was seen in 1406, when in Córdova the remnant of the Judería was again assailed by the mob, hundreds of Jews were slain and their houses were sacked and burnt. It is true that the king ordered the magistrates to punish the guilty and expressed his displeasure by a fine of twenty-four thousand doblas on the city, but he had, the year before, in the Córtes of 1405, assented to a series of laws depriving the Jews at once of property and of defence, by declaring void all bonds of Christians held by them, reducing to one-half all debts due to them and requiring a Christian witness and the debtor's acknowledgement for the other half, annulling their privileges in the trial of mixed cases and requiring the hateful red circle to be worn except in travelling, when it could be laid aside in view of the murders which it invited.[337]

This was cruel enough, yet it was but a foretaste of what was in store. In 1410, when the Queen-regent Doña Catalina was in Segovia, there was revealed a sacrilegious attempt by some Jews to maltreat a consecrated host. The story was that the sacristan of San Fagun had pledged it as security for a loan--the street in which the bargain was made acquiring in consequence the name of Calle del Mal Consejo. The Jews cast it repeatedly into a boiling caldron, when it persistently arose and remained suspended in the air, a miracle which so impressed some of them that they were converted and carried the form to the Dominican convent and related the facts. The wafer was piously administered in communion to a child who died in three days. Doña Catalina instituted a vigorous investigation which implicated Don Mayr, one of the most prominent Jews in the kingdom, whose services as physician had prolonged the life of the late king. He was subjected to torture sufficient to elicit not only his participation in the sacrilege but also that he had poisoned his royal master. The convicts were drawn through the streets and quartered, as were also some others who in revenge had attempted to poison Juan de Tordesillas, the Bishop of Segovia. The Jewish synagogue was converted into the church of Corpus Christi and an annual procession still commemorates the event. San Vicente Ferrer turned it to good account, for we are told that in 1411 he almost destroyed the remnants of Judaism in the bishopric.[338]

The affair made an immense impression especially, it would seem, on San Vicente, convincing him of the advisability of forcing the Jews into the bosom of the Church by reducing them to despair. At Ayllon, in 1411, he represented to the regents the necessity of further repressive legislation and his eloquence was convincing.[339] The Ordenamiento de Doña Catalina, promulgated in 1412 and drawn up by Pablo de Santa María as Chancellor of Castile, was the result. By this rigorous measure, Jews and Moors, under savage and ruinous penalties, were not only required to wear the distinguishing badges, but to dress in coarse stuffs and not to shave or to cut the hair round. They could not change their abodes and any nobleman or gentleman receiving them on his lands was heavily fined and obliged to return them whence they came, while expatriation was forbidden under pain of slavery. Not only were the higher employments of farming the revenues, tax-collecting, and practising as physicians and surgeons forbidden, but any position in the households of the great and numerous trades, such as those of apothecaries, grocers, farriers, blacksmiths, peddlers, carpenters, tailors, barbers, and butchers. They could not carry arms or hire Christians to work in their houses or on their lands. That they should be forbidden to eat, drink or bathe with Christians, or be with them in feasts and weddings, or serve as godparents was a matter of course under the canon law, but now even private conversation between the races was prohibited, nor could they sell provisions to Christians or keep a shop or ordinary for them. It is perhaps significant that nothing was said about usury. Money-lending was almost the only occupation remaining open, while the events of the last twenty years had left little capital wherewith to carry it on and the laws of 1405 had destroyed all sense of security in making loans. They were moreover deprived of the guarantees so long enjoyed and were subjected to the exclusive jurisdiction, civil and criminal, of the Christians.[340] They were thus debarred from the use of their skill and experience in the higher pursuits, professional and industrial, and were condemned to the lowest and rudest forms of labor; in fine, a wall was built around them from which their only escape was through the baptismal font. Fernando of Antequera carried the law in all its essentials to Aragon and King Duarte adopted it in Portugal, so that it ruled the whole Peninsula except the little kingdom of Navarre where Judaism was already almost extinct. It is significant that Fernando, in promulgating it in Majorca, alleged in justification the complaints of the inquisitors as to the social intercourse between Jews and Christians.[341]

While San Vicente and Pablo de Santa María were thus engaged in reducing to despair the Jews of Castile, the other great Converso, Gerónimo de Santafé, was laboring in a more legitimate way for their conversion in Aragon. He had been appointed physician to the Avignonese pope, Benedict XIII, who had been obliged to cross the Pyrenees, and who, on November 25, 1412, summoned the aljamas of Aragon to send, in the following January, their most learned rabbis to San Mateo, near Tortosa, for a disputation with Gerónimo on the proposition that the Messiah had come. Fourteen rabbis, selected from the synagogues of all Spain, with Vidal ben Veniste at their head, accepted the challenge. The debate opened, February 7, 1414, under the presidency of Benedict himself, who warned them that the truth of Christianity was not to be discussed but only sixteen propositions put forward by Gerónimo, thus placing them wholly on the defensive. Despite this disadvantage they held their ground tenaciously during seventy-nine sessions, prolonged through a term of twenty-one months. Gerónimo covered himself with glory by his unrivalled dialectical subtilty and exhaustless stores of learning and his triumph was shown by his producing a division between his opponents.[342]

During this colloquy, in the summer of 1413, some two hundred Jews of the synagogues of Saragossa, Calatayud and Alcañiz professed conversion. In 1414 there was a still more abundant harvest. A hundred and twenty families of Calatayud, Daroca, Fraga and Barbastro presented themselves for baptism and these were followed by the whole aljamas of Alcañiz, Caspe, Maella, Lérida, Tamarit and Alcolea, amounting to about thirty-five hundred souls. The repressive legislation was accomplishing its object and hopes were entertained that, with the aid of the inspired teaching of San Vicente, Judaism would become extinct throughout Spain.[343] To stimulate the movement by an increase of severity towards the recalcitrant, Benedict issued his constitution Etsi doctoribus gentium, in which he virtually embodied the Ordenamiento de Doña Catalina, thus giving to its system of terrible repression the sanction of Church as well as of State. He further forbade the possession of the Talmud or of any books contrary to the Christian faith, ordering the bishops and inquisitors to make semi-annual inquests of the aljamas and to proceed against all found in possession of such books. No Jew should even bind a book in which the name of Christ or the Virgin appeared. Princes were exhorted to grant them no favors or privileges and the faithful at large were commanded not to rent or sell houses to them or to hold companionship or conversation with them. Moreover they were prohibited to exercise usury and thrice a year they were to be preached to and warned to abandon their errors. The bishops in general were ordered to see to the strict enforcement of all these provisions and the execution of the bull was specially confided to Gonzalo, Bishop of Sigüenza, son of the great Converso, Pablo de Santa María. As the utterance of the Anti-pope Benedict, this searching and cruel legislation, designed to reduce the Jews to the lowest depths of poverty and despair, was current only in the lands of his obedience, but when his triumphant rival, Martin V, confirmed the charge confided to the Bishop of Sigüenza he accepted and ratified the act of Benedict.[344] Nay more; in 1434, Alfonso de Santa María, Bishop of Burgos, another son of the Converso Pablo, when a delegate to the council of Basle, procured the passage of a decree in the same sense.[345] The quarrel of the council with the papacy, it is true, deprived its utterance of oecumenic authority, but this deficiency was supplied when, in 1442, Eugenius IV issued a bull which was virtually a repetition of the law of Doña Catalina and of the constitution of Benedict XIII, while this was followed, in 1447, by an even more rigorous one of Nicholas V.[346] Thus all factions of the Church, however much they might wrangle on other points, cheerfully united in rendering the life of the Jew as miserable as possible and in forbidding princes to show him favor. This was symbolized when, in 1418, the legate of Martin V was solemnly received in Gerona and the populace, with inerring instinct, celebrated the closing of the great Schism and the reunion of the Church by playfully sacking the Judería, though the royal officials, blind to the piety of the demonstration, severely punished the perpetrators.[347]

***

The immediate effect of this policy corresponded to the intentions of its authors, though its ultimate results can scarce have been foreseen. The Jews were humiliated and impoverished. Despite their losses by massacre and conversion, they still formed an important portion of the population, with training and aptitudes to render service to the State but, debarred from the pursuits for which they had been fitted, they were crippled both for their own recuperation and for the benefit of the public. The economic effect was intensified by the inclusion of the Mudéjares in the repressive legislation; commerce and manufactures decayed and many products which Spain had hitherto exported she was now obliged to import at advanced prices.[348]

VICISSITUDES

On the other hand the Conversos saw opened to them a career fitted to stimulate and satisfy ambition. Confident in their powers, with intellectual training superior to that of the Christians, they aspired to the highest places in the courts, in the universities, in the Church and in the State. Wealth and power rendered them eligible suitors and they entered into matrimonial alliances with the noblest houses in the land, many of which had been impoverished by the shrinkage of the revenues derived from their Jewish subjects. Alfonso de Santa María, in procuring the decree of Basle, was careful to insert in it a recommendation of marriage between converts and Christians as the surest means of preserving the purity of the faith, and the advice was extensively followed. Thus the time soon came when there were few of the ancient nobility of Spain who were not connected, closely or remotely, with the Jew. We hear of marriages with Lunas, Mendozas, Villahermosas and others of the proudest houses.[349] As early as 1449 a petition to Lope de Barrientos, Bishop of Cuenca, by the Conversos of Toledo, enumerates all the noblest families of Spain as being of Jewish blood and among others the Henríquez, from whom the future Ferdinand the Catholic descended, through his mother Juana Henríquez.[350] It was the same in the Church, where we have seen the rank attained by the Santa Marías. Juan de Torquemada, Cardinal of San Sisto, was of Jewish descent and so, of course, was his nephew, the first inquisitor-general,[351] as was likewise Diego Deza, the second inquisitor-general, as well as Hernando de Talavera, Archbishop of Granada. It would be easy to multiply examples, for in every career the vigor and keenness of the Jews made them conspicuous and, in embracing Christianity, they seemed to be opening a new avenue for the development of the race in which it would become dominant over the Old Christians; in fact, an Italian nearly contemporary describes them as virtually ruling Spain, while secretly perverting the faith by their covert adherance to Judaism.[352] This triumph however was short-lived. Their success showed that thus far there had been no antagonism of race but only of religion. This speedily changed; the hatred and contempt which, as apostates, they lavished on the faithful sons of Israel reacted on themselves. It was impossible to stimulate popular abhorrence of the Jew without at the same time stimulating the envy and jealousy excited by the ostentation and arrogance of the New Christians. What was the use of humiliating and exterminating the Jew if these upstarts were not only to take his place in grinding the people as tax-gatherers but were to bear rule in court and camp and church?

Meanwhile the remnant of the Jews were slowly but indomitably recovering their position. It was much easier to enact the Ordenamiento de Doña Catalina than to enforce it and, like much previous legislation, it was growing obsolete in many respects. In the early days of Juan II, Abrahem Benaviste was virtually finance minister and, when the Infante Henry of Aragon seized the king at Tordesillas and carried him off, he justified the act by saying that it was because the government was in the hands of Abraham.[353] In fact there are indications of a reaction in which the Jews were used as a counterpoise to the menacing growth of Converso influence. When, in 1442, the cruel bull of Eugenius IV was received, although it scarce contained more than the laws of 1412 and the bull of Benedict XIII, Alvaro de Luna, the all-powerful favorite, not only refused to obey it but proceeded to give legal sanction to the neglect into which those statutes had fallen. He induced his master to issue the Pragmática of Arévalo, April 6, 1443, condemning the refusal of many persons to buy or sell with Jews and Moors or to labor for them in the fields, under color of a bull of Eugenius IV, published at Toledo during his absence. Punishment is threatened for these audacities, for the bull and the laws provide that Jews and Moors and Christians shall dwell together in harmony and no one is to injure or slay them. It was not intended to prevent Jews and Moors and Christians from dealing together, nor that the former should not follow industries base and servile, such as all manner of mechanical trades, and Christians can serve them for proper wages and guard their flocks and labor for them in the fields, and they can prescribe for Christians if the medicines are compounded by Christians.[354]

Thus a revulsion had taken place in favor of the proscribed race which threatened to undo the work of Vicente Ferrer and the Conversos. It was in vain that, in 1451, Nicholas V issued another bull repeating and confirming that of Eugenius IV.[355] It received no attention and, under the protection of Alvaro de Luna, the Jews made good use of the breathing-space to reconstruct their shattered industries and to demonstrate their utility to the State. The conspiracy which sent Alvaro to the block, in 1453, was a severe blow but, on the accession of Henry IV, in 1454, they secured the good-will of his favorites and even procured the restoration of some old privileges, the most important of which was the permission to have their own judges. One element in this was the influence enjoyed by the royal physician Jacob Aben-Nuñez on whom was conferred the office of Rabb Mayor.[356] In the virtual anarchy of the period, however, when every noble was a law unto himself, it is impossible to say how far royal decrees were effective, or to postulate any general conditions. In 1458, the Constable Velasco orders his vassals of the town of Haro to observe the law forbidding Christians to labor for Jews and Moors, but he makes the wise exception that they may do so when they can find no other work wherewith to support themselves. Even under these conditions the superior energy of the non-Christian races was rapidly acquiring for them the most productive lands, if we may trust a decree of the town of Haro, in 1453, forbidding Christians to sell their estates to Moors and Jews, for if this were not stopped the Christians would have no ground to cultivate, as the Moors already held all the best of the irrigated lands.[357]

The nobles had seen the disadvantage of the sternly oppressive laws and disregarded them to their own great benefit, thus raising the envy of the districts obliged to observe them, for the Córtes of 1462 petitioned Henry to restore liberty of trade between Christian and Jew, alleging the inconvenience caused by the restriction and the depopulation of the crown lands for, as trade was permitted in the lands of the nobles, the Jews were concentrating there. When further the Córtes asked that Jews should be permitted to return with their property and trades to the cities in the royal domains from which they had been expelled, it indicates that popular aversion was becoming directed to the Conversos rather than to the Jews.[358] It may be questioned whether it was to preserve the advantage here indicated or to gain popular favor, that the revolted nobles, in 1460, demanded of Henry that he should banish from his kingdoms all Moors and Jews who contaminated religion and corrupted morals and that, when they deposed him, in 1465, at Avila and elevated to the throne the child Alfonso, the Concordia Compromisoria which they dictated, annulled the Pragmática de Arévalo and restored to vigor the laws of 1412 and the bull of Benedict XIII. This frightened the Jews, who offered to Henry an immense sum for Gibraltar, where they proposed to establish a city of refuge, but he refused.[359]

The fright was superfluous for, in the turbulence of the time, the repressive legislation was speedily becoming obsolete. When the reforming Council of Aranda, in 1473, made but a single reference to Jews and Moors and this was merely to forbid them to pursue their industries publicly on Sundays and feast days, with a threat against the judges who, through bribery, permitted this desecration, it is fair to conclude that the law of 1412, if observed at all, was enforced only in scattered localities.[360] That the restrictions on commercial activity were obsolete is manifest from a complaint, in 1475, to the sovereigns, from the Jews of Medina del Pomar, setting forth that they had been accustomed to purchase in Bilbao, from foreign traders, cloths and other merchandise which they carried through the kingdom for sale, until recently the port had restricted all dealings with foreigners to the resident Jews, whereupon Ferdinand and Isabella ordered these regulations rescinded unless the authorities could show good reasons within fifteen days.[361]

With the settlement of affairs under Ferdinand and Isabella the position of the Jews grew distinctly worse. Although Don Abraham Senior, one of Isabella's most trusted counsellors, was a Jew, her piety led her to revive and carry out the repressive policy of San Vicente Ferrer and, in codifying the royal edicts in the Ordenanzas Reales, confirmed by the Córtes of Toledo in 1480, all the savage legislation of 1412 was re-enacted, except that relating to mechanical trades, and the vigor of the government gave assurance that the laws would be enforced, as we have seen in the matter of the separation of the Juderías.[362] Ferdinand's assent to this shows that he adopted the policy and, in his own dominions, by an edict of March 6, 1482, he withdrew all licenses to Jews to lay aside the dangerous badge when travelling, and he further prohibited the issuing of such licenses under penalty of a thousand florins. Another edict of December 15, 1484, recites that at Cella, a village near Teruel, some Jews had recently taken temporary residence; as there is no Judería, in order to avoid danger to souls, he orders them driven out and that none be allowed to remain more than twenty-four hours under pain of a hundred florins and a hundred lashes.[363]

DECLINE OF JUDAISM

This recrudescence of oppression probably had an influence on the people, for there came a revulsion of feeling adverse to the proscribed race, inflamed by the ceaseless labors of the frailes whose denunciatory eloquence knew no cessation. Under these circumstances the Jews and Moors seem to have had recourse to the Roman curia, always ready to speculate by selling privileges, whether it had power to grant them or not, and then to withdraw them for a consideration. We shall have ample occasion to see hereafter prolonged transactions of the kind arising from the operation of the Inquisition; those with the Jews at this time seem to have been closed by a motu proprio of May 31, 1484, doubtless procured from Sixtus IV by pressure from the sovereigns, in which the pope expresses his displeasure at learning that in Spain, especially in Andalusia, Christians, Moors and Jews dwell together; that there is no distinction of vestments, that the Christians act as servants and nurses, the Moors and Jews as physicians, apothecaries, farmers of ecclesiastical revenues etc., pretending that they hold papal privileges to that effect. Any such privileges he withdraws and he orders all officials, secular and ecclesiastical, to enforce strictly the canonical decrees respecting the proscribed races.[364] Under these impulses the municipalities, which, in 1462, had petitioned to have the prescriptive laws repealed now enforced them with renewed vigor and even exceeded them, as at Balmaseda, where the Jews were ordered to depart. They appealed to the throne, representing that they lived in daily fear for life and property and begged the royal protection, which was duly granted.[365]

Subjected to these perpetual and harassing vicissitudes, the Jews had greatly declined both in numbers and wealth. An assessment of the poll-tax, made in 1474, shows that in the dominions of Castile there were only about twelve thousand families left, or from fifty to sixty thousand souls, although there were still two hundred and sixteen separate aljamas. Their weakness and poverty are indicated by the fact that such communities as those of Seville, Toledo, Córdova, Burgos, etc., paid much less than inconspicuous places prior to 1391. The aljama of Ciudad-Real, which had paid, in 1290, a tax of 26,486 maravedís, had disappeared; the only one left in La Mancha was Almagro, assessed at 800 maravedís.[366] The work of Martínez and San Vicente Ferrer was accomplishing itself. Popular abhorrence had grown, while the importance of the Jews as a source of public revenue had fatally diminished. The end was evidently approaching, but a consideration of its horrors must be postponed while we glance at the condition of the renegades who had sought shelter from the storm by adopting the faith of the oppressor.

***

The Conversos, in steadily increasing numbers, had successfully worked out their destiny, accumulating honors, wealth and popular hatred. In both Castile and Aragon they filled lucrative and influential positions in the public service and their preponderance in Church and State was constantly becoming more marked. In Catalonia, however, they were regarded with contempt and, though the boast that Catalan blood was never polluted by inter-mixture is exaggerated, it is not wholly without foundation. The same is true of Valencia, where intermarriage only occurred among the rural population. Throughout Spain, moreover, the farming of all the more important sources of revenue passed into their hands and thus they inherited the odium as well as the profits of the Jews.[367]

The beginning of the end was seen at Toledo where, in 1449, Alvaro de Luna made a demand on the city for a million maravedís for the defence of the frontier and it was refused. He ordered the tax-gatherers to collect it. They were Conversos and when they made the attempt the citizens arose and sacked and burnt not only their houses but those of the Conversos in general. The latter organized in self-defence and endeavored to suppress the disturbance but were defeated, when those who were wealthy were tortured and immense booty was obtained. In vain Juan II sought to punish the city; the triumphant citizens, with the magistrates at their head, organized a court in which the question was argued whether the Conversos could hold any public office. In spite of the evident illegality of this and of active opposition led by the famous Lope de Barrientos, Bishop of Cuenca, it was decided against the Conversos in a quasi-judicial sentence, known as the Sentencia-Estatuto which, in the bitterness of its language, reveals the extreme tension existing between the Old and New Christians. The Conversos were stigmatized as more than suspect in the faith and as in reality Jews; they were declared incapable of holding office and of bearing witness against Old Christians and those who held positions were ejected.[368] The disturbances spread to Ciudad-Real, where the principal offices were held by Conversos. The Order of Calatrava, which had long endeavored to get possession of the city, espoused the side of the Old Christians; there was considerable fighting in the streets and for five days the quarter occupied by the Conversos was exposed to pillage.[369] Thus the hatred which of old had been merely a matter of religion had become a matter of race. The one could be conjured away by baptism; the other was indelible and the change was of the most serious import, exercising for centuries its sinister influence on the fate of the Peninsula.

PERSECUTION OF CONVERSOS

The Sentencia-Estatuto threatened to introduce a new principle into public and canon law, both of which had always upheld the brotherhood of Christians and had encouraged conversions by prescribing the utmost favor for converts. Nicholas V was appealed to and responded, September 24, 1449, with a bull declaring that all the faithful are one; that the laws of Alfonso X and his successors, admitting converts to all the privileges of Christians, were to be enforced and he commissioned the Archbishops of Toledo and Seville, the Bishops of Palencia, Avila and Córdova, and the Abbot of San Fagun to excommunicate all who sought to invalidate them.[370] More than this seems to have been needed and, in 1450, he formally excommunicated Pedro Sarmiento and his accomplices as the authors of the Sentencia-Estatuto and again, in 1451, he repeated his bull of 1449. Finally, in the same year the synods of Vitoria and Alcalá condemned it and Alfonso de Montalvo, the foremost jurist of the time, pronounced it to be illegal.[371] It never, in fact, was of binding force, but the effort made to set it aside shows how dangerous a menace it was and how it expressed a widespread public opinion. It was the first fitful gust of the tornado.

Toledo remained the hot-bed of disturbance. In 1461 the martial Archbishop, Alonso Carrillo commissioned the learned Alonso de Oropesa, General of the Geronimites to investigate the cause of dissension. He did so and reported that there were faults on both sides and, at the request of the archbishop, he proceeded to write his Lumen ad Revelationem Gentium to prove the unity of the faithful, but, while he was engaged in this pious labor the inextinguishable feud broke out afresh.[372] Any chance disturbance might bring this about and the opportunity was furnished in 1467, when the canons, who enjoyed a revenue based on the bread of the town of Maqueda, farmed it out to a Jew. Alvaro Gómez, an alcalde mayor, was lord of Maqueda; his alcaide beat the Jew and seized the bread for the use of the castle; the canons promptly imprisoned the alcaide and summoned Gómez to answer. When he came the quarrel grew bitterer; the Count of Cifuentes, leader of one of the factions of the city and protector of the Conversos, espoused the cause of Gómez, while Fernando de la Torre, a leader of the Conversos, hoping to revenge the defeat of 1449, boasted that he had at command four thousand well-armed fighting men, being six times more than the Old Christians could muster. Matters were ripe for an explosion and, on July 21st, at a conference held in the cathedral, the followers of the two parties taunted each other beyond endurance; swords were drawn and blood polluted the sanctuary, though only one man was slain. The canons proceeded to fortify and garrison the cathedral, which was attacked the next day. The clergy, galled by the fire of the assailants, to create a diversion, started a conflagration in the calle de la Chapineria, which spread until eight streets were destroyed--the richest in Toledo, crowded with shops full of costly merchandise. The device was successful; the Conversos were disheartened and lost ground till, on the 29th, Cifuentes and Gómez fled, while Fernando de la Torre and his brother Alvaro were captured and hanged. The triumphant faction removed from office all their opponents and revived with additional rigor the Sentencia-Estatuto. Toledo at the time belonged to the party of the pretender Alfonso XII but, when the citizens sent to him to confirm what they had done, he refused and the city soon afterwards transferred its allegiance to Henry IV.[373] It is quite probable that, in reward for this, he confirmed the Sentencia-Estatuto for when, about the same time, Ciudad-Real revolted from Alfonso and adhered to Henry, he granted, July 14, 1468, to that city that thenceforward no Converse should hold municipal office.[374] In the all-pervading lawlessness such disturbances as those of Toledo met with neither repression nor punishment. In 1470 Valladolid saw a similar tumult, in which the Old Christians and Conversos flew to arms and struggled for mastery. The former sent for Ferdinand and Isabella who came, but the majority of the citizens preferred Henry IV and the royal pair were glad to escape.[375]

Everywhere the hatred between the Old Christians and the New was manifesting itself in this deplorable fashion. In Córdova we are told that the Conversos were very rich and had bought not only the offices but the protection of Alonso de Aguilar, whose power and high reputation commanded universal respect, while the Old Christians ranged themselves under the Counts of Cabra and the Bishop, Pedro de Córdova y Solier. Only a spark was needed to produce an explosion and an accident during a, procession, March 14, 1473, furnished the occasion. With shouts of viva la fe de Dios the mob arose and pillage, murder and fire were let loose upon the city. Alonso and his brother Gonsalvo--the future Great Captain--quelled the riot at the cost of no little bloodshed, but it burst forth again a few days later and, after a combat lasting forty-eight hours the Aguilars were forced to take refuge in the alcázar carrying with them such Conversos and Jews as they could. Then followed a general sack in which every kind of outrage and cruelty was perpetrated, until the fury of the mob was exhausted by the lack of victims. Finally Alonso came to terms with the city authorities, who banished the Conversos for ever and such poor wretches as had escaped torch and dagger were thrust forth to be robbed and murdered with impunity on the highways.[376]

Laborers from the country, who chanced to be in Córdova, carried the welcome news to neighboring places and the flame passed swiftly through Andalusia from town to town. Baena was kept quiet by the Count of Cabra, Palma by Luis Portocarrero, Ecija by Fadrique Manrique and Seville and Jerez by Juan de Guzman and Rodrigo Ponce de Leon, but elsewhere the havoc was terrible. At Jaen, the Constable of Castile, Miguel Luis de Iranzo, was treacherously murdered while kneeling before the altar; his wife, Teresa de Torres, was barely able to escape, with her children, to the alcázar, and the Conversos were plundered and dispatched. Only at Almodovar del Campo do we hear of any justice executed on the assassins, for there Rodrigo Giron, Master of Calatrava, hanged some of the most culpable. The king, we are told, when the news was brought to him, grieved much, but inflicted no punishment.[377]

On the accession of Ferdinand and Isabella, in 1474, a Converso of Córdova, Anton de Montoro, addressed to them a poem in which he gives a terrible picture of the murders committed with impunity on his brethren, whose purity of faith he asserts. Fire and sword had just ravaged the aljama of Carmona and fresh disasters were threatening at Seville and Córdova.[378] Dominicans and Franciscans were thundering from the pulpits and were calling on the faithful to purify the land from the pollution of Judaism, secret and open. It was commonly asserted and believed that the Christianity of the Conversos was fictitious, and fanaticism joined with envy and greed in stimulating the massacres that had become so frequent. The means adopted to win over the Jewish converts had not been so gentle as to encourage confidence in the sincerity of their professions and, rightly or wrongly, they were almost universally suspected. The energy with which the new sovereigns enforced respect for the laws speedily put an end to the hideous excesses of the mob, for we hear of no further massacres, but the abhorrence entertained for the successful renegades, whose wealth and power were regarded as obtained by false profession of belief in Christ, was still wide-spread, though its more violent manifestations were restrained. Wise forbearance, combined with vigorous maintenance of order, would in time have brought about reconciliation, to the infinite benefit of Spain, but at a time when heresy was regarded as the greatest of crimes and unity of faith as the supreme object of statesmanship, wise forbearance and toleration were impossible. After suppressing turbulence the sovereigns therefore felt that there was still a duty before them to vindicate the faith. Thus, after long hesitation, their policy with regard to the Conversos was embodied in the Inquisition, introduced towards the end of 1480. The Jewish question required different treatment and it was solved, once for all, in most decisive fashion.

***

EXPULSION OF JEWS CONSIDERED

The Inquisition had no jurisdiction over the Jew, unless he rendered himself amenable to it by some offence against the faith. He was not baptized; he was not a member of the Church and therefore was incapable of heresy, which was the object of inquisitional functions. He might, however, render himself subject to it by proselytism, by seducing Christians to embrace his errors, and this was constantly alleged against Jews, although their history shows that, unlike the other great religions, Judaism has ever been a national faith with no desire to spread beyond the boundaries of the race. As the chosen people, Israel has never sought to share its God with the Gentiles. There was more foundation, probably, in the accusation that the secret perversity of the Conversos was encouraged by those who had remained steadfast in the faith, that circumcisions were secretly performed and that contributions to the synagogues were welcomed.

While the object of the Inquisition was to secure the unity of faith, its founding destroyed the hope that ultimately the Jews would all be gathered into the fold of Christ. This had been the justification of the inhuman laws designed to render existence outside of the Church so intolerable that baptism would be sought as a relief from endless injustice, but the awful spectacle of the autos de fe and the miseries attendant on wholesale confiscations led the Jew to cherish more resolutely than ever the ancestral faith which served him as shield from the terrors of the Holy Office and the dreadful fate ever impending over the Conversos. His conversion could no longer be hoped for and, so long as he remained in Spain, the faithful would be scandalized by his presence and the converts would be exposed to the contamination of his society. The only alternative was his removal.

Isabella tried a partial experiment of this kind in 1480, apparently to supplement the Inquisition, founded about the same time. Andalusia was the province where the Jews were most numerous and she commenced by ordering the expulsion from there of all who would not accept Christianity and threatening with death any new settlers.[379] We have no details as to this measure and only know that it was several times postponed and that it was apparently abandoned.[380] A bull of Sixtus IV, in 1484, shows us that Jews were still dwelling there undisturbed and, when the final expulsion took place in 1492, Bernaldez informs us that from Andalusia eight thousand households embarked at Cadiz, besides many at Cartagena and the ports of Aragon.[381]

That there was vacillation is highly probable, for policy and fanaticism were irreconcilable. The war with Granada was calling for large expenditures, to which the Jews were most useful contributors and the finances were in the hands of two leading Jews, Abraham Senior and Isaac Abravanel, to whose skilful management its ultimate success was largely due. It may be that the threatened expulsion was rather a financial than a religious measure, adopted with a view of selling suspensions and exemptions, and this may also perhaps explain a similar course adopted by Ferdinand when, in May, 1486, he ordered the inquisitors of Aragon to banish all Jews of Saragossa from the archbishopric of Saragossa and the bishopric of Albarracin, in the same way as they had been banished from the sees of Seville, Córdova and Jaen.[382] The sovereigns knew when to be tolerant and when to give full rein to fanaticism, as was evinced in their treatment of renegades and Conversos at the capture of Málaga as contrasted with the liberal terms offered in the capitulations of Almería and Granada. They were prepared to listen to the counsel of those who opposed all interference with the Jewish population, in whose favor there were powerful influences at work. Isabella apparently hesitated long between statesmanship and her conceptions of duty, while Torquemada never ceased to urge upon her the service to be rendered to Christ by clearing her dominions of the descendants of his crucifiers.[383]

STIMULATION OF PREJUDICE

There was no lack of effort to inflame public opinion and to excite still further the hostility so long and so carefully cultivated. A story had wide circulation that Maestre Ribas Altas, the royal physician, wore a golden ball attached to a cord around his neck; that Prince Juan, only son of the sovereigns, begged it of him and managed to open it, when he found inside a parchment on which was painted a crucifix with the physician in an indecent attitude; that he was so affected that he fell sick and, after much persuasion, revealed the cause, adding that he would not recover until the Jew was burnt, which was accordingly done and Ferdinand consented to the expulsion of the accursed sect.[384] Then we are told that, on Good Friday, 1488, some Jews, to avenge an insult, stoned a rude cross which stood on the hill of Gano near Casar de Palomero; they were observed and denounced, when the Duke of Alba burnt the rabbi and several of the culprits; the cross was repaired and carried in solemn procession to the parish church, where it still remains an object of popular veneration.[385] It is to this period also that we may presumably refer the fabrication of a correspondence, discovered fifty years later among the archives of Toledo by Archbishop Siliceo, between Chamorro, Prince of the Jews of Spain and Uliff, Prince of those of Constantinople, in which the latter, replying to a request for counsel, tells the former "as the king takes your property, make your sons merchants that they may take the property of the Christians; as he takes your lives, make your sons physicians and apothecaries, that they may take Christian lives; as he destroys your synagogues, make your sons ecclesiastics, that they may destroy the churches; as he vexes you in other ways, make your sons officials, that they may reduce the Christians to subjection and take revenge."[386]

The most effective device, however, was a cruel one, carried out by Torquemada unshrinkingly to the end. In June, 1490, a Converso named Benito García, on his return from a pilgrimage to Compostella, was arrested at Astorga on the charge of having a consecrated wafer in his knapsack. The episcopal vicar, Dr. Pedro de Villada, tortured him repeatedly till he obtained a confession implicating five other Conversos and six Jews in a plot to effect a conjuration with a human heart and a consecrated host, whereby to cause the madness and death of all Christians, the destruction of Christianity and the triumph of Judaism. Three of the implicated Jews were dead, but the rest of those named were promptly arrested and the trial was carried on by the Inquisition. After another year spent in torturing the accused, there emerged the story of the crucifixion at La Guardia of a Christian child, whose heart was cut out for the purpose of the conjuration. The whole tissue was so evidently the creation of the torture-chamber that it was impossible to reconcile the discrepancies in the confessions of the accused, although the very unusual recourse of confronting them was tried several times; no child had anywhere been missed and no remains were found on the spot where it was said to have been buried. The inquisitors finally abandoned the attempt to frame a consistent narrative and, on November 16, 1491, the accused were executed at Avila; the three deceased Jews were burned in effigy, the two living ones were torn with red-hot pincers and the Conversos were "reconciled" and strangled before burning. The underlying purpose was revealed in the sentence read at the auto de fe, which was framed so as to bring into especial prominence the proselyting efforts of the Jews and the Judaizing propensities of the Conversos and no effort was spared to produce the widest impression on the people. We happen to know that the sentence was sent to La Guardia, to be read from the pulpit, and that it was translated into Catalan and similarly published in Barcelona, showing that it was thus brought before the whole population--a thing without parallel in the history of the Inquisition. The cult of the Saint-Child of La Guardia--El santo niño de la Guardia--was promptly started with miracles and has been kept up to the present day, although the sanctity of the supposed martyr has never been confirmed by the Holy See. Torquemada's object was gained for, though it would be too much to say that this alone won Ferdinand's consent to the expulsion, it undoubtedly contributed largely to that result. The edict of expulsion, it is true, makes no direct reference to the case but, in its labored efforts to magnify the dangers of Jewish proselytism it reflects distinctly the admissions extorted from the accused by the Inquisition.[387]

EXPULSION OF THE JEWS

With the surrender of Granada in January, 1492, the work of the Reconquest was accomplished. The Jews had zealously contributed to it and had done their work too well. With the accession of a rich territory and an industrious Moorish population and the cessation of the drain of the war, even Ferdinand might persuade himself that the Jews were no longer financially indispensable. The popular fanaticism required constant repression to keep the peace; the operations of the Inquisition destroyed the hope that gradual conversion would bring about the desired unity of faith and the only alternative was the removal of those who could not, without a miraculous change of heart, be expected to encounter the terrible risks attendant upon baptism. It is easy thus to understand the motives leading to the measure, without attributing it, as has been done, to greed for the victims' wealth, for though, as we shall see, there are abundant evidences of a desire to profit by it, as a whole it was palpably undesirable financially.

Thus the expulsion of the Jews from all the Spanish dominions came to be resolved upon. When this was bruited about the court, Abraham Senior and Abravanel offered a large sum from the aljamas to avert the blow. Ferdinand was inclined to accept it, but Isabella was firm. The story is current that, when the offer was under consideration, Torquemada forced his way into the royal presence and holding aloft a crucifix boldly addressed the sovereigns: "Behold the crucified whom the wicked Judas sold for thirty pieces of silver. If you approve that deed, sell him for a greater sum. I resign my power; nothing shall be imputed to me but you will answer to God!"[388] Whether this be true or not, the offer was rejected and, on March 30th, the edict of expulsion was signed, though apparently there was delay in its promulgation, for it was not published in Barcelona until May 1st.[389] It gave the entire Jewish population of Spain until July 31st in which to change their religion or to leave the country, under penalty of death, which was likewise threatened for any attempt to return. During the interval they were taken under the royal protection; they were permitted to sell their effects and carry the proceeds with them, except that, under a general law, the export of gold and silver was prohibited.[390]

A supplementary edict of May 14th granted permission to sell lands, leaving but little time in which to effect such transactions and this was still more fatally limited in Aragon, where Ferdinand sequestrated all Jewish property in order to afford claimants and creditors the opportunity to prove their rights, the courts being ordered to decide all such cases promptly. Still less excusable was his detaining from all sales an amount equal to all the charges and taxes which the Jews would have paid him, thus realizing a full year's revenue from the trifling sums obtained through forced sales by the unhappy exiles.[391] In Castile, the inextricable confusion arising from the extensive commercial transactions of the Jews led to the issue, May 30th, of a decree addressed to all the officials of the land, ordering all interested parties to be summoned to appear within twenty days to prove their claims, which the courts must settle by the middle of July. All debts falling due prior to the date of departure were to be promptly paid; if due to Christians by Jews who had not personal effects sufficient to satisfy them, the creditors were to take land at an appraised valuation or be paid out of other debts paid by Jews. For debts falling due subsequently, if due by Jews, the debtors had to pay at once or furnish adequate security; if due by Christians or Moors, the creditors were either to leave powers to collect at maturity or to sell the claims to such purchasers as they could find.[392] These regulations afford us a glimpse into the complexities arising from the convulsion thus suddenly precipitated and, as the Jews were almost universally creditors, we can readily imagine how great were their losses and how many Christian debtors must have escaped payment.

The sovereigns also shared in the spoils. When the exiles reached the seaports to embark they found that an export duty of two ducats per head had been levied upon them, which they were obliged to pay out of their impoverished store.[393] Moreover, the threat of confiscation for those who overstayed the time was rigorously enforced and, in some cases at least, the property thus seized was granted to nobles to compensate their losses by the banishment of their Jews.[394] All effects left behind also were seized; in many cases the dangers of the journey, the prohibition to carry coin and the difficulty of procuring bills of exchange, led the exiles to make deposits with trustworthy friends to be remitted to them in their new homes, all of which was seized by the crown. The amount of this was sufficient to require a regular organization of officials deputed to hunt up these deposits and other fragments of property that could be escheated, and we find correspondence on the subject as late as 1498.[395] Efforts were even also made to follow exiles and secure their property on the plea that they had taken with them prohibited articles, and Henry VII of England and Ferdinand of Naples were appealed to for assistance in cases of this description.[396]

The terror and distress of the exodus, we are told, were greatly increased by an edict issued by Torquemada, as inquisitor-general, in April, forbidding any Christian, after August 9th, from holding any communication with Jews, or giving them food or shelter, or aiding them in any way.[397] Such addition to their woes was scarce necessary, for it would be difficult to exaggerate the misery inflicted on a population thus suddenly uprooted from a land in which their race was older than that of their oppressors. Stunned at first by the blow, as soon as they rallied from the shock, they commenced preparations for departure. An aged rabbi, Isaac Aboab, with thirty prominent colleagues, was commissioned to treat with João II of Portugal for refuge in his dominions. He drove a hard bargain, demanding a cruzado a head for permission to enter and reside for six months.[398] For those who were near the coasts, arrangements were made for transhipment by sea, mostly from Cadiz and Barcelona on the south and Laredo on the north. To the north-east, Navarre afforded an asylum, by order of Jean d'Albret and his wife Leonora, although the cities were somewhat recalcitrant.[399] As the term approached, two days' grace were allowed, bringing it to August 2d, the 9th of Ab, a day memorable in Jewish annals for its repeated misfortunes.[400]

The sacrifices entailed on the exiles were enormous. To realize in so limited a time on every species of property not portable, with means of transportation so imperfect, was almost impossible and, in a forced sale of such magnitude, the purchasers had a vast advantage of which they fully availed themselves. An eye-witness tells us that the Christians bought their property for a trifle; they went around and found few buyers, so that they were compelled to give a house for an ass and a vineyard for a little cloth or linen: in some places the miserable wretches, unable to get any price, burnt their homes and the aljamas bestowed the communal property on the cities. Their synagogues they were not allowed to sell, the Christians taking them and converting them into churches, wherein to worship a God of justice and love.[401] The cemeteries, for which they felt peculiar solicitude, were in many places made over to the cities, on condition of preservation from desecration and use only for pasturage; where this was not done they were confiscated and Torquemada obtained a fragment of the spoil by securing, March 23, 1494, from Ferdinand and Isabella, the grant of that of Avila for his convent of Santo Tomas.[402]

The resolute constancy displayed in this extremity was admirable. There were comparatively few renegades and, if Abraham Senior was one of them, it is urged in extenuation that Isabella, who was loath to lose his services, threatened, if he persisted in his faith, to adopt still sharper measures against his people and he, knowing her capacity in this direction, submitted to baptism; he and his family had for god-parents the sovereigns and Cardinal González de Mendoza; they assumed the name of Coronel which long remained distinguished.[403] The frailes exerted themselves everywhere in preaching, but the converts were few and only of the lowest class; the Inquisition had changed the situation and San Vicente Ferrer himself would have found missionary work unfruitful, for the dread of exile was less than that of the Holy Office and the quemadero.

There was boundless mutual helpfulness; the rich aided the poor and they made ready as best they could to face the perils of the unknown future. Before starting, all the boys and girls over twelve were married. Early in July the exodus commenced and no better idea of this pilgrimage of grief can be conveyed than by the simple narrative of the good cura of Palacios. Disregarding, he says, the wealth they left behind and confiding in the blind hope that God would lead them to the promised land, they left their homes, great and small, old and young, on foot, on horseback, on asses or other beasts or in wagons, some falling, others rising, some dying, others being born, others falling sick. There was no Christian who did not pity them; everywhere they were invited to conversion and some were baptized, but very few, for the rabbis encouraged them and made the women and children play on the timbrel. Those who went to Cadiz hoped that God would open a path for them across the sea; but they stayed there many days, suffering much and many wished that, they had never been born. From Aragon and Catalonia they put to sea for Italy or the Moorish lands or whithersoever fortune might drive them. Most of them had evil fate, robbery and murder by sea and in the lands of their refuge. This is shown by the fate of those who sailed from Cadiz. They had to embark in twenty-five ships of which the captain was Pero Cabron; they sailed for Oran where they found the corsair Fragoso and his fleet; they promised him ten thousand ducats not to molest them, to which he agreed, but night came on and they sailed for Arcilla. (a Spanish settlement in Morocco), where a tempest scattered them. Sixteen ships put into Cartagena, where a hundred and fifty souls landed and asked for baptism; then the fleet went to Málaga, where four hundred more did the same. The rest reached Arcilla and went to Fez. Multitudes also sailed from Gibraltar to Arcilla, whence they set out for Fez, under guard of Moors hired for the purpose, but they were robbed on the journey and their wives and daughters were violated. Many returned to Arcilla, where the new arrivals, on hearing of this, remained, forming a large camp. Then they divided into two parties, one persisting in going to Fez, the other preferring baptism at Arcilla, where the commandant, the Count of Boron, treated them kindly and the priests baptized them in squads with sprinklers. The count sent them back to Spain and, up to 1496, they were returning for baptism—in Palacios, Bernaldez baptized as many as a hundred, some of them being rabbis. Those who reached Fez were naked and starving and lousy. The king, seeing them a burden, permitted them to return and they straggled back to Arcilla, robbed and murdered on the road, the women violated and the men often cut open in search of gold thought to be concealed in their stomachs. Those who remained in Fez built a great Jewry for themselves of houses of straw; one night it took fire, burning all their property and fifty or a hundred souls--after which came a pestilence, carrying off more than four thousand. Ferdinand and Isabella, seeing that all who could get back returned for baptism, set guards to keep them out unless they had money to support themselves.[404]

The whole world was pitiless to these wretched outcasts, against whom every man's hand was raised. Those who sought Portugal utilized the six months allotted to them by sending a party to Fez to arrange for transit there; many went and formed part of the luckless band whose misfortunes we have seen. Others remained, the richer paying the king a hundred cruzados per household, the poorer eight cruzados a head, while a thousand, who could pay nothing, were enslaved. These King Manoel emancipated, on his accession in 1495, but in 1497 he enforced conversion on all. Then in Lisbon, at Easter, 1506, a New Christian in a Dominican church, chanced to express a doubt as to a miraculous crucifix, when he was dragged out by the hair and slain; the Dominicans harangued the mob, parading the streets with the crucifix and exciting popular passion till a massacre ensued in which the most revolting cruelties were perpetrated. It raged for three days and ended only when no more victims could be found, the number of slain being estimated at several thousand.[405] The further fate of these refugees we shall have occasion to trace hereafter.

FATE OF THE EXILES

In Navarre, where the exiles had been kindly received, the era of toleration was brief. In 1498, an edict, based on that of Ferdinand and Isabella, gave them the alternative of baptism or expulsion and, at the same time, such difficulties were thrown in the way of exile that they mostly submitted to baptism and remained a discredited class, subjected to numerous disabilities.[406] Naples, whither numbers flocked, afforded an inhospitable refuge. In August, 1492, nine caravels arrived there, loaded with Jews and infected with pestilence, which they communicated to the city, whence it spread through the kingdom and raged for a year, causing a mortality of twenty thousand. Then, in the confusion following the invasion of Charles VIII, in 1495, the people rose against them; many abandoned their religion to escape slaughter or slavery; many were carried off to distant lands and sold as slaves; this tribulation lasted for three years, during which those who were steadfast in the faith were imprisoned or burnt or exposed to the caprices of the mob.[407] Turkey, on the whole, proved the most satisfactory refuge, where Bajazet found them such profitable subjects that he ridiculed the wisdom popularly ascribed to the Spanish sovereigns who could commit so great an act of folly. Though exposed to occasional persecution, they continued to flourish; most of the existing Jews of Turkey in Europe and a large portion of those of Turkey in Asia, are descendants of the exiles; they absorbed the older communities and their language is still the Spanish of the sixteenth century.[408]

When the fate of the exiles was, for the most part, so unendurable, it was natural that many should seek to return to their native land and, as we have seen from Bernaldez, large numbers did so. At first this was tacitly permitted, on condition of conversion, provided they brought money with them, but the sovereigns finally grew fearful that the purity of the faith would be impaired and, in 1499, an explanatory edict was issued, decreeing death and confiscation for any Jew entering Spain, whether a foreigner or returning exile, even if he asked for baptism, unless beforehand he sent word that he wished to come for that purpose, when he was to be baptized at the port of entry and a notarial act was to be taken. That this savage edict was pitilessly enforced is manifested by several cases in 1500 and 1501. Moreover, all masters of Jewish slaves were ordered to send them out of the country within two months, unless they would submit to baptism.[409] Spain was too holy a land to be polluted with the presence of a Jew, even in captivity.

In the absence of trustworthy statistics, all estimates of the number of victims must be more or less a matter of guess-work and consequently they vary with the impressions or imagination of the annalist. Bernaldez informs us that Rabbi Mair wrote to Abraham Senior that the sovereigns had banished 35,000 vassals, that is, 35,000 Jewish households, and he adds that, of the ten or twelve rabbis whom he baptized on their return, a very intelligent one, named Zentollo of Vitoria, told him that there were in Castile more than 30,000 married Jews and 6000 in the kingdoms of Aragon, making 160,000 souls when the edict was issued, which is probably as nearly correct an estimate as we can find.[410] With time the figures grew. Albertino, Inquisitor of Valencia, in 1534, quotes Reuchlin as computing the number of exiles at 420,000.[411] The cautious Zurita quotes Bernaldez and adds that others put the total at 400,000, while Mariana tells us that most authors assert the number of households to have been 170,000, and some put the total at 800,000 souls; Páramo quotes the figures of 124,000 households or over 600,000 souls.[412] Isidore Loeb, after an exhaustive review of all authorities, Jewish and Christian, reaches the estimate[413]--

Emigrants,	165,000
Baptized,	50,000
Died,	20,000
	235,000

and this, in view of the diminished number of Jews, as shown by the Repartimiento of 1474 (p. 125) is probably too large an estimate.

CONTEMPORARY OPINION

Whatever may have been the number, the sum of human misery was incomputable. Rabbi Joseph, whose father was one of the exiles, eloquently describes the sufferings of his race: "For some of them the Turks killed to take out the gold which they had swallowed to hide it; some of them hunger and the plague consumed and some of them were cast naked by the captains on the isles of the sea; and some of them were sold for men-servants and maid-servants in Genoa and its villages and some of them were cast into the sea.... For there were among those who were cast into the isles of the sea upon Provence a Jew and his old father fainting from hunger, begging bread, for there was no one to break unto him in a strange country. And the man went and sold his son for bread to restore the soul of the old man. And it came to pass, when he returned to his old father, that he found him fallen down dead and he rent his clothes. And he returned unto the baker to take his son and the baker would not give him back and he cried out with a loud and bitter cry for his son and there was none to deliver."[414] Penniless, friendless and despised they were cast forth into a world which had been taught that to oppress them was a service to the Redeemer.

Yet such were the convictions of the period, in the fifteenth century after Christ had died for man, that this crime against humanity met with nothing but applause among contemporaries. Men might admit that it was unwise from the point of view of statesmanship and damaging to the prosperity of the land, but this only enhanced the credit due to the sovereigns whose piety was equal to the sacrifice. When, in 1495, Alexander VI granted to them the proud title of Catholic Kings, the expulsion of the Jews was enumerated among the services to the faith entitling them to this distinction.[415] Even so liberal and cultured a thinker as Gian Pico della Mirandola, praises them for it, while he admits that even Christians were moved to pity by the calamities of the sufferers, nearly all of whom were consumed by shipwreck, pestilence and hunger, rendering the destruction equal to that inflicted by Titus and Hadrian.[416] It is true that Machiavelli, faithful to his general principles, seeks to find in Ferdinand's participation a political rather than a religious motive, but even he characterizes the act as a pietosa crudeltà.[417] So far, indeed, was it from being a cruelty, in the eyes of the theologians of the period, that Ferdinand was held to have exercised his power mercifully, for Arnaldo Albertino proved by the canon law that he would have been fully justified in putting them all to the sword and seizing their property.[418]

***

The Edict of Expulsion proclaimed to the world the policy which in its continuous development did so much for the abasement of Spain. At the same time it closed the career of avowed Jews in the Spanish dominions. Henceforth we shall meet with them as apostate Christians, the occasion and the victims of the Inquisition.

CHAPTER IV - ESTABLISHMENT OF THE INQUISITION

Much as the Conversos had gained, from a worldly point of view, by their change of religion, their position, in one respect, as we have seen, was seriously deteriorated. As Jews they might be despoiled and humiliated, confined in narrow Jewries and restricted as to their careers and means of livelihood, but withal they enjoyed complete freedom of faith, in which they were subjected only to their own rabbis. They were outside of the Church and the Church claimed no jurisdiction over them in matters of religion, so long as they did not openly blaspheme Christianity or seek to make proselytes. As soon, however, as the convert was baptized he became a member of the Church and for any aberration from orthodoxy he was amenable to its laws. As the Inquisition had never existed in Castile and was inactive in Aragon, while the bishops, who held ordinary jurisdiction over heresy and apostasy, were too turbulent and worldly to waste thought on the exercise of their authority in such matters, the Conversos seem never to have recognized the possibility of being held to account for any secret leaning to the faith which they had ostensibly abandoned. The circumstances under which the mass of conversions was effected--threats of massacre or the wearing pressure of inhuman laws--were not such as to justify confidence in the sincerity of the neophytes, nor, when baptism was administered indiscriminately to multitudes, was there a possibility of detailed instruction in the complicated theology of their new faith. Rabbinical Judaism, moreover, so entwines itself with every detail of the believer's daily life, and attaches so much importance to the observances which it enjoins, that it was impossible for whole communities thus suddenly Christianized, to abandon the rites and usages which, through so many generations, had become a part of existence itself. Earnest converts might have brought up their children as Christians and the grandchildren might have outgrown the old customs, but the Conversos could not be earnest converts, and the sacred traditions, handed down by father to son from the days of the Sanhedrin, were too precious to be set aside. The Anusim, as they were known to their Hebrew brethren, thus were unwilling Christians, practising what Jewish rites they dared, and it was held to be the duty of all Jews to bring them back to the true faith.[419]

JUDAISM OF CONVERSOS

As soon, therefore, as the Church had gained her new recruits she began to regard them with a pardonable degree of suspicion, although she seems to have made no effort to instruct them in her doctrines after hurriedly baptizing them by the thousand. In 1429 the council of Tortosa indignantly denounced the unspeakable cruelty of the Conversos who, with damnable negligence, permit their children to remain in servitude of the devil by omitting to have them baptized. To remedy this the Ordinaries were ordered, by the free use of ecclesiastical censures, and by calling in if necessary the secular arm, to cause all such children to be baptized within eight days after birth, and all temporal lords were commanded to lend their aid in this pious work.[420] The outlook, certainly, was not promising that the coming generation should be free from the inveterate Jewish errors. How little concealment, indeed, was thought necessary by the Conversos, so long as they exhibited a nominal adherence to Catholicism, is plainly shown by the testimony in the early trials before the Inquisition, where servants and neighbors give ample evidence as to Jewish observances openly followed. Still more conclusive is a case occurring, in 1456, in Rosellon, which, although at the time held in pawn by France, was subject to the Inquisition of Aragon. Certain Conversos not only persisted in Jewish practices, such as eating meat in lent, but forced their Christian servants to do likewise, and when the inquisitor, Fray Mateo de Rapica, with the aid of the Bishop of Elna, sought to reduce them to conformity, they defiantly published a defamatory libel upon him and, with the assistance of certain laymen, afflicted him with injuries and expenses.[421] It was not without cause that, when Bishop Alfonso de Santa María procured the decree of 1434 from the council of Basle, he included a clause branding as heretics all Conversos who adhered to Jewish superstitions, directing bishops and inquisitors to enquire strictly after them and to punish them condignly, and pronouncing liable to the penalties of fautorship all who support them in those practices.[422] The decree, of course, proved a dead letter, but none the less was it the foreshadowing of the Inquisition. When Nicholas V, in 1449, issued his bull in favor of the Conversos, he followed the example of the council of Basle, in excepting those who secretly continued to practise Jewish rites. In the methods commonly employed to procure conversions the result was inevitable and incurable.

What rendered this especially serious was the success of the Conversos in obtaining high office in Church and State. Important sees were occupied by bishops of Jewish blood; the chapters, the monastic orders and the curacies were full of them; they were prominent in the royal council and everywhere enjoyed positions of influence. The most powerful among them--the Santa Marías, the Dávilas and their following--had turned against the royal favorite Alvaro de Luna and, with the discontented nobles, were plotting his ruin, when he seems to have conceived the idea that, if he could introduce the Inquisition in Castile, he might find in it a weapon wherewith to subdue them. At least this is the only explanation of an application made to Nicholas V, in 1451, by Juan II, for a delegation of papal inquisitorial power for the chastisement of Judaizing Christians. The popes had too long vainly desired to introduce the Inquisition in Castile for Nicholas to neglect this opportunity. He promptly commissioned the Bishop of Osma, his vicar general, and the Scholasticus of Salamanca as inquisitors, either by themselves or through such delegates as they might appoint, to investigate and punish without appeal all such offenders, to deprive them of ecclesiastical dignities and benefices and of temporal possessions, to pronounce them incapable of holding such positions in future, to imprison and degrade them, and, if the offence required, to abandon them to the secular arm for burning. Full power was granted to perform any acts necessary or opportune to the discharge of these duties and, if resistance were offered, to invoke the aid of the secular power. All this was within the regular routine of the inquisitorial office, but there was one clause which showed that the object of the measure was the destruction of de Luna's enemies, the Converso bishops, for the commission empowered the appointees to proceed even against bishops--a faculty never before granted to inquisitors and subsequently, as we shall see, withheld when the new Inquisition was organized.[423] All this was the formal establishment of the Inquisition on Castilian soil and, if circumstances had permitted its development, it would not have been left for Isabella to introduce the institution. The Inquisition, however, rested on the secular power for its efficiency. In Spain, especially, there was little respect for the naked papal authority, while that of Juan II was too much enfeebled to enable him to establish so serious an innovation. The New Christians recognized that their safety depended on de Luna's downfall; the conspiracy against him won over the nerveless Juan II and, in 1453, he was hurriedly condemned and executed. Naturally the bull remained inoperative, and, some ten years later, Alonso de Espina feelingly complains "Some are heretics and Christian perverts, others are Jews, others Saracens, others devils. There is no one to investigate the errors of the heretics. The ravening wolves, O Lord, have entered thy flock, for the shepherds are few; many are hirelings and as hirelings they care only for shearing and not for feeding thy sheep."[424]

ALONSO DE ESPINA

To Fray Alonso de Espina may be ascribed a large share in hastening the development of organized persecution in Spain, by inflaming the race hatred of recent origin which already needed no stimulation. He was a man of the highest reputation for learning and sanctity and when, early in his career, he was discouraged by the slender result of his preaching, a miracle revealed to him the favor of Heaven and induced him to persevere.[425] In 1453 we find him administering to Alvaro de Luna the last consolations of religion at his hurried execution, and he became the confessor of Henry IV.[426] In 1454, when a child was robbed and murdered at Valladolid and the body was scratched up by dogs, the Jews were, of course, suspected and confession was obtained by torture. Alonso happened to be there and aroused much public excitement by his sermons on the subject, in which he asserted that the Jews had ripped out the child's heart, had burnt it and, by mingling the ashes with wine, had made an unholy sacrament, but unfortunately, as he tells us, bribery of the judges and of King Henry enabled the offenders to escape.[427] The next year, 1455, as Provincial of the Observantine Franciscans, he was engaged in an unsuccessful attempt to drive the Conventuals out of Segovia or to obtain a separate convent for the Observantines.[428] Thenceforth he seems to have concentrated his energies on the endeavor to bring about the forced conversion of the Jews and to introduce the Inquisition as a corrective of the apostasy of the Conversos. He is usually considered to have himself belonged to the class of Converso who entertained an inextinguishable hatred for their former brethren, but there is no evidence of this and the probabilities are altogether against it.[429]

His Fortalicium Fidei is a deplorable exhibition of the fanatic passions which finally dominated Spain. He rakes together, from the chronicles of all Europe, the stories of Jews slaying Christian children in their unholy rites, of their poisoning wells and fountains, of their starting conflagrations and of all the other horrors by which a healthy detestation of the unfortunate race was created and stimulated. The Jewish law, he tells us, commands them to slay Christians and to despoil them whenever practicable and they obey it with quenchless hatred and insatiable thirst for revenge. Thrice a day in their prayers they repeat "Let there be no hope for Meschudanim (Conversos); may all heretics and all who speak against Israel be speedily cut off; may the kingdom of the proud be broken and destroyed and may all our enemies be crushed and humbled speedily in our days!"[430] But the evil now wrought by Jews is trifling to that which they will work at the coming of Antichrist, for they will be his supporters. Alexander the Great shut them up in the mountains of the Caspian, adjoining the realms of the Great Khan or monarch of Cathay. There, between the castles of Gog and Magog, confined by an enchanted wall, they have multiplied until now they are numerous enough to fill twenty-four kingdoms. When Antichrist comes they will break loose and rally around him, as likewise will all the Jews of the Diaspora, for they will regard him as their promised Messiah and will worship him as their God, and with their united aid he will overrun the earth. With such eventualities in prospect it is no wonder that Fray Alonso could convince himself, in opposition to the canon law, that the forced conversion of the Jews was lawful and expedient, as well as the baptism of their children without their consent.[431] When such was the temper in which a man of distinguished learning and intelligence discussed the relations between Jews and Christians, we can imagine the character of the sermons in which, from numerous pulpits, the passions of the people were inflamed against their neighbors.

JUDAISM OF CONVERSOS

If open Judaism thus was abhorrent, still worse was the insidious heresy of the Conversos who pretended to be Christians and who more or less openly continued to practise Jewish rites and perverted the faithful by their influence and example. These abounded on every hand and there was scarce an effort made to repress or to punish them. The law, from the earliest times, provided the death penalty for their offence, but there was none found to enforce it.[432] Fray Alonso dolefully asserts that they succeeded by their presents in so blinding princes and prelates that they were never punished and that, when one person accused them, three would come forward in their favor. He relates an instance of such an attempt, in 1458 at Formesta, where a barber named Fernando Sánchez publicly maintained monotheism. Fortunately Bishop Pedro of Palencia had zeal enough to prosecute him, when his offence was proved and, under fear of the death penalty, he recanted, but when he was condemned to imprisonment for life so much sympathy was excited by the unaccustomed severity that, in accordance with numerous petitions, the sentence was commuted to ten years' exile. In 1459, at Segovia, a number of Conversos were by an accident discovered in the synagogue, praying at the feast of Tabernacles, but nothing seems to have been done with them. At Medina del Campo, in the same year, Fray Alonso was informed that there were more than a hundred who denied the truth of the New Testament, but he could do nothing save preach against them, and subsequently he learned that in one house there were more than thirty men, at that very time, laid up in consequence of undergoing circumcision. It is no wonder that he earnestly advocated the introduction of the Inquisition as the only cure for this scandalous condition of affairs, that he argued in its favor with the warmest zeal and answered all objections in a manner which showed that he was familiar with its workings from a careful study of the Clementines and of Eymeric's Directorium.[433]

The good Cura de los Palacios is equally emphatic in his testimony as to the prevalence of Judaism among the Conversos. For the most part, he says, they continued to be Jews, or rather they were neither Christians nor Jews but heretics, and this heresy increased and flourished through the riches and pride of many wise and learned men, bishops and canons and friars and abbots and financial agents and secretaries of the king and of the magnates. At the commencement of the reign of Ferdinand and Isabella this heresy grew so powerful that the clerks were on the point of preaching the law of Moses. These heretics avoided baptizing their children and, when they could not prevent it, they washed off the baptism on returning from the church; they ate meat on fast days and unleavened bread at Passover, which they observed as well as the Sabbaths; they had Jews who secretly preached in their houses and rabbis who slaughtered meat and birds for them; they performed all the Jewish ceremonies in secret as well as they could and avoided, as far as possible, receiving the sacrament; they never confessed truly--a confessor, after hearing one of them, cut off a corner of his garment saying "Since you have never sinned I want a piece of your clothes as a relic to cure the sick." Many of them attained to great wealth, for they had no conscience in usury, saying that they were spoiling the Egyptians. They assumed airs of superiority, asserting that there was no better race on earth, nor wiser, nor shrewder, nor more honorable through their descent from the tribes of Israel.[434]

COMMENCEMENT OF PERSECUTION

In fact, when we consider the popular detestation of the Conversos and the invitation to attack afforded by their Judaizing tendencies, the postponement in establishing the Inquisition is attributable to the all-pervading lawlessness of the period and the absence of a strong central power. The people gratified their hatred by an occasional massacre, with its accompanying pillage, but among the various factions of the distracted state no one was strong enough to attempt a systematic movement provoking the bitterest opposition of a powerful class whose members occupied confidential positions in the court not alone of the king but of every noble and prelate. Earnest and untiring as was Fray Alonso's zeal it therefore was fruitless. In August, 1461, he induced the heads of the Observantine Franciscans to address the chapter of the Geronimites urging a union of both bodies in the effort to obtain the introduction of the Inquisition. The suggestion was favorably received but the answer was delayed, and the impatient Fray Alonso, with Fray Fernando de la Plaza and other Observantines, appealed directly to King Henry, representing the prevalence of the Judaizing heresy throughout the land and the habitual circumcision of the children of Conversos.[435] The zeal of Fray Fernando outran his discretion and in his sermons he declared that he possessed the foreskins of children thus treated. King Henry sent for him and said that this practice was a gross insult to the Church, which it was his duty to punish, ordering him to produce the objects and reveal the names of the culprits. The fraile could only reply that he had heard it from persons of repute and authority, but, on being commanded to state their names, refused to do so, thus tacitly acknowledging that he had no proof. The Conversos were not slow in taking advantage of his blunder and, to crown the defeat of the Observantines, the Geronimites changed their views. Their general, Fray Alonso de Oropesa, who himself had Jewish blood in his veins, was a man deservedly esteemed; under his impulsion they mounted the pulpit in defence of the Conversos and the Observantines for the time were silenced.[436] While the labors of the fiery Fray Alonso were unquestionably successful in intensifying the bitterness of race hatred, their only direct result was seen in the Concordia of Medina del Campo between Henry IV and his revolted nobles in 1464-5. In this an elaborate clause deplored the spread of the Judaizing heresy; it ordered the bishops to establish a searching inquisition throughout all lands and lordships, regardless of franchises and privileges, for the detection and punishment of the heretics; it pledged the king to support the measure in every way and to employ the confiscations in the war with the Moors and it pointed out that the enforcement of this plan would put an end to the tumults and massacres directed against the suspects.[437] Under this impulsion some desultory persecution occurred. In the trial of Beatriz Nuñez, by the Inquisition of Toledo in 1485, witnesses allude to her husband, Fernando González who, some twenty years before, had been convicted and reconciled.[438] More detailed is a case occurring at Llerena in 1467, where, on September 17th, two Conversos, Garcí Fernández Valency and Pedro Franco de Villareal, were discovered in the act of performing Jewish ceremonies. The alcalde mayor, Alvaro de Céspedes, at once seized them and carried them before the episcopal vicar, Joan Millan. They confessed their Judaism and the vicar at once sentenced them to be burnt alive, which was executed the same day; two women compromised in the matter were condemned to other penalties and the house in which the heresy had been perpetrated was torn down.[439] In such cases the bishops were merely exercising their imprescriptible jurisdiction over heresy, but the prelacy of Castile was too much occupied with worldly affairs to devote any general or sustained energy to the suppression of Judaizers, and the land was too anarchical for the royal power to exert any influence in carrying the Concordia into effect; the Deposition of Avila, which followed in the next year, plunged everything again into confusion and the only real importance of the attempt lies in its significance of what was impending when peace and a strong government should render such a measure feasible. Yet it is a noteworthy fact that, in all the long series of the Córtes of Castile, from the earliest times, the proceedings of which have been published in full, there was no petition for anything approaching an Inquisition. In the fourteenth century there were many complaints about the Jews and petitions for restrictive laws, but these diminish in the fifteenth century and the later Córtes, from 1450 on, are almost free from them. The fearful disorders of the land gave the procuradores or deputies enough to complain about and they seem to have had no time to waste on problematical dangers to religion.[440]

***

A History of the Inquisition of Spain: Volume I
PRELIMINARY MOVEMENTS

This was the situation at the accession of Ferdinand and Isabella in 1474. Some years were necessary to settle the question of the succession, disputed by the unfortunate Beltraneja, and to quell the unruly nobles. During this period Sixtus IV renewed the attempt to introduce the papal Inquisition, for, in sending Nicoló Franco to Castile as legate, he commissioned him with full inquisitorial faculties to prosecute and punish the false Christians who after baptism persisted in the observance of Jewish rites.[441] The effort, however, was fruitless and is interesting chiefly from the evidence which it gives of the desire of Sixtus to give to Castile the blessing of the Inquisition. Ferdinand and Isabella, as we have seen, were habitually jealous of papal encroachments and were anxious to limit rather than to extend the legatine functions; they did not respond to the papal zeal for the purity of the faith and even when quiet was to a great extent restored they took no initiative with regard to a matter which had seemed to Fray Alonso de Espina so immeasurably important. In his capacity of agitator he had been succeeded by Fray Alonso de Hojeda, prior of the Dominican house of San Pablo of Seville, who devoted himself to the destruction of Judaism, both open as professed by the Jews and concealed as attributed to the Conversos. The battle of Toro, March 1, 1476, virtually broke up the party of the Beltraneja, of which the leaders made their peace as best they could, and the sovereigns could at last undertake the task of pacifying the land. At the end of July, 1477, Isabella, after capturing the castle of Trugillo, came, as we have seen, to Seville where she remained until October, 1478.[442] The presence of the court, with Conversos filling many of its most important posts, excited Fray Alonso to greater ardor than ever. It was in vain, however, that he called the queen's attention to the danger threatening the faith and the State from the multitude of pretended Christians in high places. She was receiving faithful service from members of the class accused and she probably was too much occupied with the business in hand to undertake a task that could be postponed. It is said that her confessor, Torquemada, at an earlier period, had induced her to take a vow that, when she should reach the throne, she would devote her life to the extirpation of heresy and the supremacy of the Catholic faith, but this may safely be dismissed as a legend of later date.[443] Be this as it may, all that was done at the moment was that Pero González de Mendoza, then Archbishop of Seville, held a synod in which was promulgated a catechism setting forth the belief and duties of the Christian, which was published in the churches and hung up for public information in every parish, while the priests were exhorted to increased vigilance and the frailes to fresh zeal in making converts.[444] The adoption of such a device betrays the previous neglect of all instruction of the Marranos in the new religion imposed on them.

The court left Seville and Hojeda's opportunity seemed to have passed away. Whatever alacrity the priests may have shown in obeying their archbishop, nothing was accomplished nor was the increased zeal of the frailes rewarded with success. There is a story accredited by all historians of the Inquisition that Hojeda chanced to hear of a meeting of Jews and Conversos on the night of Good Friday, March 28, 1478, to celebrate their impious rites and that he hastened with the evidence to Córdova and laid it before the sovereigns, resulting in the punishment of the culprits and turning the scale in favor of introducing the Inquisition, but there is no contemporary evidence of its truth and the dates are irreconcilable, nor was such an incentive necessary.[445] The insincerity of the conversion of a large portion of the Marranos was incontestable; according to the principles universally accepted at the period it was the duty of the sovereigns to reduce them to conformity; with the pacification of the land the time had come to attempt this resolutely and comprehensively and the only question was as to the method.

THE INQUISITION APPLIED FOR

It was inevitable that there should have been a prolonged struggle in the court before the drastic remedy of the Inquisition was adopted. The efforts of its advocates were directed, not against the despised and friendless Jews, but against the powerful Conversos, embracing many of the most trusted counsellors of the sovereigns and men high in station in the Church, who could not but recognize the danger impending on all who traced their descent from Israel. There seems at first to have been a kind of compromise adopted, under which Pedro Fernández de Solis, Bishop of Cadiz, who was Provisor of Seville, with the Assistente Diego de Merlo, Fray Alfonso de Hojeda and some other frailes were commissioned to take charge of the matter, with power to inflict punishment. This resulted in a report by the commissioners to the sovereigns that a great portion of the citizens of Seville were infected with heresy, that it involved men high in station and power, and that it spread throughout not only Andalusia but Castile, so that it was incurable save by the organization of the Inquisition.[446] The Archbishop Mendoza, doubtless disgusted with the failure of his methods of instruction, joined in these representations and they had a powerful supporter in Fray Thomas de Torquemada, prior of the Dominican convent of Santa Cruz in Segovia, who, as confessor of the sovereigns, had much influence over them and who had long been urging the vigorous chastisement of heresy.[447] At last the victory was won. Ferdinand and Isabella resolved to introduce the Inquisition in the Castilian kingdoms and their ambassadors to the Holy See, the Bishop of Osma and his brother Diego de Santillan, were ordered to procure the necessary bull from Sixtus IV.[448] This must have been shrouded in profound secrecy, for, in July, 1478, while negotiations must have been on foot in Rome, Ferdinand and Isabella convoked a national synod at Seville which sat until August 1st. In the propositions laid by the sovereigns before this body there is no hint that such a measure was desired or proposed and, in the deliberations of the assembled prelates, there is no indication that the Church thought any action against the Conversos necessary.[449] Even as late as 1480, after the procurement of the bull and before its enforcement, the Córtes of Toledo presented to the sovereigns a detailed memorial embodying all the measures of reform desired by the people. In this the separation of Christians from Jews and Moors is asked for, but there is no request for the prosecution of apostate Conversos.[450] Evidently there was no knowledge of and no popular demand for the impending Inquisition.

Sixtus can have been nothing loath to accomplish the introduction of the Inquisition in Castile, which his predecessors had so frequently and so vainly attempted and which he had essayed to do a few years previous by granting the necessary faculties to his legate. If the request of the Castilian sovereigns, therefore, was not immediately granted it cannot have been from humanitarian motives as alleged by some modern apologists, but because Ferdinand and Isabella desired, not the ordinary papal Inquisition, but one which should be under the royal control and should pour into the royal treasury the resultant confiscations. Hitherto the appointment of inquisitors had always been made by the Provincials of the Dominican or Franciscan Orders according as the territory belonged to one or to the other, with occasional interference on the part of the Holy See, from which the commissions emanated. It was a delegation of the supreme papal authority and had always been held completely independent of the secular power, but Ferdinand and Isabella were too jealous of papal interference in the internal affairs of their kingdoms to permit this, and it is an evidence of the extreme desire of Sixtus to extend the Inquisition over Castile that he consented to make so important a concession. There also was doubtless discussion over the confiscations which the wealth of the Conversos promised to render large. This was a matter in which there was no universally recognized practice. In France they enured to the temporal seigneur. In Italy the custom varied at different times and in the various states, but the papacy assumed to control it and, in the fourteenth century, it claimed the whole, to be divided equally between the Inquisition and the papal camera.[451] The matter was evidently one to be determined by negotiation, and in this too the sovereigns had their way, for the confiscations were tacitly abandoned to them. Nothing was said as to defraying the expenses of the institution, but this was inferred by the absorption of the confiscations. If it was to be dependent on the crown the crown must provide for it, and we shall see hereafter the various devices by which a portion of the burden was subsequently thrown upon the Church.

NATURE OF THE PAPAL BULL

The bull as finally issued bears date November 1, 1478, and is a very simple affair which, on its face, bears no signs of its momentous influence in moulding the destinies of the Spanish Peninsula. After reciting the existence in Spain of false Christians and the request of Ferdinand and Isabella that the pope should provide a remedy, it authorizes them to appoint three bishops or other suitable men, priests either regular or secular, over forty years of age, masters or bachelors in theology or doctors or licentiates of canon law, and to remove and replace them at pleasure. These are to have the jurisdiction and faculties of bishops and inquisitors over heretics, their fautors and receivers.[452] Subsequently Sixtus pronounced the bull to have been drawn inconsiderately and not in accordance with received practice and the decrees of his predecessors, which doubtless referred to the power of appointment and removal lodged in the crown and also to the omission of the requirement of episcopal concurrence in rendering judgment.[453] The creation of inquisitors was in itself an invasion of episcopal jurisdiction, which, from the earliest history of the institution, had been the source of frequent trouble, and where, as in Spain, many bishops were of Jewish blood and therefore under suspicion, the question was more intricate than elsewhere. With respect to this, moreover, it is observable that the bull did not confer, like that of Nicholas V, in 1451, jurisdiction over bishops in any special derogation of the decree of Boniface VIII requiring them, when suspected of heresy, to be tried by the pope.[454] Both of these questions, as we shall see, subsequently gave rise to considerable discussion.

So far the anti-Semitic party had triumphed, but Isabella's hesitation to exercise the powers thus obtained shows that the Conversos in her court did not abandon the struggle and that for nearly two years they succeeded in keeping the balance even. It is possible also that Ferdinand was not inclined to a severity of which he could forecast the economical disadvantages, for as late as January, 1482, a letter from him to the inquisitors of his kingdom of Valencia manifests a marked preference for the use of mild and merciful methods.[455] Whatever may have been the influences at work, it was not until September 17, 1480, that the momentous step was taken which was to exercise so sinister an influence on the destinies of Spain. On that day commissions were issued to two Dominicans, Miguel de Morillo, master of theology, and Juan de San Martin, bachelor of theology and friar of San Pablo in Seville, who were emphatically told that any dereliction of duty would entail their removal, with forfeiture of all their temporalities and denationalization in the kingdom, thus impressing upon them their subordination to the crown. Still there were delays. October 9th a royal order commanded all officials to give them free transportation and provisions on their way to Seville, where, as in the most infected spot, operations were to commence. When they reached the city they waited on the chapter and presented their credentials; the municipal council met them at the chapter-house door and escorted them to the city hall, where a formal reception took place and a solemn procession was organized for the following Sunday. They were thus fairly installed but apparently they still found difficulties thrown in their way for, on December 27, it was deemed necessary to issue a royal cédula to the officials ordering them to render all aid to the inquisitors.[456]

COMMENCEMENT AT SEVILLE

They had not waited for this to organize their tribunal, with Doctor Juan Ruiz de Medina as assessor and Juan Lopez del Barco, a chaplain of the queen, as promotor fiscal or prosecuting officer. To these were added, May 13, 1481, Diego de Merlo, assistente or corregidor of Seville, and the Licentiate Ferrand Yáñez de Lobon as receivers of confiscations--an indispensable office in view of the profits of persecution. All soon found plenty of work. The Conversos of Seville had not been unmindful of the coming tempest. Many of them had fled to the lands of the neighboring nobles, in the expectation that feudal jurisdictions would protect them, even against a spiritual court such as that of the Inquisition. To prevent this change of domicile a royal decree ordered that no one should leave any place where inquisitors were holding their tribunal, but in the general terror this arbitrary command received scant obedience. A more efficient step was a proclamation addressed, on January 2, 1481, to the Marquis of Cadiz and other nobles by the frailes Miguel and Juan. This proved that no error had been made in the selection of those who were to lay the foundations of the Inquisition and that a new era had opened for Spain. The two simple friars spoke with an assured audacity to grandees who had been wont to treat with their sovereigns on almost equal terms--an audacity which must have appeared incredible to those to whom it was addressed, but to which Spain in time became accustomed from the Holy Office. The great Rodrigo Ponce de Leon and all other nobles were commanded to search their territories, to seize all strangers and newcomers and to deliver them within fifteen days at the prison of the Inquisition; to sequestrate their property and confide it, properly inventoried, to trustworthy persons who should account for it to the king or to the inquisitors. In vigorous language they were told that any failure in obeying these orders would bring upon them excommunication removable only by the inquisitors or their superiors, with forfeiture of rank and possessions and the release of their vassals from allegiance and from all payments due--a release which the inquisitors assumed to grant in advance, adding that they would prosecute them as fautors, receivers and defenders of heretics.[457] This portentous utterance was effective: the number of prisoners was speedily so great that the convent of San Pablo, which the inquisitors at first occupied, became insufficient and they obtained permission to establish themselves in the great fortress of Triana, the stronghold of Seville, of which the immense size and the gloomy dungeons rendered it appropriate for the work in hand.[458]

THE FIRST AUTO DE FE

There were other Conversos, however, who imagined that resistance was preferable to flight. Diego de Susan, one of the leading citizens of Seville, whose wealth was estimated at ten millions of maravedís, assembled some of his prominent brethren of Seville, Utrera and Carmona to deliberate as to their action. The meeting was held in the church of San Salvador and comprised ecclesiastics of high rank, magistrates and officials belonging to the threatened class. Civic tumults had been so customary a resource, when any object was to be gained, that Susan naturally suggested, in a fiery speech, that they should recruit faithful men, collect a store of arms, and that the first arrest by the inquisitors should be the signal of a rising in which the inquisitors should be slain and thus an emphatic warning be given to deter others from renewing the attempt. In spite of some faint-heartedness manifested by one or two of those present, the plan was adopted and steps were taken to carry it out. When Pedro Fernández Venedera, mayordomo of the cathedral, one of the conspirators, was arrested, weapons to arm a hundred men were found in his house, showing how active were the preparations on foot. The plot would doubtless have been executed and have led to a massacre, such as we have so often seen in the Spanish cities, but for a daughter of Diego Susan, whose loveliness had won for her the name of the Fermosa Fembra. She was involved in an intrigue with a Christian caballero, to whom she revealed the secret and it was speedily conveyed to the inquisitors.[459]

Nothing could better have suited their purpose. If there had been any feeling of opposition to them on the part of the authorities it disappeared and the most important members of the Converso community were in their power. Diego de Merlo, the assistente of Seville, arrested at the bidding of the inquisitors the richest and most honorable Conversos, magistrates and dignitaries, who were confined in San Pablo and thence transferred to the castle of Triana. The trials were prompt and at the rendering of sentence a consulta de fe or assembly of experts was convoked, consisting of lawyers and the provisor of the bishopric, thus recognizing the necessity of concurrent action on the part of the episcopal jurisdiction. What justified the sentence of burning it would be difficult to say. It was not obstinate heresy for one at least of the victims is stated to have died as a good Christian; it could not have been the plot, for this, in so far as it was an ecclesiastical offence, was merely impeding the Inquisition, and even the assassins of St. Peter Martyr, when they professed repentance, were admitted to penance. It was a new departure, in disregard of all the canons, and it gave warning that the New Inquisition of Spain was not to follow in the footsteps of the Old, but was to mark out for itself a yet bloodier and more terrible career.[460]

Justice was prompt and the first auto de fe was celebrated February 6, 1481, when six men and women were burnt and the sermon was preached by Fray Alonso de Hojeda, who now saw the efforts of so many years crowned with success. He might well say nunc demittis, for though a second auto followed in a few days his eyes were not to rejoice at the holy spectacle, for the pestilence which was to carry off fifteen thousand of the people of Seville was now commencing and he was one of the earliest victims. In the second auto there were only three burnings, Diego de Susan, Manuel Sauli and Bartolomé de Torralba, three of the wealthiest and most important citizens of Seville. As though to show that the work thus begun was to be an enduring one, a quemadero, brasero, or burning-place was constructed in the Campo de Tablada, so massively that its foundations can still be traced. On four pillars at the corners were erected statues of the prophets in plaster-of-Paris, apparently to indicate that, although technically the burning was the work of secular justice, it was performed at the command of religion.[461]

THE TERM OF GRACE

Further arrests and burnings promptly followed, the wealth and prominence of the victims proving that here was a tribunal which was no respecter of persons and that money or favor could avail nothing against its rigid fanaticism. The flight of the terror-stricken Conversos was stimulated afresh, but the Inquisition was not thus to be balked of its prey; flight was forbidden and guards were placed at the gates, where so many were arrested that no place of confinement sufficiently capacious for them could be found, yet notwithstanding this great numbers escaped to the lands of the nobles, to Portugal and to the Moors. The plague now began to rage with violence, God and man seemed to be uniting for the destruction of the unhappy Conversos, and they petitioned Diego de Merlo to allow them to save their lives by leaving the pest-ridden city. The request was humanely granted to those who could procure passes, on condition that they should leave their property behind and only take with them what was necessary for immediate use. Under these regulations multitudes departed, more than eight thousand finding refuge at Mairena, Marchena and Palacios. The Marquis of Cadiz, the Duke of Medina Sidonia and other nobles received them hospitably, but many kept on to Portugal or to the Moors and some, we are told, even found refuge in Rome. The inquisitors themselves were obliged to abandon the city, but their zeal allowed of no respite; they removed their tribunal to Aracena, where they found ample work to do, burning there twenty-three men and women, besides the corpses and bones of numerous deceased heretics, exhumed for the purpose. When the pestilence diminished they returned to Seville and resumed their work there with unrelaxing ardor.[462] According to a contemporary, by the fourth of November they had burnt two hundred and ninety-eight persons and had condemned seventy-nine to perpetual prison.[463]

As novices, it would seem that the zeal of the inquisitors had plunged them into the business of arresting and trying suspects without resorting to the preliminary device, which had been found useful in the earliest operations of the Holy Office--the Term of Grace. This was a period, longer or shorter according to the discretion of the inquisitors, during which those who felt themselves guilty could come forward and confess, when they would be reconciled to the Church and subjected to penance, pecuniary and otherwise, severe enough, but preferable to the stake. One of the conditions was that of stating all that they knew of other heretics and apostates, which proved an exceedingly fruitful source of information as, under the general terror, there was little hesitation in denouncing not only friends and acquaintances, but the nearest and dearest kindred--parents and children and brothers and sisters. No better means of detecting the hidden ramifications of Judaism could be devised and, towards the middle of the year 1481, the inquisitors adopted it.[464] The mercy thus promised was scanty, as we shall see hereafter when we come to consider the subject, but it brought in vast numbers and autos de fe were organized in which they were paraded as penitents, no less than fifteen hundred being exhibited in one of these solemnities. It can readily be conceived how soon the inquisitors were in possession of information inculpating Conversos in every corner of the land. It was freely asserted that they were all in reality Jews, who were waiting for God to lead them out of the worse than Egyptian bondage in which they were held by the Christians.[465] Thus was demonstrated not only the necessity of the Inquisition but of its extension throughout Spain. The evil was too great and its immediate repression too important for the work to be entrusted to the two friars laboring so zealously in Seville. Permission had been obtained only for the appointment of three and application was made to Sixtus IV for additional powers. On this occasion he did not as before allow the commissions to be granted in the name of the sovereigns but issued them direct to those nominated to him by them, whereby the inquisitors held their faculties immediately from the Holy See. Thus by a brief of February 11, 1482, he commissioned seven--Pedro Ocaño, Pedro Martínez de Barrio, Alfonso de San Cebriano, Rodrigo Segarra, Thomás de Torquemada and Bernardo Santa María, all Dominicans.[466] Still more were required, of whose appointments we have no definite knowledge, to man the tribunals which were speedily formed at Ciudad-Real, Córdova, Jaen, and possibly at Segovia.[466a]

CIUDAD-REAL AND TOLEDO

The one at Ciudad-Real was intended for the great archiepiscopal province of Toledo, to which city it was transferred in 1485. The reason why it was first established at the former place may perhaps be that the warlike Archbishop Alonso Carrillo, whether through zeal for the faith or in order to assert his episcopal jurisdiction over heresy and prevent the intrusion of the papal inquisitors, had appointed before his death, July 1, 1482, a certain Doctor Thomás as inquisitor in Toledo. To what extent the latter performed his functions we have no means of knowing, the only trace of his activity being the production and incorporation, in the records of subsequent trials by the Inquisition of Ciudad-Real, of evidence taken by him.[467] Be this as it may the Inquisition of Ciudad-Real was not organized until the latter half of 1483. It commenced by issuing an Edict of Grace for thirty days, at the expiration of which it extended the time for another thirty days. Meanwhile it was busily employed, throughout October and November, in making a general inquest and taking testimony from all who would come forward to give evidence. In the resultant trials the names of some of the witnesses appear with suspicious frequency and the nature of their reckless general assertions, without personal knowledge, shows how flimsy was much of the evidence on which prosecutions were based. That the inquest was thorough and that every one who knew anything damaging to a Converso was brought up to state it may be assumed from the trial of Sancho de Ciudad in which the evidence of no less than thirty-four witnesses was recorded, some of them testifying to incidents happening twenty years previous. Much of this moreover indicates the careless security in which the Conversos had lived and allowed their Jewish practices to be known to Christian servants and acquaintances with whom they were in constant intercourse. The first public manifestation of results seems to have been an auto de fe held November 16th, in the church of San Pedro, for the reconciliation of penitents who had come forward during the Term of Grace.[468] Soon after this the trials of those implicated commenced and were prosecuted with such vigor that, on February 6, 1484, an auto de fe was held in which four persons were burnt, followed on the 23d and 24th of the same month by an imposing solemnity involving the concremation of thirty living men and women and the bones and effigies of forty who were dead or fugitives.[469] In its two years of existence the tribunal of Ciudad-Real burnt fifty-two obstinate heretics, condemned two hundred and twenty fugitives and reconciled one hundred and eighty-three penitents.[470]

In 1485 the tribunal of Ciudad-Real was transferred to the city of Toledo where the Conversos were very numerous and wealthy. They organized a plot to raise a tumult and despatch the inquisitors during the procession of Corpus Christi (June 2d) but, as in the case of Seville, it was betrayed and six of the conspirators were hanged, after which we hear of no further trouble there. Those who were first arrested confessed that the design extended to seizing the city gates and cathedral tower and holding the place against the sovereigns.[471]

PENITENTS IN TOLEDO

The inquisitor, Pedro Díaz, had preached the first sermon on May 24th, and, after the defeat of the conspiracy, the tribunal entered vigorously on its functions. The customary Term of Grace of forty days was proclaimed and after some delay we are told that many applied for reconciliation rather through fear of concremation than through good will. After the expiration of the forty days, letters of exccommunication were published against all cognizant of heresy who should not denounce it within sixty days--a term subsequently extended by thirty more. Another very effectual expedient was adopted by summoning the Jewish rabbis and requiring them, under penalty of life and property, to place a major excommunication on their synagogues and not remove it until all the members should have revealed everything within their knowledge respecting Judaizing Christians. This was only perfecting a device that had already been employed elsewhere. In 1484, by a cédula of December 10th, Ferdinand had ordered the magistrates of all the principal towns in Aragon to compel, by all methods recognized in law, the rabbis and sacristans of the synagogues and such other Jews as might be named, to tell the truth as to all that might be asked of them, and in Seville we are told that a prominent Jew, Judah Ibn-Verga, expatriated himself to avoid compliance with a similar demand. The quality of the evidence obtained by such means may be estimated from the fact that when, in the assembly of Valladolid, in 1488, Ferdinand and Isabella investigated the affairs of the Inquisition, it was found that many Jews testified falsely against Conversos in order to encompass their ruin, for which some of those against which this was proved were lapidated in Toledo. Whether true or false, the Toledan Inquisition reaped by these methods a plentiful harvest of important revelations. It is easy, in fact, to imagine the terror pervading the Converso community and the eagerness with which the unfortunates would come forward to denounce themselves and their kindred and friends, especially when, after the expiration of the ninety days, arrests began and quickly followed each other.[472]

The penitents were allowed to accumulate and at the first auto de fe, held February 12, 1486, only those of seven parishes--San Vicente, San Nicolás, San Juan de la leche, Santa Yusta, San Miguel, San Yuste, and San Lorenzo--were summoned to appear. These amounted to seven hundred and fifty of both sexes, comprising many of the principal citizens and persons of quality. The ceremony was painful and humiliating. Bareheaded and barefooted, except that, in consideration of the intense cold, they were allowed to wear soles, carrying unlighted candles and surrounded by a howling mob which had gathered from all the country around, they were marched in procession through the city to the cathedral, at the portal of which stood two priests who marked them on the forehead as they entered with the sign of the cross, saying "Receive the sign of the cross which you have denied and lost." When inside they were called one by one before the inquisitors while a statement of their misdeeds was read. They were fined in one-fifth of all their property for the war with the Moors; they were subjected to lifelong incapacity to hold office or to pursue honorable avocations or to wear other than the coarsest vestments unadorned, under pain of burning for relapse, and they were required to march in procession on six Fridays, bareheaded and barefooted, disciplining themselves with hempen cords.[473] The loving mother Church could not welcome back to her bosom her erring children without a sharp and wholesome warning, nor did she relax her vigilance, for this perilous process of confession and reconciliation was so devised as to furnish many subsequent victims to the stake, as we shall see hereafter.

The second auto was held on April 2, 1486, where nine hundred penitents appeared from the parishes of San Roman, San Salvador, San Cristóval, San Zoil, Sant Andrés and San Pedro. The third auto, on June 11th, consisted of some seven hundred and fifty from Santa Olalla, San Tomás, San Martin and Sant Antolin. The city being thus disposed of, the various archidiaconates of the district were taken in order. That of Toledo furnished nine hundred penitents on December 10th, when we are told that they suffered greatly from the cold. On January 15, 1487, there were about seven hundred from the archidiaconate of Alcaraz and on March 10th, from those of Talavera, Madrid and Guadalajara about twelve hundred, some of whom were condemned in addition to wear the sanbenito for life. While the more or less voluntary penitents were thus treated there were numerous autos de fe celebrated of a more serious character in which there were a good many burnings, including not a few frailes and ecclesiastical dignitaries, as well as cases of fugitives and of the dead, who were burned in effigy and their estates confiscated.[474]

TRIBUNAL OF GUADALUPE

In 1485 a temporary tribunal was set up at Guadalupe, where Ferdinand and Isabella appointed as inquisitor (under what papal authority does not appear) Fray Nuño de Arevalo, prior of the Geronimite convent there. Apparently to guide his inexperience Doctor Francisco de la Fuente was transferred from Ciudad-Real and, with another colleague, the Licentiate Pedro Sánchez de la Calancha, they purified the place of heresy with so much vigor that, within a year, they held in the cemetery before the doors of the monastery seven autos de fe in which were burnt a heretic monk, fifty-two Judaizers, forty-eight dead bodies and twenty-five effigies of fugitives, while sixteen were condemned to perpetual imprisonment and innumerable others were sent to the galleys or penanced with the sanbenito for life. These energetic proceedings do not appear to have made good Christians of those who were spared for, July 13, 1500, Inquisitor-general Deza ordered all the Conversos of Guadalupe to leave the district and not to return.[475] The same year, 1485, saw a tribunal assigned to Valladolid, but it must have met with effective resistance, for in September, 1488, Ferdinand and Isabella were obliged to visit the city in order to get it into working condition; it forthwith commenced operations by arresting some prominent citizens and on June 19, 1489, the first auto de fe was held in which eighteen persons were burnt alive and the bones of four dead heretics.[476] Still, the existence of this tribunal would seem to have long remained uncertain for, as late as December 24, 1498, we find Isabella writing to a new appointee that she and the inquisitor-general have agreed that the Inquisition must be placed there and ordering him to prepare to undertake it, and then on January 22, 1501, telling Inquisitor-general Deza that she approves of its lodgement in the house of Diego de la Baeza, where it is to remain for the present; she adds that she and Ferdinand have written to the Count of Cabra to see that for the future the inquisitors are well treated.[477] Permanent tribunals were also established in Llerena and Murcia, of the early records of all of which we know little. In 1490 a temporary one was organized in Avila by Torquemada, apparently for the purpose of trying those accused of the murder of the Santo Niño de la Guardia; it continued active until 1500 and during these ten years there were hung in the church the insignias y mantetas of seventy-five victims burnt alive, of twenty-six dead and of one fugitive, besides the sanbenitos of seventy-one reconciled penitents.[478]

The various provinces of Castile thus became provided with the machinery requisite for the extermination of heresy, and at an early period in its development it was seen that, for the enormous work before it, some more compact and centralized organization was desirable than had hitherto been devised. The Inquisition which had been so effective in the thirteenth and fourteenth centuries was scattered over Europe; its judges were appointed by the Dominican or Franciscan provincials, using a course of procedure and obeying instructions which emanated from the Holy See. The papacy was the only link between them; the individual inquisitors were to a great extent independent; they were not subjected to visitation or inspection and it was, if not impossible, a matter of difficulty to call them to account for the manner in which they might discharge their functions. Such was not the conception of Ferdinand and Isabella who intended the Spanish Inquisition to be a national institution, strongly organized and owing obedience to the crown much more than to the Holy See. The measures which they adopted with this object were conceived with their customary sagacity, and were carried out with their usual vigor and success.

ORGANIZATION

At this period they were earnestly engaged in reorganizing the institutions of Castile, centralizing the administration and reducing to order the chaos resulting from the virtual anarchy of the preceding reigns. In effecting this they apportioned, in 1480, with the consent of the Córtes of Toledo, the affairs of government among four royal councils, that of administration and justice, known as the Concejo Real de Castella, that of Finance, or Concejo de Hacienda, the Concejo de Estado and the Concejo de Aragon, to which was added a special one for the Hermandades.[479] These met daily in the palace for the despatch of business and their effect in making the royal power felt in every quarter of the land and in giving vigor and unity to the management of the state soon proved the practical value of the device. The Inquisition was fast looming up as an affair of state of the first importance, while yet it could scarce be regarded as falling within the scope of either of the four councils; the sovereigns were too jealous of papal interference to allow it to drift aimlessly, subject to directions from Rome, and their uniform policy required that it should be kept as much as possible under the royal superintendence. That a fifth council should be created for the purpose was a natural expedient, for which the assent of Sixtus IV was readily obtained, when it was organized in 1483 under the name of the Concejo de la Suprema y General Inquisicion--a title conveniently abbreviated to la Suprema--with jurisdiction over all matters connected with the faith. To secure due subordination and discipline over the whole body it was requisite that the president of this council should have full control of appointment and dismissal of the individual inquisitors who, as exercising power delegated directly from the pope, might otherwise regard with contempt the authority of one who was also merely a delegate. It thus became necessary to create a new office, unknown to the older Inquisition--an inquisitor-general who should preside over the deliberations of the council. The office evidently was one which would be of immense weight and the future of the institution depended greatly on the character of its first chief. By the advice of the Cardinal Archbishop of Toledo, Pero González de Mendoza, the royal choice fell on Thomas de Torqemada, the confessor of the sovereigns, who was one of the seven inquisitors commissioned by the papal letter of February 11, 1482. The other members of the council were Alonso Carrillo, Bishop of Mazara (Sicily) and two doctors of laws, Sancho Velasco de Cuellar and Ponce de Valencia.[480] The exact date of Torquemada's appointment is not known, as the papal brief conferring it has not been found, but, as Sixtus created him Inquisitor of Aragon, Catalonia and Valencia by letters of October 17, 1483, his commission as Inquisitor-general of Castile was somewhat antecedent.[481]

Henry Charles Lea

TORQUEMADA

The selection of Torquemada justified the wisdom of the sovereigns. Full of pitiless zeal, he developed the nascent institution with unwearied assiduity. Rigid and unbending, he would listen to no compromise of what he deemed to be his duty, and in his sphere he personified the union of the spiritual and temporal swords which was the ideal of all true churchmen. Under his guidance the Inquisition rapidly took shape and extended its organization throughout Spain and was untiring and remorseless in the pursuit and punishment of the apostates. His labors won him ample praise from successive popes. Already, in 1484, Sixtus IV wrote to him that Cardinal Borgia had warmly eulogized him for his success in prosecuting the good work throughout Castile and Leon, adding "We have heard this with the greatest pleasure and rejoice exceedingly that you, who are furnished with both doctrine and authority, have directed your zeal to these matters which contribute to the praise of God and the utility of the orthodox faith. We commend you in the Lord and exhort you, cherished son, to persevere with tireless zeal in aiding and promoting the cause of the faith, by doing which, as we are assured you will, you will win our special favor." Twelve years later, Cardinal Borgia, then pope under the name of Alexander VI, assures him in 1496, that he cherishes him in the very bowels of affection for his immense labors in the exaltation of the faith.[482] If we cannot wholly attribute to him the spirit of ruthless fanaticism which animated the Inquisition, he at least deserves the credit of stimulating and rendering it efficient in its work by organizing it and by directing it with dauntless courage against the suspect however high-placed, until the shadow of the Holy Office covered the land and no one was so hardy as not to tremble at its name. The temper in which he discharged his duties and the absolute and irresponsible control which he exercised over the subordinate tribunals can be fitly estimated from a single instance. There was a fully organized Inquisition at Medina, with three inquisitors, an assessor, a fiscal and other officials, assisted by the Abbot of Medina as Ordinary. They reconciled some culprits and burnt others, apparently without referring the cases to him, but when they found reason to acquit some prisoners they deemed it best to transmit the papers to him for confirmation. He demurred at this mercy and told the tribunal to try the accused again when the Licentiate Villalpando should be there as visitador. Some months later Villalpando came there, the cases were reviewed, the prisoners were tortured, two of them were reconciled and the rest acquitted, the sentences being duly published as final. Torquemada on learning this was incensed and declared that he would burn them all. He had them arrested again and sent to Valladolid, to be tried outside of their district, where his threat was doubtless carried into effect.[483] When such was the spirit infused in the organization at the beginning we need not wonder that verdicts of acquittal are infrequent in the records of its development. Yet withal Torquemada's zeal could not wholly extinguish worldliness. We are told, indeed, that he refused the archbishopric of Seville, that he wore the humble Dominican habit, that he never tasted flesh nor wore linen in his garments or used it on his bed, and that he refused to give a marriage-portion to his indigent sister, whom he would only assist to enter the order of beatas of St. Dominic. Still, his asceticism did not prevent him from living in palaces surrounded by a princely retinue of two hundred and fifty armed familiars and fifty horsemen.[484] Nor was his persecuting career purely disinterested. Though the rule of his Dominican Order forbade individual ownership of property and, though his position as supreme judge should have dictated the utmost reserve in regard to the financial results of persecution, he had no hesitation in accumulating large sums from the pecuniary penances inflicted by his subordinates on the heretics who spontaneously returned to the faith.[485] It is true that the standards of the age were so low that he made no secret of this and it is also true that he lavished them on the splendid monastery of St. Thomas Aquinas which he built at Avila, on enlarging that of Santa Cruz at Segovia of which he was prior and on various structures in his native town of Torquemada. Yet amid the ostentation of his expenditure he lived in perpetual fear, and at his table he always used the horn of a unicorn which was a sovereign preservative against poison.[486]

INTERNAL QUARRELS

As delegated powers were held to expire with the death of the grantor, unless otherwise expressly defined, Torquemada's commission required renewal on the decease of Sixtus IV. Ferdinand and Isabella asked that the new one should not be limited to the life of the pope, but that the power should continue, not only during Torquemada's life, but until the appointment of his successor.[487] The request was not granted and, when Innocent VIII, by a brief of February 3, 1485, recommissioned Torquemada it was in the ordinary form. This apparently was not satisfactory, but the pope was not willing thus to lose all control of the Spanish Inquisition and a compromise seems to have been reached, for when, February 6, 1486, Torquemada was appointed Inquisitor-general of Barcelona and his commission for Spain was renewed, on March 24th of the same year, it was drawn to continue at the good pleasure of the pope and of the Holy See, which, without abnegating papal control, rendered renewals unnecessary.[488] This formula was abandoned in the commissions of Torquemada's immediate successors, but was subsequently resumed and continued to be employed through the following centuries.[489]

Torquemada's commission of 1485 contained the important power of appointing and dismissing inquisitors, but the confirmation of 1486 bore the significant exception that all those appointed by the pope were exempted from removal by him, indicating that in the interval he had attempted to exercise the power and that the resistance to it had enlisted papal support. In fact, at the conference of Seville, held in 1484 by Torquemada, there were present the two inquisitors of each of four existing tribunals; from Seville we find Juan de San Martin, one of the original appointees of 1479, but his colleague, Miguel de Morillo, has disappeared and is replaced by Juan Ruiz de Medina, who had been merely assessor, while but a single one, Pero Martínez de Barrio, of the seven commissioned by Sixtus IV in 1482 appears as representing the other tribunals--the rest are all new men, doubtless appointees of Torquemada.[490] There was evidently a bitter quarrel on foot between Torquemada and the original papal nominees, who held that their powers, delegated directly from the pope, rendered them independent of him, and, as usual, the Holy See inclined to one side or to the other in the most exasperating manner, as opposing interests brought influence to bear. Complaints against Torquemada were sufficiently numerous and serious to oblige him thrice to send Fray Alonso Valaja to the papal court to justify him.[491] He seems to have removed Miguel de Morillo, who vindicated himself in Rome, for a brief of Innocent VIII, February 23, 1487, appoints him inquisitor of Seville, in complete disregard of the faculties granted to Torquemada. Then a motu proprio of November 26, 1487, suspends both him and Juan de San Martin and commissions Torquemada to appoint their successors. Again, a brief of January 7, 1488, appoints Juan Inquisitor of Seville, while subsequent briefs of the same year are addressed to him concerning the business of his office as though he were discharging his duties independently of Torquemada, but his death in 1489 removed him from the scene. The quarrel evidently continued, and at one time Fray Miguel enjoyed a momentary triumph, for a papal letter of September 26, 1491, commissions him as Inquisitor-general of Castile and Aragon, thus placing him on an equality with Torquemada himself.[492] It would be impossible now to determine what part the sovereigns may have had in these changes and to what extent the popes disregarded the authority conferred on them of appointment and removal. There was a constant struggle on the one hand to render the Spanish Holy Office national and independent, and on the other to keep it subject to papal control.

FIVE INQUISITORS GENERAL

Finally the opposition to Torquemada became so strong that Alexander VI, in 1494, kindly alleging his great age and infirmities, commissioned Martin Ponce de Leon, Archbishop of Messina, but resident in Spain, Iñigo Manrique, Bishop of Córdova, Francisco Sánchez de la Fuente, Bishop of Avila, and Alonso Suárez de Fuentelsaz, Bishop of Mondonego and successively of Lugo and Jaen, as inquisitors-general with the same powers as Torquemada; each was independent and could act by himself and could even terminate cases commenced by another.[493] It is quite probable that, to spare his feelings, he was allowed to name his colleagues as delegates of his powers, for in some instructions issued, in 1494, by Martin of Messina and Francisco of Avila they describe themselves as inquisitors-general in all the Spanish realms subdelegated by the Inquisitor-general Torquemada.[494] He evidently still retained his pre-eminence and was active to the last, for we have letters from Ferdinand to him in the first half of 1498 concerning the current affairs of the Inquisition, in which the Bishop of Lugo declined to interfere with him. The Instructions of Avila, in 1498, were issued in his name as inquisitor-general, and the assertion that he resigned two years before his death, September 16, 1498, is evidently incorrect.[495] In some respects, however, the Bishop of Avila had special functions which distinguished him from his colleagues, for he was appointed by Alexander VI, November 4, 1494, judge of appeals in all matters of faith and March 30, 1495, he received special faculties to degrade ecclesiastics condemned by the Inquisition, or to appoint other bishops for that function.[496] So long as they were in orders clerics were exempt from secular jurisdiction and it was necessary to degrade them before they could be delivered to the civil authorities for burning. Under the canons, this had to be done by their own bishops, who were not always at hand for the purpose, and who apparently, when present, sometimes refused or delayed to perform the office, which was a serious impediment to the business of the Inquisition, as many Judaizing Conversos were found among clerics.

This multiform headship of the Inquisition continued for some years until the various incumbents successively died or resigned. Iñigo Manrique was the first to disappear, dying in 1496, and had no successor. Then, in 1498, followed the Bishop of Avila, who had been transferred to Córdova in 1496. In the same year, as we have seen, Torquemada died, and this time the vacancy was filled by the appointment as his successor of Diego Deza, then Bishop of Jaen (subsequently, in 1500, of Palencia, and in 1505 Archbishop of Seville) who was commissioned, November 24, 1498, for Castile, Leon and Granada, and on September 1, 1499, for all the Spanish kingdoms.[497] In 1500 died Martin Archbishop of

Messina--apparently a defaulter, for, on October 26th of the same year, Ferdinand orders his auditor of the confiscations to pass in the accounts of Luis de Riva Martin, receiver of Cadiz, 18,000 maravedís due by the archbishop for wheat, hay, etc., which he forgives to the heirs.[498] From this time forward Deza is reckoned as the sole inquisitor-general and direct successor of Torquemada, but Fuentelsaz, Bishop of Jaen, remained in office, for, as late as January 13, 1503, an order for the payment of salaries is signed by Deza and contains the name of the Bishop of Jaen as also inquisitor-general.[499] He relinquished the position in 1504 and Deza remained as sole chief of the Inquisition until, in 1507, he was forced to resign as we shall see hereafter.

IT FRAMES ITS OWN RULES

At the time of his retirement the kingdoms of Castile and Aragon had been separated by the death of Isabella, November 26, 1504. Ferdinand's experience with his son-in-law, Philip I, and his hope of issue from his marriage in March, 1506, with Germaine de Foix, in which case the kingdoms would have remained separate, warned him of the danger of having his ancestral dominions spiritually subordinated to a Castilian subject. Before Deza's resignation, therefore, he applied to Julius II to commission Juan Enguera, Bishop of Vich, with the powers for Aragon which Deza was exercising. Julius seems to have made some difficulty about this, for a letter of Ferdinand, from Naples, February 6, 1507, to his ambassador at Rome, Francisco de Rojas, instructs him to explain that, since he had abandoned the title of King of Castile, the jurisdiction was separated and it was necessary and convenient that there should be an Inquisition for each kingdom.[500] He prevailed and the appointments of Cardinal Ximenes for Castile and of Bishop Enguera for Aragon were issued respectively on June 6 and 5, 1507.[501] During the lifetime of Ximenes the Inquisitions remained disunited, but in 1518, after his death, Charles V caused his former tutor, Cardinal Adrian of Utrecht, Bishop of Tortosa, who in 1516 had been made Inquisitor-general of Aragon, to be commissioned also for Castile, after which there was no further division. During the interval Ferdinand had acquired Navarre and had annexed it to the crown of Castile, so that the whole of the Peninsula, with the exception of Portugal, was united under one organization.[502]

***

Among other powers granted to Torquemada was that of modifying the rules of the Inquisition to adapt them to the requirements of Spain.[503] The importance of this concession it would be difficult to exaggerate, as it rendered the institution virtually self-governing. Thus the Spanish Inquisition acquired a character of its own, distinguishing it from the moribund tribunals of the period in other lands. The men who fashioned it knew perfectly what they wanted and in their hands it assumed the shape in which it dominated the conscience of every man and was an object of terror to the whole population. In the exercise of this Torquemada assembled the inquisitors in Seville, November 29, 1484, where, in conjunction with his colleagues of the Suprema, a series of regulations was agreed upon, known as the Instruciones de Sevilla, to which, in December of the same year and in January, 1485, he added further rules, issued in his own name under the authority of the sovereigns. In 1488 another assembly was held, under the supervision of Ferdinand and Isabella, which issued the Instruciones de Valladolid.[504] In 1498 came the Instruciones de Avila--the last in which Torquemada took part--designed principally to check the abuses which were rapidly developing, and, for the same purpose, a brief addition was made at Seville in 1500, by Diego Deza. All these became known in the tribunals as the Instruciones Antiguas.[505] As the institution became thoroughly organized under the control of the Suprema, consultation with the subordinate inquisitors was no longer requisite and regulations were promulgated by it in cartas acordadas. It was difficult, however, to keep the inquisitors strictly in line, and variations of practice sprang up which, in 1561, the Inquisitor-general Fernando Valdés endeavored to check by issuing the Instruciones Nuevas. Subsequent regulations were required from time to time, forming a considerable and somewhat intricate body of jurisprudence, which we shall have to consider hereafter. At present it is sufficient to indicate how the Inquisition became an autonomous body--an imperium in imperio--framing its own laws and subject only to the rarely-exercised authority of the Holy See and the more or less hesitating control of the crown.

FLIGHT OF NEW CHRISTIANS

At the same time all the resources of the State were placed at its disposal. When an inquisitor came to assume his functions the officials took an oath to assist him, to exterminate all whom he might designate as heretics and to observe and compel the observance by all of the decretals Ad abolendum, Excommunicamus, Ut officium Inquisitionis and Ut Inquisitionis negotium--the papal legislation of the thirteenth century which made the state wholly subservient to the Holy Office and rendered incapable of official position any one suspect in the faith or who favored heretics.[506] Besides this, all the population was assembled to listen to a sermon by the inquisitor, after which all were required to swear on the cross and the gospels to help the Holy Office and not to impede it in any manner or on any pretext.[507]

GENERAL SUBMISSION

It is no wonder that, as this portentous institution spread its wings of terror over the land, all who felt themselves liable to its animadversion were disposed to seek safety in flight, no matter at what sacrifice. That numbers succeeded in this is shown by the statistics of the early autos de fe, in which the living victims are far outnumbered by the effigies of the absent. Thus in Ciudad-Real, during the first two years, fifty-two obstinate heretics were burnt and two hundred and twenty absentees were condemned.[508] In Barcelona, where the Inquisition was not established until 1487, the first auto de fe, celebrated January 25, 1488, showed a list of four living victims to twelve effigies of fugitives; in a subsequent one of May 23d, the proportions were three to forty-two; in one of February 9, 1489, three to thirty-nine; in one of March 24, 1490, they were two to one hundred and fifty-nine, and in another of June 10, 1491, they were three to one hundred and thirty-nine.[509] If the object had simply been to purify the land of heresy and apostasy this would have been accomplished as well by expatriation as by burning or reconciling, but such was not the policy which governed the sovereigns, and edicts were issued forbidding all of Jewish lineage from leaving Spain and imposing a fine of five hundred florins on ship-masters conveying them away.[510] This was not, as it might seem to us, wanton cruelty, although it was harsh, inasmuch as it assumed guilt on mere suspicion. To say nothing of the confiscations, which were defrauded of the portable property carried away by the fugitives, we must bear in mind that, to the orthodox of the period, heresy was a positive crime, nay the greatest of crimes, punishable as such by laws in force for centuries, and the heretic was to be prevented from escaping its penalties as much as a murderer or a thief. The royal edicts were supplemented by the Inquisition, and it is an illustration of the extension of its jurisdiction over all matters, relating directly or indirectly to the faith, that, November 8, 1499, the Archbishop Martin of Messina issued an order, which was published throughout the realm and was confirmed by Diego Deza, January 15, 1502, to the effect that no ship-captain or merchant should transport across seas any New Christian, whether Jewish or Moorish, without a royal license, under pain of confiscation, of excommunication and of being held as a fautor and protector of heretics. To render this effective two days later Archbishop Martin ordered that suitable persons should be sent to all the sea-ports to arrest all New Christians desiring to cross the sea and bring them to the Inquisition so that justice should be done to them, all expenses being defrayed out of the confiscations.[511] These provisions were not allowed to be a dead-letter, though we are apt to hear of them rather in cases where, for special reasons, the penalties were remitted. Thus, July 24, 1499, Ferdinand writes to the Inquisitors of Barcelona that a ship of Charles de Sant Climent, a merchant of their city, had brought from Alexandria to Aiguesmortes certain persons who had fled from Spain. Even this transportation between foreign ports came within the purview of the law, for Ferdinand explains that action in this case would be to his disservice, wherefore if complaint is lodged with them they are to refer it to him or to the inquisitor-general for instructions. Again, on November 8, 1500, the king orders the release of the caravel and other property of Diego de la Mesquita of Seville, which had been seized because he had carried some New Christians to Naples--the reason for the release being the services of Diego in the war with Naples and those which he is rendering elsewhere. A letter from Ferdinand to the King of Portugal, November 7, 1500, recites that recently some New Christians had been arrested in Milaga, where they were embarking under pretext of going to Rome for the jubilee. On examination by the Inquisition at Seville they admitted that they were Jews but said that they had been forced in Portugal to turn Christians; as this brought them under inquisitorial jurisdiction, the inquisitors were sending to Portugal for evidence and the king was asked to protect the envoys and give them facilities for the purpose.[512] The same determination was manifested to recapture when possible those who had succeeded in effecting their flight. In 1496 Micer Martin, inquisitor of Mallorca, heard of some who were in Bugia, a sea-port of Africa. He forthwith despatched the notary, Lope de Vergara, thither to seize them, but the misbelieving Moors disregarded his safe-conduct and threw him and his party into a dungeon where they languished for three years. He at length was ransomed and, in recompense of his losses and sufferings, Ferdinand ordered, March 31, 1499, Matheo de Morrano receiver of Mallorca to pay him two hundred and fifty

REPRESSION OF ABUSES

It shows how strong an impression had already been made by the resolute character of the sovereigns, and how violent was the antagonism generally entertained for the Conversos, that so novel and absolute a tyranny could be imposed on the lately turbulent population of Castile without resistance, and that so powerful a class as that against which persecution was directed should have submitted without an effort save the abortive plots at Seville and Toledo. The indications that have reached us of opposition to the arbitrary acts of the Inquisition in making arrests or confiscations are singularly few. In the records of the town-council of Xeres de la Frontera, under date of August 28, 1482, there is an entry reciting that there had come to the town a man carrying a wand and calling himself an alguazil of the Inquisition; he had seized Gonçalo Caçabé and carried him off without showing his authority to the local officials, which was characterized as an atrocious proceeding and the town ought to take steps with the king, the pope and the Inquisition to have it undone.[514] Doubtless the summary acts of the Holy Office over-riding all recognized law, created such feeling in many places as we may gather from a cédula of Ferdinand, December 15, 1484, forbidding the reception of heretics and ordering their surrender on demand of the inquisitors, and another of July 8, 1487, commanding that any one bearing orders from the inquisitors of Toledo is to be allowed to arrest any person, under a penalty of 100,000 maravedís for the rich and confiscation for others,[515] but complaints were dangerous, for they could be met by threats of punishment for fautorship of heresy. Still it required considerable time to accustom the nobles and people to unquestioning submission to a domination so absolute and so foreign to their experience. As late as the year 1500 there are two royal letters to the Count of Benalcázar reciting that he had ordered the arrest of a girl of Herrera who had uttered scandals against the faith; she was in the hands of his alcaide, Gutierre de Sotomayor, who refused to deliver her when the inquisitor sent for her. The second letter, after an interval of nineteen days, points out the gravity of the offence and peremptorily orders the surrender of the girl. She proved to be a Jewish prophetess whose trial resulted in bringing to the stake large numbers of her unfortunate disciples. There is also an anticipation of resistance in a letter, January 12, 1501, to the Prior of St. John, charging him to see that no impediments are placed in the way of the receiver of the Inquisition of Jaen in seizing certain confiscated property at Alcázar de Consuegra.[516] More indicative of popular repugnance is a letter of October 4, 1502, to the royal officials of a place not specified, reciting that the people are endeavoring to have Mosen Salvador Serras, lieutenant of the vicar, removed because he had spoken well of the Inquisition and had been charged by the inquisitors with certain duties to perform; they are not to allow this to be done and are to see that he is not ill-treated.[517] In 1509 Ferdinand had occasion to remonstrate with the Duke of Alva, in the case of Alonso de Jaen, a resident of Coria, because, when he was arrested, an agent of the duke had seized certain cows and sold them and, when he was condemned and his property confiscated, Alva had forbidden any one to purchase anything without his permission. Ferdinand charges him to allow the sale to proceed freely and to account for the cows, pointing out that he had granted to him a third of the net proceeds of all confiscations in his estates.[518] This grant of a third of the confiscations was made to other great nobles and doubtless tended to reconcile them to the operations of the Inquisition. In this general acquiescence it is somewhat remarkable that, as late as 1520, when Charles V ordered Merida to prepare accommodations for a tribunal, the city remonstrated; everything there was quiet and peaceable, it said, and it feared a tumult if the Holy Office was established there, while if merely a visit was made for an inquest it would lend willing aid. Cardinal Adrian hearkened to the warning in Charles's absence and in a letter of November 27, 1520, ordered his inquisitors to settle somewhere else.[519]

FERDINAND'S BIGOTRY

At the same time it was inevitable that power so irresponsible would be frequently and greatly abused, and it is interesting to observe that, when no resistance was made, Ferdinand was, as a general rule, prompt to intervene in favor of the oppressed. Thus January 28, 1498, he writes to the inquisitors-general that recently some officials of the Inquisition of Valencia went to the barony of Serra to arrest some women who wore Moorish dress and, as they were not recognized, they were resisted by the Moors, whereupon the inquisitors proceeded to seize all the Moors of Serra who chanced to come to Valencia, so that the place was becoming depopulated. He therefore orders the inquisitors-general to intimate to their subordinates that they must find some other method whereby the innocent shall not suffer for the fault of individuals and, not content with this, he wrote directly to the Inquisitor of Valencia, instructing him to proceed with much moderation. In another case where opposition had been provoked he writes, January 18, 1499, "We have your letter and are much displeased with the maltreatment which you report of the inquisitor and his officials. It will be attended to duly. But often you yourselves are the cause of it, for if each of you would attend to his duties quietly and carefully and injure no one you would be held in good esteem. Look to this in the future, for it will displease us much if you do what you ought not, with little foundation." At the same time he charges the inquisitor not to make arrests without good cause, "for in such things, besides the charge on your conscience, the Holy Office is much defamed and its officials despised." So in a letter of August 15, 1500, to the inquisitors of Saragossa, he tells them that he has received a copy of an edict which they had issued at Calatayud; it is so sharp that if it is enforced no one can be safe; they must consider such things carefully or consult him; in the present case they will obey the instructions sent by the inquisitors-general and must always bear in mind that the only object of the Inquisition is the salvation of souls. Again, when the inquisitors of Barcelona imperiously placed the town of Perpiñan under interdict, in a quarrel arising out of a censal or ground-rent on Carcella, Ferdinand writes to them, March 5, 1501, that the town is poor and must be gently treated, especially as it is on the frontier, and he sends a special envoy to arrange the matter.[520] The wearing delays, which were one of the most terrible engines of oppression by the Inquisition, were especially distasteful to him. January 28, 1498, he writes to an inquisitor about the case of Anton Rúiz of Teruel, who had been imprisoned for five months without trial for some remarks made by him to another person about the confiscation of the property of Jaime de Santangel, though application had been made repeatedly to have the case despatched. Ferdinand orders that it be considered at once; the prisoner is either to be discharged on bail or proper punishment is to be inflicted. So, January 16, 1501, he reminds inquisitors that he has written to them several times to conclude the case between the heirs of Mossen Perea and the sons of Anton Rúiz and deliver sentence; the case has been concluded for some time but the sentence is withheld; it must be rendered at once or the case must be either delegated to a competent person or be sent to the Suprema. At the same time, whenever there was the semblance of opposition to an injustice, on the part of the secular authorities, he was prompt to repress it. The action of the Inquisition of Valencia, in confiscating the property of a certain Valenzuola, excited so much feeling that the governor, the auditor-general, the royal council and the jurados met to protest against it and in so doing said some things unpleasing to the inquisitors, who thereupon complained to Ferdinand. He wrote to the offenders, March 21, 1499, rebuking them severely; it was none of their business; if the inquisitors committed an injustice the appeal lay to the inquisitor-general, who would rectify it; their duty was to aid the Inquisition and he ordered them to do so in future and not to create scandal.[521] He was more considerate when the frontier town of Perpiñan was concerned, for in 1513, when the deputy receiver of confiscations provoked antagonism by the vigor of his proceedings and the consuls complained that he had publicly insulted Franco Maler, one of their number, Ferdinand ordered the inquisitor of Barcelona to investigate the matter at once and to inflict due punishment.[522]

His whole correspondence shows the untiring interest which he felt in the institution, not merely as a financial or political instrument, but as a means of defending and advancing the faith. He was sincerely bigoted and, when he had witnessed an auto de fe in Valladolid, he wrote, September 30, 1509, to the inquisitor Juan Alonso de Navia to express the great pleasure which it had given him as a means of advancing the honor and glory of God and the exaltation of the Holy Catholic faith.[523] Inquisitors were in the habit of sending him reports of the autos celebrated by them, to which he would reply in terms of high satisfaction, urging them to increased zeal. On one occasion, in 1512, and on another in 1513, he was so much pleased that he made a present to the inquisitor of two hundred ducats and ordered fifteen ducats to be given to the messenger.[524]

***

A quarter of a century elapsed before there was, in the Castilian kingdoms, any serious resistance to the Inquisition. The trouble which then occurred was provoked by the excesses of an inquisitor named Lucero at Córdova, which were brought to light only by the relaxation of Ferdinand's stern rule during the brief reign of Philip of Austria and the subsequent interregnum. As this affords us the only opportunity of obtaining an inside view of what was possible, under the usually impenetrable mantle of secrecy characteristic of inquisitorial procedure, it is worthy of investigation in some detail.

Córdova was somewhat unfortunate in its inquisitors; whether more or less so than other communities it would now be impossible to say. Lucero's predecessor was Doctor Guiral, Dean of Guadix, who was transferred from there to Avila, in 1499. Falling under suspicion for irregularities, a papal brief was procured commissioning the Archbishop of Toledo to investigate him--and it is noteworthy that, although the inquisitor-general had full power of appointment, punishment and dismissal, papal intervention was deemed necessary in this case. The result showed the ample opportunities offered by the position for irregular gains and for oppression and injustice. He had received 150,000 maravedís by selling to penitents exemptions from wearing the sanbenito, or penitential garment. A large amount was secured in various ways from the receiver of confiscations, who was evidently an accomplice and who, of course, received his share of the spoils. Pilfering from sequestrated property yielded something, including ninety-three pearls of great value. Through his servants he gathered rewards or percentages offered, as we shall see, for discovering concealed confiscated property. He pocketed the fines which he imposed on reconciled penitents and was therefore interested in aggravating them. He negotiated for the Conversos of Córdova an agreement under which they compounded with 2,200,000 maravedís for confiscations to which they might become liable, and for this he received from them nearly 100,000, to which he added 50,000 by enabling two of the contributors to cheat their fellows by escaping payment of their assessments to the common fund. When transferred to Avila his field of operations was less productive, but he made what he could by extorting money from the kindred of his prisoners, and he did not disdain to take ten ducats and an ass from an official of the prison for some offence committed. As the royal fisc suffered from his practices he was arrested and tried, but, unfortunately, the documents at hand do not inform us as to the result.[525]

EXCESSES OF LUCERO

His successor at Córdova, Diego Rodríguez Lucero, was a criminal of larger views and bolder type, who presents himself to us as the incarnation of the evils resultant from the virtually irresponsible powers lodged in the tribunals. Our first glimpse of him is in 1495, when he figures as inquisitor of Xeres and the recipient from Ferdinand and Isabella of a canonry in Cadiz.[526] This shows that he had already gained the favor of the sovereigns, which increased after his promotion to Córdova, September 7, 1499, where, by the methods which we shall presently see, his discoveries of apostate Judaizers were very impressive. A royal letter of December 11, 1500, cordially thanked him for the ample details of a recent despatch relating how he was every day unearthing new heretics; he was urged to spare no effort for their punishment, especially of those who had relapsed, and to report at once everything that he did. His zeal scarce required this stimulation and his lawless methods are indicated by a letter of February 12, 1501, of Ferdinand and Isabella to their son-in-law Manoel of Portugal, expatiating on the numerous heretics recently discovered in Córdova, of whom two heresiarchs, Alfonso Fernández Herrero and Fernando de Córdova had escaped to Portugal, whither Lucero had despatched his alguazil to bring them back without waiting to obtain royal letters. This was an unwarrantable act and, when the alguazil seized the fugitives, Manoel refused license to extradite them until he should have an opportunity of seeing the evidence against them. Ferdinand and Isabella declare that this would be a grievous impediment to the Holy Office and disservice to God and they affectionately entreat Manoel to surrender the accused for the honor of God and also to protect from maltreatment the officials who had aided in their capture.[527]

We may not uncharitably assume that a portion, at least, of the favor shown to Lucero may have been due to the pecuniary results of his activity. By this time the confiscations, which at first had contributed largely to the royal treasury, were considerably diminished and at some places were scarce defraying the expenses of the tribunals. To this Córdova was now an exception; that its productiveness was rapidly growing is manifest from a letter of Ferdinand, March 12, 1501, to the receiver, Andrés de Medina, stating that he learns that there is much to be done and authorizing the appointment of two assistants at salaries of 10,000 maravedís and, on January 12 and 13, 1503, orders were drawn on Córdova for 500,000 maravedís to defray inquisitorial salaries elsewhere. On the same date we have another illustration of Lucero's activity in the sudden arrest of four of the official public scriveners. As they were the depositaries of the papers of their clients, the sequestration of all their effects produced enormous complications, to relieve which Ferdinand ordered all private documents to be sorted out and put in the hands of another scrivener, Luis de Mesa. This shows how the operations of the Inquisition might at any moment affect the interests of any man and it illustrates another of the profits of persecution for, when these delinquents should be burnt or disabled from holding public office, there would be four vacancies to be eagerly contended for by those who had money or favor for their acquisition.[528]

SECRETARY CALCENA

As early as 1501 there is evidence of hostility between Lucero and the Córdovan authorities. When the receiver of confiscations, accompanied by Diego de Barrionuevo, scrivener of sequestrations, was holding a public auction of confiscated property, the alguazil mayor of the city, Gonzalo de Mayorga, ordered the town-crier, Juan Sánchez, who was crying the auction, to come with him in order to make certain proclamations. The scrivener interposed and refused to let Sánchez go; hot words passed in which Mayorga insulted the Inquisition and finally struck the scrivener with his wand of office, after which the alcalde mayor of the city, Diego Rúiz de Zarate, carried him off to prison. The inviolability of the officials of the Inquisition was vindicated by a royal sentence of September 6th, in which Mayorga, in addition to the arbitrary penance to be imposed on him by Lucero, was deprived of his office for life, was disabled from filling any public position whatever, and was banished perpetually from Córdova and its district, which he was to leave within eight days after notification. Zarate was more mercifully treated and escaped with six months' suspension from office.[529] This severity to civic officials of high position was a warning to all men that Lucero was not to be trifled with.

The unwavering support that he received from Ferdinand is largely explicable by the complicity of Juan Róiz de Calcena, a corrupt and mercenary official whom we shall frequently meet hereafter. He was Ferdinand's secretary in inquisitorial affairs, conducting all his correspondence in such matters, and was also secretary to the Suprema, and thus was able in great degree to control his master's action, rendering his participation in the villainies on foot essential to their success. How these were worked is displayed in a single case which happens to be described in a memorial from the city of Córdova to Queen Juana. The Archdeacon of Castro, Juan Muñoz, was a youth of seventeen, the son of an Old Christian mother and a Converso hidalgo. His benefice was worth 300,000 maravedís a year and he was a fair subject of spoliation, for which a plot was organized in 1505. His parents were involved in his ruin, all three were arrested and convicted and he was penanced so as to disable him from holding preferment. The spoils were divided between Cardinal Bernardino Carvajal, for whom bulls had been procured in advance, Morales the royal treasurer, Lucero and Calcena. The governor and chapter of Córdova gave the archdeaconry to Diego Vello, chaplain of the bishop, but the Holy See conveniently refused confirmation and bestowed it on Morales; Lucero obtained a canonry in Seville and some benefices in Cuenca, while Calcena received property estimated at 4,000,000 maravedís--doubtless an exaggerated figure representing the aggregate of his gains from complicity throughout Lucero's career.[530]

It was probably in 1501 that the combination was formed which emboldened Lucero to extend his operations, arresting and condemning nobles and gentlemen and church dignitaries, many of them Old Christians of unblemished reputation and limpios de sangre. It was easy, by abuse and threats, or by torture if necessary, to procure from the accused whatever evidence was necessary to convict, not only themselves but whomsoever it was desired to ruin. A great fear fell upon the whole population, for no one could tell where the next blow might fall, as the circle of denunciation spread through all ranks. Apologists from that time to this have endeavored to extenuate these proceedings by suggesting that those compromised endeavored to secure allies by inculpating in their confessions men of rank and influence, but in view of Lucero's methods and the extent of his operations such an explanation is wholly inadequate to overthrow the damning mass of evidence against him.[531]

LUCERO'S REIGN OF TERROR

His views expanded beyond the narrow bounds of Córdova, and he horrified the land by gathering evidence of a vast conspiracy, ramifying throughout Spain, for the purpose of subverting Christianity and replacing it with Judaism, which required for its suppression the most comprehensive and pitiless measures. In memorials to Queen Juana the authorities, ecclesiastic and secular, of Córdova described how he had certain of his prisoners assiduously instructed in Jewish prayers and rites so that they could be accurate in the testimony which, by menaces or torture, he forced them to bear against Old Christians of undoubted orthodoxy. In this way he proved that there were twenty-five profetissas who were engaged in traversing the land to convert it to Judaism, although many of those designated had never in their lives been outside of the city gates. Accompanying them were fifty distinguished personages, including ecclesiastics and preachers of note.[532] Of course, these stories lost nothing in passing from mouth to mouth, and it was popularly said that some of these prophetesses, in their unholy errand, travelled as drunken Bacchantes and others were transported on goats by the powers of hell.[533] A single instance, which happens to have reached us, illustrates the savage thoroughness with which he protected the faith from this assault. A certain Bachiller Membreque was convicted as an apostate Judaizer who had disseminated his doctrines by preaching. Lists were gathered from witnesses of those who had attended his sermons and these, to the number of a hundred and seven, were burnt alive in a single auto de fe.[534] The inquisitorial prisons were filled with the unfortunates under accusation, as many as four hundred being thus incarcerated, and large numbers were carried to Toro where, at the time, Inquisitor-general Deza resided with the Suprema.

The reign of terror thus established was by no means confined to Córdova. Its effects are energetically described by the Capitan Gonzalo de Avora, in a letter of July 16, 1507, to the royal secretary Almazan. After premising that he had represented to Ferdinand, with that monarch's assent, that there were three things requisite for the good of the kingdom--to conduct the Inquisition righteously without weakening it, to wage war with the Moors, and to relieve the burdens of the people--he proceeds to contrast this with what had been done. "As for the Inquisition," he says, "the method adopted was to place so much confidence in the Archbishop of Seville (Deza) and in Lucero and Juan de la Fuente that they were able to defame the whole kingdom, to destroy, without God or justice, a great part of it, slaying and robbing and violating maids and wives to the great dishonor of the Christian religion.... As for what concerns myself I repeat what I have already written to you, that the damages which the wicked officials of the Inquisition have wrought in my land are so many and so great that no reasonable person on hearing of them would not grieve."[535] When a horde of rapacious officials, clothed in virtual inviolability, was let loose upon a defenceless population, such violence and rapine were inevitable incidents, and the motive of this was explained, by the Bishop of Córdova and all the authorities of the city, in a petition to the pope, to be the greed of the inquisitors for the confiscations which they habitually embezzled.[536]

It was probably in 1505, after the death of Isabella, November 16, 1504, that the people of Córdova first ventured to complain to Deza. He offered to send the Archdeacon Torquemada who, with representatives of the chapter and the magistrates, should make an impartial investigation, but when the city accepted the proposition he withdrew it. A deputation consisting of three church dignitaries was then sent to him asking for the arrest and prosecution of Lucero. He replied that if they would draw up accusations in legal form he would act as would best tend to God's service, and, if necessary, would appoint judges to whom they could not object.[537] This was a manifest evasion, for the evidence was under the seal of the Inquisition and Deza alone could order an investigation. Apparently realizing that it was useless to appeal to Ferdinand, whose ears were closed by Calcena, their next recourse was to Isabella's daughter and successor, Queen Juana, then in Flanders with her husband Philip of Austria. Philip was eager to exercise an act of sovereignty in the kingdom, which Ferdinand was governing in the name of his daughter and, on September 30, 1505, a cédula bearing the signatures of Philip and Juana was addressed to Deza, alleging their desire to be present and participate in the action of the Inquisition and meanwhile suspending it until their approaching arrival in Castile, under penalty of banishment and seizure of temporalities for disobedience, at the same time protesting that their desire was to favor and not to injure the Holy Office. Although a circular letter to all the grandees announced this resolution and commanded them to enforce it, no attention was paid to it. Don Diego de Guevara, Philip's envoy, in fact wrote to him the following June that his action had produced a bad impression, for the people were hostile to the Conversos and there was talk of massacres like that of Lisbon.[538]

ARCHBISHOP TALAVERA

The next step of the opponents of Lucero was to recuse Deza as judge and to interject an appeal to the Holy See, leading to an active contest in Rome between Ferdinand and his son-in-law. A letter of the former, April 22, 1506, to Juan de Loaysa, agent of the Inquisition in Rome, described the attempt as an audacious and indecent effort to destroy the Inquisition which was more necessary than ever. Loaysa was told that he could render no greater service to God and to the king than by defeating it; minute instructions were given as to the influences that he must bring to bear, and he was reminded that Holy Writ permits the use of craft and cunning to perform the work of God. The extreme anxiety betrayed in the letter indicates that there was much more involved than the mere defence of Lucero and Deza; it was with Philip and Juana that he was wrestling and the stake was the crown of Castile. On the other hand, Philip, doubtless won by the gold of the Conversos, had fairly espoused their cause and was laboring to obtain for them a favorable decision from the pope. His ambassador, Philibert of Utrecht, under date of June 28th, reported that he had urged Julius II not to reject the appeal of the Marranos but the politic pontiff replied that he must reserve his decision until Ferdinand and Philip had met.[539]

Undeterred by the mutterings of the rising storm, Lucero about this time saw in Isabella's death a chance to strike at a higher quarry than he had hitherto ventured to aim at. The Geronimite Hernando de Talavera had won her affectionate veneration as her confessor and, on the conquest of Granada, in 1492, she had made him archbishop of the province founded there. He had a Jewish strain in his blood, as was the case in so many Spanish families; he was in his eightieth year, he was reverenced as the pattern and exemplar of all Christian virtues and he devoted himself unsparingly to the welfare of his flock, spending his revenues in charity and seeking by persuasion and example to win over to the faith his Moorish subjects. Yet he was not without enemies, for he had been the active agent in the reclamation by Ferdinand and Isabella, in 1480, of royal revenues to the amount of thirty millions of maravedís, alienated by Henry IV to purchase the submission of rebellious nobles and, although a quarter of a century had passed, it is said that the vengeful spirit thus aroused was still eager to encompass his ruin.[540]

Whatever may have been Lucero's motive, inquisitorial methods afforded abundant facilities for its accomplishment. He selected a woman whom he had tortured on the charge of being a Jewish prophetess and maintaining a synagogue in her house. He threatened her with further torture unless she should testify to what she had seen in Talavera's palace and on her replying that she did not know, he instructed her that an assembly was held, divided into three classes; in the first was the archbishop, with the bishops of Almería, Jaen and others; in the second, the dean and the provisor of Granada, the treasurer, the alcaide and other officials; in the third the prophetesses, the sister and nieces of Talavera, Doña María de Peñalosa and others. They agreed to traverse the kingdom, preaching and prophesying the advent of Elias and the Messiah, in concert with the prophets who were in the house of Fernan Alvárez of Toledo, where they were crowned with golden crowns.[541] All this was duly sworn to by the witness, as dictated to her by the fiscal, and formed a basis for the prosecution of Talavera and his family, doubtless supported by ample corroborative evidence, readily obtainable in the same manner. The occurrence of the name of the Bishop of Jaen suggests a further political intrigue; he was Alfonso Suárez de Fuentelsaz, the former colleague of Deza as inquisitor-general and was no doubt known as inclining to the Flemish party, as he subsequently accepted from Philip the presidency of the Royal Council.

PHILIP AND JUANA

Impenetrable secrecy was one of the most cherished principles of inquisitorial procedure, but Lucero probably desired to prepare the public for the impending blow and whispers concerning it began to circulate. Peter Martyr of Anghiera, who was attached to the royal court, wrote on January 3, 1506, to the Count of Tendilla, Governor of Granada, that Lucero, by means of witnesses under torture, had succeeded in imputing Judaism to the archbishop and his whole family and household; as there was no one more holy than Talavera, he found it difficult to believe that any one could be found to fabricate such a charge.[542] The attack commenced by arresting, in the most public and offensive manner, Talavera's nephew, the dean and the officials of his church, during divine service and in his presence, evidently with the purpose of discrediting him. The arrest followed of his sister, his nieces and his servants, and we can readily conceive the means by which even his kindred were compelled to give evidence incriminating him, as we gather from a letter of Ferdinand, June 9, 1506, to his ambassador at Rome, Francisco de Rojas, in which he says that the testimony against Talavera is that of his sisters and kindred and servants.[543] Before he could be arrested and prosecuted, however, special authorization from the Holy See was requisite, for, by a decree of Boniface VIII, inquisitors had no direct jurisdiction over bishops. For this, Ferdinand's intervention was necessary and, after some hesitation, he consented to make the application. The inculpatory evidence given by Talavera's family was sent to Rome; Francisco de Rojas procured the papal commission for his trial and forwarded it, June 3, 1506.[544]

Before it was despatched, however, Ferdinand's position had changed with the arrival in Spain of his daughter Juana, now Queen of Castile, and her husband Philip of Austria. Eager to throw off Ferdinand's iron rule and to win the favor of the new sovereigns, most of the nobles had flocked to them and with them the Conversos, who hoped to secure a modification in the rigor of the Inquisition. They had been aroused by the sufferings of their brethren in Córdova, whose cause was their own, and they were becoming an element not to be disregarded in the political situation; they had already secured a hearing in the Roman curia, always ready, as we shall see hereafter, to welcome appellants with money and to sacrifice them after payment received; they had obtained from Julius II commissions transferring from the Inquisition cognizance of certain cases--commissions which Ferdinand repeatedly asked the pope to withdraw and doubtless with success, as they do not appear in the course of events; they had even approached Ferdinand himself, while in Valladolid, with an offer of a hundred thousand ducats if he would suspend the Inquisition until the arrival of Juana and Philip. This offer, he says in a letter of June 9, 1506, to Rojas, he spurned, but we may perhaps doubt his disinterestedness when he adds that, as Philip has disembarked and is unfamiliar with Spanish affairs, he had secretly ordered Deza to suspend the operations of all the tribunals--the motive of which evidently was to create the belief that Philip was responsible for it. As for Talavera, he adds, as it would greatly scandalize the new converts of Granada, if they thought there were errors of faith in him whom they regarded as so good a Christian, he had concluded to let the matter rest for the present and would subsequently send instructions.[545] He evidently had no belief in Lucero's fabricated evidence, a fact to be borne in mind when we consider his attitude in the ultimate developments of the affair. This despatch, of course, reached Rojas too late to prevent the issuing of the commission to try Talavera, but it explains why that document was suppressed when it arrived. Deza denied receiving it; it disappeared and Talavera, in his letter of January 23, 1507, to Ferdinand, manifests much anxiety to know what had become of it, evidently dreading that it would be opportunely found when wanted.

THE INQUISITION SUCCUMBS

By the agreement of Villafáfila, June 27, 1506, Ferdinand bound himself to abandon Castile to Philip and Juana; he departed for Aragon and busied himself with preparations for a voyage to Naples, whither he set sail September 4th. Philip assumed the government and disembarrassed himself of his wife by shutting her up as unfit to share in the cares of royalty. He was amenable to the golden arguments of the Conversos and doubtless had not forgotten the contempt with which had been treated his order of the previous year to suspend the Inquisition. He therefore naturally was in no haste to revive its functions. Ferdinand's secretary Almazan writes to Rojas, July 1st, that the king and the grandees have imprisoned Juana and no one is allowed to see her; he has in vain sought to get some prelates to carry letters from her to her father, but no one ventures to do so; the grandees have done this to partition among themselves the royal power, the Conversos to free themselves from the Inquisition, which is now extinct.[546]

The people of Córdova made haste to take advantage of the situation. They sent a powerful appeal to Philip and Juana, stating that their previous complaints had been intercepted through Deza's influence and accusing Lucero of the most arbitrary iniquities.[547] They asked that all the inquisitorial officials at Córdova and Toro should be removed and the whole affair be committed to the Bishop of Leon. Philip referred the matter to the Comendador mayor, Garcilasso de la Vega and to Andrea di Borgo, ambassador of Maximilian I, two laymen, to the great scandal, we are told, of all ecclesiastics.[548] The Conversos were triumphant and the Inquisition succumbed completely. The Suprema, including Deza himself, hastened to disclaim all responsibility for Lucero's misdeeds in a letter addressed to the chapter of Córdova, in which it said that the accusations brought against him seemed incredible, for even highwaymen, when robbing their victims, spare their lives, while here not only the property but the lives of the victims were taken and the honor of their descendants to the tenth generation. But, after hearing the narrative of the Master of Toro there could no longer be doubt and to tolerate it would be to approve it. Therefore, the chapter was instructed to continue to prevent these iniquities, and their majesties would be asked to apply a remedy and to punish their authors.[549] The remedy applied was to compel Deza to subdelegate irrevocably to Diego Ramírez de Guzman, Bishop of Catania and member of the Council of State, power to supersede Lucero and revise his acts, which was confirmed by a papal brief placing in Guzman's hands all the papers and prisoners in Córdova, Toro and Valladolid.[550] Lucero endeavored to anticipate this by burning all his prisoners so as to get them out of the way, but after the auto de fe was announced there came orders from the sovereigns which fortunately prevented the holocaust.[551]

The relief of the sufferers seemed assured, but the situation was radically changed by the sudden death of Philip, September 25, 1506, for although Juana was treated nominally as queen, she exercised no authority. Deza promptly revoked Guzman's commission, of which the papal confirmation seems not to have been received; he took possession of the prisoners at Toro and sent the Archdeacon of Torquemada to Córdova to do the same, but Francisco Osorio, the representative of Guzman, refused to obey. The people of Córdova were in despair. It was in vain that they sent delegations to Deza and petitioned the queen to save them. Deza was immovable and the queen refused to act in this as in everything else. The chapter, every member of which was an Old Christian, proud of his limpieza, assembled on October 16th to consider the situation. Some of the most prominent dignitaries of the Church had already been arrested by Lucero and had been treated by him as Jewish dogs; he had asserted that all the rest, and most of the nobles and gentlemen of the city and of other places, were apostates who had converted their houses into synagogues; in view of the impending peril, it was unanimously resolved to defend themselves, while the citizens at large declared that they would sacrifice life and property rather than to submit longer to such insupportable tyranny.[552]

PERSECUTION RENEWED

If the eclipse of the royal authority had enabled Deza to restore Lucero to power it also afforded opportunity for forcible resistance. The grandees of Castile were striving to recover the independence enjoyed under Henry IV, and a condition of anarchy was approaching rapidly. The two great nobles of Córdova, the Count of Cabra, Lord of Baena and the Marquis of Priego, Lord of Aguilar and nephew of the Great Captain, were nothing loath to listen to the entreaties of the citizens, especially as the marquis had been summoned by Lucero to appear for trial. Meetings were held in which formal accusations of Lucero and his promotor fiscal, Juan de Arriola, were laid before Padre Fray Francisco de Cuesta, comendador of the convent of la Merced, who seems to have assumed the leadership of the movement. He pronounced judgement, ordering Lucero and the fiscal to be arrested and their property to be confiscated. Under the lead of Cabra and Priego the citizens arose to execute the judgement. On November 9th they broke into the alcázar, where the Inquisition held its seat, they seized the fiscal and some of the subordinates and liberated the prisoners, whose recital of their wrongs excited still more the popular indignation, but no blood was shed and Lucero saved himself by flight.[553] The whole proceeding appears to have been orderly: a commission of ecclesiastics and laymen was appointed, to which the kinsmen and friends of the prisoners gave security that they should be forthcoming for trial as soon as there should be a king in the land to administer justice. This engagement was duly kept and their temporary liberation under bail was justified on the ground that many of them had been incarcerated for six or seven years and that all were in danger of perishing by starvation, for they were penniless, their property having been confiscated and Deza having ordered the receiver of confiscations not to provide for them.[554]

When the news of this uprising reached Deza he promptly, November 18th, commissioned his nephew, Pedro Juárez de Deza, Archbishop-elect of the Indies, to prosecute and punish all concerned, while by his orders the tribunal of Toledo intercepted and threw into prison Doctor Alonso de Toro, sent by the city to present its case to the queen. Other envoys, however, bore instructions to ask for the removal of Deza and the prosecution of Lucero and his officials, coupled with the intimation that steps had been taken to convoke all the cities of Andalusia and Castile to devise measures of protection against the intolerable tyranny of the Inquisition.[555] This plan seems to have been abandoned but, early in January, 1507, the Bishop of Córdova, Juan de Daza, in conjunction with the clerical and secular authorities, sent a solemn appeal to the pope, asking him to appoint Archbishop Ximenes and the Bishop of Catania or of Málaga, with full power to investigate and to act, and this they accompanied, January 10th, with a petition to Ferdinand, who was still in Naples, to support their request to the pope.[556] Deza, however, continued to command Ferdinand's unwavering support and the result was seen in the prompt and uncompromising action of Julius II. He wrote to Deza that the Jews, pretending to be Christians, who had dared to rise against the Inquisition, must be exterminated root and branch; no labor was to be spared to suppress this pestilence before it should spread, to hunt up all who had participated in it and to exercise the utmost severity in punishing them, without appeal, for their crimes.[557]

Thus stimulated and encouraged, Lucero resumed his activity and the liberated prisoners were surrendered to him. Peter Martyr writes from the court, March 7, 1507, to Archbishop Talavera, that his sister and his nephew the Dean of Granada, Francisco Herrera--who had doubtless been released in the rising of November 9th--had been thrown in prison in Córdova. Talavera himself, moreover, was put on trial before the papal nuncio, Giovanni Ruffo, and assessors duly commissioned by the pope, showing that Ferdinand's scruples as to scandalizing the people of Granada had vanished in the fierce resolve to vindicate Lucero and that the missing papal brief had been duly found. Peter Martyr describes his earnest efforts to convince the judges of Talavera's holy life and spotless character, to which they replied that all this might be true but their business was to ascertain the secrets of his heart.[558] By the time the evidence was sent to Rome, however, his conviction was no longer desired; the testimony was pronounced to be worthless and Pascual de la Fuente, Bishop of Burgos, who was in attendance on the curia, was an earnest witness in his favor.[559] The papal sentence was acquittal and this apparently carried with it the exoneration of his kindred--but it came too late. On May 21st Peter Martyr exultingly writes to him that the dean and his sister with their mother and the rest of his innocent household had been set free, but already he had gone to a higher tribunal. On Ascension-day (May 13th) he had walked, bareheaded and barefooted, in the procession through the streets of Granada, when a violent fever set in and carried him off the next day. He had accumulated no treasure, having spent all his revenues on the poor; he left no provision for his family and the Bishop of Málaga charitably gave to his sister a house in Granada to shelter her old age. His reputation for sanctity is seen in the accounts which at once were circulated, with universal credence of the miracles wrought by him in curing the sick.[560]

POLITICAL INTRIGUES

The reaction in favor of the Inquisition, led by Ferdinand and Julius II, had evidently been short-lived, for the political situation dominated everything and king and pope found it advisable to yield. Juana was keeping herself secluded with the corpse of her husband and was refusing to govern. The rival factions of the two grandfathers of Charles V, Maximilian I and Ferdinand, each striving for the regency during his minority, were both desirous of the support of the Conversos and thus the question of the Córdovan prisoners attained national importance as one on which all parties took sides. Ximenes, the Duke of Alva and the Constable of Castile, the heads of Ferdinand's party, held a conference at Cavia and listened to the complaints against Deza, for which they promised to find a remedy. The friends of the prisoners, however, seemed more inclined towards the faction of Maximilian; they offered money to defray the expenses of troops to be sent to Spain to resist Ferdinand's return and it was currently rumored that four thousand men were gathered in a Flemish port ready to embark. It is not easy to penetrate the secret intrigues culminating in the settlement which gave the regency to Ferdinand, but Ximenes, who represented him, took advantage of the situation, with his usual skill, to further his own ambition, which was to gain the cardinal's hat and Deza's position as inquisitor-general.[561] For the former of these Ferdinand had made application as early as November 8, 1505, and had repeated the request October 30, 1506; it was granted in secret consistory, January 4, 1507, and was published May 17th.[562] For the latter, the complaints of the Conversos afforded substantial reasons; we have seen that Córdova had petitioned the pope to commission Ximenes as its judge and his appointment would help to pacify the troubles. Ferdinand at length recognized that Deza's sacrifice was inevitable, and the way was made easy for him, as he was allowed to resign. On May 18th Ferdinand writes to Ximenes from Naples that he had received Deza's resignation and had taken the necessary steps to secure for him the succession; he has two requests to make--that he shall foster piety and religion by appointing only the best men and that he shall exercise the utmost care that nothing shall be allowed to impair Deza's dignity.[563] The commission as inquisitor-general was duly issued on June 5, 1507.

LUCERO'S VICTIMS RELEASED

The hatred excited by Lucero had been too wide-spread and the friends of the prisoners were too powerful to be satisfied with the mere substitution of Ximenes for Deza, and there was evidently an understanding that the matter was not to be dropped. As early as May 1st, Peter Martyr writes that it is reported that the imprisoned witnesses, corrupted by Lucero, are to be released and that he will expiate with due punishment his unprecedented crimes.[564] Some such promise was probably necessary for the pacification of the land, but the delay in its performance is significant of protection at the fountain-head of justice. It assumed at first the shape of an action brought by the chapter and city of Córdova before the pope, charging Lucero with the evil wrought by his suborning some witnesses and compelling others by punishment to testify that the plaintiffs were heretics. Julius II commissioned Fray Francisco de Mayorga as apostolic judge to try the case, and, on October 17, 1507, he decreed that Lucero be imprisoned and held to answer at law. Nothing further was done, however, and the impatient citizens addressed a memorial to Queen Juana, asking her to send some one to inform himself about it and report to her.[565] The action of the apostolic judge seems to have been regarded as a mere formality; the months passed away and it was not until May 18, 1508, that the Suprema took independent cognizance of the matter, when Ximenes and his colleagues, except Aguirre, all voted that Lucero should be arrested.[566] Peter Martyr intimates more than once that numbers of the Suprema were suspected of complicity with Lucero and assures us that the Council did not act without thorough investigation of numerous witnesses and interminable masses of documents, revealing an incredible accumulation of impossible and fantastic accusations contrived to bring infamy on all Spain.[567]

It was apparently the first time that an inquisitor had been thus publicly put on trial for official malfeasance and the opportunity was improved to render the spectacle a solemn one, fitted not only to satisfy the national interest felt in the case but to magnify the office of the accused by the scale of the machinery employed to deal with him. Lucero was carried in chains to Burgos, where the court was in residence, and was confined in the castle under strict guard. Ximenes assembled a Congregacion Católica, composed of twenty-one members besides himself, including a large portion of the Royal Council, the Inquisitor-general of Aragon and other inquisitors, several bishops and various other dignitaries--in short, an imposing representation of the piety and learning of the land.[568] After numerous sessions, presided over by Ximenes, sentence was rendered July 9, 1508, and was published August 1st, at Valladolid, whither the court had removed, in presence of Ferdinand and his magnates and a great concourse assembled to lend solemnity to this restoration of the honor of Castile and Andalusia, which had been so deeply compromised by the pretended revelations extorted by Lucero. This weighty verdict declared that there were no grounds for the asserted existence of synagogues, the preaching of sermons and the assemblies of missionaries of Judaism or for the prosecution of those accused. The witnesses--or rather prisoners--were discharged and everything relating to these fictitious crimes was ordered to be expunged from the records. To complete the vindication of the memory of the victims, Ferdinand ordered the rebuilding of the houses which had been torn down under the provisions of the canon law requiring the destruction of the conventicles of heresy.[569] By implication, the acquittal of the prisoners convicted Lucero, but all this was merely preliminary to his trial.

REACTION--ESCAPE OF LUCERO

Ferdinand's hand had been forced; he had been obliged to yield to public opinion, but his resolve was inflexible to undo as far as he could the results reached by Ximenes. In October he visited Córdova, where he rewarded some officials of the tribunal by grants out of the confiscated estates, which should have been restored when the proceedings were annulled. It is true that the judge of confiscations, Licenciado Simancas, was suspended, but in November, 1509, he was ordered to resume his functions and to act as he had formerly done. We happen to know that, in 1513, the house of the unfortunate Bachiller Membreque was still in possession of the Inquisition. There was no relief for those who had suffered. When the new inquisitor, Diego López de Cortegano, Archdeacon of Seville, revoked Lucero's sentence on the Licenciado Daza, who had been penanced and his property confiscated, the purchasers who had bought it complained to Ferdinand and he expressed his wrath by promptly dismissing the inquisitor and ordering all the papers in the case to be sent to the Suprema for review and action. The vacancy thus created was not easy to fill, for when, in September, 1509, Ferdinand offered the place to Alonso de Mariana he declined, saying that it would kill him, but he agreed to take the tribunal of Toledo, and it was not until February, 1510, that the Licenciado Mondragon was transferred from Valladolid to take Cortegano's place. In fact, the interests involved in the confiscations were too many and too powerful for the victims to obtain justice. Martin Alonso Conchina had been condemned by Lucero to reconciliation and confiscation; when the pressure was removed he revoked his confession as having been extorted by threats and fear, whereupon the confiscated property was placed in sequestration awaiting the result. Unluckily for him one of the items, a ground-rent of 9000 mrs. a year had been given, in April, 1506, to the unprincipled secretary Calcena, with the result that one of the new inquisitors, Andrés Sánchez de Torquemada, promptly arrested Conchina, tried him again, convicted him and sentenced him to perpetual imprisonment, so that the confiscation held good and the ground-rent, with all arrears, was confirmed to Calcena by a royal cédula of December 23, 1509. There seems to have still been some obstacle to this reaction in the episcopal Ordinary, Francisco de Simancas, Archdeacon of Córdova for, in February, 1510, Ferdinand wrote to the bishop that, without letting it be known that the order came from the king, he must be replaced with some one zealous for the furtherance of justice and, a month later, this command was peremptorily repeated. It is true that the extravagant wickedness of Lucero was scarce to be dreaded, but, with a tribunal reconstructed under such auspices, the people of Córdova could not hope for justice tempered with mercy and its productive activity is evidenced by the large drafts made, in 1510, on its receiver of confiscations. We may assume that Ximenes looked on this with disfavor for, in a letter to Ferdinand, after his return from the expedition to Oran in 1509, he supplicates that the decision of the Congregation be maintained for he has never infringed it and never intends to do so.[570]

As for the author of the evil, Lucero himself, he was sent in chains to Burgos with some of his accomplices. Ximenes, as inquisitor-general, had full power, as we have seen, to dismiss and punish them but, for some occult reason, a papal commission for their trial was applied for. This caused delay under which Ferdinand chafed, for he wrote, September 30, 1509, to his ambassador complaining that it caused great inconvenience and ordering him to urge the pope to issue it at once so that it could be sent by the first courier.[571] When it came, it empowered the Suprema to try the case and Ferdinand, who warmly espoused Lucero's cause, expressed his feelings unequivocally in a letter of April 7, 1510--"the prisoners say that they have been long in prison and those who informed against them have gone to Portugal or other parts, and others have been burnt or penanced as heretics, showing clearly that they testified falsely, and they supplicate me to provide that their trial be by inquisitorial and not by accusatorial process, so that they shall not be exposed to greater infamy than hitherto by dead or perjured witnesses, especially as the law provides that the trial be summary and directed only to reach the truth. There is great compassion for their long imprisonment and suffering, wherefore I beg and charge you to look well into the matter and treat it conscientiously and with diligence for its speedy termination, with which I shall be well pleased."[572]

INQUISITORIAL METHODS

In spite of this urgency the trial dragged on, much delay being caused by the difficulty of finding an advocate willing to undertake Lucero's defence. The Suprema selected the Bachiller de la Torre, but he declined to serve and Ferdinand, on May 16th, expressed his fear that no one would assume the duty. July 19th he writes that Lucero complains that he still has no counsel and he suggests that, if none of the lawyers of the royal court can be trusted, Doctor Juan de Orduña of Valladolid be called in and his fees be paid by the Inquisition. The suggestion was adopted and, on August 20th, Ferdinand wrote personally to Orduña ordering him to take charge of the defence and see that Lucero suffered no wrong, and at, the same time, he wrote to the University of Valladolid to give Orduña the requisite leave of absence. Under this royal pressure, and considering that the adverse witnesses had been largely burnt or frightened into flight, it is perhaps rather creditable to the Suprema that it ventured to dismiss Lucero, without inflicting further punishment on him. He retired to the Seville canonry, which he had acquired by the ruin of the Archdeacon of Castro, and there he ended his days in peace. In 1514, Ferdinand manifested his undiminished sympathy by a gift of 15,000 mrs. to Juan Carrasco, the former porter of the tribunal of Córdova, to indemnify him for losses and sufferings which he claimed to have endured in the rising of 1506.[573] Yet before we utterly condemn him for his share in this nefarious business we should make allowance for the influence of Lucero's accomplice, his secretary Calcena, who was always at hand to poison his mind and draft his letters. To the same malign obsession may doubtless also be attributed an order of Charles V, in 1519, requiring the Córdovan authorities to bestow the first vacant scrivenership on Diego Marino, who had been Lucero's notary.[574]

***

That Lucero was an exceptional monster may well be admitted, but when such wickedness could be safely perpetrated for years and only be exposed and ended through the accidental intervention of Philip and Juana, it may safely be assumed that the temptations of secrecy and irresponsibility rendered frightful abuses, if not universal at least frequent. The brief reign of Philip led other sorely vexed communities to appeal to the sovereigns for relief, and some of their memorials have been preserved. One from Jaen relates that the tribunal of that city procured from Lucero a useful witness whom for five years he had kept in the prison of Córdova to swear to what was wanted. His name was Diego de Algeciras and, if the petitioners are to be believed, he was, in addition to being a perjurer, a drunkard, a gambler, a forger and a clipper of coins. This worthy was brought to Jaen and performed his functions so satisfactorily that the wealthiest Conversos were soon imprisoned. Two hundred wretches crowded the filthy gaol and it was requisite to forbid the rest of the Conversos from leaving the city without a license. With Diego's assistance and the free use of torture, on both accused and witnesses, it was not difficult to obtain whatever evidence was desired. The notary of the tribunal, Antonio de Barcena, was especially successful in this. On one occasion he locked a young girl of fifteen in a room, stripped her naked and scourged her until she consented to bear testimony against her mother. A prisoner was carried in a chair to the auto de fe with his feet burnt to the bone; he and his wife were burnt alive and then two of their slaves were imprisoned and forced to give such evidence as was necessary to justify the execution. The cells in which the unfortunates were confined in heavy chains were narrow, dark, humid, filthy and overrun with vermin, while their sequestrated property was squandered by the officials, so that they nearly starved in prison while their helpless children starved outside. Granting that there may be exaggeration in this, the solid substratum of truth is clear from the fact that the petitioners only asked that the tribunal be placed under the control of the Bishop of Jaen--that bishop being Alfonso Suárez de Fuentelsaz, one of Torquemada's inquisitors, who had risen to be a colleague of Deza. He had not been a merciful judge, as many of his sentences attest, yet the miserable Conversos of Jaen were ready to fly to him for relief.[575]

A memorial from Arjona, a considerable town near Jaen, illustrates a different phase of the subject. It relates that a certain Alvaro de Escalera of that place conspired with other evil men to report to the inquisitors of Jaen that there were numerous heretics in Arjona, so that when confiscations came to be sold they could buy the property cheap. In due time an inquisitor came with the notary Barcena. No Term of Grace was given, but the Edict of Faith was published, frightening the inhabitants with its fulminations unless they testified against their neighbors. Then a Dominican preached a fiery sermon to the effect that all Conversos were really Jews, whom it was the duty of Christians to destroy. The inquisitors then sent for the slaves of the Conversos, promising them liberty if they would testify against their masters and assuring them of secrecy. The notary followed by traversing the town with Escalera and his friends, proclaiming that there was a fine of ten reales on all who would not come forward with testimony, and the exaction of the fine from a number had a quickening influence on the memories of others. Then a house to house canvass was made for evidence; the women were told that it was impossible that they should not know the Jewish tendencies of their neighbors; they could give what evidence they pleased for their names would not be divulged; they were not obliged to prove it, for the accused had to disprove it. Those who would not talk were threatened that they would be carried to Jaen and made to accuse their neighbors, and, in fact, a number were taken and compelled to give evidence in prison. Then the inquisitors departed with the accumulated testimony; there was peace in Arjona for three months and the Conversos recovered from their fright. Suddenly one night there arrived the notary, the receiver and some officials; they quietly aroused the regidores and alcaldes and made them collect a force of armed men who were stationed to guard the walls and gates. When morning came the work of arresting the suspects was commenced; their property was sequestrated, their houses locked and their children were turned into the street, while the officials carried off their prisoners, who were thrust into the already crowded gaol of Jaen. The confiscations were auctioned off and those who had plotted the raid had ample opportunity of speculating in bargains.576

Still other methods are detailed in a memorial from Llerena, the seat of one of the older tribunals with jurisdiction over Extremadura. It stated that for many years the Inquisition there had found little or nothing to do, until there came a new judge, the Licenciado Bravo. He was a native of Fregenal, a town of the province, where he had bitter law-suits and active enmities; he had had two months' training under Lucero at Córdova and he came armed with ample evidence gathered there. On his arrival, without waiting for formalities or further testimony, he made a large number of arrests and sent to Badajoz where he seized forty more and brought them to Llerena. They were mostly men of wealth whose fortunes were attractive objects of spoliation, and Bravo took care of his kindred by appointing them to positions in which they could appropriate much of the sequestrated property. The treatment of the prisoners was most brutal, and when his colleague, Inquisitor Villart, who was not wholly devoid of compassion, was overheard remonstrating with him and saying that the death of the captives would be on their souls, Bravo told him to hold his peace, for he who had placed him there desired that they should all die off, one by one. The petitioners were quite willing to be remitted to the tribunal of Seville or to have judges who would punish the guilty and discharge the innocent, but they earnestly begged, by the Passion of Christ, that they should not be left to the mercy of Inquisitor-general Deza. Orders, they said, had been given to him to mitigate in some degree the sufferings of the people of Jaen, which he suppressed and replaced with instructions to execute justice. What this meant we may gather from a last despairing appeal, by the friends of the prisoners of Jaen, to Queen Juana; a junta of lawyers, they said, had been assembled, a scaffold of immense proportions was under construction; their only hope was in her and they entreated her to order that no auto de fe be held until impartial persons should ascertain the truth as to the miserable captives.577 Juana was in no condition to respond to this agonized prayer, and we may safely assume that greed and cruelty claimed their victims. These glimpses into the methods of the tribunals elucidate the statements of the Capitan Avora as to the desolation spread over the land by the Inquisition.

***

It would seem that these fearful abuses were creating a general feeling of hostility to the institution and its officials, for Ferdinand deemed it necessary to issue a proclamation, January 19, 1510, calling upon all officials, gentlemen and good citizens to furnish inquisitors and their subordinates with lodgings and supplies at current prices and not to maltreat or assail them, under penalty of 50,000 maravedís and punishment at the royal discretion. A month later, February 22d, we find him writing to the constable of Castile that inquisitors are to visit the districts of Burgos and Calahorra, and he asks the constable to give orders that they may not be impeded. Somewhat similar instructions he gave in March to the provisor and corregidor of Cuenca, when the inquisitors of Cartagena were preparing to visit that portion of their district, as though these special interpositions of the royal power were requisite to ensure their comfort and safety in the discharge of their regular duties. Even these were sometimes ineffectual as was experienced, in 1515, by the inquisitor Paradinas of Cartagena, who, while riding on his mule in the streets of Murcia, was set upon, stabbed and would have been killed but for assistance, while the assassins escaped, calling forth from Ferdinand the most emphatic orders for their arrest and trial.578

XIMENES ATTEMPTS REFORM

Yet, however rudely the Inquisition may have been shaken, it was too firmly rooted in the convictions of the period and too energetically supported by Ferdinand to be either destroyed or essentially reformed. When he died, January 23, 1516, his testament, executed the day previous, laid strenuous injunctions on his grandson and successor Charles V--"As all other virtues are nothing without faith, by which and in which we are saved, we command the said illustrious prince, our grandson, to be always zealous in defending and exalting the Catholic faith and that he aid, defend and favor the Church of God and labor, with all his strength, to destroy and extirpate heresy from our kingdoms and lordships, selecting and appointing throughout them ministers, God-fearing and of good conscience, who will conduct the Inquisition justly and properly, for the service of God and the exaltation of the Catholic faith, and who will also have great zeal for the destruction of the sect of Mahomet."579

With his death, during the absence of his successor, the governing power was lodged in the hands of Inquisitor-general Ximenes. From the papal brief of August 18, 1509, alluded to above, we may infer that he had already endeavored to effect a partial reform, by dismissing some of the more obnoxious inquisitors, and he now made use of his authority to strike at those who had hitherto been beyond his reach. Aguirre was one of these and another was the mercenary Calcena, concerning whom he wrote to Charles, December, 1516, that it was necessary that they should in future have nothing to do with the

Inquisition in view of their foul excesses. Another removal, of which we chance to have cognizance, was that of Juan Ortiz de Zarate, the secretary of the Suprema. Whatever were the failings of the inflexible Ximenes, pecuniary corruption was abhorrent to him and, during the short term of his supremacy in Castile, we may feel assured that he showed no mercy to those who sought to coin into money the blood of the Conversos.[580] With his death, however, came a speedy return to the bad old ways. Adrian of Utrecht, though well-intentioned, was weak and confiding. When appointed Inquisitor-general of Aragon, he had made Calcena, February 12, 1517, secretary of that Suprema and, after the death of Ximenes we find Calcena acting, in 1518, as royal secretary of the reunited Inquisition, a position which he shared with Ugo de Urries, Lord of Ayerbe, another appointee of Adrian's, who long retained that position under Charles V. Aguirre had the same good fortune, having been appointed by Adrian to membership in the Suprema of Aragon and resuming his position in the reunited Inquisition after the death of Ximenes. His name occurs as signed to documents as late as 1546, when he seems to be the senior member.[581]

Ferdinand's dying exhortation to his grandson was needed. Charles V, a youth of seventeen, was as clay in the hands of the potter, surrounded by grasping Flemish favorites, whose sole object, as far as concerned Spain, was to sell their influence to the highest bidder. During the interval before his coming to take possession of his new dominions, he fluctuated in accordance with the pressure which happened momentarily to be strongest. The Spaniards who came to his court gave fearful accounts of the Inquisition, which they said was ruining Spain, and we are told that his counsellors were mostly Conversos who had obtained their positions by purchase.[582] In his prologue to his subsequent abortive project of reform, Charles says that while in Flanders he received many complaints about the Inquisition, which he submitted to famous men of learning and to colleges and universities, and his proposed action was in accordance with their advice.[583] Ximenes was alive to the danger and it was doubtless by his impulsion that the Council of Castile wrote to Charles that the peace of the kingdom and the maintenance of his authority depended on his support of the Inquisition.[584] A more adroit manoeuvre was the advantage which he took of the death, June 1, 1516, of Bishop Mercader, Inquisitor-general of Aragon. It would probably not have been difficult for him to have reunited the Inquisitions of the two crowns under his own headship, but he took the more politic course of urging Charles to nominate his old tutor, Adrian of Utrecht, then in Spain, as his representative, and to secure for him the succession to Mercader's see of Tortosa. Charles willingly followed the advice; July 30th he replied that in accordance with it he had written to Rome for the commission; November 14th Pope Leo commissioned Adrian as Inquisitor-general of Aragon, and we shall see hereafter how complete was the ascendancy which he exercised over Charles in favor of the Holy Office.[585]

COMPLAINTS OF THE CORTES

Meanwhile Charles continued to vacillate. At one time he proposed to banish from his court all those of Jewish blood, and sent a list of names in cypher with instructions to report their genealogies, to which the Suprema of Aragon replied, October 27, 1516, with part of the information, promising to furnish the rest and expressing great gratification at his promises of aid and support in all things.[586] Then there came a rumor that he proposed to abolish the suppression of the names of witnesses, which was one of the crowning atrocities of inquisitorial procedure. For this there must have been some foundation for, March 11, 1517, Ximenes sent to his secretary Ayala a commission as procurator of the Inquisition at Charles's court, with full power to resist any attempt to restrict or impede it, and he followed this, March 17th, with a letter to Charles, more vigorous than courtly, telling him that such a measure would be the destruction of the Inquisition and would cover his name with infamy; Ferdinand and Isabella, when in straits for money during the war with Granada, had refused 1,200,000 ducats for such a concession, and Ferdinand had subsequently rejected an offer of 400,000.[587]

OFFERS OF THE NEW CHRISTIANS

It can readily be imagined that, in spite of the character of Ximenes, the death of Ferdinand and the uncertainty as to the views of the distant sovereign had sensibly diminished the awe felt for the Inquisition. There is an indication of this in a complaint made by the Suprema, in September, 1517, that, when it moved with the court from place to place, the alcaldes of the palace refused to furnish mules and wagons to transport its books and papers and personnel, or, at most, only did so after all the other departments of the government had been supplied.[588] There is significance also in a tumult occurring in Orihuela, in 1517, when the inquisitors of Cartagena made a visitation there, obliging the Licenciado Salvatierra to invoke the royal intervention.[589] The Conversos, though decimated and impoverished, still had money and influence and the abuses which Ximenes had not been able to eradicate still excited hostility. When Charles, after his arrival in Spain, in September, 1517, held his first Córtes at Valladolid in 1518, the deputies petitioned him to take such order that justice should be done by the Inquisition, so that the wicked alone should be punished and the innocent not suffer; that the canons and the common law should be observed; that the inquisitors should be of gentle blood, of good conscience and repute and of the age required by law, and, finally, that episcopal Ordinaries should be judges in conformity with justice.[590] Although drawn in general terms this formal complaint indicates that the people felt the Holy Office to be an engine of oppression, for the furtherance of the private ends of the officials, to the disregard of law and justice. Charles made reply that he would consult learned and saintly men, with whose advice he would so provide that injustice should cease and meanwhile he would receive memorials as to abuses and projects of reform. The deputies made haste to give him ample information as to the tribulations of his subjects and the injury resulting to his dominions, and the outcome of the consultations of his advisers was a series of instructions to the officials of the Inquisition which, if carried into effect, would have deprived the Holy Office of much of its efficiency for persecution as well as of its capacity for injustice. Peter Martyr tells us that the New Christians, to procure this, gave to the high chancellor, Jean le Sauvage, who was a thoroughly corrupt man, ten thousand ducats in hand, with a promise of ten thousand more when it should go into effect, but that, fortunately for the Inquisition, he fell sick towards the end of May and died early in July.[591] The Instructions had been finally engrossed and lacked only the signatures; they were drawn in the names of Charles and Juana and were addressed not only to the officials of the Inquisition but to those of the state and secular justice, but nothing more was heard of them, for the new chancellor, Mercurino di Gattinara, was a man of different stamp, and Charles as yet was swayed by the influences surrounding him. The elaborate project is therefore of no interest except as an acknowledgement, in its provisions for procedure, of the iniquity of the inquisitorial process as we shall see it hereafter, and, in its prohibitory clauses, that existing abuses exaggerated in every way the capacity for evil of the system as practised. Thus it prohibited that the salaries of the inquisitors should be dependent on the confiscations and fines which they pronounced, or that grants should be made to them from confiscated property or benefices of those whom they condemned, or that sequestrated property should be granted away before the condemnation of its owners; that inquisitors and officials abusing their positions should be merely transferred to other places instead of being duly punished; that those who complained of the tribunals should be arrested and maltreated; that those who appealed to the Suprema should be maltreated; that inquisitors should give information to those seeking grants as to the property of prisoners still under trial; that prisoners under trial should be debarred from hearing mass and receiving the sacraments; that those condemned to perpetual prison should be allowed to die of starvation.[592] The general tenor of these provisions indicate clearly what a tremendous stimulus to persecution and injustice was confiscation as a punishment of heresy, how the whole business of the Inquisition was degraded from its ostensible purpose of purifying the faith into a vile system of spoliation, and how those engaged in it were inevitably vitiated by the tempting opportunity of filthy gains.

Although Charles, on the death of his chancellor, dropped the proposed reform, he seems to have recognized the existence of these evils. When his Inquisitor-general, Cardinal Adrian, was elevated to the papacy in 1522, he sent from Flanders his chamberlain La Chaulx to congratulate him before he should leave Spain, and among the envoy's instructions was the suggestion that he should be careful in his appointments and provide proper means to prevent the Inquisition from punishing the innocent and its officials from thinking more about the property of the condemned than the salvation of their souls--a pious wish but perfectly futile so long as the methods of the institution were unchanged, and its expenses were to be met and its officials enriched by fines and confiscations.[593]

The sufferers had long recognized this and offers had more than once been vainly made to Ferdinand to compound for the royal right of confiscation--offers of which we know no details. With the failure of the comprehensive scheme of reform, this plan was revived and, before Charles left Spain, May 21, 1520, to assume the title of King of the Romans, a formal proposition was made to him to the effect that if justice should be secured in the Inquisition, by appointing judges free from suspicion who should observe the law, so that the innocent might live secure and the wicked be punished and the papal ordinances be obeyed, there were persons who would dare to serve him as follows. Considering that greed is the parent of all evils; that it is the law of the Partidas that the property of those having Catholic children should not be confiscated[594] and further that the royal treasury derived very little profit from the confiscations, as they were all consumed in the salaries and costs of the judges and receivers who enriched themselves, his Majesty could well benefit himself by a composition and sale of all his rights therein, for himself and his descendants for ever, obtaining from the pope a bull prohibiting confiscations and pecuniary penances and fines. If this were done the parties pledged themselves to provide rents sufficient, with those that Ferdinand had assigned towards that purpose, to defray all the salaries and costs of the Inquisition, on a basis to be defined by Charles. Moreover, they would pay him four hundred thousand ducats--one hundred thousand before his departure and the balance in three equal annual payments at the fair of Antwerp in May. Or, if he preferred not to do this in perpetuity, he could limit the term, for which two hundred thousand ducats would be paid, in similar four instalments. For the collection of the sum to meet these engagements there must be letters and provisions such as the Catholic king gave for the compositions of Andalusia, and it must be committed in Castile to the Archbishop of Toledo (Cardinal de Croy), and in Aragon to the Archbishop of Saragossa (Alfonso de Aragon) from whose decisions there was to be no appeal. But to furnish the necessary personal security for the fulfilment of this offer, it was significantly added that it would be necessary for the king and Cardinal Adrian to give safe-conducts to the parties, protecting them from prosecution by the Inquisition and these must be issued in the current month of October so that there might be time to raise the money.[595] It is scarce necessary to say that this proposition was unsuccessful. Charles was under the influence of Cardinal Adrian and Adrian was controlled by his colleagues. It was asking too much of inquisitors that they should agree to allow themselves to be restricted to the impartial administration of the cruel laws against heresy, to be content with salaries and forego the opportunities of peculation. It was also in vain that the Córtes of Coruña, in 1520, repeated the request of those of Valladolid for a reform in procedure.[596] Charles sailed for Flanders leaving his subjects exposed to all the evils under which they had groaned so long. There were still occasional ebullitions of resistance for, in 1520, when the tribunal of Cuenca arrested the deputy corregidor it gave rise to serious troubles and Inquisitor Mariano of Toledo was despatched thither with his servants and familiars to restore peace, a task which occupied him for five months.[597]

A still further project for mitigating the rigors of the Inquisition was laid before Charles in 1520, apparently after his arrival in Flanders. This proposed no payment, but suggested that the expenses should be defrayed by the crown, which should wholly withdraw the confiscations from the control of the inquisitors. With this were connected various reforms in procedure--revealing the names of witnesses, allowing the accused to select his advocate and to see his friends and family in presence of the gaoler, the punishment of false witness by the talio, the support of wife and children during the trial from the sequestrated property and some others.[598] There would seem also, about 1522, to have been a further offer to Charles of seven hundred thousand ducats for the abandonment of confiscation, but it does not appear what conditions accompanied it.[599] It was all useless. The grasp of the Inquisition on Spain was too firm and its routine too well established for modification.

In the revolt of the Comunidades, which followed the departure of Charles, the affairs of the Inquisition had no participation. Some ten years later, however, in 1531, the tribunal of Toledo came upon traces of an attempt to turn the popular movement to account in removing one of the atrocities of inquisitorial procedure. The treasurer, Alfonso Gutiérrez, is said to have spent in Rome some twelve thousand ducats in procuring a papal brief which removed the seal of secrecy from prisons and witnesses. He endeavored to secure for his scheme the favor of Juan de Padilla, the popular leader, by a loan of eight hundred ducats on the pledge of a gold chain, but Padilla, while accepting the loan, prudently refused to jeopardize his cause by arousing inquisitorial hostility.[600]

What Gutiérrez failed to obtain was sought for again from Charles V in 1526. About this time commenced the efforts to subject the Moriscos of Granada to the Holy Office and apparently in preparation for this Granada was separated from Córdova and was favored with a tribunal of its own, transferred thither from Jaen. The frightened inhabitants made haste to petition Charles to do away with the secrecy which was so peculiarly provocative of abuses. They pointed out that a judge, if licentiously disposed, had ample opportunity to work his will with the maidens and wives brought before him as prisoners and even with those merely summoned to appear, whose terror betrayed that they would dare to offer no resistance. In the same way the notaries and other subordinates, who were frequently unmarried men, had every advantage with the wives and daughters of the prisoners, eagerly seeking to obtain some news of the accused, immured incomunicado in the secret prison, from which no word could escape, and ready, in their despairing anxiety, to make any sacrifice to learn his fate. Or, if the officials preferred, they could sell information for money and all this was so generally understood that these positions were sought by evil-minded men in order to gratify their propensities. Bad as was this, still worse was the suppression of the witnesses' names in procuring the conviction of the innocent while facilitating the escape of the guilty. The memorial assumes, what was practically the fact, that the only defence of the accused lay in guessing the names of the adverse witnesses and discrediting and disabling them for mortal enmity, and it pointed out how, in diverse ways, this facilitated miscarriage of justice. It did not confine itself to argument, however, but added that the little kingdom of Granada would pay fifty thousand ducats for the removal of secrecy from the procedure and prisons of the Inquisition, and that a very large sum could be thus obtained from the other provinces of Spain.[601] The only possible answer to the reasoning of the memorial was that the faith would suffer by any change, but this always sufficed and the Inquisition continued to shroud its acts in the impenetrable darkness which served to cover up iniquity and give ample scope for injustice.

***

A History of the Inquisition of Spain: Volume I
NAVARRE

When Charles had returned to Spain and again held the Córtes at Valladolid, in 1523, they repeated the petitions of 1518 and 1520, adding that nothing had been done. They further suggested that inquisitors should be paid salaries by the king and not draw their pay from the proceeds of their functions, and that false witnesses should be punished in accordance with the Laws of Toro. This shows that the old abuses were felt as acutely as ever, but Charles merely replied that he had asked the pope to commission as inquisitor-general the Archbishop of Seville, Manrique, whom he had especially charged to see that justice was properly administered. Again, in 1525, the Córtes of Toledo complained of the excesses of the inquisitors and the disorders committed by the familiars and asked that the secular judges might be empowered to restrain abuses, but they obtained only a vague promise that, if abuses existed, he would have them corrected.[602] It required no little courage for deputies to arraign the Inquisition publicly in the Córtes, and it is not surprising that the hardihood to do so disappeared with the recognition of the fruitlessness of remonstrance.

Thus all efforts proved futile to mitigate or ameliorate inquisitorial methods, and the Holy Office, in its existing form, was firmly established in Castile for three centuries momentous to the Spanish people.

When Ferdinand, in 1512, made the easy conquest of Navarre he presumably no longer had hope of issue by his Queen Germaine, to whom he could leave the kingdoms of his crown of Aragon. To avoid, therefore, for the new territory the limitations on sovereignty imposed by the Aragonese fueros, in the Córtes of Burgos, in 1515, he caused Navarre to be incorporated with the crown of Castile.[603] Its Inquisition thus finally became Castilian, although at first it was scarce more than a branch of that of Saragossa.

When the Castilian invaders under the Duke of Alva occupied Pampeluna they found there the Dominican friar, Antonio de Maya, armed with a commission as inquisitor, issued by his provincial and confirmed by the pope. The office had doubtless been a sinecure under the House of Albret, but the transfer of the land to the Catholic king gave promise of its future usefulness, for the little kingdom had served as an asylum for refugees from the rest of Spain. The good fraile lost no time in obtaining from Alva permission to exercise his office and in despatching an envoy to Ferdinand at Logroño to secure the royal confirmation and suggest the necessity of appointing a staff of salaried officials. Besides, the episcopal vicar-general of Pampeluna was seeking to exercise the office, and the king was asked to order him not to interfere. Ferdinand, with his usual caution, wrote on September 30, 1512, to the Duke of Alva, as captain-general, and to the Bishop of Majorca as governor, expressing his earnest desire to forward the good work and desiring information as to the character of Maya; meanwhile, if the inquisitors of Saragossa sent to claim fugitives, they were to be promptly surrendered.

No further action was taken for a year, during which Fray Maya did what he could in the absence of assistance. At length a royal letter of September 26, 1513, to the Marquis of Comares, lieutenant and captain-general, announced that Inquisitor-general Mercader had appointed as inquisitors Francisco González de Fresneda, one of the inquisitors of Saragossa, and Fray Antonio de Maya, to whom the customary oath of obedience was to be taken; the only other official designated was Jaime Julian, as escribano de secuestras, with a salary of 2500 sueldos. Further delays, however, occurred and, on December 21st, the king wrote to Fresneda to lose no time in going to Pampeluna with his officials, where he would find Maya awaiting him. On the 24th a proclamation announced that Leo X had ordered the continuance of the Inquisition in all the kingdoms of Spain and especially in that of Navarre, wherefore in order that dread of loss of property might not deter those conscious of guilt from coming forward and confessing, the king granted release from confiscation to all who would confess and apply for reconciliation within the Term of Grace of thirty days which the inquisitors would announce. As a preparation for those who should disregard this mercy, already, on the 22d, Martin Adrian had been commissioned to the important office of receiver of the confiscations which were expected to supply the funds for the machinery of persecution and, on January 1, 1514, he was empowered to pay himself a salary of 6000 sueldos and one of 3000 to Fray Maya. As nothing is said about the salaries of the other officials, they presumably were carried on the pay-roll of the tribunal of Saragossa. The process of manning the new Inquisition was conducted with great deliberation. It was not until July 13, 1514, that receiver Adrian was informed that Bishop Mercader had appointed Juan de Villena as fiscal, or prosecuting officer, to whom a salary of 2500 sueldos was to be paid. The close connection of the tribunal of Pampeluna with that of Aragon is seen in the fact that Adrian was also notary of the Inquisition of Calatayud and continued in service there for which he received his accustomed salary. Juan de Miades, also, the alguazil of Saragossa, was put in charge of the prison at Pampeluna, for which he was allowed an additional salary of 500 sueldos, until, October 15, 1515, Bernardino del Campo, of Saragossa, was appointed gaoler at Pampeluna with a salary of 500 sueldos. We also hear of Miguel Daoyz, notary del secreto of Saragossa acting for the Inquisition of Pampeluna. This may partly be attributable to Ferdinand's policy, as expressed, March 23, 1514, in a letter to the Marquis of Comares, that the officials must not be Navarrese, for he had elsewhere experienced the disadvantage of employing natives. More urgent, however, was the pressure of economy, for the Pampeluna Inquisition had apparently little to do; Navarre had never had a population of Moors and Jews comparable to that of the southern kingdoms and the refugees there doubtless hastened their departure as soon as the shadow of the Inquisition spread over the land, although one of the earliest orders of Ferdinand to Comares, December 21, 1513, had been to place guards secretly at all ports and passes to prevent their escape. How little material existed for the Holy Office is manifested by the fact that the confiscations did not pay the very moderate expenses and in May, 1515, it was necessary to transfer from Valencia two hundred ducats to enable Martin Adrian to meet the necessary charges. In September, 1514, we find the inquisitors making a visitation of their district and, in the following month, Fray Maya returned to the seclusion of his convent, but of the actual work of the tribunal we hear little. It is true that a letter of the Suprema, October 11, 1516, respecting the collection of a penance of 300 ducats imposed on Miguel de Sant Jaime shows that occasionally a lucrative prize was secured, but chances of this kind must have been few for, in 1521, Cardinal Adrian, in view of the necessities of the tribunal, ruthlessly cut down the salaries of all the officials. Its authority cannot have been well assured for, in 1518, the Viceroy, Duke of Najera, expresses doubts whether a sentence of sanbenitos, pronounced on Rodrigo de Osca and his wife, of Pampeluna, can be enforced, in view of their numerous kindred, to which the Suprema replies by instructing him to see that nothing is allowed to impede it. Little as it had to do, the business of the tribunal was delayed by its imperfect organization. In 1519 eight citizens of Pampeluna complained to the Suprema that, for trifling causes, their fathers and mothers, wives and brothers, were in the prison of the Inquisition, where three of them had died and the rest were sick. They had been detained for seven or eight months, although their cases were finished, awaiting consultores from Saragossa to vote on them, wherefore the petitioners asked that decisions be reached without further delay and that, when discharged, the prisoners should not be ruined by pecuniary penances greater than their substance, as had occurred on previous occasions. The Suprema, January 12, 1519, forwarded this petition to the inquisitors with instructions that, within fifteen days, one of them should bring to Saragossa all the cases concluded, to be duly voted on, while the remainder were to be finished as soon as possible and within fifteen days thereafter to be similarly brought to Saragossa for decision. As in this letter the Council describes itself as entrusted with the business of the Inquisition in all the kingdoms and lordships of the crown of Aragon and Navarre, it shows that the latter still remained subject to the section of the Suprema pertaining to Aragon.

While the tribunal of Pampeluna was thus of little service for its ostensible objects, it was turned to account politically in the perturbations which followed the death of Ferdinand, January 23, 1516. Jean d'Albret, supported by France, naturally made an effort to recover his dominions, but his ineffective siege of Saint-Jean-Pied-du-Port, and the defeat and capture of the Marshal of Navarre at Roncesvalles, speedily put an end to the invasion. It was important for the Spanish government to ascertain the extent to which assistance had been pledged to him by his former subjects. The Inquisition was unpopular among them and would undoubtedly have been overthrown had d'Albret succeeded, so that an investigation into those concerned in the movement could come within an elastic definition of its functions, while its methods fitted it admirably to obtain the information desired. Accordingly a cédula of April 21, 1516, instructed the inquisitors to spare no effort, in every way, to discover the names of those engaged in the affair and to obtain all the information they could about the whole matter. This probably did not increase the popularity of the Holy Office and the French invasion of 1521 offered an opportunity, which was not neglected, of expressing in action the hostility of the people. After the expulsion of the enemy, reprisals were in order which Cardinal Adrian committed to the Precentor of Tudela. Apparently he was not sufficiently vigorous in the work for, in 1523, we find the Suprema stimulating him to greater activity.[604]

Spanish domination being thus assured, the Navarrese tribunal became useful chiefly as a precaution to prevent the subject kingdom from continuing to be an asylum for heretics. It had been shifted from Pampeluna to Estella and thence to Tudela, where, in 1518, the Suprema instructs the inquisitors to find a suitable building, in order to relieve the monastery of San Francisco in which the tribunal was temporarily lodged. Some years later there was talk of returning it to Pampeluna, but finally it was recognized as having a district inadequate to its support, while the monarchy felt itself strong enough to disregard the old boundaries of nationality. At some time prior to 1540, Calahorra, with a portion of Old Castile, was detached from the enormous district of Valladolid and was made the seat of a tribunal of which the jurisdiction extended over Navarre and Biscay. About 1570 this was transferred to Logroño, on the boundary between Old Castile and Navarre, and there it remained, as we shall have occasion to see, until the dissolution of the Holy Office.[605]

CHAPTER V - THE KINGDOMS OF ARAGON

The Crown of Aragon comprised the so-called kingdoms of Aragon and Valencia, the principality of Catalonia, the counties of Rosellon and Cerdana, and the Balearic Isles, with the outlying dependencies of Sicily, Sardinia and Corsica. Although marriage had united the sovereigns of Castile and Aragon, the particularism born of centuries of rivalry and frequent war kept the lands jealously apart as separate nations and Ferdinand ruled individually his ancestral dominions. What had been accomplished in Castile for the Inquisition had therefore no effect across the border and the extension of the Spanish organization there was complicated by the character of the local institutions and the fact that the papal Inquisition was already in existence there since its foundation in the middle of the thirteenth century.

Aragon had not undergone the dissolving process of Castilian anarchy which enabled Ferdinand and Isabella to build up an absolute monarchy on the ruins of feudalism. Its ancient rights and liberties had been somewhat curtailed during the tyrannical reigns of Ferdinand of Antequera and his successors, but enough remained to render the royal power nominal rather than real and the people were fiercely jealous of their independence. The Córtes were really representative bodies which insisted upon the redress of grievances before voting supplies and, if we may believe the Venetian envoy, Giovanni Soranzo, in 1565, the ancient formula of the oath of allegiance was still in use: "We, who are as good as you, swear to you who are no better than we, as to the prince and heir of our kingdom, on condition that you preserve our liberty and laws and if you do otherwise we do not swear to you."[606]

In dealing with a people whose liberties were so extensive and whose jealousy as to their maintenance was so sensitive, Ferdinand was far too shrewd to provoke opposition by the abrupt introduction of the Inquisition such as he had forced upon Castile. His first endeavor naturally was to utilize the institution as it had so long existed. This, although founded as early as 1238, had sunk into a condition almost dormant in the spiritual lethargy of the century preceding the Reformation, and in Aragon, as in the rest of Europe, it appeared to be on the point of extinction. It is true that, in 1474, Sixtus IV had ordered Fra Leonardo, the Dominican General, to fill all the tribunals of the Holy Office and he had complied by appointing Fray Juan as Inquisitor of Aragon, Fray Jaime for Valencia, Fray Juan for Barcelona and Fray Francisco Vital for Catalonia, but we have no record of their activity.[607] So little importance, indeed, was attached to the functions of the Inquisition that in Valencia, where in 1480 the Dominicans Cristóbal de Gualbes and Juan Orts were inquisitors, they held faculties enabling them to act without the concurrence of the episcopal representative--an unexampled privilege, only explicable on the assumption that the archbishop declined to be troubled with matters so trivial. The archbishop at the time was Cardinal Rodrigo Borgia, papal vice-chancellor, better known as Alexander VI, who speedily woke up to the speculative value of his episcopal jurisdiction over heresy, when the fierce persecution, which arose in Andalusia in January, 1481, with its attendant harvest of fines and compositions, showed that a similar prospect might be anticipated in his own province. Accordingly a brief of Sixtus IV, December 4, 1481, addressed to the inquisitors, withdrew their faculties of independent action and went to the other extreme by directing them in future to do nothing without the concurrence of the vicar-general, Mateo Mercader, senior archdeacon of Valencia.[608]

REVIVAL OF OLD INQUISITION

In reviving and stimulating to activity this papal institution, Ferdinand was fully resolved to have it subjected to the crown as completely as in Castile. Hitherto it had been a Dominican province, with inquisitors holding office at the pleasure of the Dominican authorities and his first step therefore was to procure, in 1481, from the Dominican General, Salvo Caseta, a commission to Fray Gaspar Juglar to appoint and dismiss inquisitors at the royal will and pleasure.[609] This gave him control over the personnel of the Inquisition, but to render it completely dependent and at the same time efficient, it was necessary that the appointees should be well paid and that the pay should come from the royal treasury. A hundred years earlier, Eymerich, the Inquisitor of Aragon, had sorrowfully recorded that princes were unwilling to defray the expenses, because there were no rich heretics left whose confiscations excited their cupidity; the Church was equally disinclined, so that, in the absence of regular financial support, the good work languished.[610] Now, however, greed and fanaticism joined hands at the prospect of wealthy Conversos to be punished and Ferdinand, by a rescript of February 17, 1482, provided ample salaries for the manning of the tribunal of Valencia, with all the necessary officials.[611] We may reasonably assume that he commenced there in the anticipation of meeting less obstinate resistance than in the older and stronger provinces of Aragon and Catalonia. He was, however, not yet fully satisfied with his control over appointments and he applied to Sixtus IV for some larger liberty, but the pope, who was beginning to recognize that the Castilian Inquisition was more royal than papal, refused, by a brief of January 29, 1482, alleging that to do so would be to inflict disgrace on the Dominicans to whom it had always been confided.[612]

The reorganized tribunal speedily produced an impression by its activity. The Conversos became thoroughly alarmed; opposition began to manifest itself, while the more timid sought safety in flight. A certain Mossen Luis Masquo, one of the jurats of Valencia, made himself especially conspicuous in exciting the city against the inquisitors and in stimulating united action in opposition by the Estates of the kingdom. A letter to him from Ferdinand, February 8, 1482, censures him severely for this and vaguely threatens him with the royal wrath for persistence. Another letter of the same date to the Maestre Racional, or chief accounting officer of the kingdom, shows that the severity with which the property of those arrested was seized and sequestrated was arousing indignation, for it explains the necessity of this so that not a diner shall be lost; if the inquisitors have not power to do this, it shall be conferred on them.[613] The Maestre Racional had suggested that for those who should spontaneously come forward and confess a form of abjuration and reconciliation might be adopted which should spare them the humiliation of public penance while still keeping them subject to the penalties of relapse. To this, after consultation with learned canonists, Ferdinand assented and sent him the formula agreed upon, with instructions that it should appear to be the act of the local authorities and not his--doubtless to prevent his Castilian subjects from claiming the same exemption from the humiliating penitential processions in the autos de fe.[614]

PAPAL INTERFERENCE

Allusions in this correspondence to special cases of arrests and fugitives and sequestrations show that Ferdinand was succeeding in moulding the old Inquisition as he desired and that it was actively at work, when suddenly a halt was called. In the general terror it is presumable that the Conversos had recourse to the Holy See and furnished the necessary convincing arguments; it may also be conjectured that Sixtus was disposed, by throwing obstacles in the way, to secure the recognition of his profitable but disputed right to entertain appeals and that he was unwilling, without a struggle, to lose control of the Inquisition of Aragon as he had done with that of Castile. There are traces also of the hand of Cardinal Borgia seeking to recover his episcopal jurisdiction over heresy in Valencia. Whatever may have been the impelling cause, the first move of Sixtus was to cause the Dominican General, Salvo Caseta, to withdraw the commission given to Fray Gaspar Juglar to appoint inquisitors at Ferdinand's dictation. At this the royal wrath exploded in a letter to the General, April 26, 1482, threatening the whole Order with the consequences of his displeasure; Gualbes and Orts had done their duty fearlessly and incorruptibly, while Fray Francisco Vital--appointed to Catalonia by the Dominican General--had been taking bribes and had been banished the kingdom; he will never allow inquisitors to act, except at his pleasure; even with the royal favor they can accomplish little in the face of popular opposition and without it they can do nothing; meanwhile Gualbes and Orts will continue to act. This heated epistle was followed, May 11th, by one in a calmer mood, asking that Juglar's commission be renewed or another one be issued, failing which he would obtain papal authority and overslaugh the Dominican Order.[615]

PAPAL INTERFERENCE

The next move by Sixtus was the issue, April 18, 1482, of the most extraordinary bull in the history of the Inquisition--extraordinary because, for the first time, heresy was declared to be, like any other crime, entitled to a fair trial and simple justice. We shall have abundant opportunity to see hereafter how the inquisitorial system, observed since its foundation in the thirteenth century, presumed the guilt of the accused on any kind of so-called evidence and was solely framed to extort a confession by depriving him of the legitimate means of defence and by the free use of torture. It was also an invariable rule that sacramental confession of heresy was good only in the forum of conscience and was no bar to subsequent prosecution. There was brazen assurance therefore in Sixtus's complaining that, for some time, the inquisitors of Aragon had been moved not by zeal for the faith but by cupidity; that many faithful Christians, on the evidence of slaves, enemies and unfit witnesses, without legitimate proofs, had been thrust into secular prisons, tortured and condemned as heretics their property confiscated and their persons relaxed to the secular arm for execution. In view of the numerous complaints reaching him of this, he ordered that in future the episcopal vicars should in all cases be called in to act with the inquisitors; that the names and evidence of accusers and witnesses should be communicated to the accused, who should be allowed counsel and that the evidence for the defence and all legitimate exceptions should be freely admitted; that imprisonment should be in the episcopal gaols; that for all oppression there should be free appeal to the Holy See, with suspension of proceedings, under pain of excommunication removable only by the pope. Moreover, all who had been guilty of heresy should be permitted to confess secretly to the inquisitors or episcopal officials, who were required to hear them promptly and confer absolution, good in both the forum of conscience and that of justice, without abjuration, on their accepting secret penance, after which they could no longer be prosecuted for any previous acts, a certificate being given to them in which the sins confessed were not to be mentioned, nor were they to be vexed or molested thereafter in any way--and all this under similar pain of excommunication. The bull was ordered to be read in all churches and the names of those incurring censure under it were to be published and the censures enforced if necessary by invocation of the secular arm; while finally all proceedings in contravention of these provisions were declared to be null and void, all exceptions from excommunication were withdrawn and all conflicting papal decrees were set aside.[616] It is evident that the Conversos had a hand in framing this measure and they could scarce have asked for anything more favorable. In fact Ferdinand in December, 1482, writes to Luis Cabanilles, Governor of Valencia, that he learns that Gonsalvo de Gonsalvo Royz was concerned in procuring the bull for the Conversos: he is therefore to be arrested at once and is not to be released without a royal order, while Luis de Santangel, the royal escribano de racion, will convey orally the king's intentions concerning him.[617]

In this elaborate and carefully planned decree Sixtus formally threw down the gage of battle to Ferdinand and announced that he must be placated in some way if the Inquisition of Aragon was to be allowed to perform its intended functions. That it was simply a tactical move--rendered doubly advantageous by liberal Converso payment--and that he is to be credited with no humanitarian motives, is sufficiently evident from his subsequent action and also from the fact that the bull was limited to Aragon and in no way interfered with the Castilian tribunals. Ferdinand promptly accepted the challenge. He did not await the publication of the bull but addressed, on May 13th, a haughty and imperative letter to Sixtus. He had heard, he said, that such concessions had been made, which he briefly condensed in a manner to show that his information was accurate, and further that the inquisitors Gualbes and Orts had been removed, at the instance of the New Christians who hoped for more pliable successors. He refused to believe that the pope could have made grants so at variance with his duty but, if he had thus yielded to the cunning persuasions of the New Christians, he, the king, did not intend ever to allow them to take effect. If anything had been conceded it must be revoked; the management of the Inquisition must be left to him; he must have the appointment of the inquisitors, as only through his favor could they adequately perform their functions; it was through lack of this royal power that they had hitherto been corrupted and had allowed heresy to spread. He therefore asked Sixtus to confirm Gualbes and Orts and the commission to Gaspar Juglar, or to give a similar commission to some other Dominican, for he would permit no one to exercise the office in his dominions except at his pleasure.[618]

Sixtus seems to have allowed five months to elapse before answering this defiance, but in the meanwhile the Inquisition went on as before. Ferdinand had formed in Valencia a special council for the Holy Office and this body ventured to remonstrate with him about the confiscations and especially the feature of sequestration, by which, as soon as an arrest was made, the whole property of the accused was seized and held; this was peculiarly oppressive and the council represented that it violated the fueros granted by King Jaime and King Alfonso, but Ferdinand replied, September 11th, that he was resolved that nothing belonging to him should be lost but should be rigidly collected, while what belonged to others should not be taken. Another letter of September 6th to the Governor Luis Cabanilles refers to an arrangement of a kind that became frequent, under which the Conversos agreed to pay a certain sum as a composition for the confiscations of those who might be proved to be heretics.[619]

CRISTOBAL GUALBES

At length, on October 9th, Sixtus replied to Ferdinand in a manner to show that he was open to accommodation. The new rules, he said, had been drawn up with the advice of the cardinals deputed for the purpose; they had scattered in fear of the impending pestilence but, when they should return to Rome, he would charge them to consider maturely whether the bull should be amended; meanwhile he suspended it in so far as it contravened the common law, only charging the inquisitors to observe strictly the rules of the common law--the "common law" here being an elastic expression, certain to be construed as the traditional inquisitorial system.[620] Thus the unfortunate Conversos of Aragon, as we shall see hereafter were those of Castile, were merely used as pawns in the pitiless game of king and pope over their despoilment and the merciful prescriptions of the bull of April 18th were only of service in showing that, in his subsequent policy, Sixtus sinned against light and knowledge. What negotiations followed, the documents at hand fail to reveal, but an understanding was inevitable as soon as the two powers could agree upon a division of the spoil. It required a twelvemonth to effect this and in the settlement Ferdinand secured more than he had at first demanded. It was no longer a question of commissioning a fraile to appoint inquisitors at his pleasure, but of including in the organization of the Castilian Inquisition the whole of the Spanish dominions. On October 17, 1483, the agreement was ratified by a bull appointing Torquemada as inquisitor of Aragon, Valencia and Catalonia, with power to appoint subordinates. In this, with characteristic shamelessness, Sixtus declares that he is only discharging his duty as pope, while his tender care for the reputation of the Dominicans is manifested by his omitting to prescribe that the local inquisitors should be members of that Order, the only qualification required being that they should be masters in theology.[621]

During the interval, prior to this extension of Torquemada's jurisdiction, there was an incident showing that Sixtus had yielded the appointment of inquisitors, while endeavoring to retain the power of dismissing them. Cristóbal Gualbes, who was acting in Valencia to the entire satisfaction of Ferdinand, became involved in a bitter quarrel with the Archdeacon Mercader for whom, as we have seen, Cardinal Borgia had obtained a papal brief, virtually constituting him an indispensable member of the tribunal--a power which he doubtless used speculatively to the profit of Borgia and himself. It is to the interference of Gualbes with these worthies that we may reasonably attribute the action of Sixtus, who wrote, May 25, 1483, to Ferdinand and Isabella that the misdeeds of Gualbes merited heavy punishment, but he contented himself with removing him and asked them to fill his place with some fitting person on whom he in advance conferred the necessary powers. He evidently felt doubtful as to their acquiescence, for he wrote on the same day to Iñigo Archbishop of Seville, asking him to use his influence to induce the sovereigns to concur in this.[622] Ferdinand was not inclined to abandon Gualbes for, in a letter of August 8th, he orders the Maestre Racional of Valencia to pay to "lo devot religios maestre Gualbes" forty libras to defray his expenses in coming to the king at Córdova and in order that he might without delay return to work.[623] In the final settlement however Gualbes was sacrificed, for when Torquemada was made Inquisitor-general of Aragon, Sixtus expressly forbade him from appointing that son of iniquity Cristóbal Gualbes who, for his demerits, had been interdicted from serving as inquisitor.[624]

***

If Ferdinand imagined that he had overcome the resistance of his subjects by placing them under the Castilian Inquisition with Torquemada at its head, he showed less than his usual sagacity. They had been restive under the revived institution conducted by their own people and the intense particularism of the Aragonese could not fail to arouse still stronger opposition to the prospect of subjection to the domination of a foreigner such as Torquemada, whose sinister reputation for pitiless zeal gave assurance that the work would be conducted with greater energy than ever.

VALENCIA

In Castile the introduction of the Inquisition had been done by the arbitrary power of the crown; in Aragon the consent of the representatives of the people was felt to be necessary for the change from the old to the new and a meeting of the Córtes was convoked at Tarazona for January 15, 1484. Ferdinand and Isabella arrived there on the 19th and remained until May, when the opening of the campaign against Granada required their presence elsewhere. Torquemada was there ready to establish the tribunals; what negotiations were requisite we do not know, though we hear of his consulting with persons of influence, and an agreement was reached on April 14th. It was not until May 7th, however, that Ferdinand issued from Tarazona a cédula addressed to all the officials throughout his dominions, informing them that with his assent the pope had established the Inquisition to repress the Judaic and Mahometan heresies and ordering that the inquisitors and their ministers should be honored and assisted everywhere under pain of the royal wrath, of deprivation of office and of ten thousand florins.[625]

Under the plenary powers of Torquemada's commission, steps were taken to reorganize the Inquisition and adapt it to the active discharge of its duties. Tribunals were to be established permanently in Valencia, Saragossa and Barcelona with new men to conduct them. Gualbes was disposed of by the enmity of Sixtus IV. Orts still figures in an order for the payment of salaries, April 24, 1484, and, on May 10th, Ferdinand, writing from Tarazona, says that he is there and will be sent to Saragossa, but he never appeared at the latter place, though he was not formally removed from office until February 8, 1486, by Innocent VIII, when he was styled Inquisitor of Valencia and Lérida.[626]

In the Spring of 1484 Torquemada appointed, for Valencia, Fray Juan de Epila and Martin Iñigo, but the popular resistance and effervescence were such that their operations were greatly delayed. The jurats, or local authorities, prevented the opening of their tribunal and, by the advice of Miguel Dalman, royal advocate fiscal, presented an appeal to the Córtes of the kingdom, imploring their intervention. The Córtes had assembled and all four brazos or Estates united in remonstrances against the threatened violation of the fueros and privileges of the land and threw every impediment in the way of the inquisitors. All this we learn from a series of letters despatched, July 27th, by Ferdinand to the various officials, from the governor down, in which he gives free vent to his wrath and indignation, declaring his will to be unchangeable, threatening with punishment and dismissal all who resist it and pronouncing as frivolous the argument that the Inquisition was an invasion of the privileges of the land. At the same time he wrote to the inquisitors informing them of his proposed measures, instructing them to perform their duties without fear and cautioning them to observe the fueros and privileges and to show clemency and mercy, in so far as they could with a good conscience, to those who confessed their errors and applied for reconciliation.[627]

Energetic and determined as was the tone of these letters they produced no effect upon the obstinate Valencians. The Córtes and the city joined in sending a deputation to the king to remonstrate against the proposed violation of their rights. The Maestre Racional stood by and did nothing to remove the dead-lock. Even the Royal Council of Valencia prevented the inquisitors from opening their tribunal, on the ground that they were foreigners while, by the fueros, none but natives could exercise official functions. All this produced another explosion of royal anger under date of August 31st. Ferdinand roundly scolded his officials and threatened punishment proportioned to the gravity of the offence; the reasons alleged by the envoys and the council were brushed aside as untenable; he ordered the governor to set the inquisitors at work, without caring what the Córtes might do or what the people might say, and he exhorted the inquisitors to lose no time in performing their duties.[628] The struggle continued but at length opposition was broken down and, on November 7, 1484, the inquisitors were able formally to assume their functions by preaching their sermon de la fe and publishing their edicts. Although they were thus in shape to carry on the business of the tribunal, the usual solemnities were omitted and they did not venture to exact, from the secular and ecclesiastical dignitaries, the customary oaths--all of which Ferdinand subsequently ordered to be performed.[629]

Scarcely had the inquisitors commenced operations when Borgia's representative, the Archdeacon Mateo Mercader, was the cause of fresh trouble. Discord arose between him and Juan de Epila which threatened to have even more serious results than his quarrels with Gualbes, which had compromised the attempt to revive the old Inquisition. Ferdinand's patience was exhausted and so serious did he consider the situation that he despatched his secretary, Antonio Salavert, to Valencia armed with peremptory orders to Mercader and the governor. The former was required to make over his episcopal functions to Martí Trigo, another vicar-general, to surrender the bull of December 4, 1481, delegating to him inquisitorial powers, and no longer to meddle in any way with the Holy Office. In case of disobedience, the governor was instructed, without a moment's delay, to order him under pain of five thousand florins, to depart within twenty-four hours for the royal court and to be beyond the frontier of Valencia within six days; if he failed in this all his temporalities were to be seized to defray the fine and further contumacy was to be met by banishing him from the kingdom as a disobedient rebel. The inquisitors were also told no longer to summon him to their deliberations and not to allow him to take part in their action.[630] All this was in flagrant violation of the fueros of the land and independence of the Church and shows what latitude Ferdinand allowed himself when the Inquisition was concerned. It was successful however and we hear no more of Mercader, though it was not until February 8, 1486, that the curia assented to this arbitrary illegality by withdrawing his commission along with those of the old inquisitors.[631]

Still, Valencia was not disposed to allow to the Inquisition the untrammelled exercise of its powers or to render to it the assistance required of all the faithful. The nobles continued for some months to offer resistance and when this was nominally broken down it continued in a passive form. To meet it, Ferdinand, in a letter of August 17, 1485, ordered Mossen Joan Carrasquier, alguazil of the Inquisition, at the simple bidding of the inquisitors, to arrest and imprison any one, no matter how high in station. For this he was not to ask the concurrence of any secular authority, for the whole royal power was committed to him and all officials, under pain of two thousand gold florins, and other arbitrary punishment, were required to lend him active assistance. Even this infraction of the royal oath to respect the liberties of the subject did not suffice, for another letter of January 23, 1486, states that the nobles continued to give refuge in their lands to fugitives from the Inquisition, even to those condemned and burnt in effigy, wherefore they were summoned, under their allegiance and a penalty of twenty thousand gold florins, to surrender to the alguazil all whom he might designate and to aid him in seizing them. About the same time Ferdinand placed the royal palace of Valencia at the service of the Inquisition and ordered to be built in it the necessary prisons. His own officials apparently had by this time been taught obedience for in March, 1487, he writes to the governor warmly praising their zeal.[632] To stimulate this, on July 28, 1487, he issued a safe-conduct, taking under the royal protection all the officials of the Inquisition, their families and goods; all royal officials, from the highest to the lowest, were required, under pain of five thousand florins and the king's wrath, to assist them and to arrest whomsoever they might designate.[633]

ARAGON

Still, there were occasional ebullitions of resistance which were met with prompt and effective measures. In 1488 the Lieutenant-general of the kingdom ventured to remove by force, from the inquisitorial prison, a certain Domingo de Santa Cruz, condemned for heresy, and was at once summoned by Torquemada to answer for his temerity. Ferdinand at the same time wrote to him severely to come without delay and, that the kingdom might not be without a governor, sent him a commission in blank to fill in with the name of a deputy to act during his absence or until the king should otherwise provide; moreover, all who had assisted in the removal of the prisoner were to be forthwith arrested by the inquisitors.[634] So, when in 1497 the notaries of Valencia claimed that the notaries of the Holy Office had no power to certify documents concerning the sales of confiscated property and other similar business and summoned them before the secular authorities, Ferdinand threatened them with severe punishment, besides the prosecution by the inquisition to which they were liable for impeding it, for it was not subject to any of the laws or privileges of the land. He also wrote to the Duke of Segorbe, his lieutenant-general, to support the Inquisition; the fiscal of the Suprema presented a clamosa claiming that those guilty of this action were excommunicate and liable to the penalties for fautorship of heresy, and the inquisitor-general forwarded this to them with a summons to appear within fifteen days and defend themselves.[635] The Inquisition was so sacred that a mere attempt to decide at law a question of business was a crime involving heavy penalties. Ferdinand's sharp rebuke, in 1499, when a case of confiscation, involving peculiar hardship, provoked the royal officials and local magistrates to meet and draw up a protest in terms unflattering to the tribunal has already been referred to. It was probably one of the results of this that, on June 28, 1500, the inquisitors summoned all the officials and the Diputados before them and, when all were assembled, read to them the apostolic letters and those of the king respecting the tribunal and its fees and required all present to take the oath of obedience, which was duly acceded to without objections.[636] The unintermitting pressure of the throne was thus finally effective and, in spite of its fueros, the little kingdom was brought under the yoke.

The tribunal had been active and efficient. Already, in June, 1488, a list of those reconciled under the Edicts of Grace amounted to 983 and, among these, no less than a hundred women are described as the wives or daughters of men who had been burnt. Those included in this enumeration were given assurance that their property would not be subject to confiscation--unless it had already been sequestrated--and that they could effect sales and make good titles. Apparently inquisitorial zeal disregarded this assurance for these penitents applied for and obtained its confirmation, May 30, 1491.[637] Of course they had been subjected to heavy fines under the guise of pecuniary penance and we can readily imagine how large was the sum thus contributed to the coffers of the Inquisition, to which as yet these fines enured.

OPPOSITION IN SARAGOSSA

The parent state of Aragon proper seemed at first sight to present an even more arduous problem than Valencia. The people were proud of their ancient liberty and resolute in its maintenance, through institutions sedulously organized for that purpose. The Conversos were numerous, wealthy and powerful, occupying many of the higher offices and intermarried with the noblest houses and, in the fate of their brethren of Castile, they had ample warning of what was in store for them. In the revival of the old Inquisition, Valencia was the scene of action and we hear little of Gualbes and Orts beyond its boundaries. The acceptance, however, by the Córtes of Tarazona, in the Spring of 1484, of Torquemada's jurisdiction, of course included Aragon; he lost no time in organizing a tribunal in Saragossa, by the appointment, May 4th, as inquisitors of Fray Gaspar Juglar and of Maestre Pedro Arbués, a canon of the cathedral, with the necessary subordinates and, by May 11th, the appointments for a full court were completed, as we learn by an order for the payment of the salaries.[638] The expense was large but it was already provided for; Torquemada must himself have employed his leisure in acting as inquisitor for, on May 10th, an auto de fe was held in the cathedral in which four persons were penanced and subjected to confiscation.[639] Gaspar Juglar in this appointment obtained his reward for the services he had rendered as a nominator of inquisitors, but he did not long enjoy it; he disappears almost immediately, poisoned, as it was said, by the Conversos in some rosquillas or sweet cakes.[640] No time was lost in getting to work. Ferdinand had written from Tarazona, May 10th, that the Edict of Grace which had been resolved upon was not to be published, but that proceedings should go on as if it had been proclaimed and had expired, thus depriving the Conversos of the opportunity of coming forward for confessing, and explaining the absence at Saragossa of the long lists of penitents that we find elsewhere.[641] Thus, although some time must have been required for the members of the tribunal to assemble, by June 3d it was ready for another auto, held in the courtyard of the archiepiscopal palace. This time it was not bloodless, for two men were executed and a woman was burnt in effigy.[642]

No more autos were held in Saragossa for eighteen months. Thus far the people had been passive; they had accepted the action of the Córtes of Tarazona, apparently under the impression that the new Inquisition would be as inert as the old had so long been, but, as they awoke to the reality, an opposition arose which called a halt and Arbués never celebrated another auto. Not only the Conversos but many of the Old Christians denounced the Inquisition as contrary to the liberties of the land. The chief objections urged against it were the secrecy of procedure and the confiscation of estates and, as these were the veriest commonplaces of inquisitorial business, it shows how completely the old institution had been dormant. So many Conversos were lawyers and judges and high officials that they had abundant opportunity to impede the action of the tribunal by obtaining injunctions and decisions of the courts as to confiscations, which they regarded as the most assailable point, believing that if these could be stopped the whole business would perish of inanition.[643]

To overcome this resistance, resort was had to the rule compelling all who held office to take the oath of obedience to the Inquisition. On September 19th, the royal and local officials were assembled and solemnly sworn to maintain inviolably the holy Roman Catholic faith, to employ all their energies against every one of whatever rank, who was a heretic or suspect of heresy or a fautor of heresy, to denounce any one whom they might know to be guilty and to appoint to office no one suspect in the faith or incapacitated by law. A few days later the same oath was taken by the Governor of Aragon, Juan Francisco de Heredia and his assessor, Francisco de Santa Fe, son of that Geronimo de Santa Fe the convert, who had stimulated the popular abhorrence of Judaism. Other nobles were subsequently required to take the oath, and it was gradually administered to all the different Estates. Then, in November, followed Torquemada's assembly of inquisitors at Seville, whose instructions were duly transmitted to Aragon for observance, although Aragon had not been represented in the conference. Thus far the tribunal seems to have had no definite quarters, but it was now settled in some houses between the cathedral and the archiepiscopal palace, convenient to the ecclesiastical gaol.[644]

Agitation grew stronger and those who deemed themselves in danger began to seek safety in flight, whereupon Ferdinand, on November 4th, issued orders to the authorities of the three kingdoms to adopt whatever means might be necessary to prevent the departure of all who were not firm in the faith. The effort proved ineffective, as it was decided to be in violation of the fueros, but the Inquisition was superior to the fueros and Ferdinand instructed the inquisitors to issue an edict forbidding any one to leave the kingdom without their license, under pain of being held as a relapsed heretic in case of return, and this scandalous stretch of arbitrary power he sarcastically said that he would enforce so that the object might be attained without infringing on the liberties of the kingdom.[645]

RESISTANCE IN TERUEL

The rich Conversos offered large amounts to the sovereigns if they would forego the confiscations, but the proposition was rejected. A heavy sum was subscribed to propitiate the curia, but the arrangement by which the land was subjected to Torquemada was too recent to be changed. The lieutenant of the Justicia of Aragon, Tristan de la Porta, was urged to prohibit the Inquisition altogether, but in vain. Then the Four Estates of the realm were called together to deliberate on a subject which involved the liberties of the whole land. To forestall their action Ferdinand, on December 10th, addressed a circular letter to the deputies and to the leading nobles, entreating them affectionately to favor and aid the inquisitors of Saragossa and Teruel, but this had no influence and a solemn embassy was sent to remonstrate with him. To their representations he answered, disposing of their arguments by assuming practically that he was only the agent of the Church in enforcing the well-known principles of the canons. The essence of his answer is embodied in responding to their demand that the Inquisition be carried on as in times past, for in any other way it violated the liberties of the kingdom. "There is no intention" he said "of infringing on the fueros but rather of enforcing their observance. It is not to be imagined that vassals so Catholic as those of Aragon would have demanded, or that kings so Catholic would have granted, fueros and liberties adverse to the faith and favorable to heresy. If the old inquisitors had acted conscientiously in accordance with the canons there would have been no cause for bringing in the new ones, but they were without conscience and corrupted with bribes. If there are so few heretics as is now asserted, there should not be such dread of the Inquisition. It is not to be impeded in sequestrating and confiscating and other necessary acts, for be assured that no cause or interest, however great, shall be allowed to interfere with its proceeding in future as it is now doing."[646]

Meanwhile there had been, at Teruel, a more open resistance to the Inquisition, in which the inflexible purpose of the monarch to enforce obedience at any cost was abundantly demonstrated. Simultaneously with the organization of the Saragossa tribunal, Fray Juan Colivera and Mossen Martin Navarro were sent to Teruel with their subordinates to establish one there. Teruel was a fortified city of some importance, near the Castilian border, the capital of its district, although it was not elevated into a separate bishopric until 1577. When the reverend fathers appeared before the gates, the magistrates refused them entrance and they prudently retired to Cella, a village about four leagues distant, whence they fulminated an edict excommunicating the magistrates and casting an interdict on the town. From the venal papal court Teruel had no difficulty in procuring letters in virtue of which the dean, Francisco Savistan, and Martin de San Juan, rector of Villaquemada, absolved the excommunicates and removed the interdict, nor is it likely that any success attended Ferdinand's order to his son, the Archbishop of Saragossa, to send to his official at Teruel secret instructions to seize the two priests and hold them in chains. The town sent a supplication to him by Juan de la Mata and Micer Jaime Mora, but he only ordered them to send home a peremptory command to submit, under pain of such punishment as should serve as a perpetual example. This he also communicated to the Governor of Aragon, Juan Fernández de Heredia, with instructions to take it to Teruel and read it to the magistrates, when, if they did not yield, a formal summons to appear before him was to be read to each one individually--all of which was doubtless performed without effect. Ferdinand had also ordered the envoys not to leave the court, but they fled secretly and his joy was extreme when, six months later, Juan de la Mata was captured by Juan Garcés de Marzilla.

The next step of the Inquisition was a decree, October 2, 1484, confiscating to the crown all the offices in Teruel and pronouncing the incumbents incapable of holding any office of honor or profit--a decree which Ferdinand proceeded to execute by stopping their salaries. It was in vain that the Diputados of Aragon interceded with him; he replied curtly that the people of Teruel had nothing to complain of and were guilty of madness and outrage. Then the inquisitors took final action, which was strictly within their competence, by issuing a letter invoking the aid of the secular arm and summoning the king to enable them to seize the magistrates and confiscate their property. To this he responded, February 5, 1485, with an Executoria invocationis brachii sæcularis, addressed to all the officials of Aragon, requiring them and the nobles to assemble all the horse and foot that they could raise and put them at the service of the inquisitors, under a captain whom he would send to take command. Under pain of the royal wrath, deprivation of office, a fine of twenty thousand gold florins and discretional penalties, they were ordered to seize all the inhabitants of Teruel and their property and deliver them to the inquisitors to be punished for their enormous crimes in such wise as should serve for a lasting example. The people of Cella, also, were ordered to deliver their castle to the inquisitors to serve as a prison and to make all repairs necessary for that purpose. Apparently the response of Aragon to this summons was unsatisfactory for Ferdinand, in defiance of the fuero which forbade the introduction of foreign troops into the kingdom, took the extreme step of calling upon the nobles of Cuenca and other Castilian districts contiguous to the border, to raise their men and join in the holy war, while the receiver of confiscations was ordered to sell enough property to meet the expenses. Whether this formidable array was raised or not, the documents do not inform us, nor of the circumstances under which Teruel submitted, but it had braved the royal will as long as it dared and it could not hold out against the forces of two kingdoms. By April 15th Ferdinand was in position to appoint Juan Garcés de Marzilla, the captor of Juan de la Mata, as assistente or governor of Teruel, with absolute dictatorial powers, and the spirit in which he exercised them may be gathered from his declaration that he did not intend to allow fueros or privileges to stand in the way. The lot of the inhabitants was hard. Ferdinand ordered Marzilla to banish all whom the inquisitors might designate, thus placing the whole population at their mercy, and their rule must have been exasperating, for, in January, 1486, Ferdinand reproaches Marzilla because his nephew, who had aided in the capture of la Mata, had recently attempted to slay the alguazil of the Inquisition. Presumably the inquisitorial coffers were filled with the fines and confiscations which could be inflicted at discretion on the citizens for impeding the Inquisition. During the long struggle Teruel had been at the disadvantage that the surrounding country supported the inquisitors, won over through an astute device by which the inquisitors, while at Cella, had guaranteed, on the payment of certain sums, the remission of all debts and the release of all censos or bonds and groundrents, which might be due to heretics who should be convicted and subjected to confiscation in Teruel. All debtors were thus eager for the success of the inquisitors and for the punishment of heresy among the money-lending Conversos of the town.[647]

***

Meanwhile, in Saragossa, the Conversos were growing desperate. All peaceful means of averting the fate that hung over them had failed and events at Teruel demonstrated the futility of resistance. The bolder spirits began to whisper that the only resource left was to kill an inquisitor or two, when the warning would deter others from incurring the hazard. They knew that secret informations were on foot gathering from all sources testimony against them all. Inquisitor Arbués was almost openly said to be ready to pay for satisfactory evidence, and the life and fortune of every man was at the mercy of the evil-minded.[648] Sancho de Paternoy, the Maestre Racional of Aragon, when on trial, admitted to prejudice against Juan de Anchias, secretary of the tribunal, because he had enquired of a Jewish tailor whether Paternoy had a seat in the synagogue.[649] Suspense was becoming insupportable; the project of assassination gradually took shape and, when the friends of the Conversos at the royal court were consulted, including Ferdinand's treasurer Gabriel Sánchez, they approved of it and wrote that if an inquisitor was murdered it would put an end to the Inquisition.[650]

At first the intention was to make way not only with Pedro Arbués but with the assessor, Martin de la Raga, and with Micer Pedro Francés, and a plot was laid to drown the assessor while he was walking by the Ebro, but he chanced to be accompanied by two gentlemen and it was abandoned.[651] The whole attention of the conspirators was then concentrated on Arbués. Maestre Epila, as he was commonly called, was not a man of any special note, though his selection by Torquemada indicates that he was reputed to possess the qualities necessary to curb the recalcitrant Aragonese, and we are told that he was an eloquent preacher. He possessed the gift of prophecy, if we may believe the story that he foretold to his colleague Martin García that he would reach the episcopate, for García, in 1512, became Bishop of Barcelona, but such foresight is not necessary to explain his reluctance to accept the inquisitorship, for, although this was always a promising avenue to promotion, the post was evidently to be an arduous one.[652] His hesitation was overcome and we have seen how energetically he commenced his new career, yet the interruptions which supervened had prevented him from accomplishing much and he fell a victim rather to fear than to revenge.

ASSASSINATION OF ARBUES

The conspirators were evidently irresolute, for the plot was long in hatching, but the secret was wonderfully well kept, considering that the correspondence respecting it was extensive. Rumors however were not lacking and, as early as January 29, 1485, Ferdinand wrote to the Governor of Aragon that a conspiracy was on foot and that a large sum was being raised to embarrass the Inquisition in every way, yet at the same time he thanked the jurats for their zeal in aiding the inquisitors.[653] If suspicion was then aroused, it slumbered again and for six months meetings were held without being discovered. It was determined to raise fund for hiring assassins and three treasurers were appointed. Juan de Esperandeu, a currier, known as a desperate man, whose father had been arrested, undertook to find the bravos and hired Juan de la Badía for the purpose. In April or May, 1485, an attempt was made on the house where Arbués lodged, but the men were frightened off and the matter was postponed for several months. At length, on the night of September 15th, Esperandeu went to the house of la Badía and wakened him; together they returned to Esperandeu's, where they found the latter's servant Vidau Durango, a Frenchman, with Mateo Ram, one of the leaders of the plot, his squire Tristanico Leonis and three others who were masked and who remained unknown. They all went to the cathedral and entered by the chapter door, which was open on account of the service of matins. Arbués was kneeling in prayer between the high altar and the choir, where the canons were chanting; he knew that his life was threatened, for he wore a coat of mail and a steel cap, while a lance which he carried was leaning against a pillar. La Badía whispered to Durango "There he is, give it to him!" Durango stole up behind and, with a back-stroke, clove his neck between his armor. He rose and staggered towards the choir, followed by la Badía, who pierced him through the arm, while Mateo Ram was also said to have thrust him through the body. He fell; the assassins hurried away and the canons, alarmed at the noise, rushed from the choir and carried him to his house near by, where surgeons were summoned who pronounced the wounds to be mortal. He lay for twenty-four hours, repeating, we are told, pious ejaculations, and died on September 17th, between 1 and 2 A.M. Miracles at once attested his sanctity. On the night of the murder the holy bell of Villela tolled without human hands, breaking the bull's pizzle with which the clapper was secured. His blood, which stained the flagstones of the cathedral, after drying for two weeks, suddenly liquefied, so that crowds came to dip in it cloths and scapulars and had to be forcibly driven off when he was buried on the spot where he fell: when the conspirators were interrogated by the inquisitors, their mouths became black and their tongues were parched so that they were unable to speak until water was given to them. It was popularly believed that when, in their flight, they reached the boundaries of the kingdom, they became divinely benumbed until seized by their captors. More credible is the miracle, reported by Juan de Anchias, that their trials led to the discovery of innumerable heretics who were duly penanced or burnt.[654] Pecuniarily the affair had not been costly; the whole outlay had been only six hundred florins, of which one hundred was paid to the assassin.[655]

REVULSION OF FEELING

Like the murder of Pierre de Castelnau in Languedoc, this crime turned the scale. Its immediate effect was to cause a revulsion of popular feeling, which hitherto had been markedly hostile to the Inquisition. The news of the assassination spread through the city with marvellous rapidity and before dawn the streets were filled with excited crowds shouting "Burn the Conversos who have slain the inquisitor!" There was danger, in the exaltation of feeling, not only that the Conversos would be massacred but that the Judería and Morería would be sacked. By daylight the archbishop, Alfonso de Aragon, mounted his horse and traversed the streets, calming the mob with promises of speedy justice. A meeting was at once called of all the principal persons in the city, which resolved itself into a national assembly and empowered all ecclesiastical and secular officials to proceed against every one concerned with the utmost vigor and without observing the customs and fueros of the kingdom.[656] For some days the Conversos continued to flatter themselves that with money they would disarm Ferdinand's wrath; they had, they said, the whole court with them and the sympathies of all the magnates of the land,[657] but they miscalculated his shrewd resolve to profit to the utmost by their blunder and the consequent weakness of their friends. The royal anger, indeed, was much dreaded and the Diputados, a few days later, wrote to the king reporting what had been done; the criminals had already scattered in flight; the city had offered a reward of five hundred ducats; the judges had written to foreign lands to invoke aid in intercepting the fugitives and both city and kingdom would willingly undergo all labor and expense necessary to avenge the crime. A proclamation was also issued excommunicating all having knowledge of the conspiracy who should not within a given time come forward and reveal what they knew.[658]

It was probably in consequence of the murder that Ferdinand and Isabella succeeded in obtaining, from Innocent VIII, papal letters of April 3, 1487, ordering all princes and rulers and magistrates to seize and deliver to the Inquisition of Spain all fugitives who should be designated to them, thus extending its arms everywhere throughout Christendom and practically outlawing all refugees; no proof was to be required, simple requisition sufficed, the surrender was to be made within thirty days and safe-conduct assured to the frontier, under pain of excommunication and the penalties for fautorship of heresy. Fortunately for humanity this atrocious attempt to establish a new international law by papal absolutism was practically ignored.[659]

THE INQUISITION AT WORK

There was one case however in which its punitive clauses seem to have been invoked. Several of the accomplices in the assassination found refuge in Tudela, a frontier city of Navarre and on January 27, 1486, Ferdinand wrote to the magistrates there affectionately requesting that, if the inquisitors should send for the accused, all aid should be rendered, seeing that he had given orders to obey such requisitions throughout his own kingdoms. This application was unsuccessful and in May he repeated it imperiously, threatening war upon them as defenders of heretics.[660] The condition of the perishing kingdom of Navarre, under the youthful Catherine and Jean d'Albret, was not such as to protect it from the insults of a sovereign like Ferdinand and the inquisitors presumed so far as to instruct Don Juan de Ribera, then in command of the frontier, to carry the royal threats into execution. That prudent officer refused to make war upon a friendly state without the protection of an express order bearing the signatures of Ferdinand and Isabella, whereupon, on June 30th, the inquisitors complained of him to the king. He was in Galicia, suppressing a rising of the Count of Lemos and reducing the lawless nobles to order and from Viso, July 22d, he replied that he would at once have sent the order but that he had brought with him all the frontier troops; as soon as his task was accomplished he would send back forces with orders to Don Juan to make war on Tudela in such fashion as to compel it to do what was requisite for the service of God.[661] A letter of the same date to Torquemada states that the inquisitors have asked for letters of marque and reprisal against Tudela on account of Luis de Santangel, but this must be preceded by a carta requisitoria, which he instructs Torquemada to prepare and send to him when he will execute it.[662] It was not until the end of November that the sovereigns returned to Salamanca and it is presumable that the campaign against Tudela was postponed until the Spring. Of course the fugitives had long before sought some safer asylum, but the papal brief of April 3, 1487, could be enforced against the magistrates and they endured the humiliation of submitting to the tribunal of Saragossa. At an auto de fe held March 2, 1488, the alcalde and eight of the citizens appeared and performed penance.[663]

Ferdinand recognized the opportunity afforded by the assassination of Arbués and was resolved to make the most of it. Prominent among the means for this was the stimulation of the popular veneration of the martyr. On September 29, 1486, his solemn exequies were celebrated with as much solemnity as those of the holiest saint; a splendid tomb was built to which his remains were translated, December 8, 1487; a statue was erected with an inscription by the sovereigns and over it a bas-relief representing the scene of the murder. During a pestilence, in 1490, the city ordered a silver lamp, fifty ounces in weight, to be placed before the tomb and another silver lamp to burn day and night.[664] His cult as a saint was not allowed to await the tardy recognition of the Holy See.

The conspirators miscalculated when they imagined that his murder would deter others from taking his place. There was no danger for inquisitors now in Aragon and the tribunal of Saragossa was promptly remanned and enlarged for the abundant harvest that was expected.[665] It was not long in getting to work and on December 28, 1485, an auto was celebrated in which a man and a woman were burnt.[666] The tribunal was removed to the royal palace-fortress outside of the walls, known as the Aljafería, as an evidence that it was under the royal safeguard and Ferdinand proclaimed that he and his successors took it under their special protection.[667] Strict orders were sent to the Estates of the kingdom and to the local officials to suppress summarily all resistance to the confiscations, which were becoming so extensive that the receiver at Saragossa had his hands full and was empowered to appoint deputies throughout the land to attend to the work in their respective districts.[668]

In the prevailing temper pursuit was hot after the murderers of Arbués and the avengers were soon upon their track. There were some hair-breadth escapes, and much curious detail, for which space fails us here, will be found in the Memoria de diversos Autos in the Appendix, some of it showing that there were powerful secret influences in favor of individuals. One party, consisting of the chief contriver of the plot, Juan de Pedro Sánchez and his wife, Gaspar de Santa Cruz and his wife, Martin de Santangel, García de Moras, Mossen Pedro Mañas and the two Pedro de Almazan, effected their escape by way of Tudela, for which, as we have seen, that city was held responsible, and the Lord of Cadreyta, an ancestor of the Dukes of Alburquerque, was penanced for giving them shelter and receiving sixty florins in payment.[669]

PUNISHMENT OF THE ASSASSINS

Although by decree both secular and ecclesiastical courts were empowered to punish the guilty, the prosecutions seem to have been left altogether to the Inquisition and it had the satisfaction of burning the effigies of the fugitives. Many, however, paid the penalty in their persons. Vidau Durango was soon caught at Lérida, when he made no difficulty in revealing the details of the plot and the names of the accomplices. The work of retribution followed and was continued for years. In the auto of June 30, 1486, Juan de Pedro Sánchez was burnt in effigy; Vidau Durango was treated mercifully, doubtless in consideration of his communicativeness; his hands were cut off and nailed to the door of the Diputacion, or House of Diputados, and it was not until he was dead that he was dragged to the market-place when he was beheaded and quartered and the fragments were suspended in the streets. The punishment of Juan de Esperandeu was more harsh; he was dragged while living to the portal of the cathedral when his hands were cut off; he was then dragged to the market-place, beheaded and quartered, as in the case of Durango. On July 28th Caspar de Santa Cruz and Martin de Santangel were burnt in effigy and Pedro de Exea, who had contributed to the fund, was burnt alive. On October 21st, Maria de la Badía was burnt as an accessory. On December 15th an auto was hastily arranged; Francisco de Santa Fe, assessor of the Governor of Aragon and son of the great Converso Jeronimo de Santa Fe, was fatally compromised in the conspiracy; hopeless of escape he threw himself from the battlement of the tower in which he was confined and was dashed to pieces and the same day his remains were burnt and his bones, enclosed in a box, were cast into the Tagus as though it was feared that they would be venerated as those of a martyr. Juan de la Badía eluded his tormentors in even more desperate fashion. An auto was arranged for January 21, 1487, in which he was to suffer; in his cell the day before he broke in pieces a glass lamp and swallowed the fragments, which speedily brought the death he craved; the next day his corpse was dragged and quartered and the hands were cut off and on the same occasion there were burnt in effigy as accomplices Pedro de Almazan the elder, Anton Pérez and Pedro de Vera. On March 15th Mateo Ram, who superintended the murder, had his hands cut off and was then burnt, with Joan Francés, who was suspected of complicity and the effigies of three accomplices, Juan Ram, Alonso Sánchez and García de Moras. August 8th, Luis de Santangel, who was one of the chief conspirators, was beheaded in the market-place, his head was set upon a pole and his body was burnt.[670]

Thus the ghastly tragedy went on for years, as the ramifications of the conspiracy were explored and all who were remotely connected with it were traced. It was not until 1488 that Juan de la Caballería was placed on trial, the wife of Caspar de la Caballería having testified that her husband told her that Juan had offered him five hundred florins to kill the inquisitor. Juan admitted having learned from Juan de Pedro Sánchez that there was a fund for the purpose and that he had mentioned it to Gaspar but concluded that Gaspar had not sufficient resolution for the deed; he died in gaol in 1490 and his body was burnt in the auto of July 8, 1491, while Gaspar was penanced in that of September 8, 1492.[671] In this latter auto Sancho de Paternoy, Maestre Racional of Aragon, was penanced with perpetual imprisonment. His trial had been a prolonged one; he had been repeatedly tortured and had confessed privity to the murder and had then retracted wholly, saying that he knew nothing about it and that he had spent the night of the assassination in the palace of the archbishop. His guilt was not clear; he had powerful friends, especially Gabriel Sánchez, Ferdinand's treasurer, and he was punished on mere suspicion.[672] Any expression of satisfaction at the murder was an offence to be dearly expiated. Among the crimes for which Pedro Sánchez was burnt, May 2, 1489, this is enumerated and it was one of the chief accusations brought against Brianda de Bardaxi, but, though she admitted it under torture she retracted it afterwards; it could not be proved against her and she was let off with a fine of a third of her property and temporary imprisonment.[673] The assassination gave the Inquisition ample opportunity to make a profound impression and it made the most of its good fortune.[674]

RAVAGES OF THE INQUISITION

The Inquisition thus had overcome all resistance and Aragon lay at its mercy. How that mercy was exercised is seen in the multitude of victims from among the principal Converso families which were almost extinguished by the stake or by confiscation. The names of Caballería, Sánchez, Santangel, Ram and others occur with wearying repetition in the lists of the autos de fe. Thus of the Santangel, who were descended from the convert Rabbi Azarías Ginillo, Martin de Santangel escaped to France and was burnt in effigy; Luis de Santangel, who had been knighted by Juan II for services in the war with Catalonia, was beheaded and burnt as we have seen. His cousin, Luis de Santangel, Ferdinand's financial secretary, who advanced to Isabella the 16,000 or 17,000 ducats to enable Columbus to discover the New World, was penanced July 17, 1491. He still continued in the royal service but he must have been condemned again for, after his death, about 1500, Ferdinand kindly made over his confiscated property to his children, including a thousand ducats of composition for the confiscation of Micer Tarancio. There was yet another Luis de Santangel, who married a daughter of Juan Vidal, also a victim of the Inquisition, and who finally fled with her to France, after which he was burnt in effigy. Juan de Santangel was burnt in 1486. Juan Tomás de Santangel was penanced, August 12, 1487. A brother of Juan was the Zalmedina de Santangel who fled to France and was burnt in effigy March 17, 1497. Gabriel de Santangel was condemned in 1495. Gisperte and Salvador de Santangel were reconciled at Huesca in 1499. Leonardo de Santangel was burnt at Huesca, July 8, 1489, and his mother two days afterwards. Violante de Santangel and Simon de Santangel, with Clara his wife, were reconciled at Huesca. Micer Miguel de Santangel of Huesca was reconciled March 1, 1489.[675] To estimate properly this terrible list we must bear in mind that "reconciliation" involved confiscation and disabilities inflicted on descendants which were almost equivalent to extinguishing a family. In 1513 Folsona, wife of Alonso de Santangel, petitioned Ferdinand saying that her husband, Alonso de Santangel, thirty years before, had fled from the Inquisition and his property had been confiscated, leaving her in poverty with four young children; she had withheld eighty libras of his effects and had spent them; now her conscience impelled her to confess this and to sue for pardon which the king graciously granted "with our customary clemency and compassion." One of these four children seems to be an Augustin de Santangel of Barbastro, son of Alonso, who as late as 1556, obtained relief from the disabilities consequent on his father's condemnation.[676]

There was in Aragon no Converso house more powerful than the descendants of Alazar Usuf and his brothers who took the name of Sánchez and furnished many officials of rank such as treasurer, bayle, dispenser mayor, etc. Of these, between 1486 and 1503, there were burnt, in person or in effigy, Juan de Pedro Sánchez, Micer Alonso Sánchez, Angelina Sánchez, Brianda Sánchez, Mossen Anton Sánchez, Micer Juan Sánchez, and, among the Tamarit, with whom they were allied by marriage, Leonor de Tamarit and her sister Olalía, Valentina de Tamarit and Beatríz de Tamarit. Of the same family there were penanced Aldonza Sánchez, Anton Sánchez, Juan de Juan Sánchez, Luis de Juan Sánchez, Juan Sánchez the jurist, Martin Sánchez, María Sánchez and Pedro Sánchez.[677] It is unnecessary to multiply examples of what was going on in Spain during those dreadful years, for Aragon was exceptional only in so far as the industrious notary, Juan de Anchías, kept and compiled the records that should attest the indelible stain on descendants. There is something awful in the hideous coolness with which he summarizes the lists of victims too numerous to particularize: "The Gómez of Huesca are New Christians and many of them have been abandoned to the secular arm and many others have been reconciled"; "The Zaportas and Benetes of Monzon ... many of them have been condemned and abandoned to the secular arm."[678]

CATALONIA

RESISTANCE

Catalonia had of old been even more intractable than her sister kingdoms and fully as jealous of her ancient rights and liberties. The Capitols de Cort, or fueros granted in the successive Córtes, were ordered to be systematically arranged and fairly written out in two volumes, one in Latin and the other in Limosin; these volumes were to be kept in the Diputacion, secured by chains but open to the public, so that every citizen might know his rights. Whenever the king or his officials violated them by edict or act, the Diputados--a standing committee of the Córtes--were instructed to oppose by every lawful means the invasion of their liberties until the obnoxious measure should be withdrawn.[679]

Apparently forewarned as to Ferdinand's designs, Catalonia had manifested her independence by refusing to send representatives to the Córtes of Tarazona in January, 1484, alleging that it was illegal to summon them beyond the boundaries of the principality.[680] The Catalans had thus escaped assenting to the jurisdiction of Torquemada, but this in no way hindered Ferdinand from sending, May 11th, to Juan de Medina, his receiver of confiscations at Barcelona, a list of salaries similar to that drawn up at the same time for Saragossa, although the names of appointees were left in blank.[681] The citizens met this by sending him a consulta affirming their rights and meanwhile prevented the old inquisitors from manifesting any increase of activity. To this Ferdinand replied from Córdova, August 4th, expressing his extreme dissatisfaction. They need not, he assured them, be alarmed as to their privileges and liberties, for the Inquisition will do nothing to violate them and will use no cruelty but will treat with all clemency those who return to the faith. Further remonstrance, he adds, will be useless for it is his unchangeable determination that the Inquisition shall perform its work and opposition to it will be more offensive to him than any other disservice.[682]

The Catalans were obdurate to both blandishments and threats. Barcelona claimed, as a special privilege, derived directly from the Holy See, that it had a right to an inquisitor of its own and that it could not be subjected to an inquisitor-general. It already had its inquisitor in the person of Juan Comte, who apparently gave the people no trouble and served as a convenient impediment to the extension of Torquemada's jurisdiction, especially as he held a papal commission. To meet this obstacle Ferdinand wrote, October 12th, to his ambassador at Rome, that the inquisitors were not doing their duty, wherefore he earnestly requested that, at the earliest possible moment, further power be granted to him and to Isabella and Torquemada to appoint and remove at pleasure officials who should be full inquisitors and not merely commissioners, as the franchises of the cities provide that they shall not be subjected to commissioners.[683] The Catalan Conversos doubtless understood how to counteract with the curia the king's desires, for nine months later, July 9, 1485, Ferdinand again wrote to his auditor apostólico that the Inquisition in Aragon, Catalonia and Valencia was much impeded by the papal commissions granted to Dominican masters of theology and other persons, and that he must at once procure a bull revoking all commissions to act as inquisitors, especially those of Fray Juan Comte of Barcelona and Archdeacon Mercader of Valencia; Torquemada must have a fresh appointment for the Aragonese kingdoms and especially as inquisitor of Barcelona, with faculty to subdelegate his powers.[684] It is possible that Cardinal Borgia's interest in his Vicar-general Mercader neutralized the efforts of Ferdinand's agents, for six months passed away without the request being granted and, in January, 1486, the king ventured the experiment of sending two appointees of Torquemada, the Dominicans Juan Franco and Guillen Casells, with an Executoria pro Inquisitoribus apud Cataloniam, addressed to all the officials, who were ordered under pain of five thousand gold florins to receive and convey them safely, to aid them in their work, to arrest and imprison in chains whomsoever they might designate and to inflict due punishment on all whom they might abandon to the secular arm.[685] This energetic movement was as fruitless as its predecessors and some weeks later an order was issued to the inquisitors at Saragossa to reimburse, from the pecuniary penances in their hands, the expenses of the cleric who had been sent to Barcelona and also to pay fifty libras each to Esteban Gago, sent there as alguazil and Jaime Millan as notary, in order to provide for their support.[686] At the same time Ferdinand expressed the hope that the Barcelonese tribunal would soon be in working order, and in this he was not wholly disappointed.

BARCELONA SUBMITS

Innocent VIII yielded at last and, by a brief of February 6, 1486, under pretext that they had been too zealous, he removed all inquisitors holding papal commissions--in Aragon Juan Colivera, Juan de Epila, Juan Franco and Guillen Casells, in Valencia Juan Orts and Mateo Mercader and in Barcelona Juan Comte; he appointed Torquemada as special inquisitor for Barcelona, with power of subdelegation and, apparently to prepare for expected resistance, he authorized the Bishops of Córdova and Leon and the Abbot of St. Emelian of Burgos to suppress all opposition, especially on the part of Juan Comte, while he expressly set aside the privileges of the city.[687] In spite of this formidable missive nearly eighteen months elapsed before Barcelona was reduced to submission, and Torquemada's final appointee, Alonso de Espina, was able to enter the city. When at last he succeeded, July 5, 1487, we are told that the Lieutenant-general of the Principality, the Bishops of Urgel, Tortosa and Gerona and many gentlemen and citizens sallied forth to greet him, but there is no mention made of the Diputados, or the local magistracy, or the canons joining in the reception, and it was not until July 30th that the municipal officials took the oath of obedience to him.[688]

He probably still found obstacles in his path, for it was not until December 14th that the first procession of penitents took place, consisting only of twenty-one men and twenty-nine women, followed, a week later, by another in which the participants were scourged.[689] The smallness of these numbers, as the result of five months' work, showed that the Edict of Grace had met an ungrateful response and the first public auto, celebrated January 25, 1488, furnished only four living victims and the effigies of twelve fugitives. As already remarked elsewhere, the fear spread abroad by the advent of the Inquisition, after so long a struggle, caused the greater part of those who had reason for fear to seek safety in flight, in spite of the edicts forbidding expatriation. During the whole of the year 1488 the number of burnings amounted only to seven and in 1489 there were but three. It was doubtless owing to the lukewarmness of the local magistracy that, in the earlier autos, the sufferers were spared the extreme penalty of concremation and were mercifully strangled before the pile was lighted.[690] In fact, a royal cédula of March 15, 1488, ordering afresh all officials to render aid and support to the Inquisition, under penalty of two thousand florins, would seem to argue no little slackness on their part.[691]

The jurisdiction of the tribunal of Barcelona was extensive, comprehending the dioceses of Barcelona, Tarragona, Vich, Gerona, Lérida, Urgel and Elna; the inquisitors were industrious and visited many portions of their territory, for we have record, during the remainder of the century, of autos de fe held in Tarragona, Gerona, Perpignan, Balaguer and Lérida, but as late as November 18, 1500, Ferdinand complains that in Rosellon the Inquisition had not yet been put fairly in operation and that no effort had been made to secure the confiscations.[692]

SUPREMACY OF THE INQUISITION

The imperiousness with which the inquisitors exercised their authority to break the independent spirit of the Catalans is well illustrated by a trifling but significant incident in 1494. The city of Tarragona had established a quarantine against Barcelona on account of pestilence. On June 18th the inquisitor, Antonio de Contreras, with all his officials, presumably fleeing from the pest, presented himself at the gates and demanded admittance. The vicar-general of the archbishop, the canons and the royal and local officials came to meet him and explained the situation, asking him to remain in some convenient place in the neighborhood for some days. His reply was to give them the delay of three Misereres in which to open their gates under pain of major excommunication and interdict, whereupon they left him, after interjecting an appeal to the Holy See. He recited the Miserere thrice, commanded his notary to knock at the gate and then fulminated his censures, with an additional order that no notary but his own should make record of the affair. He then withdrew to the neighboring Dominican convent, whence he sent his excommunication to be affixed to the town-gates. While at supper, Ciprian Corte, a scrivener, came and served him with a notice of the appeal to Rome and was seized and confined in the convent prison. During the night the vicar-general with a crowd of citizens surrounded the convent in a fashion so threatening that the scrivener was released. It was not until July 18th that the inquisitor entered Tarragona, when he suspended the excommunication and interdict and took testimony as to the affair, banishing a man who said that Vich had similarly refused to break a quarantine for an inquisitor. Finally, on September 5th all the dignitaries, ecclesiastical and secular, with the leading citizens, were assembled in the chapel of the chapter, in presence of the inquisitor and of Don Juan de Lanuza, the Lieutenant-general of Catalonia. There they humbly begged for pardon and absolution and offered to undergo any penance that he might inflict; he made them swear obedience to him and appointed the following Sunday for the penance, when they were all obliged to attend mass as penitents, with lighted candles in their hands, thus incurring an indelible stigma on themselves and their posterity.[693]

Men who wielded their awful and irresponsible power in this arbitrary fashion were not to be restrained by law or custom and from their tyranny there was no appeal save to the king, who was resolved that no one but himself should check them. He had already, by a cédula of March 26, 1488, forbidden all secular officials, from the lieutenant-general down, from taking cognizance of anything concerning the subordinates and familiars of the Holy Office, under penalty of the royal wrath and a fine of two thousand florins and when, in 1505, the Diputados of Catalonia were involved in some trifling quarrel with the inquisitors and represented to Ferdinand that their jurisdiction was in derogation of the constitution of the land, he sternly replied that the jurisdiction of the faith and the execution of its sentences pertained to the Inquisition; that this jurisdiction was supreme over all others and that there was no fuero or law that could obstruct it.[694] This fateful declaration became practically engrafted upon Spanish public law.

It was impossible that such irresponsible power should not be abused and there speedily commenced a series of complaints from the Catalan authorities which, as we shall see hereafter, continued with little intermission until the revolt of 1640. At the present time, however, Ferdinand showed a disposition to curb the abuses inevitable under the system and, in letters of August 16th and 20th and September 3, 1502, to the inquisitors of Barcelona, he enclosed a memorial from the Diputados of Catalonia, accompanying it with a severe rebuke. The chief source of complaint that the receiver of confiscations bought up claims and prosecuted them through the irresistible machinery of the tribunal. In a sample instance Francí Ballester made over to the receiver for 100 libras a debt of 228 due by Juan de Trillo which was then collected through the Inquisition. Ferdinand said that he had frequently forbidden this practice and he ordered the inquisitors to excommunicate the receiver if he persisted in it. The receiver then contented himself with a smaller profit and proceeded, in the case of the confiscated estate of a certain Mahul, to collect from it debts for a commission of ten per cent., whereby the creditors with the weakest claims got most of the money. Again Ferdinand prohibited this, September 9th, ordering all funds to be paid in to the tabla of Barcelona, for equitable distribution among the creditors and all commissions to be refunded.[695] At the same time there was no talk of the only effective way of cutting up these practices by the roots--that of discharging the knavish receiver. This tenderness for official malfeasance continued throughout the career of the Inquisition and prevented any effective reform.

THE BALEARIC ISLES

Majorca claimed to be a separate and independent kingdom, governed by its own customs and only united dynastically with Catalonia. In 1439 it complained that its franchises were violated by the queen-regent when she summoned citizens to appear before her on the mainland, for they were entitled to be tried nowhere but at home, and her husband Alfonso V admitted the justice of this and promised its observance for the future.[696] The frequent repetition of this privilege shows how highly it was prized and it rendered necessary a separate tribunal for the Balearic Isles. This had long been in operation under the old institution and the inquisitor at this period was Fray Nicolas Merola who was as inert as his brethren elsewhere. The records of his office show that under him there were no relaxations; that in 1478 there were four Judaizers reconciled; in 1480, one; in 1482, two and in 1486, one. He was probably stimulated to greater energy by the prospect of removal, for in 1487 the number increased to eight.[697]

It was not until the following year, 1488, that the new Inquisition was introduced, when Fray Merola was replaced by the doctors Pedro Pérez de Munebrega and Sancho Martin.[698] Their Edict of Grace was so successful that three hundred and thirty-eight persons came forward, confessed and were reconciled, August 18, 1488, in addition to sixteen reconciled, August 13th, after trial. Evidently the prosperous Converso population recognized that the new institution was vastly more efficient than the old. There must undoubtedly have been some popular effervescence, of which the details have not reached us, for the inquisitors were removed and replaced by a native, Fray Juan Ramon, but, if the change calmed the agitation it did not diminish the activity of the tribunal, for the records of the year 1489 show seven autos in which there were ten reconciliations, forty-four relaxations in effigy, one of bones exhumed and six in person. A momentary pause followed, for, in 1490, we find only the reconciliation of ninety-six penitents, March 26th, under the Edict of Grace. Then, in 1491, another Edict was published, of which, on July 10th and 30th, a hundred and thirty-four persons availed themselves, besides two hundred and ninety of those already reconciled in 1488 and 1490, who had relapsed and were readmitted as a special mercy. In addition to these the records of 1491 show numerous autos in which there were fifty-seven reconciliations, eighteen relaxations in effigy and eighteen in person. As elsewhere, the delay in introducing the new Inquisition had given opportunity for flight and for some years the chief business of the tribunal was the condemnation of fugitives. Thus, in an auto of May 11, 1493, there were but three relaxations in person to forty-seven in effigy and, in one of June 14, 1497, there was no living victim, the bones of one were burnt and the effigies of fifty-nine.[699]

As usual these proceedings against the dead and absent were productive of abundant confiscations and the fears of descendants were thoroughly aroused lest some aberration of an ancestor should be discovered which would sweep away their fortunes. This gave rise to the expedient of compositions, of which we shall see more hereafter, as a sort of insurance against confiscation. In the present case a letter from Ferdinand, January 28, 1498, to the inquisitor and the receiver announces that these people are coming forward with offers and he orders the officials to make just and reasonable bargains with them and report to him, when he will decide what is most to his advantage. In this and other ways the operations of the tribunal were beginning to bring in more than its expenses, for, February 2, 1499, there is an order given on the receiver Matheo de Morrano to pay to the receiver of Valencia two hundred gold ducats to cancel some debts that were pressing on the royal conscience, followed soon after by other orders to pay four hundred and fifty ducats to the royal treasury and fifty florins to the nunnery of Santa Clara of Calatayud. The confiscating zeal of the officials was stimulated, February 21, 1498, by an allowance to Morrano of three thousand sueldos, in addition to his salary, in reward of his eminent services and another, March 2d, of a hundred libras mallorquines to the notary Pere Prest. It was not always easy to trace the property which the unfortunates naturally sought to conceal and a liberal offer of fifty per cent. was made to informers who should reveal or discover it.[700]

DISCONTENT

It was as difficult to reconcile the Mallorquins as the Catalans to the new Inquisition. In 1517 the Suprema was obliged to order the viceroy not to maltreat the officials or obstruct them in the performance of their duty, and at the same time, the inquisitors were instructed to proceed against him if he did not cease to trouble them. Apparently he did not heed the warning for, in 1518, the inquisitor was formally commanded to prosecute him. What followed we have no means of knowing, but apparently the viceroy had full popular sympathy, for soon afterwards there was a rising, led by the Bishop of Elna, whose parents had been condemned by the tribunal. The inquisitor fled and the populace was about to burn the building and the records, when the firmness of the Bishop of Majorca, at the risk of his life, suppressed the tumult. It was probably this disturbance that called forth, in 1520, an adjuration from the Suprema to the viceroy and the ecclesiastical and secular authorities, not to permit the ill-treatment of the inquisitor and other officials. It was impossible, however, to preserve the peace and, in 1530, we find the viceroy, his assessor and officials, under excommunication as the result of a competencia or conflict of jurisdiction. Even more significant was the imprisonment and trial, in 1534, of the regent or president of the royal high court of justice, resulting in the imposition, in 1537, of a fine so excessive that the Suprema ordered its reduction.[701] This was but the beginning and we shall see hereafter how perpetual were the embroilments of the tribunal with both the civil and the ecclesiastical authorities.

***

With more or less resistance the new Inquisition was thus imposed on the various provinces subject to the crown of Aragon. The pretence put forward to secure its introduction, that it in no way violated the fueros and liberties of the land, was soon dropped and, as we have seen, it was boldly pronounced to be superior to all law. For awhile this was submitted to in silence, but the ever-encroaching arrogance of the officials, their extension of their jurisdiction over matters unconnected with the faith and their abuse of their irresponsible prerogatives aroused opposition which at length found opportunity for expression. In 1510 the representatives of Aragon, Catalonia and Valencia were, for the first time, assembled together in the Córtes of Monzon. They came with effusive enthusiasm, stimulated by the conquest of Oran and Algiers and the desire to retrieve the disaster of Gerbes and they voted for Ferdinand the unprecedented servicio or tax-levy of five hundred thousand libras, obtaining in return the abolition of the Santa Hermandad.[702] Yet even this enthusiasm did not prevent murmurs of discontent, and complaints were made that the Inquisition assumed jurisdiction over cases of usury, blasphemy, bigamy, necromancy and the like and that the privileges and exemptions enjoyed by the officials led to their unnecessary multiplication, rendering the tribunals oppressive to those who bore the burdens of the state. Ferdinand eluded reform by promising it for the future and the Córtes were dissolved without positive action.[703] When they next met at Monzon, in 1512, they were in a less confiding mood and it is probable that popular agitation must have assumed a threatening aspect, sufficient to compel Ferdinand to yield to their demands. An elaborate series of articles was drawn up, or rather two, one for Aragon and the other for Catalonia, nearly identical in character, which received the royal assent. It is significant that, with the exception of a clause as to appeals, these articles do not concern themselves with the prosecution of heresy but are confined to the excesses with which the tribunals and their underlings afflicted the faithful.

THE CONCORDIA OF MONZON

The reform demanded by Catalonia embraced thirty-four articles, a few of which may serve to suggest the abuses that had grown so rankly. An especial grievance was the multiplication of officials--not only those engaged in the work of the tribunal but the unsalaried familiars scattered everywhere and the servants and slaves of all concerned, who all claimed the fuero, or jurisdiction of the Inquisition, with numerous privileges and exemptions that rendered them a most undesirable element in society. It was demanded that the number of familiars in Catalonia should be reduced to thirty-four, whose names should be made known; that under the guise of servants should be included only those actually resident with their masters or employers; that no one guilty of a grave offence should be appointed to office; that the privilege of carrying arms should be restricted to those who bore commissions, in default of which they could be disarmed like other citizens; that the claim to exemption from local taxes and imposts be abandoned; that officials caught flagrante delicto in crime should be subject to arrest by secular officials without subjecting the latter to prosecution; that civil suits should be tried by the court of the defendant; that the common clause in contracts by which one party subjected himself to whatever court the other might name should be held not to include the Inquisition; that the rule forbidding officials to engage in trade should be enforced; that officials buying claims or property in litigation should not transfer the cases to the Inquisition, nor use it to collect their rents; that inquisitors should not issue safe-conducts except to witnesses coming to testify; that in cases of confiscation, when the convict had been reputed a good Christian, parties who had bought property from him, had paid their debts to him or had redeemed rent-charges, should not lose the property or be obliged to pay the debts a second time; that the dowry of a Catholic wife should not be confiscated because her father or husband should be subsequently convicted of heresy; that possession for thirty years by a good Catholic should bar confiscation of property formerly owned by those now convicted of heresy and that the inquisitors should not elude this prescription of time by deducting periods of war, of minority, of ignorance of the fisc and other similar devices; that the inquisitors should withdraw their decree prohibiting all dealings with Conversos, which was not only a serious restraint of trade but involved much danger to individuals acting through ignorance. As regards the extension of jurisdiction over subjects unconnected with heresy, the Inquisition was not in future to take cognizance of usury, bigamy, blasphemy, and sorcery except in cases inferring erroneous belief. Remaining under excommunication for a year involved suspicion of heresy and the Edict of Faith required the denunciation of all such cases to the Inquisition, but as there were innumerable decrees of ipso facto excommunications and others which were privately issued, it was impossible to know who was or was not under the ban, wherefore the tribunal was not to take action except in cases where the censure had been publicly announced. The extent to which the inquisitors had carried their arbitrary assumption of authority is indicated by an article forbidding them in the future from interfering with the Diputados of Catalonia or their officials in matters pertaining to their functions and the rights of the State and in the imposts of the cities, towns, and villages. The only reform proposed as to procedure is an article providing that appeals may lie from the local tribunal to the inquisitor-general and Suprema, with suspension of sentences until they are heard. But there is a hideous suggestiveness in the provision that, when perjured testimony has led to the execution of an innocent man, the inquisitors shall do justice and shall not prevent the king from punishing the false witnesses.

The independence of the Inquisition, as an imperium in imperio, is exhibited in the fact that its acceptance was deemed necessary to each individual article, an acceptance expressed by the subscription to each of Plau a su Reverendissima senyoria, the senyoria being that of Inquisitor-general Enguera. To confirm this he and the inquisitors were required to swear in a manner exhibiting the profound distrust entertained of them. The oath was to observe each and every article; it was to be taken as a public act before a notary of the Inquisition, who was to attest it officially and deliver it to the president of the Córtes, and authentic copies were to be supplied at the price of five sueldos to all demanding them. All future inquisitors, whether general or local, were to take the same oath on assuming office and all this was repeated in various formulas so as to leave no loop-hole for equivocation. Ferdinand also took an oath promising to obtain from the pope orders that all inquisitors, present and future should observe the articles and also that, whenever requested by the Córtes, the Diputados or the councillors of Barcelona, he would issue the necessary letters and provisions for their enforcement.[704] This was the first of the agreements which became known as Concordias--adjustments between the popular demands and the claims of the Holy Office. We shall have frequent occasion to hear of them in the future, for they were often broken and renewed and fresh sources of quarrel were never lacking. The present one was not granted without a binding consideration, for the tribunal of Barcelona was granted six hundred libras a year, secured upon the public revenues.[705]

MERCADER'S INSTRUCTIONS

If the Catalans distrusted the good faith of king and inquisitor-general they were not without justification, for the elaborate apparatus of oaths proved a flimsy restraint on those who would endure no limitation on their arbitrary and irresponsible authority. At first Ferdinand manifested a desire to uphold the Concordia and to restrain the inquisitors who commenced at once to violate it. The city of Perpignan complained that the prescription of time was disregarded and that the duplicate payment of old debts was demanded, whereupon Ferdinand wrote, October 24, 1512, sharply ordering the strict observance of the terms agreed upon and the revocation of any acts contravening them.[706] Before long however his policy changed and he sought relief. For potentates who desired to commit a deliberate breach of faith there was always the resource of the authority of the Holy See which, among its miscellaneous attributes, had long assumed that of releasing from inconvenient engagements those who could command its favor, and Ferdinand's power in Italy was too great to permit of the refusal of so trifling a request. Accordingly on April 30, 1513, Leo X issued a motu proprio dispensing Ferdinand and Bishop Enguera from their oaths to observe the Concordia of Monzon.[707]

The popular demands, however, had been too emphatically asserted to be altogether ignored and an attempt was made to satisfy them by a series of instructions drawn up, under date of August 28, 1514, by Bishop Luis Mercader of Tortosa, who had succeeded Enguera as inquisitor-general. These comprised many of the reforms in the Concordia, modified somewhat to suit inquisitorial views, as, for instance, the number of armed familiars permitted for Barcelona was twenty-five, with ten each for other cities. From Valladolid, September 10th, Ferdinand despatched these instructions by Fernando de Montemayor, Archdeacon of Almazan, who was going to Barcelona as visitor or inspector of the tribunal. It was not until December 11th that they were read in Barcelona in presence of the inquisitors and of representatives of Catalonia. The latter demanded time for their consideration and a copy was given to them. Another meeting was held, January 10, 1515, and a third on January 25th, in which the instructions were published and the inquisitors promised to obey them. There is no record that the Catalans accepted them as a fulfilment of the Concordia and, if they were asked to do so, it was merely as a matter of policy. In a letter of January 4th to the archdeacon, Ferdinand assumes that the assent of the Catalans was a matter of indifference; the instructions were to be published without further parley and no reference to Rome was requisite as the privileges of the Inquisition were not curtailed by them.[708]

Subsequent Córtes were held at Monzon and Lérida, where the popular dissatisfaction found expression in further complaints and demands, leading to some concessions on the part of Ferdinand. The temper of the people was rising and manifested itself in occasional assaults, sometimes fatal, on inquisitorial officials, to facilitate the punishment of which Leo X, by a brief of January 28, 1515, authorized inquisitors to try such delinquents and hand them over to the secular arm for execution, without incurring the "irregularity" consequent on judgements of blood.[709] Ferdinand was too shrewd to provoke his subjects too far; he recognized that the overbearing arrogance of the inquisitors and their illegal extension of their authority gave great offence, even to the well-affected, and he was ready to curb their petulance. A case occurring in May, 1515, shows how justifiable were the popular complaints and gave him opportunity to administer a severe rebuke. It was the law in Aragon that, when the Diputados appointed any one as lieutenant to the Justicia, if he refused to serve they were to remove his name from the lists of those eligible to public office. A certain Micer Manuel, so appointed, refused to serve and to escape the penalty procured from the inquisitors of Saragossa letters prohibiting, under pain of excommunication, the Diputados from striking off his name. This arbitrary interference with public affairs gave great offence and Ferdinand sharply told the inquisitors not to meddle with matters that in no way concerned their office; the Diputados were under oath to execute the law and the letters must be at once revoked.[710] Finally he recognized that the demands of the Córtes of Monzon had been justified and that he had done wrong in violating the Concordia of 1512. One of his latest acts was a cédula of December 24, 1515, announcing to the inquisitors that he had applied to the Holy See for confirmation of the agreements made and sworn to in the Córtes of Monzon and Lérida; there was no doubt that this would speedily be granted, wherefore he straitly commanded, under pain of forfeiture of office, that the articles must not be violated in any manner, direct or indirect, but must be observed to the letter; the inquisitor-general had agreed to this and would swear to comply with the bull when it should come.[711]

FURTHER DEMANDS

Ferdinand died January 23, 1516, followed in June by Inquisitor-general Mercader. Leo X probably waited to learn whether the new monarch Charles desired to continue the policy of his grandfather. It is true that he had dispensed Ferdinand and Enguera from their oaths in view of the great offence to God and danger to conscience involved in the observance of the Concordia, but a word from the monarch was sufficient to overcome his scruples. What Ferdinand had felt it necessary to concede could not be withheld when, in the youth and absence of Charles, his representatives could scarce repress the turbulent elements of civil discord. Accordingly Leo confirmed all the articles of both the Catalan and Aragonese Concordias by the bull Pastoralis officii, August 1, 1516, in which he declared that the officials of the Inquisition frequently transgressed the bounds of reason and propriety in their abuse of their privileges, immunities and exemptions and that their overgrown numbers reduced almost to nullity the jurisdiction of the ordinary ecclesiastical and secular courts. This action, he says, is taken at the especial prayer of King Charles and Queen Juana and all inquisitors and officials contravening its prescriptions, if they do not, within three days after summons, revoke their unlawful acts, are subject to excommunication latæ sententiæ, deprivation of office and perpetual disability for re-employment, ipso facto. Moreover the Archbishops of Saragossa and Tarragona were authorized and required, whenever called upon by the authorities, to compel the observance of the bull by ecclesiastical censures and other remedies without appeal, invoking if necessary the secular arm.[712]

Thus, after four years of struggle, the Concordias of 1512 were confirmed in the most absolute manner and the relations between the Inquisition and the people appeared to be permanently settled. The inquisitors however, as usual, refused to be bound by any limitations. They claimed, and acted on the claim, that the papal bull of confirmation was surreptitious and not entitled to obedience and that both the Concordias and the Instructions of Bishop Mercader were invalid as being restrictions impeding the jurisdiction of the Holy Office.[713] On the other hand the people grew more restive and increased their demands for relief. The occasion presented itself when Charles came to Spain to assume possession of his mother's dominions. At Córtes held in Saragossa, May, 1518, he received the allegiance of Aragon and swore to observe the fueros of the Córtes of Saragossa, Tarazona and Monzon. Money was soon wanted to supply the reckless liberality with which he filled the pouches of his greedy Flemings, and towards the end of the year he summoned another assembly to grant him a subsidio. It agreed to raise 200,000 libras but coupled this with a series of thirty-one articles, much more advanced than anything hitherto demanded in Aragon--in fact copied with little change from those agreed to in Castile by Jean le Sauvage and abandoned in consequence of his death--articles which revolutionized inquisitorial procedure and assimilated it to that of the secular criminal courts. Charles, in these matters was now wholly under the influence of his former tutor and present inquisitor-general Cardinal Adrian. He wanted the money, however, and he gave an equivocal consent to the articles; it was, he said, his will that in each and all the holy canons should be observed, with the decrees of the Holy See and without attempting anything to the contrary. If doubts arose the pope should be asked to decide them; if any one desired to accuse inquisitors or officials, he could do so before the inquisitor-general, who would call in counsellors and administer justice, or, if the crime appertained to the secular courts, he would see that justice was speedy. This declaration, with the interpretation to be put on each and every article by the pope, he promised under oath to observe and enforce and he further swore not to seek dispensation from this oath or to avail himself of it if obtained.[714] The people were amply justified in distrusting their rulers, for Charles subsequently instructed the Count of Cifuentes, his ambassador at Rome, to procure the revocation of the articles and a dispensation from his oath to observe them.[715]

Charles had thus shuffled off from his shoulders to those of the pope the responsibility for this grave alteration in inquisitorial procedure which, by forcing the Holy Office to administer open justice, would have diminished so greatly its powers of evil. The question was thus transferred to Rome and the Córtes lost no time in seeking to obtain from Leo X the confirmation of the articles. A letter requesting this was procured from Charles and was forwarded to Rome with a copy of the articles and of Charles's oath, officially authenticated by Juan Prat, the notary of the Córtes. The papers were sent to Rome by a certain Diego de las Casas, a Converso of Seville who, as his subsequent history shows, must have been amply provided with the funds necessary to secure a favorable hearing.

STRUGGLE IN SARAGOSSA

The situation was one which called for active measures on the part of the Inquisition. The Córtes dissolved January 17, 1519, and a letter of the 22d, from the Suprema to the Inquisitor of Calatayud, shows that already steps had been taken to prosecute all who had endeavored to influence them against the Inquisition or who had made complaints to Charles or Adrian.[716] A more effective and bolder scheme was to accuse Juan Prat of having falsified the series of articles sent to Rome. Charles had appointed a commission, consisting of the Archbishop of Saragossa, Cardinal Adrian and Chancellor Gattinara, to consider all matters connected with the Inquisition; to them Prat had submitted the articles which they returned to him with a declaration, which must have been an approval as its character was studiously suppressed in the subsequent proceedings. Notwithstanding this the Saragossa inquisitors, Pedro Arbués and Toribio Saldaña promptly reported to Charles, who had left Saragossa for Barcelona, that Prat had falsified the articles and Charles, from Igualada, February 4th, replied ordering them to obey the instructions of Cardinal Adrian and collect evidence as to the falsifications which they claimed to have discovered. They postponed action, however, for some weeks until the archbishop had left the city and did not arrest Prat until March 16th. Their investigation revealed some trivial irregularities but nothing to invalidate the accuracy of the articles transmitted to Rome, yet on the 18th they communicated to the Suprema the results of their labors as though the whole record was vitiated and Prat had been guilty of falsification. A way thus was opened to escape from the engagements entered into with the Córtes. A series of articles was drawn up, signed by Gattinara, which was sent to Rome as the genuine one and urgent letters were despatched, April 30th, to all the Roman agents, the pope and four of the cardinals in the Spanish interest, stating that the official copy was falsified, the genuine one was that bearing Gattinara's name, the honor of God was involved and the safety of the Catholic faith and no effort was to be spared to secure the papal confirmation of the right articles.

To justify this it was necessary that Prat should be convicted and punished. Apparently fearing that this could not be accomplished in Saragossa, Cardinal Adrian ordered the inquisitors to send him to Barcelona for trial, in ignorance that this was in violation of one of the dearest of the Aragonese privileges forbidding the deportation of any citizen against his will. This aroused a storm and the leading officials of Church and State interposed so effectually with the inquisitors that Prat was allowed to remain in the secret prison of the Aljafería. The quarrel was now assuming serious proportions; not only was the kingdom aflame with this attempted violation of its privileges but it was universally believed that Charles had granted all the demands of the Córtes in return for the servicio and his interference with the papal confirmation was bitterly resented. The Diputados summoned the inquisitors to obey the Concordia of 1512, as confirmed by the bull of August 1, 1516, while awaiting confirmation of the new Concordia and at the same time they called the barons and magnates of the realm to a conference at Fuentes, whence, on May 9th, they sent to Charles a remonstrance more emphatic than respectful, with an intimation that the servicio would not be collected until Prat should be released, the pretext being that the papers relating to it were in his office.

To this Charles responded loftily, May 17th, that for no personal interest would he neglect his soul and conscience nor, to preserve his kingdom, would he allow anything against the honor of God and to the detriment of the Holy Office. Under threat of excommunication and other severe penalties he ordered the Diputados not to convoke the Estates of the realm or to send envoys to him; he would comply with the Concordia and had already asked its confirmation of the pope--the fact being that he had on May 7th written to Rome--and this he repeated May 29th--to impede the confirmation of the official Concordia and to urge that of his own version. There was a rumor that the Estates on May 14th had resolved to take Prat from the Aljafería by force and to meet this, on May 17th, he sent the Comendador García de Loaisa to Saragossa with instructions to arm the Cofradia of San Pedro Martir--an association connected with the Inquisition--to raise the people and to meet force with force. The authorities were to be bullied and told that the king would assert his sovereign authority and that nothing should prevent the extradition of Prat. In the hands of his ghostly advisers he was prepared to risk civil war in defence of the abuses of the Inquisition. There was fear that the inquisitors might be intimidated into releasing Prat and Cardinal Adrian took the unprecedented step of writing directly to the gaoler of the Aljafería instructing him to disobey any such orders.

In spite of this assertion of absolutism, Charles's orders were treated with contempt. The Córtes met at Azuaga, refused to obey his angry commands to disperse and sent to him Don Sancho de la Caballería with the unpleasant message that the servicio would be withheld until he should grant justice to the kingdom. His finances, in the hands of his Flemish favorites, were in complete disorder. The Emperor Maximilian had died January 22d and the contest for the succession, against the gold of Francis I, was expensive. Moreover, in expectation of the servicio, Chièvres had obtained advances at usurious interest so that the expected funds were already nearly exhausted and, as soon as the electoral struggle ended in Charles's nomination, June 28th, there came fresh demands for funds to prepare for his voyage to assume his new dignity. Chièvres therefore eagerly sought for some compromise to relieve the dead-lock, but the Aragonese on the one hand and Cardinal Adrian on the other were intractable. The high-handed arrest of Prat had fatally complicated the situation.

Charles yielded in so far as to order that Prat should not be removed from the kingdom and several tentative propositions were made as to the trial of Prat which only show how little he and his advisers realized the true condition of affairs. With wonted Aragonese tenacity the Diputados adhered to the position that the accuracy of the record should not be called in question and that the only point to be determined was whether the Inquisition rightfully had any jurisdiction in the matter. At the same time, to show that they were not seeking to elude payment of the servicio they agreed on September 7th to levy it, at the same time begging Charles to release Prat.

They were probably led to make this concession by a victory which they had gained in Rome. Both sides had been vigorously at work there, but the Aragonese had the advantage that Leo X at the moment was incensed against the Spanish Inquisition because of the insolent insubordination of the Toledo tribunal in the case of Bernardino Díaz, of which more hereafter. His own experience showed him of what it was capable and the request of the Córtes for the confirmation of the Concordia was to a great extent granted by three briefs, received August 1st, addressed respectively to the king, to Cardinal Adrian and to the inquisitors of Saragossa, reducing the Inquisition to the rules of the common law. Charles did not allow the briefs to be published and, when the Diputados presented to the inquisitors the one addressed to them, they refused to obey it without instructions from Adrian, whereupon, on August 8th, the Diputados applied to Rome for some further remedy.

Although the briefs were thus dormant they became the central point of the contest. On September 24th, Charles despatched to Rome Lope Hurtado de Mendoza as a special envoy with long and detailed instructions. He had been advised, he said that the pope intended to issue a bull revoking all inquisitorial commissions, save that of Cardinal Adrian; that in future the bishops with their chapters in each see were to nominate two persons of whom the inquisitor-general was to select the fittest and present him to the pope for confirmation; the acts of these inquisitors were to be judicially investigated every two years, and their procedure was to conform to the common law and to the canons. The elaborate arguments which Charles urged against each feature of this revolutionary plan show that it was not a figment but was seriously proposed with likelihood of its adoption. Moreover he said that influences were at work to secure the removal of the sanbenitos of convicts from the churches, against which he earnestly protested; Ferdinand had refused three hundred thousand ducats offered to him to procure this concession. In conclusion Charles declared that no importunity should shake his determination to make no change in the Inquisition and he significantly expressed his desire to preserve the friendship of his Holiness.

What secret influences were at work to effect a complete reversal of papal policy it would be vain to guess, but Mendoza had scarce time to reach Rome when he procured a brief of October 12th, addressed to Cardinal Adrian. In this Sadoleto's choicest Latinity was employed to cover up the humiliation of conscious wrong-doing, in its effort to shift the responsibility to the shoulders of others. Charles's letters and Mendoza's message had enlightened him as to the intentions of the king with regard to the preservation of the faith and the reform of the Inquisition. He promised that he would change nothing and would publish nothing without the assent of the king and the information of the inquisitor-general, but he dwelt on the complaints that reached him from all quarters of the avarice and iniquity of the inquisitors; he warned Adrian that the infamy of the wickedness of his sub-delegates redounded to the dishonor of the nation and affected both him and the king; he was responsible and must seek to preserve his own honor and that of the king by seeing that they desist from the insolence with which they disregarded the papal mandates and rebelled against the Holy See.

While thus the three briefs were not revoked they were practically annulled. The indignation of the Aragonese at finding themselves thus juggled was warm and found expression, January 30, 1520, in discontinuing the collection of the servicio. Charles was now at Coruña, preparing for his voyage to Flanders and thither, on February 3d, the Diputados sent Azor Zapata and Iñigo de Mendoza to procure the liberation of Prat and to urge Charles to obtain the confirmation of the Concordia. To liberate Prat without a trial was tacitly to admit the correctness of his record, yet, on April 21st, Cardinal Adrian issued an order for the fiscal to discontinue the prosecution and for the inquisitors to "relax" Prat. This order was presented May 1st to the inquisitors, but the word "relaxation" was that used in the delivery of convicts to the secular arm for burning; Prat stoutly refused to accept it and remained in prison.

Charles embarked May 21st and the rest of the year 1520 was spent in endeavors by each side to obtain the confirmation of their respective formulas of the Concordia and in fruitless attempts by Charles to have the three briefs revoked. Though unpublished and virtually annulled they were the source of great anxiety to the Inquisition. The correspondence between Charles and his Roman agents shows perpetual insistance on his part and perpetual promises and evasions by the pope, sometimes on the flimsiest pretexts for postponement, the secret of which is probably to be found in a report by Juan Manuel, the Spanish ambassador, on October 12th, that the pope was promised 46,000 or 47,000 ducats if he could induce the king to let the briefs stand. Thus it went on throughout the year and, when Leo died, December 1, 1521, the briefs were still unrevoked.

A year earlier, however, December 1, 1520, he had confirmed the Concordia, in a bull so carefully drawn as not to commit the Holy See to either of the contesting versions. It was limited to the promises embraced in Charles's oath and, as regards the articles, it merely said that the canons and ordinances and papal decrees should be inviolably observed, under pain of ipso facto excommunication, dismissal from office and disability for re-appointment. Either side was consequently at liberty to put what construction it pleased on the papal utterance.

Charles meanwhile had been growing more and more impatient for the servicio so long withheld; he had written to Adrian and also to the inquisitors, ordering that the Concordia of Monzon (1512) and that of Saragossa, according to his version, should be strictly obeyed, so that the abuses thus sought to be corrected should cease and the people should pay the impost. The inquisitors dallied and seem to have asked him what articles he referred to for he replied, September 17th, explaining that they were those of Monzon and Saragossa, the latter as expressed in the paper signed by Adrian and Gattinara. When, therefore, he received the papal confirmation of December 1st he lost no time in writing, December 18th, to Adrian and the inquisitors announcing it and ordering the articles to be rigidly observed without gloss or interpretation, so that the abuses and disorders prohibited in them may cease, but he was careful to describe the articles as those agreed upon at Monzon and lately confirmed at Saragossa in the form adopted by Adrian and Gattinara.

The Aragonese, on the other hand, adhered to their version. The bull of confirmation seems to have reached Saragossa through Flanders, accompanied by a letter from Charles and it was not until January 15, 1521, that the Diputados wrote to Adrian enclosing the royal letter and a copy of the bull. In obeying it, he conceded the Aragonese version of the Concordia, though with a bad grace. From Tordesillas, January 28th, he wrote to the Diputados and the inquisitors that the bull must be obeyed although it might properly be considered surreptitious, as it asserted that Charles had sworn to the fictitious articles inserted by Juan Prat, for which the latter deserved the severest punishment. In spite of this burst of petulance, however, he practically admitted Prat's innocence by ordering his liberation and, on February 13, 1521, the order was carried in triumph by the governor, the Diputados and a concourse of nobles and citizens to the Aljafería and solemnly presented to the inquisitors, who asked for copies and, with these in their hands, said that they would do their duty without swerving from justice and reason. So well satisfied were the Aragonese that to show their gratitude they had already, on January 18th, ordered the cities and towns to pay all current imposts as well as the suspended subsidio within thirty-five days. It may be added that finally Cardinal Adrian recognized the innocence of Prat in the most formal manner, in a letter of April 20th to the inquisitors, imposing silence on the fiscal and ordering the discharge of Prat and his securities.[717]

STRUGGLE IN BARCELONA

Triumph and gratitude were alike misplaced. Cardinal Adrian had followed his letter of January 28th with another of the 30th to the inquisitors, instructing them that the papal confirmation must be construed in accordance with the sacred canons and the decrees of the Holy See, so that they could continue to administer justice duly and he encouraged them with an ayuda de costa or gratuity.[718] They went on imperturbably with their work; not only was the Concordia of Saragossa never observed but that of Monzon was treated as non-existent and we shall see hereafter that, towards the close of the century, the Inquisition coolly asserted that the latter had been invalidated when Leo X released Ferdinand from his oath to observe it and that the former had never been confirmed and that there was no trace of either having ever been observed. The Inquisition, in fact, was invulnerable and impenetrable. It made its own laws and there was no power in the land, save that of the crown, that could force it to keep its engagements.

***

Meanwhile the obstinacy of the Catalans, which detained the impatient Charles in Barcelona throughout the year 1519, secured, nominally at least, the formal confirmation by both Charles and Adrian, of the Monzon Concordia of 1512 with additions. One of these provided that any one who entered the service of the Holy Office while liable to a civil or criminal action, should still be held to answer before his former judge, and that criminal offences, unconnected with the faith, committed by officials should be exclusively justiciable in the civil courts. This struck at the root of one of the most serious abuses--the immunity with which the Inquisition shielded its criminals--and scarcely less important to all who had dealings with New Christians was another article providing that property acquired in good faith, from one reputed to be a Christian, should be exempt from confiscation in case the seller should subsequently be convicted, even though the thirty years' prescription should still exist.[719]

The agreement was reached January 11, 1520, but experience of the faithlessness of the Inquisition had made the Catalans wary. They were about to grant a servicio to Charles and they sought a guarantee by addressing to him a supplication that he should make Cardinal Adrian swear to the observance of the Concordia of 1512 and the new articles and that he should procure within four months from the pope a bull of confirmation, in which the Bishops of Lérida and Barcelona should be appointed conservators, with full power to enforce the agreement. They offered to pay two hundred ducats towards the cost of the bull and they demanded that they should retain twenty thousand libras of the servicio until the bull should be delivered to the Diputados. The same condition was attached to a liberal donation of twelve thousand libras which they made to the Inquisition--probably a part of the bargain. Meanwhile Charles was to give orders that the inquisitors should be bound by the articles and, in case of infraction, satisfaction for such violations should be deducted from the twenty thousand libras. In due time, August 25th, Leo X executed a formal bull of confirmation of the articles of 1512 and 1520 and appointed the Bishops of Lérida and Barcelona as conservators.[720]

ABUSES CONTINUE

What was the value of the Concordia thus solemnly agreed to and liberally paid for, with its papal confirmation and conservators, was speedily seen when, in 1523, the authorities of Perpignan became involved in a quarrel with Inquisitor Juan Naverdu over the case of the wife of Juan Noguer. They complained of an infraction of the Concordia and applied to the Bishop of Lérida for its enforcement. He appointed Miguel Roig, a canon of Elna, as the executor of his decision, who issued letters ordering the inquisitor and his secretary to observe the Concordia, under pain of excommunication, and to drop the cases which they were prosecuting. Appeal was also made to Rome and letters were obtained from Clement VII. Charles, however, intervened and obtained another brief, January 6, 1524, annulling the previous one and transferring the matter to Inquisitor-general Manrique. The result was that nearly all the magistrates of Perpignan--the consuls and jurados with their lawyers and Miguel Roig--were obliged to swear obedience in all things to the Inquisition, were exposed to the irredeemable disgrace of appearing as penitents at the mass and were subjected to fines from which the Holy Office gathered in the comfortable sum of 1115 ducats.[721] The motto of the Inquisition was noli me tangere and it administered a sharp lesson to all who might venture, even under papal authority, to make it conform to its agreements.

It was in vain that the sturdy subjects of the crown of Aragon struggled and gained concessions, paid for them and fenced them around with all the precautions held sacred by public law. The inquisitors felt themselves to be above the law and all the old abuses continued to flourish as rankly as ever. About this time the Córtes of the three kingdoms, by command of Charles, addressed to Inquisitor-general Manrique a series of sixteen grievances, repeating the old complaints--the extension of jurisdiction over usury, blasphemy, bigamy and sodomy; the acceptance by the inquisitors of commissions to act as conservators in secular and ecclesiastical cases and profane matters; their arresting people for private quarrels and on trivial charges and insufficient evidence, leaving on them and their descendants an ineffaceable stain, even though they were discharged without penance; their multiplication of familiars and concealing their names, appointing criminals and protecting them in their crimes and finally their overbearing and insulting attitude in general. In answer to this the inquisitor-general contented himself with asserting that the laws were obeyed and asking for specific instances of infraction and the names of the parties--secure that no one would dare to come forward and expose himself to the vengeance of the tribunal.[722] Again, in 1528 at the Córtes of Monzon, we find a repetition of grievances--the abuse of confiscations, the cognizance of usury and other matters disconnected with heresy and general inobservance of the articles agreed upon. To the petition that he remedy these and procure from the inquisitor-general an order to his subordinates to conform themselves to the Concordias, Charles returned the equivocating answer "His majesty will see that the inquisitor-general orders the observance of that which should be observed, removing abuses if there are any."[723]

The imperial attitude was not such as to discourage the audacity of the inquisitors and, at the Córtes of Monzon in September, 1533, the deputies of Aragon presented to Inquisitor-general Manrique, who was present, two series of grievances. One of these he promptly answered by characterizing some of the demands as impertinent, scandalous, and illegal, and others as not worthy of reply. The other series was referred to Charles and was not answered until December. It commenced by asking that the Concordia confirmed by Leo X, in 1516, should be observed, to which the reply was that such action should be taken as would comport with the service of God and proper exercise of the Inquisition. The request that the inquisitors confine themselves to matters of faith was met with the assertion that they did so, except when under orders from their superiors. To the demand that the dowries of Catholic wives should not be confiscated, the dry response was that the laws should be observed. In this cavalier spirit the rest of the petition was disposed of, and the whole shows how completely the Holy Office was emancipated from any subjection to the laws which had cost such struggles to obtain and which had been paid for so largely.[724]

While Manrique and the Suprema were at Monzon, they were called upon to take action with regard to troubles at Barcelona between the inquisitor, Fernando de Loazes and the magistrates and Diputados. These had been on foot for some time. A letter of Charles from Bologna, February 25, 1533, to Loazes assures him of his sympathy and support and, in September, the Suprema at Monzon resolved to send a judge thither to prosecute and punish the offenders for their enormous delinquencies.[725] What were the merits of the quarrel do not appear, but it was doubtless provoked by the overbearing arrogance of Loazes for, at the Córtes of Monzon, the Catalans represented to Charles that the pretensions of the inquisitor impeded the course of justice in matters involving the regalías or prerogatives of the crown, and asked to have him prosecuted by the Bishop of Barcelona. Charles thereupon addressed to Loazes a letter January 16, 1534, forbidding him in future to interfere with the royal judges, as no one could claim exemption from the royal jurisdiction. At the same time he instructed his lieutenant for Aragon, Fadrique de Portugal, Archbishop of Saragossa, to enforce this mandate. It was not long before Loazes had the opportunity of manifesting his contempt for these expressions of the royal will. One of the consuls holding the admiralty court of Barcelona was hearing a case between two merchants, Joan Ribas and Gerald Camps: a quarrel ensued between them; Ribas with his servant Joan Monseny struck Camps in the face and then drawing his sword, threatened the consul's life. This was a scandalous offence to the dignity of the crown under whose protection the court was held. By order of the Archbishop and royal council the culprits were arrested and thrown in prison, but Ribas was a familiar of the Inquisition and Loazes presented himself before the archbishop in full court and claimed him. The letters of Charles V were read and his claim was rejected, whereupon, on June 13th, he issued a mandate demanding the surrender to him of Ribas and forbidding all proceedings against him under pain of excommunication.[726] What was the termination of this special case we have no means of knowing, but Loazes did not suffer by reason of his audacity. In 1542 he was made Bishop of Elna, whence he passed by successive translations through the sees of Lérida, Tortosa and Tarragona, dying at last, full of years and honors in 1568 as Archbishop of Valencia.

**

It is not worth while at present to pursue these disputes which reveal the character of the Inquisition and the resistance offered to it by the comparatively free populations subject to the crown of Aragon. We shall have ample opportunity hereafter to note the persistant arrogance of the inquisitors under the royal favor, the restlessness of the people and the fruitlessness of their struggle for relief from oppression. The Holy Office had become part of the settled policy of the House of Austria. The Lutheran revolt had grown to enormous proportions and no measures seemed too severe that would protect the faith from an enemy even more insidious and more dangerous than Judaism. The system grew to be an integral part of the national institutions to be uprooted only by the cataclysm of the French Revolution and the Napoleonic war. At what cost to the people this was effected is seen in the boast, in 1638, of a learned official of the Inquisition that in its favor the monarchs had succeeded in breaking down the municipal laws and privileges of their kingdoms, which otherwise would have presented insuperable obstacles to the extermination of heresy, and he proceeds to enumerate the various restrictions on the arbitrary power of the secular courts which the experience of ages had framed for the protection of the citizen from oppression, all of which had been swept away where the Inquisition was concerned, leaving the subject to the discretion of the inquisitor.[727]

BOOK II - RELATIONS WITH THE STATE

CHAPTER I - RELATIONS WITH THE CROWN

What gave to the Spanish Inquisition its peculiar and terrible efficiency were the completeness of its organization and its combination of the mysterious authority of the Church with the secular power of the crown. The old Inquisition was purely an ecclesiastical institution, empowered, it is true, to call upon the State for aid and for the execution of its sentences, but throughout Christendom the relations between Church and State were too often antagonistic for its commands always to receive obedience. In Spain, however, the Inquisition represented not only the pope but the king; it practically wielded the two swords--the spiritual and the temporal--and the combination produced a tyranny, similar in character, but far more minute and all-pervading, to that which England suffered during the closing years of Henry VIII as Supreme Head of the Church.

While thus its domination over the people was secure and unvarying, its relations with the royal power varied with the temperament of the sovereign. At times it was the instrument of his will; at others it seemed as though it might almost supplant the monarchy; it was constantly seeking to extend its awful authority over the other departments of State, which struggled with varying success to resist its encroachments, while successive kings, autocratic in theory, sometimes posed as arbitrators, sometimes vainly endeavored to enforce their pacificatory commands, but more generally yielded to its domineering spirit.

FERDINAND'S CONTROL

When Ferdinand consented to the introduction of the Inquisition, it was no part of his policy to permit the foundation of an institution which should be independent of the royal authority. He who sought to forbid in Spain the residence of papal nuncios and legates was not likely to welcome the advent of a new swarm of papal delegates, whose power over life and property would carry unchecked to every corner of the land the influence of Rome. Accordingly, as we have seen, he conditioned the admission of the Inquisition on the concession of the power of appointment and dismissal and he flatly told Sixtus IV that he would permit none but appointees of his own to exercise the office of inquisitor. As the institution developed and became more complex he nominated to the pope the individual to whom the papal delegation as inquisitor-general should be given and he appointed the members of the Suprema, which became known as the Consejo de su Magestad de la Santa General Inquisicion. Although the papal commission granted to the inquisitor-general faculties of subdelegating his powers and appointing and dismissing his subordinates, thus rendering his action indispensable, Ferdinand was careful to assert his right to control all appointments and to assume that at least they were made with his assent and concurrence. In 1485 the sovereigns had no scruple in appointing at Guadalupe the inquisitors who made such havoc among the apostates.[728] August 8, 1500, he writes to the Bishop of Bonavalle that he had determined to commit to him the office of inquisitor in Sardinia, for which the commission and subdelegation will be despatched to him by the inquisitors-general; he can appoint an assessor and notary, but the other officials will be sent from Spain. A letter of the same date to the Lieutenant-general of Sardinia announces the appointment by the inquisitors-general "con nuestra voluntad y consentimiento," which was the ordinary formula employed, even in such petty cases as when he advised Pedro Badía, receiver of confiscations at Barcelona, March 13, 1501, that they had appointed Gregorio Zamarado as portero or apparitor of that tribunal, in place of Guillen Donadou and that he is to receive the same wages.[729] Although the participation of the inquisitor-general was indispensable, Ferdinand customarily assumed his acquiescence as a matter of course; he would make the appointment and then ask affectionately for the subdelegation of power.[730] As regards subordinate positions, Torquemada recognized the royal participation when, in 1485, he instructed inquisitors that they could fill vacancies temporarily "until the king and I provide for them." As a rule, it may be said that Ferdinand rarely troubled himself about subordinates, but had no hesitation in assuming full power when he saw fit, as in writing to an inquisitor, March 21, 1499, "we order you to appoint, as by these presents we appoint, Juan de Montiende as fiscal in your tribunal."[731]

If he thus controlled appointments he was equally concerned in dismissals. We find him writing, April 22, 1498, to an inquisitor of Saragossa, who had discharged an official at Calatayud, to reinstate him, as he had done good service with danger to his person, and on September 19, 1509, ordering Diego López de Cortegano, Inquisitor of Córdova, to cease his functions at once and return to his benefice--though this latter order was countersigned by the members of the Suprema.[732] It would be superfluous to adduce additional examples of the control thus exercised over the personnel of the Inquisition--a control which remained inherent in the crown although, as we shall see, often allowed to become dormant.

In all save spiritual matters, Ferdinand considered the Inquisition to be merely an instrument to carry out his will, though it must be added that this arose from his anxiety that it should be perfected in every way for the work in hand, and there is absolutely no evidence, in his enormous and confidential correspondence, that he ever used it for political purposes, even in the stormiest times when struggling with unruly nobles. Every detail in its organization and working was subject to his supervision and, amid all the cares of his tortuous policy, extending throughout Western Europe, and the excitement of his frequent wars, he devoted the minutest care to its affairs. When, in December 1484, Torquemada issued his supplementary instructions, he was careful to state that he did so by command of the sovereigns, who ordered them to be observed. So in subsequent instructions, issued in 1485, Torquemada orders the inquisitors to write to him and to Ferdinand about everything that should be reported; the king provides their salaries promises them rewards; if there is anything that the king ought to remedy he is to be written to.[733] That, in fact, the was recognized as controlling the Inquisition is seen in all the efforts of the Córtes, appealing to him to obtain a modification of its rigors, although, as we have seen, the Concordia of 1512 was held to require the assent of Inquisitor-general Enguera to render it binding, with subsequent confirmation by the pope and though, in later times, the monarchs found it convenient to throw upon the inquisitor-general the responsibility of rejecting the demands of their subjects.

Ferdinand was too self-reliant to deem it necessary to assert his power consistently on all occasions. In a subsequent chapter we shall see that he submitted to the inconveniences arising from an excommunication threatened by Torquemada on receivers of confiscations who honored royal drafts in preference to paying salaries. He had no scruples in making Torquemada join with him in grants of money or in settling competing claims on the debts due to a condemned heretic; he sometimes allowed his cédulas to be countersigned by members of the Suprema, especially in the later periods; indeed, toward the end of his reign, this became so habitual that in letters of November 25th and December 10, 1515, he explained that his orders were to be obeyed although not so authenticated, because none of the members happened to be at hand; he sometimes delayed answering applications for instructions until he could consult the inquisitor-general, but the mere application to him shows that he was regarded as the ultimate arbiter. In fact, in a case in which some prisoners named Martínez had appealed to him, he replies to the inquisitors, September 30, 1498, and March 2, 1499, that the inquisitors-general send instructions and it is his will that these should be executed, thus implying that his confirmation was requisite.[734]

***

Whatever participation he might thus allow to the head of the Inquisition, when he saw fit he asserted his arbitrary control and he by no means deemed it necessary to communicate with the tribunals through the inquisitor-general but frequently issued his commands directly. May 14, 1499, he writes to an inquisitor to have a certain confiscated property sold at an appraised value to Diego de Alcocer, no matter what instructions he may have from the inquisitors-general or what orders to the contrary. Even for trifles he took them sharply to task, as when, May 17, 1511, he vigorously rebuked one for sending Bachiller Vazquez to him on an affair which could have been as well settled by letter with much less expense. He was fully aware that the power of the Inquisition rested on his support and when there was the slightest opposition to his will he had no hesitation in saying so, as when, in a letter of July 22, 1486, to the inquisitors of Saragossa, he tells them that, although they have the name, it is to him and to Isabella that the Holy Office owes its efficiency; without the royal authority they can do little and, as they recognize his good intentions, they must not interfere with his orders.[735]

These instances illustrate the minute and watchful care which he exercised over all the details of the Holy Office. Nothing was too trivial to escape his vigilant attention, and this close supervision was continued to the end. The receiver of Valencia consults him about a carpenter's bill of ninety sueldos for repairs on the royal palace occupied by the tribunal and Ferdinand tells him, May 31, 1515, that he may pay it this time, but it is not to be a precedent. On January 18th of the same year he had written to the receiver of Jaen that he learns that the audience-chamber is ill-furnished and that the vestments for mass are lacking or worn out, wherefore he orders that what the inquisitors may purchase shall be paid for.[736]

***

Ferdinand's control over the Inquisition rested not only on the royal authority, the power of appointment, his own force of character and his intense interest in its workings, but also on the fact that he held the purse-strings. He had insisted that the confiscations should enure to the crown, and he subsequently obtained the pecuniary penances. The Inquisition had no endowment. One could easily have been provided out of the immense sums gathered from the victims during the early years of intense activity but, although some slender provision of the kind was at times attempted, either the chronic demands of the royal treasury or a prudent desire to prevent the independence of the institution rendered these investments fragmentary and wholly inadequate. Thus the expenses of the tribunals and the salaries of the officials were in his hands. Nothing could be paid without his authorization and the accounts of the receivers of confiscations, who acted as treasurers, were scrutinized with rigid care. He regulated the salary of every official and his letter-books are full of instructions as to their payment. Besides this, it was the Spanish custom to supplement inadequate wages with ayudas de costa, or gifts of greater or less amount as the whim of the sovereign or the deserts of the individual might call for. In time, as we shall see, this became a regular annual payment, subject to certain conditions but, under Ferdinand, it was still an uncertainty, dependent upon the royal favor and the order of the king was requisite in each case, even including the Suprema and its officials.[737] The crown thus held the Holy Office at its mercy and the recipients of its bounty could not resent its control.

INDEPENDENCE IN MATTERS OF FAITH

Yet in this perpetual activity of Ferdinand in the affairs of the Inquisition it is to be observed that he confined himself to temporal matters and abstained from interference with its spiritual jurisdiction. In his voluminous correspondence, extending, with occasional breaks, over many years, the exceptions to this only serve to prove the rule. I have met with but two and these fully justified his interference. In 1508 the leading barons of Aragon complained that the inquisitors were persecuting the Moors and were endeavoring to coerce them to baptism. As they had no jurisdiction over infidels, he rebuked them severely, telling them that conversion through conviction is alone pleasing to God and that no one is to be baptized except on voluntary application. So, when some had been converted and had been abandoned by their wives and children, he ordered the inquisitors to permit the return of the latter and not to coerce them to baptism.[738] The other case was that of Pedro de Villacis, receiver of Seville, a man who possessed Ferdinand's fullest confidence. No name occurs more frequently in the correspondence and he was entrusted with the management of an enormous and most complicated composition, in which the New Christians of Seville, Córdova, Leon, Granada and Jaen agreed to pay eighty thousand ducats as an assurance against confiscation. While deeply immersed in this the tribunal of Seville commenced to take testimony against him. On hearing of this Ferdinand was astounded; he expressed indignation that such action should be taken without consulting him and ordered all the original papers to be sent to him for consideration with the Suprema, pending which and future orders nothing further was to be done.[739]

This was an extreme case. There are others which prove how useless it was to rely upon the royal favor in hopes of interposition. Thus Ferdinand's vice-chancellor for Aragon was Alonso de la Caballería, a son of that Bernabos de la Caballería whose Çelo de Cristo contra los Judíos has been referred to above (p. 115). The father's orthodox zeal did not preserve his children from the Inquisition and their names and those of their kindred frequently occur in the records. Alonso had already passed through its hands without losing his position. In December, 1502, his brother Jaime was arrested by the tribunal of Saragossa, and Alonso ventured to ask Ferdinand's intervention in his favor and also for himself in case he should be involved and be subjected to another trial. Ferdinand replied, December 23d, expressing regret and the hope that all would turn out as he desired; if Alonso's case comes up again he shall be tried by Deza himself who can be relied upon to do exact justice. A second application from Alonso brought a reply, January 3, 1503, reiterating these assurances and promising a speedy trial for his brother, about whom he writes to the inquisitors. In effect, a letter to them of the same day alludes, among other matters, to Jaime's case, with the customary injunctions to conduct it justly so as not to injure the Inquisition and assuring them that if they do so they shall not be interfered with. How little the appeal to Ferdinand benefited the accused is seen in the result that Jaime was penanced in an auto de fe of March 25, 1504.[740]

In one respect Ferdinand showed favoritism, but he did so in a manner proving that he recognized that the royal power could not of itself interfere with the exercise of inquisitorial jurisdiction. Notwithstanding his settled aversion to papal intervention, he procured a series of curious briefs to spare those whom he favored from the disgrace of public reconciliation and penance and their descendants from disabilities. So many of his trusted officials were of Jewish lineage that he might well seek to shield them and to retain their services. Thus, in briefs of February 11, 1484, and January 30, 1485, Innocent VIII recites that he is informed that some of those involved in this heresy would gladly return to the faith and abjure if they could be secretly reconciled, wherefore he confers on the inquisitors faculties, in conjunction with episcopal representatives, to receive secretly, in the presence of Ferdinand and Isabella, fifty persons of this kind to abjuration and reconciliation. A subsequent brief of May 31, 1486, recites that he learns that the sovereigns cannot always be present on these occasions, wherefore he grants for fifty more similar power to be exercised in their absence but with their consent. Then, July 5, 1486, the same is granted for fifty more, even if testimony has been taken against them, with the addition of the removal of disabilities and the stain of infamy in favor of their children and moreover it authorizes the secret exhumation and burning of fifty bodies--doubtless the parents of those thus favored. These transactions continued, for there are similar letters of November 10, 1487, and October 14, 1489, each for fifty persons and fifty bodies, to be nominated by the king and queen, and possibly there were subsequent ones that have not reached us.[741] It was doubtless under letters of this kind that, on January 10, 1489, Elionor and Isabel Badorch were secretly reconciled in the royal palace of Barcelona.[742]

INSISTENCE ON JUSTICE

These apparently trivial details are of interest as revealing the basis on which the Inquisition was established and from which it developed. They also throw light on the character of Ferdinand, whose restless and incessant activity made itself felt in every department of the government, enabling his resolute will to break down the forces of feudalism and lay the foundation of absolute monarchy for his successors. It would be doing him an injustice, however, to dismiss the subject without alluding to his anxiety that the Inquisition should be kept strictly within the lines of absolute justice according to the standard of the period. Trained in the accepted doctrine of the Church that heresy was the greatest of crimes, that the heretic had no rights and that it was a service to God to torture him to death, he was pitiless and he stimulated the inquisitors to incessant vigilance. He was no less eager in gathering in every shred of spoil which he could lawfully claim from the confiscation of the victims, but, in the distorted ethics of the time, this comported with the strictest equity, for it was obedience to the canon law which was the expression of the law of God. There can have been no hypocrisy in his constant instructions to inquisitors and receivers of confiscations to perform their functions with rectitude and moderation so that no one should have cause to complain. This was his general formula to new appointees and is borne out by his instructions in the innumerable special cases where appeal was made to him against real or fancied injustice. His abstinence from intrusion into matters of faith limited such appeals to financial questions, but these, under the cruel canonical regulations as to confiscations, were often highly complicated and involved the rights of innocent third parties. His decisions in such cases are often adverse to himself and reveal an innate sense of justice wholly unexpected in a monarch who ranked next to Cesar Borgia in the estimation of Machiavelli. An instance or two, taken at random out of many, will illustrate this phase of his character. July 11, 1486, he writes to his receiver at Saragossa "Fifteen years ago, Jaime de Santangel, recently burnt, possessed a piece of land in Saragossa and did not pay the ground-rent on it to García Martinez. By the fuero of Aragon, when such rent is unpaid for four years the land is forfeited. You are said to hold the land as part of the confiscated estate of Santangel and for the above reason it is said to belong to Martínez. You are therefore ordered to see what is justice and do it to Martínez without delay and if you have sold the land, the matter must be put into such shape that Martínez may obtain what is due." In a similar spirit, when Caspar Roig, of Cagliari, deemed himself aggrieved in a transaction arising out of a composition for confiscation, Ferdinand writes to the inquisitor of Sardinia, March 11, 1498, "As it is our will that no one shall suffer injustice, we refer the case to you, charging you at once to hear the parties and do what is just, so that the said Gaspar Roig shall suffer no wrong.... You will see that the said Gaspar Roig shall not again have to appeal to us for default of justice."[743]

***

It was inevitable that, when this powerful personality was withdrawn, the royal control over the Inquisition should diminish, especially in view of the inability of Queen Juana to govern and the absence of the youthful Charles V. The government of Spain practically devolved upon Ximenes, who was Inquisitor-general of Castile, while his coadjutor Adrian speedily obtained the same post in Aragon. After the arrival of Charles and the death of Ximenes, Adrian became chief of the reunited Inquisition and his influence over Charles in all matters connected with it was unbounded. The circumstances therefore were peculiarly propitious for the development of its practical independence, although theoretically the supremacy of the crown remained unaltered.

POWER OF APPOINTMENT

Thus the Suprema, of which we hear little under Ferdinand, at once assumed his place in regulating all details. The appointing power, even of receivers, who were secular officials, accountable only to the royal treasury, passed into its hands. Thus a letter of Ximenes, March 11, 1517, to the receiver of Toledo, states that there are large amounts of uncollected confiscations, wherefore he is directed to select a proper person for an assistant and send him to the Suprema to decide as to his fitness, so that Ximenes may appoint him with its approval.[744] Still, the nominating power remained technically with the crown and, when Charles arrived, he was assumed to exercise it as Ferdinand had done, however little real volition he may have displayed. In a letter of December 11, 1518, concerning the appointment of Andrés Sánchez de Torquemada as Inquisitor of Seville, Charles is made to say that, being satisfied of Torquemada's capacity, he had charged him to accept the office and that with his assent Adrian had appointed him. In another case, where an abbot, to whom Adrian had offered the inquisitorship of Toledo, had declined the office, Charles writes, September 14, 1519, charging him to accept it.[745] That Adrian could not act alone was recognized for, after Charles left Spain, in May, 1520, questions arose on the subject and, by letters patent of September 12th, he formally empowered Adrian, during his absence, to appoint all inquisitors and other officials.[746]

Whether formal delegations of the appointing power were subsequently made does not appear, but practically it continued with the inquisitor-general, subject to an uncertain co-operation of the Suprema, whose members countersigned the commissions, while, with the subordinate positions in the tribunals, the inquisitors were sometimes consulted, their recommendations received attention and their remonstrances were heard. The various factors are illustrated in a letter of the Suprema, August 24, 1544, to the inquisitors of Saragossa who had furnished a statement of the qualifications of various aspirants for the vacant post of notario del juzgado. In reply the Suprema states that its secretary, Hieronimo Zurita, had recommended Martin Morales; it had advised with the inquisitor-general who had appointed him, but it will bear in mind Bartolomé Malo and will give him something else.[747]

So far as I am aware, Philip II never interfered with this exercise of the appointing power. That he threw the whole responsibility on the inquisitor-general and disclaimed any concurrence for himself is apparent in a series of instructions, May 8, 1595, to the new inquisitor-general, Geronimo Manrique. He orders him to observe the utmost care to select fit persons for all positions without favoritism and, although it is his duty to appoint inquisitors and fiscals, he should communicate his selections in advance to the Suprema, as his predecessors had always done, because some of the members may be acquainted with the parties and prevent errors from being made.[748] That a supervisory power, however, was still recognized in the crown is seen in a consulta of June 21, 1600, presented to Philip III, by Inquisitor-general Guevara, lamenting the unfitness of many of the inquisitors. With the habitual tenderness manifested to unworthy officials he did not propose to dismiss them but to make a general shifting by which the best men should be made the seniors of the tribunals. To this the king replied with a caution about discrediting the Inquisition and a suggestion that the parties shifted should be made to ask for the change; he also called for their names and the reasons, because he ought to be informed about all the individuals.[749]

This indicated a desire to resume the close watchfulness of Ferdinand which had long since been forgotten in the turmoil and absences of Charles V and the secluded labors of Philip II, over despatches and consultas. A bureaucracy was establishing itself in which the various departments of the government were becoming more or less independent of the monarch and Philip for the moment appeared disposed to reassert his authority, for, in 1603, we are told that he made many appointments of inquisitors, fiscals, and even of minor officials.[750] If so, he was too irresolute, feeble, and fitful to carry out a definite line of policy for when, in 1608, he issued the customary instructions to a new inquisitor, Sandoval y Rójas, he merely repeated the injunctions of 1595, with the addition that transfers should also be communicated to the Suprema.[751] Yet in one case he even exceeded Ferdinand by intervening in a case of faith. When he went to Toledo with his court to witness the auto de fe of May 10, 1615, he asked to see the sentence of Juan Cote, penanced for Lutheranism, and made some changes in the meritos, or recital of offences, altered the imprisonment to perpetual and irremissible and added two hundred lashes. The tribunal consulted the Suprema, which approved the changes on the supposition that the inquisitor-general had participated in them, but the day after the auto Cote was informed that the Suprema had mercifully remitted the scourging.[752]

***

Philip IV, in 1626, on the death of Inquisitor-general Pacheco, asked the Suprema to suggest the instructions to be given to the new incumbent and was advised to repeat those of 1608. He virtually admitted the power of appointment to be vested in that office when, in the same year, the Córtes of Barbastro petitioned that in Aragon all the officials of the tribunals should be Aragonese and he replied that he would use his authority with the inquisitor-general that a certain portion of them should be so.[753] Notwithstanding his habitual subservience to the Inquisition, however, he reasserted his prerogative, in 1640, by appointing the Archdeacon of Vich as Inquisitor of Barcelona and he followed this, in 1641 and 1642, by several others, even descending to the secretaryship of Lima which he gave to Domingo de Aroche.[754] This brought on a struggle, ending in a compromise in which the inquisitor-general was sacrificed to the Suprema. Papal intervention was deemed to be necessary and a brief was procured in March, 1643, under which Philip, by decree of July 2, ordered that in future, in all vacancies of positions of inquisitor and fiscal, the inquisitor-general and Suprema should submit to him three names from which to make selection. The Suprema thus recognized was satisfied, but Sotomayor, the inquisitor-general, was obstinate. In June, Philip had called for his resignation, which he offered after some hesitation and expressed his feelings in a protest presenting a sorry picture of the condition of the Holy Office. The present disorders, he said, had arisen from the multiplication of offices, whereby their character had depreciated and, as the revenues were insufficient for their support, they were led to improper devices. The Suprema had been powerless for, on various occasions, the king had rewarded services in other fields by the gifts of these offices, when no consideration could be given to character, and he had also been forced to make appointments by commands as imperative as those of the king--an evident allusion to Olivares.[755]

Sotomayor's successor, Arce y Reynoso, conformed himself to these new rules and, until his death in 1665, he submitted all appointments and transfers to the king. Philip survived him but three months and, under the regency which followed and the reign of the imbecile Carlos II, the inquisitor-general resumed the power of appointment without consultation. So completely was the royal supervision forgotten that the instructions to Inquisitor-general Rocaberti, in 1695, repeat the old formula of 1608.[756] In this, the injunction of consulting the Suprema was displeasing to the Holy See, after its intervention in the affair of Froilan Díaz (of which more hereafter) had caused it to take sides in the quarrel over the respective powers of the inquisitor-general and the Suprema. As the commission of the former was a papal grant, it held that no restriction could be placed on him and, when Vidal Marin was appointed, Clement XI sent to him August 8, 1705, urgent instructions to uphold the dignity of his office which had exclusive authority in the premises.[757]

The command was too agreeable not to be obeyed and, from this time, the unrestricted power of appointment was in the hands of the inquisitor-general. About 1765, a writer tells us that all salaried offices were filled by him alone. If the king wished to gratify some one with a position he would signify his desire to the inquisitor-general that such person should be borne in mind at the first vacancy and the royal wish was respected, in the absence of special objection. If such there were it was reported to the king and his decision was awaited.[758] With the tendency to assert the prerogative, under Carlos III, this was called in question, in 1775, when the royal Camara scrutinized the brief commissioning Felipe Bertran as inquisitor-general, but the protest was merely formal; the appointing power remained undisturbed; it survived the Revolution and continued until the Inquisition was suppressed.[759]

***

THE INQUISITOR-GENERALSHIP

Of vastly greater importance was the power of selecting and virtually dismissing the inquisitor-general and this the crown never lost. In fact this was essential to its dignity, if not to its safety. Had the appointment rested with the pope, either the Inquisition would of necessity have been reduced to insignificance or the kingdom would have become a dependency of the curia. Had the Suprema possessed the power of presenting a nominee to the pope, the Inquisition would have become an independent body rivalling and perhaps in time superseding the monarchy. Yet, after the death of Ferdinand, Cardinal Adrian, when elected to the papacy, seemed to imagine that Ferdinand's privilege of nomination had been merely personal and that it had reverted to him. February 19, 1522, he wrote to Charles that a successor must be provided; after much thought he had pitched on the Dominican General but had not determined to make the appointment without first learning Charles's wishes. If the Dominican was not satisfactory, Charles could name some one else, for which purpose he suggested three other prelates. Charles replied from Brussels, March 29th, assuming the appointment to be in his hands, but ordered his representative Lachaulx to confer with Adrian. He was in no haste to reach a decision and it was not until July 13, 1523, that he instructed his ambassador, the Duke of Sessa, to ask the commission for Alfonso Manrique, Bishop of Córdova, on whom he had conferred the post of inquisitor-general and the archbishopric of Seville.[760]

The records afford no indication of any question subsequently arising as to the power of the crown to select the inquisitor-general. It was never, however, officially recognized by the popes, whose commissions to the successive nominees bore the form of a motu proprio--the spontaneous act of the Holy See--by which, without reference to any request from the sovereign, the recipient was created inquisitor-general of the Spanish dominions and was invested with all the faculties and powers requisite for the functions of his office.[761] No objection seems to have been taken to this until Carlos III exercised a jealous care over the assertion and maintenance of the regalías against the assumptions of the curia. The first appointment he had occasion to make was that of Felipe Bertran, Bishop of Salamanca, after the death of Inquisitor-general Bonifaz. December 27, 1774, was despatched the application to the papacy for the commission, carefully framed to avoid attributing to the latter any share in the selection or appointment and merely asking for a delegation of faculties, accompanied with instructions to the ambassador Floridablanca to procure for Bertran a dispensation from residence at his see during his term of office. Clement XIV had died, September 22, 1774, and the intrigues arising from the suppression of the Jesuits delayed the election of Pius VI until February 15, 1775, but on February 27th the commission and dispensation were signed. March 25th, Carlos sent the commission to the royal Camara for examination before its delivery to Bertran and the Camara reported, April 24th, that its fiscal pronounced it similar to that granted to Bonifaz in 1755, but that it did not express as it should the royal nomination and had the form of a motu proprio; he also objected to its granting the power of appointment and further that some of the faculties included infringed on the royal and episcopal jurisdictions, while the clauses on censorship conflicted with the royal decrees. Under these reserves the brief was ordered to be delivered to Bertran; whether or not a protest was made to the curia does not appear, but if it was it was ineffective for the same formula was used in the commission issued to Inquisitor-general Agustin Rubin de Cevallos, February 17, 1784.[762]

**

It may be assumed as a matter of course that the king had no power to dismiss an inquisitor-general who held his commission at the pleasure of the pope, but the sovereign had usually abundant means of enforcing a resignation. Whether that of Alfonso Suárez de Fuentelsaz, in 1504, was voluntary or coerced is not known, but the case of Cardinal Manrique, the successor of Adrian, shows that if an inquisitor-general was not forced to resign he could be virtually shelved. Manrique, as Bishop of Badajoz, after Isabella's death, had so actively supported the claims of Philip I that Ferdinand ordered his arrest; he fled to Flanders, where he entered Charles's service and returned with him to Spain, obtaining the see of Córdova and ultimately the archbishopric of Seville.[763] Perhaps he incurred the ill-will of the Empress Isabella soon after his appointment, for we find him complaining, January 23, 1524, to Charles that when in Valencia she had ordered the disarmament of the familiars and the arrest of Micer Artes, a salaried official of the Inquisition, violations of its privileges for which he asked a remedy.[764] In 1529, he gave more serious cause of offence. When Charles sailed, July 28th, to Italy for his coronation, he placed under charge of the empress Doña Luisa de Acuña, heiress of the Count of Valencia, until her marriage should be determined. There were three suitors--Manrique's cousin the Count of Treviño, heir apparent of the Duke of Najera, the Marquis of Astorga and the Marquis of Mayorga. The empress placed her ward in the convent of San Domingo el Real of Toledo, where Manrique abused his authority by introducing his cousin; an altar had been prepared in advance and the marriage was celebrated on the spot. The empress, justly incensed, ordered him from the court to his see until the emperor should return and turned a deaf ear to the representations by the Suprema, December 12th, of the interference with the holy work of the Inquisition and the discredit cast upon it. It was probably to this that may be referred the delay in his elevation to the cardinalate, announced March 22, 1531, after being kept in petto since December 19, 1529. On Charles's return, in 1533, he was allowed to take his place again, but he fell into disgrace once more in 1534, when he was sent back to his see where he died at an advanced age in 1538. Still, this was not equivalent to dismissal; he continued to exercise his functions and his signature is appended to documents of the Inquisition at least until 1537.[765] Yet while thus dealing with the inquisitor-general the crown could exercise no control over the tribunals. The empress was interested in the case of Fray Francisco Ortiz, arrested April 6, 1529, by the tribunal of Toledo, and she twice requested the expediting of his trial for which, October 27, 1530, she alleged reasons of state, but the tribunal was deaf to her wishes as well as to those of Clement VII who interposed July 1, 1531, and the sentence was not rendered until April 17, 1532.[766]

There was no occasion for royal interference with Inquisitors-general Tavera, Loaysa or Valdés. If the latter was forced to resign, in 1566, it was not by order of Philip II but of Pius V for his part, as we shall see hereafter, in the prosecution of Carranza, Archbishop of Toledo. So if Espinosa, in 1572, died in consequence of a reproof from Philip II, it was not for official misconduct and merely shows the depth of servility attainable by the courtiers of the period. The reign of the feeble Philip III however afforded several instances that the royal will sufficed to create a vacancy. He had scarce mounted on the throne as a youth of twenty, on the death of Philip II, September 13, 1598, before he sought to get rid of Inquisitor-general Portocarrero, who had, it is said, spoken lightly of him, or had incurred the ill-will of the favorite, the Duke of Lerma. To effect this, a bull was procured from Clement VIII requiring episcopal residence; Portocarrero was Bishop of Cuenca, a see reputed to be worth forty thousand ducats a year, but he preferred to abandon this and made fruitless efforts at Rome to be permitted to do so. He left Madrid in September, 1599, for Cuenca and died of grief within a twelve-month, refusing to make a will because, as he said, he had nothing to leave but debts that would take two years' revenue of his see to pay.[767] His successor, Cardinal Fernando Niño de Guevara fared no better. He was in Rome at the time of his appointment and did not take possession of his office until December 23, 1599, but already in May, 1600, there were rumors that he was to be superseded by Sandoval y Rojas, Archbishop of Toledo. Yet, in 1601, he was made Archbishop of Seville and he sought to purchase Philip's favor by a gift of forty thousand ducats and nearly all his plate. This was unavailing and, in January, 1602, he was ordered to reside in his see, when he dutifully handed in his resignation.[768] Juan de Zuñiga, who succeeded, had a clause in his commission permitting him to resign the administration of his see in the hands of the pope, but the precaution was superfluous for he died, December 20, 1602, after only six weeks' enjoyment of the office, for which he had sacrificed thirty thousand ducats a year from his see. He was old and feeble and his death was attributed to his coming in winter from a warm climate to the rigors of Valladolid, then the residence of the court.[769]

***

The question of non-residence was happily solved, for a time at least, by selecting as the next incumbent Juan Bautista de Azevedo, Bishop of Valladolid, the seat of the court. He was a person of so little consequence that the appointment aroused general surprise until it was recalled that he had been a secretary of Lerma. When the court removed to Madrid, in 1606, he was obliged to choose between the two dignities and his resignation of the bishopric was facilitated by granting him a pension of twelve thousand ducats on the treasury of the Indies, besides which, as Patriarch of the Indies, he had a salary of eight thousand.[770] His death soon followed, in 1608, when Sandoval y Rojas, the uncle of Lerma, obtained the position without sacrificing his primatial see of Toledo, a dispensation for non-residence being doubtless easily obtained by such a personage.

Sandoval was succeeded, in 1619, by Fray Luis de Aliaga, a Dominican who had been Lerma's confessor. In 1608 Lerma transferred him to the king, over whom his influence steadily increased, although his doubtful reputation is inferable from the popular attribution to him of the spurious continuation of Don Quixote, published in 1614 under the name of Avellaneda--a work of which the buffoonery and indecency are most unclerical.[771] Though he owed his fortune to Lerma, he joined, in 1618, in causing his patron's downfall in favor of Lerma's nephew, the Duke of Uceda, and during the rest of Philip's reign Uceda and Aliaga virtually ruled and misgoverned the land, filling the offices with their creatures, selling justice and intensifying the financial disorders which were bringing Spain to its ruin. When Philip IV succeeded to the throne, March 31, 1621, under tutelage to his favorite Olivares, their first business was to dismiss all who had been in power under the late king. The secular officials were easily disposed of, but the papal commission of the inquisitor-general rendered him independent of the king; he did not manifest the accommodating disposition of Portocarrero and Guevara and, as he was not a bishop, he could not be ordered to his see. It illustrates the anomalous position of the Inquisition, as part of an absolute government, that for some weeks the question of his removal was the subject of repeated juntas and consultations, but finally, April 23d, Philip wrote, ordering him to leave the court within twenty-four hours, for the Dominican Convent of Huete, where his superior would give him further instructions. He obeyed, but he refused the bishopric of Zamora and the continuance of his ecclesiastical revenues as the price of his resignation. The only method left was to obtain from Gregory XV the withdrawal of his delegated powers by representing his unworthiness, his guilty complicity with Uceda and Osuna and Philip III's reproach to him on his death-bed for misguiding his soul to perdition. Gregory listened favorably and Aliaga seems to have recognized the untenableness of his position and to have resigned, although no evidence of it exists. All we know is that Andrés Pacheco, Bishop of Cuenca, was appointed as his successor in February, 1622, and took possession of the office in April. Even after this Aliaga was an object of apprehension. In June, 1623, he came to Hortaleza, which was within a league or two of Madrid. Immediately the court was in a flutter; the king held earnest consultations; his propinquity was regarded as dangerous and he could not be allowed to return, as he had asked, to his native Aragon, which was in a chronically inflammable condition, while in Valencia his brother was archbishop; nor could he be allowed to leave the kingdom, possessing as he did so intimate a knowledge of state secrets. There were messages and active correspondence and finally he was allowed to settle in Guadalajara with ample means, where his remaining three years of life passed in obscurity. Llorente tells us that proceedings were commenced against him for propositions savoring of Lutheranism and materialism, which were discontinued after his death, a device doubtless adopted to keep him in retirement.[772]

***

Andrés Pacheco, who succeeded him in 1622, prudently resigned his see of Cuenca and, in spite of his audacious enforcement of inquisitorial claims, was allowed to hold the office until his death, April 7, 1626.[773] There was no haste in filling the vacancy, for it was not until August 6th that Olivares replied to the king's order to report in writing the best persons to fill the office. He named four, covertly indicating his preference for Cardinal Zapata, who had resigned the archbishopric of Burgos in 1605 and at the time was governor of that of Toledo. Philip followed the suggestion by an endorsement on the paper, which was a singularly informal appointment, remarking at the same time that the choice should not be made public until his successor at Toledo was selected.[774] His resignation of the office, in 1632, is commonly attributed to a request from the king, but this is by no means certain. He was more than eighty years of age and for some time had been talking of resigning; already in 1630 the Suprema alludes in a consulta to the publicity of his intention of relieving himself of the charge. Possibly at the end some gentle pressure may have been used, but when, September 6, 1632, the commission of his successor arrived, his parting with the king was in terms of mutual respect and good feeling. His retirement was softened by continuing to him his full salary and perquisites, amounting to 1,353,625 mrs. (3620 ducats) which, as the Suprema never had enough revenue for its desires, was not cordially welcomed.[775]

His successor, the Dominican Fray Antonio de Sotomayor, was Archbishop of Damascus in partibus and confessor of the king. He was already in his seventy-seventh year and, when he had held his office for eleven years, his infirmities and incapacity became more evident to others than to himself. Early in 1643 the fall of Olivares deprived him of support, his opposition to the king in the matter of appointments still further weakened his position and in June he was requested to resign in view of his advanced age and to preserve his health. He was much disturbed and consulted friends, who advised him to obey, but he still held on, saying that they might await his death. Greater pressure was applied to which he yielded. June 20th he made a formal notarial attestation of his desire to be relieved on account of his great age and the next day he sent in an ungracious resignation, followed, on the 24th by one addressed to the pope. His successor, Diego de Arce y Reynoso, Bishop of Plasencia, was already on the spot, exercising some of the functions, but Urban VIII hesitated to confirm the change and required explanations. It was not until September 18th that the commission of Arce y Reynoso was expedited and it only reached Madrid November 7th. Sotomayor was "jubilated" with half his salary of nine thousand ducats, which he enjoyed for five years longer.[776]

Arce y Reynoso, as we shall see, when embroiled with Rome in the prosecution of Villanueva, Marquis of Villalva, was obliged to resign his see of Plasencia, December 2, 1652, in order to retain his inquisitor-generalship. He continued in office until his death, June 20, 1665, followed by that of Philip, September 16th. During this interval, Philip gave the appointment to Pascual of Aragon, son of the Duke of Cardona and serving at the time as Viceroy of Naples. He promptly sailed for Spain and, though he is said to have resigned without acting, there are documents of October and November, 1665, which show that he performed the functions of the office.[777] He obtained the see of Toledo March 7, 1666, and desired to retain the inquisitor-generalship, but the Queen-regent, Maria Ana of Austria, compelled him to resign, in order to fill the place with her confessor and favorite the German Jesuit, Johann Everardt Nithard.[778]

***

Nithard, in 1668, boasted that he had had charge of the queen's conscience for twenty-four years, during which she had kept him constantly with her. He had thus moulded her character from youth and, as she was weak and obstinate, he had rendered himself indispensable. Her selection of him as inquisitor-general provoked lively opposition, which even reverence for royalty could not repress; protests were presented, leading to prolonged and heated discussion, but resistance was in vain.[779] He was appointed October 15, 1666, and speedily became the ruler of the kingdom which he misgoverned. The general dissatisfaction thus aroused was stimulated by the jealousy of the frailes, who had been accustomed to see Dominicans as royal confessors and whose hatred of the Company of Jesus was exacerbated by his combination of that position with the inquisitor-generalship. He was accused of filling the Holy Office with Jesuit calificadores, under whose advice he managed it, and with accumulating for himself pensions amounting to sixty thousand ducats a year. Spain at the time had a pinchbeck hero in the person of the second Don Juan of Austria, son of Philip IV by a woman known as la Calderona; he stood high in popular esteem, for he had the reputation of suppressing the Neapolitan revolt of 1648 and of ending the Catalan rebellion by the capture of Barcelona in 1652. Between him and Nithard there inevitably arose hostility which ripened into the bitterest hatred. To get him out of the country, he was given command of an expedition about to sail for Flanders; he went to Coruña but refused to sail; he was ordered to retire to Consuegra, whither a troop of horse was sent to arrest him, but he had fled to Catalonia, leaving a letter addressed to the queen in which he said that the execrable wickedness of Nithard had forced him to provide for his safety; his refusal to sail had been caused by his desire to remove from her side that wild beast, so unworthy of his sacred office; he did not propose to kill him for he did not wish to plunge into perdition a soul in such evil state, but he would devote himself to relieving the kingdom of this basilisk, confident that the queen would recognize the service thus rendered to the king.

    This letter and a similar one of November 13th were widely circulated and inflamed the popular detestation of Nithard. Don Juan stood forward as the champion of the people against the hated foreigner and continued to issue inflammatory addresses. Letters came pouring into the court, from the cities represented in the Córtes, praying the queen to accede to his demands but, though her councillors wavered, she stood firm. December 3d she wrote to him to return to Consuegra or to come near to Madrid, where negotiations could be carried on. While taking advantage of this he avoided the trap by writing that, as his life was endangered, her envoy, the Duke of Osuna, had furnished him with a guard of three companies of horse--about 250 men in all. With this escort he started from Barcelona by way of Saragossa. It was in vain that orders were sent from the court to insult him on the road. Everywhere his journey was like a royal progress. Nobles and peoples gathered to applaud him and, in Saragossa even the tribunal of the Inquisition bore a part, while the students carried around the effigy of a Jesuit and burnt it before the Jesuit house, forcing the rector to witness it from the window.

    As he drew near to Madrid with his handful of men, Nithard called on the nobles of his party to assemble with their armed retainers, but the Council of Regency prohibited this. Don Juan was in no haste; on February 9th he reached Junquera, some ten leagues from Madrid and, on the 22d, he was at Torrejon de Ardoz, about five leagues distant. Imminent danger was felt that if he advanced the populace would rise and murder the ministers to whom they attributed their sufferings, and all idea of resistance was abandoned. Nithard induced the papal nuncio to see Don Juan, February 24th, and ask further time for negotiation but at 9 P.M. the nuncio returned with word that Nithard must leave Spain at once. The Royal Council sat until 10 P.M. and reached the same conclusion. The next day the city was in an uproar; people carried their valuables to the convents for safe keeping and a mob assembled around the palace, where the Junto de Gobierno drew up a decree that Nithard must depart within three hours. It bore that he had supplicated permission to leave and in granting it the queen, to express her satisfaction with his services, appointed him ambassador to Germany or to Rome as he might elect, with retention of all his offices and salaries. The queen signed this and the Archbishop of Toledo and the Count of Peñaranda were deputed to carry it to Nithard, who received it without a trace of emotion and placed himself at their disposal. It was arranged that they should call for him at 6 P.M. The archbishop and the Duke of Maqueda came with two coaches and Nithard entered, carrying with him nothing but his breviary. Thrice, in the streets, the howling mob threatened an attack, but were deterred by the sight of a cross with which the archbishop had prudently provided himself. They drove him to Fuencarral, about two leagues from the city and left him at the house of the cura. The next day he went to San Agustin, about ten leagues distant, where he lingered for awhile in the vain hope of recall.

***

    Don Juan fell back to Guadalajara, where terms were agreed upon, the principal articles being that Nithard should immediately resign all his offices and never return to Spain and that Diego de Valladares, Don Juan's special enemy, should have nothing to do in any matter affecting him. Nithard accordingly went to Rome, but he had no commission to show and no instructions. He reported this to the Council of State, which told him to urge the definition by the Holy See of the Immaculate Conception. The queen endeavored by a subterfuge to obtain for him a cardinal's hat, which had been promised to Spain, but failed. He still hoped for a return to his honors, stimulated by the correspondence of his confidential agent, the Jesuit Salinas, but a letter warning him not to resign the inquisitor-generalship, for things were tending towards his return, with a lodging in the queen's palace, chanced to fall into the hands of the nuncio, who placed it where it would do the most good. The result was a peremptory order for him to resign in favor of Valladares, who had been nominated as his successor. When this was handed to him by San Roman, the Spanish ambassador, he is said to have fainted and not to have recovered his senses for an hour. The coveted cardinal's hat was bestowed on Portocarrero, Dean of Toledo, and when the news of this reached the queen it threw her into a tertian fever. The Jesuit General Oliva, seeing Nithard thus stripped of his offices and offended at his arrogance, ordered him to leave Rome and he retired to a convent, but he was amply provided with funds and, for some years at least, he was carried on the books of the Suprema and received his salary regularly. Moreover, in 1672, the queen procured from Clement X what Clement IX had persistently refused and Nithard was created Archbishop of Edessa and cardinal.[780]

Valladares had received his appointment September 15, 1669. It was not until 1677 that he resigned his see of Plasencia and he held the inquisitor-generalship until his death, January 29, 1695. He was succeeded by Juan Thomás de Rocaberti, Archbishop of Valencia, for whom Innocent XII, at the request of Carlos II, granted a dispensation from residence, conditioned on his making proper provision for the spiritual and temporal care of his see.[781] He died June 13, 1699, and his successor, Alfonso Fernández de Aguilar, Cardinal of Córdova, followed him September 19th, the very day that his commission arrived, after a brief illness and not without grave suspicions of poison.[782] The choice then fell on Balthasar de Mendoza y Sandoval, Bishop of Segovia, who became involved, as we shall see, in a deadly quarrel with his colleagues of the Suprema over the case of Fray Froilan Díaz. In the confusion of the concluding months of the disastrous reign of Carlos II, who died November 1, 1700, Mendoza made the mistake of embracing the Austrian side; his arbitrary action, in the case of Froilan Díaz, served as a sufficient excuse for his removal and Philip V, apparently in 1703, ordered him to return to his see. He is generally said to have resigned in 1705 but, in the papal commission, March 24, 1705, for his successor Vidal Marin, Clement XI states that he has seen fit to relieve Mendoza of the office because his presence is necessary at Segovia.[783] Vidal Marin served till his death in 1709 and so did his successor Riva-Herrera, Archbishop of Saragossa, who, however, enjoyed his dignity for little more than a year.

***

Philip V had brought to Spain the Gallicanism and the principles of high royal prerogative which were incompatible with the pretensions of the curia and the quasi-independence of the Inquisition. With the Bourbons there opens a new era in the relations between the crown and the Holy Office. Yet in his first open trial of strength, Philip's fatal vacillation, under the varying influences of his counsellors, confessors and wives, left him with a dubious victory. In 1711 he selected as inquisitor-general Cardinal Giudice, Archbishop of Monreal in Sicily, a Neapolitan of much ambition and little scruple. The recognition of the Archduke Charles as King of Spain by Clement XI, in 1709, had caused relations to be broken off between Madrid and Rome. Philip dismissed the nuncio, closed the tribunal of the nunciatura and forbade the transmission of money to Rome. There was talk in the curia of reviving the medieval methods of reducing disobedient monarchs to submission and Philip, to prepare for the struggle, ordered, December 12, 1713, the Council of Castile to draw up a statement of the regalías which would justify resistance to the demands of the curia and to the jurisdiction exercised by nuncios. It was a quarrel which had been in progress for a century and a half, now breaking out fiercely and then smothered, but none the less bitter. The Council entrusted the task to its fiscal, Melchor Rafael de Macanaz, a hard-headed lawyer, fully imbued with convictions of royal prerogative, whose report was, in general and in detail, thoroughly subversive of Ultramontanism and consequently most distasteful to the curia.[784] When it was presented to the council, December 19th, Don Luis Curiel and some others prevented a vote and asked for copies that they might consider the matter maturely. Copies were given to each member, consideration was postponed and on February 14, 1714, Molines, the ambassador at Rome, reported that copies had been sent there by Curiel, Giudice and Belluga, Bishop of Murcia. Although it was a secret state paper, the curia issued a decree condemning it and, coupled with it, an old work, Barclay's reply to Bellarmine and a French defence of the royal prerogative by Le Vayer, attributed to President Denis Talon. Such a decree could not be published in Spain without previous submission to the Royal Council, but Giudice was relied upon to evade this. He was nothing loath, for he had an old quarrel with Macanaz, who had prevented his obtaining the archbishopric of Toledo, his enmity being so marked that at one time Philip, to separate them, had sent Macanaz to France with the title of ambassador extraordinary, but without functions. At the moment Giudice was ambassador to France and the decree was sent to him; he declined to act unless assured of the protection of the courts of Rome and Vienna and, on receiving pledges of this, he signed it, July 30th as inquisitor-general and sent it to the Suprema for publication. Four of the members promptly signed it and had it published at high mass in the churches on August 15th. This created an immense sensation and exaggerated accounts were circulated of the errors and heresies contained in the unknown legal argument which Macanaz had prepared in the strict line of his duty.

When Philip was informed the next day of this audacious proceeding he called into consultation his confessor Robinet and three other theologians, who submitted on the 17th an opinion in writing that the Suprema should be required to suspend the edict and that Giudice should be dismissed and banished. The Suprema obeyed, excusing itself on the pretext that it had supposed, as a matter of course, that Giudice had submitted the edict to the king. He was not satisfied with this and dismissed three of them, but they refused to surrender their places. Then he summoned a meeting of the Council of Castile, pointing out that, if such things were permitted, the kingdom would be reduced to vassalage under the Dataria and other tribunals of the curia; the Council was not to separate until every member had recorded his opinion as to the measures to be taken. Seven of them voted for dismissing and banishing

Giudice, while four showed themselves favorable to the Inquisition. Meanwhile, on the 17th, Philip had despatched a courier to Paris summoning Giudice to return and informing Louis XIV of the affair. The latter, recognizing that the decree was an assault on the French as well as the Spanish regalías, refused to Giudice a farewell audience and sent his confessor Le Tellier to tell him that, were he not certain that Philip would punish him condignly, he would do so himself. When Giudice reached Bayonne he was met by an order not to enter Spain until the edict should be revoked. He replied submissively, enclosing his resignation, whereupon Philip commanded him to return to his archbishopric--a command which he did not obey. Felipe Antonio Gil de Taboada was appointed inquisitor-general and, on February 28, 1715, his commission was despatched from Rome; probably the Suprema interposed difficulties for he never served; he obtained the post of Governor of the Council of Castile, to be rewarded subsequently with the archbishopric of Seville.[785]

***

Meanwhile there was a court revolution. María Luisa of Savoy, Philip's wife, died February 11, 1714. The Princesse des Ursins, who had accompanied her to Spain and had become the most considerable personage in the kingdom, desired to find a new bride whom she could control. Giulio Alberoni, an adroit Italian adventurer, was then serving as the envoy of the Duke of Parma and persuaded her that Elisabeth Farnese, the daughter of his patron, would be subservient to her, and the match was arranged. December 11, 1714, Elisabeth reached Pampeluna and found Alberoni there ready to instruct her as to her course and his teaching bore speedy fruit. Des Ursins had also hastened to meet the new queen and was at Idiaguez, not far distant, where she received from the imperious young woman an order to quit Spain. Alberoni, who was in league with Giudice and hated Macanaz, painted him to Elisabeth in the darkest colors and his ruin was resolved upon.

He had been pursuing his duty as Fiscal-general of the Council of Castile; in July, 1714, he had occasion to make another report on the notorious evils of the Religious Orders, pointing out the necessity of their reform and asserting that the pope is not the master of ecclesiastical property and spiritual profits. Some months later he was called upon to draw up a complete reform of the Inquisition, suggested doubtless by the pending conflict, for which an occasion was found in an insolent invasion of the royal rights by the tribunal of Lima. The Council of Indies complained that the latter had removed from the administration of certain properties indebted to the royal treasury the person appointed by the Chamber of Accounts, on the plea that the owner was also a debtor to the Inquisition. Philip V thereupon ordered Macanaz, in conjunction with D. Martin de Miraval, fiscal of the Council of Indies, to make a report covering all the points on which the Holy Office should be reformed. The two fiscals presented their report November 14, 1714, exhaustively reviewing the invasions of the royal jurisdiction which, as we shall see hereafter, were constant and audacious, and their recommendations were framed with a view of rendering the Inquisition an instrument for executing the royal will, to the subversion of the jealously-guarded principle that laymen should be wholly excluded from spiritual jurisdiction.[786]

In the reaction wrought by Elisabeth and Alberoni, Macanaz was necessarily sacrificed. Philip, notoriously uxorious, speedily fell under the domination of his strong-minded bride and Alberoni became the all-powerful minister. Giudice, who had been loitering on the borders, was recalled and, on March 28, 1715, Philip abased himself by signing a most humiliating paper, evidently drawn up by Giudice, reinstating the latter and apologizing for his acts on the ground of having been misled by evil counsel.[787] Alberoni and Giudice, however, were too ambitious and too unprincipled to remain friends. Their intrigues clashed in Rome, the one to obtain a cardinal's hat, the other to advance his nephew. Alberoni had the ear of the queen and speedily undermined his rival. Giudice was also tutor of the young prince Luis; on July 15, 1716, he was deprived of the post and ordered to leave the palace and, on the 25th, he was forbidden to enter it. He fell into complete disfavor and shortly left Spain for Rome, where he placed the imperial arms over his door. His resignation must have followed speedily for, on January 23, 1717, the tribunal of Barcelona acknowledges receipt of an announcement from the Suprema that the pope has at last acceded to the reiterated requests of Cardinal Giudice to be allowed to resign and has appointed in his place D. Joseph de Molines, as published in a royal decree of January 9th.[788] Alberoni obtained the coveted cardinalate but his triumph was transient. He replaced the king's confessor, Father Robinet with another Jesuit, Father Daubenton, who soon intrigued against him so successfully and so secretly that the first intimation of his fall was a royal order, December 5, 1719, to leave Madrid within eight days and Spain in three weeks. He vainly sought an audience of Philip and was forced to obey.[789]

***

Although the episode of Giudice is thus closed, the fate of Macanaz is too illustrative of inquisitorial methods and of royal weakness to be passed over without brief mention. He had incurred the undying hatred of the Inquisition simply in discharge of his duty as an adviser of the crown, with perhaps an excess of zeal for his master and an intemperate patriotism that strove to restore its lost glories to Spain. It was impossible to continue him in his high function while recalling Giudice and, as a decent cover for banishment, he was allowed, in March, 1715, to seek the waters of Bagnères for his health, when he departed on an exile that lasted for thirty-three years to be followed by an imprisonment of twelve. Giudice promptly commenced a prosecution for heresy, sufficient proof of which, according to the standards of the Holy Office, was afforded by his official papers. As he dared not return, his trial in absentia resulted, as such trials were wont to do, in conviction, and he seems to have been sentenced to perpetual exile with confiscation of all his property, including even five hundred doubloons which the king was sending to him at Pau through a banker of Saragossa. All his papers and correspondence in the hands of his friends were seized and his brother, a Dominican fraile, whom the king had placed in the Suprema, was arrested in the hope of obtaining incriminating evidence.[790]

Thenceforth he led a life of wandering exile, so peculiar that it is explicable only by the character of Philip. He was in constant correspondence with high state officials and was frequently entrusted with important negotiations. Sometimes he was under salary, but it was irregularly paid and for the most part he had to struggle with poverty. When the Infanta María Ana Vitoria was sent back to Spain from France, in 1725, he was commissioned to attend her to the border and from there he went as plenipotentiary to the Congress of Cambray, with the comforting assurance that the king was endeavoring to put an end to the affair of the Inquisition--an effort apparently frustrated by the influence of Père Daubenton.[791] It was possibly with a view to overcome this fatal enmity that he occupied his leisure, between 1734 and 1736, in composing a defence of the Inquisition from the attacks of Dr. Dellon and the Abbé Du Bos. In this he had nothing but praise for its kindliness towards its prisoners, its scrupulous care to avoid injustice, the rectitude of its procedure and the benignity of its punishments. Beyond these assertions, the defence reduces itself to showing that, from the time when the Church acquired the power to persecute, it has persecuted heretics to the death and that the heretics in their turn have been persecutors--propositions readily proved from his wide and various stores of learning and sufficient to satisfy a believer in the semper et ubique et ab omnibus.[792] Ten years later, when Fernando VI ascended the throne in 1746, Macanaz addressed him a memorial on the measures requisite to relieve the misery of Spain and in this he superfluously urged the maintenance of the Inquisition in all its lustre and authority.[793] In spite of all this it was unrelenting and his entreaties to be allowed to return were fruitless.

In 1747 he was sent to the Congress of Breda where he mismanaged the negotiations, deceived, it is said, by Lord Sandwich. Relieved and ordered, in 1748, to present himself to the Viceroy of Navarre at Pampeluna, after some delay he was carried to Coruña and immured incomunicado in a casemate of the castle of San Antonio, a prison known as a place of rigorous confinement. Even the authorities there compassionated him and, at their intercession, he was removed to an easier prison and permitted the use of books and writing materials. Here, during a further captivity of twelve years, the indomitable old man occupied himself with voluminous commentaries on the Teatro crítico of Padre Feyjoo and the España sagrada of Florez, with many other writings and memorials to the king. It was not until the death of the latter, in 1760, that Elisabeth of Parma, the regent and the cause of his misfortunes, liberated him with orders to proceed directly to Murcia. At Leganes he was greeted by his wife and daughter, with whom he went to Hellin, his birth-place, where he died on the following November 2d, in his ninety-first year.[794]

***

There is no record of any further exercise of royal control over inquisitors-general until, in 1761, Clement XIII saw fit to condemn the Catechism of Mesengui for its alleged Jansenism in denying the authority of popes over kings. The debate over it in Rome had attracted the attention of all Europe and the prohibition of the book was regarded as a general challenge to monarchs. Carlos III had watched the discussion with much interest, especially as the work was used in the instruction of his son. He expressed his intention of not permitting the publication of the prohibition but, by a juggle between the nuncio and the inquisitor-general, Manuel Quintano Bonifaz, an edict of condemnation was hastily drawn up of which copies were given to the royal confessor on the night of August 7th. They did not reach the king at San Ildefonso until the morning of the 8th, who at once despatched a messenger to Bonifaz ordering him to suspend the edict and recall any copies that might have been sent out. Bonifaz replied that copies had already been delivered to all the churches in Madrid and forwarded to nearly all the tribunals; to suppress it would cause great scandal, injurious to the Holy Office, wherefore he deeply deplored that he could not have the pleasure of obeying the royal mandate. Carlos was incensed but contented himself with ordering Bonifaz to absent himself from the court; he obeyed and, in about three weeks, made an humble apology, protesting that he would forfeit his life rather than fail in the respect due to the king. Carlos then permitted him to return and resume his functions and, when the Suprema expressed its gratitude, he significantly warned it to remember the lesson.[795] He took warning himself and, on January 18, 1762, he issued a pragmática systematizing the examination of all papal letters before issuing the royal exequatur which permitted their publication.[796]

Carlos III had no further occasion to exercise his prerogatives but it was otherwise with Carlos IV. His first appointee, Manuel Abad y la Sierra, Bishop of Astorga, who assumed office May 11, 1793, had but a short term, for he was requested to resign in the following year. His successor, Francisco Antonio de Lorenzana, Archbishop of Toledo, who accepted the post September 12, 1794, was not much more fortunate, although his enforced resignation, in 1797, was decently concealed under a mission to convey to Pius VI the offer of a refuge in Majorca. He was followed by Ramon José de Arce y Reynoso, Archbishop of Saragossa, who resigned March 22, 1808, four days after the abdication of Carlos IV in the "tumult of lackeys" at Aranjuez, probably to escape his share of the popular odium directed against the favorite Godoy.[797] During the short-lived revival of the Inquisition under the Restoration, its dependence on the royal power was too great for differences to arise that would provoke assertions of the prerogative.

***

THE SUPREMA

The relations of the crown with the Suprema were originally the same as with the other royal councils. The king appointed and removed at will although, as the members came to exercise judicial functions, it was necessary for the inquisitor-general to delegate to them the papal faculties which alone conferred on them jurisdiction over heresy. Ferdinand exercised the power of appointment and removal and, as his orders were requisite for the receivers of confiscations to pay their salaries, it is scarce likely that anyone had the hardihood to raise a question.[798] We have seen how he forced the members to accept as a colleague Aguirre though he was a layman, how Ximenes when governor of Castile removed him and Adrian reinstated him. The earliest formula of commission that I have met is of the date of 1546; it bears that it is granted by the inquisitor-general, who constitutes the appointee a member and invests him with the necessary faculties, and it is moreover countersigned by the other members.[799] In this there is no allusion to any nomination by the king, although the appointment lay in his hands. In 1573 the Venitian envoy Leonardo Donato so states, adding that the popes felt very bitterly the fact that they had no participation in it; they had repeatedly tried to secure the membership of some one dependent upon them, such as the nuncio, but Philip would not permit it; the council did nothing without his consent, tacit or expressed.[800] At some period, not definitely ascertainable, the custom arose of the inquisitor-general presenting three names from among which the king made selection. At first the number of members was uncertain, but it came to be fixed at five, in addition to the inquisitor-general. To these Philip II added two from the Council of Castile; as these were sometimes laymen, he finally had scruples of conscience and, in his instructions to Manrique de Lara, in 1595, he tells him that when there are fitting ecclesiastics in the Council of Castile they are to be proposed to him for selection; if there are not, it is to be considered whether a papal brief should be procured to enable them to act in matters of faith.[801] These adventitious members came to be known as consejeros de la tarde, as they attended only twice a week and in the afternoon sessions of the body, where its secular business was disposed of, and thus they took no share in matters of faith. Their salary was one-third that of the others.

The royal authority was emphatically asserted when, in 1614, Philip III ordered that a supernumerary place should be made for his confessor Fray Aliaga, with precedence over his colleagues and a salary of fifteen hundred ducats; also that when the royal confessor was a Dominican he should always have this place and, when he was not, that it should be given to a Dominican. The Suprema accepted Aliaga but demurred to the rest, when Lerma peremptorily ordered it to be entered on the records; there were murmurings followed by submission. After the accession of Philip IV, he ordered the Council to make out a commission for his confessor, the Dominican Sotomayor, to which there was ineffectual opposition.[802] The rule held good. Soon after the Inquisition was reorganized under the Restoration, Fernando VII, July 10, 1815, appointed his confessor, Cristóbal de Bencomo, a member to serve without salary for the time but with the reversion of the first vacancy and all the honors due to his predecessors; he had the seat next to the dean and when the latter died, February 16, 1816, he took his position and salary.[803] Philip V ordered that a seat should always be occupied by a Jesuit; this of course lapsed with the expulsion of the Jesuits in 1767, after which Carlos III, in 1778, provided that the Religious Orders should have a representative by turns.[804]

***

The royal power of appointment was not uncontested and gave rise to frequent debates. Philip IV sometimes yielded and sometimes persisted; occasionally the question was complicated and papal intervention was hinted at.[805] A decisive struggle came in 1640, in which the Suprema chose its ground discreetly. It suited Olivares to appoint Antonio de Aragon, a youthful cleric and the second son of the Duke of Cardona. Anticipating resistance, Philip announced the nomination imperiously; Don Antonio must be admitted the next day as he was about to start for Barcelona and any representations against it could be made subsequently. The Suprema replied that the inquisitor-general could not make the appointment and if he did so it would be invalid; Don Antonio was less than thirty years old; the canons require an inquisitor to be forty, although Paul III had reduced for Spain, the age to thirty; members of the Suprema were inquisitors and it was only as such that they sat in judgement without appeal in cases of faith. To this Philip rejoined that Olivares would report the efforts he had made to quiet his conscience in view of the great public good to result from the appointment, wherefore he expected that possession would be given to Don Antonio without delay. Matters went so far that the Duchess of Cardona wrote to her son to abandon the effort but the royal command prevailed; he obtained the position and in the following year he was made a member of the Council of State; he was already a member of the Council of Military Orders and the whole affair gives us a glimpse of how Olivares governed Spain.[806] Having thus asserted his prerogative, Philip, in 1642 and the early months of 1643, made four appointments without consultation. The remonstrances of the Suprema must have been energetic for Philip yielded and, in a decree of June 26 (or July 2), 1643, he agreed that the old custom of submitting three names should be renewed, with the innovation that the Suprema should unite in making the recommendations. Against this the inquisitor-general protested, but in vain. It was probably to make an offset to these royal nominees that, November 10, 1643, the inquisitor-general and Suprema asked that their fiscal should have a vote, which Philip refused.[807] The rule continued of submitting three names for selection, but the participation of the Suprema in this seems to have been dropped. The royal control, moreover asserted itself in the case of Froilan Díaz when, by decree of November 3, 1704, Philip V reinstated three members, Antonio Zambrana, Juan Bautista Arzeamendi and Juan Miguélez, who had been arbitrarily ejected and jubilado by Inquisitor-general Mendoza, ordering moreover that they should receive all arrears of salary.[808]

***

While thus the crown continued to exercise the right of selecting the heads of the Inquisition, its practical control was greatly weakened by one or two changes which established themselves. Of these perhaps the most important was the claim of the Suprema to interpose itself between the king and the tribunals, so that no royal commands to them should be obeyed unless they should pass through it, thus rendering the inquisitors subject to itself alone and not to the sovereign. In a government theoretically absolute this was substituting bureaucracy for autocracy and, when the example was followed, though at a considerable distance, by some of the other royal councils, it at times produced deadlocks which threatened to paralyze all governmental action.

We have seen that, towards the end of Ferdinand's reign, his letters to the tribunals were sometimes countersigned by members of the Suprema, but that this was not essential to their validity and, when there was an attempt to establish such a claim, he was prompt to vindicate his authority. A royal cédula of October 25, 1512, gave certain instructions as to the manumission of baptized children of slaves whose owners had suffered confiscation. There was no question of faith involved, but when, in 1514, Pedro de Trigueros applied to the inquisitors of Seville to be set free under it, they refused on the ground that it had not been signed by the Suprema. He appealed to Ferdinand who promptly ordered the inquisitors to obey it; if they find Pedro's story to be true they are to give him a certificate of freedom and meanwhile are to protect him from his master, who was seeking to send him to the Canaries for sale.[809] The claim which Ferdinand thus peremptorily rejected was persistently maintained during the period of confusion which followed his death. Whether it received positive assent from Charles is more than doubtful, although the Suprema so asserts in a letter of July 27 1528, ordering inquisitors to examine whether a certain royal cédula had been signed by its members, for the kings had ordered that none should be executed in matters connected with the Inquisition unless thus authenticated--thus basing the claim on the royal will and not on any inherent right of the Holy Office.[810] So complete was the autonomy thus established for the organization that a carta acordada or circular of instructions May 12, 1562, tells the tribunals that, if an inquiry from the king comes to them through any other council, they are to reply that if the king desires the information it will be furnished to him through the inquisitor-general or the Suprema.[811]

***

The far-reaching importance of this principle can scarce be exaggerated. One of its results will be seen when we come to consider the complaints and demands of the Córtes and find that fueros directed against inquisitorial aggressions, in purely civil matters, when agreed to by the king were invalid without confirmation by the inquisitor-general. A single instance here will suffice to show the working of this. In 1599 various demands of the Córtes of Barcelona were conceded by Philip III. One regulated the number of familiars, which Philip promised that he would induce the inquisitor-general to put into effect, within two months if possible. Another provided that all officials, save inquisitors, should be Catalans; he agreed to charge the inquisitor-general and Suprema to observe this and he would get it confirmed by the pope. Another was that, in the secular business of the tribunal, the opinion of the Catalan assessor should govern, because he would be familiar with the local law; this he accepted and promised, in so far as it concerned the inquisitor-general and Suprema, to charge them to give such orders to the tribunal. Another was that commissioners and familiars should not be "religious," to which his reply was the same. Another required the inquisitor-general to appoint a resident of Barcelona to hear appeals in civil cases below five hundred libras; this he said was just and he would charge the inquisitor-general to do so. After this, in fulfilment of his plighted word, he addressed the inquisitor-general in terms almost supplicatory "I charge you greatly that for your part you condescend and facilitate that what they have supplicated may be put in execution, in conformity with what I have conceded and decreed in each of these articles, which will give me particular contentment." Not the slightest attention was paid to this request and, on May 6, 1603, Philip repeated it "As until now it is understood that not a single thing contained in it has been put in execution and, as I desire that it be enforced, I ask and charge you to condescend to it and help and facilitate it with the earnestness that I confidently look for."[812] This second appeal was as fruitless as the first and the Catalans gained nothing. It is true that, in 1632, the Barcelona tribunal, in a memorial to Philip IV, asserted that Philip III had only assented to these articles to get rid of the Catalans and that he wrote privately to the pope asking him not to confirm them.[813]

This case may have been mere jugglery and collusion, but in general it by no means followed that royal decrees sent to the Suprema for transmission were forwarded. If it objected, it would respond by a consulta arguing their impropriety or illegality, and this would, if necessary, be repeated three or four times at long intervals until, perhaps, the matter was forgotten or dropped or some compromise was reached. The privilege that all instructions must be transmitted through the Suprema was therefore one of no little importance and it was insisted upon tenaciously. There was a convenient phrase invented which we shall often meet--obedecer y no cumplir--to obey but not to execute, which was very serviceable on these occasions. In 1610 the Suprema argued away a cédula of Philip III as invalid because it had been despatched through the Council of State and the king was repeatedly told to his face that the laws required his cédulas to be countersigned by the Suprema in order to secure their execution. This was done to Philip IV, in 1634, when he intervened in a quarrel and, in 1681 to Carlos II when there were difficulties threatened with foreign nations arising from abuses committed in examining importations in search of forbidden books.[814] As the questions calling for royal interposition as a rule affected only the wide secular and not the spiritual jurisdiction of the Inquisition, this created conditions unendurable in any well-organized government.

***

Another change which conduced greatly to the independence of the Inquisition was the control which it acquired over its finances. We have seen that, under Ferdinand, the confiscations and pecuniary penances belonged to the crown and that the salaries and expenses were paid by his orders. The finances of the Inquisition will be discussed hereafter and meanwhile it suffices to say that, after his death and the exuberant liberality of Charles to his Flemish favorites during his first residence in Spain, the diminishing receipts from these sources caused them to be virtually assigned to defraying the expenses of the Inquisition and they were no longer regarded as a source of supply to the royal treasury. Still, the money belonged to the crown and the Inquisition enjoyed it only under the authority and by virtue of the bounty of the sovereign.

FINANCIAL INDEPENDENCE

The growth of control over income and of virtual financial independence was gradual and irregular. Even Ferdinand, in his watchful care over his receivers of confiscations, felt the need of some central auditor and it seemed natural that he should be an official of the Suprema. Accordingly as early as 1509 we find a "contador general" in that position. In 1517 there are two officers, a contador and a receiver-general and, in 1520, the two are merged into one.[815] When, in 1513, Bishop Mercader was made inquisitor-general of Aragon he desired a statement from all receivers of their receipts and payments and of the property remaining in their hands and Ferdinand ordered them to comply, alluding to it as usual on the entrance of a new inquisitor-general.[816] This inevitably ripened into the transfer to that official of the control over receivers which Ferdinand had exercised, so that in place of being royal officials they became virtually officers of the Inquisition and eventually were designated as treasurers. By 1544 we find the Suprema to be the final court of revision of all the receivers of the local tribunals, whose accounts were rendered to it and audited by it.[817]

Still, in theory the money belonged to the crown and its disbursement could only be made under royal authority. The order for the payment of the ayuda de costa of the Suprema, July 21, 1517, was drawn in the name of la reyna y el rey--Juana and Charles.[818] After Charles reached Spain, in September of that year he made grants from the confiscations with a profusion that threatened to bankrupt the Inquisition, and if we find Adrian and the Suprema also occasionally issuing orders for payments it was undoubtedly under powers granted by Charles.[819] When Charles left Spain, May 20, 1520, he gave Adrian a general faculty for this purpose, but it seems to have been called in question, for he found it necessary to send from Brussels, September 12th, a cédula to all receivers confirming it and stating that Adrian's orders, signed by members of the Suprema, would be received as vouchers by the auditor-general. Under this the Suprema exercised full authority over the funds collected by all the receivers and disposed of them at its pleasure. When Charles returned he presumably resumed control and, after his marriage with Isabel of Portugal, during his frequent absences, he left the power in her hands until her death May 1, 1539.[820] When he saw fit, moreover, he claimed and received a share of the spoils. A letter of Cardinal Manrique, June 17, 1537, shows that a portion of the proceeds of a certain auto de fe had been paid to him and another of October 11th, of the same year, addressed to him at the Córtes of Monzon, reinforces an appeal not to sacrifice the interests of the Inquisition to the Aragonese demands, with the welcome news that the receiver of Cuenca had arrived with the ten thousand ducats for which he had asked from the confiscations of that tribunal.[821]

Charles's hasty departure in November, 1539, to quell the insurrection of Ghent left matters in some confusion. The Suprema, on March 20, 1540, wrote to Chancellor Granvelle that cédulas for the salaries, under the crown of Aragon, were always signed by the emperor and that the inquisitor-general could not do it; they had sent him a power for execution similar to that given to Cardinal Adrian but he had refused to sign it, saying that they could do as under Cardinal Manrique, forgetting that there had been the empress who always signed the cédulas, wherefore they ask him to get the emperor to sign the power. He doubtless did so, for an order, June 12th, on the receiver of Valencia to send fifteen hundred ducats for the salaries of the Suprema purports to be by virtue of a special power granted by their majesties. On Charles's return he again assumed control and when he went to Italy, in 1543, he left Philip as regent, while during the absence of Philip there were successive regents who signed cédulas as called for by the Suprema.[822]

Yet, in spite of these formalities, the control of the crown was becoming scarcely more than nominal. It is true that, in 1537, Cardinal Manrique declared that he could not increase salaries without the royal assent but, when the crown undertook any exercise of power, the little respect paid to its commands is seen in the fate of an application made in 1544, by Juan Tomás de Prado, notary of the tribunal of Saragossa, to Prince Philip for an ayuda de costa of three hundred ducats. Philip ordered his prayer to be granted, but the death of Inquisitor-general Tavera served as a convenient pretext for disregarding the command. It was repeated, for the same amount, January 11, 1548, and finally, on June 4th, Inquisitor-general Valdés authorized the payment of a hundred ducats.[823]

***

To perfect the absolute control of the confiscations, thus gradually assumed, it was necessary to keep the crown in ignorance of their amount. Its right to them was incontestable, and the Inquisition deliberately abused the confidence reposed in it when their collection was left in its hands. The less the king was allowed to know, the less likely he was to claim his share and the policy was adopted of deceiving him. As early as 1560 we have evidence of this in a letter to the inquisitors of Sicily instructing them, when reporting autos de fe to the king, to suppress all statements as to the confiscations, but to report them to the Suprema so that it may determine how far to inform him. This was doubtless a general mandate to all the tribunals; it was repeated in instructions of 1561 and we shall see that it became a settled practice.[824] This systematic concealment was the more indefensible from the fact that the Inquisition was now obtaining funds from other sources than confiscations. We shall see hereafter how it utilized the scare caused by the discovery of Protestantism in Valladolid and Seville in 1558, with the plea of additional expenses thus caused, to obtain from Paul IV a levy of a hundred thousand gold ducats on the revenues of the clergy and the more permanent endowment of a canonry to be suppressed for its benefit in every cathedral and collegiate church. A large portion of the inquisitors, moreover already held canonries and other benefices for which, under a brief of Innocent VIII, February 11, 1485, they were dispensed for non-residence.[825] The burden of the Holy Office was thus thrown largely on the ecclesiastical establishment, which remonstrated and resisted but was compelled to submit. It could thus look with equanimity on the shrinkage of the confiscations. In Valencia, an agreement was reached, in 1571, by which the Moriscos compounded for them with an annual payment to the tribunal of twenty-five hundred ducats.[826] The Judaizing heretics had been largely eliminated, especially the more wealthy ones, and it was not until some years after the conquest of Portugal, in 1580, that the influx of Portuguese New Christians brought a new and profitable harvest.

All this tended to the financial independence of the Inquisition although the crown by no means abandoned its claim on the confiscations. A book of receipts given by the royal representative in Valencia for the proceeds of the confiscations in 1593 shows that, under the financial pressure of the time, Philip II was reasserting his rights.[827] The treasury was empty when Philip III succeeded to the throne in 1598 and, among his expedients to raise money, he ordered the receivers of the tribunals to send to him all the funds in their hands, promising speedy repayment. The Suprema had no faith in the royal word and instructed the tribunals to retain enough to meet their own wants. The obedience of the tribunals was by no means prompt and the Suprema was obliged to order Valencia to comply with the royal demand and to furnish an oath that no money was left.[828]

In the earlier years of Philip IV the tendency of the Inquisition to emancipate itself from royal control grew rapidly. We shall see hereafter that when, in 1629, the king called for a statement of salaries and perquisites the Suprema equivocated and suppressed nearly all the information required. Still more significant was its attitude respecting the colonial tribunals, which the king supported under an annual expenditure of thirty thousand pesos, with the understanding that this should cease when the confiscations should become sufficient. These, which had been small at first, rapidly increased in the seventeenth century and were enormous between 1630 and 1650, when the whole trading communities of Peru and Mexico were shattered, enabling the tribunals to make permanent investments that rendered them wealthy, besides sending heavy remittances to the Suprema, which moreover seized the goods and credits in Seville of the colonial Judaizers. In addition to this, in 1627, a prebend in each cathedral was suppressed for the benefit of the tribunals. Yet the salaries were still demanded of the royal treasury and the repeated efforts of Philip III and Philip IV, from 1610 to 1650, to obtain statements of the receipts from confiscations and pecuniary penances were completely baffled. That was an inviolable secret which no royal official was allowed to penetrate. It is true that the colonial tribunals, on their side, adopted the same policy in concealing, as far as they could, from the Suprema the extent of their own gains.[829]

DEMANDS OF THE CROWN

Yet, in the ever-increasing distress of the crown, demands were made upon the Inquisition, as on all other departments of government, demands which it was forced to meet. Thus, for the ten years, 1632 to 1641 inclusive, an annual sum of 2,007,360 mrs. was required of it, to aid in defraying the cost of garrisons and fleet, and a statement of October 11, 1642, shows that it had paid the aggregate of 11,583,110 in vellon and 18,700 in silver, leaving a balance still due of 8,474,790.[830] Evidently there was good reason for concealing its revenues. In the frightful confusion of the finances which followed the revolution of Portugal and the revolt of Catalonia, in 1640, while Spain was heroically battling for existence against France and its rebellious subjects, the demands were varied and incessant--sometimes for sums so small as to reveal the absolute penury of the State--and Philip's impatient urgency, as he chafed under the dilatoriness of the responses, shows the desperate emergencies in which he was involved. In 1643 a royal decree of February 16th ordered all officials to send their silver plate to the mint, a watch being kept and a report made so as to see that each sent a quantity proportioned to his station. To a complaint of delay in performance the Suprema replied that those who had sent in their silver could get no satisfaction from the mint--the delays were such that the promptitude required by the king was impossible.[831]

Even more arbitrary was the seizure, in 1644 at Seville, of a remittance of 8676 ducats in silver, a remittance from the colonial tribunals to the Suprema. In protesting against this the Suprema, February 29th, gave a deplorable account of its condition, owing to the demands made upon it by the king. On the 10th he had called upon it for 16,000 ducats which it would be wholly unable to raise if deprived of the silver that had been seized. It was already short in 7,724,843 mrs. of its annual expenses and the provincial tribunals were short 5,318,000, for it had impoverished them to meet the royal demands. Last year it had sold a censo of 18,000 ducats belonging to the tribunal of Saragossa, which was beseeching its return. It had also given the king 10,000 ducats for the cavalry and to raise this amount it had taken the sequestrations in the tribunal of Seville--a sacred deposit--including 20,000 ducats' worth of wool, the owners of which, having been acquitted, were besieging it for their money. This dolorous plaint was effective in so far that the seizure at Seville was credited on account of the demand for 16,000 ducats.[832] How much of it was true we can only guess, for the Inquisition had means of raising money outside of its judicial functions. When, in 1640, the king summoned its familiars and officials to render military service like the nobles, the Suprema arranged that they should buy themselves off, and from this source was chiefly raised 40,000 ducats expended on two companies of horse, in return for which, by a cédula of September 2, 1641, the king promised to maintain inviolate the privileges and exemptions of the familiars and officials.[833]

These instances, out of many, will suffice to show how the crown, in its days of distress, was recouping itself for abandoning the spoils of the heretics. In time these special and arbitrary demands were systematized into an annual requirement of fifty horses, estimated at an outlay of about 5500 ducats and the raising and equipping of two hundred foot, costing 8000 ducats. The Suprema was in no wise prompt in meeting these demands; a cédula of June 24, 1662, tells it that what is due for the present year as well as the previous arrears, must be paid at once, otherwise an inventory of its property must be given to the president of the treasury, who will raise the money on it.[834] Subsequently there was a feeble attempt to return some of these contributions and, in each of the years 1673 and 1674, a trifling payment was made of 10,000 reales vellon, but, in 1676, the Suprema stated to Carlos II that in all it had furnished for remounts of horses 90,000 ducats vellon and 10,000 in silver and that its total assistance to the crown had amounted to no less than 800,000 pesos, equivalent to over 500,000 ducats, to accomplish which the salaries in many tribunals had been unpaid and vacancies of necessary offices had remained unfilled.[835] Still, as we shall have occasion to see, the Suprema always had money, not only for an undiminished pay-roll but for perquisites and amusements.

CLAIM ON THE CONFISCATIONS

The crown could not accept this assistance, however grudgingly rendered, without a sacrifice of its supremacy and the Inquisition came to treat with it as with an independent body. About this time the Suprema happens to mention, in a letter to the tribunal of Lima, that it had lent the king 40,000 pesos, of which 10,000 came from Peru and 30,000 from Mexico and that the Count of Medellin had become security for the return of the loan, as though it were a banker dealing with a merchant.[836] Yet all parties knew that these colonial remittances were derived from confiscations, the ownership of which the crown had never relinquished. This is the more noteworthy because, about this time, the king suddenly asserted his claims on some large sums which could not be wholly concealed. In 1678 the tribunal of Majorca unexpectedly made a successful raid on the whole New Christian population of Palma and, in the early months of 1679, there were more than two hundred penitents reconciled. As they constituted the active trading element of the place the confiscations were enormous and the affair attracted too much attention to be hidden. As soon as the news came of the arrests, the king wrote, May 20, 1678, to the viceroy to look carefully to the sequestrations because, in case of confiscation, the proceeds belonged to the treasury. The Suprema, however, made him hold his hands off with direful threats and kept control of the liquidation. After the condemnations, a consulta of July 5, 1679, shows that 50,000 pesos had already been paid to the king, but that the Inquisition was resolved to have its full share. In November the king acceded to a compromise under which 200,000 pesos were to be used to endow certain tribunals and to cancel certain loans made to him by the Inquisition--probably those just alluded to. The balance coming to him was estimated at 250,000 pesos but, in the handling of the assets and the settlements with creditors, the property melted away till the Suprema reported that it barely sufficed to meet the portion assigned to the Inquisition and finally, in 1683, the king had to content himself with 18,000 pesos spent on the fortifications of Majorca and the payment to him of 2000, which the Suprema assured him that it advanced at considerable risk to itself.[837]

The secretiveness so carefully observed undoubtedly had its advantages or it would not have been so persistently claimed as a right. In a consulta of 1696 the Count of Frigiliana states that, when he was viceroy of Valencia, he had in vain endeavored to get from the tribunal a statement of its affairs and he asked the king whether or not the Inquisition possessed the privilege of rendering no account of its assets and income.[838] At length the quarrel between Inquisitor-general Mendoza and his colleagues, in the case of Froilan Díaz, and his banishment to his see in 1703, gave opportunity for royal intervention and investigation. The War of Succession had deranged the finances of the Inquisition and it had appealed to the king for help. He required a statement of the pay-rolls, investments and revenues of all the tribunals, which was furnished March 9, 1703, after which, on May 27th, he issued a decree declaring that he must put an end to the abuses and disorders which had crept into the administration and disbursement of its property, in order to relieve the embarrassment of which it complained. He therefore annulled all commissions and appointments without obligation of service, granted by the inquisitor-general, whether within or outside of Spain. The papers of all jubilations, new places and gratuities created or granted since the time of Valladares (1695) were to be placed in his hands. In no case thereafter should the inquisitor-general jubilate any official of the Suprema or local tribunal without consulting him, and any such act issued without a previous royal order was declared void. No ayuda de costa or grant exceeding thirty ducats vellon, for a single term, was to be made without awaiting his decision and this decree was to be placed in the hands of all receivers or treasurers for their guidance. It was so transmitted June 8th, with strict orders for its observance. This was a resolute assertion of the royal control over the finances of the Inquisition and it held good, in theory at least, however much it may have been eluded in practice. About the middle of the eighteenth century a systematic writer describes it as still in force and states that no salaries can be increased without the royal approval. It so continued to the end and, under the Restoration, an order from the king, countersigned by the Suprema, was requisite for any extraordinary disbursement.[839]

FINES AND PENANCES

Philip also reasserted and made good the right of the crown to the confiscations, by claiming a percentage of the rentals of all confiscated property, but he listened to appeals from the tribunals and, in 1710, we hear of Saragossa and Valencia being practically restored to their enjoyment, a liberality which was doubtless followed with regard to the others. In 1725 Valencia expressed its fear that the alliance with Austria against England, France and Prussia would result in its having to restore the confiscations, and the blow seems to have fallen for, in 1727, the suprema, in a consulta of December 9th, describing the poverty of Saragossa, attributes it to the king having taken away the confiscations which he had granted. With the gradual amelioration in the Spanish finances, this source of revenue must have been restored, for, in 1768, the Inquisition is described as enjoying the confiscations which the pious liberality of the monarchs had bestowed.[840]

***

There were other sources of revenue--rehabilitations or dispensations from the sanbenito and disabilities, commutations of punishment and the pecuniary penances known as penas y penitencias. All these will be considered hereafter, but a few words may be said as to the latter in their relation with the royal authority.

The penitents who were reconciled under Edicts of Grace were not subject to confiscation, but were punished with fines under the guise of pecuniary penance, at the discretion of the inquisitor. We have seen (pp. 169-70) how numerous these were and we can conjecture how large were the sums thus exacted, for penances of a half or a third of the penitent's property were not uncommon. Similar fines also usually accompanied sentences that did not embrace confiscation and formed a continual although fluctuating source of revenue. Sometimes there were special officials for their collection but, when this was entrusted to the receivers of confiscations, they were instructed to keep a separate account of them, as the two funds were held to be essentially different and, as a rule, were to be employed for different purposes.

In the earliest Instructions of 1484, these pecuniary penances are said to be imposed as a limosna, or alms, to aid the sovereigns in the pious work of warring with the Moors, but, in the Instructions issued a few months later by Torquemada, this is modified by ordering them to be placed in the hands of a trustworthy person and reports to be made to him or to the king, in order that they may be spent on the war or in other pious uses or in paying the salaries of the Inquisition.[841] Both the destination and the control of these funds were thus left undetermined and they so continued for some years. In 1486 we find Ferdinand giving orders for sums from this source for various uses--for the war with Granada, to pay the salaries of a lay judge, to pay expenses of a tribunal of the Inquisition, to repay Luis de Santangel for advances made to tribunals; in one case his tone is apologetic and he asks Torquemada to confirm the order, in others his command is absolute.[842]

This indicates the uncertainty which existed both as to the use and the control of the pecuniary penances. So long as lasted the war with Granada, whatever was taken by the crown might be regarded as devoted, directly or indirectly, to that holy object, but when the conquest was achieved, in January, 1492, that excuse no longer existed and doubtless the inquisitors looked with jealousy upon the diversion to secular objects of the proceeds of their pious labors. The confiscations unquestionably belonged to the crown, but the penances were spiritual funds which for centuries had always enured to the Church. There must have been a sustained effort to withhold them from the royal acquisitiveness, to which Ferdinand was not disposed to yield, for he procured from Alexander VI, February 18, 1495, a brief directing the inquisitors to hold all such moneys subject to the control of the sovereigns, to be disposed of at their pleasure. Even this was resisted and Ferdinand and Isabella complained to the pope that they were unable to compel an accounting of the sums received or to collect the amounts, to correct which Alexander issued another brief, March 26, 1495, commissioning Ximenes, then Archbishop of Toledo, to enforce accounting and payment by excommunication and other censures.[843]

***

This was equally ineffective. There was a privacy and simplicity in the imposition and collection of a penance very different from the procedure of sequestration and confiscation, and Ferdinand, at least for a time, abandoned the struggle. This is manifested by a clause in the Instructions of 1498, enjoining on inquisitors not to impose penances more heavily than justice requires in order to insure the payment of their salaries,[844] and the principle was formally recognized by Ferdinand and Isabella in a cédula of January 12, 1499, reciting that, although they held a papal brief placing at their disposal all moneys arising from penances, commutations and rehabilitations, yet they grant to the inquisitors-general all collections from these sources, both in Castile and Aragon, to be used in paying salaries, disbursements being made only on their order.[845]

Ferdinand, however, was not disposed to relax, on any point, his control over the Inquisition and, on April 10th of the same year, we find him forbidding the levying of penances on the members of a town-council for fautorship of heresy--doubtless a speculative infliction for some assumed neglect in arresting suspects. In 1501 his renunciation is already forgotten and he is making grants from the penances as absolutely as ever--even empowering Inquisitor-general Deza to use those of Valencia, to the extent of a hundred ducats a year for the salary of Jaime de Muchildos, the Roman agent of the Inquisition.[846] So, in 1511, we find him granting to Enguera, Inquisitor-general of Aragon, a thousand libras out of the penances to defray the expenses of his bulls for the see of Lérida and authorizing him to pay from them an ayuda de costa of two hundred ducats to Joan de Gualbes, a member of the Aragonese Suprema. Then, in 1514, he places all the penances unreservedly at the disposal of Inquisitor-general Mercader to be employed on the salaries and other necessary expenses of the Inquisition of Aragon. This seems to have been final. After his death, instructions sent to the tribunal of Sicily assume that the inquisitor-general has sole and absolute control. It was the same in Castile. Instructions issued by Ximenes, in 1516, direct the receiver-general, who was an officer of the Suprema, to collect the penances from the receivers of the tribunals, who were to keep them in a separate account and not to disburse them without an order from the inquisitor-general. After this we find the Suprema in full control.[847]

There is virtually no trace of any interference subsequently by the crown, and the Inquisition found itself in possession of an independent and by no means inconsiderable source of revenue which it could levy, almost at will, from those who fell into its hands. The only exception to this that I have met is that Philip IV, in his financial distress, by a decree of September 30, 1639, claimed and collected twenty-five per cent. of fines, but he scrupulously limited this to those inflicted in cases not connected with the faith--that is, in the exercise of the royal jurisdiction, civil and criminal, enjoyed by the Inquisition in matters concerning familiars and other officials.[848]

***

IRRESPONSIBILITY

Though, as we have seen, the independence of the Inquisition, as a self-centered and self-sustaining institution in the State, varied with the temper and the necessities of the sovereign, there was a time when it seemed as though it might throw off all subjection and become dominant. But for the prudence of Ferdinand, in insisting upon the power of appointment and dismissal, this might have happened in the temper of the Spanish people, trained to an exaltation of detestation of heresy which to us may well appear incomprehensible. There is no question that, under the canon law, kings, like their subjects, were amenable to the jurisdiction of the Inquisition and that they held their kingdoms on the tenure not only of their own orthodoxy but of purging their lands of heresy and heretics. The principles which had been worked so effectually for the destruction of the Houses of Toulouse and of Hohenstaufen and under which Pius V released the subjects of Queen Elizabeth from their allegiance, in 1570, were fully recognized in Spain as vital to the faith.[849] But beyond this the Spaniards, in the exuberance of their religious ardor, boasted that their national institutions conditioned orthodoxy as necessary to their kingship. Even when the seventeenth century was well advanced, a learned and loyal jurisconsult tells us that, from the time of the sixth Council of Toledo, in 638, their monarchs had imposed on themselves the law that, if they fell into heresy, they were to be excommunicated and exterminated; that Ferdinand, in 1492, had renewed this law and that he had instituted that most severe tribunal the Inquisition and had sanctioned that, in view of the Toledan canon, all kings in future should be subject to it.[850] Even Spanish loyalty could not have been relied upon to sustain a king suspect of heresy, against the claims of the Holy Office to try him in secret, and suspicion of heresy was a very elastic term. Impeding the Inquisition came within its definition and any effort to curb the arrogant extension of its powers could readily be so construed, as Macanaz found to his sorrow. The fact that the Inquisition possessed such power must have had its influence more than once on the mind of the sovereign when engaged in debate with his too powerful subject and perhaps explains what appears to us occasionally a pusillanimous yielding.

The monarchs had guarded the Inquisition against all supervision and all accountability to the other departments of government. Within its own sphere it was supreme and irresponsible and its sphere, owing to the exemption from the secular courts accorded to all connected with it in however remote a degree, covered a large area of civil and criminal business, besides its proper function of preserving the purity of the faith. In this self-centered independence it stood alone. Even the spiritual jurisdiction of the Church, so jealously guarded, had become subject to the recurso de fuerza, which, like the French appel comme d'abus, gave to those who suffered wrong an appeal to the Council of Castile.[851] But even from this the Inquisition was exempt. A decree of Prince Philip, in 1553, was its ægis and was constantly invoked. This was addressed to all the courts and judicial officers of the land and affirmed, in the most positive terms, the sole and exclusive jurisdiction of the Inquisition in all matters within its competence, civil or criminal, concerning the faith or confiscations--and faith was a convenient term covering the impeding of the Inquisition in all that it wanted to do. Philip recited that repeated cédulas of Ferdinand and Isabella and of Charles V had asserted this and now he reaffirmed and enforced it. No appeals from its tribunals were to be entertained, for the only appeal lay to the Suprema, which would redress any wrong, for it, by delegation from the crown and the Holy See, had exclusive cognizance of such matters. If therefore anything concerning the Inquisition should be brought before them they must decline to entertain it and must refer it back to the Holy Office.[852]

The Inquisition was not content to enjoy these favors as a revocable grace from the crown but, in a consulta of December 22, 1634, it advanced the claim that this decree was a bargain or compact between two powers which could not be in any way modified without mutual consent.[853] This was emphasized in a printed argument in 1642, asserting that that transaction could only become of binding force by the consent of both parties--the king and the inquisitor-general--and the king had no power to change it of his own motion, as it was an agreement. Even were it admitted to be a concession granted by the crown, this would make no difference, for a privilege conceded to one who is not a subject (as the Inquisition in the present case) and accepted by the latter becomes a contract which the prince cannot revoke.[854]

EFFORTS AT INDEPENDENCE

We shall see hereafter the use made of this by the Inquisition in its daily quarrels with all the other jurisdictions, but a single case may be cited here to indicate how it utilized this position to render itself virtually independent. There was a long-standing debate over canonries in the churches of Antequera, Málaga and the Canaries, which it claimed to be suppressed for its benefit under the brief of January 7, 1559, but which the royal Camara asserted to belong to the patronage of the king, whose rights of appointment were not curtailed by the brief. A suit on the subject, commenced in 1562, was not yet decided when, about 1611, the king filled vacancies in Málaga and the Canaries. This provoked a discussion, during which, without awaiting settlement, the inquisitors excommunicated the appointees-- and an inquisitorial excommunication could be removed only by him who had fulminated it, by the inquisitor-general or by the pope. In 1611 the king ordered the appointees to be absolved and mandates signed by him to that effect were addressed to the inquisitors of Málaga and the Canaries. The Suprema complained loudly of this as an unheard of violation of the rights of the Holy Office and refused obedience. In 1612 it declared that, when the appointees abandoned the prebends which they had usurped, they should be absolved and not before. On February 12th, in a consulta to the king, it argued that its power had always been so great and so independent of all other bodies in the State that the kings had never allowed them to interfere with it, directly or indirectly; it determined for itself everything relating to itself, consulting only with the king and permitting no interference of any kind. Its determination prevailed over the weakness of the king who ordered the Camara to desist from its pretensions and not to despoil the Holy Office.[855]

These somewhat audacious assertions of independence were chiefly stimulated by the perpetual quarrels arising from the exclusive jurisdiction, civil and criminal, exercised by the Inquisition over its thousands of employees and familiars and their families, which kept the land in confusion. This is a subject which will require detailed consideration hereafter and is only referred to here because of its development into the exaggerated pretensions of the Inquisition to emancipate itself from all control. When Ferdinand granted this fuero it was understood on all hands to be a special deputation of the royal jurisdiction and as such liable at any time to modification or revocation. Ferdinand himself, in a cédula of August 18, 1501, alluded to it as such--the inquisitors enjoyed it just as the corregidors did.[856] So, in the Concordia of Castile, in 1553, defining the extent of this jurisdiction, the inquisitors are specially described as holding it from the king, and Philip II, Philip III and Philip IV repeatedly alluded to it as held during the royal pleasure.[857] There was no thought of disputing this until the seventeenth century was well advanced. The Suprema itself, in papers of 1609, 1619, 1637 and 1639 freely admitted that its temporal jurisdiction was a grant from the king, while its spiritual was a grant from the pope.[858]

Apparently the earliest departure from this universally conceded position was made, in 1623, by

Portocarrero in an argument on a clash of jurisdictions in Majorca, wherein he sought to prove that the civil and criminal jurisdiction of the Inquisition over its subordinates was ecclesiastical and derived from the pope.[859] About the same time, in an official paper, a similar claim was advanced, based on the papal briefs authorizing Torquemada and his successors to appoint, dismiss and punish their subordinates.[860] These were mere speculations and attracted no attention at the time. We have just seen that as late as 1639 the Suprema made no claims of the kind but two years later, in 1641, it suddenly adopted them in the most offensive fashion. There was a competencia, or conflict of jurisdiction, between the tribunal of Valladolid and the chancillería or high royal court; the Council of Castile had occasion to present several consultas to the king, in one of which it said that the jurisdiction exercised in the name of the king by the Inquisition was temporal, secular and precarious and could not be defended by excommunication. Thereupon the Suprema assembled its theologians who pronounced these propositions to be false, rash and akin to heretical error; armed with this opinion the fiscal, or prosecuting officer, accused the whole Council of Castile, demanded that its consulta be suppressed and that its authors be prosecuted. Theoretically there was nothing to prevent such action, which would have rendered the Inquisition the dominating power in the land, but the Suprema lacked hardihood; even the habitual subservience of Philip IV was revolted and he told the inquisitor-general that he had done ill to lend himself to a question contrary to the sovereignty of the monarch and to the honor of the highest council of the nation.[861]

***

In spite of this rebuff, having once asserted the claim that its temporal jurisdiction was spiritual and not secular, the Inquisition adhered to it. The prize was worth a struggle, for it would have put the whole nation at its mercy. It would have deprived the king of powers to check aggression and to protect his subjects from oppression for, as Portocarrero had pointed out, although princes have authority to relieve their subjects when aggrieved by other secular subjects, they have none when the oppressors are ecclesiastics, exempt by divine law from their jurisdiction.[862] To win this the Inquisition persisted in its claim. In 1642, on the occasion of a competencia in Granada, there appeared, under its authority, a printed argument to prove that the temporal jurisdiction of the Holy Office was a grant from the Holy See, which had power to intervene in the internal affairs of States and that it had merely been acquiesced in and confirmed by the kings.[863] Again, in a notorious case occurring in Cuenca in 1645, the inquisitors argued that their temporal jurisdiction was ecclesiastical and papal, with which the king could not interfere.[864] But the audacity with which these pretensions were pushed culminated in a consulta presented by the Suprema, March 31, 1646, to Philip IV, when he was struggling against the determination of the Córtes of Aragon to curb the excesses of the Inquisition.

In this paper the Suprema asserted that the civil and political jurisdiction is inferior to the spiritual and ecclesiastical, which can assume by indirect power whatever is necessary for its conservation and unimpeded exercise, without being restricted by secular princes. The royal prerogative is derived from positive human law or the law of nations; the supreme power of the Inquisition is delegated by the Holy See for cases of faith with all that is requisite, directly or indirectly, for its untrammelled enjoyment; this is of divine law and, as such, is superior to all human law, to which it is in no way subject. The very least that can be said is that princes are bound to admit this, and though they have a right to concede no more than is requisite, the decision as to what is requisite rests with the ecclesiastical authority, which is based on divine law. Any departure from these principles, under the novel pretext that the king is master of this jurisdiction, with power to limit or abrogate, is dangerous for the conscience and very perilous as leading to the gravest errors.[865] It would be difficult to enunciate more boldly the theory of theocracy, with the Inquisition as its delegate and the crown merely the executor of its decrees.

These pretensions were not realized and the king was not reduced to insignificance, but his power was seriously trammelled by the bureaucracy of which the Suprema was the foremost and most aggressive representative. Its quasi-independence led to emulation by the other great departments of the State and though their success was not so marked, it was sufficient in all to render the government incredibly cumbersome and inefficient and to paralyze its action by wasting its strength in efforts to keep the peace between the rival and warring bodies. In these bickerings and dissensions the power of the crown decreased and the theoretically autocratic monarch found himself unable to enforce his commands. Philip IV recognized this fatal weakness, but his efforts to overcome the evil were puerile and inefficient. October 15, 1633, he sent to the Suprema, and presumably to the other councils, a decree setting forth emphatically that the slackness of obedience and disregard of the royal commands had been the cause of irreparable damage to the State and must be checked if the monarchy were to be preserved from ruin. It was his duty, under God, to prevent this; he had unavailingly represented it repeatedly to his councillors and now he proposed to make out a schedule of penalties, to be incurred through disobedience, scaled according to the gravity of each offence. This was to be completed within twenty days and he called upon the Suprema to give him the necessary information that should enable him to tabulate the matters coming within its sphere of action.

***

    This grotesque measure, calling upon offenders to define their offences for the purpose of providing condign punishment, was received by the Suprema with a cool indifference showing how lightly it regarded the royal indignation. There was nothing, it said in reply, within its jurisdiction which imperilled the monarchy, for its function was to preserve the monarchy by preserving the unity of religion. As for obedience, it was of the highest importance that the royal commands should be obeyed and the laws provided punishments for all disobedient vassals. But the canon and imperial laws and those of Spain deprived of their places judges, who executed royal cédulas issued against justice and the rights of parties, for it was assumed that such could not be the royal intention and that they were decreed in ignorance, so that they were suspended until the prince, better informed, should provide justice. Therefore when councillors opposed cédulas which would work great injury to the jurisdiction and immunities of the Holy Office, it was only to prevent innovation and it was in the discharge of duty that this was represented to the king. The Suprema therefore prayed him that, before determining matters proposed by other councils, they should be submitted to it as heretofore so that, after hearing the reasons of both sides, he might determine according to his pleasure.[866] Thus with scarcely veiled contempt the Suprema told him that it would continue to do as it had done and the very next year, as we have seen, it boldly informed him that none of his commands respecting the Inquisition would be obeyed until it should have confirmed them--commands, be it remembered, that in no case affected its action in matters of faith, for all the trouble arose from its encroachments on secular affairs.

    The character of Philip IV ripened and strengthened under adversity and, in the exigencies of the struggle with Catalonia and Portugal, he developed some traits worthy of a sovereign. Although he meekly endured the insolence of the Suprema in 1646 and labored strenuously with the Córtes of Aragon to prevent the reform of abuses, he yet, as we have seen, insisted on the right to supervise appointments. He doubtless asserted his authority in other ways for the Suprema abated its pretensions that its civil and criminal jurisdiction was spiritual and papal. In an elaborate consulta of March 12, 1668, during a long and dreary contest, in which the tribunal of Majorca was involved, it repeatedly refers to its enjoying the royal jurisdiction from the king, showing that it had abandoned the attempt to render itself independent of the royal authority.[867]

REASSERTION OF ROYAL SUPREMACY

    Under the imbecile Carlos II and his incapable ministers, the domineering arrogance of the Inquisition increased and, as we shall see hereafter, it successfully eluded a concerted movement, in 1696, of all the other councils, represented in the Junta Magna, to reduce its exuberance. With the advent of the House of Bourbon, however, it was forced to recognize its subordination to the royal will in temporal matters, in spite of the temporary interference of Elisabeth Farnese in favor of Inquisitor-general Giudice. We have already seen indications of this and shall see more; meanwhile a single instance will suffice to show how imperiously Philip V, under the guidance of Macanaz, could impose his commands. In 1712 there was an echo of the old quarrel over the so-called suppressed canonries of Antequera, Málaga and the Canaries (p. 342). The suit, commenced in 1562, had never been decided and had long been suspended. The trouble of 1612 had been quieted by allowing the Inquisition to enjoy the canonries, not as a right, but as a revocable grant from the crown; excesses committed by the inquisitors in collecting the fruits led to the resumption of the benefices and then, by a transaction in 1622, they were restored under the same conditions. Such was the position when a violent quarrel arose in the Canaries between the tribunal and the chapter. The former questioned the accuracy of the accounts rendered to it and demanded the account books. This the chapter refused but offered to place the books in the accounting room of the cathedral, allowing the officials of the tribunal free access and permission to make what copies they desired. There was also a subsidiary quarrel over the claim that, when the secretary of the tribunal went to the chapter, he should be entitled to precedence. With their customary violence the inquisitors publicly excommunicated and fined the dean and treasurer of the chapter and moreover they took under their protection the Dominican Joseph Guillen, Prior of San Pedro Martir, who was a notary of the tribunal. He circulated a defamatory libel on the chapter which laid a complaint before his superior, the Provincial; the latter commenced to investigate, when the tribunal inhibited him from all cognizance of the matter. Then there came a mandate from the Dominican General to the Provincial, relegating Fray Guillen to a convent and ordering a president to be appointed for San Pedro Martir, whereupon the tribunal required the Provincial to surrender this mandate and all papers concerning the affair, under pain of excommunication and two hundred ducats. The sub-prior of San Pedro Martir was forced to assemble the brethren, whom the inquisitors ordered to disobey the commands of the General and not to acknowledge the president appointed under his instructions, thus violating the statutes of the great Dominican Order and the principle of obedience on which it was based. They further excommunicated the Provincial in the most solemn manner; they took by force Fray Guillen from the convent and paraded the streets in his company; the whole community was thrown into confusion and to prevent recourse to the home authorities they forbade, under heavy penalties, the departure of any vessel for Teneriffe, through which communication was had with Spain. In all this there was nothing at variance with the customary methods of asserting the lawless supremacy of the Inquisition over the secular and spiritual authorities, but Philip V ordered Giudice, September 30, 1712, to put an end to these excesses and, on October 11th, the Suprema reported that it had ordered the inquisitors to desist. If it did so, they paid no attention to its commands. Then, June 11, 1713, he addressed a peremptory order to Giudice to revoke all that had been done in the Canaries, to recall the inquisitors, to dismiss them and give them no other appointments. The Suprema replied, July 18th, enclosing an order which it proposed despatching; this displeased him as not in compliance with his commands and he insisted on their complete fulfilment. Still there was evasion and delay and when, in July, 1714, the Canary chapter presented to the tribunal royal orders requiring the removal of the excommunications and the remission of the fines, the inquisitors not only refused obedience but commenced proceedings against the notaries who served them. The Suprema professed to have sent orders similar to those of the king, but it evidently had been playing a double game. Philip therefore, November 1, 1714, addressed the inquisitor-general, holding the Suprema responsible for the prolonged contumacy of the inquisitors; he ordered it to deliver to him the originals of all the correspondence on the subject and required the inquisitor-general to issue an order for the immediate departure from the islands of the inquisitors and fiscal, without forcing the governor to expel them, as he had orders to do so in case of disobedience. Moreover, if the Suprema should not, within fifteen days, deliver all the documents, so that the king could regulate matters directly with the tribunal, the old suspended suit would be reopened and such action would be taken as might be found requisite. This was a tone wholly different from that to which the Inquisition had been accustomed under the Hapsburgs; the evasions and delays of the Suprema, which had so long been successful, proved fruitless. The struggle was prolonged, but the royal authority prevailed in the end, although, when the inquisitors reached Spain, in the summer of 1715, Giudice had been restored to office and Philip weakly permitted them to be provided for in other tribunals and to curse fresh communities with their lawless audacity.[868]

We shall hereafter have occasion to see how, under the House of Bourbon, with its Gallican ideas as to royal prerogative, the subordination of the Inquisition became recognized, while its jurisdiction was curtailed and its influence was diminished.

CHAPTER II - SUPEREMINENCE

When the Inquisition, as we have seen, arrogated to itself almost an equality with the sovereign, it necessarily assumed supremacy over all other bodies in the State. Spain had been won to the theory, assiduously taught by the medieval Church, that the highest duty of the civil power was the maintenance of the faith in its purity and the extermination of heresy and heretics. The institution to which this duty was confided therefore enjoyed pre-eminence over all other departments of the State and the latter were bound, whenever called upon, to lend it whatever aid was necessary. To refuse to assist it, to criticise it, or even to fail in demonstrations of due respect to those who performed its awful functions, were thus offences to be punished at its pleasure.

Allusion has already been made (p. 182) to the oath required of officials at the founding of the Inquisition, pledging obedience and assistance, whenever an inquisitor came to a place to set up his tribunal. This was not enough, for feudalism still disputed jurisdiction with the crown, and the inquisitor was directed to summon the barons before him and make them take not only the popular oath but one promising to allow the Inquisition free course in their lands, failing which they were to be prosecuted as rebels.[869] As the tribunals became fixed in their several seats, when a new inquisitor came he brought royal letters, addressed to all officials, from the viceroy down, commanding them, under penalty of five thousand florins, to lend him and his subordinates what aid was necessary and to obey his mandates in making arrests and executing his sentences, and this was published in a formal proclamation, with sound of trumpets, by the viceroy or other royal representative.[870] This was not an empty formality. When, in 1516, the Corregidor of Logroño, the Comendador Barrientos, a knight of Santiago, ventured to assert that the familiars were not to be assisted in making an arrest the inquisitors excommunicated him and ordered him to seek the inquisitor-general and beg for pardon, which was granted only on condition of his appearance in a public auto de fe, after hearing mass as a penitent, on his knees and holding a candle, after which he was to be absolved with stripes and the other humiliations inflicted on penitents.[871] This was not merely an indignity but a lasting mark of infamy, extending to the kindred and posterity.

OATHS OF OBEDIENCE

As though this were not sufficient, at a somewhat later period, the officials of all cities where tribunals were established were required to take an elaborate oath to the inquisitors, in which they swore to compel every one within their jurisdiction to hold the Catholic faith, to persecute all heretics and their adherents, to seize and bring them before the Inquisition and to denounce them, to commit no public office to such persons nor to any who were prohibited by the inquisitors, nor to receive them in their families; to guard all the pre-eminences, privileges, exemptions and immunities of the inquisitors, their officials and familiars; to execute all sentences pronounced by the inquisitors and to be obedient to God, to the Roman Church and to the inquisitors and their successors.[872] In this, the clause pledging observance of the privileges and exemptions of the officials was highly important for, as we shall see hereafter, the privileges claimed by the Inquisition were the source of perpetual and irritating quarrels with the royal and local magistrates. It was an innovation of the middle of the sixteenth century, for Prince Philip, in a letter of December 2, 1553, to the tribunal of Valencia, says that he hears it requires the royal officials to swear to maintain the privileges, usages and customs of the Inquisition; this he says is a novelty and, as he does not approve of innovations, he asks what authority it has for such requirement. To this the answer was that every year, when the municipal officials enter upon their duties, they come and take such an oath and the records showed that this had been observed for a hundred years without contradiction. This seems to have silenced his objections and the formula became general. The Valencia Concordia, or agreement of 1554, simply provides that the secular magistrates shall take the accustomed oath and what that was is doubtless shown by the one taken, in 1626, by the almotacen, or sealer of weights and measures, when he came to the Inquisition and swore on the cross and the gospels to observe the articles customarily read to the royal officials and to guard the privileges of the Holy Office and defend it with all his power.[873]

Even all this was insufficient to emphasize the universal subordination. At all autos de fe, which were attended by the highest in the land as well as by the lowest, and at the annual proclamation of the

Edict of Faith, to which the whole population was summoned, a notary of the Inquisition held up a cross and addressed the people: "Raise your hands and let each one say that he swears by God and Santa Maria and this cross and the words of the holy gospels, that he will favor and defend and aid the holy Catholic faith and the holy Inquisition, its ministers and officials, and will manifest and make known each and every heretic, fautor, defender and receiver of heretics and all disturbers and impeders of the Holy Office, and that he will not favor, or help, or conceal them but, as soon as he knows of them, he will denounce them to the inquisitors; and if he does otherwise that God may treat him as those who knowingly perjure themselves: Let every one say Amen!"[874] When the sovereign was present at an auto this general oath did not suffice and he took a special one. Thus, at the Valladolid auto of May 21, 1559, the Inquisitor-general Valdés administered it to the Regent Juana and at that of Madrid, in 1632, Inquisitor-general Zapata went to the window at which Philip IV was seated, with a missal and a cross, on which the king swore to protect and defend the Catholic faith as long as he lived and to aid and support the Inquisition--an oath which was then duly read aloud to the people.[875] Thus the whole nation was bound, in the most solemn manner, to be obedient to the Inquisition and to submit to what it might assert to be its privileges.

How purely ministerial were the functions of the public officials in all that related to the Inquisition, even under Philip V, was illustrated when, at Barcelona, in an auto de fe, June 28, 1715, a bigamist named Medrano was sentenced to two hundred lashes to be inflicted on the 30th. On the 29th word was sent to the public executioner to be ready to administer them, but the Viceroy, the Marquis of Castel-Rodrigo, forbade the executioner to act until he should give permission, holding that no public punishment should be inflicted until he should be officially notified of the sentence. There were hasty conferences and debates, lasting to nearly midnight, and it was not until 7 A.M. of the 30th that the marquis gave way and the sentence was executed. The tribunal reported the affair to the Suprema, which replied in the name of the king, diplomatically thanking the marquis and rebuking his legal adviser, who was told that it was his duty and that of all officials to be obedient to the Inquisition.[876]

As a perpetual reminder of this subordination, there appears to have been kept in the royal chancellery the formula of a letter addressed to all viceroys and captains-general. This recited the invaluable services of the Inquisition in clearing the land of infinite heretics and preserving it from the convulsions afflicting other nations, thus rendering its efficiency one of the chief concerns of the crown. Therefore the king charges his representatives emphatically to honor and favor all inquisitors, officials and familiars, giving them all the necessary aid for which they may ask and enforcing the observance of all the privileges and exemptions conceded to them by law, concordias, royal cédulas, use and custom and in any other way, so that the Holy Office may have the full liberty and authority which it has always enjoyed and which the king desires it to retain. A copy of this was sent to all the viceroys in 1603 and, as I have chanced to find it again addressed, in 1652, to the Duke of Montalto, then Viceroy of Valencia, it was presumably part of the regular instructions furnished to all who were appointed to these responsible positions.[877]

***

POWER TO CRIPPLE OPPONENTS

In the interminable conflicts through which the Inquisition established its enjoyment of the powers thus conferred, the inquisitor was armed, offensively and defensively, in a manner to give him every advantage. He could, at any moment, when involved in a struggle with either the secular or ecclesiastical authorities, disable his opponent with a sentence of excommunication removable only by the Holy Office or the pope and, if this did not suffice, he could lay an interdict or even a cessatio a divinis on cities, until the people, deprived of the sacraments, would compel submission. It is true that, in 1533, the Suprema ordered that much discretion should be exercised in the use of this powerful weapon, on account of the indignation aroused by its abuse, but we shall have ample opportunity to see how recklessly it was employed habitually, without regard to the preliminary safeguards imposed by the canons.[878] On the other hand, the inquisitor was practically immune. His antagonists were mostly secular authorities who had no such weapon in their armories and, when he chanced to quarrel with a prelate, he usually took care to be the first to fulminate an excommunication, and then unconcernedly disregarded the counter censures as uttered by one disabled from the exercise of his functions, for the anathema deprived its subject of all official faculties. It had the contingent result, moreover, that he who remained under excommunication for a year could be prosecuted for suspicion of heresy.[879]

There was another provision which rendered it even more formidable as an antagonist. In matters of faith and all pertaining directly or indirectly thereto, its jurisdiction was exclusive. In the extensive field of civil and criminal business, of which it obtained cognizance through the immunities of its officials and, in the frequent quarrels arising from questions of ceremony and precedence, no court, whether secular or spiritual, had power to inhibit any action which it might see fit to take. By special papal favor, however, it had power to inhibit their action and thus to cripple them on the spot. This extraordinary privilege, with power to subdelegate, appears to have been first granted in the commissions issued, in 1507, to Ximenes and Enguera as inquisitors-general respectively of Castile and Aragon and was repeated in those of Luis Mercader and Pedro Juan Poul in 1513.[880] For a considerable time this clause disappears from the commissions, but, towards the close of the century, it again finds place, in a more detailed and absolute form in that granted to Manrique de Lara, after which it continued in those of his successors to the end. It confers the power of inhibiting all judges, even of archiepiscopal dignity, under pecuniary penalties and censures to be enforced by the invocation of the secular arm and of absolving them after they shall have submitted and obeyed.[881] This proclaimed to the world that the Inquisition outranked all other authorities in Church and State and the power was too often exercised for its existence to be ignored or forgotten. This superiority found practical expression in the rule that, in the innumerable conflicts of jurisdiction, all secular and ecclesiastical judges must answer communications from inquisitors in the form of petition and not by letter. If they replied to commands and comminations by letter they were to be fined and proceedings were to be commenced against them and their messengers, and they were required to withdraw and erase from their records all such letters which were held to be disrespectful to the superiority of the Holy Office.[882]

ASSERTION OF SUPERIORITY

It was an inevitable inference from this that there was no direct appeal from whatever a tribunal might do except to the Suprema, which, though it might in secret chide its subordinates for their excesses, customarily upheld them before the world. The sovereign, it is true, was the ultimate judge and, in occasional cases, he interposed his authority with more or less effect, but the ordinary process was through a competencia, a cumbrous procedure through which, as we shall see, the Inquisition could wrangle for years and virtually, in most cases, deny all practical relief to the sufferers.

Another weapon of tremendous efficacy was the power of arrest, possessed at will by inquisitors during the greater portion of the career of the Inquisition. Even to gratify mere vindictiveness, by simply asserting that there was a matter of faith, the inquisitor could throw any one into the secret prison. The civil magistrate might thus abuse his authority with little damage to the victim, but it was otherwise with the Inquisition. In the insane estimate placed on limpieza de sangre, or purity of blood, the career of a man and of his descendants was fatally narrowed by such a stain on his orthodoxy; it mattered little what was the outcome of the case, the fact of imprisonment was remembered and handed down through generations while the fact of its being causeless was forgotten. In the later period, when the Suprema supervised every act of the tribunals, the opportunities for this were greatly restricted, but during the more active times the ill-will of an inquisitor could at any moment inflict this most serious injury and the power was often recklessly abused in the perpetual conflicts with the secular authorities. The ability thus to destroy at a word the prospects in life of any man was a terrible weapon which goes far to explain the awe with which the inquisitor was regarded by the community.

That the inquisitor should assume to be superior to all other dignitaries was the natural result of the powers thus concentrated in him. Páramo asserts that he is the individual of highest authority in his district, as he represents both pope and king; and the Suprema, in a consulta addressed to Philip V, in 1713, boasted that its jurisdiction was so superior that there was not a person in the kingdom exempt from it.[883] The haughty supremacy which it affected is seen in instructions issued in 1578 that inquisitors, when the tribunal is sitting, are not to go forth to receive any one, save the king, the queen or a royal prince and are not, in an official capacity, to appear in receptions of prelates or other public assemblies, and this was virtually repeated in 1645, when they were told not to visit the viceroy or the archbishop or accept their invitations, for such demonstrations were due only to the person of the king.[884] Exception however, was probably taken to this for a carta acordada of March 17, 1648, lays down less stringent rules and specifies for each tribunal, according to the varying customs of different places, the high officials whom the inquisitor is permitted to visit on induction into office and on occasions of condolence or congratulation.[885]

In the social hierarchy the viceroys and captains-general stood next to the king as representing, in their respective governments, the royal person. To outrank these exalted personages was not beyond inquisitorial ambition. In 1588 there was great scandal in Lima, when the inquisitors claimed precedence over the Count of Villar, the Viceroy of Peru, and carried their point by excommunicating him, but Philip II, in a cédula of March 8, 1589, took them severely to task for their arrogance and added that the viceroy was equally to blame for yielding, as he represented the royal power. This lesson was ineffectual and some years later another method was tried of asserting superiority. In 1596, the Captain-general of Aragon complained to the king that, in the recent auto de fe, the inquisitors had refused to give him the title of Excellency. To this Philip replied, February 6, 1597, that it was unreasonable for them thus to affect equality with his personal representative; they must either concede to him the title of Excellency or themselves be treated as vuestra merced, in place of muy ilustres or señoria, and therefore he could attend the next auto.[886]

***

This asserted superiority of the Inquisition was very galling to the bishops, who argued that the Holy Office had been founded only four hundred years before, as an aid to their jurisdiction, and they resented bitterly the efforts of the resolute upstarts to claim higher privileges and precedence. The Inquisition, however, was an organized whole, with sharp and unsparing methods of enforcing its claims and protected in every way from assault, while the episcopate was a scattered and unwieldy body, acting individually and, for the most part, powerless to defend the officials, through whom it acted, from those who claimed that everything concerning themselves was a matter of faith of which they had exclusive cognizance. The serious conflicts over jurisdiction will be considered in a subsequent chapter; here we are concerned merely with questions of etiquette and ceremonial. Seen through the perspective of the centuries, these quarrels, which were conducted with frantic eagerness, seem trivialities unworthy of record, but their significance was momentous to the parties concerned, as they involved superiority and inferiority. The hundred years' quarrel over precedence in Rome, between the ambassadors of France and Spain, which was not settled until 1661 by the triumph of France, had a meaning beyond a mere question of ceremony. In Spain these debates often filled the land with confusion. All parties were tenacious of what they conceived to be their rights and were ready to explode in violence on the smallest provocation. The enormous mass of letters and papers concerning the seats and positions of the inquisitors and their officials at all public functions--whether seats should be chairs or benches and whether they were to have canopies, or cushions, or carpets, shows that these were regarded as matters of the highest moment, giving rise to envenomed quarrels with the ecclesiastical and secular dignitaries, requiring for their settlement the interposition of the royal authority. The inquisitors were constantly arrogating to themselves external marks of superiority and the others were disputing it with a vehemence that elevated the most trivial affairs into matters of national importance, and the attention of the king and the highest ministers was diverted from affairs of state to pacify obscure quarrels in every corner of the land.

It would be futile to enter into the details of these multitudinous squabbles, but one or two subjects in dispute may be mentioned to illustrate the ingenuity with which the Inquisition pushed its claims to superiority. Towards the middle of the seventeenth century it demanded that, when there was an episcopal letter or mandate to be published in the churches and also an edict or letter of the Inquisition, the latter should have precedence in the reading. This was naturally regarded as an effort to show that the inquisitorial jurisdiction was superior to the episcopal and it led to frequent scandals. In 1645, at Valencia, on Passion Sunday, a secretary of the tribunal endeavored to read letters of the inquisitors before one of the archbishop's, but, by the latter's order, the priest refused to give way, whereupon the inquisitors arrested him: the matter was carried up to the king, who ordered the priest to be discharged in such wise that there should be no record of his prosecution and that his good fame should be restored. Soon after this, in Saragossa on a feast-day in the cathedral, a priest commenced to read an archiepiscopal letter, but before he had finished more than a few lines, a secretary of the Inquisition mounted the other pulpit and began reading a letter of the Inquisition; the priest was so disturbed that he stopped, whereupon the archbishop, Juan Cebrian, ordered his arrest, but he pleaded his surprise and confusion and the archbishop relented. In 1649 a more determined effort was made by the Saragossa tribunal. August 15th the parish priest of the cathedral read certain archiepiscopal letters at the accustomed time and was followed by the secretary of the Inquisition with others of the inquisitors. Two days later the priest was summoned before the tribunal and was made to swear secrecy as to orders given to him. The result showed what were his instructions, for the next Sunday, having archiepiscopal letters to read, he waited until the secretary read those of the inquisitors. Some days later similar secret orders were given to the priest of Nuestra Señora del Pilar and when, on October 11th, he commenced reading an archiepiscopal letter, an officer of the Inquisition seized him by the arm and forced him to read first those of the tribunal. Archbishop Cebrian addressed memorials to the king, September 7th and 21st and October 12th asking his protection to preserve the archiepiscopal jurisdiction; the Council of Aragon presented a consulta supporting him, on which the wearied monarch made an endorsement, deploring the evil results of such conflicts and telling the Council to write to the archbishop not to proceed to extremities but to seek some adjustment similar to that by which, a short time before, Cardinal Moscoso in Toledo had caused an inquisitorial letter to be read on a different day, to which the tribunal must be made to conform.[887]

***

The persistence with which the Inquisition maintained any claim once advanced is illustrated by its endeavor to introduce change in the ritual of the mass favorable to its assumption of superiority. It was the custom that the celebrant should make a bow to the bishop, if present, and in his absence, to the Eucharist. In 1635, at Valladolid, the inquisitors required that when the Edict of Faith was read the bow should be made to them and, on the refusal of the officiating canon, they arrested him and the dean who upheld him and held them under heavy bail. This aroused the whole city and brought a rebuke from the king, who ordered them to discharge the bail and not to abuse their jurisdiction. Unabashed by this the effort was made again at Compostella, in 1639, and duly resisted; the king was again obliged to examine the question and, after consultation with learned men, decided that the chapter was in the right and that the inquisitors had the alternative of absenting themselves from the reading. Two rebuffs such as this should have sufficed but, in 1643, after careful preparation, another attempt was made at Córdova, which produced a fearful scandal. Neither side would yield; the services were interrupted; the inquisitors endeavored to excommunicate the canons, but the latter raised such a din with howls and cries, the thunder of the organ, the clangor of bells and breaking up the seats in the choir, that the fulmination could not be heard. Even the inquisitors shrank from the storm and left the church amid hisses, with their caps pulled down to their eyes, but they lost no time in commencing a prosecution of the canons, who appealed to the king, in a portentous document covering two hundred and fifty-six folio pages. Philip and his advisers at the moment had ample occupation, what with the dismissal of Olivares, the evil tidings from Rocroy and the rebellions in Catalonia and Portugal, but they had to turn aside to settle this portentous quarrel. A royal letter of June 16, 1643, ordered the inquisitors to restore to the canons certain properties which they had seized and to remove the excommunications, while reference to similar decisions at Compostella, Granada and Cartagena shows how obstinate and repeated had been the effort of the Holy Office. Notwithstanding this the tribunal of Córdova refused obedience to the royal mandate and a second letter, of September 28th from Saragossa, where Philip was directing the campaign against Catalonia, was required. This was couched in peremptory terms; the excommunications must be removed and, for the future, the Roman ceremonial must be observed, prescribing that in the absence of the bishop, the reverence must be made to the sacrament.[888]

QUESTIONS OF CEREMONY

While thus steadily endeavoring to encroach on the rights of others, the Inquisition was supersensitive as to anything that might be reckoned as an attempt by other bodies to assert superiority, and it vindicated what it held to be its rights with customary violence. When the funeral solemnities of Queen Ana, of Austria were celebrated in Seville, in 1580, a bitter quarrel about precedence in seats arose between the tribunal, the royal Audiencia or high court and the city authorities, when the former arbitrarily suspended the obsequies until consultation could be had with Philip II, then in Lisbon, engaged in the absorption of Portugal. He regulated the position which each of the contending parties should occupy and the postponed honors were duly rendered. Matters remained quiescent until a similar function became necessary, after the death of Philip in 1598. The city spent weeks in costly preparations and the catafalque erected in the cathedral was regarded as worthy of that magnificent building. November 29th was fixed for the ceremonies; on the vigil, the regent, or president judge of the Audiencia, sent a chair from his house to the place assigned to him, but the chapter protested so vigorously against the innovation that he was obliged to remove it. The following morning, when the various bodies entered the church at half-past nine, the benches assigned to the judges and their wives were seen to be draped in mourning. This was at once regarded as an effort on their part to establish pre-eminence and excited great indignation. The services commenced and during the mass the inquisitors sent word to the cabildo, or city magistracy, that it should order the mourning removed. After some demur, the cabildo sent its procurador mayor, Pedro de Escobar, with a notary and some alguaziles to the Audiencia, bearing a message to the effect that if the drapery were not removed, the inquisitors and the church authorities were agreed that the ceremonies should be suspended. He was told not to approach and on persisting he and his followers were arrested and thrown into the public gaol. The inquisitors then sent their secretary with a message, but he too was kept at a distance when he mounted the steps of the catafalque and cried out that the tribunal excommunicated the three judges, Vallejo, Lorenzana and Guerra, if they did not depart. A second time he came with a message, which he was not allowed to deliver, and again he mounted the steps to declare all the judges excommunicated and that they must leave the church in order that the services might proceed, for the presence of excommunicates was a bar to all public worship. This was repeated again by the fiscal, when the Audiencia drew up a paper declaring the acts of the tribunal to be null and void and ordering it to remove the censure under pain of forfeiting citizenship and temporalities, but the scrivener sent to serve it was refused a hearing and on his persisting was threatened with the pillory. The alcalde of the city endeavored to calm the inquisitors, but Inquisitor Zapata replied furiously that if St. Paul came from heaven and ordered them to do otherwise they would refuse if it cost them their souls.

Meanwhile there were similar trouble and complications among the church authorities. The vicar-general, Pedro Ramírez de Leon, ordered the services resumed, under pain, for the dean and officiating priest, of excommunication and of a thousand ducats; the precentor and canons appealed to the pope, but the vicar-general published them in the choir as excommunicates. The celebrant, Dr. Negron, was sought for, but he had prudently disappeared in the confusion and could not be found. It was now half-past twelve and the canons sent word to the Audiencia that they were going and it could go. To leave the church, however, would seem like an admission by the judges that they were excommunicate and they grimly kept their seats. The cabildo of the city and the tribunal were not to be outdone and the three hostile groups sat glaring at each other until four o'clock, when the absurdity of the situation grew too strong and they silently departed. Meanwhile the candles had been burning until five hundred ducats' worth of wax was uselessly consumed.

So complicated a quarrel could of course only be straightened out by the king to whom all parties promptly appealed. The judges proved that they had not draped their benches as a sign of pre-eminence but had proposed that the same be done by the cabildo and the tribunal. As far as regards the latter, the royal decision was manifested in two cédulas of December 22d. One of these told the inquisitors that they had exceeded their jurisdiction in excommunicating the judges, whom they were to absolve ad cautelam and they also had to pay for the wasted wax. The other ominously ordered the inquisitors Blanco and Zapata to appear at the court within fifteen days and not to depart without licence. At the same time, on December 21st the suspended obsequies were duly celebrated.[889]

SUPERIORITY TO LAW

It will be seen from these cases that the only appeal from inquisitorial aggression lay to the king and that, even when the inquisitors were wholly in the wrong and the royal decision was against them, no steps were taken to keep them within bounds for the future. The altered position of the Holy Office under the Bourbons was therefore significantly indicated by a decision of Fernando VI in 1747. At the celebration in Granada, on September 11th, of his accession, the chancillería, or great high court of New Castile, observed that the archbishop occupied a chair covered with taffety, outside of his window overlooking the plaza, and that the inquisitors had cushions on their window-sills. It sent messengers to request the removal of these symbols of pre-eminence and, on receiving a refusal in terms of scant respect, it stopped the second bull-fight and put an end to the ceremonies. The matter was referred to the king, when the Suprema, in a memorial of solemn earnestness, argued that the Inquisition had for centuries been in the uncontested enjoyment of the privilege of which it was now sought to be deprived. It was the highest tribunal, not only in Spain but in the world, as it had charge of the true religion, which is the foundation of all kingdoms and republics. The time had passed for this swelling self-assertion. Full discussion was devoted to the momentous question and, on October 3d, Fernando issued a decree which proclaimed to Spain that the Holy Office was no longer what it had been. This was to the effect that, as the chancillería represented the royal jurisdiction, and thus indirectly the king himself, it was entitled to pre-eminence in all such celebrations and in those of the royal chapel; it was justified in its action and thereafter no such signs of dignity as canopies, cushions, ceremonial chairs and the like should be used in its presence. In case of attempts to do so, one of the alcaldes del crimen with his officers should remove them and punish any workmen in setting them up.[890]

***

The Inquisition and its members were protected in every way from subjection to local laws and regulations. An edict of Charles V, in 1523, forbade all municipalities or other bodies from adopting statutes which should in any way curtail their privileges or be adverse to them and, if any such should be attempted he declared them in advance to be null and void.[891] This in fact, was only expressing and enforcing the canon laws enacted in the frenzied efforts to suppress heresy in the thirteenth century and still in vigor. A constitution of Urban IV (1261-5) declares invalid the laws of any state or city which impede, directly or indirectly, the functions of the Inquisition, and the bishop or inquisitor is empowered to summon the ruler or magistrates to exhibit such statutes and compel him by censures to revoke or modify them.[892] While this was designed to prevent the crippling of the Inquisition by hostile legislation, it inferred a superiority to law and was construed in the most liberal way, as was seen in a struggle in Valencia which lasted for nearly two centuries. A police regulation for the improvement of the market-place ordered the removal of all stands for the display of goods under the arcades of the houses. One house belonged to the tribunal; its tenant was the worst offender, and he obstinately kept his stand and appealed to the tribunal for protection against the law. This protection was accorded with such vigor in 1603, that the saintly Archbishop, Juan de Ribera, who was also captain-general, vainly endeavored to secure obedience to the law. Until the close of the eighteenth century the tribunal thus successfully defied the Real Junta de Policia, consisting of the captain-general, the regente and other high officials. At length, in 1783, Carlos III issued a royal declaration that no one should be exempt from obedience to orders of police and good government and that all such cases should be adjudicated by the ordinary courts without admitting the competencias with which the Holy Office habitually sought to tire out those who ventured to withstand its aggressiveness. Under this, in 1791, the nuisance in Valencia was abated, when the tribunal apologized to the Suprema for yielding and excused itself in virtue of the royal declaration of 1783. It had held out as long as it could, but times had changed and even the Inquisition was forced to respect the law.[893] Madrid had been earlier relieved from such annoyance, for a royal cédula of 1746, regulating the police system of the capital, has a clause evidently directed at the Inquisition for it declares that no exemption, even the most privileged, shall avail in matters concerning the police, the adornment and the cleanliness of the city.[894]

INVIOLABILITY

The lawlessness thus fostered degenerated into an arbitrary disregard of the rights of others, leading to a petty tyranny sometimes exercised in the most arbitrary and capricious manner. Inquisitor Santos of Saragossa was very friendly with the Licenciado Pedro de Sola, a beneficed priest of the cathedral, and Juan Sebastian, who were good musicians and who gathered some musical friends to sing complins with them on Holy Saturday at Santa Engracia, where the inquisitors spent Holy Week in retreat. Santos used to send his coach for them and entertain them handsomely, but when, in 1624, he became Bishop of Solsona, although the singing continued, the coach and entertainment ceased and the musicians went unwillingly. Finally, in 1637, some of them stopped going; the inquisitors sent for them and scolded them which made them all indignant. Then, in 1638, the secretary Heredia was sent to order them to go and when the chapel master excused them, with an intimation that they ought to be paid, Heredia told them the tribunal honored them sufficiently in calling for them. They did not go and, when Easter was over, two of them, beneficed priests, were summoned and, after being kept waiting for three hours, were imprisoned in a filthy little house occupied by soldiers and were left for twelve hours without bedding, food or drink. The next day they managed to communicate with the chapter, but it was afraid to interfere and, after six days of this confinement, they were brought before the tribunal and informed that they had the city for a prison, under pain of a hundred ducats, and were made to swear to present themselves whenever summoned. As they went out they saw two more brought in--the chapel-master and a priest. At last the chapter plucked up courage to address a memorial to the king through the Council of Aragon, which added the suggestion that he should order the inquisitor-general to see to the release of the musicians and the prevention of such extortion. May 11th Philip referred this to the Suprema which, after a month's delay, replied, June 14th, that, desiring to avoid controversy with the church of Saragossa, it had ordered the tribunal to pay the musicians in future, to release any that were in prison and to return whatever fines had been imposed.[895] When petty tyranny such as this could be practised, especially on the privileged class of priests, we can appreciate the terrorism surrounding the tribunals.

***

Another distinction contributed to the supereminence claimed by the Inquisition--the inviolability which shielded all who were in its service. From an early period the Church had sought to protect its members, whose profession was assumed to debar them from the use of arms, by investing them with a sanctity which should assure their safety in an age of violence. Throughout the middle ages no canon was more frequently invoked than Si quis suadente diabolo, which provided that whoever struck a cleric or monk incurred an anathema removable only by personal appearance before the pope and accepting his sentence.[896] More than this was asked for by the Inquisition, for the greater portion of its officials were laymen. They were no more exposed to injury or insult than those of the secular courts, but it was assumed that there was a peculiar hatred felt for them and that their functions in defending the faith entitled them to special security. We shall see hereafter that the Inquisition obtained jurisdiction in all matters connected with its officials, but this, while enabling it to give them special protection, had the limitation that judgements of blood rendered ecclesiastics pronouncing them "irregular." In cases of heresy this had long been evaded by a hypocritical plea for mercy, when delivering convicts to the secular arm for execution, but it was felt that some special faculties were requisite in dealing with cases of mere assault or homicide and a motu proprio was procured from Leo X, January 28, 1515, empowering inquisitors to arrest any one, even of the highest rank, whether lay or clerical, who strikes, beats, mutilates or kills any minister or official of the Inquisition and to deliver him to the secular arm for punishment, without incurring irregularity, even if it results in effusion of blood.[897] The Holy Office thus held in its own hands the protection of all who served it.

This was rendered still more efficient by subsequent papal action. Irritated at some resistance offered to the Roman Inquisition, Pius V published, April 1, 1569, the ferocious bull Si de protegendis, under which any one, of whatever rank, who should threaten, strike or kill an officer or a witness, who should help a prisoner to escape or make way with any document or should lend aid or counsel to such act, was to be delivered to the secular judge for punishment as a heretic--that is to say, for burning--including confiscation and the infamy of his children.[898] Although this was intended for Italy, the Spanish Inquisition speedily assumed the benefit of it; it was sent out October 16th and it was annually published in the vernacular on Holy Thursday.[899]

***

Thus all concerned in the business of the Holy Office were hedged around with an inviolability accorded to no other class of the community. The inquisitors themselves were additionally protected against responsibility for their own malfeasance by the received theory that scandal was more to be dreaded than crime--that there was inherent in their office such importance to religion that anything was better than what might bring that office into contempt. Francisco Peña, in treating of this, quotes the warning of Aquinas as to cardinals and applies it to the punishment of inquisitors; if scandal has arisen, they may be punished; otherwise the danger to the reputation of the Holy Office is greater than that of impunity to the offender.[900] The tenderness, in fact, with which they were treated, even when scandal had arisen, was a scandal in itself. Thus, when the reiterated complaints of Barcelona caused a visitation to be made there, in 1567, by de Soto Salazar, and his report confirmed the accusations, showing the three inquisitors to be corrupt, extortionate and unjust, the only penalty imposed, in 1568, was merely suspension for three years from all office in the Inquisition. Even this was not enforced, at least with regard to one of them, Dr. Zurita, for we chance to meet him as inquisitor of Saragossa in 1570. He does not seem to have reformed, for his transfer thence to Sardinia, the least desirable of the tribunals, can only have been in consequence of persistent misconduct.[901] The tribunals naturally showed the same mercy to their subordinates, whose sole judges they were, and this retention in office of those whom unfitness was proved was not the least of the burdens with which the Inquisition afflicted Spain.

What rendered this inviolability more aggravating was that it extended to the servants and slaves of all connected with the Holy Office. About 1540 a deputy corregidor of Murcia, for insulting a servant of the messenger of the tribunal, was exposed to the infamy of hearing mass as a penitent.[902] In 1564, we find Dr. Zurita, on circuit through his district, collecting evidence against Micael Bonet, of Palacio de Vicio, for caning a servant boy of Benet Modaguer, who held some office in the Inquisition, and the case was sent to Barcelona for trial, which shows that it was regarded as serious. So, in 1568, for quarrelling with a servant of Micer Complada, who styled himself deputy of the abogado fiscal at Tarragona, the Barcelona tribunal, without verifying Complada's claims to office, threw into prison Gerónimo Zapata and Antonio de Urgel and condemned Zapata to a fine of thirty ducats and six months' exile and Urgel to ten ducats and three months.[903] In Murcia, Sebastian Gallego, the servant of an inquisitor, quarrelled with a butcher over some meat, when they exchanged insults. The secular judge arrested both but the tribunal claimed them, prosecuted the butcher and banished him from the town.[904] Such cases were of frequent occurrence and it is easy to conceive how galling was the insolence of despised class thus enabled to repay the contempt with which it was habitually treated.

ENFORCEMENT OF RESPECT

When the honor of slaves was thus vindicated inquisitors were not apt to condone any failure, real or imaginary, in the respect which they held to be their due, and the offender was made to feel the awful authority which shrouded the tribunal and its judges. As their powers were largely discretional, with undefined limits, the manner in which they were exercised was sometimes eccentric. In 1569, for instance, the Jesuits of Palermo prepared for representation in their church a tragedy of St. Catherine and, on October 4th, they gave a private rehearsal to which were invited the viceroy and principal dignitaries. The inquisitor, Juan Biserra, came as one of the guests and finding the door closed knocked repeatedly without announcing himself or demanding admittance. The janitor, thinking it to be some unauthorized person, paid no attention to the knocking and Biserra departed, highly incensed. When the Jesuits heard of it, the rector and principal fathers called on him to apologize, but, after keeping them waiting for some time he refused to see them. The public representation was announced for October 8th; the church was crowded with the nobility awaiting the rising of the curtain, when a messenger from Biserra notified the Jesuits that he forbade the performance, under pain of excommunication and other penalties at his discretion, until after the piece should have been examined and approved by him. The audience was dismissed and the next day the MS. was sent to Biserra who submitted it to Dominican censors. Although they returned it with their approval he discovered in it two objectionable points, so absurdly trifling as to show that he wanted merely to make a wanton exhibition of his power. The censors replied to his criticism and he finally allowed the performance to proceed. We may not unreasonably assume that this may have been one of the freaks for which Biserra was suspended in

1572, on the report made of him by the visitor Quintanilla. Then, with customary tenderness, he was employed in the responsible post of visitor at Barcelona, where he died soon afterwards.[905]

The sensitiveness to disrespect and the terrorism which its arbitrary punishment diffused through the community were well illustrated when, in 1617, Fray Diego Vinegas preached the Lenten sermons in the Hospital of N. Señora de la Gracia of Saragossa. He was a distinguished Benedictine, who had held high offices in his Order, and his eloquence on this occasion brought in alms amounting to eight thousand crowns. On January 21st the inquisitors sent him a message to come to them the next day at 2 P.M., to which he replied in writing that he was indisposed and closely occupied with his sermons; if they wished to order him to preach the Edict of Faith, he held himself already charged to do so and begged them to excuse his coming. A second message the same day told him to come at the same hour another day, when he would be told what was wanted of him, to which he answered that he would come but that if it was only to order him to preach the sermon he would return at once to Castile, without again mounting the pulpit. Whether anything underlay this somewhat mysterious action does not appear; the significance of the affair lies in the fact that it at once became a matter of general public concern. When that same night the governor of the Hospital heard of it he recognized the injury that would accrue to the institution and to the whole city and forthwith reported it to the viceroy, who commissioned the Licentiate Balthasar Navarro to undo the mischief. The result of his labors was that the inquisitors declared that as Fray Vinegas pleaded indisposition they would excuse him from preaching the Edict of Faith. The affair appeared to be settled and Vinegas begged permission to call on the two inquisitors, Santos and Salcedo, and pay them the Easter compliments. They graciously acceded and on Easter Monday he waited on them, exculpated himself, and begged their pardon for having been prevented by indisposition from preaching the Edict, all of which they accepted with great courtesy. The community breathed freer, for some vindication of the honor of the Inquisition had been expected. The inquisitors however had been consulting the Suprema and vengeance was at hand. The next day, Tuesday, was the last of the series of sermons; Vinegas preached successfully to a crowded church when, on descending from the pulpit, he was arrested by an alguazil of the Inquisition, dragged through the crowd like a heresiarch attempting escape, thrown into a coach and carried to the Aljafería. There he was placed on a bench like a criminal, interrogated as one and then, without being listened to, was sentenced to perpetual deprivation of the honors of the Inquisition (preaching at autos, the edicts, etc.) and reprimanded with the utmost severity. The mark of infamy thus inflicted was indelible and the scandal was immense. The people flocked in crowds to the viceroy in the greatest excitement and he had much ado to quiet them by promising that it should be remedied. Vinegas applied for the reinstatement of his honor to the Council of Aragon, which replied that it had no jurisdiction; then he applied to the Suprema, which refused to hear him. He sent a memorial to the king, who referred it to the Council of Aragon and he continued his efforts for more than a year but it does not appear that he ever obtained relief.[906]

***

As a rule, any criticism of the justice of the Inquisition and any complaint by one who had passed through its hands were offences to be punished with more or less severity. To this, however, there was an exception in a case the singularity of which deserves mention. Perhaps the most distinguished Franciscan theologian of his day was Miguel de Medina. He fell under suspicion of Lutheranism, was arrested and tried and died during trial, May 1, 1578, in the secret prison of Toledo after four years of detention. Another Franciscan, Francisco Ortiz, espoused his cause so zealously that, in a public sermon in 1576 he pronounced the trial to be unjust, for it was the work of a conspiracy among his brother frailes; the arrest was a mortal sin, as though it were St. Jerome or St. Augustin, and the inquisitor-general (Espinosa) who had signed the warrant was in hell unless he had repented; the inquisitors were ashamed and were seeking to avert the disgrace from themselves, when they ought to be punishing the perjury of those who had testified. This was flat blasphemy against the Holy Office, and it is not easy to understand why the daring fraile escaped, when tried by the tribunal of Toledo, with a reprimand administered privately in the audience-chamber and a prohibition to enter Madrid without permission--a sentence which was duly confirmed by the Suprema.[907] We shall see hereafter that another Fray Francisco Ortiz, for a similar offence, did not escape so easily.

***

These were the defences thrown around the Inquisition to secure its effectiveness in its supreme function of maintaining religious unity, and these were the efforts which it made to secure the recognition of the supremacy to which it aspired. It was an institution suddenly introduced into an established ecclesiastical and secular hierarchy, which regarded the intruder with natural jealousy and dislike and resented its manifest resolve to use its spiritual authority for their humiliation. Its arrogant self-assertion led it into frequent mistakes in which even its royal protectors could not justify it, but it gradually won its way under the Hapsburgs. The advent of the Bourbons brought into play a new theory as to the relations between Church and State and the civil authorities were able in time to vindicate their equality and independence. We shall have the opportunity of following this struggle, in which religion was in no way concerned, for the defence of the faith was a pretext under which the Holy Office sought to arrogate to itself control over a constantly widening area of secular affairs, while claiming release from secular obligations.

CHAPTER III - PRIVILEGES AND EXEMPTIONS

Before the Revolution introduced the theory of equality, class privileges were the rule. The public burdens were eluded by those best able to bear them and were accumulated on the toilers. The mortmain lands held by the Church were exempt from both taxation and military service and, though Philip V, in the Concordat of 1737, obtained the privilege of taxing such as might subsequently be acquired, the repeated decrees for its enforcement show the impossibility of enforcing it.[908] The complete immunity of ecclesiastics from taxation was emphatically asserted by Boniface VIII in the bull Clericis laicos and, although this was revoked by the Council of Vienne in 1312, care was taken to enunciate the principle as still in vigor.[909] Yet in the kingdoms of Aragon they were subject to all imposts on sales, to import and export dues and other local taxation and, when resistance was offered to this, Charles V procured from Adrian VI, in 1522, and from Clement VII, in 1524, briefs confirming their liability.[910] Hidalguia, or gentle blood, conferred a multiplicity of privileges, including exemption from taxation, royal and local, with certain exceptions that were largely evaded, and the labrador--the peasant or commoner--was distinctively known as a pechero or tax-payer.[911] That in such a social order the Inquisition should seek for its members all the exemptions that it could grasp was too natural to excite surprise, though it might occasionally provoke resistance.

As regards freedom from taxation, the subject is complicated by questions concerning royal and local imposts, by the varying customs in the different provinces, and by the distinction between the active officials of the tribunals, known as titulados y asalaridos, and the more numerous unsalaried ones, who were only called upon occasionally for service, such as familiars, commissioners, notaries, consultors and censors. Their rights were loosely defined and were subject to perpetual variation by conflicting decisions in the contests that were constantly occurring with the secular authorities, provoked by habitual antagonism and the frequent imposition of new taxes, raising new questions. Ferdinand wrote sharply, April 13, 1504, to the town-council of Barcelona, when it attempted to subject the officials of the tribunal to the burdens borne by other citizens, in violation of the pre-eminences and exemptions of the Holy Office, and he warned them to desist, in view of the judicial measures that would be taken. Yet, in 1508, we find him writing still more sharply to that tribunal, scolding it because it had taken from the house of the alguazil of the Bailía a female slave and, without waiting for formal judgement, had sold her without paying the royal impost of twenty per cent., a disregard of the regalías not permitted to them. They had also issued an order on the custom-house to pass free of duty certain articles for an inquisitor, which was against all rule for, even if the goods were needed for the support of the officials, it was a matter for the farmers of the revenue to decide, and the issuing of such passes would be fruitful of fraud and loss.[912]

TAXATION

These instances indicate the uncertainties of the questions that were constantly arising in the intricate system--or lack of system--of Spanish taxation. To follow the subject in detail would be an endless and unprofitable task. I have collected a considerable number of more or less contradictory decisions of this early period, but the only deductions to be drawn from them are the indefiniteness of the exemption and the earnestness of the effort made to extend it by the Inquisition. The matter evidently was one in which there were no recognized rules and, in 1568, Philip II undertook to regulate it, at least in so far as concerned royal taxation. He defined for each tribunal the officials who were to be exempted from all taxes, excise and assessments, and forbade their exaction under pain of fifty thousand maravedís and punishment at the royal discretion, but this exemption was granted only during his good pleasure, so that he retained full control and admitted no privilege as inherent in the Inquisition. His enumeration moreover comprised only the titulados y asalariados, holding commissions from the Suprema and in constant service, and omitted the familiars and others who greatly exceeded them in numbers.[913]

This attempt at settlement left the matter still undefined and provocative of endless strife. It said nothing as to local taxes; these and the royal taxes were often indistinguishable, or so combined that they could not be separated; the unsalaried officials were not specifically declared to be taxable and were always striving for exemption, and when, in the growing needs of the monarchy, new taxes were imposed, there came ever fresh struggles conducted with the customary violence of the Inquisition. May 10, 1632, the Royal Council earnestly represented to Philip IV that it had already laid before him certain excesses of the inquisitors of Cuenca to which he had not seen fit to reply. Now the corregidor of Cuenca has reported other excesses requiring immediate remedy, for they have issued an order, under pain of excommunication and other penalties, that the collector of the excise on wine, imposed for the pay of the troops, shall not collect it of the salaried officials of the tribunal although they are laymen and subject to it. They pretended that they were not liable to the alcavala (tax on sales) but they were defeated in the suit on this before the Council of Hacienda. And if this is permitted all the other tribunals will attempt the same, and with their exemption will come that of their servants and kindred and connections of all kinds, with frauds and concealment as usual, resulting in increase of charge to other vassals and damage to the treasury, for it seems as though the sole object of the inquisitors is to diminish the royal patrimony.[914] Similar troubles attended the levying of the servicio de millones, an exceedingly unpopular impost on wine, meat, vinegar and other necessaries.[915]

**

When, in 1631, the tax of media añata, or half a year's salary levied on appointees to office, was imposed there was a discussion as to whether it was applicable to the Inquisition. This was settled in the affirmative and the Suprema made no objection, for its collection was taken from the Sala de Media Añata and was given to Gabriel Ortiz de Sotomayor, appointed by Inquisitor-general Zapata and when he, in the course of a few years, became Bishop of Badajoz, the business was intrusted to the inquisitor-general himself. For awhile the payments were made with some regularity, but in 1650, an investigation showed that for a long while it had been quietly allowed to drop and, as it was in the hands of the inquisitor-general, there were no means of enforcing an accounting. For a year Arce y Reynoso eluded the efforts of the Sala de Media Añata to obtain information and finally, May 17, 1651, the king ordered him peremptorily to pay his own media añata (due since 1643), to make the other officials do so and to furnish the required information to the Sala. On receiving this he said there were difficulties in making ecclesiastics like inquisitors pay, but he would consult the Suprema and reply in July. July passed away and the Sala again applied to him, when he replied that, as concerned the familiars and other secular officials, orders had already been given and collections made, but as to clerics there were scruples about which he would advise with the king. He failed to do so and in October the king was urged to repeat his demand for immediate payment. The outcome of the affair was that ecclesiastics were exempted and laymen had to pay, while familiars, who had no salaries, were assessed nine ducats--so Arce y Reynoso succeeded in eluding his tax. Collection, moreover, from the laymen was not easy and, January 28, 1654, the Suprema issued general instructions to deduct it without exception from the salaries. This only transferred the indebtedness from the individuals to the receivers or treasurers of the tribunals, who seem to have been equally slow to pay and, in 1655, an inquisitor in each tribunal of Castile and the colonies was designated to collect the money from the treasurer and remit it at once.[916] It is safe to assume that the receipts were trivial and the whole business affords an illustration of the methods by which the revenues of Spain were frittered away before reaching the treasury. Whether productive or not, however, the media añata remained until the end a permanent charge upon the lay officials. In Valencia, in 1790, it had for ten years amounted to an annual average of ten libras.[917]

With regard to local taxation, contests were renewed at every new impost with varying success, and a single case will elucidate the character of these struggles. In 1645 the Córtes of Valencia agreed to furnish for six years twelve hundred men to garrison Tortosa, reserving the right to impose whatever duties or excise might be necessary to defray the expense. In order that the clergy might be included the assent of Archbishop Aliaga was sought, which he granted with difficulty and only on condition that, within eight months, a confirmatory papal brief should be obtained, which was duly accomplished. To meet the charge an excise, known as the sisa del corte was levied on all goods cut for garments. The tribunal refused to submit to this and pointed to its contributions to a loan of twenty thousand ducats made by the Inquisition to the king in 1642, and to its payment since 1643 of five per cent. of the salaries for the maintenance of certain mounted men. The city yielded for a while and then a compromise was made; the ecclesiastics at the time were paying eighteen deniers on the libra (7-1/2 per cent.) while the officials of the tribunal were to be taxed only six deniers (2-1/2 per cent.). To maintain their principle of exemption, however, for some years they had their garments made in the name of other ecclesiastics and paid the eighteen deniers, but in 1659 they grew tired of this and paid the six deniers for themselves, first registering a protest that it was without prejudice to their privileges and exemptions. This continued until 1668, when suddenly, on June 19th, the fiscal of the tribunal summoned the collectors of the sisa del corte to pass freely, within twenty-four hours, the cloth cut for the garments of Benito Sanguino, the alcalde mayor, under pain of five hundred ducats. On the 21st the syndics of the city and the collectors interjected an appeal to the king, in spite of which the next day the mandate was repeated, this time giving twelve hours for obedience and adding excommunication to the fine. Another appeal was interposed and the regent of the Audiencia applied for a competencia, or orderly method of settling disputes, as provided in the Concordia, but notwithstanding this the next day the excommunications were published and the names of the collectors were affixed to the doors of the cathedral as under the anathema of the Church.[918] The final outcome is of little moment; the interest of the affair lies in its illustration of the persistence of the Inquisition and the violence of its methods.

In this respect the case is not exceptional. The formularies of the Inquisition contained a full assortment of arbitrary mandates which it employed, in place of seeking the legal courses prescribed in the Concordias, by which the king and the Córtes sought to preserve the peace. One of these, drawn in the name of the tribunal of Llerena, addressed to the governor and magistrates, recites that complaint has been made of the imposition on officials and familiars of a new octroi on meat and proceeds to assert that, by immemorial custom and royal cédulas, the commissioned officials are exempted from paying any taxes, excise, imposts and assessments, whether royal or local or otherwise; the magistrates are commanded within two hours to desist from the attempt, under pain of major excommunication and a fine of a hundred thousand maravedís for the governor or his deputy and of fifty thousand for subordinates, with the threat, in case of disobedience, of prosecution with the full rigor of law. Moreover the secretary or notary of the city is ordered within the two hours to bring to the tribunal and surrender all papers concerning the assessment on the officials, under pain of excommunication and ten thousand maravedís.[919] Such were the peremptory commands habitually employed, the arrogance of which rendered them especially galling.

***

Not only were these fulminations ready for use when the case occurred, but there were formulas drawn up in advance to prevent any attempted infraction of the privileges claimed by the officials. Thus this same collection has one addressed to the corregidor and magistrates of a town where a fair is to be held, reciting that an official of the tribunal proposes to send thither a certain number of cattle bearing his brand, which he swears to be of his own raising and, as he is exempt from paying alcavala, tolls, ferriages, royal servicio and all other assessments and dues and, as he fears that there may be an attempt to impose them, therefore all officials and collectors are ordered, under pain of major excommunication and two hundred ducats, to abstain from all such attempts, with threats of further punishment in case of disobedience.[920] The enormous advantage which the official thus possessed is plain, as well as the door which it opened to fraud. That the claim was groundless appears by a memorial presented to the Suprema in 1623, in response to a call by Inquisitor-general Pacheco on his colleagues for suggestions as to the better government and improvement of the Inquisition--a remarkable paper to which reference will frequently be made hereafter. On this point it states that, in some tribunals, the officials are exempted from paying the alcavala on the products of their estates, while in others they are not. In some, a portion of the officials have dexterously secured exemption, while others have been compelled to pay, by judicial decision, as there is no basis for such claims. If there is no right or privilege of exemption, it is not seen how the officials can conscientiously escape payment, or how the inquisitors can defend them in evading it, besides the numerous suits thence arising which occupy the time of the tribunals. To cure this it is suggested that the king grant exemptions to all, for there are not more than two or three in each tribunal to be thus benefited.[921] This suggestion was not adopted, but the claim was persisted in with its perpetual exasperation and multiplicity of litigation.

The large numbers of the unsalaried officials, especially the familiars, rendered the question of their exemption of considerably greater importance. They had no claim to it, but they were persistently endeavoring to establish the right and for the most part they were supported by the tribunals in the customary arbitrary fashion. In the futile Concordia of Catalonia in 1599, it was provided that levies and executions for all taxes and imposts could be made on familiars and commissioners by the ordinary officers of justice. In the memorial to Clement VIII asking for the disallowance of this Concordia, the Suprema proved learnedly, by a series of canons from the fourth Council of Lateran down, that the cruce-signati (whom it claimed to correspond with the modern familiars) were exempt. It even had the audacity to cite the Concordia of 1514, which in reality denied their exemption, and it assumed with equal untruth that this was the universal custom in Spain.[922] Yet, in a consulta of December 30, 1633, the Suprema tacitly excluded the unsalaried officials when it argued that there were not, exclusive of ecclesiastics, more than two hundred officials in Spain entitled to the exemption.[923]

***

Still, the Inquisition fought the battle for the unsalaried officials with as much vigor as for the salaried. In 1634 the levying of a few reales on a familiar of Vicalvero, on the occasion of the voyage to Barcelona of the Infante Fernando, was resisted with such violence by the tribunal of Toledo, that finally the king had to intervene, resulting in the banishment and deprival of temporalities of a clerical official and the summoning to court of the senior inquisitor.[924] In 1636, Philip IV, to meet the extravagant outlays on the palace of Buen Retiro, levied a special tax on all the towns of the district of Madrid. In Vallecas the quota was assessed on the inhabitants, among whom was a familiar who refused to pay, when the local alcaldes levied upon his property. He appealed to the Suprema which referred the matter to the tribunal of Toledo and it arrested the alcaldes and condemned them in heavy penalties. Then the Alcaldes de Casa y Corte, the highest criminal court, intervened and arrested the familiar, whereupon the Suprema twice sent to the Sala de los Alcaldes, declaring them to be excommunicated, but the bearer of the censure was refused audience. On this the Suprema, with the assent of the Council of Castile, sent a cleric to arrest the alcaldes and convey them out of the kingdom, and on March 12th, in all the churches of Madrid, they were published as excommunicate and subject to all the penalties of the bull in Coena Domini.[925] What was the outcome of this the chronicler fails to inform us, but the Council of Castile took a different view of the question when, in 1639, one of its members, Don Antonio Valdés, who had been sent to Extremadura as commissioner to raise troops, was publicly excommunicated by the tribunal of Llerena because, in assessing contributions for that purpose, he had not exempted its officials and familiars. The Council thereupon appealed to Philip, who ordered the decree expunged from the records and that a copy of the royal order should be posted in the secretariate of the tribunal.[926]

Yet it was about this time that the claim in behalf of unsalaried officials seems to have been abandoned, for, in 1636, 1643 and 1644 the Suprema issued repeated injunctions that in the existing distress the royal imposts and taxes must be paid. In 1646 it ordered the tribunal of Valencia not to defend two familiars in resisting payment and in the same year the Córtes of Aragon gained a victory which subjected them to all local charges.[927]

With the advent of the Bourbons the salaried officials found a change in this as in so much else. In the financial exigencies of the War of Succession they were subjected to repeated levies. Philip V called upon them for five per cent. of their salaries and then for ten per cent. to which they were forced to submit. In 1712 a general tax was laid of a doubloon per hearth, which was assessed in each community according to the wealth of the individual. There were no exemptions and appeals were heard only by the provincial superintendents of the revenue. The sole concession obtained by the Suprema was that, where officials of the Inquisition were concerned, the local tribunal could name an assessor to sit with the superintendent and it warned the tribunals that any interference with the collection would be repressed with the utmost severity.[928] Salaries, however, were held to be subject only to demands from the crown for, when Saragossa in 1727 endeavored to include them in an assessment for local taxation, Philip, in response to an appeal from the Suprema, decided that those of the Inquisition, in common with other tribunals, should be exempt, but that real and personal property, including trade, belonging to officials, should be held liable to the tax.[929]

Towards the close of the eighteenth century various documents show that all ideas of resistance and all pleas of exemption had been abandoned. The Holy Office submitted to ordinary and extraordinary exactions and the Suprema warned the tribunals that the assessments were wholly in the hands of the royal officers and that it had no cognizance of the matter. The calls were frequent and heavy, as when, in 1794, four per cent. was levied on all salaries of over eight hundred ducats, and three months later a demand was made of one-third of the fruits of all benefices and prebends, which was meekly submitted to and statements were obediently rendered.[930] Under the Restoration, the Inquisition was less tractable. In 1818 an incometax was levied and was imposed on all salaries, including those of the Suprema, which at once prepared for resistance. There seems to have been a prolonged struggle with a successful result for, on November 17th, it issued a circular enclosing a royal order which conceded exemption.[931]

***

The exemption from taxation, which included import and export dues or merchandise and provisions required for officials and prisoners, led to the claim of other privileges and to not a few abuses. It was not confined to sea-ports and frontier towns, for the jealous particularism of the kingdoms, dynastically united, kept up their antagonistic policy towards each other and intercourse between them was subjected to regulations similar to those of foreign trade. The exemption from these, as well as from the octroi duties of the towns, was a most important privilege, capable of being turned to account in many ways besides diminishing the expenses of the officials.

CUSTOMS DUTIES

We have seen that Ferdinand, in 1508, prohibited the issue of orders to pass goods free, but nevertheless it continued. When, in 1540, Blas Ortiz went to take possession of his office as inquisitor of Valencia, the Suprema furnished him with a pass addressed to all customs officials permitting him to cross the frontiers with three horses and four pack-mules; he could be required to swear that what he carried was his private property and was not for sale, but all further interference was hidden under pain of excommunication and a hundred ducats.[932] It was not only on such occasions, however, that the customhouses were thus eluded. Before the introduction of regular posts, the constant communications between the tribunals and with the Suprema were carried by couriers or by muleteers, and the mysterious secrecy which shrouded all the operations of the Holy Office furnished an excuse for preventing any risk that these sacred packages should be examined. All bearers of letters therefore, even when they had loaded mules, were furnished with passes forbidding, under excommunication and fine, any unpacking or investigation of what they carried.[933] The facilities thus offered for contraband trade are obvious and their value can only be appreciated through a knowledge of the elaborate system of import and export duties and prohibitions of import and export which characterize the policy of the period.[934] Complaints were fruitless, for when the Council of Hacienda issued letters against certain familiars in the Canaries, detected in importing prohibited goods, Philip II, February 11, 1593, ordered the letters to be recalled and that no more should be issued.[935]

There were few things concerning which there was more jealousy than the transfer of grain from one Spanish kingdom to another, and when it was permitted there were duties, either import or export or perhaps both. Deficient harvests, in one province or another, were not infrequent and the tribunals were constantly seeking special relief by obtaining permits to violate the laws, or by violating the laws without permits. Many instances of this could be cited, but it will suffice to recount the experience of the Valencia tribunal in endeavoring to obtain wheat from Aragon. For this it had special facilities, for the Aragonese districts of Teruel and Albarracin were subject to it, but, on the other hand, Aragon was especially firm in prohibiting the exportation of wheat. In 1522 the tribunal undertook to bring some wheat from Aragon and threatened the frontier officials with excommunication if they should interfere. In spite of this they detained it, when the inquisitor published the censures and imprisoned a guard whom he caught, whereupon the Aragonese Diputados remonstrated, saying that if the emperor or pope wanted wheat from Aragon he applied for licence, and begging the inquisitor to keep within his jurisdiction and release the guard. Then an accommodation was reached and the tribunal was permitted to bring in thirty cahizes (about one hundred bushels), on condition of removing any excommunication that might exist, but it repudiated its side of the agreement and summoned the officials to appear and receive penance. This exhausted the patience of the Diputados; they ordered the wheat to be stopped or, if it had gone forward to be followed and captured with the mules bearing it; the inquisitor might do what he pleased, but they would employ all the forces of the kingdom and enforce respect for the laws. The position in which the inquisitor had placed himself was so untenable that the inquisitor-general issued an order forbidding tribunals to take anything out of Aragon in violation of the prohibitions.[936]

IMPORTATION OF WHEAT

The effect of this rebuff was evanescent. The tribunal persisted and by false pretences established a claim which, in 1591, the Suprema warned it to use with moderation as the Council of Aragon was making complaint. As usual no attention was paid to this and, in 1597, Philip II was compelled to interfere because the tribunal was issuing to excess letters authorizing the export of wheat from Teruel-- an abuse which was doubtless abundantly profitable.[937] If this brought any amendment it was transient. On June 16, 1606, the Diputados represented to the tribunal that they were bound by their oaths of office, under pain of excommunication, to enforce the laws prohibiting the export of wheat; that, in spite of these laws, large quantities were carried to Valencia, to the destruction and total ruin of the land, by individuals armed with licences issued by the tribunal, wherefore they prayed that no more licences be issued. No attention was paid to this and on January 8, 1607, they wrote again, stating that the abuse was increasing and that they must appeal to the king and the Suprema for its suppression. This brought an answer to the effect that the tribunal was more moderate than it had previously been and would continue to be so as it would find convenient, without prejudice to the rights conceded to it by the royal cédulas and, as it was occupied in the service of God, it could reasonably exercise those rights. The asserted rights under which it had so long nullified the laws of Aragon were a conscious fraud for, when it complained to the Suprema of the interference of the Diputados with its immemorial privilege and enclosed the royal cédula conferring it, the Suprema pointed out that this referred only to Castile and not to Aragon; the complaints of the Diputados had been listened to and all that could be done was to invoke the good offices of the Saragossa tribunal to obtain permission to get fifteen hundred bushels per annum. The Saragossa inquisitors willingly lent their aid, but in vain. They wrote, June 6, 1608, that they had brought to bear all their influence on the Diputados who declared that the fuero prohibiting the export of grain was too strict for them to violate it. A correspondence ensued with the Suprema which ordered the tribunal, February 8, 1610, to abstain, as previously ordered, but if, in any year, there should be special necessity, it might report the quantity required when instructions would be given. This imposed silence on it until 1618, when another attempt was made to overcome the obstinacy of the Diputados; it had abstained, the tribunal said, for some years from issuing licences, in consequence of the great abuses and excesses of those to whom they were granted, but now the sterility of the land causes great inconveniences and it asks that the fruits of its prebends in Aragon and its rents be invested in wheat allowed to be exported. The Diputados however wisely refused to open the door; the law to which they had sworn imposed heavy penalties for its infraction and they were compelled to refuse. This was probably effectual, as far as concerned Aragon, for we happen to find the tribunal, in 1631, obtaining from the king licence to import two hundred and fifty bushels from Castile.[938]

EVASION OF OCTROI DUTIES

This narrative is instructive in more ways than one. The pretence of necessity in the service of God was as fraudulent as the claims put forward. The whole business was purely speculative and the licences were doubtless sold to the highest bidder through all these years. The Valencian tribunal was at no time in need of wheat from Aragon or Castile, for it had ample privileges at home for all its wants and it was working these local privileges for a profit to some one. Among other public-spirited acts of Ximenes was the founding, in 1512, of an alhondiga, or public granary, in Toledo so that, as we are told in 1569, in times of scarcity the citizens could procure supplies at moderate prices.[939] It was probably owing to this that other cities, including Valencia, formed establishments of the kind, monopolizing the traffic in wheat, to which the citizens resorted day by day for their provision. When a loss occurred in the business, from a surplus over the demand or from spoiling of the grain, it was assessed upon the citizens, under the name of pan asegurado, but, in 1530, the magistrates relieved the officials of the tribunal from sharing this burden and the exemption is enumerated, in 1707, as still among its privileges.[940] Another privilege, which it shared with the viceroy and the archbishop, was that the baker who served it was the second one allowed every morning to enter the granary and select a sack of wheat (trigo fuerte) of five and a half bushels and every week a cahiz (3-1/2 bushels) of trigo candeal, without payment save a small tax known as murs y valls--evidently for the maintenance of the city defences. This he baked and distributed the bread among the officials and to the prison, in allotted portions, and what was over he sold--showing that the tribunal not only got its wheat gratuitously but more than it needed, to somebody's profit. The amount must have been considerable, for the bakers complained of the unfair competition of the favored baker and, in 1609, the city endeavored to put an end to the abuse, but without success. The matter slumbered until 1627, when the city obtained a royal cédula abolishing the privilege of taking the wheat, but obedience to this was refused because it had been issued without preliminary notice to the other side and without a junta or conference between the Suprema and the Council of Aragon. Then the city ordered the baker no longer to go to the granary for wheat and the aggrieved Suprema complained loudly to the king, urging him to consider the services to God and the tonsure of the inquisitors and not to allow these holy labors to be interrupted by the necessity of going personally to the granary. To this Philip replied by ordering the fueros to be observed, which was virtually a confirmation of his cédula, but this seems to have been similarly disregarded, for, in 1628 we find the city again endeavoring to put an end to the collateral abuse of the sale of the surplus bread and the tribunal busily engaged in gathering testimony to prove that this had publicly been the custom from time immemorial. In proving this, however, it also proved unconsciously how fraudulent had been the claim that it had been in need of wheat from Aragon.[941]

This commercial development of the Inquisition led it to utilize its exemption from taxation and octroi duties by opening shops for the necessaries of life, causing violent quarrels with the cities whose revenues were impaired and whose laws were ostentatiously disregarded. Among a number of cases of this in the records, a series of occurrences in Saragossa will illustrate this phase of the activity of the Holy Office. A large part of the local revenues of the city was derived from a monopoly of wine, meal and provisions and no citizen was allowed to bring these articles within the gates. The Aljafería, occupied by the tribunal, was situated a few hundred feet beyond the walls; the inquisitors assumed that they were not bound by the municipal regulations; they introduced what they pleased into the town and the authorities complained that they maintained in the Aljafería a public meat-market, a tavern and a shop where citizens could purchase freely to the infinite damage of the public revenues. The Córtes of 1626 demanded that affairs should be reduced to what they had been prior to the troubles of 1591, when the Aljafería was garrisoned with soldiers, giving rise to profitable trade, but the Suprema prevented the royal confirmation of the acts of the Córtes and the matter was left open. This led to troubles which came to a head, September 21, 1626, when a load of wine for the tribunal on entering the city was seized under the law by the guard and taken to the house of one of the jurados or town-councillors. At once the inquisitors issued letters demanding its release under pain of excommunication and a thousand ducats. The jurados lost no time in forming the competencia, which, in accordance with the existing Concordia, was the method provided for deciding such contests, but the inquisitors refused to join in it, asserting that there could be no competencia, as it was a matter of faith and impeding the Inquisition in the exercise of its functions. They arrested and imprisoned one of the guards, notwithstanding that he had letters of manifestacion from the court of the Justicia of Aragon--a species of habeas corpus of the highest privilege in Aragon, which was traditionally venerated as the palladium of popular liberty--and the next day they seized three more who were likewise manifestados. The incensed magistrates applied to the Justicia and to the Diputados, to release by force the prisoners from the Aljafería and there was prospect of serious disorder. The Governor of Aragon, however succeeded in getting himself accepted as umpire by both sides and temporarily quieted them by the compromise that the wagon, mules and wine should be delivered to him, that the prisoners should be surrendered through him to the city and that the comminatory letters should be withdrawn, all this being without prejudice to either party. He wrote earnestly to the king, pointing out the imminent danger of an outbreak and the necessity of a decision that should avert such perils for the future; if the assumption that such questions were matters of faith were admitted, the inquisitors could refuse all competencias, which would annul the Concordia and destroy the royal jurisdiction. The city also addressed him, saying that the inquisitors had refused to abstain from further action pending his decision and if these pretensions were admitted they would be unable to pay him the servicio which had been granted.[942]

SALT AND BAKE-OVEN

This resulted in a compromise, agreed upon between the Suprema and the Council of Aragon, under which the city obligated itself to supply the tribunal with meat, wine and ice. It was impossible however to compel the Inquisition to observe compacts. Fresh complaints arose, the nature of which is indicated by a decree of Philip IV, June 17, 1630, requiring the Suprema to order the inquisitors to keep to the agreement and not to sell any portion of the provisions furnished and further to stop the trade carried on in some little houses in the Aljafería where the municipal supervisors could not inspect them. This resulted in a fresh agreement of December 7, 1631, under which the city bought for three thousand crowns the casa de penitencia, or prison for penitents, and engaged to maintain in it shops to the sale of meat and ice to the inhabitants of the Aljafería at the prices current in the town.[943]

Probably this quieted the matter, but before long the irrepressible inquisitors started another disturbance. The salt-works of Remolinos and el Castellon belonged to the royal patrimony and were farmed out under condition that no other salt should be sold or used in Saragossa and some other places under heavy fines. To enforce this there were commissioners empowered to investigate all suspected places, even churches not being exempt. In 1640 a party in the city was found to be selling salt and confessed that he obtained it from the gardener of the Aljafería. The commissioner, Baltasar Peralta, went there with a scrivener and in the gardener's cottage they found two sacks, one empty, the other nearly full of salt, with a half-peck measure. They announced the penalty to the gardener's wife and proceeded to enforce it in the customary manner by seizing pledges--in the present case, three horses. The inquisitor, who had doubtless been sent for, came as they were leading the horses away, forced the surrender of the horses and salt and told them that they should deem themselves lucky if they were not thrown in prison. Thereupon the royal advocate-fiscal of Aragon, Adrian de Sada, reported the case to the king, adding that it was learned that the coachman of one of the inquisitors was selling salt from the salt-works of Sobradiel. He pointed out that, if the servants of the Inquisition could sell salt freely and the royal officials be deterred by threats from investigation, the revenue would be seriously impaired, for no one would venture to farm the salt-works, and he asked for instructions before resorting to proceedings which might disturb the public peace, as had happened on previous occasions. The matter was referred to the Council of Aragon, which advised the king to issue imperative commands that the inquisitors should not obstruct the detection and punishment of frauds, for their cognizance in no way pertained to the Holy Office.[944]

The Saragossa tribunal had a still more prolonged and bitter dispute with the city over the bake-oven of the Aljafería. This belonged to the crown and, at some time prior to 1630, Philip IV made it over to the tribunal which was pleading poverty. Its use of the privilege soon brought it into conflict with the city, but a complicated arrangement respecting it was included in the agreement of December 7, 1631, requiring the baker to purchase at least seventy bushels of wheat per month from the public granary, with certain restrictions as to the places whence he could procure further supplies. In 1649 we chance to learn that the oven was farmed out for six thousand reales per annum and in 1663, a lively conflict arose because the tribunal had granted a lease which was not subject to the restrictions of 1631. Then again, in 1690, the trouble broke out afresh, each side accusing the other of violating the agreement. All the authorities, from the king and viceroy down, were invoked to settle it; there were fears of violence but, May 1, 1691, the tribunal reported to the Suprema that a compromise had been reached on satisfactory terms.[945]

The independent spirit of Aragon caused it to suffer less from the mercantile enterprises of the Inquisition than the more submissive temper of Castile. In 1623 there was a flagrant case in Toledo, arising from a butcher-shop established by the tribunal in violation of the municipal laws. Its violent methods triumphed and Don Luis de Paredes, an alcalde de corte, sent thither to settle the matter, was disgraced for attempting to restrain it. This called forth an energetic protest from the Council of Castile, which boldly told the king that he should not shut his eyes to the fact that the inquisitors were extending their privileges to matters beyond their competence, with such prejudice to the public weal that they were making themselves superior to the laws, to the government and to the royal power, trampling on the judges, seizing the original documents, forcing them to revoke their righteous acts, arresting their officials and treating them as heretics because they discharged their duty.[946]

SEIZURE OF PROVISIONS

In procuring provisions, whether for consumption or sale, besides the freedom from local imposts, the Inquisition had the further advantage of employing coercive methods on unwilling vendors and of disregarding local regulations and prohibitions. As early as 1533 the Aragonese, at the Córtes of Monzon, took the alarm and petitioned that the statutes of the towns, when short of bread-stuffs and provisions, should be binding on officials of the Inquisition, to which the emperor's reply was the equivocating one customary when evading confirmation.[947] The significance of this is manifested by a carta acordada of 1540, authorizing the tribunals to get wheat in the villages for their officials and prisoners and, if the local magistrates interfere, to coerce them with excommunication. Yet inquisitorial zeal in using this permission sometimes overstepped the bounds and, in this same year, the Suprema had occasion to rebuke a tribunal which had issued orders to furnish it with wheat under pain of a hundred lashes, for it was told that, in rendering such extra-judicial sentences, it was exceeding its jurisdiction.[948] How bravely the Suprema itself overcame all such scruples was manifest when laws of maximum prices, and the heavy discount on the legal-tender spurious vellon coinage, rendered holders of goods unwilling to part with them at the legal rates. It issued, February 14, 1626, to its alcalde, Pedro de Salazar, an order to go to any places in the vicinage and embargo sheep and whatever else he deemed necessary, sufficient for the maintenance of the households of the inquisitor-general and of the members and officials, paying therefore at the rates fixed by law, to effect which he was empowered to call for aid on all royal justices, who were required to furnish all necessary aid under penalty of major excommunication latæ sententiæ and five hundred ducats. So again, on April 11, 1630, Salazar was ordered to go anywhere in the kingdom and seize six bushels of wheat, in baked bread, for the same households, paying for it at the established price, and all officials, secular, ecclesiastical and inquisitorial, were required to assist him under the same penalties.[949] This was an organized raid on all the bakeries of Madrid, and Salazar was more scrupulous than the average official of the time if he did not turn an honest penny by taking bread on his own account at the legal rate and selling it at the current one.[950]

The tribunal of Valencia enjoyed another privilege in the important matter of salt, the royal monopoly of which rendered it so costly to the ordinary consumer. Every year the tribunal issued an order to the farmers of the salt-works, commanding them, under pain of excommunication and fifty ducats, to deliver to the receiver of confiscations twelve cahizes (about forty-two bushels) of refined salt, at the price of eight reales the cahiz, and the custom-house officials were summoned, under the same penalties, to let it pass without detention or trouble for the service of God. The salt was duly apportioned among the officials at this trivial price, each inquisitor getting four bushels down to the messengers who received two-thirds of a bushel, and even jubilado officials had their portion. When or how this originated is unknown; in 1644 it seems established as of old date and it continued until 1710, when the new dynasty brought it to a sudden conclusion. The Council of Hacienda reported it to the king, as though it were a novelty just discovered, pointing out that the eight reales were less than the cost of transport from the works to the magazines; that the manufacture was a monopoly of the regalías and the price charged was in no respect a tax or impost, but was regulated by the necessities of the national defence; that no other tribunal in Spain, secular or ecclesiastic, made such a demand, while the publication of censures against royal officials was dangerous in those calamitous times. This aroused Philip, who ordered a prompt remedy. The Suprema no longer ventured an opposition or remonstrance, but wrote immediately to Valencia expressing its surprise; the demand must be withdrawn at once; if any censures had been published they must be revoked and no such demonstration should have been made without previous consultation.[951]

It would be superfluous to adduce further examples of the manner in which the tribunals abused their power for unlawful gains and benefits, and we can readily conceive the exasperation thus excited, even among those most zealous in the extermination of heresy.

BILLETING TROOPS

Few of the privileges claimed by the Inquisition gave rise to more bickering and contention than its demand that all connected with it should be exempt from the billeting of troops and the furnishing of bagages or beasts of burden for transportation. The subject is one of minor importance, but it furnishes so typical an illustration of inquisitorial methods that it is worthy of examination somewhat in detail. Under the old monarchy the yantar or droit de gîte, or right to free quarters, was an insufferable burden. Almost every Córtes of Leon and Castile, from the twelfth century complained of it energetically, for it was exercised, not only by the royal court in its incessant peregrinations, but by nobles and others who could enforce it, and it was accompanied by spoliation of every kind, while the impressment of beasts of burden was an associated abuse and even the lands of the Church were not exempt.[952] The more independent Aragonese were unwilling to submit to it, and a fuero of the Córtes of Aleañiz, in 1436, provided that the courtiers and followers of the king should pay all Christians in whose houses they lodged.[953] When the Inquisition was founded and was to a great extent peripatetic, its officials apparently claimed free quarters, for a clause in the Instructions of 1498 provides that where a tribunal was set up they should pay for their accommodations and provide their own beds and necessaries.[954] When travelling, a decree of Ferdinand, October 21, 1500, repeated in 1507, 1516, 1518, 1532, and 1561, provided that they should have gratuitous lodging and beds, with food at moderate prices.[955] The frequent repetition of this indicates that it aroused opposition and, in 1601, when the inquisitor of Valencia was ordered to go at once on a visitation of Tortosa, he was told not to oppress the city by demanding free quarters but to lodge decently in a monastery or in the house of some official.[956]

Furnishing free quarters however was different from enjoying them. The old abuses gradually disappeared with the settled habitations for kings and tribunals, but the change in military organization, with standing armies, gave rise to others which, if more occasional, were also more oppressive--the billeting of troops. When Louis XIV resorted to the dragonnades--the quartering of dragoons on Huguenot families--as an effective coercion to conversion, it shows how severe was the infliction. The rebellion of Catalonia, in 1640, had for its proximate cause the outrages committed by troops quartered for the winter in places insufficient for their support, culminating in their burning the churches of Riu de Arenas and Montiró.[957] The massacre in Saragossa, December 28, 1705, of the French troops in the service of Philip V, had the same origin.[958]

As the pay of Spanish armies was habitually in arrears and the commissariat system imperfect, it can be realized how valuable was the privilege of exemption from entertaining these uninvited guests and providing them with transportation when they departed. In the war with Portugal, in 1666, Galicia suffered so seriously that we are told a company of cavalry was worth to its captain two thousand ducats in ransoms, from outrage.[959] That the Inquisition should claim such exemption was to be expected, for it was one of the privileges of hidalgos, but the earliest allusion to it that I have met occurs in 1548, when Inquisitor-general Valdés ordered that no billets must be given on houses occupied by inquisitors or officials, even though not their own or during their absence, for their clothes were in them.[960] What authority he had to issue such a command it might be difficult to say, but it indicates that the exemption was an innovation and, as it refers only to salaried officials, it infers that the numerous unsalaried ones were not entitled to the privilege, which is further proved by the fact that, in the Castilian Concordia of 1553, regulating the exemptions of familiars, there is no allusion to billeting. The action of Valdés, however, settled the matter as far as the salaried officials were concerned and even the Aragonese Córtes of 1646, which greatly limited the claims of the Inquisition, admitted that they had the same privileges as hidalgos.[961]

***

The determination with which this was enforced is seen in a case in 1695, when Inquisitor Sanz y Múñoz of Barcelona threatened with excommunication and a fine of two hundred libras the town-councillors of Manlleu if they should assign quarters in a country-house belonging to the portero of the Inquisition, although it was occupied by a peasant who worked on the land. The councillors appealed for protection to the Audiencia, or royal court, which invited the inquisitor to settle the matter amicably in the prescribed form of a competencia, but he treated the overture with such contempt that he promptly issued a second mandate, under the same penalties, and summoned the councillors to appear before him as having incurred them. The Audiencia made another attempt at pacification to which he replied that he proposed at once to declare the councillors as publicly excommunicated. The Diputados of Catalonia thereupon protested vigorously to the king that, while all the rest of the people were patriotically united in aiding the war, and the gentry had voluntarily foregone their privilege of exemption, the officials and familiars of the Inquisition were exciting tumults and riots in their efforts to extend exemptions to those who had no claim.[962]

    The chief trouble arose with the unsalaried officials, especially the multitudinous familiars, who had no claim to exemption. The Barcelona tribunal seems to have started it, for one of the complaints made to de Soto Salazar, on his visitation of 1567, was that the inquisitors forbade the quartering of soldiers in the houses of familiars; in his report he suggested that it should be done when necessary and the Aragonese Concordia of 1568 followed this idea by prohibiting inquisitors to support familiars in refusing to receive men assigned to them when there were no other houses to receive them.[963] There was evidently no recognized exemption but a steady effort to establish one, while the familiars complained that the hatred felt for them led to their being oppressed with billets when others went free. To remedy this Philip II, in a cédula of February 21, 1576, ordered that no discrimination should be made against them, but that they should be placed on an equality with justicias and regidores who were not called upon to furnish quarters until all other houses were occupied. Complaints continued and he advanced a step, February 22, 1579, by decreeing that for three years, in towns of upwards of five hundred hearths, familiars should be exempt from billeting and furnishing transportation; in smaller towns, one-half should be exempted and where there was but one he should be exempt. This was renewed frequently for three years at a time and as frequently was overlooked, but this made little difference for we are told by an experienced inquisitor that it was always assumed to be in force and, when a familiar complained of a billet, the tribunal would issue a mandate ordering his relief within three hours under a penalty of 100,000 mrs.; if the exemption was in force, a copy of the cédula was included in the mandate, if it was not it still was quoted as existing in the archives of the tribunal.[964]

    There were few questions which gave rise to more embroilment than this. Both sides were unscrupulous; the privilege excited ill-will, it was evaded by the authorities wherever possible and the tribunals were kept busy in defending their familiars with customary violence. At length, in 1634, the necessities of the state were pleaded by Philip IV as his reason for withdrawing all exemptions--a measure which he was obliged to repeat more than once.[965] It is somewhat remarkable therefore that, when the Córtes of Aragon, in 1646, succeeded in greatly abridging the privileges of familiars, they were included with the salaried officials in the exemption from billets. This did not avail them much for we are told that, in the changes effected by the Córtes, the terror felt for the Inquisition was so greatly diminished that there was scant ceremony in imposing on its officials; that the familiars were singled out to have two or three soldiers quartered on them and when they complained the tribunal ventured no more than to instruct its commissioner to use persuasion.[966] Catalonia was not so fortunate and strife continued with the usual bitterness. As a frontier province, in war time it was occupied with troops and there were abundant opportunities for friction. In 1695 the Diputados complained that, as the only mode of escaping billets was to become a familiar, many had themselves appointed, although there was already an innumerable multitude, and that even when the local magistrates were compelled to receive soldiers, the familiars refused, in contempt of the royal orders.[967]

***

    The War of Succession brought fresh necessities and the change of dynasty was unfavorable to the Inquisition in this as in so much else. A royal decree of February 11, 1706, abolished all exemptions but, as a favor to the Inquisition, four of its officials were excepted in towns and twenty in cities that were seats of tribunals. The Suprema accepted this cheerfully but, when a decree of January 19, 1712, revoked all exemptions, it remonstrated and was told that, while the king recognized the claims of the Inquisition to all the privileges granted by his predecessors, the existing urgency required the withdrawal of all exemptions and, as the law was absolute, he could make no exceptions. Although this covered the salaried officials, it seems to have been the familiars who complained the loudest; possibly now that the tribunals could no longer protect them they were exposed to special discrimination. It was a question of money, however, rather than of hardship, for a system of composition had been developed under which by paying the cuartel or utensilio--an assessment proportioned to the wealth of the individual--the billet was escaped.[968] When the urgency of immediate peril was passed these decrees were either withdrawn or became obsolete. The claim of exemption revived and with it the active efforts of the tribunals to protect those whose exemptions were disregarded and to punish the officials who disregarded them.[969]

    In 1728 Philip V made a well-intentioned attempt to relieve the oppression of the poor arising from the numerous classes of officials who claimed exemption from the common burdens, including the billeting of troops. As for the familiars, he says, who all claim exemptions and give rise to disturbances, attacks on the local magistrates, with excommunications and other penalties, and perpetual competencias, all this must cease. Yet he admits their exemption and only insists that it must be confined to the number allowed by the Concordia of 1553; that limitation had never been observed and the inquisitors had appointed large numbers in excess of it, in spite of perpetual remonstrance, and Philip now ordered that tribunals should not issue certificates to more than the legal number and should not take proceedings against the local magistrates.[970] As usual the royal orders were disregarded. The tribunal of Valencia threatened with excommunication and fine the magistrates of Játiva and San Mateo, at the instance of some familiars on whom soldiers had been quartered, and, on learning this, Philip addressed the Suprema in 1729 stating that the records showed that familiar were entitled to no exemption; even if they were, the tribunal had exceeded its powers in employing obstreperous methods in defiance of the royal decrees. There must be no competencia; the Valencia tribunal must be notified not to exceed its jurisdiction and the Suprema itself must observe the royal orders. After the delay of a month, the Suprema forwarded the royal letter to Valencia, sullenly telling the tribunal to report what could be done and not to act further without orders.[971]

For two centuries the Inquisition had been accustomed to obey or to disregard the royal decrees at its pleasure and to tyrannize over the local authorities. The habit was not easily broken and it was hard to conform itself to the new order of things. A formulary of about 1740 contains a letter to be sent to magistrates granting billets on familiars, couched in the old arrogant and peremptory terms and threatening excommunication and a fine of two hundred ducats. Familiars, it says, are not to furnish quarters and beasts of burden, except in extreme urgency when no exemptions are permitted, and this it assumes to be in accordance with the royal decrees, including the latest one of November 3, 1737.[972] I can find no trace of a decree of 1737 and we may assume that it was this obstinacy of the Inquisition that induced Philip, in 1743, to reissue his decree of 1728 with an expression of regret at its inobservance and the disastrous results which had ensued; he added that, when the houses of the non-exempt were insufficient for quartering troops, they could be billeted on hidalgos and nobles.[973]

BEARING ARMS

The Inquisition still adhered to its claims, but Carlos III taught it to abandon its comminatory style. When, in 1781, the authorities of Castellon de la Plana billeted troops on familiars, the Valencia tribunal adopted the more judicious method of persuading the captain-general that they were to be classed with hidalgos and he issued orders to that effect. This did not please Carlos III, who brushed aside the claim to exemption by a peremptory order that the familiars of Castellon de la Plana should subject themselves to the local government in the matters of billets and that there should be no change until he should issue further commands.[974]

This would seem in principle to abrogate all claims to exemption, but Spanish tenacity still held fast to what it had claimed and, in 1800, when José Poris, a familiar of Alcira, complained that the governor had quartered on him an officer of the regiment of Sagunto, the Valencia tribunal took measures for his relief.[975] The times were adverse to privilege, however, and in 1805 the Captain-general of Catalonia sent a circular to all the towns stating that familiars were not exempt. The magistrates accordingly compelled them to furnish quarters and beasts of burden, and, when the tribunal complained to the captain-general and adduced proofs in support of its claims, he responded with the decrees of 1729 and 1743, which he assumed to have abrogated the exemption and he continued to coerce the familiars. The same process was going on in Valencia and, when that tribunal applied to Barcelona for information and learned the result, it ordered its familiars to submit under protest. Then followed a royal cédula of August 20, 1807, limiting strictly what exemptions were still allowed; the Napoleonic invasion supervened and under the Restoration I have met with no trace of their survival.[976]

***

Another privilege which occasioned endless debate and contention was the right of officials and familiars to bear arms, especially prohibited ones. This was a subject which, during the middle ages, had taxed to the utmost the civilizing efforts of legislators, while the power assumed by inquisitors to issue licences to carry arms, in contravention of municipal statutes, was the source of no little trouble, especially in Italian cities.[977] The necessity of restriction, for the sake of public peace, was peculiarly felt in Spain, where the popular temper and the sensitiveness as to the pundonor were especially provocative of deadly strife.[978] It would be impossible to enumerate the endless series of decrees which succeeded each other with confusing rapidity and the repetition of which, in every variety of form, shows conclusively how little they were regarded and how little they effected. Particular energy was directed against armas alevosas--treacherous weapons--which could be concealed about the person. In the Catalan Córtes of 1585, Philip II denounced arquebuses, fire-locks and more especially the small ones known as pistols, as unworthy the name of arms, as treacherous weapons useless in war and provocative of murder, which had caused great damage in Catalonia and had been prohibited in his other kingdoms. They were therefore forbidden, not only to be carried but even to be possessed at home and in secret, and against this no privilege should avail, whether of the military class or official or familiar of the Inquisition or by licence of the king or captain-general, under penalty for those of gentle blood of two years' exile, for plebeians of two years' galley-service, and for Frenchmen or Gascons of death, without power of commutation by any authority. Three palms, or twenty-seven inches of barrel, was the minimum length allowed for fire-arms in Catalonia and four palms in Castile. Philip IV, in 1663, even prohibited the manufacture of pistols and deprived of exemptions and fuero those who carried them, while as for poniards and daggers, Philip V, in 1721, threatened those who bore them with six years of presidio for nobles and six years of galleys for commoners.[979]

***

These specimens of multitudinous legislation, directed against arms of all kinds, enable us to appreciate how highly prized was the privilege of carrying them. In an age of violence it was indispensable for defence and was equally desired as affording opportunities for offence. That the Inquisition should claim it for those in its service was inevitable and it had the excuse, at least during the earlier period, that there was danger in the arrest and transportation of prisoners and in the enmities which it provoked, although this latter danger was much less than it habitually claimed. The old rules, moreover, were well known under which no local laws were allowed to interfere with such privilege,[980] and the Inquisition had scarce been established in Valencia when the question arose through the refusal of the local authorities to allow its ministers to carry arms. Ferdinand promptly decided the matter in its favor by an order, March 22, 1486 that licences should be issued to all whom the inquisitors might name--for the time had not yet come in which the inquisitors themselves issued licences.[981] Probably complaints arose as to the abuse of the privilege for the instructions of 1498, which were principally measures of reform, provided that, in cities, where bearing arms was forbidden, no official should carry them except when accompanying an inquisitor or alguazil.[982] As indicated by this, policy on the subject was unsettled and it so remained for a while. November 14, 1509, Ferdinand ordered that the ministers of the Sicilian Inquisition should not be deprived of their arms; June 2, 1510, he thanked the Valencia tribunal for providing that its officials should go unarmed, for, by the grace of God, there is no one now who impedes or resists the Inquisition and, if there were, the royal officials or he in person will provide for it; then, in about three months, on August 28th, he wrote to the Governor of Valencia that the salaried officials of the tribunal, with their servants and forty familiars should enjoy all the prerogatives of the Holy Office and were not to be deprived of their arms.[983]

We see in all this traces of general popular opposition to exempting inquisitorial officials from the laws forbidding arms-bearing. This was stimulated by the difficulty of preventing the exemptions from being claimed by unauthorized persons without limit, leading Catalonia, in the Concordia of 1512, to provide that officials bearing arms could be disarmed, like other citizens, unless they could show a certificate from the tribunal, and further that the number of familiars for the whole principality should be reduced to thirty, except in cases of necessity.[984] Although this Concordia was not observed, Inquisitor-general Mercader, in his instructions of August 28, 1514, admitted the necessity of such regulations by prohibiting the issue of licences to bear arms; by reducing the overgrown number of familiars to twenty-five in Barcelona and ten each in Perpignan and other towns, by permitting the disarmament of those who could not exhibit certificates and by endeavoring to check the fraud of lending these certificates by requiring them to swear not to do so and keeping lists whereby they could be identified.[985]

The right of arming its familiars, thus assumed by the Inquisition was by no means uncontested. We have seen how the Empress Isabella when in Valencia, in 1524, ordered the arms taken from them and broken, leading to a protest from Inquisitor-general Manrique, who asserted this to be a privilege enjoyed since the introduction of the Inquisition. In spite of this Charles V, by a cédula of August 2, 1539, ordered inquisitors to prohibit the use of arms by familiars.[986] The matter remained a subject of contest for some years more. In 1553 there were quarrels concerning it between the Valencia tribunal and the local authorities, but the Concordia of 1554 admitted the right unreservedly.[987]

By this time, in fact, it was generally recognized, but this, in place of removing a cause of discord only intensified and multiplied it. The right to bear arms could scarce be held to include weapons which were prohibited to all by general regulations, yet the authorities had no jurisdiction over familiars to enforce them. Thus when flint-lock arquebuses were prohibited and the Viceroy of Valencia included familiars in a proclamation on the subject, in 1562, Philip II called him to account, telling him that the order must come from the inquisitors and, in 1575 he repeated this to the Viceroy of Catalonia.[988] The Suprema might decide that familiars were included in prohibitory decrees and that inquisitors must issue the necessary orders, as it did, in 1596, with regard to one respecting daggers and in 1598 to one forbidding fire-locks and pistols at night,[989] but the tribunals had no police to enforce these orders and, when the secular authorities undertook to do so, inquisitors were prompt to resent it, in their customary fashion, as a violation of the immunities of the Holy Office.

***

Henry Charles Lea

Even more fruitful of trouble was the fact that it was impossible to make the inquisitors respect the limitations imposed by the Concordias on the number of familiars and consequently to obey the rule of furnishing lists of them to the authorities so that they might be known. Appointments were lavished greatly in excess of all possible needs and without informing the magistrates--often, indeed, without keeping records in the archives. The familiar might or might not carry with him the evidence of his official character but, whether he did so or not, his arrest or disarmament was violently resented, and the ordinary citizen when caught offending was apt to claim that he was a familiar in hopes of being released. How exasperating to the civil authorities was the situation may be gathered from a case occurring in Barcelona, in 1568. The veguer, on his nightly rounds, arrested Franco Foix, whom he found armed with a coat of mail, sword, buckler and dagger. The culprit claimed to be a familiar and the veguer obediently handed him over to the tribunal. He proved not to be one, but, instead of returning him, the inquisitors fined him in forty-four reales for their own benefit (presumably as a penalty for personating an official) and restored to him his forfeited arms.[990] When the laws were thus openly set at defiance, conditions were eminently favorable for quarrels, even without the violent mutual animosity everywhere existing between the tribunals and the civil authorities; collisions were correspondingly frequent and were fought to the bitter end.

It would be wearisome to multiply cases illustrating the various phases of these quarrels which occupied the attention of the king and his councils in their settlement. A single one will suffice to show the spirit in which they were conducted on both sides. In 1620, by order of the tribunal of Valencia, acting in its secular capacity and not in a matter of faith, the commissioner at Játiva arrested a man and sent him to Valencia under the customary guard of relays of familiars. One of these named Juan López, armed with a prohibited flint-lock, was conveying him, on February 23d, when at Catarroja, about a league from the city, some armed alguaziles, in the service of Dr. Pedro Juan Rejaule, a judge on the criminal side of the Audiencia, arrested him, taking away his weapon and carrying him to Dr. Rejaule's house. Disregarding his documents, Rejaule told him that he could not be released without giving bail to present himself to the viceroy and, as he was unable to furnish it he was handed as a prisoner to the local magistrates. On learning the event the inquisitors applied to the regent of the Audiencia who ordered the release of López, which was effected and Rejaule visited the tribunal, admitted that he had been in error and promised in future to observe all necessary respect. In spite of this the inquisitors proceeded to try him for impeding the Inquisition, ordered him to keep his house as a prison under pain of three hundred ducats, and threw into the secret prison as though they were heretics, the four alguaziles who had made the arrest. When notice of this was served on Rejaule he protested that the inquisitors were not his judges and that he would appeal, whereupon the additional indignity was inflicted upon him of posting two guards in his house with orders to keep him in sight.

***

This produced a crisis. The viceroy assembled in his palace all three salas or branches of the Audiencia, where the matter was fully discussed and it was resolved to release Rejaule and hold the two guards as hostages for the imprisoned alguaziles. At 2 A.M. Dr. Morla went with halberdiers furnished by the viceroy, seized and handcuffed the guards and brought Rejaule to his brother judges. At the same time a scrivener of the court had been sent to the inquisitor Salazar with a message from the viceroy to the effect that, as the offence had not been in a matter of faith, Rejaule was justiciable only by the king; if the Inquisition held otherwise a competencia could be formed; the Audiencia had decided that Rejaule and the alguaziles must be released and the guards be held until this was done. The scrivener also presented a petition of appeal to the pope, or to whomsoever was judge, and demanded apostolos or letters to that effect. To this Salazar replied in writing that the arrests had been made for matters incident to and dependent upon affairs of the faith, in which the Inquisition had exclusive jurisdiction and could admit no competencia; he could say no more as to the cause of the arrests without violating the secrecy of the Inquisition and incurring excommunication and he begged the viceroy not to interfere in a matter concerning so greatly the service of God and the king. At 4 A.M. the scrivener returned with this reply to where the viceroy and judges were waiting. At the magic word "faith," however fraudulently employed, all opposition vanished. By six o'clock Dr. Morla had taken Rejaule back to his house and had replaced the guards and, at the same time, the scrivener bore to the inquisitors a note from the viceroy saying that, as they had certified that it was a matter of faith, the Audiencia had restored everything to its previous condition and he offered not only not to impede the Inquisition but to show it all aid and favor.

The case was thus transferred to the court, where the Suprema on one side and the Council of Aragon on the other, struggled for a favorable decision from Philip III. The former evidently felt the weakness of the claim that the faith was involved, but it argued that impeding the Inquisition in any way conferred jurisdiction on it and Aliaga, in his double capacity of inquisitor-general and royal confessor, added a bitter complaint as to the manner in which the Inquisition was abused and maltreated. To this the king replied that he wished the affair treated with the customary moderation and mercy of the Holy Office, especially as it was not directly a matter of faith, and whatever sentence the Suprema resolved upon for Rejaule and the other inculpated parties must be submitted to him before publication. Besides, he ordered a junta of two members each of the Suprema and the Council of Aragon to be formed and to devise a plan for the avoidance of future contention. This assumed Rejaule's guilt and awarded the victory to the Suprema, but it was not satisfied and presented a consulta representing the perilous condition of the Valencia tribunal, which necessitated the punishment of the delinquents as a warning, but Philip merely repeated his former decision.[991]

What was Rejaule's fate we have no means of knowing, but his career was evidently blasted, whatever may have been the so-called mercy exhibited. As for the perilous position of the tribunal insisted on by the Suprema, it seems to be set forth in a Petition of the syndic of the College of Familiars, February 25, 1616, complaining of arrests and ill-treatment and asking the tribunal to take evidence on the subject. It accordingly did so, but while the testimony was ample as to the existence of ill-feeling towards the familiars, in substance it amounted only to their being deprived at night of daggers and bucklers which were prohibited weapons, and it does not appear that any action was taken in consequence. Complaints continued and another petition of October 30, 1626, asked that an envoy be sent to the Suprema, for which the familiars would defray the cost, for unless some relief was had they would resign in a body, as their position only exposed them to wrong and insult and their privileges were set at naught.[992]

The difficulty of enforcing the laws on the people was intensified by the privileges claimed by the familiars. They were by no means peaceable folk and the unprivileged class naturally regarded it as a hardship to be restricted to the use of swords when these gentry were so much more efficiently armed. The Suprema as a rule supported its satellites. For ten years, from 1574, it resisted, in Aragon, the enforcement on familiars of a royal decree against carrying prohibited weapons at night, although the Concordia of Aragon in 1568 provided that familiars should obey the laws respecting arms and that inquisitors should not protect them in violations. Members of all the Royal Councils were involved in the discussion, as though it were the weightiest affair of state and it was not until 1584 that the Suprema was induced to issue the necessary orders, which it was obliged to repeat in 1592.[993]

Another illustration of its attitude occurs with respect to a pragmática of great severity against the use of fire-arms, issued by Philip III, March 14, 1613, pronouncing the mere discharge of a weapon to be a capital offence, whether death ensued or not. It abrogated all privileges and exemptions and conferred on the royal courts full jurisdiction in such cases, and all this was accepted and its observance enjoined by the Suprema. This met with such scant obedience that the Council of Aragon in a consulta of July 31, 1632, called the king's attention to the evils existing from the exemption of familiars and suggested that they should not be permitted to decline the jurisdiction of the courts for crimes committed with fire-arms. It was doubtless in consequence of opposition by the Suprema that it was not until September 30, 1633, that Philip IV, in a cédula addressed to the Viceroy of Valencia, ordered that, with the assent of the Councils of Aragon and of the Inquisition, the pragmática of 1613 must be strictly observed by which all exemptions were disallowed and offenders were triable and punishable by the royal courts; the Inquisition must withdraw from all pending competencias and the cases be carried to conclusion by the Audiencia. The Suprema must have consented unwillingly to this, for it labored with the wavering monarch and, on November 8th, he wrote withdrawing the cédula and ordering the suspension of all cases before the Audiencia. A few weeks later he yielded to other influences and annulled the last letter, but added that his orders of September 30th must be executed impartially, for the Inquisition complained that it was enforced only against its officials and in such case he would give it a free hand again. December 27th the Suprema sent this to the Valencia tribunal with formal instructions to obey it, but added a confidential letter saying that efforts would not be relaxed to persuade the king to remit all such cases back to them; meanwhile an agreement had been obtained from the Council of Aragon that all sentences by the Audiencia should be referred to it before execution and the tribunal must watch them closely and send such reports as would enable the Suprema to obtain favorable action on them.[994]

For this endless strife, for the habitual disregard of the laws by familiars, the Suprema was primarily responsible. It was perfectly acquainted with the innumerable edicts specifying prohibited weapons and forbidding the carrying of them after night-fall; it acquiesced, ostensibly at least, in the subjection of these offences to the royal courts and yet it encouraged familiars in the belief that it had power to override all laws and could confer licence to violate them. The formula of commission which it caused to be issued to familiars contained a clause granting them full liberty to carry arms, offensive and defensive, publicly and secretly, by day or by night, and ordering all secular officials to abstain from interference with them, in virtue of holy obedience and under penalty of excommunication and of fifty thousand maravedís applicable to the expenses of the Holy Office.[995] It could not be fuller or more explicit; there are no exceptions as to the character of arms or allusion to the jurisdiction in these cases granted by the king to the royal courts. When one branch of the government thus resolutely placed itself in opposition to the sovereign and encouraged its subordinates to resist the laws and the constituted authorities, peace was impossible and conflicts were inevitable. Yet the illegality of all this was admitted when, in 1634, the familiars of Valencia held a meeting to assess themselves for a donation to be offered to the king, in return for a privilege to bear arms, and the Suprema instructed the tribunal to aid the movement, and again when, in 1638, a fruitless offer was made by them of twelve thousand ducats for the revocation of legislation on the subject.[996]

***

To crown all this, the Suprema, in 1657, reached the audacity of arguing that the right of familiars to bear arms was imprescriptible and could not be abrogated by any prince, for it would impede the Inquisition in the free exercise of its functions, wherefore it denied that any competencia could be formed in such cases; the secular authorities had no jurisdiction and there could not even be a discussion about their claim to interfere.[997] Philip IV had the weakness to submit to these extravagant claims, in 1658, and to decide that the Suprema alone had cognizance in such matters. The case in which this occurred was that of Jaime Espejo, alcaide of the penitential prison of Valencia, arrested for carrying pistols and it has interest for us because in it the inquisitor, Don Antonio de Ayala Verganza, argues away all the royal decrees and pragmáticas as not meaning what they said and proves it by citing a vast number of cases in which, when carried up to the king, he overruled his own legislation, invariably deciding in favor of the Inquisition and against his own jurisdiction. He could sometimes be brought to issue wholesome general regulations, but, when it came to their execution, the ever-present dread of interfering with the service of God overwhelmed him.[998]

Yet Philip promptly reversed himself for, in a despairing effort to put an end to these interminable quarrels, he was induced to issue a royal letter, December 23, 1659, declaring that the cognizance of infractions of the laws respecting prohibited arms lay with the royal jurisdiction and that no competencias should be formed in these cases. When this letter was alleged by the royal court, in the case then pending of Joseph Navarro, a familiar arrested for carrying a pistol, the Inquisition in reply airily cast aside the pragmática of 1613, and its confirmation in 1633, by asserting that both before and after those laws it had always exercised jurisdiction over these cases, as was notorious to every one-- which was all doubtless true. As for the recent letter of 1659, it had not been issued with the assent of the Suprema; being thus irregularly issued it should not be regarded as valid, until the king should be supplicated to modify it, and until this was done the accused should be surrendered to it or he could be released under bail to both jurisdictions.[999] The vacillating monarch probably yielded again; whether he did so or not mattered little to the Holy Office, which regarded his decrees so lightly. The miserable business of quarrelling over the multiplication of the laws went on and, in 1691, Carlos II found it necessary again to prohibit the carrying of pistols and armas cortas and to deprive offenders of their claims to jurisdiction, even if they were familiars or salaried officials of the Inquisition.[1000]

Several cases in the earlier years of Philip V seem to indicate that this matter was an exception to the general limitation of the privileges of the Holy Office and that there was a tendency to admit its claims.[1001] Their final extinction, however, was not far off. In 1748, Fernando VI prohibited all officials of tribunals, including the Inquisition, from carrying cut-and-thrust weapons any kind; exclusive jurisdiction in the enforcement of this was reserved for the secular courts and all claims to fuero were abolished. He confirmed and extended this by proclamations of 1749, 1751 and 1754, with penalties of six years in the mines for commoners and six years service in presidio for nobles. In another of 1757 he regretted the non-observance of these laws and ordered their irremissible enforcement without privilege of fuero. This legislation was supplemented by Carlos III, in 1761, who included in the prohibition all fire-arms of less than four palms length of barrel, although he conceded to gentlemen the use of holster pistols when on horseback but not when on mule-back.[1002] Yet the Inquisition continued to issue the old form of commissions granting unlimited license, until the magistrates of Seville and Alcalá la Real refused to recognize them when, in 1777, it admitted its altered position by a modification which granted the right to carry non-prohibited weapons, but only when on duty for the Holy Office, and contented itself with exhorting the secular authorities not to interfere with this.[1003]

***

MILITARY SERVICE

In somewhat ludicrous contrast with the belligerent spirit, indicated by the earnest desire to carry arms, was the claim that all connected with the Inquisition were exempt from military service. In its relations with the State the Holy Office recognized no duties of citizenship; it only claimed privileges. That the salaried officials, regularly employed in the tribunals, should enjoy such exemptions was merely in accordance with old custom, for a law of Juan II, in 1432, specifically released from the obligation of service nearly all officials, including even physicians, surgeons and schoolmasters.[1004] That this should apply to the Inquisition seems to have been assumed as a matter of course in its early days but, in 1560, the corregidor of Córdova summoned the officials and familiars to appear in the musters; they all claimed exemption, when the inquisitor-general upheld the appeal of the officials but denied that of the familiars. Similar questions arose in Murcia in 1563 and 1575, in which a similar distinction was drawn.[1005] In Valencia, the familiars had probably been more successful, for an article in the Concordia of 1568 provides that they must serve their turns in guarding the coasts and that inquisitors shall not defend them in seeking exemptions under pretext of their office.[1006] The same question arose in Majorca and was settled by a law providing that familiars refusing to perform guard-duty on their appointed days could be compelled by the royal officials.[1007] Thus by common consent at this time salaried officials were exempted while the claims of familiars were rejected.

In the troubles of the seventeenth century, when the very existence of Spain was threatened, the question as to officials as well as familiars came up again and the Suprema sought to protect both classes. In 1636 and 1638, the corregidors of various cities refused to except the officials when making up the lists for conscription, but Philip IV decided that they were exempt.[1008] As the danger increased, in 1640, with the rebellions in Catalonia and Portugal, and the resources of the kingdom were strained to the utmost, all claims were disregarded. By a cédula of September 7, 1641, Philip declared this to be a religious war, as the rebels were allied with nations infected with heresy. Inquisitor general Sotomayor was required to summon all officials and familiars to organize and serve and was clothed with power to enforce it. No protest was made against this, for it was a financial rather than a military move; arrangements were made to commute service for cash and the Suprema was thus aided in meeting the royal demands for contributions.[1009]

This was only a temporary truce. Philip, in a letter of February 22, 1644, to Inquisitor-general Arce y Reynoso, reported that the attitude of the officials had excited much dissatisfaction in Galicia; he therefore ordered that no exemptions be admitted and no excuses be received. To this the Suprema responded with bitter complaints that in Saragossa the lot had fallen on a messenger of the tribunal and the widow of a notary, who were told that they must furnish substitutes, all of which was in violation of the privileges of the Inquisition, crippling it in its pious labors so essential to the faith and reducing it in popular esteem to a level with other institutions. Unstable as usual where the Holy Office was concerned, Philip abandoned his position and admitted that salaried officials were not liable to serve or to furnish substitutes, which the Suprema promptly conveyed to the tribunals, cautioning them not to employ excommunication in collisions with the royal officials until after obtaining its permission.[1010]

Even in this hour of supreme need the liability of familiars was contested. Philip endeavored to placate the Suprema by assigning them to garrison duty, but it remonstrated, asserting that the Inquisition could not perform its functions if wholly deprived of them, and the cause of religion was higher than any other. It therefore asked that no place should be left without one, in small towns there should be two and in larger places four. To this Philip assented, on condition that those exempted should contribute to those who served, but the Suprema demurred; every one could avoid service who could pay the assessment, so this would be giving the familiars no special privileges; there could be no question that favors shown to the Inquisition would contribute to success in the war, for experience had demonstrated that the more sovereigns had fostered it the more fortunate they had been. However just was the argument it was fruitless; Philip adhered to his decision, but when the corresponding decrees were issued, the Council of Castile remonstrated in its turn and the distracted monarch was involved in a fresh discussion between the two.[1011]

RIGHT TO HOLD PUBLIC OFFICE

The Suprema carried its point that those exempted should not contribute to those conscripted and the arrangement remained in force. It was repeated in a carta acordada of January 14, 1668, and, when, in 1681, a question arose in Tembleque, the Suprema cautioned the Toledo tribunal not to issue more letters of exemption than the settlement permitted, in order to avoid competencias which only serve to render the Holy Office hateful and to imperil its other privileges.[1012] Carlos III seems to have been more liberal when, in 1767, he included, in an elaborate list of those exempt from military service, the ministers and dependents of the Inquisition who were relieved from billets under the decree of May 26,

1728, which, it will be remembered, granted the privilege to the number of familiars allowed under the old Concordias. Carlos IV was more exacting for, in 1800, when regulating the conscription in minute detail, he granted exemption only to the titular officials and took special care to exclude familiars and other dependents.[1013] This continued to the end. September 14, 1818, the Suprema communicated to the tribunals a decision of the king that, in order to secure exemption from conscription, it was not necessary to exhibit a royal commission, but one from the inquisitor-general or Suprema sufficed.[1014] Evidently the local tribunals were no longer allowed to issue certificates of exemption.

***

The right of officials and familiars to hold secular offices raised questions that caused no little debate. It was evidently of advantage to the Inquisition that those who were bound to it and enjoyed its exemptions should be in positions of influence where they could guard its privileges and promote their extension. On the other hand, for these very reasons, the people were jealous of office-holding by its ministers and dreaded to have their local authorities relieved of responsibility through their claim on the fuero or jurisdiction of the Inquisition. Had these local positions been elective, popular good sense could have averted the danger, but they were awarded by lot, the names of those deemed eligible being placed in a bolsa or bag--a process known as insaculacion--and drawn forth.[1015]

The earliest instance I have met of a refusal to include officials of the Inquisition among the eligibles occurs in 1503, when Ferdinand wrote to his Lieutenant-general of Majorca that he was astonished to learn that the names of Pere Prat, his son Pere Prat, Carman Litra and Gerónimo Serma had not been insacculated because they held office in the Inquisition; it should rather be a recommendation; they must not be thus dishonored and their names must at once be put in the bolsa.[1016] Doubtless Ferdinand's watchfulness preserved this privilege for officials during his life, but subsequently popular feeling must have manifested itself by their exclusion, for, in 1523, Charles V forbade it in an edict and he followed this by a special pragmática, May 30, 1524, asserting their eligibility to public office in all his dominions and for all future time, under pain of the royal wrath and of two thousand florins, but he provided that they should not be entitled to the jurisdiction of the Inquisition for official malfeasance.[1017] Notwithstanding this, Philip II was obliged to issue special instructions on the subject to Sardinia in 1552 and to Navarre in 1558.[1018]

In this, as in so much else, the Catalans were especially intractable. Córtes of the three kingdoms of Aragon were held in 1553, in which Catalonia alone took up the matter and adopted a law, confirmed by Prince Philip, prescribing that no bayle or his lieutenant, or judge, or scrivener could be a familiar, nor could he accept office after his term of service had expired.[1019] This received scant obedience, nor did the Inquisition pay attention to the clause in the pragmática of 1524 depriving it of cognizance of official malfeasance. One of the complaints of the royal Audiencia to de Soto Salazar, in his visitation of the Barcelona tribunal in 1566, was that it assumed jurisdiction in all such cases. Salazar recommended that this should be forbidden, for it impeded the proper administration of the towns, and officials could not be punished for violating local ordinances about bread, vineyards, meadows, breaking irrigating canals to water their lands, and multitudinous other derelictions.[1020]

***

Catalonia refused to accept the Concordia of 1568 and, in 1585, the Córtes re-enacted the provisions of 1553 in an enlarged form, including almost all offices, and subjecting violation to a penalty of two hundred ducats, which was confirmed by Philip II.[1021] This seems to have been enforced for, in 1586, a memorial from the Bishop of Segovia says that in Catalonia the names of all officials of the Inquisition were removed from the lists of eligibles, that commissioners and familiars were resigning and that every day withdrawals were received from applicants, so that the tribunal would be crippled and the Córtes could have contrived nothing more damaging.[1022] The Catalans held good, despite the earnest efforts of the Holy Office, which declared long afterwards that this was the severest blow that it had ever received. In the Córtes of 1599 the battle was renewed after elaborate preparations by the inquisitors. On June 30th the king presented a series of articles, in response to those submitted to him by the Córtes, and among them was one declaring officials and familiars eligible to all offices, but the Catalans would have none of it. In the elaborate memorial presented to Clement VIII by the Suprema against the work of the Córtes, it complained bitterly of the laws of 1553 and 1585 as diminishing notably the authority of the Inquisition and causing great lack of officials, so many having ignominiously resigned, while others could not be found to replace them.[1023]

Again, when the Córtes were about to assemble in 1626, the Barcelona tribunal implored the Suprema to use its utmost exertions for the repeal of the law of 1585, for no person of consideration would accept office and it was obliged to appoint those of low condition, which was fatal to its authority. The Córtes yielded in so far as to adopt an article throwing open the offices, provided incumbents were justiciable by the civil courts for a long series of offences, but the whole legislation of the Córtes came to naught through lack of the royal confirmation.[1024] When the question was coming up again in the Córtes of 1632, earnest appeals were made to the Suprema to have the obnoxious law of 1585 repealed. The condition of the Inquisition in Catalonia was represented as most deplorable by reason of it. In a memorial to the king it was stated that in Barcelona there were but four or five familiars, and they were mechanics, ineligible to public office; there was not a single advocate of the accused, nor an ecclesiastical consultor, so greedy was every one for public office. Throughout the principality there was the same dearth--familiars only in miserable villages, destitute of tempting positions, and those were of base condition, for in fact the barons would endure none other in their lands. The Suprema was urged to bring the matter before the Rota and it submitted the question to its fiscal, but he wisely reported that, although a favorable result was to be anticipated, yet it was expedient to set the example of recourse to Rome which might result in other matters being carried thither with damage to the jurisdiction of the Holy Office.[1025]

Thus Catalan pertinacity triumphed. When, in 1667, Pedro Momparler, familiar at Alconer, asked permission to resign, in order to accept the office of bayle, and his request was referred to the Suprema, it replied that it should be denied on account of the evil influence of his example, but it added that if he should renounce his familiarship before the royal justice for the term of his office, the inquisitors should pretend ignorance.[1026]

***

In Majorca, frequent alterations of the law show that it was subject to active debate and that preponderance shifted from one side to the other. In 1637 it was decided that none of those connected with the Inquisition could hold public office; then, in 1643, they were allowed to do so, in positions where they had not to vote or to give counsel; again, in 1660, the prohibition was made absolute; then, in 1662, royal letters of January 11th and March 4th removed the prohibition, provided they would previously renounce all claim to the jurisdiction of the Inquisition. These letters afford a remarkable illustration of the vacillation of the monarch and of the extent to which bureaucracy had crippled his autocracy--only this time it was the Council of Aragon which imitated the methods of the Suprema. The latter body was dissatisfied with the arrangement and addressed to the king a consulta, April 5, 1663, asking its suspension and that a junta of the two councils should be called to consider the subject. Philip promptly acceded and, on April 10th, ordered the Council of Aragon to write to that effect to the viceroy. The command was not obeyed and, on September 19th, the Suprema asked him to remedy the omission, whereupon he asked the council to state its reasons and, on its doing so, he again ordered it, October 3d, to execute his decree of April 10th. It was still recalcitrant and, on March 19, 1664, the Suprema represented the delay to the king who the next day called upon the council to render an exact account of what it had done, replied that in conformity with his commands it had written on October 3, 1663, copy of which enclosed. This proved to be merely copies of the letters of 1662 which had given rise to the debate, showing that it had deliberately nullified his orders. In view of all this the Suprema, July 24, 1664, asked the king to insist on literal compliance and that a copy of the despatch of the Council of Aragon to the viceroy should be furnished to it. This proved to be merely a duplicate of that of October 13, 1663, with the date altered to April 6, 1664. Then the Suprema again asked the king peremptorily to order exact obedience and he replied that he had done so. Meanwhile the Viceroy and the inquisitor of Majorca had been playing at cross-purposes in consequence of the contradictory despatches received by each.[1027] Such a method of carrying on an organized government seems incredible and, trivial as was the question at issue, a case such as this throws light on one of the causes of Spanish decadence. The question itself, after all this trouble, apparently remained unsettled, for, in 1673, there was a competencia over Gabriel Berga, a knight of Santiago and a familiar, when the tribunal contended that he could not renounce its jurisdiction.[1028]

It would be superfluous to follow out in detail the vicissitudes of this matter in the other provinces of Spain, where it gave abundant occasion for quarrels conducted with customary vehemence. It seems to have settled itself into the rule that officials and familiars were eligible to public office but that, during their terms of service, they were not entitled to the jurisdiction of the Inquisition. Such, we are told in 1632, was the practice in Castile, Aragon and Valencia.[1029] Yet still there were disputes for, about the middle of the seventeenth century, a formula is given for use when a familiar is prevented from taking office. This sets forth at much length that, if familiars are refused office, no one will take the position, which will inflict great detriment on the faith; it cites the royal cédulas, it sets aside opposing arguments by showing that for all malfeasance in office the familiar will be subject to the royal jurisdiction and finally it orders his immediate induction in his post under penalty of excommunication and of five hundred ducats; no further notice will be given and all further action will be published in the halls of the Inquisition, which will be full legal notice to all parties concerned.[1030] I have met with no further legislation on the subject and presumably some arrangement of this kind was in force to the end.

***

It was highly inconsistent but, at the same time, thoroughly in keeping with the spirit of the Inquisition in its dealings with the public, that while it vindicated so energetically the right of its officials to hold honorable and lucrative posts, it claimed for them the privilege to refuse to serve in those which were onerous. In the municipalities there were a certain number of these latter, entailing unremunerative labor and responsibility which no one could refuse to accept when his name was drawn from the bolsa. The officials claimed to be insaculated for the desirable positions but not for the undesirable ones. That such a claim could be made and sustained is a forcible illustration of the power of the Inquisition.

RIGHT TO REFUSE OFFICE

There is no allusion to this in the earlier Concordias and no specific grant that I have been able to find. It seems to have been merely a gratuitous assumption on the part of the Inquisition, asserted with its customary persistence. A noteworthy case growing out of it occurred, in 1622, in the town of Lorca (Murcia) where a familiar refused to serve in the office of collector of the alcavala, or tax on sales, and was imprisoned for contumacy. The inquisitors of Murcia demanded his liberation and excommunicated the alcalde mayor for refusing to obey. This failing, they prepared to arrest him and called upon the corregidor of Murcia, Pedro de Porres, for assistance. On his refusal they excommunicated him and then laid an interdict on the city of Murcia. The citizens appealed to their bishop, Fray Antonio Trejo, who remonstrated with the tribunal and, finding this unavailing, issued an edict declaring the interdict invalid. Bishops were not subject to inquisitorial jurisdiction, even for heresy, without special papal faculties, but the inquisitor-general, Andres Pacheco, was the most audacious and inexorable assertor of inquisitorial omnipotence and he did not hesitate to condemn the episcopal edict, to publish the condemnation in all the churches, to fine the bishop in eight thousand ducats and to summon him, under pain of four thousand more, to appear within twenty days and answer to the action brought against him by the fiscal as an impeder of the Inquisition. The bishop and chapter sent the dean and a canon to represent them, but, without a hearing, they were thrown incomunicado into the secret prison, excommunicated and the censure published in all the churches. The inquisitors imprisoned the parish priest of Santa Catalina for disregarding the interdict and the whole ecclesiastical body of Murcia became involved. Finally, through the intervention of the king and the pope, the bishop was absolved, but the Inquisition reaped a rich harvest of fines. Those of the bishop, dean and some of the canons were kept by the Suprema, while the local tribunal, in addition to inflicting terms of exile, of from one to eight years, secured from José Lucas, the episcopal secretary, a thousand ducats, from Alonso Pedriñan, the fiscal, eight hundred and, from thirteen other priests and dignitaries of the church, sums ranging from fifty to one hundred and fifty--in all, an aggregate of 3272 ducats.[1031]

A claim enforced so relentlessly was dangerous to dispute and even the Aragonese Concordia of 1646, which registered a triumph over the Holy Office, admitted the right of salaried officials and familiars to decline onerous offices.[1032] In time, however, there seems to have come a slight modification of the claim. About 1750 we have the formula of a mandate, issued at the instance of a familiar, forbidding, under pain of excommunication and of two hundred ducats, the authorities of a town from including him among those liable to serve in any of the minor offices, nor in any of the more important ones until every other inhabitant has served his turn.[1033]

***

It is not difficult to understand the origin of the claim that the buildings of the Inquisition and the houses of its officials were sanctuaries into which the officers of justice could not penetrate without special permission. The asylum afforded to criminals in churches was an old established practice throughout Europe to which Spain was no exception. Even as late as 1737 the papal sanction was deemed necessary to except from this certain crimes, such as murder, highway robbery and high treason.[1034] Asylum was also afforded by the feudal rights which debarred royal officers of justice from intruding on lands of nobles, and the withdrawal of this right in Granada is cited as one of the causes of the agitation leading to the rebellion of 1568.[1035] In Aragon this was developed so far that a law of Jaime I, in the Córtes of Huesca in 1247, which still continued in force, gave to the houses of infanzones, or gentlemen, the same right of asylum as that possessed by churches.[1036]

It is therefore somewhat remarkable that the claim of affording asylum was not made at the outset by the Inquisition, especially in view of the importance attached to the secrecy which shrouded all its operations. Yet, until the middle of the sixteenth century, such claims when made were authoritatively repudiated. Inquisitor-general Tavera writes, September 3, 1540, a sharp letter to the inquisitors of Seville saying that he is informed that recently certain murderers had been received and protected in the castle of Triana, occupied by the tribunal, and that the officers of the royal justice had not been allowed to search for them; the punishment of delinquents should be in no way impeded and no occasion be given for complaint; the gates of the castle must be kept shut so that criminals cannot take refuge there.[1037] So, in 1546, among instructions from the Suprema to the tribunal of Granada, is an order that no criminals or debtors shall find refuge in the Inquisition, nor be allowed to sleep there nor between the gates; the janitor must eject them and, if they will not go, report it to the inquisitors for proper action.[1038] This shows that the abuse was commencing but that it was disapproved and the same is seen in the Valencia Concordia of 1554, which says that, as the Inquisition has no privileges as an asylum, it cannot protect those who take refuge there.[1039]

RIGHT OF ASYLUM

Evidently the local tribunals were claiming a right which the central authority disallowed; they were moreover claiming it not only for the building of the Inquisition but for the houses of officials and familiars. Among the malfeasances of the Barcelona tribunal, reported in 1567 by de Soto Salazar, were cases of this kind. When the bayle of Perpignan sought to arrest some culprits they were sheltered by Pedro de Roca, a familiar, in his house and he resisted the bayle who came with a posse to arrest them; Roca accused the bayle and his men for this; they were imprisoned for a long while by the Barcelona inquisitors and were condemned to fines and exile. So when the bayle of Sens, with a posse, broke into the house of Vicente Valele, who was merely a temporary commissioner, to arrest some culprits who had taken refuge there, he accused them and they were all imprisoned.[1040]

The rapidity with which the abuse developed in Valencia is manifested by a comparison of the Concordias of 1554 and 1568. The former, as we have seen, admits that the Inquisition could offer no asylum, while the latter is obliged to forbid the lower officials and familiars from putting the arms of the Inquisition on their houses; all such must be removed and their houses shall not have immunity from the officers of justice--evidently the officials found profit in harboring thieves and murderers and the tribunal supported them.[1041] In Barcelona a sort of compromise was reached by which, on application to the tribunal, one of its ministers was sent with the officers of justice to enter houses of officials where criminals had taken refuge, but the Córtes of 1599 complained that this delay afforded time for escape and, in the abortive Concordia enacted there, a clause provided that this should not be necessary and that, in case of resistance, houses could be entered. It shows how slow was the Suprema to assert a right of asylum that, in its protest to Clement VIII, it accepts this article on the ground that the Inquisition never has impeded the pursuit and arrest of malefactors.[1042] In time, however, it overcame these scruples and, in 1632, it issued repeated orders that the officers of justice should not be allowed to enter the houses of officials. Philip IV countermanded this, but the Suprema presented a consulta saying that there was no objection when the pursuit was flagrante delicto; prisoners, however, were frequently confined in the houses of officials and an unlimited right of entry might be abused to obtain communication with them in violation of the all-important secrecy of the Holy Office. As usual, the vacillating monarch yielded and, in 1634, issued a decree restricting the right of search to cases of hot pursuit.[1043]

It is remarkable that the Aragonese Concordia of 1646, imposed by the Córtes on Philip, which in so many ways restricted the privileges of the Inquisition, recognized this doubtful one in the fullest manner. As the ministers, it says, of so holy an office should enjoy certain honors and pre-eminence, it orders that they, including familiars, shall have as to their houses the same privileges as caballeros and hijosdalgo--which, as we have seen, included the right of asylum.[1044] As regards the buildings of the Inquisition itself, a scandalous case occurring in 1638 shows how far it had travelled since Tavera rebuked the tribunal of Seville. In Majorca the Count of Ayamano, at the head of a band of assassins, committed the sacrilege of escalading the walls of a convent for the purpose of murdering his wife who had sought refuge there. Philip ordered every effort made to arrest him and his accomplices, but he escaped to Barcelona with eight of them and all found asylum in the Inquisition, in the apartments of his uncle, the Inquisitor Cotoner. It affords a curious insight into the conditions of the period to see that this created a situation impenetrable to the highest authorities of the land. Philip called a junta of two members each of the Suprema and Council of Aragon to devise how the criminals could be captured without scandal or quarrel with the Inquisition. The result of their deliberations seems to be a letter from the Suprema to Cotoner telling him that, if he wanted to help his nephew, it should be outside and not inside of the Inquisition, in order to avoid the troubles ensuing on an attempt of the royal officers to remove him. The imperturbable Cotoner was not to be scared by this gentle warning and a fortnight later the Suprema enclosed to him a royal decree telling him that he would see the untoward results of sheltering his nephew. As complete satisfaction was demanded he was ordered to report in full all details, including his motives in harboring one who was put to the ban, especially when the latter was not a familiar.[1045] Unfortunately we do not know how the affair ended, but when the Suprema, in place of dismissing Cotoner, inquired as to his motives, we may assume that the asylum offered by the Inquisition saved the forfeit life of the criminal by some compromise.

***

The immunity of the houses of officials became generally recognized, with the proviso that permission of search would be granted by inquisitors if special application was made to them, when they preserved their jurisdiction by sending one of their people to accompany the officers of justice. An exception which proved the rule however was made in favor of the administrators of the tax on tobacco, to whom general letters were given empowering them to search the houses of officials for contraband tobacco. Even this was argued away by the Suprema in 1728, when it asserted that semi-proof in advance was necessary to justify search and full proof to give jurisdiction.[1046]

***

It is evident from the above that the Holy Office, with its claims for special privileges and exemptions and its methods for enforcing their recognition, was a very disturbing factor in the body politic. Yet the greatest source of conflict lay in the exclusive jurisdiction which it sought to establish over all who were connected with it, not only between themselves but between them and the rest of the community. This engrossed so large a portion of its activity and was the cause of such perpetually recurring trouble that its consideration requires a chapter to itself.

CHAPTER IV - CONFLICTING JURISDICTIONS

The principal source of strife between the Inquisition and the other authorities arose from its claim to exclusive competence in all cases involving those connected with it and their dependents. This gave rise to perpetual conflicts, conducted with the utmost tenacity, which filled the land with confusion and, in many cases, rendered the administration of justice a mockery. For two centuries the monarchs vainly endeavored to keep the peace by repeated efforts to define the boundaries between the rival jurisdictions and the methods of settling their differences. The tireless efforts, on the one side, of the Holy Office to extend its authority and increase its emoluments caused it constantly to violate compacts, while the jealousy of the civil magistracy on the other and its natural desire to repel intrusion rendered it prompt to use whatever means lay in its power. The struggle was unequal against the superior weapons furnished by papal faculties and against the royal favor which was with the Inquisition, but the conflict was maintained with marvellous constancy, supported by popular sympathy, and the time of the king and his advisers was frittered away in deciding a continuous stream of petty quarrels, growing out of trivial incidents, but assuming portentous proportions through the violent methods which had aggravated them.

To understand the claim of the Inquisition to exclusive cognizance of the cases of its subordinates it is necessary to bear in mind the benefit of clergy, through which, from the early middle ages, all clerics were exempted from the jurisdiction of the laity and were subjected wholly to the spiritual courts. This amounted virtually to immunity for crime, both because those courts were debarred from rendering judgements of blood and because of the inevitable favoritism manifested to those of their own cloth.[1047] As civilization advanced the disorders caused by a class, thus emboldened in wrong-doing by impunity, were the source of constant solicitude to rulers and were deplored by right-thinking churchmen. In this, Spain was no exception. In a project of instructions drawn up by a Spanish bishop for the delegates to the Lateran Council in 1512, the crimes and scandals perpetrated by married clerks and those in the lower orders, through expectation of immunity, are dwelt upon as reasons for a change; there were daily conflicts between the spiritual and secular courts, leading to interdicts cast on cities and some universal legislation by the Church was desirable.[1048] No such remedy was adopted, and when the Council of Trent gave promise of reform, the Spanish prelates, in contrast with the Inquisition, which made every effort to extend its jurisdiction over offenders, proposed in 1562 to the council that married clerks wearing secular habits should not enjoy protection from secular justice.[1049] In 1544, Fernando de Aragon, when Viceroy of Valencia, declared that his principal trouble lay with the Church, of which the chief object was to protect evil-doers and liberate them from his justice, an opinion in which he was heartily seconded by the saintly Tomás de Vilanova, then recently appointed archbishop.[1050]

LATITUDE IN SECULAR AFFAIRS

Yet the marked aversion in Spain to ecclesiastical encroachment led to repeated enactments restraining spiritual jurisdiction within strict limits. In a series of laws, dating from the fourteenth to the sixteenth century, Henry II, Juan II, Henry IV, Ferdinand and Isabella and Charles V endeavored by the severest penalties to repress its inevitable tendency to extend itself, whether by seizure of the persons or property of the laity or by entertaining cases between laymen. Ferdinand and Isabella, in 1493, even threatened half confiscation and perpetual exile from Spain for all who, under any pretext, aided ecclesiastical judges in taking prisoners from secular officials or who assisted them in any way.[1051] In addition to this was the recurso de fuerza through which appeal lay to the royal courts or to the Sala de Gobierno whenever the spiritual courts refused an appeal or heard secular cases or those in which laymen were concerned.[1052] It is necessary to bear in mind this tendency and these restrictions on ecclesiastical jurisdiction to estimate properly the latitude obtained by the Inquisition in purely secular affairs.

Whether, at its inception, the Inquisition enjoyed the prerogative of exclusive cognizance of cases involving its officials it would be impossible now to say. They were mostly laymen and as such were subject to the secular courts, while, in the popular opposition elicited by their proceedings, especially in the Aragonese kingdoms, there might be anticipated danger that they would be terrorized or prosecuted unless protected by being reserved for judgement by their own tribunals. The earliest mandate to this effect that I have met is a cédula of Ferdinand, March 26, 1488, addressed to all the officers of justice in Catalonia ordering them, under penalty of two thousand florins and the royal wrath, to take no cognizance of anything concerning the ministers and familiars of the Inquisition; all their acts in such cases are declared invalid, and any one whom they may have arrested is at once to be transferred to the tribunal, showing that, at least in Catalonia, no such exemption from secular justice had previously been recognized.[1053]

Yet in this unlimited decree Ferdinand had overlooked details which necessarily presented themselves in practice. Was this exemption from secular jurisdiction confined to the titulados y asalariados or did it extend to the unsalaried commissioners and familiars, receiving no pay, pursuing their customary avocations and only called upon for occasional service? There was also a question about the servants of officials, for an abuse of the spiritual courts had included those of clerics. Then it might be asked whether the protection accorded to the person of the official extended to his property in civil suits, with the wide avenue thus opened to abuses of many kinds. There was, moreover, a well-settled principle of law that the accuser or plaintiff must seek the court of the defendant; if, in violation of this, the official could enjoy what was known as the active fuero as well as the passive--that is, if he as plaintiff could bring suit or prosecution before his own tribunal--his power of offence would be vastly increased, together with his opportunities for tyrannizing over all around him.

These were questions which had to be decided. It would seem that the inquisitors construed their powers in the most liberal fashion, giving rise to abuses which called for repression and a limitation of their jurisdiction. The reformatory Instructions of 1498, accordingly, order them not to defend officials and their servants in civil cases and only officials in criminal actions, a rule repeated in a carta acordada of May 4th of the same year.[1054] This excluded servants wholly and deprived officials of the fuero in civil matters, but it was soon modified by Ferdinand, in a letter of January 12, 1500, to the Catalonia tribunal, ordering it not to interfere with the royal court in a certain suit, and expressing the rule that the plaintiff must seek the court of the defendant.[1055] It was impossible however to restrain inquisitors from exceeding their jurisdiction and he was obliged, August 20 1502, to repeat his injunctions to the same tribunal, in consequence of complaints from the Diputados. The inquisitors were roundly taken to task for lending themselves to the schemes of the receiver in buying up debts and claims and then collecting them through the tribunal; they were told that they must defend none but salaried officials actually in service; if they are plaintiffs in civil suits they must apply to the court of the defendants, while if they are defendants the plaintiffs must seek the tribunal. To evoke other cases, he says, causes great scandal and will lead to troubles which must be prevented. A fortnight later he emphasized this about a civil case which they had evoked from the royal court; they must remit it back and not have to be written to again as he would not tolerate such proceedings.[1056] Thus familiars and servants were not entitled to the fuero, or inquisitorial jurisdiction, while salaried officials enjoyed it, active and passive, in criminal actions and only passive in civil suits.

INTERFERENCE WITH COURSE OF JUSTICE

Unduly favorable as was this to the Inquisition, the tribunals paid no attention to its limitations; they welcomed all who sought their judgement seat, and the desire for it of those who had no claim on it shows that they had a reputation of selling justice. One or two cases will exemplify this and show how good were the grounds of complaint by the people. There was a certain Juan de Sant Feliu of Murviedro, whose father and mother-in-law had been condemned for heresy, and to whom Ferdinand had kindly granted their confiscations, including the dowry of his wife. In 1505 the town of Murviedro farmed out to him and his wife the impost on meat for 11,100 sueldos a year; he died and, in the settlement of his account, he was found to owe the town a hundred and fifty libras, which it proceeded to collect from his sons in the court of the governor. Under pretext that his property had been confiscated and restored, they appealed in 1511 to the tribunal of Valencia, which promptly evoked the case and inhibited the court from further action, whereupon the town complained to Ferdinand who ordered the case remitted to the governor. Unabashed by this, in 1513, Sant Feliu's heirs on the same pretext obtained the intervention of the tribunal in another case, in which Doña Violante de Borja had sued them for 7500 sueldos which she had entrusted to him to invest in a censo of the town of Murviedro; the censo had been paid off and he had concealed the fact and kept the money. Judgement was given against them, when the inquisitors interposed and prohibited the royal court from further action. Ferdinand expressed much indignation at their interference with justice in a matter wholly foreign to their jurisdiction and ordered the prohibition to be withdrawn. Even more arbitrary was the action, in 1511, of the Majorca tribunal, when Pedro Tornamirandez sued the heirs of Francisco Ballester for some cattle and obtained judgement in the court of the royal lieutenant, whereupon the heirs appealed to the inquisitor who evoked the case and forbade further proceedings in the secular court. None of the parties had any connection with the Inquisition and there was not even the pretext of confiscation; it was a mere wanton interference with the course of justice, only explicable by some illicit gain, and when Ferdinand's attention was called to it he ordered the inquisitor to revoke his action.[1057] If, under Ferdinand's incessant vigilance the Inquisition thus boldly prostituted its powers, we can appreciate how well-founded, under his careless successors, were the complaints of those who suffered under wrongs perpetrated under the pretence of serving God.

In the Catalan Concordia of 1512 there was an attempt to do away with some of these abuses and the bull Pastoralis officii of Leo X, confirming the Concordia, marks another stage in the development of the fuero. No one, he said, could be cited save in his own ordinary court at the instance of an official or familiar; if it were attempted, all acts concerning it were invalid and the inquisitors must condemn the plaintiff in double the expenses and damage; if any official bought property in suit, or on which a suit was expected, he could be cited before a court not his own and if he claimed property under seizure by a secular judge, the latter could disregard all inhibitions issued by inquisitors; moreover inquisitors should have no cognizance in matters concerning the private property of officials. While thus striking at some of the more flagrant abuses of the fuero, Leo opened the door to worse ones by admitting familiars and the commensals or servants of officials to participation in the immunities of the Inquisition.[1058] The bull, in fact, is in accordance with the Instructions of 1514, as issued by Inquisitor-general Mercader, and we shall see how completely the restrictive clauses were ignored while those admitting familiars and servants were developed.[1059]

IMMUNITY OF SERVANTS

The question as to familiars and servants was not absolutely settled for some years. It is true that, in 1515 at Logroño, when the corregidor arrested Martin de Viana, a servant of the secretary Lezana, and refused to surrender him to the tribunal, he and his deputy and alguazil were excommunicated and the Suprema on appeal subjected them all to fines and humiliating penance.[1060] On the other hand, in 1516 at Valladolid, when Alonso de Torres, servant of Inquisitor Frias, was thrown into the royal prison, the inquisitor did not reclaim him but procured the interposition of the Suprema, which ordered him to be released on bail and then, after nine months had passed without a charge being brought against him, he procured a royal cédula for the release of his bondsmen.[1061] Whatever doubts may have existed on the subject were removed, in 1518, by a cédula of Charles V, reciting that in Jaen the secular courts assumed cognizance of criminal cases concerning officials and familiars and their servants, which was contrary to the privileges of the Holy Office, wherefore he forbade it strictly for the future.[1062] After this the Inquisition had no hesitation in insisting on its rights. When, in 1532, the corregidor and officials of Toledo were excommunicated for punishing the servant of an inquisitor and the Empress-regent Isabel wrote to the tribunal to absolve them, the Suprema instructed it not to obey her.[1063] She learned the lesson and, in 1535, when ordering some servants of inquisitors and familiars to be remitted to the Inquisition, she said it was accustomed to have their cases, both civil and criminal, and it was her pleasure that this should be observed.[1064]

The civil authorities were somewhat dilatory in recognizing the immunity of servants, and cases continued to occur in which the tribunals vindicated their jurisdiction energetically. About 1565 two officers of the royal justice in Barcelona arrested a servant of Inquisitor Mexia in a brothel where he was quarrelling with a woman, for which they were thrown into the secret prison as though they were heretics and were banished for three months, while the judge of the royal criminal court, who had something to do with the matter, was compelled to appear in the audience-chamber and undergo a reprimand in the presence of the assembled officials of the tribunal. The virtual immunity for offenders resulting from the privilege is illustrated by the case, in the same tribunal, of Pedro Juncar, servant of the receiver, who murdered the janitor of the Governor of Catalonia; the governor arrested him but was forced to surrender him to the tribunal, which discharged him with a sentence of exile for a year or two and costs.[1065] The influence on social order of conferring immunity on such a class can readily be conceived.

The privilege of the fuero was not confined to servants but was extended in whatever direction the ingenuity and perseverance of the tribunal could enforce it. Penitents who were fulfilling their terms of penance were claimed and the claim was confirmed, in 1547, by Prince Philip. In Valencia and Barcelona the workmen employed on the buildings of the Inquisition were given nominal appointments under which they claimed immunity. In Lima the tribunal complained to the viceroy of the arrest of a bricklayer who was working for it, but it got no satisfaction. In Barcelona the tribunal granted inhibition with censures on the civil court, in which the brother of a familiar was suing a merchant on a protested bill of exchange.[1066]

***

IMMUNITY OF FAMILIARS

We have seen the limitations imposed by Ferdinand and the bull Pastoralis officii and the reiteration of the principle that the plaintiff must seek justice in the court of the defendant. As far as regards Castile, Charles V had overthrown this in criminal matters for both officials and familiars. Civil cases remained in a somewhat undetermined state, especially concerning familiars, the inquisitors endeavoring to grasp as far as they could both the active and passive fuero. When, in 1551, complaints came from Valencia that the tribunal was collecting debts for familiars, Inquisitor-general Valdés wrote that he did not know how this had come to pass and called for precise information as to when it had commenced and generally as to the method observed in the civil cases, active and passive, of familiars, so that he could answer Prince Philip.[1067] There was a good deal of uncertainty about the whole subject; the courts were restive and the situation was becoming strained. In the endeavor to settle it, Charles, in 1542, reissued his edict of 1518 with a sobre carta emphatically commanding its strict observance and forbidding the secular courts from any cognizance of the criminal cases of officials or familiars.[1068] This did not mend matters. The courts persisted in exercising jurisdiction over familiars, the recurso de fuerza was freely invoked and competencias multiplied. Both sides appealed to Charles, who was in Germany, and this time the opponents of the Inquisition gained the advantage. Prince Philip, as regent, issued a cédula, May 15, 1545, in which he described how laymen, subject to the secular courts, obtained immunity for their crimes on pretext of being familiars; how the tribunals, in defending them, cast excommunications on the officers of justice, through which scandals and disquiet were daily increasing, and the course of justice was impeded. The familiars were in no way entitled to immunity from the secular courts, as they were not officials, although a different custom existed in Aragon and the inquisitors pretended to it in Castile, under the cédula of 1518 and the sobrecédula of 1542, but these were both irregular, not having been despatched by the Council and Secretariat of Castile as is customary and necessary. Therefore in order that delinquent familiars may not remain unpunished and be induced to commit crimes by the prospect of immunity, the emperor ordered the matter to be thoroughly discussed and meanwhile the cédulas of 1518 and 1542 to be suspended, in conformity with which they are declared to be suspended, inquisitors are ordered no longer to take cognizance of the cases of familiars and the secular courts are instructed to prosecute them in accordance with the laws.[1069]

The Inquisition did not acquiesce tamely in this defeat, which was aggravated by the secular courts interpreting it as giving them jurisdiction over officials as well as familiars. It protested and resisted and showed so little obedience that the Córtes of Valladolid, in 1548, asked that it should be compelled to confine itself to its proper functions in matters of faith.[1070] Quarrels and recursos de fuerza continued and finally the whole question was referred to a junta consisting of two members each from the Suprema and Council of Castile. The representatives of the Inquisition conceded that it had been in fault in appointing too many familiars and in claiming for them all the exemptions of salaried officials; those of the Council admitted that the courts had erred in interfering with civil and criminal cases properly appertaining to the Holy Office. Mutual concessions were made, resulting in what was known as the Concordia of Castile, March 10, 1553--an agreement which the Inquisition admitted, a century later, that neither side had observed.[1071]

THE LAW IN CASTILE

The Concordia was silent as to the salaried officials, thus leaving them in possession of the active and passive fuero in both civil and criminal cases. It devoted itself wholly to the familiars who, in this as in so much else, were the leading source of trouble. After regulating, as we shall see hereafter, their number and character, it defined that in civil cases they should be subject wholly to the secular courts. For the greater crimes, moreover, cognizance was also reserved exclusively to the courts, the list comprising treason, unnatural crime, sedition, violating royal safe-conducts, disobedience to royal mandates, treachery, rape, carrying off women, highway robbery, arson, house-breaking and crimes of greater magnitude than these, as well as resistance or formal disrespect to the royal courts. Those who held office were also amenable to the courts for official malfeasance. This left only petty offences subject to inquisitorial jurisdiction and for these familiars were liable to arrest by secular magistrates, subject to being immediately transferred to the Inquisition. For doubtful cases it was provided that, when the lay judge and inquisitor could not agree, there should be no contention, but the evidence was to be sent to the court of the king, where two members each of the Suprema and Council of Castile should decide as to the jurisdiction; for this a majority was required and, in case of equal division of votes, the matter went to the king for final decision. No appeal from this was allowed and meanwhile the accused was retained in the prison to which he had been consigned at arrest.[1072] This process of adjudicating disputes became known as competencia, the details of which will be considered hereafter.

Whatever concession the Inquisition made in thus surrendering a portion of its jurisdiction over familiars was more than compensated by what was evidently part of the agreement, the issue on the same day of Philip's cédula addressed to all judicial bodies forbidding them to entertain appeals of any kind from the acts of the Holy Office (p. 341). It thus secured complete autonomy; it was rendered self-judging, responsible to the king alone, and the populations were surrendered wholly to its discretion.

As far as regards Castile, the Concordia of 1553 was final. It is true that the royal cédula of Aranjuez, April 28, 1583, extended its principles to the salaried officials, but there is no trace of the observance of this.[1073] Another point was subjected to a temporary modification. The absolute denial of justice in allowing inquisitors to have their civil suits decided by their own tribunals attracted attention, after nearly a century, and the Suprema, February 18, 1641, ordered that these cases should be referred to it, when, if it deemed proper, it would commission the tribunal to hear them, but this slender restriction seems to have elicited so active an opposition that it was withdrawn within three months by a counter order of May 14th, restoring to the inquisitors the power of sitting in judgement on their own cases.[1074] It is easy to conceive the amount of oppression and wrong which they could thus inflict.

With these trivial exceptions the Concordia remained the law in Castile. In 1568 Philip II issued a cédula stating that it had not been observed, wherefore he ordered strict compliance with it and, as late as 1775 Carlos III treats it as being still in force and to be respected by all parties.[1075] If Philip, however, expected peace between the rival and jealous jurisdictions, as the result of the Concordia, he deceived himself. Both were eager for quarrel and opportunities to gratify combative instincts were not lacking. The secular courts resented the intrusion of the Inquisition, which was careful to keep antagonism active by the insulting arrogance of its methods, whenever a question arose between them. There was ample field for contention, for not only were the excepted crimes loosely defined, giving rise to many nice questions, but the Inquisition acutely argued that before the royal courts could assume possession of a case the crime must be fully proved, for the familiar was entitled to the fuero until his guilt was ascertained, thus keeping in its own hands all the vital parts of the process and excluding the secular justices.[1076] Then the circle of excepted cases was enlarged, not only for familiars but for salaried officials, by various edicts from time to time, as we have seen with regard to pistols and discharging fire-arms. Another instance was a cédula of Philip II, in 1566, including among exceptions the violation of royal pragmáticas, which was put to the test, in 1594, when the Chancellery of Granada prosecuted a notary of the tribunal for wearing a larger ruff than was allowed by a sumptuary pragmática; the tribunal excommunicated the judges but, when the case was carried up to the Suprema and Council of Castile, the Chancellery was justified.[1077] In the frenzied efforts to maintain the value of the worthless vellon coinage, Philip IV, by repeated edicts between 1631 and 1660, deprived familiars and salaried officials of the fuero in cases of demanding more than the legal premium for the precious metals or of counterfeiting or importing base money.[1078] Frauds on the revenue from tobacco also deprived all offenders of exemptions, by a pragmática of 1719, but it was difficult to enforce and had to be repeated in 1743, after which at last Inquisitor-general Prado y Cuesta, in 1747, ordered the tribunals to obey it.[1079]

***

VALENCIA

Although Navarre was under the crown of Castile, the Concordia of 1553 was not extended to it until 1665, by a royal cédula of May 9th. The questions which agitated the rest of Spain seem to have rarely presented themselves there, for we hear little of them in that quarter, although, in 1564, the tribunal of Logroño complained of the intrusion of the secular courts on its jurisdiction and there were, as we shall see hereafter, occasional collisions on the subject of witchcraft, which was mixti fori.[1080]

***

The kingdoms of the Crown of Aragon were the scenes of much greater trouble than those of Castile, in delimiting the boundaries of the rival jurisdictions, for they still had institutions which could remonstrate against abuses and struggle for their removal. We have seen how recalcitrant they were when the Inquisition was introduced and how vigorously they struggled against the abuses which followed. In the Concordias of 1512 and 1520 they secured certain paper guarantees, but these were brushed aside by the Inquisition with customary ill-faith. Irritation and hostility became chronic, with the result that they were denied some of the slender alleviations vouchsafed to Castile, on the ground that the character of the population and the neighborhood of the heretics of France rendered it necessary that the Holy Office should be fortified with greater privileges than in the rest of Spain.

Of the three kingdoms Valencia was the one which gave the least trouble in this matter. Yet a case occurring in 1540 is highly significant of the terrorism under which the royal judges discharged their duties. Dr. Ferrer of Tortosa, one of the judges, appealed to Inquisitor-general Tavera, representing that in the previous year he had condemned to death a murderer, who had fully deserved it. Now that the inquisitor had come his enemies represent that the culprit was a familiar, although he had never claimed to be one, and it is currently reported that the inquisitor is about to prosecute him (Ferrer). If he is in fault in the matter he will cheerfully submit to punishment, but he begs not to be subjected to the infamy of a trial. To this appeal the Suprema responded by ordering the inquisitor to send it such evidence as he may gather and to await a reply before taking action.[1081] It is evident that all criminal judges lived in an atmosphere of dread lest at any moment the honest discharge of their functions might precipitate them into a disastrous conflict with the tribunal. It justifies the complaints of the Córtes of 1547 and 1553, the latter of which declared that the inquisitors exceeded their jurisdiction, intervening in many affairs, both civil and criminal, that had no connection with heresy. This caused great disturbance of justice and contentions between the jurisdictions, in which the tribunal assumed to be supreme and to define the limits of its own power. Great as were these evils they were daily increasing and were becoming intolerable, wherefore the Córtes prayed that the subject be investigated and a clear definition be made between the royal jurisdiction and that of the Inquisition.[1082]

***

This resulted in a junta of the members of the Suprema and of the Council of Aragon, who agreed upon a Concordia, published by Prince Philip, May 11, 1554. In this he recited that, in consequence of the great numbers of familiars and their endeavoring to have all their cases, civil and criminal, tried by the tribunal, which sought to protect them in this against the claims of the royal judges, there had arisen many contentions in which the whole of the Audiencia had been excommunicated. To put an end to this unseemly strife he had caused the junta to be held, with the result of the following articles, which he ordered both sides to observe, the royal officials under pain of a thousand florins, and the inquisitors as they desired to please him and the emperor. In this the first point was the reduction of the excessive number of familiars; in the city of Valencia they were not to exceed one hundred and eighty; in towns of more than a thousand hearths there might be eight, in those of over five hundred six, in smaller places four, except that in the coast towns there might be two more. Lists of all appointees were to be furnished to the magistrates, both to check excess and to identify individuals. In civil suits they were to enjoy the passive fuero but not the active; if in contracts they renounced this privilege the condition held good, while, if the other party agreed to accept the jurisdiction of the Inquisition, he could not be cited before it. In criminal cases, the Inquisition had sole cognizance with respect to officials, their servants and families and to familiars but not to their wives, children and servants. When contests arose with secular courts, mild measures were to be used and excommunication be avoided as far as possible. When a familiar entered into a treaty of peace and truce, it was to be executed before an inquisitor and, if it contained a condition of death for violation, the inquisitor, in case of such violation, was to relax the culprit to the secular arm to be put to death. Familiars who were in trade were not to enjoy the fuero for frauds or violations of municipal laws and officials holding public office were liable to the secular courts for malfeasance therein.[1083]

This would appear to grant to the Inquisition all that it had any excuse for asking, but it was impossible to bind the inquisitors to any compact, or to observe any rules. A letter to them from the Suprema, in September, 1560, reminds them that it had already ordered them, in the case of Juan Sánchez, to deprive him of his familiarship, to withdraw their inhibitions and censures, and to remit the affair to the secular judge, in spite of which they had gone forward and rendered sentence; now, as Sánchez is not a familiar, they must positively send the case back to the ordinary courts.[1084] When such persistence in injustice existed, it is not surprising that, at the Córtes of Monzon, in 1564, the deputies of Valencia, like those of Aragon and Catalonia, presented a series of complaints, bearing chiefly on abuses of jurisdiction. We happen to have a view of the situation by an impartial observer, the Venetian envoy, Giovanni Soranzo, in his relation of 1565, which is worth repeating, although we must bear in mind that it was impossible for a Venetian statesman to give Philip II credit for the honest fanaticism which underlay his character. After alluding to the privileges of the Aragonese kingdoms, he proceeds "The king uses every opportunity to deprive them of these great privileges and, knowing that there is no easier or more certain method than through the Inquisition, he is continually increasing its authority. In these last Córtes the Aragonese prayed that the Inquisition should take cognizance of no cases save those of religion and said that they grieved greatly that it embraced infinite things as distant as possible from its jurisdiction and they presented many cases not pertaining in any way to its duties. In truth at present the Inquisition interposes in everything, without respect to any one of whatever rank or position, and we may say positively that this tribunal is the real master which rules and dominates all Spain. The king replied that the Inquisition was not to be discussed in the Córtes, when they all arose and threatened to depart without finishing any other business, if the king did not wish them to discuss a matter of so much importance to them. The king quieted them by promising that, when he returned to Castile, he would listen to their complaints and would not fail to grant the appropriate relief. But undoubtedly he did this so that the Córtes should end without a revolt, his intention being to increase rather than to diminish the importance of the Inquisition, clearly recognizing it as the means of maintaining his reputation and of keeping the people in obedience and terror."[1085]

***

  Soranzo's account of the Córtes is not wholly complete. When Philip promised relief after his return to Castile, the deputies replied that they did not choose to be convoked in Castile and that they would go no further with the subsidio which he wanted until they were satisfied. The sessions were prolonged; the patience of the deputies outwore his own and he promised that he would have a visitation made of the tribunals of the three kingdoms and then, in concert with their Diputados, issue a new series of regulations.[1086] The promise was kept. Francisco de Soto Salazar, a member of the Suprema, was sent, in 1566, with full powers and instructions to investigate all abuses, but especially those connected with jurisdiction in matters not of faith. In Valencia his attention was particularly called to a practice of appointing deputy inquisitors and officials and investing them with the privilege of the fuero as well as mechanics employed on the palace of the Inquisition and houses of the officials and also to the overgrown number of familiars and their character.[1087] In Catalonia, especially, he found much to criticize, as we shall have occasion to see hereafter, for he performed his mission thoroughly and conscientiously; he listened to all complaints, investigated them and bore back to the Suprema full reports which bore hardly on the methods of all the tribunals. Prolonged debates ensued between the Suprema, the Council of Aragon and the Diputados and finally, in 1568, a new Concordia was issued. It is significant that it no longer was a royal decree but bore the shape of instructions from Inquisitor-general Espinosa and the Suprema to the tribunals, and the king only appeared in it as communicating it to his representatives and ordering its observance under pain of a thousand florins, coupled with commands to favor and reverence the Inquisition and its officials, to give them all necessary aid and to protect and defend their privileges.

  The Concordia thus granted to Valencia confirmed that of 1554 and ordered its observance, adding a number of special provisions, highly suggestive of the abuses which had flourished. As affording a view in some detail of the causes of popular irritation and of the remedies sought, I subjoin an abstract of the articles bearing on the subject.

> Outside of the city the local magistrates are to have cognizance of civil cases of familiars involving less than twelve libras.
>
> Familiars of other districts settling in Valencia lose the fuero, but retain it if the residence is temporary.
>
> The number of familiars is to be reduced to that provided in 1554, weeding out the least desirable.
>
> They must present themselves with their commissions to the local magistrates in order to be entered on the lists, without which they forfeit their exemption.
>
> The provision depriving those in trade of the fuero, for frauds and offences committed in their business, which has not been observed, is to be enforced.
>
> Crimes committed prior to appointment are not entitled to the fuero.
>
> No cleric or religious or powerful noble or baron is to be appointed.
>
> Consultors are not to be considered as officials, but only persons holding commissions from the inquisitor-general, to whom may be added a steward of the prison and two advocates of prisoners.
>
> In future the servants of officials must really be servants living with them and receiving regular wages in order to be protected by the inquisitors.

Inquisitors are not to interfere, at the petition of an official or familiar, with the regulations of the college of surgeons.

Any familiar who is a carpenter and who brings lumber from the sierra of Cuenca shall not be protected by the inquisitors, but shall be left for judgement to the secular court.

Outside of cases of heresy inquisitors must not interfere with the execution of justice by the royal judges under pretext that culprits have committed offences pertaining to them, but in such cases the judges shall be notified and allowed to execute justice, after which the inquisitors can inflict punishment. In case of heresy, however, a prisoner can be demanded, to be returned after trial, provided he is not sentenced to relaxation.

Familiars are not to be protected in the violation of municipal regulations, nor, during pestilence, in the refusal to observe the regulations for the avoidance of contagion; they must submit for inspection the goods which they bring in and the royal judges shall not be prevented from imposing the penalties provided in the royal pragmática.

Commissioners shall not form competencias with secular or ecclesiastical judges, nor shall their assistants enjoy greater privileges than familiars.

Persons temporarily employed to make arrests, or to read the edicts, or as procurators, etc., shall not be defended by the inquisitors.

As the inquisitorial district of Valencia comprehends Teruel in Aragon and Tortosa in Catalonia, those places are not to be exempted from the Concordia under the pretext that the Concordia of 1554 spoke of the kingdom of Valencia.

The widows of officials, while remaining unmarried, enjoy both civil and criminal fuero, but not their children and families as has been the case, but widows of familiars are deprived of it and are not to be defended by the inquisitors.

The judge employed by the inquisitors to hear the cases of officials and familiars is to be dismissed; such cases are to be heard by the inquisitors outside of the regular hours of service and for this they are to charge no fees.

Servants and families of salaried officials are only to have the passive fuero in civil cases, like familiars.

Inquisitors are no longer to defend familiars in matters of the apportionment of irrigating waters, injuries to harvests, vineyards, pastures, forests, furnishing of lights, licences for building, street-cleaning, road-mending and furnishing provisions.

Inquisitors are not to publish edicts with excommunication for the discovery of debts, thefts or other hidden offences committed against officials and familiars, nor such edicts against any delinquents save in cases of heresy.

Persons arrested, except for heresy, are not to be confined in the secret prison but in the public one, where they can confer with their counsel and procurators, and they are to be allowed to hear mass and receive the sacraments.

Familiars holding office are not to be defended for official frauds or malfeasance, but the secular authorities are to be freely allowed to administer justice.

Inquisitors shall not give safe-conducts to persons outlawed or banished by the royal judges, except in cases of faith and then only for the time necessary to appear before them.

When any official or familiar, in criminal or civil cases not of faith, has consented tacitly or explicitly to the secular jurisdiction or has pleaded clergy, the inquisitors shall not protect him nor inhibit the secular judges. And if any official or familiar inherits property in litigation the case shall remain in the court where it is pending.

As familiars in civil cases have only the passive and not the active fuero there shall no longer, as heretofore, be artifices employed, such as pretended criminal prosecutions and interdicts, to obtain cognizance of such cases, but they shall be conducted in the court of the defendant.

When a suit between outsiders has been decided, if any official or familiar intervenes to prevent the execution of the decision, on the pretext that he is in possession of the property at issue or a part of it, the inquisitors shall not support him in it.
[Sidenote: VALENCIA]

If an outsider commits a crime while in company with an official or familiar, or is an accomplice in a crime committed by an official or familiar, the inquisitors shall not have cognizance of his case but only of that of the official or familiar.

When a grave crime has been committed by or against a familiar the inquisitors shall not send a judge to take testimony or punish, with salary by the day, but shall avoid expense by making a commissioner gather the evidence.

Inquisitors shall no longer enforce contracts of peace and truce unless they have been entered into before them or by their order.

Inquisitors shall not have cognizance of contracts between outsiders because of a clause submitting them to the fuero, nor of cases of donations or cession to officials or familiars.

Inquisitors shall not protect widows of officials and familiars in refusing to pay imposts and contributions.

When inquisitors have to summon secular judges before them it must be only in cases where it is unavoidable and then only with great consideration.

If a bankrupt is a familiar the inquisitors have cognizance, but not in the case of an outsider under pretext that an official or familiar is a creditor.

Familiars shall not make arrests or other execution of justice without orders from inquisitors.

Inquisitors shall not proceed against the priors and officials of guilds and confraternities who levy upon a familiar, who is a member, for dues under the rules of the association, or when a familiar has had the administration of a church or hermitage or hospital and is sued for debts or contributions due.[1088]

The other prayers and demands of the Córtes were rejected, but those which were granted sufficiently indicate the abusive manner in which the tribunal had extended its jurisdiction, how that jurisdiction was admittedly used to protect officials and familiars in violations of law, and how intolerable was the influence on municipal and commercial life of letting loose on the community a class who were beyond the reach of justice. We can readily understand the eagerness of the lawless and unscrupulous to obtain positions which secured for them such privileges and why it was impossible to restrain inquisitors within the prescribed limits of their appointing power.

After protracted effort the Valencians had thus obtained promise of substantial relief, but as usual it was a promise only made to be broken. How little intention there was of enforcing the reform was promptly revealed for, when the authorities naturally ordered the new Concordia to be printed so that the courts and rural magistrates could be guided by it in their dealings with the officials and familiars, the inquisitors at once ordered the printers to suspend work and appealed to the king, who commanded that all copies should be surrendered.[1089] Although the settlement was permanent and remained in force until the end, it apparently never was published for general information. At the moment it was regarded as greatly limiting the secular jurisdiction of the tribunal, and the worthy Valencian inquisitor, Juan de Rojas, says that he is ashamed to allude to its depressed and weakened condition, which has worked great injury to the faith.[1090] His grief was superfluous; the tribunal was not accustomed to be bound by law and its methods of enforcing its assumed prerogatives were difficult to resist. In 1585 the Córtes had a fresh accumulation of grievances which, by order of the king, the Suprema sent to the inquisitors with orders to report the method of meeting them most advantageous to the Holy Office.[1091]

***

If space permitted abundant cases could be cited to show the justice of these complaints. In fact, the correspondence between the Suprema and the tribunal, during the last fifteen years of the sixteenth century, is largely devoted to cases of competencias arising from crimes of all descriptions committed by familiars and to the punishments inflicted by the tribunal, the heaviest of which is the galleys, in two or three cases. Sometimes the charges are dismissed and as a whole the criminals seem to have escaped so lightly that prosecution only served to encourage their lawlessness.[1092] There was no improvement as time went on and a case occurring in 1632 is worth alluding to as illustrating the results of the fuero and the spirit in which it was administered by the tribunal. Don Martin Santis was murdered by pistol shots, while returning with some Dominican frailes in a coach from the Grao of Valencia to the city. Four notorious familiars, Pedro Rebert, Joan Ciurana, Jaime Blau and Calixto Tafalla, were suspected and were arrested by the Audiencia. The tribunal claimed them, a competencia was formed and the case came up before the Suprema and the Council of Aragon. The Marquis of los Velez, the viceroy, took advantage of it to represent to Philip IV the disorders and scandals caused by the criminal familiars who were protected by the Inquisition. This paper was referred to the Council of Aragon which, on July 21st, presented a consulta on the subject. There is, it says, no peace or safety to be hoped for in Valencia unless there is reform in the selection of familiars, for there is no crime committed there in which they are not principals or accomplices, in the confidence of escape through the intervention of the tribunal, since there is no one, however guilty he may be of atrocious crime, who is not speedily seen walking the streets in freedom. In all disturbances, familiars are recognized as ringleaders and their object in gaining appointment is only to enjoy immunity for their crimes. In Valencia, Pedro Revert, Joan Ciurana and Sebastian Adell, all familiars, are the chief disturbers of the peace. So in Villareal, a place notorious for murders, Jaime Blau has been the moving spirit. In Benignamin, where there are constant outbreaks, the leaders of the factions are Gracian España, Martin Barcela and others, likewise familiars. It is the same in Orihuela with Juan García de Espejo and others. Scarce anywhere is there trouble in which familiars are not concerned and they daily become more insolent through impunity, for the inquisitors never punish with the requisite severity. One result is that it is almost impossible to procure evidence against these malefactors, in consequence of witnesses knowing that they will shortly be released and will avenge themselves. Justice cannot be administered and still greater evils are to be anticipated if the king does not provide a remedy. If it is difficult to revise the Concordia and introduce the necessary provisions, at least the king can order that these familiars be dismissed and greater care be exercised in new appointments. All the viceroys have recognized these impediments to justice, for these people only seek exemption from the secular courts in order to be free to commit crimes.

We might imagine much of this to be exaggeration were not its truth tacitly admitted by the Suprema, when transmitting it to Valencia with instructions for information on which to base a reply. There is no rebuke or exhortation to amendment, but the inquisitors are told to act with the utmost caution and secrecy; to report the number of familiars in Valencia and how many are unmarried; to give details as to the cases cited by the Council of Aragon and what punishments were inflicted; what was the record of those inculpated in the murder of Don Martin Santís; covertly to obtain statistics of crime in Valencia for the last ten years, committed by those not exempt, the punishments inflicted by the royal court and whether these were subsequently remitted; whether, when familiars were tried by the tribunal, accomplices were prosecuted in the royal courts, and if so what sentences were pronounced; also to make secret investigation as to promises made to familiars by the judges to let them off easily if they would not claim the fuero, and finally to furnish a list of cases in which the tribunal has punished its officials for trifling offences. Altogether the effort was evidently much less to offer a justification than to make a tu quoque rejoinder. Apparently the statistics asked of the tribunal were unsatisfactory, for there was no use made of them in the answer presented October 6th, in which, after seeking to explain away the assertions of the viceroy and Council of Aragon, the Suprema accused the secular courts and their officials of perpetual prosecution of familiars, who were arrested on the slightest suspicion, assumed to be guilty and then forced by cruel treatment to renounce the fuero. The suggestions for reform were airily brushed aside. To dismiss delinquent familiars would be almost impossible, in view of its effect upon their families and kindred. To enquire of the royal officials as to the character of aspirants for appointment was inadmissible, as it would admit them to participation in a matter with which they had nothing to do. The true cure for the troubles would be to secure the Inquisition in its rights by forbidding the secular courts from assuming any jurisdiction over familiars. In short it was a passionate outburst, precluding all hope of amendment, to which the king replied by telling the Suprema to see that the tribunal did not employ violent measures against the royal officials, but report to him any excess for his action. Evidently nothing was to be hoped for from him and indeed he had written on August 6th to the viceroy that the case must take its regular course as a competencia and the inquisitors must not use inhibitory censures or summon the judges to appear before them. The result was the usual one that the tribunal obtained cognizance of the case; one, at least, of the accused, Jaime Blau, was found guilty, for we have his insufficient sentence, condemning him to exile and a fine of three hundred ducats--a sentence which goes far to explain the eagerness of the inquisitors to extend their jurisdiction, for they rarely inflicted corporal punishments on their delinquent officials, when pecuniary ones were so much more profitable.[1093]

***

The same spirit was shown when, in 1649, disturbances between armed bands led Philip IV to order the Suprema to instruct the inquisitors that familiars and officials participating in these brawls, or lending aid to peacebreakers, should not enjoy the fuero and that the tribunal should not defend them or interfere with the course of justice. Instead of obeying, the Suprema replied that it suspended the order until the king should be better informed. It then proceeded with a long argument to show that the faith would be imperilled by such abridgement of the privileges of the Holy Office. Besides, these factional contests had always been customary in Valencia and it was impossible to avoid favoring one side or the other, for these armed bands demanded whatever they wanted--money, or food or clothes--and people were forced to give it at the risk of having their harvests burnt or their throats cut. The consulta ended with the impudent suggestion that in future it would be much better for the king, before issuing such decrees, to communicate to the Suprema the consultas of the other councils on which they were based so that a junta could be formed and the matter be debated.[1094]

Evidently the Suprema held that this semi-savage state of society should be encouraged by favoring the factionists and, under such conditions, amelioration was impossible. Rivalry of jurisdiction paralyzed the law and there was perpetual friction over the veriest trifles, for the tribunal was always on the watch to resist the minutest infraction of its prerogatives or disregard of its dignity. When, in 1702, Jacinto Nadal, a familiar of Onteniente, received a summons to appear before Don Pedro Domenech, a criminal judge of the Audiencia, he at once appealed to the tribunal which sent word, on May 29th, that he had been under arrest since March 25th and the papers in any charge against him must be surrendered to it. It turned out that Domenech only wanted him to enter security for his son and, when this was done, the inquisitors complained that Nadal had done wrong in going to the judge after appealing to them, and that Domenech had not treated them with proper respect, so that some months were required to arrange a truce between them.[1095]

***

Aragon was a source of greater trouble than Valencia. The popular spirit was more independent, it had resisted the introduction of the Inquisition until the murder of San Pedro Arbués had rendered further opposition impossible, it had been cheated of the fruits of the tenacity of Juan Prat and it possessed an institution peculiar to itself, designed to limit the encroachments of the sovereign power and well adapted to restrain the arrogance of anything less formidable than the mingled spiritual and temporal jurisdiction of the Holy Office.

ARAGON

The origin of the court of the Justicia of Aragon was fondly attributed by the Aragonese to the legendary times of the kingdom of Sobrarve and there is fair probability in the theory of the latest writer on the subject that it was derived by the Christians from the conquered Moors.[1096] In the thirteenth century the Justicia was already judge between the king and his subjects; every precaution was taken to render him independent; he was irremovable by the king and even his resignation was void; he could accept no office from the king; he was not liable to arrest and in a case of prosecution the Córtes sat in judgement on him; every person in the kingdom was required to obey his commands, to respect his decisions and to aid in their enforcement. His court consisted of his assessors or lieutenants, originally appointed by him, but subsequently by the king. The Córtes of 1528 increased the number to five, submitting fifteen names to Charles V, who selected five, while the rest were placed in a bolsa and drawn as vacancies occurred. They were virtually the equals of the Justicia, for the assent of a majority was required in all judgements and all precautions were taken to secure their independence.[1097] It is true that, in spite of the inviolability of the Justicia, there were cases on record in which Justicias had been made way with and that, on the suppression of the rising caused by Antonio Pérez, in 1591, the Justicia, Juan de Lanuza, was beheaded without trial, and in the ensuing Córtes of Tarazona the appointment of both Justicia and lieutenants was surrendered to the king.[1098] Nevertheless the court of the Justicia was regarded by the Aragonese with the greatest pride and reverence, as the safeguard of their liberties and the highest expression of judicial authority existing in the world; it was the bond that united the state and the foundation of its tranquillity. When the Justicia authorized the cry of Contrafuero! Viva la Libertad y ayuda á la Libertad! it summoned every citizen to sally forth in arms to defend the liberties of the land. Moreover, he had the power of withholding from execution all papal decrees, and his authority in ecclesiastical matters in general caused him to be popularly termed the married pope.[1099]

So far as we are concerned, the power of the court was exercised through two processes, the manifestacion and the firma. The former was a kind of habeas corpus, under which a person had to be produced before it, either to be liberated on bail or to be confined in the carcel de manifestados--a special prison over which even the king had no jurisdiction. The summons of a manifestacion had to be obeyed, even if the subject were on the gallows with the halter around his neck, or if it was addressed to the highest secular or spiritual court of the land. It was a privilege to which every citizen was entitled; when, in 1532, Charles V sent orders that Don Pedro de Luna should be deprived of it, he was not obeyed, and a special envoy was sent to him in Germany, asking the prompt withdrawal of the command as, until the return of the messenger, the land would be in great suspense. The firma was of various kinds, but in general it was of the nature of an injunction, stopping all proceedings and summoning the parties before the court of the Justicia, where their cases would be determined, and it was especially useful in preventing arbitrary arrests and seizure of property. Failure to obey a firma was promptly followed by seizure of temporalities and, under a fuero of King Martin, it could be served on the king himself. One was served on Charles V, at Valladolid, and again one on the papal nuncio and, when the latter disregarded it, his temporalities were sequestrated. Such a jurisdiction could not fail to come into collision with the Inquisition, against which its powers were frequently invoked, and the favorite device of the tribunal, of evading service by closing its doors, was unavailing, for attaching the firma to the gates was held to be legal service. In 1561, the Justicia granted a manifestacion to Don Juan Francés del Ariño, in a case not of faith; the tribunal prepared to answer by fulminating excommunications, but the court issued a monitorio against it, when a settlement was reached which both parties considered satisfactory. In the same year, when the inquisitors arrested Bartolomé Garate, secretary of the court, it served a monitorio upon them and, in 1563, it did the same for the censures issued against Augustin de Morlanes, of the criminal council of the Audiencia. In 1626, when Pedro Banet, secretary of the tribunal, was accused of the murder of Juan Domingo Serveto, the action of the inquisitors led to the issue against them of a firma and monitorio, under which their temporalities were seized and this was followed by another firma, prohibiting the use of excommunication.[1100]

***

Under such institutions, animated by such a spirit, it was inevitable that the extension of the temporal jurisdiction of the Holy Office should provoke a bitter and prolonged conflict. We have seen the early struggles of this; how concessions were wrung from monarch and Inquisition, to be disregarded by them as soon as the momentary pressure had passed, and how the remonstrances of the Córtes of 1528 and 1533 were contemptuously brushed aside. The grievances were real and the Suprema knew them to be such, but the policy was invariable of denying their existence and refusing amendment when asked for by the sufferers. The temper in which complaints were heard was significantly manifested when, in 1533, the Córtes of Monzon adopted certain articles and presented them to Inquisitor-general Manrique and the Suprema, with the request that they should be adopted. Thereupon Miguel de Galbe, fiscal of the tribunal of Lérida, addressed to Manrique a formal accusation, naming four members of the Córtes, who seem to have been the committee deputed to communicate with the Suprema, asking that they and all who had advocated the articles should be prosecuted as fautors of heretics and impeders and disturbers of the Inquisition, while the articles in question should be publicly torn and burnt as condemned and suspect of heresy, injurious to the honor of God and prejudicial to the Holy Office.[1101] Parliamentary discussion had doubtless been warm and freedom of debate and legislation was contrary to the principles of the Holy Office. Possibly it was the unpleasant experience of the Suprema on this occasion that led it to keep away from the Córtes of Monzon in 1537 and to order the inquisitors to do likewise or, if their duties called them there, to keep silent. Thus, when the Córtes asked the emperor to make the Inquisition obey the laws, he was able to promise accordingly and then the Suprema could subsequently argue it away in a consulta.[1102]

The remedial decree of Prince Philip, in 1545, was limited to Castile, and Aragon was coolly told that its customs were different. Abuses continued unchecked and at the Córtes of Monzon, in 1547, a long series of grievances was presented to the inquisitor-general, as though the crown had ceased to be a factor. The bull Pastoralis officii, by which Leo X had confirmed the Concordia of 1512, had limited the number of familiars to ten permanent ones in Saragossa and ten temporary ones elsewhere as needed, in place of which the number was between five hundred and a thousand; the bull had prescribed that they should be married men of good character, in place of which many were bandits and homicides and of notoriously evil life; the bull had ordered dismissal for officials and familiars who did not pay their debts or who engaged in trade, whereas the fuero was held to cover debts contracted and offences committed prior to appointment; when they became bankrupt they took refuge with the tribunal and the creditors were unpaid; if they were creditors of a bankrupt they seized all the assets and others got nothing; men procured appointments in order to revenge themselves in safety on their enemies; it was impossible to collect debts of them and this protection was extended even to women. A woman who claimed that her father had been a familiar was thus defended from her creditors; the brother of a notary of the tribunal, who had committed an offence, caused the aggrieved parties to be arrested and the inquisitors held them until they were forced to a compromise. How little hope there was of redress for all this is visible in the contemptuous indifference with which Inquisitor-general Valdés answered the several articles. As to bandits and homicides being made familiars, he said the Inquisition had need of all kinds of officials for its various functions, and as to the specific complaints the stereotyped answer was that any one deeming himself aggrieved could appeal to the Suprema and get justice.[1103]

The Concordia of 1553 was applicable to Castile alone and that of 1554 to Valencia. Aragon remained without the slender alleviation provided for in the latter, for the adjustments of 1512 and 1521 were treated as non-existent. At the Córtes of 1563-4 the complaints were so vivacious that, as we have seen, Philip promised investigation which resulted in the Concordia of 1568. The formula for Aragon was virtually the same as the combined Valencia Concordias of 1554 and 1568, the evils with which the two kingdoms were afflicted being virtually the same. As usual, familiars were the class that excited the bitterest hostility. Their commissions were all to be called in and then sixty were to be appointed for Saragossa, while the other towns were assigned from eight to one or two according to population. Their character was to be closely scrutinized and all bandits, homicides, criminals, powerful nobles, frailes and clerics were to be excluded, and no one was to enjoy the fuero whose name was not on lists presented to the magistrates. They were to have, in criminal matters, the active and passive fuero but in civil suits only the passive; it was the same with servants of officials, while officials themselves had active and passive in both civil and criminal. The utmost caution and moderation was prescribed in the employment of inhibitions and excommunications of the royal judges, and the royal alguazils were not to be arrested save in cases of grave and notorious infraction of inquisitorial rights.[1104]

***

The Concordia did not bring concord. In 1571 there arose a bitter dispute between the tribunal and the court of the Justicia, in which excommunications were freely used and, in December, the Diputados appealed to Pius V to evoke the case and remove the censures, but he told them to go to the inquisitor-general. After the death of Pius, the kingdom insisted with Gregory XIII and, in December, 1572, obtained from him a brief committing the case to the Suprema or to Ponce de Leon the new inquisitor-general, but, at the same time, he ordered that some remedy be found to prevent the inquisitors from abusing the privileges conceded to them by the canons and the popes.[1105] The next year, 1573, formal complaints were made by the kingdom of infractions of the Concordia and, by 1585, aggravation had reached a point that the Córtes asked for a new concordia. Philip promised to send a person to Saragossa to gather information as to grievances alleged against certain inquisitors and officials, after which arrangements were made for the drafting and acceptance or rejection of a new agreement, but there is no trace of any resultant understanding.[1106] Quarrelling necessarily continued with little intermission. In 1613 the removal of the name of Juan Porquet, a familiar, from insaculacion, by the royal commissioner of Tamarit, gave rise to a great disturbance which was long remembered and, in 1619, there was a clash between the tribunal and the captain-general, which caused much scandal, resulting in the governor being summoned to Madrid, where he was kept for four years.[1107]

Thus it went on until, in 1626, the Córtes were again assembled. It was known that demands for relief would be made and the Suprema asked Philip to submit to it whatever articles were proposed, in reply to which he assured it that there should be no change to its prejudice, but that he would procure its increase of privilege.[1108] The chief business of the Córtes was the questions connected with the Inquisition. Philip was not present and his representative, the Count of Monterrey, did not feel empowered to grant the demands made. The only absolute action taken was to adopt as a fuero or law the Concordia of 1568, which hitherto had only the authority of the orders of the king and inquisitor-general. As regards reform, it was left to a commission, consisting on one side of royal appointees and on the other of four delegates named by each of the four brazos or estates. The commission framed a series of fourteen articles, by no means radical in their character, but Philip procrastinated in confirming or rejecting them; the Suprema, in 1627, appealed to Rome to withhold papal sanction and they were quietly allowed to drop, on the pretext that the Concordia of 1568, now erected into law, would suffice to prevent future grounds of complaint. How futile this was is apparent from a conflict which occurred during the sitting of the commission. The assessor of the governor, as was his duty, entered the house of the secretary of the tribunal, flagrante delicto, for a most treacherous murder attributed to him. Although his obligation to do this was notorious, arrest of subordinates followed on both sides and the indignant people were with difficulty restrained from a tumult. The royal officials at once took steps to form a competencia, in conformity with the Concordia which had just been erected into a law; this required all proceedings to be suspended but the inquisitors excommunicated the assessor, refusing to join in the competencia because, as they asserted, the case was an evident one, thus assuming that they could set aside all law by merely declaring that a case was evident.[1109]

***

The Inquisition had never been restrained by the Concordia and now that it had again baffled the Córtes it was still less inclined to submit to restraint. Quarrels continued as virulent as before, a single example of which will illustrate its invincible tendency to extend its jurisdiction on all possible pretexts. Berenguer de San Vicente of Huesca, in 1534, had founded in that city the College of Santiago and when, in 1538, the municipality added an endowment of more than six thousand ducats, he made the magistrates its patrons. In 1542 he procured from Charles V a cédula, confirmed by the pope, making the inquisitors of Aragon visitors or inspectors of the college, during the royal pleasure and so long as they should perform their functions loyally and well. This supervisory function they stretched in course of time to bring the college and all its members under their jurisdiction, although in 1643 it was asserted that the last visitation had been made in 1624. This power they exercised in most arbitrary fashion. When an attempt was made to burn the college and the town offered a reward for the detection of the incendiary, they interposed with the threat of an interdict and frightened the citizens into submission. In 1643 a pasquinade against some of the inhabitants led to the prosecution of the rector of the college, Dr. Juan Lorenzo Salas, who promptly procured letters from the tribunal inhibiting further proceedings and demanding all the papers. The patience of Huesca was exhausted. It declared its position to be intolerable, for the students appealed to the fuero in all disputes with the townsmen, and the result of the stimulus thus given to that turbulent element was driving away the population and every one lived in apprehension of some terrible event. To gain relief it applied to the Audiencia for a competencia but was told that this was impossible, whereupon it obtained from the court of the Justicia a firma prohibiting the inquisitors from acting; they refused to allow it to be served when it was put on the gate of the Aljaferia with notice that if answer was not made within thirty days it would be followed with exile and seizure of temporalities. The Suprema ordered the inquisitors to answer by excommunicating all concerned. Philip was then in Saragossa, on his way to Catalonia to put himself at the head of his army, for the disgrace of Olivares had forced him to govern as well as to reign, but he was compelled to distract his thoughts with these miserable squabbles. The Council of Aragon appealed to him to require the inquisitors to show cause why they should not be deprived of the visitation and to impose silence on all until he should reach a decision; the Audiencia rendered an opinion that the court of the Justicia could not refuse to issue the firma and, if the complainant insisted on its service, it must be served if the whole power of the kingdom had to be called upon. On the other hand the Suprema declared that the service of the firma was unexampled and urged the king to support the Inquisition in a matter on which depended the ruin or the preservation of the monarchy, for it would be better to close the Holy Office than to expose its jurisdiction to such disgrace, while in these calamitous times favor shown to the Inquisition would placate God and insure the success of his arms. Philip's reply was long and maundering, irresolute between his reverence for the Inquisition and his fear of alienating in his extremity the Aragonese by violating their most cherished privileges. If Huesca would desist from the service of the firma he would order the tribunal to form a competencia. Huesca, however, was intractable; its very existence, it asserted, was at stake and it begged the king not to interfere with the legal remedies to which it had been forced and, in conveying this reply to the king, the Council of Aragon warned him that it could not prevent Huesca from serving the firma, as this would be a notorious violation of the law on the point regarded by the kingdom as most essential. Yet, after all, the question was evaded by the device of appointing as visitor of the college the inquisitor Juan Llano de Valdés, who succeeded in reaching an agreement with the city. It would seem that thereafter special visitors were nominated for, in 1665, we hear of such an appointment issued to Inquisitor Carlos del Hoya and it may be doubted whether Huesca gained much.[1110]

    These disturbances mark the highest point reached by the Inquisition in Aragon as regards its temporal jurisdiction. How little cause of complaint it really had, and how Aragon, in spite of its sturdy independence, had endured greater abuses than those permitted in Castile, is evinced in a suggestion made by the Suprema, February 11, 1643, in response to a demand from the king to devise some new source of raising money for the bankrupt treasury. This was that if he would grant to the familiars of Castile the same privileges of active and passive fuero enjoyed by those of Aragon, they would cheerfully contribute to a considerable assessment, with the added advantage of diminishing the competencias which caused so much trouble and loss of time.[1111] Such a proposal affords the measure of the wrongs inflicted on society by those who profited by their exemption from the secular courts, for even the more limited privileges of the Castilian familiars rendered the position one to be eagerly sought, in spite of the considerable cost of proving the condition precedent of limpieza, or purity of blood. These evils were vastly aggravated by the fact, as we shall see hereafter, that the tribunals never regarded the limitation on numbers prescribed by the Concordias, but filled the land with these privileged persons who, for the most part, turned to the best account the protection of the Holy Office.

***

    That Aragon should be permanently restive under this adverse discrimination was inevitable and the time had come when it could dictate in place of supplicating. Since the Córtes of 1626 twenty years elapsed before Philip found himself constrained to assemble them again. The situation was desperate; the Catalan rebellion bade fair to end in the permanent alienation of the Principality to France, and it was not wise to impose too severe a strain on the loyalty of Aragon, when the Córtes met September 20, 1645, for a session of fifteen months. In preparation for the struggle, the Suprema presented to the king, September 30th, an elaborately argued memorial in which it told him that the calamities of the war should lead him to greater zeal in fortifying the Inquisition with new graces and privileges, so as to win the favor of God, whose cause they served and from whom alone was relief to be expected. It was therefore asked that whatever demands on the subject should be presented should be reserved for discussion with the inquisitor-general and Suprema.[1112] Philip doubtless made the desired promise, but the Aragonese had too often found their hopes frustrated in this manner to submit to it again under existing circumstances.

    The Córtes lost no time in presenting their petition on the subject, which asked for radical reform in all the Aragonese kingdoms. The jurisdiction of the Inquisition was to be confined to cases of faith and to civil and criminal actions between its officials. In certain mixed cases, such as bigamy, unnatural crime, sorcery, solicitation and censorship it should have jurisdiction cumulative with the appropriate secular and spiritual courts. A number of minor points were added, including a demand that all inquisitors and officials should be natives and it was significantly stated that the petition was presented thus early in order that it might be granted, so that the Córtes could proceed more heartily with the servicio that was asked for. This paper was submitted to the Suprema which replied in a long consulta, March 31, 1646, arguing that the Inquisition had been introduced into Aragon without law and was independent of all law. It proceeded to demonstrate, as we have seen (p. 345), that its temporal jurisdiction was inalienable and that the Concordias were compacts which could not be modified without its consent. The officials were so abhorred that it would be impossible for them to perform their duties if they were not thus protected. If the Córtes should stubbornly insist, the king was urged, like Charles V in 1518, to remember his soul and his conscience, and to prefer the loss of part of his dominions rather than consent to anything contrary to the honor of God and the authority of the Inquisition.[1113]

    The policy of the Suprema was to carry the war into Africa, and it followed this manifesto with another demanding that the court of the Justicia should be prohibited from issuing firmas and manifestaciones in cases concerning the Inquisition. Both sides asked for more than they expected to get and, when the Córtes answered these papers, June 20th, after numerous citations to disprove the arguments of the Suprema and an exposition of the hardships caused by the existing system, they opened the way to a compromise by pointing out that Castile for nearly a hundred years had enjoyed what Aragon had vainly prayed for, and concluded by suggesting that the best settlement would be to confer on Aragon the Concordia of Castile which had been thoroughly discussed by lawyers and its practical working determined and understood.[1114]

Finally the demands of the Córtes were formulated in a series of twenty-seven articles, which were prudently declared to be law, whether confirmed or not by the inquisitor-general. Of these the essential ones deprived familiars of the active and passive fuero in civil suits, of the active in criminal cases, and excepted certain specified crimes in the passive. Servants of salaried officials were put on the same footing in criminal matters. The number of both familiars and salaried officials was limited to four hundred and fifty in the whole kingdom and those who held office were deprived of the fuero for official malfeasance; in cases not of faith the use of torture was prohibited as well as confinement in the secret prison; all cases, whether civil or criminal, were to be concluded within two years; fraudulent alienation of property to officials, so as to place it under the fuero, was declared invalid; all persons or bodies, in case of violation of these provisions, had the right to avail themselves of all remedies known to the laws of the land, while to the tribunal was reserved the power to employ censures and other legal processes. A concession was made by granting to both officials and familiars the right of asylum in their houses, relief from billeting, exemption from arrest for debt, capacity to hold office and freedom from tolls, ferriages, etc. In return for this the Córtes were liberal with the servicio, agreeing to keep in the field two thousand foot and five hundred horse for four years, paying them two reales a day, while the king should find them in food, arms and horses.[1115]

***

In these conditions there was nothing affecting the faith or restricting the persecution of heresy; nothing save a prudent regard for the peace and protection of society from the intolerable burden of gangs of virtual bandits clothed in inviolability. Yet Philip resisted to the last extremity these reasonable concessions, which merely placed Aragon on the same footing as Castile. We are told that he declared that he cherished the Inquisition as the apple of his eye and that he exhausted every means to preserve its privileges. He offered to concede everything else that was asked; he endeavored to win the Aragonese by bribing them with royal grants and graces, of which three hundred and sixty were published in a single day, with the names of the recipients, but nothing could overcome the hatred felt for the Holy Office and the brazos were immovable. In his perplexity he appealed to his usual counsellor, the mystic Sor María de Agreda, affirming his determination to uphold the Inquisition, and he must have been surprised when that clear-sighted woman advised him to compromise, for a quarrel with Aragon might turn it to the side of Catalonia and lead to the permanent disruption of the monarchy. Even this failed to move him. He endeavored to depart for Madrid, but deputation after deputation was sent to the convent of Santa Engracia where he was lodged, insisting on his confirmation of the articles and detaining him for two or three days while his coach stood ready at the gate, until at last he yielded, seeing that there was no alternative. The writer who records this adds that the people rejoiced and since then in Aragon, where the Inquisition had stood higher than elsewhere, for an inquisitor was regarded with more reverence than an archbishop or a viceroy, it has so fallen in estimation that some say that all is over with it. The officials and familiars feel this every day in the withdrawal of their privileges and exemptions, and it is palpable that in all that does not concern the faith, the ancient powers of the tribunal of Aragon are prostrated.[1116]

It was not long before the sullen yielding of the Inquisition to the changed situation was manifested in a case which did not tend to restore it to reverence. Inquisitor Lazaeta was involved in an intrigue with a married woman of San Anton, whose husband, a Catalan named Miguel Choved, grew suspicious and pretended to take a journey. Lazaeta fell into the trap. October 27, 1647, he went to the house at nightfall, leaving his coach in hiding behind the shambles; the coachman waited for him in vain, for the injured husband had entered by a side-door and given him a sword-thrust of which he died in the street, while stumbling forward in search of his coach. The woman escaped and Choved disappeared, but some demonstration was necessary and the tribunal arrested one Francisco Arnal as an accessory. The court of the Justicia issued a manifestacion in his favor, when the inquisitors complained of the interference with their functions of such orders and that the tribunal could not be maintained if they were to be banished and their temporalities be seized whenever they judged that a case was not comprehended within the fueros. To this the Council of Aragon replied that the court of the Justicia always acted with great caution and that, in the present case, Arnal had renounced the manifestacion and had been returned to the tribunal, which had found him innocent and had discharged him. The Suprema insisted that it would be better to remove the tribunal from Aragon than to have it subjected to such insults, to which the Council rejoined that there was no admission of firmas and manifestaciones except in matters not of faith; if the inquisitors would keep within their just limits, such troubles would be avoided, while, if they exceeded them, the kingdom must avail itself of the remedies provided by the laws.[1117] Now in this case the tribunal was strictly within its rights under the Concordia and its abstention from excommunication and interdict indicates how thoroughly it was humbled.

Another grievance of the Inquisition shows how completely the tables were turned. September 23, 1648, the Suprema represented in a consulta that the tribunal had been notified to reduce the number of its officials and familiares to the prescribed four hundred and fifty, which had not been done under the plea that the number was insufficient, that the Concordia did not order the dismissal of the overplus and that the incumbents could not be deprived of their rights. Still there was little doubt that persistent refusal would lead the Diputados to obtain a firma compelling a selection and until this was done no familiar would be allowed to enjoy their privileges--in fact a number of towns had already assumed this position and others were taking steps to obtain firmas. The Suprema endeavored to show the illegality of this on the ground that the Concordia of 1646 was not valid in the absence of confirmation by the inquisitor-general. Philip submitted this to the Council of Aragon and merely transmitted its answer, in non-committal fashion, to the Suprema for its information. This took the ground that only the secular and royal jurisdiction was concerned; the king had confirmed the laws which provided that the acquiescence of the inquisitor-general was unnecessary; if parties were aggrieved they could apply to the court of the Justicia.[1118]

***

Under these conditions, the laws of 1646, by restricting the tribunal to its proper functions, were a severe blow to its predominance, diminishing the terror which it inspired and affecting in some degree its finances. The continual suits brought before it had afforded a rich harvest of fees for its officials and the fines imposed had been a resource to its treasury. All this fell off greatly and, in 1649, the Suprema reminded Philip that, in 1646, it had predicted this result and he had promised indemnification by a fixed income to be paid by Aragon or by the royal treasury; although it did not regard the laws as binding in the absence of confirmation by the inquisitor-general, and had resisted their execution in every way, still they were executed and the officials were suffering keenly from their diminished fees, wherefore it asked the king to grant to the four notaries and messengers eight hundred ducats a year out of the fund for the Catalan refugees. This demand, and the impudent assertion of the nullity of the laws which he had approved, provoked Philip into one of his rare assertions of kingship. The Catalan fund, he replied, could not be touched; he would listen to other suggestions for the relief of the incumbents but not of their successors; he was master of the secular jurisdiction granted to the Inquisition for his service and could make laws and abrogate them at his pleasure.[1119]

Philip had learned a lesson and the laws of 1646 were duly executed. When, in 1677, there was another convocation of the Córtes of Aragon, the Suprema, in a suppliant tone contrasting strongly with its former arrogance, begged Carlos II to influence them to condescend to a modification. It gave a most dolorous account of the condition of the Saragossa tribunal resulting from that legislation. It forebore to discuss whether the officials had given just cause of complaint, but the total destruction of the Inquisition was curing one malady by introducing a worse one, and the Inquisition of Aragon had been destroyed. The number of officials was reduced below that at the time of its foundation, and its poverty was so great that wages were unpaid and the tribunal would probably have to be abandoned. The treasurer was compelled to collect its income and debts through the court of the Justicia, where it was impossible for him to carry on so many suits, so that only those paid whose consciences compelled them. The reduction of the officials impeded its usefulness; possibly there were fewer culprits but certainly there were fewer convictions--less in Aragon than in the other provinces--and a single one who escaped correction was a matter of greater consequence to God than the enjoyment of the fuero by five hundred persons. It was impossible to fill the allotted number of familiares, for the fuero in criminal matters left to them was rather a disadvantage, for they died in prison owing to the interminable delays in settling the numerous competencias, while other defendants were released on bail. At the same time the deprivation of the active fuero exposed them to the effects of the general hatred felt for them. It was inconceivable that, in so pious a nation, this hatred could be caused by their functions, but its existence was a matter of experience and, in the absence of protection, the risks to which it exposed them prevented men from seeking the position. The Inquisition did not desire jurisdiction, but it could not exist without revenue and officials, and it therefore prayed the king that proper measures of relief be discussed in the Córtes, or a junta could be formed from both parties and a new Concordia be framed. Even allowing for customary exaggeration, this paper shows how greatly the Inquisition had outgrown the functions for which it had been imposed upon the people.

The concessions asked for were singularly moderate--that the treasurer should not be required to make collections through the court of the Justicia, that more familiares be allowed--though it had just been said that they could not be had--that they be admitted to bail during competencias, and a timid suggestion respecting the firma and manifestacion. The time, however, was not propitious even for demands so modest. The youthful Carlos II had just relegated his mother to a convent and her favorite

Valenzuela to the Philippines; all power was in the hands of Don Juan of Austria, who held the inquisitor-general Valladares to be his personal enemy. The appeal of the Suprema was received unsympathetically and it seems to have gained nothing. That the Aragonese were content with the situation appears from the fact that the only complaint made by the Córtes regarded the non-observance of a law of 1646 prescribing the number of natives to be employed by the tribunal, and this arose merely from greed of office, for they suggested that, for each foreigner appointed in Aragon, an Aragonese should have a corresponding berth in a tribunal elsewhere.[1120]

CATALONIA

The legislation of 1646 remained a finality. As late as 1741 the Suprema remonstrated against the Audiencia of Saragossa for impeding the jurisdiction of the tribunal by employing the firma, which, with customary disingenuousness, it characterized as an innovation.[1121]

***

Catalonia was as intractable as Aragon, while its more pronounced spirit of independence rendered it particularly troublesome. Although it lacked the institution of the Justicia, it had a somewhat imperfect substitute in the Banch Royal, or King's Bench, which was used in the appeals por via de fuerza from the spiritual courts. The Audiencia summoned the ecclesiastical judge before it and his disregard of the summons was followed by a decree of banishment and seizure of temporalities. The inquisitors denied their liability to this, the Catalans asserted it, and the endeavor to enforce it was a serious cause of quarrel. It was not without influence, for a memorial, in 1632, from the inquisitors complains that the Duke of Maqueda, when viceroy in 1592, had employed it against the tribunal, since when the veneration felt for the latter had greatly declined, and a complaint of the Catalan authorities to Carlos II, in 1695, describes it as the sole refuge and protection of the people from the oppression of the inquisitors and ecclesiastical judges.[1122]

We have already seen the Concordia reached in 1512, abolishing most of the then existing abuses; how it was sworn to by king, inquisitor-general and inquisitors, and how a similar oath was to be taken by all future inquisitors; how Leo X obligingly released them all from their oaths; how Ferdinand, just before his death, accepted the conditions, in December, 1515, and the complaisant pontiff, in the bull Pastoralis officii, confirmed them, and how Barcelona, in return, bound itself to a yearly subvention of six hundred ducats. It is well to recall these facts in view of the bare-faced denials with which subsequently the Catalan complaints of non-observance were persistently met. Even while the papal dispensation from the oaths was still in force, the Instructions issued by Inquisitor-general Mercader, in 1514, prescribed rules which, if observed, would have removed the leading causes of complaint. Any official or familiar committing a crime deserving of corporal punishment was to be denounced to him, when he would dismiss the culprit and punish the inquisitor who tolerated it. The civil suits of officials were to be brought in the court of the defendant; if the official was plaintiff, all proceedings before an inquisitor were pronounced invalid and both official and inquisitor were to be punished; even when both parties to a contract agreed to accept the forum of the tribunal, inquisitors were forbidden, under pain of punishment, to entertain the case. Secular officials could arrest familiars caught in the act. Officials were forbidden to engage in trade, even through third parties, and were deprived of the fuero for all matters thence arising, and similarly if they purchased claims subject to suits, nor could they employ other officials to collect debts connected with their private estates.[1123] Although these Instructions were in force for only a year or two, they have interest as manifesting Ferdinand's purpose that the Holy Office should not be distracted from its legitimate functions or be used to oppress his subjects or to minister to private greed. He could, at the same time, believe that it required special privileges, for it did not as yet inspire awe in so turbulent a population. In that same year, 1514, at Lérida, the inquisitor Canon Antist was besieged in his house and the assailants were with difficulty beaten off, after which they defiantly walked the streets, uttering challenges to his defenders.[1124]

A further victory was gained by the Catalans at the Córtes of Monzon in 1520, when, on December 28th, Cardinal Adrian, in the most solemn manner, not only swore to observe the articles of 1512 but presented for attestation a document from Queen Juana and Charles V, promising investigation and redress of charges brought against certain officials, and enacting that, to prevent such abuses for the future, all offences disconnected with the faith, committed by officials, should be tried by the ordinary courts, thus depriving them of the much-prized criminal passive fuero. This, too, Adrian swore to observe when the necessary papal confirmation should be obtained--a confirmation which the Inquisition probably had sufficient influence to prevent, as there appears to be no further trace of it.[1125]

***

The articles of 1512 thus were a compact in which the Catalans, the king, the Inquisition and the pope all joined in the most solemn manner, pledging all future inquisitors to swear to them. For a while this latter clause was observed. Fernando Loazes, who was inquisitor of Barcelona for twenty years from about 1533, took the oath, but he was promptly involved in a quarrel with the magistrates in which Juan de Cardona, Bishop-elect of Barcelona, was induced, as papal commissioner, to prosecute him for perjury, and after that no inquisitor took the oath.[1126] In this they were wise for they emancipated themselves completely from the Concordia. The Córtes of 1547 complained of the inordinate multiplication of familiars, over the thirty allowed by it, and of the neglect to furnish lists or other means for their identification, together with other infractions, but Prince Philip replied that he would consult the Suprema and would reach appropriate conclusions, which of course ended the matter.[1127] How completely the provisions of the Concordia were ignored is manifest in 1551, when Catalina Murciana asked relief in the veguer's court from suits brought against her in the Inquisition by the fiscal, the Abbot of Besalú, when she was entitled to her own court. On refusal of redress by the inquisitor, Juan Arias, a monitorio was obtained from the Banch Reyal, whereupon Arias threw the officials of the veguer's court into prison and kept them there. The matter was carried up to the Royal Councils with the result that the judges of the Audiencia were ordered to erase all record of the affair from their dockets and appear in person before the inquisitor to report to him that it was duly expunged.[1128]

Thus supported by the monarch, the tribunal exercised its powers at discretion without regard to compacts. The report, in 1561, by Inquisitor Gaspar Cervantes of the visitation which he had just completed, describes the disorders which had long reigned in all departments. The last visitation had been made in 1550 and its recommendations had been wholly ignored. It had ordered a reduction in the number of familiars and that lists of them be sent to the Suprema, which had not been done; in fact the tribunal itself had kept no correct register; it had a hundred and eight names recorded for Barcelona, but when they were ordered to present their papers under penalty of being dropped, only sixty-eight of these came forward, while there were thirty-one who were not registered. The number, he said, should be reduced and more care be exercised in the selection; many of the laymen were bandits and the clerics were men of bad character, who sought the office to obtain exemption from their prelates. All this resulted in so much secular business that it seemed to be the real duty of the tribunal and that nothing else was attended to--in fact there was so little to do in matters of faith that the inquisitors could well be spared from Barcelona and employ themselves in visiting their district. All this is explicable by the exorbitance of the fees charged, about which there was much complaint. There was no authorized fee-bill. In civil cases the inquisitors charged from two and a half to ten per cent. on the amount at issue, depending on its magnitude, with a maximum of seventy-five libras; in criminal cases they received nothing but had the opportunity of inflicting fines. The officials had fees for every act, drawing and copying papers, serving notices, summoning witnesses, levying executions, etc., etc., and there was a standing quarrel between the notaries of the three departments--of the secreto, or tribunal of faith, of sequestrations and of the juzgado, or court of confiscations--as to which should have the business.[1129]

***

That the Córtes of Monzon, in 1563-4, should protest energetically against these abuses was natural. Indeed, a Catalan named Gaspar Mercader carried the protest so far as to say, among other odious things, that the Inquisition had been introduced only for a limited time which had expired and that it should be abolished, for which the tribunal arrested, tried and punished him.[1130] In spite of this interference with the freedom of debate, the general disaffection, as we have seen, led to the visitation of de Soto Salazar. In Barcelona he found that not the slightest attention had been paid to the orders of the Suprema based on the report of Cervantes. Advocates, familiars and commissioners continued to be appointed in profusion, without investigation as to fitness. When an inquisitor visited his district he carried with him blank commissions which he distributed at will. All these, with their families, were protected and defended by the tribunal in civil and criminal cases, nor was this all, for it would seem that any one who claimed the fuero, whether he was entitled to it or not, was admitted and, in the absence of lists filed with the magistrates, the latter had no means of resisting the arrogant and peremptory demand of the tribunal to surrender cases. Instances were given which showed that the tribunal was a court where justice--or rather injustice--was bought and sold and there had been no reform in the excessive fees which had scandalized Cervantes.[1131]

That it should be hated was inevitable. In 1566, Govilla, Bishop of Elna, defending himself for acts committed when he was inquisitor of Barcelona, declared that the Inquisition was even more odious in Catalonia than elsewhere.[1132] This hatred sometimes expressed itself more forcibly than by complaints. In 1567, the evocation of a case, which the local authorities claimed as their own, led to the fiercest excitement which the viceroy fruitlessly sought to allay and appealed to Philip II for his immediate interposition. Disregarding the inviolable secrecy of the Inquisition, the Diputados, with the veguer, forced their way into the palace, penetrated to the audience-chamber where the inquisitors were trying a case, and inventoried and sequestrated everything, even to the private property of the Inquisitor Padilla in his apartments--apparently a seizure of temporalities under an order of the Banch Royal. Even more flagrant was the insult committed when the messenger and the secretary were conveying from Perpignan to Barcelona two government officials accused of impeding the Inquisition and also a prisoner under a charge of heresy. Near Gerona, one of the Diputados, at the head of an armed band, seized the whole party and carried them back to Perpignan, where they were paraded through the streets with blare of trumpets, as though criminals on the way to execution, and were then cast into prison, where they lay until discharged without accusation. This was a most serious assault on the dignity of the Holy Office and even worse was permitting the escape of the heretic, but it was obliged to submit without vindicating its authority.[1133]

Such being the temper of the Catalans and such the provocation to meet lawlessness with lawlessness, it is not surprising that, when the Concordia of 1568 was prepared for the three kingdoms, Catalonia would have none of it. When, in September, it was submitted to the Diputados, they were incensed and proposed to send envoys to the king to remonstrate against it. There was a universal outcry that it was contrary to the constitution and privileges of the land; they would observe it in so far as it was in their favor, but as to the rest they were ready to lose life, property and children rather than to submit to it. In February, 1569, the inquisitors wrote that the people would not be content until they had driven the Inquisition from the land; as for themselves they proposed to go on as they had previously done until the Concordia should be accepted, to which the Suprema cordially assented.[1134]

***

This attitude of mutual defiance was not conducive to peace. In 1570, there arose a quarrel so bitter that the Diputados invoked the protection and interposition of Pius V, and he urged Philip II to come to some understanding with them, in view of possible serious consequences. Philip took the position that they were so excited and so obstinate that any concessions would lead only to further demands, but he asked the pope to dismiss the envoys, referring them to him with recommendation for favorable consideration, so that anything that he might yield would be to the Holy See and not to recalcitrant subjects. The situation was critical; the rebellion of Granada was exhausting his resources, there was acute apprehension of attack by a Turkish fleet and the Catalans were soon afterwards called upon to contribute to the defence of the coasts, but if any concessions were enforced on the Inquisition they have left no traces. In fact, the Venetian envoy, Leonardo Donato, in his relation of 1573, states that, after the Catalans had spent a hundred thousand ducats in these efforts, the Inquisition imprisoned those who had been most active in the matter and that they subsequently refused to leave the prison without a formal declaration that they had not been arrested for heresy.[1135] Dissension naturally continued. In 1572 we hear of a demand from the Diputados that the inquisitors should show them their commissions and take an oath to obey the constitution of Catalonia, because they held rents on the Diputacion; the inquisitors acceded to the first of these and were rebuked by the Suprema because it was a demand that had been persistently refused before and they must not do it again. Then, in 1574, there came a complaint from all the cities that familiars refused obedience to the local laws respecting prices, pasturage and other matters as required under the Concordia, to which the Suprema superciliously replied by instructing the inquisitors that, as the people had rejected the Concordia, they need not observe it.[1136] Then, in 1585, as we have seen (p. 416) the Córtes obtained an advantage in excluding familiars and officials from public offices.

In this spirit of undisguised hostility both sides were aligned for a decisive struggle in the Córtes of 1599, under the new royalty of the youthful Philip III. As the Catalan efforts failed and the Inquisition was left in possession of its usurped powers, the details of the contest have no interest except as an exhibition of shameless duplicity, by which the king tricked his vassals. They hoped to win favor by a subsidio of a million libras to the king and a hundred thousand to his bride, besides shrewdly granting ten thousand to the Marquis of Denia (soon to become Duke of Lerma) and six thousand to the Vice-chancellor of Aragon,[1137] but they reaped nothing but deceit. Long discussions resulted in a series of articles, divided into two categories, to one of which Philip gave unqualified assent and to the other his assent as far as concerned himself, with a promise to procure that of the inquisitor-general and pope. It was proposed to withhold the pension of six hundred libras granted in 1520, if the papal confirmation were not procured within a year, but Philip declared that no such guarantee was necessary, for the letters which he had ordered to be written to the pope were so strong that no influence could counteract them. His despatches to his ambassador were sent through the Diputados in order to satisfy them, but they assuredly were not allowed to see others which instructed the ambassador to be circumspect in urging the matter. He also sent word to the inquisitor-general that the delivery of these despatches had been delayed in order to give him time to express his views. The Suprema, in appealing to Clement VIII to withhold confirmation, did not hesitate to say that Philip had endeavored to escape under cover of the inquisitor-general and pope and had finally signed only in so far as concerned himself. Indeed, in a subsequent official paper, it was unblushingly asserted that he had done so only to get rid of the Catalans. Under these influences it is needless to say that the confirmation never came and the subsidio was the only practical result of the labors of the Córtes.[1138]

One of the articles required the execution of the Concordia of 1520, which embraced that of 1512, the fulfilment of which the Catalans had never ceased to demand, and the manner in which these solemn compacts were argued away is instructive. In 1566, Govilla, Bishop of Elna, who had been inquisitor of Barcelona, calmly asserted that the articles of 1512 had been revoked as prejudicial to the free exercise of the Inquisition. The Suprema, in urging Clement VIII to refuse confirmation of the new Concordia of 1599, argued that the transactions of 1512 and 1520 were invalid through simony, as the Córtes had obtained the assent of Ferdinand in 1516 (sic) and of Charles in 1520 by conditioning subsidios on it. Leo's bull of condemnation in 1513 was relied upon and that of confirmation in 1516 was dismissed as obreptitious and surreptitious. So Cardinal Adrian's action in 1520 was represented as conditional on confirmation by the Holy See, and as in no way binding on the Inquisition. So, in 1632, the Barcelona tribunal drew up a statement to be laid before Philip IV by the Suprema, adroitly mixing up the affairs of Aragon and Catalonia and telling him that the Córtes of 1518 demanded the revival of the articles of 1512, that Charles refused to swear to them, that Juan Prat interpolated others, for which he was imprisoned and that the effort failed. In transmitting this the Suprema added that the fact that the Córtes never ceased to demand the enforcement of the articles showed that they had never been observed.[1139] From first to last it was a history of deception, in which kings conspired with inquisitors to betray their subjects, without even the excuse that the faith was concerned in these details of secular jurisdiction.

***

The Catalan temper was not soothed by the disappointment of 1599, and the refusal of redress prompted resort to forcible measures. There was a contest in 1608 in which the Banch Reyal uttered a sentence of banishment against the inquisitors; a vessel was made ready for their deportation but, when the day came, they barred their door and hung over it a portière of black velvet to which was attached a crucifix. The city showed its piety by placing candles in front of the sacred emblem and the chapter sent priests to pray before it. No one ventured to disturb it; the Diputados, the chapter and the city authorities interposed, and an accommodation was reached.[1140] A more savage quarrel arose, in 1611, in consequence of the veguer disarming the coachman of an inquisitor. The city authorities seized the temporalities, laid siege to the palace of the Inquisition, sentenced the inquisitors to banishment and proclaimed it with trumpets through the streets. This they justified to the king by telling him that the Holy Office had been instituted for a limited term which had expired, so that it should be abolished in Catalonia and the cognizance of matters of faith be restored to the episcopal courts, all of which, we are told, gave his majesty much concern.[1141]

Mutual detestation did not diminish and, when the Córtes of 1626 were approaching, the inquisitors anxiously urged the Suprema to impress upon the king that the peace and preservation of Catalonia depended upon the maintenance of their temporal jurisdiction. The deputies, they said, were holding daily juntas and accumulating stores of documents from the archives, asserting that the time had expired for which the Inquisition was instituted, and if they accomplish their intention they will destroy it wholly. That they were really alarmed is visible in their asking the Suprema to secure some compromise. The Suprema duly represented the danger to Philip IV, who in reply gave assurance that no prejudicial change would be approved, for his unceasing desire was to promote the exaltation of the Inquisition. After the Córtes had assembled, the tribunal reported, June 27th, that they had drawn up a series of articles effectually disabling the jurisdiction of the Inquisition and that they declare that they will not vote a subsidio until the king shall have confirmed them. The articles deemed so obnoxious scarce amounted to more than the Concordia of Castile so long in force, save provisions that the inquisitors should be Catalans and should take an oath to obey the laws, and that disputes of jurisdiction should be settled by a junta consisting of an inquisitor, a judge of the Audiencia and the Bishop of Barcelona. Moderate as they were, Philip kept his promise and referred them, September 23d, to Diego de Guzman, Archbishop of Seville, acting head of the Suprema in the vacancy of the inquisitor-generalship, so that, on the adjournment of the Córtes, the whole matter remained suspended.[1142]

An attempt at compromise was made in what was known as the Concordia of Cardinal Zapata, arranged, December 24, 1630, between him as inquisitor-general and the Council of Aragon. This made no substantial change in the jurisdiction of the Inquisition but was directed chiefly to restraining the misuse of excommunication on the one side and the recourse to the Banch Reyal on the other, by providing that all disputed cases should be settled by competencias conducted according to the received form of procedure, under penalty for a first offence of five hundred ducats on the tribunal refusing, and suspension from office for a second. This left untouched the roots of trouble and accomplished little, in consequence, it is said, of the delays and evasions of the inquisitors, and frequent recourse continued to the Banch Reyal, especially by creditors.[1143]

The Córtes of 1626 had not been dissolved and they met again in 1632 to conclude their unfinished business. As usual, the tribunal and the Suprema prepared for the struggle by earnest appeals to Philip, who responded with assurances of special care in all that concerned the Inquisition. The Suprema had the hardihood to tell him that the Concordia of 1512, on which the Catalans based their claims, had never been confirmed, but it was within the truth when it said that it had never been observed. It declared moreover that the articles framed by the Córtes would so prostrate the tribunal that it would have to cease its functions. A memorial by the secretary of the tribunal, Miguel Rodríguez, gives a deplorable account of the social condition of Catalonia, where the barons and gentlemen, the cities and church foundations, he says, possessed excessive powers and where the bishops were also barons. The hostility of the nobles and cities to the familiars was manifested by the daily murders committed on them and their children and the burning of their houses. But for the protection of the Inquisition they would be exterminated, for its jurisdiction was the only one respected. Fathers endured the murder of their sons, sons that of their fathers and wives that of their husbands, for fear of greater evils and, in addition to this, was the turbulent temper of the population. The viceroys had nominal power, but it was exercised only on the common folk and not on the powerful, whom no one dared to accuse or to bear witness against. All this busy preparation was superfluous; the Córtes were dissolved without gaining their object.[1144]

The Inquisition, as usual, had triumphed, but peace was impossible between the incompatible claims of rival jurisdictions. In 1637 the Suprema complained of the continuous series of troubles and of the disregard of the Concordia of Zapata. This time the offender was the viceroy, the powerful Duke of Cardona, who had imprisoned a familiar for carrying a pistol and refusing to surrender it, and had arrested two servants of the receiver, fining one and discharging the other. When the tribunal sent to him a priest bearing a monitorio with excommunication, he shut the priest up, incomunicado, in a room of the palace. Then he invited to dinner the fiscal of the tribunal and shut him up likewise. He ordered the inquisitor to withdraw the excommunication and, on his refusal, he pronounced sentence of banishment, posted four hundred men around the Inquisition and made ready a vessel to carry him to Majorca. The inquisitor assembled five bishops who declared that Cardona had incurred the excommunication of the bull Si de protegendis and the inquisitor so declared him, though for the avoidance of scandal he forbore to publish it. Under the intervention of the bishops the sentences of banishment and excommunication were mutually withdrawn, and the viceroy released the priest and fiscal, boasting that he had carried his point. Thereupon the Suprema asked the king to execute on Cardona the penalties of the Concordia of Zapata and greater ones in view of his unprecedented acts and also that the ipso facto censures of the canon Si quis suadente and the bull Si de protegendis be published in order that he might seek the salvation of his soul. To this the weary king could only reply by deprecating these unseemly quarrels and ordering that viceroys should not try the cases of familiars--Cardona apparently having undertaken to do this only because there was no other authority that ventured to do so, although the offence was one which forfeited the fuero.[1145] Soon after this, in 1639, a still more serious trouble broke out in Tortosa, in which the magistrates were involved and the people rose against the Inquisition, but while this was in progress the Catalan rebellion broke out and prudence counselled abstention from severe measures of repression.[1146]

Whatever share the Inquisition may have had in stimulating the disaffection that led to the rebellion, the unredressed grievances which so excited the Córtes nowhere appear on the surface. The proximate cause, as has been stated above, was the burning of the churches of Montiró and Rio de Arenas by the Neapolitan troops quartered on the people; some consecrated hosts were found reduced to coals and the peasants, who had suffered from the outrages of the unpaid soldiery, rose in arms, cut them off in detail, styled themselves the Exercit Christiá and bore on their banners the Venerable Sacrament, with the legend "Senor judicau vostra causa" and claimed that their object was to protect the people and defend the Catholic faith. In fact, the Inquisition was invited to prosecute the guilty authors of the sacrilege and undertook to do so, but of course the culprits could not be identified and it was reduced to excommunicating them in bulk. It was against the representatives of the king that the initial riots of June 7 and 8, 1640, were directed, when the judges of the royal Audiencia and the Viceroy, the Count of Santa Coloma, were murdered. The inquisitors at once proffered their services to the Diputados and, at the request of the latter, they wrote to the king and inquisitor-general praising the efforts of the Diputados to preserve peace, not knowing that for months they had been organizing the rebellion in correspondence with France. When too, in September, a tax was laid to put the land in a state of defence, the assent of the tribunal was asked as to levying it on familiars.[1147]

There was thus no open hostility towards the Inquisition, but, at the same time, there was no respect for its inviolability. When the mob rose again on Christmas day, to put to death all Castilians, there was a report that two thousand of them were concealed in the Inquisition. Led by a coachman of one of the inquisitors, the people broke into the Inquisition, maltreated the officials, hanged some of them, emptied the money chests and found in the secret prison a solitary Castilian on trial for heresy. Him they carried to the town-council who returned him to the tribunal and garroted the coachman.[1148]

When, on January 23, 1641, terms of submission to France were concluded, the Inquisition was provided for. Having cut loose from Spain, it was impossible to permit the tribunal to remain subject to the Suprema in Madrid, and the clause respecting it was that all inquisitors and officials should be Catalans, jurisdiction should be restricted to matters of faith, and it should be directly under the Roman Congregation of the Holy Office.[1149] Still the inquisitors remained at their posts; for five months they had had no word from the Suprema; they expected to be called upon to take the oath of allegiance to King Louis and they sent their secretary, Juan de Eraso, to Madrid for instructions, suggesting that they had better move to Tarragona or Tortosa. Philip ordered them to remain and they resolutely obeyed, but the situation grew constantly worse and, on November 7th, they made another appeal, representing their danger, their destitution, their inability to perform their functions, and their expectation that they would be forced to kiss the hands of the Marshal de Brézé, the approaching French governor. This was confirmed by Don Antonio de Aragon, who had just returned from Barcelona; on two occasions the mob had set fire to the Inquisition and heresy was rampant, for many of the French troops were Calvinists and Calvinism was openly preached. The Suprema characteristically debated the question under four heads--Shall the Inquisition be removed to Tarragona or Tortosa? Shall the inquisitors kiss the hands of the French governor? Does their lack of means to prosecute relieve them from prosecuting native or French heretics? Shall testimony against such heretics be taken in Madrid and action be based on it? After elaborate discussion the fourth question was decided in the affirmative and the other three in the negative. Juan de Mañozca was appointed to gather testimony in Madrid, and the inquisitors were told to stand their ground and do their duty, using censures and interdict if necessary. If driven from the town, they were to carry with them the records so as to be able to work elsewhere.[1150]

One of the inquisitors, Dr. Cotoner, had left Barcelona for his home in Majorca. The other two, with most of the officials, stood to their post and, in August, 1643, they were called upon to utter fearful curses on unknown parties supposed to have committed a sacrilegious theft of consecrated hosts.[1151] Towards the end of September, however, they were expelled, to give place to a native tribunal, and it was done with a refinement of cruelty. There were ten in all--seven subordinates and the son of one of them, besides the two inquisitors--who had stood faithful to their duty. They were put on board a vessel, with orders to land them in Portugal, which, like Catalonia, was in revolt against Spain. Although the crew consisted of Catalans and Frenchmen, they were persuaded to put into Cartagena, with a promise of being allowed to sell their cargo there. The reception of the refugees was most inhospitable; the vessel was seized and the cargo and effects of passengers and crew were embargoed: much red tape had to be cut and it was not until December that the conclusion was reached that the crew had rendered an essential service exposing them to punishment by the rebels, wherefore the vessel was released and they were allowed to dispose of the cargo.[1152]

The refugees were without salaries or resources and it was not without difficulty and delay that the Suprema, professing its own inability to help them, secured from Philip some moderate ayudas de costa to keep them alive. Then, in March, 1644, it ordered them to open a tribunal at Tarragona, at the same time representing to the king that this would cost forty-five hundred ducats in silver for the first year, and four thousand annually thereafter, which might be supplied from the two millions of maravedís coming from the tribunal of Cartagena--apparently some recent large confiscation--as otherwise they would die of starvation. They were doubtless thus provided for and did what they could to restore the old-time dread of the Holy Office. It had sadly diminished in these evil days for, in this same year, 1644, in the neighboring town of Tortosa, Inquisitor Roig of Valencia complained that, on reaching there during his visitation, the magistrates did not come to receive him, they assigned him no lodgings and they refused to publish his proclamation.[1153]

***

Meanwhile, in accordance with the terms arranged with France, the Catalans had organized a national Inquisition. Doctor Paulo Ferran and Doctor Joseph Pla were appointed and application was made for the usual papal faculties. These were granted and, when the briefs were received, September 26, 1643, they were installed and the Castilians were expelled. The new tribunal had not much to do. It did not meddle with the Calvinists in the French armies, but it vindicated its authority by an auto de fe, celebrated February 23, 1644, in which one victim was garroted and burnt and there were two penitents. There was another, November 7, 1647, in which there was an execution for unnatural crime and six men and five women penitents, mostly for bigamy and sorcery. The only other evidence of activity that I have met is an investigation ordered by Pla, at the request of the parish priest of Pineda, resulting in the trial of Anthoni Morell.[1154]

When the troubles of the Fronde compelled Mazarin to withdraw the French armies, the rebellion collapsed, in spite of the obstinate determination of the Catalans to sever relations with Castile. When Barcelona surrendered, October 11, 1652, Catalonia was left at the mercy of the conqueror, but Philip, with true statesmanship, restored it to its ancient privileges and liberties, save a few exceptions which have no bearing on our subject.[1155] Inquisitor Pla had lingered at Gerona, continuing his functions in virtue of his papal brief. He was found there by the Marquis of Olias y Mortara, who only ventured to suspend him and wrote to the king, October 12, 1652, for instructions, adding that the prompt re-establishment of the Inquisition would conduce greatly to the pacification of the land. The Council of Aragon, November 16th, approved of this and the next day Philip instructed the inquisitor-general to make the appointments and despatch the inquisitors at once.[1156] There were financial difficulties, however. January 18, 1653, the Suprema reported the appointments; the infection of heresy by the French promised much work, but there was an utter lack of money; the tribunal would cost six thousand ducats a year, while its resources were but two thousand, for the separation of Roussillon lost it a thousand and it had two thousand more in Barcelona loans which were incollectable; there was prospect however of large confiscations, for many Catalans had fled to France who would be prosecuted and, on the strength of this, the king was asked for four thousand a year.[1157] The adjustment of these questions probably required time, for it was not until August 2d that the new inquisitors took possession of their office, riding in state through the city, with drums and trumpets and the standard of the Holy Office, followed by all the familiars and officials of Barcelona, and making public proclamation in the customary places. The next day, Sunday, the Edict of Faith was read and on Monday they commenced their functions. Of the Catalan inquisitors, Pla died within a few days and Ferran was arrested at night as were many others, some of whom were sent to France and others were deported to Majorca. Apparently their official acts were not recognized, for familiars of their appointment continued for some years to apply for reinstatement.[1158]

***

No sooner was the tribunal re-established than the old troubles recommenced. Abuses must have been flagrant to call forth from Philip, June 2, 1661, a cédula ordering the exact observance of the Concordias and restraining the excessive use of excommunication.[1159] The quarrels which arose were prolonged and complicated by every possible device. On February 15, 1664, Juan Matheu, actual receiver and acting alguazil mayor of the tribunal, was murdered. On most slender suspicion, the next day, it arrested Joseph Guimart and Joseph Massart; the Audiencia claimed the case and the tribunal refused to enter into a competencia until the Banch Reyal threatened the inquisitors with banishment. Then they averted the preliminary conference by questions of etiquette, repeatedly disregarding the orders of the Suprema, until the intervention of the queen-regent enforced obedience. The conference was at last held and the papers were transmitted to the Suprema and Council of Aragon to decide as to the jurisdiction. While this was pending, the inquisitors started another trouble. They had confined the prisoners in the secret prison as though guilty of heresy. This was a grievous hardship and the queen ordered them transferred to the common prison; the inquisitors reported that this had been done and then, on pretext of information as to a plot to escape, brought them back to the secret prison. When the Suprema heard of this it wrote in a tone of mingled anger and fear, lest it should be discovered by the Council of Aragon; the prisoners must be moved back again; the affair had become too important, the Council of Aragon had made too many efforts and the queen imputed it all to the Suprema as they would see by her enclosed order. Then the competencia was suspended by the escape of the prisoners, March 9, 1666, and the last we hear of the matter is their negotiation for a pardon, in 1668, on terms of which the viceroy advised the acceptance, in order to avoid decision of the competencia. It was doubtless so settled, for competing jurisdictions had brought the administration of justice into such shape that it was better to let criminal accusations remain untried than to decide between the rival claims.[1160]

These quarrels were not merely occasional but were continuous and perpetual. A letter of June 18, 1667, happens to mention that there were then four or five competencias delayed by the question whether in the conferences the royal judge should bring his own notary.[1161] Perverted ingenuity was constantly devising new points over which strife could be created. Prisoners on trial in the royal gaols were sometimes borrowed by the tribunal to be prosecuted for blasphemy or other trivial offence against the faith. In 1666 a case of this kind gave rise to a question as to the exact form of receipt to be given for the body of the culprit, when it was pushed to such a point that the Suprema ordered the excommunication of all the judges of the Audiencia, and the Council of Aragon complained to the queen-regent about the oppressive abuse of censures and asked her to provide that for the future the mutual obligations of the two tribunals should be equal and reciprocal.[1162]

***

When the Inquisition took such pains to make itself detested, one is scarce surprised to learn, from a complaint of the Suprema in 1677, that in Barcelona it had so fallen in public esteem that it was able to procure but one familiar and that the alguazil mayor had asked to be relieved from carrying his wand of office, for no noble was willing to be seen walking with him when he bore it.[1163] This hostility it continued carefully to cultivate. In December, 1695, the Diputados and judges addressed to Carlos II a complaint of the multiplied excesses of the tribunal, which trampled on the laws and liberties of the land, causing such scandals that they could no longer be endured in silence. This had been especially the case since Bartolomé Antonio Sans y Muñoz had been inquisitor, whose methods can be appreciated by a single example. Captain-general Marquis of Gastañara, had imprisoned a Frenchman named Jaime Balle, on a matter of state, Spain being at the time at war with France, with strict orders to keep him incomunicado. Muñoz suddenly demanded an opportunity of taking testimony of him. Gastañara was absent and no one had authority to violate his instructions, but the regent of the royal chancery and the gaoler offered, if Muñoz would declare it to be a matter of faith, to endeavor to find some means of compliance. This assurance he refused to give, even verbally, and he threatened the regent with excommunication. The Audiencia invited him to a conference, which he refused and it then cited him before the Banch Reyal, with the customary warning of banishment and seizure of temporalities. Muñoz responded, December 29th, with a mandate to the regent ordering him, under pain of excommunication, to allow the deposition of the prisoner to be taken and he followed this, within an hour, with an excommunication published in all the pulpits and affixed to all the church-doors. The next day this was re-aggravated and the regent was publicly cursed with the awful anathema formulated for hardened and impenitent sinners. The Audiencia rejoined with the decree of banishment and seizure of temporalities, under the customary term of fifteen days. The tribunal answered this with a threat of interdict on the city; it convoked all the superiors of the religious Orders and arranged with the clergy for a great procession when it should take its departure. It kept its doors closed and even refused to receive the messengers of Gastañara, who had hastened back to Barcelona, but he delayed further action until he should communicate with Madrid and receive the royal orders. When they came, on January 11, 1696, he was at Montealegre, a couple of leagues from the city; they were sent to him by a special courier and he returned the next morning and made secret arrangements for their execution. At 2 P.M. he sent word to Muñoz that he wished to see him on the king's service. At 4.30 P.M. Muñoz came, bringing the fiscal with him. A scrivener was introduced who read to him the king's order, which he said he was ready to obey. Gastañara told him that he must start at once; a coach was at the door to which he was escorted with all honor; lackeys with flambeaux were ready and a guard of twenty-five musketeers. Gastañara gave him money and he was provided with all comforts, even to a courteous gentleman as a companion to enforce all proper respect for him. As he was leaving the palace, his violent temper burst forth in regrets that he had not been allowed time to cast the interdict on the city. He was driven to the embarcadero, placed on board a vessel that had been made ready and was conveyed to the nearest Valencian port. It is symptomatic of Spanish conditions that in war-time the captain-general was obliged to abandon all other duties and devote a day to kidnapping a troublesome priest, and this is emphasized by the fact that the inquisitor-general rewarded the conduct of Muñoz by appointing him to one of the most desirable tribunals of Spain.[1164] Possibly this affair may have influenced Carlos II in reissuing, in 1696, his father's injunction of 1661 to observe the Concordias exactly and to be more sparing of excommunications.[1165]

Philip V was scarce seated on the throne when he found himself confronted with the eternal question of Catalan hostility towards the tribunal. A consulta of the Suprema, October 16, 1701, warns him that the inquisitors of Barcelona report that, in the Córtes about to assemble, efforts will be made to limit its usefulness and he is exhorted to follow the example of his predecessors.[1166] Whatever was done was of little consequence for, in the war which broke out soon afterwards, Catalonia enthusiastically acknowledged the Archduke Charles as Carlos III and became the stronghold of the Austrian party. The situation of the rebellion of 1640-52 was duplicated. The tribunal was withdrawn, but seems to have been replaced by a local organization, for an article of the Córtes of 1706, duly approved by the Austrian Carlos, regulating the insaculacion for public office, recognizes its certificates respecting its officials.[1167] Of course it could exercise no jurisdiction over the heretic English allies; it has left no traces of its activity and was replaced by a revival of the episcopal cognizance of heresy. As to places beyond the control of the Austrian party, a provision of the Suprema, March 16, 1706, extended the jurisdiction of the Saragossa tribunal over all that should be recovered from the enemy until such time as the Inquisition of Barcelona should be re-established.[1168] The desperate resistance of the Catalans postponed this until 1715, and when the tribunal was reinstated it found in the secret prison two captives, Juan Castillo a bigamist and Mariana Costa accused of sorcery, both of them confined by order of the vicar-general of the diocese.[1169] As all the liberties and privileges of Catalonia were abolished by the conquerors, its subsequent relations with the Inquisition offer no special characteristics.

***

MAJORCA-CASTILE

Majorca had no Concordia and its tribunal was free to claim what extent of jurisdiction it saw fit, limited only by the resistance of the civil authorities, which, as we have seen, was energetically expressed at an early period. As defined by Portocarrero, in 1623, in practice it asserted complete jurisdiction, active and passive, in civil and criminal cases, over its salaried and commissioned officials and their families; over familiars, in criminal matters, active and passive; in civil, passive only, with exclusion of their families.[1170] The occasion of his book was a violent struggle between the viceroy and the tribunal, which presents the ordinary features of these contests for supremacy between rival departments of the government. In a search for arms in the house of Juan Zuñez, receiver of confiscations, some were found. The viceroy at once arrested him, sentenced him to leave the island within twenty-four hours and shipped him away. The inquisitor promptly excommunicated the viceroy; the royal fiscal appealed; the viceroy and royal judges summoned the inquisitor to a conference preparatory to a competencia or to appear in the Banch Reyal and defend his proceedings. On his refusal the Banch Reyal pronounced sentence of banishment and seizure of temporalities, which was published with sound of drum and trumpet. They also issued an edict declaring the censures null and void and ordering the clergy to disregard them; they refused to consider themselves excommunicated, they attended mass and apparently had the support of the people and clergy, for no attention was paid to the interdict cast on the city by the inquisitor.[1171] What was the final result does not appear, nor does it much matter; the significance in these affairs is the spectacle presented to the people of lawless collisions between the representatives and exponents of the law.

In Majorca the most impressive cases of this kind occurred between the Inquisition and the ecclesiastical courts and will be considered hereafter. It suffices here to say that broils with the secular authorities were constant and contributed their share to occupy and distract the attention of the central government. It would be superfluous to enumerate those of which the details have chanced to reach us; they would merely prove that, considering their small size and scanty population, the Balearic Isles were not behind their continental sisters of Aragon in adding to the perplexities of the monarchy.

***

This somewhat prolonged recital of the struggles of the kingdoms of the Crown of Aragon gives an opportunity of realizing the stubborn resistance, to the arrogant pretensions of the Inquisition, of provinces which still retained institutions through which public opinion could assert itself. The people of the kingdoms of Castile had been reduced to submission under the absolutism of the House of Austria and, though they might at times complain, they could make no effective efforts to ameliorate their position. When, in 1579 and again in 1583, the Córtes of Castile complained of the arrest and immurement in the secret prisons of individuals in every quarrel with an official of the Inquisition, to the permanent disgrace of families, Philip II merely replied that he would make inquiry and take such action as was fitting.[1172] The only resource was to raise contests in individual cases and these were frequent enough and violent enough to prove that there was the same spirit of opposition to inquisitorial encroachment and the same pervading discontent with the abuses flourishing so rankly under inquisitorial protection. Instances of this could be cited almost without limit, but one or two will suffice as examples of the multiform aspect of these quarrels and the temper in which they were fought over. It should be borne in mind that, in these struggles as in those of Aragon, there was no question of freedom of conscience and no desire to limit the effectiveness of the Holy Office as the guardian of purity of faith. The Castilian, like the Catalan, looked with exultation on the triumph over heresy in the autos de fe, and he desired only to set bounds to the intrusion of the Inquisition on the field of secular justice.

A History of the Inquisition of Spain: Volume I
CASTILE

The chancellery of Granada was the supreme tribunal of New Castile as that of Valladolid was of Old Castile. The alcaldes of its Sala del Crimen constituted the highest criminal court, from which there was no appeal save to God. April 15, 1623, the alcalde mayor, after five days' trial, condemned Gerónimo Palomino, an habitual criminal and rufian, to two hundred lashes and six years of galleys for various offences, including sundry blasphemies; on the 24th, the Sala confirmed the sentence and ordered its execution. On the same day the Inquisition served two notices on the alcalde mayor prohibiting his cognizance of the case, as some of the alleged crimes concerned the faith, over which it had exclusive jurisdiction, and it demanded the surrender of the accused and of all the papers under the customary comminations. The alcalde mayor responded by calling for a competencia and offering to deliver Palomino for trial on any charges of heresy, if record were made that he was already a galley-slave to be returned to the royal prison. The next day the tribunal sent to the prison and claimed him, on the pretext that the case had been transferred to it, whereupon the alcaide of the prison surrendered him without orders from the judges. When the latter heard of this they also learned that the transfer had been effected through the efforts of the prisoner's friends and liberal bribery of the officials of the tribunal, who had been active in getting him out of prison. After satisfying themselves of this by investigation, they ordered the arrest of four laymen--a notary, a messenger and two familiars--and they further imprisoned in their houses the alcalde mayor and alcaide of the prison for acting without informing the Sala. The tribunal concluded Palomino's trial within forty-eight hours, sentencing him to hear a mass in the audience chamber, and it appears that it returned him. It further commenced proceedings against the alcaldes, summoning them to liberate the officials within three hours under pain of excommunication. The alcaldes protested against this and demanded a competencia, as provided under the Concordia, but the next day they were excommunicated in all the churches and this was followed by an interdict laid on the city. This forced a compromise by which the prisoners were liberated, subject to rearrest in case the competencia should result in justifying the alcaldes, and the latter were absolved from the censures. The matter seemed to be settled, but all parties had counted without the impetuous and aggressive Inquisitor-general Pacheco. Without awaiting further information, and in disregard of the laws prescribing peaceful settlement by competencias, he had evoked the case to himself and acted upon it off-hand. Two days after the absolution, the inquisitors reimposed the excommunication by his command, and notices were served on the alcaldes and their alguazil mayor to appear before him within fifteen days to stand trial. Against this they protested and, on their failure to appear, they were not only excommunicated afresh but anathematized in all the churches. The scandal had thus assumed national proportions.[1173]

The alcaldes were the direct and highest judicial representatives of the king, but such was Philip's subserviency to the Inquisition that he would not permit a competencia following the regular course but took the affair into his own hands. The President of the Council of Castile, in remitting to the royal favorite Olivares, July 4, 1623, a memorial from the Council, declared that the condition to which the chancellery of Granada was reduced, owing to the methods of the Inquisition, was the most ignominious that had ever been heard of in Spain, especially considering how slight was the cause of all this disquiet, for, when everything was settled it was again enkindled at the mandate of the inquisitor-general. As the matter was in the king's hands, the Council could do nothing but appeal to his majesty, with all the disadvantages under which it labored in combating the inquisitor-general; had its hands been free it might already have conquered, to the benefit of the royal jurisdiction and service of the king, for every day brought greater disturbance to the Republic.[1174]

In spite of this appeal, Philip decided in favor of the Inquisition and the humiliation of the chancellery was complete. Yet Pacheco was not satisfied with victory and proceeded to trample on the vanquished. In the course of the quarrel, Gudiel de Peralta, one of the judges, and Matias González de Sepúlveda, the fiscal of the court, had drawn up legal arguments in its justification. These Pacheco submitted to his censors, who of course discovered latent heresies lurking in them, whereupon he ordered them to be suppressed as heretical and announced his intention of proceeding rigorously against the authors. The Council, on October 7th, again appealed to Philip. The accused, it said, had only defended the royal jurisdiction in a perfectly legitimate manner; the inquisitor-general should not have attacked royal officials and inflicted irreparable injury on them and their posterity by denouncing them as heretics, without consulting the king. He was begged to intervene and order Pacheco to suspend proceedings, while a junta of the two Councils should consider the papers and decide what course should be taken.[1175] It is probable that in some such way this indefensible attempt was suppressed, for neither of the inculpated names appear in the Expurgatory Index of Zapata, in 1632.

It would seem difficult to set bounds to the power of an organization which could thus arbitrarily employ the censures of the Church on any department of the government, without being subject to control save to that of a king docile to its exigencies. Yet the Suprema, which always sustained the tribunals in their wanton excesses, adopted their quarrels and fought them unsparingly to the end, was thoroughly conscious of their wrong-doing. While this conflict was in progress, it issued a carta acordada, April 23d, earnestly exhorting the tribunals to maintain friendly relations with the royal officials and not to waste time in dissensions to the neglect of their duties in matters of faith; competencias were always to be admitted and no censures were to be employed without consulting the Suprema, unless delay was inadmissible.[1176]

***

How nugatory were these counsels of moderation, under the dominance of such a man as Pacheco, was soon afterwards manifested in a still more scandalous outbreak in Seville, under his direction, in 1625. The assistente or governor, Fernando Ramírez Fariñas, himself a member of the Council of Castile and a man of high consideration, was excommunicated and thus prevented from concluding a negotiation for a donation to the king of eighty thousand ducats; his alguazil, an honorable man, was wounded and was shut up in prison to keep him out of the hands of the tribunal, which declared that he was wanted on a matter of faith, thus covering him and his family with infamy. The king and Olivares were besieged by Pacheco on the one hand and the Council of Castile on the other. The king, as usual, sided with the Inquisition and the President of the Council tendered his resignation with the suggestion that his office had better be given to Pacheco who, by holding both positions, could cover up these scandals, while the royal jurisdiction could scarce be reduced to greater degradation. It is no wonder that Olivares, in a letter to the president, declared himself to be the most unfortunate of men, for he could satisfy nobody; his best course would be to ask the king to let him abandon the management of affairs; when the kingdom was in such straits that he could scarce take time to breathe in devising remedies, his efforts were wasted in competencias and he concluded with the despairing declaration that he lost his senses in thinking over it without knowing what to say.[1177]

The statesmen who were guiding the destinies of Spain in those perilous times might well groan under the superfluous burden of deciding these contests over trifles so ferociously waged, but they were not to be spared. Arce y Reynoso was not so violent as Pacheco but he was equally obstinate and was determined to emancipate the Inquisition wholly by relieving it from royal supervision. There was an instructive case at Cuenca, in 1645, where the corregidor, Don Alonso Muñoz de Castilblanque sent a band of assassins to murder a woman with whom he had illicit relations, together with a priest named Jacinto. The crime created great excitement, but Muñoz was a contador, or accountant of the tribunal, and as such a titular official. He presented himself before the inquisitors who assumed his case and promptly excommunicated the judge who attempted to prosecute him. Philip had the matter investigated and was told that both the woman and the priest had been killed. He sent to the Suprema a decree ordering the removal of the excommunication and the delivery of the criminal to the Council of Castile, to be tried by the judge which it had appointed, for the inquisitors could not properly punish so atrocious a crime without incurring irregularity. This was clear and peremptory enough, but, in place of obeying it, Arce y Reynoso replied, May 4, 1645, that this would be a great and unheard of violation of the rights of the Holy Office. The woman was not dead but was in Valencia, where the tribunal was busily collecting evidence; to hand Muñoz over to the secular judges for trial and execution would incur the same irregularity as sentencing him; the case would be tried by the Suprema, which had a wide range of suitable penalties that did not infer irregularity; meanwhile Muñoz would be safely guarded and he trusted that the king would not set so pernicious an example.

When Philip rejected this appeal and repeated his order, a learned and elaborate argument was prepared to show that he had no power to interfere. It took the ground, to which we have already referred, that the temporal jurisdiction of the Inquisition over its officials was a grant from the papacy; it was exclusive and unlimited and no secular ruler could deprive the Holy Office of it; the pope had power to make this grant and the king had none to remove this or any other case from its cognizance, for he was not supreme over the ecclesiastical and papal jurisdiction--the truth being that the papal commissions to the inquisitor-general conferred power to remove and punish subordinates but said nothing as to its being exclusive, and equally fallacious was the citation of three authorities whose utterances had no bearing on the question at issue.[1178] This audacious reliance on the ignorance of Philip and his secular advisers was successful. Philip made one or two efforts more, but Arce y Reynoso held good. A memorial, in 1648, on the general subject, from a member of the Council of Castile, tells the king that his repeated commands in the case of Muñoz had been disobeyed and that, although the criminal had so long been in the hands of the inquisitors, he had not yet been sentenced, which he held to be clear proof that their aim was to defend their officials from the royal justice and not to punish them.[1179]

***

How liberal was the construction placed on this term of titular official was illustrated when, in 1622, at Toledo, the corregidor arrested the butcher of the tribunal for intolerable frauds on the public. The inquisitor demanded the prisoner and the papers, published the corregidor in all the churches as excommunicate, seized the alguazil and apparitor who had made the arrest, cast them into the secret prison, tried them as if for heresy, shaved their heads and beards and banished them and refused to their families any evidence that would preserve their posterity from infamy. There was danger of a rising in Toledo against the Inquisition, but it was averted; the Council of Castile protested and a junta was held which adopted measures to prevent a repetition of such outrages but, as usual, no attention was paid to them.[1180]

It would be superfluous to multiply examples of the perennial struggle which was distracting the energies of the government and weakening the respect for law in every quarter of Spain. Each tribunal contributed its share, and there was an unending stream of cases pouring into Madrid for settlement. Each side blamed the other for this anomalous condition. In 1632, the Suprema, in defending the tribunal of Valencia for its protection of criminal familiars, bitterly complained that the object of the Concordias was the relief of the tribunals, the punishment of offenders, the quick despatch of cases, and the diminished oppression of pleaders, but that this had been converted into perpetual strife, regardless of forms and rules of procedure.[1181] For this it was itself primarily to blame, for though there were doubtless faults on both sides, the cases recorded in the reports and the arguments of the Inquisition show that it was the chief offender. Its aggressive powers were too much greater than those of its adversaries, and its methods were too sharp, for the secular authorities often to risk the consequences of being in the wrong.

***

THE SPIRITUAL COURTS

There was another direction in which the Holy Office sought to interfere with the administration of justice. So complete is the independence of secular authority claimed by the Church for those in holy orders, that a licence from a bishop is held to be necessary before a cleric can obey a summons to appear as a witness in a lay court, even in civil cases.[1182] The Inquisition included this among the exemptions of all connected with it, whether lay or clerical, and even extended it to familiars. The privilege seems generally to have been conceded, as respects the salaried officials but, as applied to familiars, it was too grotesque not to excite opposition. The Concordia of 1568, as we have seen, provided that familiars should testify before secular judges without requiring licence from inquisitors and that the latter should not prohibit them from so doing, which infers that it was an abuse requiring correction and also that officials were conceded to enjoy the exemption. The power to summon a witness necessarily includes that of coercing him to testify, and this was exercised by imprisoning recalcitrants, which came to be regarded as an infraction of privilege. In 1649, in the case of Claudio Bolano, a familiar imprisoned for refusing to give evidence, the tribunal of Valencia formed a competencia, pending which he was released under bail to both jurisdictions. The question was of difficult solution and the competencia dragged on for ten years without settlement. Then, in 1659, the same thing occurred and another competencia was formed, in which the most that the Inquisition would concede was that, when the evidence was indispensable, a notary should be sent to the familiar's house to take it in secret, basing this upon the danger to which witnesses were exposed in the violent factions of the time.[1183] The question, however, was settled, in 1699, in the case of Felipe Bru. At Játiva, on August 14, 1698, Don Luis Salzedo, Lord of Pamis, was shot and killed when standing at a window of his house. Don Vicente Monserrat, judge of the Audiencia of Valencia, found Bru, who was a familiar, a contumacious witness. He was first given the town as a prison, then his house, and finally was confined in chains. He appealed to the tribunal, which ordered his release within three days, under pain of excommunication and five hundred ducats. A competencia was formed which, in November, 1699, was decided in favor of the royal jurisdiction. It was probably in consequence of this discussion that, on July 15th, a royal decree was issued compelling familiars to give evidence in secular courts. Even this did not abate the pretensions of the Inquisition for when, in 1702, Joseph Pérez of Montesa, a familiar, was ordered, under penalty of a thousand ducats, not to leave that town because a deposition was wanted from him, he appealed to the tribunal of Valencia which, with the usual threats, commanded the revocation of the order. On this being refused, Pérez went to Valencia and had himself incarcerated in the secret prison, where he was inaccessible. The Audiencia pursued the matter, there was considerable correspondence and preparations for a competencia, but finally the affair was settled by sending Pérez to the house of the regent of the Audiencia, where he made his deposition. To the end, however, the tribunal maintained the position that, if any constraint was used, it would resist and protect the familiar unless a competencia decided to the contrary.[1184]

***

It was not the secular courts alone that had these perpetual conflicts with the Inquisition. Like Ishmael, its hand was against every man and every man's hand was against it--but, in fact, this was to a great extent the case between all the different jurisdictions among which the various classes of society were parcelled out by their several privileges and exemptions. Next to the royal courts ranked the spiritual courts in the number and complexity of debatable questions with the Inquisition. With these there were two sources of contention, for they not only claimed by prescriptive right exclusive jurisdiction in all temporal matters over all who wore the tonsure, but there was a broad field for discussion in the somewhat hazy delimitation of spiritual offences justiciable by one or the other. This latter subject will engage our attention hereafter; at present we are concerned only with the questions arising from the personnel of the Holy Office. Notoriously lax as were the episcopal courts with offenders of the cloth, the Inquisition had the reputation of still greater indulgence with those who were under its protection; clerics who were also officials therefore preferred its tribunals, giving rise to frequent quarrels in which the inquisitors treated their clerical opponents as remorselessly as they did the secular officials and judges. The episcopal Ordinaries, provisors and vicars-general contended that they had, except in cases of faith, exclusive jurisdiction over all clerics; that the temporal jurisdiction of the Inquisition was a royal grant which could not supersede the canon law and that the papal commissions only gave faculties for punishing official malfeasance. To this unanswerable argument the inquisitors paid little heed and the prelates were worse off than the judges for these at least had the Councils of Castile or Aragon to struggle for them, but the Councils admitted that they had no standing in ecclesiastical quarrels. The natural recourse of the prelates for protection was to Rome, but this was a subject of intense jealousy, traditional in the Spanish monarchy, and Philip III, in a cédula of January 21, 1611, addressed to all the prelates of his dominions, told them that they must appeal only to the Suprema and forbade them to carry any case to the Holy See.[1185]

***

There could thus be no competencia; the conflicts between the two jurisdictions were one-sided and were conducted by the tribunals with the same overbearing arrogance as that displayed towards secular magistrates. The first summons on the provisor or vicar-general inhibited him, under pain of excommunication and a heavy fine, from further action, ordering him, within twenty-four hours, to remit the case to the Inquisition and to discharge the prisoner under bail to present himself before the tribunal, while the notary was required to surrender all the papers. If this was not obeyed, it was followed by another, commanding obedience within six hours, in default of which all beneficed priests were required, under similar penalties, to publish the provisor and notary as excommunicates and to place their names on the lists as such. A circular letter was also addressed to all priests, chaplains and sacristans of the district, to admonish all persons, within six hours and under pain of excommunication, to avoid the provisor and notary, to make no pleadings before them, to hold no communication with them and not to furnish them with bread or wine, fish or flesh, while a public edict to the same effect was issued to all the people. In case of continued obduracy, these measures were promptly followed by an edict to all the clergy, ordering them to anathematize the provisor and notary with tolling bells and extinguished candles, proclaiming them accursed of God and his saints--"accursed be the bread that they eat and the bed on which they sleep and the beasts on which they ride, and may their souls perish in hell like the candles in the water: let them be comprehended in the sentence of Sodom and Gomorrha and of Dathan and Abiram, whom the earth swallowed for disobedience, and may all the curses of Psalm Deus laudem meam (Ps. CVIII, a fearful commination) light on them!" If this did not suffice within twenty-four hours, an interdict followed, tolling bells and performing divine service in low tone with locked doors, until otherwise ordered. In case this failed, the last step was a cessatio a divinis, or cessation of church services in the city where the offenders lived, in order to coerce them with popular clamor.[1186] It was difficult for either lay or clerical officials to contend with opponents who wielded such weapons as these.

The irresponsible exercise of such powers inevitably led to their abuse. In the Concordia of 1568 it is highly suggestive to find a clause forbidding inquisitors to issue, as they have been accustomed, to familiars and officials, general inhibitions protecting them from the ecclesiastical courts; such inhibitions are to be special and issued only in each case as it may occur. Equally significant is another which says that in no case belonging by law to the provisor shall the inquisitor intervene against his will.[1187] The strained relations resulting between the ecclesiastical body and the Holy Office are alluded to in the project of reform, presented to the Suprema in 1623, which says that the clerical commissioners and their notaries bring about many conflicts with the ecclesiastical judges and, as there are no Concordias, the inquisitors are wont to arrogate to themselves greater jurisdiction than belongs to them, which causes much murmuring and resentment of the prelates and clergy. The writer piously wishes that this could be avoided, but he evidently has no remedy to propose.[1188]

A conflict caused by one of these local notaries in 1609 amply justified the murmurs of the prelates. The priest of Cabra, who occupied the almost nominal position of local notary, was a notorious incestuous concubinarian, who had not for eight years celebrated mass or recited prayers. The provisor of Córdova commenced a prosecution and threw him into the episcopal gaol, when he claimed the fuero of the Inquisition. The provisor had been on friendly terms with the three inquisitors and sought an amicable settlement of the matter when, by a trick, they obtained possession of the papers and inhibited him from further proceedings. He appealed to the Suprema and was excommunicated. Four times the Suprema ordered the inquisitors to abandon the case and remove the censure, but they persistently disobeyed. All the officials of the episcopal court were ordered to hold no communication with him, which threw the whole business of the diocese into confusion, for the bishop was absent and the provisor was his representative. The culprit escaped from the episcopal gaol and was harbored by the tribunal. Passion was becoming acute; a band of familiars and officials broke into the episcopal palace and endeavored to carry off the provisor, but he was rescued by the canons in a dilapidated condition and took to his bed. Then the inquisitors pronounced the magic word--a matter of faith--which brought to their aid the corregidor and municipal authorities, who came with a troop of soldiers and carried him off on his bed, to the sound of drums and trumpets. He was taken to the Inquisition and confined for two months in a small cell, tried without opportunity for defence and sentenced to forfeit his office of provisor, to four years of banishment and other penalties, and copies of the sentence were circulated throughout the city. The bishop had sought to come to his rescue by excommunicating the inquisitors; they disregarded the censures, threatened to prosecute him if he did not remove them and did prosecute some of the canons as conspiring against the Inquisition, because they had been elected by the chapter to aid the bishop in defending the provisor.[1189]

**

Such a sentence against a church dignitary of high rank required confirmation by the Suprema, which must have been given, for appeal was made to Philip III. He rendered some satisfaction by dismissing and banishing all secular officials who had been concerned in the arrest and wounding of the provisor, but the inquisitors, whose mere tools they had been, were left undisturbed.[1190] Yet it was impossible that an affair which had aroused the attention of all Spain should pass without an attempt to prevent the recurrence of such scandals. There had been a threat, and possibly more than a threat, to appeal to Rome in defence of the bishop and clergy of Córdova, which led to the cédula of January 21, 1611, alluded to above, restricting their recourse to the Suprema. In urging this the Suprema, in a consulta of November 15, 1610, admitted that these troubles arose from the aggressions of the tribunals and their unnecessary multiplication of nominal officials; it had recently issued three cartas acordadas on the subject and had written to all the bishops asking reports of such excesses so as to remedy them. Philip in reply authorized the Suprema to draft such a cédula as it desired but ordered it to be so framed as not to encourage the inquisitors, who were every day intervening in matters beyond their competence for the purpose of extending their jurisdiction; it was this that gave rise to these troubles, nor would they cease till the cause was removed.[1191]

Thus it was admitted on all hands that the fault lay with the tribunals, yet the wrong committed by that of Córdova remained unredressed and unpunished. Philip permitted himself, in spite of his better judgement, to be persuaded to cut off all recourse to the court of last resort in Rome, and some nominal relief must be offered to the oppressed churches and prelates. The memorial from Córdova had concluded with a prayer for some law to prevent these discords and to maintain the episcopal jurisdiction over the clergy, as the king had promised in a letter transmitted through the Council of Castile. The promise was kept after a fashion, though not until after a delay which shows how prolonged was the resistance encountered. In a carta acordada of November 28, 1612, the tribunals were informed that in order that the ministers of the Inquisition may not sin through confidence of impunity, and to prevent the conflicts which disturb the peace, the Suprema has resolved that in the cases of unsalaried clerical officials, the episcopal ordinaries shall have exclusive jurisdiction over offences relating to clerical duties and offices, to simony and spiritual matters, while inquisitors shall have cumulative jurisdiction with the ordinaries, depending on priority of action, in public and scandalous offences, such as incontinence, usury, gambling and the like.[1192] This remained in force nominally at least, until the last, but the allusion to the perpetual troubles arising from this source, in the project presented to the Suprema in 1623, shows how futile it was in curbing the aggressions of the tribunals.

Throughout Peninsular Spain the episcopal jurisdiction was thus left defenceless to the encroachments of the Inquisition, but the Church of Majorca was fortunate in obtaining the protection of Rome, leading to a series of conflicts, waged on less unequal terms, which are worth consideration as revealing a peculiar phase in these affairs. There was a long-standing quarrel between the cathedral canons and the Inquisition. In 1600, one of the former, Pere Enseñat, assisted in the escape of a man who had wounded a familiar, whereupon the inquisitor, Francisco de Esquinel, threw him in prison and made him give bail in three hundred ducats. In 1605, another canon, Francisco Sanceloni, had a verbal altercation with Bernardo Luis Cotoner, advocate of prisoners, for which Esquinel imprisoned him, tried him and condemned him in the costs, with his past incarceration as a punishment. The indignant canons addressed a strong remonstrance to the Suprema. They had an old privilege, confirmed by the Council of Trent (Sess. XXV, De Reform. cap. 6) that they could be arrested only by the Ordinary sitting in judgement with two of their number; in matters of faith they admitted subjection to the Holy Office, but they claimed exemption in civil and criminal cases. The number of familiars and officials, and their petulance arising from the protection of the tribunal, rendered it impossible to be always incurring the expense and dangers of appeals to Rome for the preservation of their privileges. This was ineffective and, in the course of another outbreak in 1630, there was a correspondence between the Congregation of the Roman Inquisition and the nuncio at Madrid respecting an appeal from the canons. In this the nuncio reported that he had applied to Inquisitor-general Zapata, who promised to instruct the inquisitor not to molest the canons.[1193]

***

If he did so, he was disobeyed as usual and, in 1636, a canon named Domenge was involved in a civil suit before the tribunal, resulting in a judgement against him of five thousand reales, the execution of which he resisted by force. This brought on him a prosecution, in spite of protests interjected by the bishop and chapter, which was carried on appeal to the Suprema, where he was condemned in seven hundred reales which he paid. Meanwhile, notwithstanding the cédula of 1611, the bishop and chapter had applied to Rome for a brief declaring that the canons were subject to the Inquisition only in matters of faith. The question was exhaustively discussed, in the Congregation of the Holy Office, with Luis de los Infantes, the Roman agent of the Inquisition. The conclusion reached was that the Majorca tribunal had no jurisdiction over the canons save in matters of faith and this was duly embodied in the brief Cum sicut dilecti, March 31, 1642, which is preserved in the Bullarium. It names the bishop and dean or treasurer as executors, with power to inflict censures and to invoke if necessary the aid of the secular arm. It was received in Majorca with general rejoicing; it was printed and circulated and a syndicate was formed by the clergy to obtain, without regard to expense, a similar one for the whole ecclesiastical body, an effort which was successful in the following September.

The brief was duly served on the inquisitor, who refused to recognize it as not having been transmitted through the Suprema; besides he asserted that it was surreptitious and obreptitious as having been granted without a hearing of the other side and moreover it was in derogation of the bull Si de protegendis. In a consulta of December 11th, the Suprema represented energetically to Philip IV the manner in which his predecessors had compelled the surrender of papal letters adverse to the Inquisition; it asked him to have the present one suppressed and to instruct the prelates that all cases of difference must be referred to it, that no recourse be had to Rome, under the penalties decreed by Ferdinand, that the Viceroy of Majorca be required to compel the chapter to desist and that the ambassador to Rome be instructed to obtain the revocation of the obnoxious letters.

Unluckily for the Suprema the times were unpropitious. Majorca was too near to rebellious Catalonia for the imperious methods of the Holy Office to be judicious. Philip replied that the revival of Ferdinand's laws would cause trouble and the remedy sought must be practicable. The inquisitor of Majorca had been guilty of gross excesses and must be ordered to exercise moderation, and he suggested a junta of members of the Suprema and Council of Aragon to devise a Concordia. Whether such compromise was reached does not appear; if it was, subsequent events show that it was not observed by either side and no reference to it occurs. The papal briefs were maintained and ten years later, after the collapse of the Catalan rebellion, instructions of April 23, 1652, to an ambassador departing for Rome, order him to labor for their revocation; their evil example was contagious; the Knights of St. John in Majorca were seeking to obtain a similar favor through the Maltese ambassador, which must be resisted in every way, for it would be followed by all the other Orders.[1194]

The Suprema continued to treat the papal briefs as surreptitious and, in 1658, Arce y Reynoso enjoyed a momentary triumph in a contest by summoning the vicar-general to Madrid and forcing him to come.[1195] Under the feebler government of the queen-regent, his successor Nithard was not so fortunate, in a fierce quarrel which involved the whole island in confusion and embroiled the rival departments of the government. May 9, 1667, on a feast-day, in the church of San Francisco, Don Jorje Dameto struck his son-in-law, Don Joseph Vallejo, with a crutch, causing effusion of blood and thus polluting the church. Both gentlemen were familiars. The inquisitor, before noon-day, ordered the arrest of both; in the afternoon Bishop Manjarre cited Dameto to appear for sacrilege and violation of the church. The rival jurisdictions locked horns and proceeded to extremities. The viceroy and Audiencia, with the bulk of the community, sided with the bishop, but disturbances were commencing and they repeatedly urged postponement of action until the government could be heard from, but the inquisitor refused. The bishop published him as excommunicate, anathematized him and caused the psalm of malediction to be repeatedly sung against him, but the inquisitor continued to celebrate mass, exhibited himself conspicuously in public, forbade the bishop entrance into his own church and threatened to suspend his sacerdotal functions. On August 29th the bishop assembled a synod where arrangements were made to send an envoy to Rome to prosecute the case, with a printed statement of all the proceedings, a copy of which was furnished to the Council of Aragon.

***

From Madrid, Nithard imperiously summoned the bishop to appear before him and plead his case. Under the canon law, the Inquisition had no jurisdiction over bishops, without a special delegation of papal faculties, and Manjarre was justified in declaring the summons null and void. Although, as an ecclesiastical question, the Council of Aragon had no direct competence, still as the peace of Majorca was seriously threatened and the viceroy was involved, it took a hand in the matter and thus were presented the gravest questions with regard to the relations of the Inquisition with the episcopate, with the Holy See, and with the secular authorities.

Secure in the blind obedience of the queen, Nithard adopted the most aggressive attitude, and the queen submissively did whatever he required, for he assured her that the case was the most serious that had arisen since the foundation of the Inquisition and that, on its rightful decision, depended the preservation or extinction, not alone of the Majorca tribunal, but of all those under the crown of Aragon. To emphasize this he summoned the bishop to appear before him, personally or by procurator, within a term designated, in default of which he would be prosecuted in contumacia. To this the queen, in October, added her commands to the Council of Aragon; as the preservation of the Catholic faith required the maintenance of the authority of the Inquisition, the Council was ordered to write to the bishop to comply with the summons, and to the viceroy to assist the tribunal if necessary; the bishop must not appeal to Rome and if he had done so the letters must be intercepted and placed in her hands.

The Council of Aragon did not obey. It held the matter until January 21, 1668, when it presented a consulta warning the queen of the consequences of her action and pointing out that the pope was the sole judge of bishops in important cases, as were provincial synods in trivial matters. Nithard, however, was superior to the Council of Trent, and the Suprema commenced a criminal prosecution of Bishop Manjarre, while, on February 5th, an answer was prepared for the Council of Aragon, couched in a tone of bitterness and scarcely veiled contempt, which showed how fierce were the passions at work. The queen was assured that her action was in accordance with all previous royal provisions and she was asked to order the Council of Aragon to obey and not to interfere hereafter with ecclesiastical controversies. Before this missive was delivered, however, news came from Majorca that the culprit Dameto had withdrawn his appeal to the tribunal and had applied for absolution to the bishop, who considered the whole matter as settled. This was a staggering blow from which it took Nithard a month to recover, but finally he sent the consulta of February 5th with a postscript of March 12th, arguing that a subject cannot impair his judge's jurisdiction by accepting another and consequently that the situation was unaltered.

The queen of course adopted this view and repeated her orders, but again the Council disobeyed her and presented, March 18th, a consulta adjuring her in solemn terms to reflect calmly, for she was making the inquisitor-general a judge of all the bishops in her dominions, not only as to conflicts of jurisdiction but also as to criminal accusations, without his holding faculties from the pope, while, at the same time, she was forbidding appeals to the Holy See which was the only proper judge. She was warned that it was impossible to exaggerate the importance of the questions at issue and she was implored, before making so momentous a decision, to consult the Councils of Castile, Italy and the Indies, for the interests of the whole monarchy were involved as well as the supreme power of the pope. To this her reply was merely a repetition of her former orders and a demand for a duplicate of the letters of the Council to the Viceroy. For the third time it disobeyed her and sent none and there are intimations that it was engaged in arousing the whole Spanish episcopate to a sense of the impending danger.

Then the affair suddenly assumed another phase. On March 7th the queen had written to her ambassador in Rome to procure the abstention of the pope from the matter, but, on that very day, the Congregation of the Inquisition, with the approval of the pope, had pronounced invalid the censures fulminated by the inquisitor. It was late in May before this was communicated to the queen by the nuncio, who said that the pope had recognized the gravity of the assault by an inquisitor on the episcopal dignity and the magnitude of the ensuing scandal, and had caused the whole subject to be carefully considered by the Congregation with the above result. The pope had felt deeply, not only the indignity offered to the episcopal office, but also that the fiscal of the Inquisition had applied to the queen to summon the bishop before it, solely on the ground of his having appealed to the Holy See. In the name of the pope the nuncio therefore asked the queen to order inquisitors not to proceed against bishops and to reject the application of the fiscal.

Even this did not shake the determination of Nithard to reduce the episcopate to subjection. A long and argumentative consulta was presented to the queen, proving that the papal decision was surreptitious and therefore invalid, and that anyhow the decrees of the Roman Inquisition had no currency in Spain. The old prohibitions of appeals to Rome were invoked and the queen was told that one of the most precious jewels of the Spanish crown was at stake, for, unless the regalías were preserved, the Inquisition must disappear, delinquents would be unpunished, religion would suffer and, with the loss of its unity, there would no longer be obedience to the throne. The queen was therefore urged to stand firm; the prosecution of the bishop must not be suspended and the Council of Aragon must be forced to obey the royal commands.

Nithard was ready to risk an open breach with the Holy See in his audacious ambition to render the Inquisition supreme in the Spanish Church. How far the queen would have suffered herself to be carried in the execution of his plans cannot be told, as the documents fail us here. His career, however, was drawing to a close. In February, 1669, he was driven from Spain amid universal execration, yet the prosecution of Bishop Manjarre was not abandoned, for the Inquisition was not accustomed openly to admit defeat. It dragged until his death, December 26, 1670, when it was quietly dropped.[1196]

Practically the intervention of Rome gave the victory to the Mallorquins, of which they took advantage. In 1671 there arose another quarrel over a fine incurred by a canon who was also a consultor of the tribunal. Both sides exchanged excommunications and Inquisitor-general Valladares, profiting by his predecessor's experience, showed moderation. On the plea that it was a matter of government rather than of jurisdiction, the Suprema ordered the tribunal to abandon the case and remove the censures imposed on the canons, but the latter were not content with this and procured from the Roman Holy Office a decree declaring invalid the censures of the inquisitors and valid those of the executors of the brief. The Council of Aragon communicated this to the queen who submissively signed a letter, January 25, 1672, to the chapter, expressing her confidence that in its use they would pay fitting attention to the peace and advantage of the Church.[1197]

The Inquisition was not accustomed to defeat and it chafed under this, as was shown when, in 1690, a quarrel arose because a priest of Minorca, named Juan Bruells, used insulting words to the commissioner, Rafael Pons. For this he was prosecuted and the case threw all the islands into confusion. The viceroy, the Audiencia and the clergy all united against the Inquisition. The Ordinary of Minorca, as executor of the brief of 1642, forcibly released Bruells, forbade the inquisitor to proceed and, on his disobeying, excommunicated him. About this time the Mallorquin tribunal had claims to consideration arising from its vigorous proceedings against Judaizers and the large resultant confiscations. The Suprema espoused its cause with the usual energy and, in repeated consultas to Carlos III, denounced the papal briefs as surreptitious and invalid, full of defects and nullities. The feeble king issued repeated commands for the prosecution of Bruells and the surrender of the briefs, but no one paid attention to them. The Mallorquin clergy procured from the Congregation of the Inquisition a decree validating the censures pronounced by the Ordinary and annulling those of the inquisitor; the pope confirmed this but subsequently suspended it at the earnest solicitation of the Spanish ambassador, at the same time ordering his nuncio to make the king understand that the Congregation had supreme power to decide all questions of jurisdiction. The affair did not result to the satisfaction of the Inquisition for the last we hear of it is a bitter complaint by the Suprema, March 11, 1693, of the contumacious Mallorquins and the miserable condition to which they had reduced the Inquisition. In Minorca, the clergy and their dependents were so hostile that Pons could not find a church in which to celebrate mass, while the officials were shunned as excommunicated heretics.[1198]

***

MILITARY ORDERS

Another jurisdiction with which there were occasional quarrels was that of the army, for soldiers were exempt from the secular courts. In such competencias settlements were made by a junta of two members each of the Suprema and the Council of War, with final reference to the king in case of disagreement. I have happened to meet with but few cases of this and they seem never to have attained the importance of those with the secular and ecclesiastical courts. One occurred in 1629, arising from disputes with the garrison that had occupied the Aljafería since the troubles of 1591. A somewhat curious case was that of Don Fernando Antonio Herrera Calderon, of Santander, who was alguazil and familiar and who resigned, in 1641, from his military company, although warned that, by so doing during hostilities, he would be tried by the Council of War. It naturally claimed him and the Suprema endeavored to protect him.[1199] It would seem that, towards the end of the eighteenth century, the exemption of the military was causing special troubles, for a royal cédula of February 9, 1793, declares that, to put an end to them, in future the military judges shall have exclusive cognizance of all cases, civil and criminal, in which soldiers are defendants, except inheritances, and that no tribunal or judge of any kind shall form a competencia concerning them under any pretext.[1200]

***

There was yet another independent jurisdiction with which the Inquisition occasionally came into collision. In Spain the Military Orders formed so important a body that, among the State Councils, there was one of Orders, which had exclusive jurisdiction over their members. It will be recalled that one of Ferdinand's most efficient measures to ensure the peace of the kingdom was to obtain the perpetual administration of those of Santiago, Calatrava and Alcántara, while the queen assumed that of Montesa. Yet he was not disposed to favor their claims of exemption in temporal matters from the jurisdiction of the Inquisition. A letter of September 15, 1515, to the tribunal of Jaen, says that certain confiscations involve property held by knights of the three Orders who may claim exemption and refuse to plead before the judge of confiscations; if so they are not to be listened to and, if necessary, are to be prosecuted with the full rigor of the law.[1201]

In civil and criminal matters the members of the Orders asserted exemption from the jurisdiction of the Inquisition, leading to disputes more or less acrimonious. In 1609, at Córdova, Don Diego de Argoté, a Knight of Santiago, with levelled pistol, prevented the arrest of one of his servants by officials of the tribunal. A competencia resulted which, when carried up to Philip III, was decided by him in favor of the Council of Orders. To this the Suprema replied in a consulta, fortelling the entire destruction of the Inquisition in case the decision was allowed to stand and so worked on Philip that he reversed his decree and allowed the Suprema to prosecute the culprit.[1202] The complication caused by these class privileges is illustrated in the case alluded to above, occurring in 1648, at Cuenca, of Muñoz de Castilblanque for the murder of the priest Jacinto. He was a Knight of Calatrava which led to an additional competencia, when the junta could not agree and the king had to decide.[1203]

In their contests with the Orders, the tribunals were apt to exhibit the same unscrupulous spirit as in those with other contestants. In Majorca Doctor Ramon Sureda, canon, chancellor and judge of competencias, was likewise conservator of the Military Orders. In 1657 he complained that, in conflicts of jurisdiction, the inquisitor would not form competencias with him in order that the papers might take the regular course of transmission for settlement by the Suprema and Council of Orders. The king and queen therefore, as administrators of the Orders, instructed him in such case to send to the inquisitor three successive messages and report them and their replies to the Council; if, in spite of this, the tribunal continued to prosecute the case, he was to proceed against the inquisitor and the viceroy was to render him all proper support. The inquisitor ingeniously evaded this in the case of Gaspar Puygdorfilio, a Knight of Santiago, in 1661, by refusing to receive any messages, saying that he received them only from the viceroy. Sureda's report of this was left unnoticed and the inquisitor adopted the same device, in 1662, in the case of Francisco de Veri, a Knight of Montesa, prosecuted for wounding a familiar who had drawn a sword upon him. He refused to receive messages and proceeded to sequestrate Veri's property, including his crops and cattle. To save them from destruction the viceroy interposed and the Council of Orders appealed to the queen, as administrator of the Order, to take some action that should enable such questions to be settled peaceably, but apparently without result.[1204]

***

As though the exempted classes were not numerous and troublesome enough, there was a project, in 1574, of adding another which, if carried into effect, would have altered the destiny of Spain by subjecting it eventually to the Inquisition and reducing the nominal monarch to the position of a roi fainéant under a Mayor of the Palace. It is a most impressive illustration of the spirit of the age that such a project should have been formulated, that it received enthusiastic support and that a sovereign so jealous of his prerogative as Philip II should have even allowed it to be debated, much less have let it assume a menacing shape and have given it serious consideration. A Military Order was to be established under the name of Santa María de la Espada Blanca, with a white sword as a symbol, like the red sword of Santiago. At its head was to be the inquisitor-general, to whom all members were to swear allegiance and whose orders in peace and war all were to obey. To him likewise they were to assign their property, receiving back at his hands what was necessary for their support, and after death their widows were to be pensioned by him. They were to be exempt from all jurisdiction save his, which was to be delegated to priors appointed in all the provinces. The ostensible object was the defence of the faith and of Spain, for which they were at any time liable to be called to the field, or to serve in garrison, under the orders of the inquisitor-general. Thus the Inquisition was to be furnished with an organized force, sworn to blind obedience and released from all other obligations. The only requisite for membership was limpieza, or purity of blood, free from all taint of Judaic or Moorish contamination, or descent from those who had been sentenced for heresy. At this period limpieza was becoming a popular mania; the cost of proving it through four generations was considerable, and there was strong temptation in the promise that the expenses of all applicants would be defrayed from the common fund.

The project may seem to us too wild to merit a thought, but it responded so perfectly to the temper of the time that it was enthusiastically adopted by the provinces of Castile, Leon, Biscay, Navarre, Aragon, Valencia, Catalonia, Asturias and Galicia. Procurators from these provinces submitted it to Philip for his approval and were supported by representatives of forty-eight noble houses and of the archiepiscopal sees of Toledo, Santiago, Seville, Saragossa, Valencia, Tarragona and Granada. It was debated earnestly and at much length, but the argument of Pedro Vinegas de Córdova decided its fate. He pointed out the troubles which were already arising on the subject of limpieza, causing jealousies, hatreds and contentions, to be increased enormously if the population was thus to be divided into two classes; also the fact that the royal courts would have left to their jurisdiction only the New Christians, while the Old Christians would have their special judges and, if the comparatively few existing familiars caused such all-pervading troubles, what the effect would be of increasing without limit the number of the exempt. On the one hand the ambitious and able men among the New Christians, being thus cast out, would foment disaffection and disturbance; on the other, if the old Military Orders had been a source of danger to the monarchy, what would be the effect of creating a new one, united and vastly more numerous and subject as vassals to an inquisitor-general, whose power was already so great, and who would control the property and have jurisdiction over all members, while in case of rebellion the frontiers and strongholds would be in his hands? This reasoning was unanswerable; Philip ordered all papers connected with the project to be surrendered; he imposed perpetual silence on its advocates and wrote to the ecclesiastical and secular bodies to abandon it, for justice and protection would never be lacking.[1205]

***

We shall probably do no injustice to the Inquisition in attributing to the profits accruing from the exercise of its temporal jurisdiction the ruthless vigor with which the tribunals sought to vindicate and extend it. The remarks of the Visitor Cervantes with regard to Barcelona, in 1561 (p. 468), indicate how lucrative it could be made and how welcome was the addition of fees and fines to the somewhat meagre salaries of the officials. This explains the reckless violence which became habitual in the conduct of quarrels, because this not only was an assurance to the parties concerned as to the vigor with which they were defended, but it also served to discourage the secular authorities from resisting encroachments. It also explains the multiplication of the unsalaried officials such as familiars, commissioners and their notaries, assessors, deputies etc., which no laws or Concordias or regulations could restrain, for each one was a possible source of profit to the tribunal and a probable cause of disturbance in his vicinage, through the comfortable assurance of immunity from the law.

EVILS OF THE SYSTEM

The natural result of this was that unprofitable business was neglected for profitable, and the suppression of heresy was postponed to the trial of civil and criminal cases which yielded fees. We have seen how Cervantes reported that in Barcelona this seemed to be the real duty of the tribunal and that there was nothing else to be attended to; his animadversions produced no amendment and, in 1567, de Soto Salazar repeated the complaint.[1206] This continued unchecked. The project of reform presented to the Suprema, in 1623, expresses the wish that other tribunals would follow the example of Saragossa, where one of the inquisitors was delegated every four months to conduct this business, so that prisoners on trial for heresy could have their cases despatched and not be kept languishing interminably in prison, which, as we shall see, was one of the sorest abuses inflicted on them.[1207] This pious wish was fruitless and the records of the Inquisition for the following century show how large a portion of its activity was devoted to these cases and to the competencias incessantly springing from them.

One feature which aggravated the oppression in these matters, especially in civil suits, was not only the favoritism which inevitably inclined the tribunal to the side of its own people, but the fact that the inquisitors were usually strangers, unfamiliar with the local laws and customs peculiar to each province, which they presumed to interpret and enforce. This justified the frequent demands that inquisitors should be natives--demands which received no attention, for the appointing power thought only of their qualifications as judges of the faith while, to the mass of the population, their duties in this respect were of small account in comparison with their activity in their temporal jurisdiction. Another well-grounded source of complaint was that the inquisitorial habits of secrecy could not be wholly overcome; the parties and their counsel were not allowed to be present, as in the royal courts; witnesses were examined by the inquisitor on lists of interrogatories furnished to him, and there was no cross-examination; written arguments were presented to him which he handed to the other side for reply and the procedure, in both civil and criminal cases, was assimilated as nearly as might be to the secret trials for heresy which was the inquisitorial ideal of the dispensation of justice. The cases were decided by the inquisitors in session together, on a majority vote. In the sixteenth century there was no appeal to the Suprema, even when the vote was not unanimous, but, in 1645, a writer assumes that either side could appeal.[1208]

We have seen how tenaciously the kingdoms of Aragon struggled against the evils of the system. Castile felt them equally but it had not the same institutions and could only remonstrate. The Córtes of Madrid, in 1607-8, represented that those of 1579 and 1586 had petitioned for the reform of the abuses arising from the temporal jurisdiction of the Inquisition to the great injury of the kingdom; that Philip II had promised relief, but had died without granting it, and therefore the request was now repeated in view of the increasing evils. Especially was attention called to the cruelty of imprisoning ordinary offenders, for the people could not distinguish and imagined all prisoners to be heretics, thus entailing infamy upon them and disqualifying them for marriage, wherefore it was asked that they be confined in the public gaols. Philip III promised to do what was proper and of course did nothing. The Córtes of 1611 repeated the petition, with similar lack of result.[1209]

***

The Council of Castile, the highest tribunal in the land, in a consulta of 1631, represented forcibly the existing evils, especially the prodigal use of censures under which corregidores and other magistrates lay under excommunication for months together, while individuals were impoverished by the long delays in settling competencias. It urged the remedy of permitting appeals to the Council por via de fuerza, in cases not of faith and this it repeated in 1634, 1669 and 1682.[1210] More outspoken was a memorial presented, in 1648, to Philip by a member of the Council, on the abuses of the criminal jurisdiction, those in civil cases being treated in a separate paper. The writer alludes to having repeatedly made the same representations orally and in writing; he dwells upon the interminable delays and other obstacles which impede justice and discourage sufferers from seeking it. The resultant immunity creates audacious criminals; the number of familiars and of soldiers who never serve in the field has increased so greatly that nothing is seen but crimes and the offenders are unpunished. Everywhere men of the most dissolute type and the largest fortunes seek appointment so as to enjoy immunity; the royal revenues are defrauded and prohibited goods are imported, while no corregidor or alcalde dares to curb them, for they are at once excommunicated by the inquisitors, even to casting interdicts over whole communities. Those who suffer remain without redress, so that those who are able are led to take it into their own hands, for they can get it nowhere else. Justice is trampled under foot; there is no alguazil who dares to make an arrest, or scrivener to draw up papers, so many have been slain or wounded for so doing and the death of an alguazil is held at naught, as though the officers of justice were common enemies. If the king would re-establish the jurisdiction of the royal courts there would be an end to the excommunications with which the inquisitors defend their delinquents, as though they were vessels of the Temple; the time of the Councils and of the king would not be consumed by these perpetual competencias and the plagues would cease wherewith God afflicts these kingdoms for the injustice, the violence and the dissolute life of the people.[1211]

These warnings and remonstrances fell on deaf ears. The Suprema was skilled to work upon the piety of the king, and to promise him relief from perils if he would placate God by increasing the privileges of the Inquisition, the very existence of which depended upon its ability to protect its familiars from the law and from the universal hatred in which they were held.

After the fall of Inquisitor-general Nithard, there was a bustling attempt to check the enormous evils admitted to exist. In 1677 Carlos II deprecated the abuses common, both in excessive charges and in forcing his pious subjects to submit by censures which deprived them of the consolations of religion. He declared excommunication to be illegal in matters connected exclusively with laymen and temporal possessions, and forbade its employment, a command which he addressed to the Suprema in 1678 with directions to enforce it and which he repeated in 1691, but without effect.[1212] Then a more comprehensive effort was made to effect a radical reform. In 1696, Carlos was induced to assemble what was known as the Junta Magna, consisting of two members each of the Councils of State, of Aragon, of Castile, of Italy, of Indies and of Orders. The decree creating it recites the disturbance and interference with justice, the continual collisions and competencias between the Inquisition and the courts over question of jurisdiction and privileges, and the necessity of establishing some fixed principles and rules to avert these troubles for the future and to preserve the Holy Office in the love and reverence of the people, without its interfering in matters foreign to its venerable purpose. The Junta was to meet at least once a week and it was furnished with materials from the records of all the Councils, through which it obtained a thorough insight into the evils to be remedied. These labors resulted in a memorial known as the Consulta Magna, drawn up by Doctor Joseph de Ledesma of the Council of Castile.

**

It constituted a terrible indictment of the abuse, by the Inquisition, of the temporal jurisdiction bestowed on it by the sovereigns, with ample proof of flagrant cases and incidents. Then followed a consideration of possible remedies, of which the most indispensable was declared to be the prohibition of censures, which were so formidable that no one could resist them. Persons arrested for offences not of faith should be confined in the royal prisons to save them from the indelible disgrace of the secret prison. The recurso de fuerza should be admitted when excommunication was used in temporal cases. The fuero should be withdrawn from the servants and commensals of officials whose insolence gave occasion to arrests and censures causing dissensions that scandalized the whole kingdom. It was admitted that familiars now gave little trouble, save in Majorca, where there was no Concordia, but the salaried officials were the source of infinite contention and they should be put on the footing of familiars. A grievance of the greatest magnitude was the interminable delay in the settlement of competencias, during which prisoners languished in confinement and excommunicates could not obtain absolution; this could be averted if the Concordias and royal orders were enforced. As all attempts to curb the Inquisition had proved useless, and in spite of them it had continually increased its abuses, the ultimate remedy of depriving it wholly of the royal jurisdiction might be found necessary, but meanwhile these milder measures might be tried in hope of relief.[1213] These proposed remedies, it will be seen, were moderate enough and in no way limited the Inquisition in its ostensible functions as the preserver of the faith.

This was the most formidable assault that the Inquisition had experienced, coming as it did from the combined forces of all the other organizations of the State, under the auspices of the king, but it was easily averted. Llorente tells us that Inquisitor-general Rocaberti, working through the royal confessor Froilan Diaz, who was ex-officio a member of the Suprema, and also Rocaberti's subject in the Dominican Order, succeeded in inducing Carlos to consign the consulta to the limbo in which reposed so many previous memorials.[1214] The manner in which this was effected was simple enough. In 1726 Don Santiago Augustin Riol drew up for Philip V a report on the creation and organization of the state councils, in which he states that the consulta was submitted to the Council of Castile for its action; this was delayed by the illness of the governor of the Council; when he returned to duty the matter was forgotten and the consulta disappeared so completely that, when Philip V called for it, in 1701, no copy could be found in the archives, as appeared from a certificate furnished by the archivist.[1215]

***

This narrow escape did not teach moderation. In 1702 the Valencia tribunal refused even to join in a competencia over a case in which it entertained a suit brought to collect the interest on a censo, by the widow of an alguazil mayor as guardian of her children. It was in vain that the regent of the Audiencia pointed out that, under the Concordia of 1568, the widow of an official only enjoyed the fuero as defendant and not as plaintiff and that the children had no claim whatever, and cited precedents that had been so decided; the tribunal was stubborn and would not even admit that the question could be carried up to the Suprema and Council of Aragon for decision.[1216] It was not long after this, however, that the Suprema was obliged to admit that reforms in the methods of the Holy Office were essential. In its carta acordada of June 27, 1705, is embodied a rebuke of the recklessness with which the tribunals undertook the defence of their officials, resulting in the universal complaints of the abuse of its jurisdiction, so that it was popularly said that everything was made a caso de Inquisicion, to the disrepute of its officials and their families. Therefore, unless the jurisdiction was indisputable, the Suprema must be consulted before assuming the defence, amicable adjustments must always be sought and friendly relations be maintained with the royal officials, thus avoiding competencias which ordinarily arose from passionate conflicts over trifles.[1217]

CURTAILMENT OF PRIVILEGES

These were wise admonitions to which as usual scant attention was paid, but in time the tribunals were made to recognize the change which had come in with the Bourbons. There was a highly illustrative case in 1720, at Toledo, where Don Pedro Paniagua, contador or auditor of the tribunal, received in October twenty sacks of cocoa from Cadiz. In the intricate details of the Spanish system of internal imposts, it would be impossible now to say whether he had observed the formalities requisite in the transmission of merchandise, but the local authorities assumed that there was a violation of law and also an infraction of quarantine, imposed in August, owing to an epidemic in Marseilles. The corregidor was prompt; at 2 A.M. of the day following the arrival of the cocoa, he searched Paniagua's country house and at 9 A.M. his town house and sequestrated the cocoa. The inquisitors responded by imprisoning the civic guards who had been employed. A fortnight later, another visit paid to Paniagua's house showed that five sacks of the sequestrated article had been removed, whereupon he was confined in the royal prison. Then the inquisitors proceeded against the corregidor and alcalde mayor with censures, and aggravated them so energetically that in twenty-four hours they had an interdict and cessatio a divinis in four parishes of the city. These active demonstrations, however suited to the seventeenth century, were out of place in the eighteenth. As soon as news of them reached Madrid, hurried orders were despatched by the Suprema to remove the interdict, absolve the officials and release the guards, and when the formal report came from the tribunal the orders were repeated, with the addition that the senior inquisitor should start for Madrid within twenty-four hours. Prior to receiving this the inquisitors had written to Inquisitor-general Camargo lamenting his abandonment of them and the dishonor inflicted on the tribunal; they blushed to be accomplices in this ruin and they tendered their resignations. The answer to this was sending the senior Inquisitor of Madrid to take charge of the tribunal, with orders to the two remaining inquisitors to report in Madrid but, on learning that they had obeyed the first orders, they were allowed to remain in Toledo.

How strong had been the pressure exerted on the Suprema to produce this action may be inferred from a protest in which, a month later, it poured forth to Philip V its bitterness of soul. The corregidor had violated the privileges and immunities of the Inquisition; the inquisitors had been perfectly justified in their action, although too speedy in aggravating the censures; they had been humiliated, while the corregidor and his underlings were boasting of their triumph over the Inquisition and of depriving it of the rights granted by the popes and the kings of Spain. The Suprema therefore asked that the senior inquisitor be allowed to return to Toledo, that Paniagua be released by the hands of the inquisitors, that his cocoa be restored and that the corregidor and alcalde mayor be duly punished. This accomplished nothing and two months later it again appealed to the king for the release of Paniagua and the restoration of the senior inquisitor, but this time it professed its zeal to see that in future the tribunals should practise more moderation.[1218] The lesson was a hard one, but it had a still harder one, in 1734, when Philip decided that a salaried official should be tried by the ordinary courts.[1219]

Step by step the old-time privileges were being curtailed. Soon after the accession of Fernando VI, some trouble arose at Llerena over the taxation of familiars. It seems to have been aggravated in the usual manner and, when it reached the king, it was of a character that induced him to issue a decree, October 5, 1747, by which the Council of Castile was given jurisdiction over the officials of the Inquisition. This called forth a heated remonstrance, dated November 1st, which must have proceeded from the Inquisitor-general Prado y Cuesta, for no other subject would have dared thus to address his sovereign. The writer tells him that the decree is unworthy of his name and his faith, nor is it well that the world should see him, in the first year of his reign, discharge such a thunderbolt against the Holy Office, such as it had never received since its foundation, leaving it prostrated by the shock. He affirms before God, and would wish to write it with his blood, that the service of Jesus Christ and the prosperity of the king and his kingdoms require that the decree be returned to the royal hands, without a copy being allowed to remain.[1220]

Although this decree was not effective as to the salaried officials, the Inquisition was falling upon evil days. It no longer inspired the old-time awe; it was no longer striving to extend its prerogatives, but was fighting a losing battle to maintain them. A writer of about this period deplores its decadence; its commissioners and familiars serve without pay and the only reward for their labors and the cost of making their proofs of limpieza is the exemptions of pure honor granted by the kings, but now scarce one of these is observed and no fit persons seek the positions, although they are much needed, for there are not a tenth part of those allowed by the Concordias.[1221] There is probably some truth in this, for Inquisitor-general Prado y Cuesta, in appointing, at the request of the tribunal of Valencia, Fray Vicente Latorre as calificador or censor, asks why, when there are so many learned canons and professors in Valencia, who formerly were eager in seeking the position, it had now fallen so greatly in estimation.[1222]

COMPETENCIAS

It was difficult for the Inquisition to reconcile itself to the tendencies of the age and several cases, about this time, in which the tribunal of Valencia refused even to admit competencias, asserting that its combined ecclesiastical and royal jurisdictions rendered it the sole judge of all that concerned its officials, show that the old spirit still lingered and found expression whenever it dared.[1223] Carlos III, however, was even more assertive of the royal prerogative than his brother Fernando. We have seen his orders of 1763 concerning municipal and police regulations which included the prohibitions of carrying concealed weapons and exporting money, in all of which familiars were wholly removed from the jurisdiction of the Inquisition, and in 1775 a competencia in Córdova caused him emphatically to order the inviolable observance of this decree.[1224] All this led to the change in the commissions of familiars as regards carrying arms, which was brought about, in 1777, by the authorities of Alcalá la Real and Seville refusing to register commissions issued by the tribunals of Toledo and Seville, because they were not in accordance with the new regulations. In place, as of old, of blustering and coercing the magistrates, the Suprema collected from all the tribunals the formulas employed by them and framed a new one, phrased in a very different spirit and in accordance with the royal edicts.[1225]

***

That the endless quarrels which we have been considering ought to be settled in an amicable manner was so self-evident that, from an early period, persistent efforts had been made to accomplish it, resulting in the "competencia" so frequently alluded to above. Originally it would seem that there was no established procedure and that the Inquisition settled for itself all questions arising with the magistrates. After the first opposition had been broken down these were not numerous, until the attribution of the fuero to the officials, and the enormous multiplication of familiars and other unsalaried officers, gave occasion for collisions with the courts. The earliest attempt that I have met to provide a method of settlement is a cédula, issued about 1535 by the empress-regent in the absence of Charles V, ordering that, when there was a dispute about jurisdiction, the president and judges of the royal court should meet the inquisitors and arrange matters harmoniously, so that it should not be known that there had been a difference between them. It was in conformity with this that, in 1542, when Joaquin de Tunes was tried in Barcelona for the murder of Juan Ballell, a familiar, the inquisitor, Miguel Puig, held a conference with the regent and judges of the royal chancellery, prior to the arrest, and the custody of the accused was settled without difficulty. It was impossible, however, to preserve peace between classes mutually jealous, and we have seen (p. 435) the troubles which Prince Philip endeavored to settle by the cédula of May 15, 1545. This favored the royal jurisdiction and produced complaints from the Suprema as when, in 1548, it represented to Charles V that in Granada the judges made the cédula a pretext to intervene in the business of the tribunal, whenever any one made a complaint, requiring the inquisitors to interrupt their work and come to the Audiencia, when they were ordered not to proceed and, if this was disobeyed, the judges raised a great disturbance. All this would cease if the old rule were restored that any one feeling aggrieved must appeal to the Suprema where he would get justice.[1226] Prince Philip's cédula of 1553 settled this as far as concerned matters of faith, but neither it nor the Castilian Concordia of the same year could prevent disputes over the immunities of the officials and familiars which the Inquisition was persistently endeavoring to extend. The Concordia, however, endeavored to provide for the settlement of these by the process described above (p. 436) which became technically known as competencia. It is remarkable that, in the Valencia Concordia of 1554, there is no such provision, but in that of 1568, for the Aragonese kingdoms, it appears in the slightly different form that the regent of the Audiencia and the senior inquisitor should consult and endeavor to come to some agreement. If they could not do so, the regent was to send his side of the case to the Council of Aragon and the inquisitor his to the Suprema, when the king would arrange how the matter should be decided.[1227] The two formulas were combined in practice and remained the established method of settling conflicts of jurisdiction.

This should have produced peace but we have seen that it only gave occasion for fresh subjects of discord. The inquisitors were restive under any restraint on their arbitrary methods and already in 1560, a carta acordada of November 14th warns them that they are not to proceed with censures against the judges, when the latter offer competencias, but are to send the papers to the Suprema and await the result, under a penalty of twenty ducats for every infraction of the rule.[1228] The inquisitors however avoided competencias as far as they could and, when obliged to concede them, the opportunity was taken of humiliating the royal judges and make them feel their inferiority in a manner most galling to men so tenacious of the respect due to position and so insistent on courtesy. When de Soto Salazar reports of the inquisitors of Barcelona that, when they had occasion to notify the lieutenant of the king or the regent of the Audiencia, they sent a messenger to summon him and then kept him waiting in the antechamber and that sometimes they called the judges before them and scolded them without cause, we can readily appreciate the intensity of the hatred thus excited.[1229]

***

So, when the Inquisition established its formula for competencias, they were sedulously framed to be as arrogantly insulting as possible. The first mandate inhibits peremptorily the judge from action and orders him to remit the case to the tribunal within twenty-four hours. If an arrest has been made the prisoner is to be discharged on bail to present himself before the inquisitors and any property seized or sequestrated is to be released. If the secular judge has any reason to allege to the contrary he is to present himself in person or by procurator to the tribunal, which will render justice, and all this is under holy obedience and the threat of major excommunication and a heavy fine. If there are any papers in the case the scrivener is ordered to surrender them, and the accuser or plaintiff is to appear within a time specified and receive justice, in default of which the case will be heard without him and without further notice. Then, if a reply is made to this alleging reasons for not obeying, a second mandate is issued pronouncing them insufficient and ordering the first one to be obeyed within a specified time under the above penalties. If the judge then proposes a competencia, a mandate is sent to him reciting the previous ones and saying that, to avoid, troubling the higher powers, he is ordered to surrender all papers and suspend all action, or the excommunication and fine will be enforced on his person and property. The next mandate accepts the competencia, states that the tribunal is ready to forward its papers and orders the judges to send their side within twelve days, adding a threat of excommunication and fine if any additional testimony be taken in the case. All this is phrased in the most mandatory fashion as of a superior addressing a subordinate and all these missives are ordered to be returned to the tribunal. If, after a competencia was formed, the familiar or official accepted the jurisdiction of the secular court, he was deprived of his commission. As we have frequently seen, there was no hesitation, at any stage of the proceedings, to excommunicate the judges, to anathematize them and to lay an interdict on the city, followed by a cessatio a divinis.[1230]

In addition to the gratification of thus humiliating the magistrates, there was also in this truculence the object of rendering the process so offensive as to make them shrink from resisting the encroachments of the Inquisition. When this failed the tribunal had abundant sources of annoyance in raising interminable questions of precedence and formalities, which were sometimes fought so bitterly and long as virtually to supersede the original case. The points that could be raised were endless. In 1602, the Count of Benavente, then Viceroy of Valencia, issued letters ordering a conference over the arrest of Gerónimo Falcon; the tribunal surrendered him, admitting that the case did not pertain to it, but demanded that the viceroy and chancellery should cancel the letters on their records and, on refusal, it excommunicated the regent. The matter was carried up to the Suprema and Council of Aragon, when the king decided that the letters must be expunged and it was done in presence of a secretary of the Inquisition. The same humiliation had been inflicted on the count's father, when he was viceroy, and also on the Duke of Segorbe.[1231]

This arrogance continued until Carlos III, in his decree of 1775, informed the Inquisition that the royal jurisdiction which it exercised was on precisely the same level as that of his judges and magistrates; there must be entire equality between them; all threats of excommunication and fines must be abandoned; there must be free interchange of papers, mutual courtesy and no assumption of superiority. It was difficult for the tribunals to abandon the formulas which flattered their vanity and a second command was necessary, issued in 1783, on the occasion of a prolonged conflict of the Valencia tribunal with the alcalde of Consentaina. This finally produced obedience and the Suprema transmitted the royal order to Valencia with instructions for its observance.[1232]

***

MODERATION UNDER THE RESTORATION

While this doubtless diminished the exasperation of these conflicts, it did not check their frequency. They continued to be a constant source of trouble and it was from a desire to diminish this, as well as to extend its authority, that the Suprema, in 1806, forbade the tribunals from instituting them without submitting the case to it and receiving its approval.[1233] When, under the Restoration, the Inquisition was revived, in 1814, the officials naturally claimed the fuero, active and passive, civil and criminal, and Fernando VII, in the decision of a case carried up to him from Seville, announced, February 15, 1815, in no uncertain tones, that they should be protected in its enjoyment, but the cases appear to be rare and the aggressive spirit had disappeared.[1234] When, in Seville, the creditors of Francisco de Paula Esquivol complained of him to the tribunal, in place of defending him, it promptly dismissed him, June 27, 1815, an action which was confirmed by the Suprema.[1235] Even more significant was a case, in 1816, when in Seville Lorenzo Ayllon abused a priest while celebrating mass and endeavored to seize the sacrament, and the secular authorities arrested and proceeded to try him. In such a case there could be no question as to the jurisdiction of the Inquisition, but there was no disturbance, and when the tribunal claimed his transfer to the secret prison the Suprema interposed and ordered that he should be allowed to remain in the public gaol, a detainer being lodged to prevent his discharge during his trial--a concession to the royal jurisdiction which would have petrified Pacheco or Arce y Reynoso.[1236]

There was the same disposition to avoid coming to extremes with the spiritual courts. In 1816 the provisor of the see of Tuy prosecuted Joseph Metzcler for impious, execrable and sacrilegious blasphemies. The tribunal of Santiago applied, in a courteous note, to the provisor for the papers and received a reply without signature. This the Suprema directed it to return and explain that there was no desire to invade the episcopal jurisdiction, but as the blasphemous propositions and acts of Metzcler might be heretical, of which the Inquisition had exclusive cognizance, it must insist on seeing the evidence to extract what appertained to it, after which the papers would be returned. It seems to have obtained the evidence for, on October 15, 1817, it voted to imprison Metzcler, as soon as his trial by the provisor should be ended, but the Suprema instructed it not to wait for this, as the jurisdiction of the Inquisition was privileged.[1237]

***

There was one peculiarly irritating feature in the position of the Inquisition in these quarrels, which exacerbated them greatly and often neutralized all efforts to maintain harmony--the power which it arrogated to itself of refusing to form competencias on the ground that its rights were too clear to admit of debate. Thus it held that the salaried and titular officials, with their families and servants, were so wholly beyond all secular jurisdiction that it refused to entertain any proceedings in contest of their claims. It was in vain that Philip III, by a royal letter of 1615, declared that if inquisitors refused a conference, on the ground that the matter was too clear to justify it, the regent of the chancellery should form a competencia and forward the papers as usual.[1238] It was equally useless for Philip IV to decree, in 1630, that when a contention was started by either party, the other must entertain it, no matter how clear it might be, under pain, for a first offence, of five hundred ducats and, for a second, of suspension during the royal pleasure. To ensure the imposition of the fine, each Council was to give the other faculties for its collection from offenders, but, when the Suprema forwarded this decree to the tribunals, with orders for its strict observance, it added significantly that it did not apply to cases of salaried and titular officials, though no such exception was made in the decree. It knew that Philip would never summon courage to enforce his law and it was right. When, in 1633, the Council of Aragon endeavored to collect such a fine, the Suprema interposed, asserting that it could only be done by consent of both Councils, which was, in effect, to invalidate the law, and Philip himself violated it, in 1634, when Augustin Vidal, messenger of the tribunal of Valencia, was arrested by the royal court for the murder of Juan Alonso Martínez, a Knight of Santiago and Bayle of Alicante. The tribunal demanded him and refused a competencia, when Philip weakly ordered him to be surrendered "for this time and without prejudice to my royal jurisdiction."[1239]

REFUSAL OF COMPETENCIAS

The Inquisition carried its point. Philip, by decisions of 1645 and 1658, admitted that there could be no competencias in the case of salaried officials and the Suprema enforced these decisions by a carta acordada of August 7, 1662, pointing out that they must not be entertained where such officials were concerned; at the same time tribunals were warned to exercise moderation and not to employ censures without consulting it, unless delay was inadmissible.[1240] Even Philip however had to intervene against the consequences of his own acts, in 1664, when the portero of the tribunal of Logroño killed in his house a priest, apparently through jealousy. The alcalde mayor prosecuted the murderer and arrested his wife; the tribunal excommunicated the alcalde and cast an interdict on the town. The Council of Aragon formed a competencia and claimed that during it the censures should be raised according to custom, but the Suprema refused on the ground that there could be no competencia. Philip was appealed to and ordered the censures raised for the unanswerable reason that as judges under excommunication could not hold their courts, if it were allowed thus to paralyze all judicial business it would have arbitrary control over all cases and frustrate all legal remedies.[1241] This decision was disregarded. It seems extraordinary that any community would endure for centuries the indefinite stoppage of the administration of justice, constantly occurring through the reckless abuse of the power of excommunication, as when, in 1672, we find the queen-regent applying to the inquisitor-general to know how she is to answer the complaints of the town of Logroño at the prolonged suspension of the powers of the corregidor who lay under excommunication, seeing that there is no conclusion of the competencia which has been so long pending.[1242]

The Inquisition evidently aggravated as far as it could the public distress as a means of establishing its claims. In an effort to limit the abuse of refusing competencias, there was a junta formed, in 1679, from the Suprema and Council of State with the assistance of some theologians. This admitted that there could be no competencia in the cases of salaried officials, except when they held public office and were prosecuted for malfeasance, but it laid down the rule that, when the Suprema refused a competencia, the Council of State could appeal to the king who could appoint a junta to decide this secondary question. A limited time was allowed to the Suprema to state its reasons for refusal and during a competencia the accused was to be liberated on bail and all censures were to be raised.[1243] This removed some of the hardships, but the Suprema seems to have sought to evade it by sullenly refusing to form the juntas with the Royal Councils, for another decree of Carlos II ordered it to attend when summoned so that these affairs might be settled.[1244] It was in vain that, in 1730, the Council of Castile urged that competencias be admitted in all cases, for Philip V decided that the agreement of 1679 should stand.[1245] Probably not much was gained in the latest attempt to settle these perennial quarrels by Carlos IV in 1804, who ordered that when a conflict arose between a royal court and a tribunal, in a matter not of faith concerning an official, the court should refer the case to the governor of the Royal Council and the tribunal to the Suprema. These should then select an examiner who was to report to the Secretaría de Gracia y Justicia for the royal decision.[1246]

***

PROTRACTED DELAYS

The evils of the system were admitted on all hands, but it was so vicious in principle that remedies were impossible. The customary juntas of two members each from the Suprema and the Council of Castile or of Aragon was at best a clumsy device, onerous on the Councils and usually leading only to procrastination. To systematize it, in 1625, a permanent Junta Grande de Competencias was formed of two members from each Council, whose duty it should be to despatch all cases, and rules for it were framed in April, 1626, but it was short-lived. In 1634 Philip IV ordered the formation of a junta of two members each of the Suprema and Council of Castile to formulate a plan of relief, but, on June 9th of that year, the Suprema reported that it had never been able to accomplish a meeting of the Junta. Then, in 1657, the Junta Grande was resuscitated and we meet with an allusion to it in 1659, but it appears to have been abandoned soon afterwards.[1247] Ingenuity was at fault to alleviate the evils inseparable from the permanent antagonism between the rival jurisdictions. Of these evils the one most keenly felt was the interminable delay in the settlement of cases. The councils from which the members were drawn were crowded with their more legitimate business; there was rarely accord in the junta; the matter would be argued without expectation of agreement; each side would be obstinate; perhaps the case would be referred to the king or years would pass before a settlement would be reached; perhaps, indeed, it would be silently dropped without a decision, especially when a decision might be undesirable because one or both sides feared a troublesome precedent. Meanwhile the case remained petrified in the condition existing at the time the competencia was formed. Until the so-called Concordia of 1679 permitted the release of prisoners on bail, if any one had been arrested, he remained in prison, perhaps to die there as sometimes occurred. In 1638 the Inquisition complained of this, when its officers happened to be the prisoners, for competencias were always slow of settlement and the work of the tribunals was crippled for lack of their ministers, while their poverty precluded their giving adequate salaries to substitutes.[1248] It was not until 1721 that a remedy for this procrastination was sought by Philip V in a decree reciting the long delays and the frequency of cases remaining undecided by reason of a dead-lock in the junta, wherefore in future when a junta was formed, he was to be notified in order that he might appoint a fifth member, thus assuring a majority.[1249] It does not seem however that this accomplished its purpose and, when Carlos III consolidated the cumbrous framework of government by instituting the Junta de Estado, composed of the ministers of the several departments, Floridablanca enumerates, among the benefits accruing, the expediting of cases of competencia and avoiding the interminable delays caused by the etiquette of the tribunals and the intrigues of the parties concerned.[1250]

***

I have dwelt thus in detail on this subject, not only because it absorbed so large a portion of the activity of the Inquisition, but because of its importance in the relations between the Holy Office and the other institutions of Spain and in explaining the detestation which the Inquisition excited. If the people regarded it as a whole with awe and veneration, as the bulwark of the Catholic faith, their hatred was none the less for its members, and the perpetual struggle against the tremendous odds of its power, supported by the unflinching favor of the Hapsburgs, bears equal testimony to the tenacity of the Spanish character and to the magnitude of the evils with which the Inquisition afflicted the nation.

CHAPTER V - POPULAR HOSTILITY

The preceding chapters illustrate some of the causes that provoked popular hatred of the Inquisition, but these were by no means all. It enjoyed, as we have said, enthusiastic support in the exercise of its appropriate functions in defending the faith, but apart from this, it had infinite ways of exciting hostility. This was the inevitable result of entrusting irresponsible power to men, for the most part overbearing and arrogant, who owed obedience only to the Suprema and who early learned that, while it might disapprove of their acts, it always supported them against complaints and, while it might administer rebuke in secret, it hesitated long before it would compromise the asserted infallibility of the Holy Office by dismissal or any other public demonstration. There was no other power to call them to account and they could rely upon its indulgence. This indulgence they extended to their subordinates, over whom, indeed, they had not the power of removal, and the consequence was that the whole body thoroughly earned the detestation of the people by the abuse of their privileges, creating irritation which was none the less exasperating because its causes might be trivial. The situation finds expression in a carta acordada of October 12, 1561, in which the Suprema begs the tribunals, for the love of God, to inflict no wrong or oppression for, since they are accused when they do right, what is to be expected when they give just grounds of complaint?[1251]

Whether just or not, grounds of complaint were never lacking. The power of the inquisitor had practically scarce any bounds but his own discretion, and the temptation to its abuse was irresistible to the kind of men who mostly filled the position. In the memorial of Llerena to Philip and Juana, in 1506, complaint is made that the officials seized all the houses that they wanted and in one case, when some young orphan girls did not vacate as quickly as ordered, they fastened up the street-door and the occupants were obliged to make an opening in order to leave it.[1252] The same spirit was shown to parties not quite so defenceless in 1642, when its exhibition in Córdova nearly provoked a disastrous tumult. There was a vacant house which Juan de Ribera, one of the inquisitors, talked of renting, but he went to Murcia without taking it. On his return he found that it had been leased to a son of Don Pedro de Cardenas, one of the veinticuatros, or town-councillors. He sent for Cardenas and asked whether he knew that he had engaged the house. Cardenas professed ignorance, adding that, if he had not moved his family into it, he would abandon it. Ribera ordered him to leave it and, on his refusal, the tribunal took up the quarrel by serving on him a notice to quit. As he did not obey, it cited him to appear and forced him to give security. His kinsmen and friends rallied around him and promised to sustain him by force; the matter became town-talk and the tribunal felt its honor engaged to sustain its commands by violence. It assembled the two companies of soldiers which it kept in the alcázar, while the caballeros armed themselves and guarded the house. The corregidor appealed to the tribunal not to drench the city in blood by exposing the poor civic militia to the swords of the gentlemen, and it consented to carry the matter to the king. The Council of Castile ordered that the tenant be maintained in possession, while the Suprema instructed the tribunal not to yield a jot, but to eject him by whatever means it could.[1253] What was the outcome does not appear, but the case illustrates the extent to which the Inquisition magnified its powers and the determination with which it employed them.

ABUSES

It was impossible to prevent these lawless abuses. The Suprema might scold and threaten but, as it rarely punished and always protected the offenders, its restraining efforts amounted to little. The visitadores, or inspectors, duly reported disorders, and instructions would be issued to reform them, but to these the inquisitors paid little respect. There is no reason to suppose that the Barcelona tribunal was worse than any other and a series of reports of visitations there gives us an insight into the evils inflicted on the people. In 1544, Doctor Alonso Pérez sent in a report in consequence of which the Suprema roundly rebuked all the subordinates, except the judge of confiscations. All but two were defamed for improper relations with women; all accepted presents; all made extra and illegal charges; all neglected their duties and most of them quarrelled with each other. The fiscal was especially objectionable for his improper conduct of prosecutions and for appropriating articles belonging to the tribunal; he refused to pay his debts; he arrested a candle-maker for not furnishing candles as promptly as he demanded; when a certain party bought some sheep from a peasant and was dissatisfied with his bargain, the fiscal cited the peasant, asserted that the purchase money was his and forced the peasant to take back the sheep and return the money. Yet the Suprema was too tender of the honor of the Holy Office to dismiss a single one of the peccant officials. It ordered them to be severely reprimanded, a few debts to be paid and presents to be returned and uttered some vague threats of what it would do if they continued in their evil courses.[1254]

The natural result of this indulgence appears in the next visitation by the Licenciado Vaca, in 1549. The same abuses were flourishing, with the addition that the inquisitor, Diego de Sarmiento, had accepted the position of commissioner of the Cruzada indulgence and had appointed as its preachers and collectors the commissioners and familiars of the tribunal, to the great oppression and vexation of the people, whose dread of the Holy Office prevented complaints. Sarmiento was dismissed in 1550, but in 1552 he was reappointed to Barcelona; the fiscal and notary, who were specially inculpated, were suspended for six months and the gaoler, for ill-treatment of prisoners, was mulcted in one month's wages.[1255] In 1561 another visitation was made by Inquisitor Gaspar Cervantes, whose report was exceedingly severe on the disorders of the tribunal and drew from the Suprema an energetic demand for their reform.[1256] This produced no amendment, the tribunal went on undisturbed until the complaints of the Córtes of 1564 led to another and more searching investigation by de Soto Salazar, in 1566. There were not only abuses of all kinds in the trials of heresy but numerous cases in which, as the Suprema told them, they had no jurisdiction. Apparently they were ready to put their unlimited powers at the disposal of all comers and imprisoned, fined and punished in the most arbitrary manner, gathering fees, commissions and doubtless bribes and selling injustice to all who wanted it, while the dread of their censures prevented opposition or remonstrance. In these cases which were not of faith, the accused were often seized in the churches, where they had sought asylum, as though they were wanted for heresy and the repeated instances in which the Suprema orders their names stricken from the records points to one of the most cruel results of this reckless abuse of jurisdiction, for it inflicted on the sufferer, his kindred and posterity, an infamy unendurable to the Spaniard of the period. The long and detailed missive which the Suprema addressed to the tribunal, as the result of Salazar's report, gives a most vivid inside view of the abuses naturally springing from unrestrained autocracy, which, by the absolute and impenetrable secrecy of its operations, was relieved from all responsibility to its victims or to public opinion. The Suprema takes every official in turn, from inquisitors down to messengers, specifies their misdeeds and scores them mercilessly, showing that the whole organization was solely intent on making dishonest gains, on magnifying its privileges and on tyrannizing over the community, while the defence of the faith was the baldest pretext for the gratification of greed and evil passions. Yet all this was practically regarded as quite compatible with the duties of the Inquisition. The three inquisitors, Padilla, Zurita and Mexia, were suspended for three years and were then sent to repeat their misdeeds elsewhere and the two former were in addition fined ten ducats apiece.[1257] That an institution possessing these powers and exercising them in such fashion, should be regarded with terror and detestation was inevitable. We shall see hereafter how it shrouded all its acts in inviolable secrecy and how it rightly regarded this as one of the most important factors of its influence, and we can understand the mysterious dread which this inspired, while, at the same time, it released the inquisitor and his subordinates from the wholesome restraint of publicity.

***

The smothered hostility thus excited was always ready for an explosion when opportunity offered to gratify it. In the desire to stimulate the breeding of horses, a royal pragmática, in 1628, prohibited the use of mules for coaches. The inquisitors of Logroño, in the full confidence that no one would venture to interfere with them, persisted in driving with mules and when the corregidor, Don Francisco Bazan, remonstrated and threatened to seize a coach, they told him it would be his ruin. He did not venture, but, in 1633, he procured from the Council of Castile an order that no coaches should be used in Logroño, under pretext that they damaged certain shops projecting on the principal street. The fiscal of the tribunal undertook to meet this by asserting that it had a special privilege from the king concerning coaches, but when Bazan promised to obey, it was not forthcoming. The Suprema took up the quarrel and represented to Philip IV the hardship inflicted on the inquisitors, too old and feeble for the saddle; the compassionate king endorsed on the consulta the customary formula of approval--"I have so ordered"; the Suprema then applied to the Council of Castile for a corresponding order and several communications passed without result. Another consulta was presented to the king, who endorsed it "I have so ordered again," but the Council of Castile was still evasive. Then the Logroño authorities offered to the Bishop of Calahorra permission to use coaches and intimated to the inquisitors that, if they would apply for a licence, it would be given. The Suprema forbade them thus to recognize the local magistracy, as they had royal authority, whereupon they resumed the use of their coaches; the alguazil of the corregidor arrested one of their coachmen and they excommunicated the corregidor. The king, December 9, 1633, ordered him to be absolved, to which, on December 30th, the Suprema replied that he would be absolved if he made application. The Council of Castile presented to the king a consulta, arguing that ecclesiastics and inquisitors alike owed obedience to the laws and that the corregidor had acted with great moderation. February 5, 1634, the king enquired what had been done with the corregidor, but it was not until December 16th that the Suprema condescended to reply, complaining bitterly of the slight put upon the Inquisition, when the whole safety of the monarchy depended upon its labors. Finally, on February 15, 1635, the Council of Castile sent to the Suprema a licence for the use of coaches in Logroño, at the same time intimating that its tax of media añata had not been paid. In the course of the quarrel the Council presented a very forcible consulta to the king which exhibits the light in which the Inquisition was regarded by the highest authorities of the State. It represented that everywhere the inquisitors and their officials, under color of privileges that they did not possess, were causing grave disorders. They were vexing and molesting the corregidors and other ministers of the king, oppressing them with violent methods and frightening them with threats of punishment in order to deter them from defending the royal jurisdiction. Thus crimes remained unpunished, justice became a mockery and the king's vassals were afflicted with what they were made to suffer in their honor, their lives, their fortunes and their consciences.[1258]

***

Trivial quarrels such as this, developed until they distracted the attention of the king and his advisers, were constantly breaking out and bear testimony to the antagonistic spirit which was all-pervading. A long-standing cause of dissension in Logroño may be taken as a type of what was occurring in many other places. Local officials there, as elsewhere, had a perquisite in the public carnicería, or shambles, of dividing among themselves the vientres or menudos--the chitterlings--of the beasts slaughtered. It was not unnatural that the inquisitors and their subordinates should seek to share in this, but the claim was grudgingly admitted, as it diminished the portions of the town officers, and it led to bickerings. In 1572 Logroño complained to the Suprema that, while it was willing to give to each inquisitor the menudo of a sheep every week, the inferior officials, down to the messengers, claimed the same and, when there was not enough to go round, they caused the slaughter of additional sheep, in order to get their perquisite. As the population was poor, living mostly on cow-beef, and meat would not keep in hot weather, this caused much waste, wherefore the town begged that during the four hot months the inferior officials should be content with what the town officers received and during the other eight months it would endeavor to give them more. To this the Suprema graciously assented, but, in 1577, there was another outbreak, to quiet which the Suprema ordered the enforcement of the agreement. In 1584 trouble arose again and still more in 1593 and in 1601 it reached a point at which the tribunal summoned all the staff of the carnicería and scolded them roundly, giving rise to great excitement. Then in 1620 there was a worse outbreak than ever, owing to the refusal of the regidor to give to one of the inquisitors two pairs of sheep's stones asked for on the plea that he had guests to breakfast. The angry inquisitor, thus deprived of his breakfast relish, induced the tribunal to summon the regidor before it and severely reprimand him, thus not only inflicting a grave stigma on him, but insulting the town, of which it complained loudly to the Suprema.[1259] It is easy to understand how trifles of the kind kept up a perpetual irritation, of which only the exacerbations appear in the records.

The privileges of the markets, in fact, were a source of endless troubles. It was recognized that both secular and ecclesiastical officials were entitled to the first choice and to be served first. Those of the Inquisition claimed the same privilege, not only in cities where there was a tribunal, but also where the scattered commissioners and notaries resided. That this was frequently resisted is shown by the formula of mandate to be used in such cases, addressed to the corregidor or alcaldes, setting forth that the rights in this respect of the aggrieved party had not been respected and that in future he should have the first and best (after the secular and ecclesiastical officials had been served) of all provisions that he required, at current prices, and this under penalty of twenty thousand maravedís, besides punishment to the full rigor of the law.[1260] It does not appear that there really was any legislation entitling the Inquisition to this privilege, but in the frequent troubles arising from its assertion, the inquisitors acted with their customary truculence. A writer, in 1609, who deprecates these quarrels, suggests as a cure that the king issue a decree that the representatives of the Inquisition shall have preference in purchasing and, at the same time, he tells of a case in Toledo where a regidor, who told the steward of the tribunal to take as many eggs as he wanted, but no more, was arrested and prosecuted, and of another in Córdova, where a hidalgo, who had bought a shad and refused to give it up to an acquaintance of a servant of an inquisitor, was punished with two hundred lashes and sent to the galleys.[1261] In 1608 the Suprema issued an injunction that purveyors of inquisitors should take nothing by force, the significance of which lies rather in the indication of existing abuses than in its promise of their removal.[1262] The claim of preference was pushed so far that in Seville, in 1705, there arose a serious trouble because the servant of an inquisitor detained boat-loads of fish coming to market, in order to make his selection, and it required a royal cédula of March 26, 1705, forbidding inquisitors to detain fish or other provisions on the way, or to designate by banderillas the pieces selected for themselves.[1263] When we consider the character of the slaves and servants thus clothed with authority to insult and browbeat whomsoever they chose, in the exercise of such functions, we can conceive the wrath and indignation stored up against their masters in the thousands of cases where fear prevented an explosion. It is true that the Suprema issued instructions that all purveyors should behave themselves modestly and give no ground of offence and that no one should be summoned or imprisoned for matters arising out of provisions, but as usual these orders were disregarded. Insolence would naturally elicit a hasty rejoinder which, as reported by the servant to his master, would imply disrespect towards the Holy Office, and severe punishment would be justified on that account.

***

Perhaps less irritating but more serious in its effects was the use made of the fuero by those engaged in trade. Inquisitor-general Deza, in 1504, issued a stringent prohibition against any salaried official having an interest, direct or indirect, in any business. Daily experience, he said, showed how much opprobrium and disturbance it brought upon the Inquisition, wherefore he decreed that it should, ipso facto, deprive the offender of his position and subject him to a fine of twenty thousand maravedís; he should cease to be an official as soon as contravention occurred and the receiver, under pain of fifty ducats, should cut off his salary. All officials cognizant of such a case should notify the inquisitor-general within fifteen days, under pain of major excommunication, and this order was to be read in all tribunals in presence of the assembled officials.[1264]

OFFICIALS AS TRADERS

The severity of this regulation indicates the recognized magnitude of the evil, and its retention in the compilation of Instructions shows that it was considered as remaining in force. Like all other salutary rules, however, it was slackly enforced from the first and the Catalans took care to have the prohibition embodied in the bull Pastoralis officii. It gradually became obsolete. A royal decree of August 9, 1725, in exempting from taxation the salaries of officials of the tribunal of Saragossa, adds that, if they possess property or are in trade, those assets are taxable, showing that their ability to trade was recognized.[1265] How aggravating was the advantage which they thus enjoyed can be gathered from a Valencia case of about 1750. Joseph Segarra, the contador of the tribunal, entered into partnership with Joseph Miralles, a carpenter, to bring timber from the Sierra de Cuenca. In the settlement Segarra claimed from Miralles a balance of 1779 libras; they entered into a formal agreement to accept the arbitration of Doctor Boyl, but Segarra rejected the award and Miralles sought to enforce it in the royal court. Then the tribunal intervened, asserting the award to be invalid because Segarra could not divest the Inquisition of its jurisdiction and it refused the request of the regent for a conference and a competencia.[1266] Evidently it was dangerous to have dealings with officials; they always had a winning card up the sleeve, to be played when needed.

As regards the great army of familiars, it was of course impossible to prevent them from trading. In fact traders eagerly sought the position in view of the advantages it offered of having the Inquisition at their backs, whether to escape payment of debts or to collect claims or to evade customs dues, or in many other ways, not recognized by the Concordias but allowed by the tribunals. The Suprema occasionally warned the inquisitors not to appoint men of low class, such as butchers, pastry-cooks, shoemakers and the like, or traders whose object was protection in their business,[1267] but no attention was paid to this; a large portion of the familiars was of this class, and the space occupied in the formularies by forms of levy and execution and sale and other similar matters shows how much business was brought to the tribunals by the collection of their claims.[1268] The opportunities thus afforded for fraudulent dealings, for evading obligations and for enforcing unjust demands were assuredly not neglected and may be reckoned among the sources of the animosity felt for everyone connected with the Holy Office.

In the remarkable paper presented, in 1623, to the Suprema by one of its members, many of the abuses of the Inquisition are attributed to the indifferent character and poverty of the officials. It would be well, the writer says, to appoint none but clerics, holding preferment to support themselves and unencumbered with wife and children. They would not, when dying, leave penniless families, which obliges the inquisitor-general to give to the children their fathers' offices, thus bringing into the tribunals men who cannot even read; an increase of salaries, also, would relieve them of the necessity of taking bribes under cover of fees, and thus would put a stop to the popular murmurs against them. The inquisitors moreover should have power of removal, subject to confirmation by the Suprema, for now their hands are tied; their subordinates are unruly and uncontrollable. The greatest injury to the reputation of the Holy Office arises from its bad officials, who recognize no responsibility. No one should be appointed to office, or as a familiar, who is a tailor, carpenter, mason or other mechanic; it is these people who cause quarrels with the secular authorities, for they have little to lose and claim to be inviolable. In short, if we may believe the writer, the whole body of the tribunals, except the inquisitors, was rotten; none of the officials, from the fiscals down, were to be trusted, for all were eagerly in pursuit of dishonest gains, robbing the Inquisition itself and all who came in contact with it, and to this he attributed its loss of public respect and confidence.[1269]

COMPLAINTS OF FEUDALISM

Matters did not improve, for the Suprema always defended the tribunals from all complaints, and its tenderness towards delinquents assured them of virtual impunity. At length, as we have seen, in 1703, Philip V made an attempt at reform. It was probably owing to this pressure that, in 1705, the Suprema issued a carta acordada prohibiting a number of special abuses and pointing out that, in regard to the proprieties of life, neither inquisitors nor officials obeyed the Instructions, consorting with improper persons and intervening in matters wholly foreign to their duties, thus rendering odious the jurisdiction of the Holy Office.[1270] From various incidents alluded to above it is evident that this produced little amendment but, when the vacillation of Philip V was succeeded by the resolute purpose of Carlos III and his able ministers, the power of the Inquisition to oppress was greatly curbed.

***

It was not alone the commonalty that had reason to complain of the extended jurisdiction claimed by the Inquisition. The feudal nobles, whose rights were already curtailed by the growth of the royal power, were restive under the interjection of this new and superior jurisdiction, which recognized no limitations or boundaries and interfered with their supremacy within their domains. Thus in 1553, the Duke of Najera complained that, in his town of Navarrete, the commissioner of the Inquisition had insulted his alcalde mayor and then, with some familiars, had forcibly taken wheat from his alguazil. Inquisitor-general Valdés wrote to the tribunal of Calahorra to investigate the matter and punish the officials if found in fault; the alcalde and alguazil were not to be prosecuted save for matters pertaining to the Inquisition and this not only in view of its proper administration but because he desired to gratify the duke.[1271]

A still more serious cause of complaint, to which the nobles were fully alive, was the release of their vassals from jurisdiction by appointment to office. In 1549, the Countess of Nieva appealed to Valdés, setting forth that Arnedo was a place belonging to the count; it was within three leagues of Calahorra and there had never been a familiar there until recently Inquisitor Valdeolivas had appointed some peasants in order to enfranchise them from the jurisdiction of their lord. It was not just that, while the count was absent from the kingdom on the king's service, his peasants should be thus honored in order that they might create disturbance in the villages and interfere with the feudal jurisdiction.[1272] It may well be doubted whether her request for the revocation of the commissions was granted, but that her prevision of trouble was justified is seen in a case before the tribunal of Barcelona, in 1577, in which Don Pedro de Queral, lord of Santa Coloma, a powerful noble of Tarragona, endeavored to secure the punishment of two of his vassals, Juan Requesens, a miller, and his cousin Vicente. They were both familiars and seem to have been the leaders of a discontented opposition which rendered Don Pedro's life miserable. The trees in his plantations were cut down, his arms, over the door of his bayle in Santa Coloma, were removed and defaced, libellous coplas against him were scattered around the streets, but the cousins, being familiars, were safe from his wrath. Don Pedro died but the trouble continued between his widow, the Countess of Queral and a new generation of Requesens, who succeeded to their fathers' office of familiars. Finally, in 1608, she succeeded in convicting Juan Requesens of malicious mischief, but her only satisfaction was that he was reprimanded, warned and sentenced to pay the costs, amounting to 115-1/2 reales.[1273] Such a case shows how feudalism was undermined and we can conceive how nobles must have writhed under the novel experience of rebellious vassals clothed with inviolability.

A History of the Inquisition of Spain: Volume I
PERSISTENT ANTAGONISM

It is easy therefore to understand the detestation felt for the Inquisition by all classes--laymen and ecclesiastics, noble and simple. It was fully aware of this and constantly alleged it to the king when defending the tribunals in their quarrels, and when urging enlarged privileges as a protection against the hatred which it had excited. In its appeals against the curtailment of its jurisdiction in Aragon, it did not hesitate to admit that it had been hated there from the beginning and that its officials were so abhorred that they would not be safe if exposed to secular justice and, even as late as 1727, it repeated the assertion of the persistent hostility of the Aragonese.[1274] In Logroño, the inquisitors reported to the Suprema, in 1584, that it was a common saying among the people that their life consisted in discord with the tribunal and that it was death to them when there was peace.[1275] It was the same in Castile. The Córtes, in 1566, when encouraging Philip II to constrain the Flemings to admit the Inquisition, gave as a reason that his success there was necessary to the peaceful maintenance of the institution in Spain, thus intimating that, if the Flemings rejected it, the Castilians would seek to follow their example.[1276] In the same year the familiars alleged that the detestation in which they were held led them to be singled out for especial oppression in the billeting of troops and, in 1647, the Suprema declared that nothing seemed sufficient to repress the hatred with which they were regarded, in support of which it instanced an unjust apportionment, in Cuenca, of an assessment of a forced loan.[1277] This hostility continued to the last, even though the decadence of the Inquisition in the eighteenth century diminished so greatly its powers of oppression. A defender of the institution, in 1803, commences by deprecating the hatred which had pursued it from the beginning; even in the present age, he says, of greater enlightenment, there is crass ignorance of its essential principles and a mortal opposition to its existence.[1278]

***

Thus, notwithstanding the Spanish abhorrence of Jews and heretics, the dread which the Inquisition inspired was largely mingled with detestation, arising from its abuse of its privileges in matters wholly apart from its functions as the guardian of the faith.

APPENDIX

I - LIST OF TRIBUNALS

The permanent tribunals of the Spanish Inquisition were Toledo, Seville, Valladolid, Corte (Madrid), Granada, Córdova, Murcia, Llerena, Cuenca, Santiago (Galicia), Logroño and Canaries, under the crown of Castile, and Saragossa, Valencia, Barcelona and Majorca under the crown of Aragon. In addition were Sicily, Sardinia, Mexico, Lima and Cartagena de las Indias, which lie beyond the scope of the present work.

This distribution of the forces of the Inquisition was not reached until experience had shown the most effective centres of action. Numerous more or less temporary tribunals were erected and many changes occurred in the apportionment of territory. The following list makes no pretension to absolute completeness but contains the result of such allusions as I have met in the documents.

***

ALCARAZ. For some years there was a tribunal fixed at Alcaraz. In 1495 Alonso Hernandez, presented for a canonry, is qualified as Inquisitor of Alcaraz and, in 1499, Alonso de Torres is appointed as inquisitor there.[1279]

ARMY AND NAVY. The fleet organized for the Catholic League which won at Lepanto seemed to require a tribunal to preserve it from heresy and Philip II procured from Pius V a brief of July 23, 1571, authorizing the inquisitor-general to appoint an inquisitor for each army of Philip II, whether by land or sea.[1280] The first appointment under this seems to have been Rodrigo de Mendoza, Inquisitor of Barcelona, whose commission as Inquisidor de las Galeras is dated March 21, 1575, together with one for his notary, Domingo de Leon, and instructions as to his duties.[1281] He was succeeded by Gerónimo Manrique, who celebrated an auto de fe in Messina. After him was Doctor Juan Bautista de Cardona, but merely as commissioner, who served for two years, when Páramo, writing in 1598; tells us that the fleets were scattered and the office ceased to exist.[1282] If so, it was revived for, in 1622, we are told that Fray Martin de Vivanco, chaplain of the galleys of Sicily, was appointed Inquisidor del Mar and, in 1632, it is stated that when a Principe del Mar was appointed he took with him an inquisitor and officials and all prisoners arrested by them were delivered to the nearest tribunal when the galleys made port.[1283]

In later times the inquisitor-general was "Vicario géneral de los Reales Ejercitos de Mar y Tierra" and as such appointed sub-delegates to accompany the army, with the necessary powers. The jurisdiccion castrense enjoyed by military men did not exempt them in matters of faith from the Inquisition, but the subdelegados castrenses seem to have possessed no judicial powers, and debate arose, in 1793 and again in 1806, whether they or the episcopal Ordinaries should be called in to vote with the inquisitors in the cases of soldiers.[1284]

AVILA. When Torquemada built his convent of San Tomas in Avila he provided accommodations for an Inquisition and, in 1590, the prisoners accused of the murder of the Santo Niño de la Guardia were transferred thither from the tribunal of Segovia for trial. It continued to exist for some years and had connection with Segovia, for, June 9, 1499, Francisco González of Fresneda and Juan de Monasterio were appointed inquisitors of Avila and Segovia, residing sometimes in one city and sometimes in the other.[1285]

BALAGUER. There were autos de fe celebrated in Balaguer, August 15, 1490 and June 10, 1493, but these were held by the inquisitors of Barcelona as they did in Tarragona, Gerona, Perpignan and other places in their district. In 1517, however, there would seem to be a tribunal there for a letter of the Suprema relates to the murder of the assessor of the Inquisition of Balaguer. If so, it was probably withdrawn in consequence for, in 1518, the inquisitors of Barcelona are ordered to publish edicts against those who molest the clergy of Balaguer for observing the interdict cast upon the town.[1286]

BARBASTRO. As early as 1488 there was a tribunal with inquisitors at Barbastro, but, in 1521, it was suppressed and incorporated with Saragossa.[1287]

BARCELONA. Established in 1486. It claimed jurisdiction over the free Republic of Andorra, which was included by Arevalo de Zuazo in his visitation of 1595. Long after Roussillon and Cerdagne had been retroceded to France, the Barcelona inquisitors in 1695 still styled themselves "Inquisidores Apostólicos ... en el Principado de Cataluña y su partido, con los Condados do Rosellon y Cerdaña y los Valls de Aran y Andorra."[1288] See LÉRIDA, TARRAGONA, TORTOSA, BALAGUER.

BURGOS. There was originally a tribunal in Burgos but, in the redistricting by Ximenes it was included in Valladolid. In 1605, Philip III transferred the tribunal to Burgos, with orders to the inquisitors to eject any occupants of buildings that they might find suited to their purposes. In 1622 it was still rendering yearly reports of cases to the Suprema but, probably about 1630, it returned to Valladolid. When, in 1706, Madrid was captured by the Allies under Galloway and Las Minas, the court fled to Burgos, carrying the Inquisition thither, but its stay was short and it soon returned to the capital.[1289]

CADIZ. See XERES.

CALAHORRA. A tribunal was established here as early as 1493, when it celebrated an auto at Logroño. In 1499 it alternated between Calahorra and Durango. In the redistricting by Ximenes in 1509 it was incorporated with Durango, but was soon re-established. Cédulas of 1516, 1517, and 1520 indicate that at this time it was the tribunal of the enormous district of Valladolid, but in 1522 the Inquisition of Navarre was extended over Calahorra; then Navarre and Calahorra were separated, but in 1540 there was a redistribution, and Navarre and the Basque Provinces were added to Calahorra. In 1560 a part of the territory of Burgos was set off from Valladolid and added to Calahorra and, in 1570, the seat of the tribunal was definitely moved to Logroño, q. v.[1290]

CALATAYUD. Calatayud was the seat of an intermittent tribunal at least from the year 1488 for, in 1502, Ferdinand speaks of Joan de Aguaviva who for fourteen years had served it as barber-surgeon whenever it resided in Calatayud and one of the first presentations to a prebend, in 1488, was Martin Márquez, described as fiscal of the Inquisition of Calatayud. A letter of the Suprema, Jan. 22, 1519, addressed to the "Inquisitor of Calatayud" shows that it was still in existence, but it must soon afterwards have been merged into Saragossa.[1291]

CANARIES. The zeal of Diego de Muros, Bishop of Canaries, did not wait for the extension of the Spanish Inquisition over his diocese, but led him to establish an episcopal one by proclamation of April 28, 1499. It was not until 1504 that Inquisitor-general Deza sent Bartolomé López de Tribaldos thither to establish a tribunal at Las Palmas, which seems to have commenced business Oct. 28, 1505. It continued thus to the end.[1292]

CARTAGENA. See MURCIA.

CIUDAD REAL. A letter of Ferdinand, Nov. 8, 1483, announces the appointment of Licenciados Costana and de Balthasar as inquisitors for Ciudad Real. May 10, 1485, Ferdinand announces the transfer of Costana to Toledo, to which place the tribunal was removed.[1293]

CÓRDOVA. A tribunal was established in Córdova as early as 1482, at the instance of its bishop, the New Christian Alonso de Burgos. Its district comprised the bishoprics of Córdova and Jaen, the Abadia de Alcalá la Real, the Adelantamiento de Cazorla, with Ecija and Estepa, to which Granada was added after the conquest.[1294] See GRANADA and JAEN.

CORTE. The tribunal of Madrid was technically known as Corte. Madrid, originally a town of no special importance, belonged to the province of Toledo and was naturally under the jurisdiction of its tribunal. As the royal residence under Philip II and eventually the capital of the kingdom (except during the brief transfer to Valladolid, 1600-1606) it furnished a large part of the business of Toledo. Toledan inquisitors came there to make investigations and even to try cases, of which we have examples in 1590 and 1592.[1295] Something more than this was felt to be needed and the Suprema adopted the plan of calling inquisitors from other places to commence prosecutions and act under its instructions, of which the Licenciado Flores, Inquisitor of Murcia, in 1593, and Cifontes de Loarte, Inquisitor of Granada, in 1615, are examples.[1296] The presence of the inquisitor-general who did not hesitate to take action in emergencies, and that of an experienced commissioner, together with the frequent sojourn of one of the Toledo inquisitors enabled speedy action to be taken when requisite, as occurred in 1621 and again in 1624 and seemed to render superfluous the organization of a special tribunal.[1297]

Yet the want of it was felt, especially with the influx of Portuguese New Christians who multiplied in the capital. As the pressure increased Toledo furnished two assistant inquisitors to reside in Madrid, thus establishing a kind of subordinate court, but in 1637 it was reported that the establishment of a tribunal was positively resolved upon, with the added comment that this would sorely vex the Toledans.[1298] To their natural opposition is doubtless to be attributed the postponement of what, to a Spaniard of the period, would seem a necessity to the capital. It cannot have been long after this that one was organized for, in the matter of the confiscation of Juan Cote, commenced in Toledo, we find it, September 10, 1640, sitting in Madrid, with Francisco Salgado and Juan Adam de la Parra as inquisitors. In the same year they suggested that the case of Benito de Valdepeñas, on which they were engaged, should be sent to Toledo as more convenient for the witnesses, which was accordingly done.[1299] Toledan influence is doubtless responsible for the action of Arce y Reynoso, soon after his accession in 1643, in suppressing the new tribunal and restoring the business to Toledo.[1300] The pressure, however, became too great and Arce y Reynoso was obliged to reverse his action. The date of the re-establishment may safely be assumed as 1650, for a list of penitents, reconciled by Corte from the beginning, starts with three in 1651 and their trials can scarce have been commenced later than 1650.[1301] Yet the relations between Toledo and Madrid continued intimate; in 1657, Lorenzo de Sotomayor styles himself as "Inquisidor Apostólico de la Inquisicion de la Ciudad y Reyno de Toledo y asistente de Corte;" to the end of the century the former always alluded to Corte as a despacho or office and not as a tribunal, and Corte seems to have sent its convicts to Toledo for their sentences to be published in the autos de fe.[1302] Its jurisdiction was strictly limited to the city, while the surrounding country remained with Toledo. In some respects its organization was peculiar. About 1750 we are informed that its inquisitors were drawn from other tribunals who continued them on their pay-rolls, their places being taken by appointees who served without salary until a vacancy occurred. Selection to serve in Corte was regarded as a promotion, leading to a place in the Suprema or to a bishopric, although the incumbent drew only the salary from his former tribunal with a Christmas propina of a hundred ducats. It had no receiver; the Suprema paid its expenses and presumably collected its fines and confiscations.[1303]

CUENCA. Murcia and Cuenca were originally under one tribunal. Some trouble apparently arose, possibly connected with the episcopal Ordinaries, for Ximenes ordered, January 22, 1512, that cases originating in Murcia should be taken to Cuenca to be voted on and vice versa. Llorente says that in 1513 they were separated and Cuenca formed an independent tribunal, but documents as late as 1519 show them still connected, until, in 1520, we find Cuenca celebrating an auto. A letter of March 7, 1522, states that the pope has given to Cuenca the see of Sigüenza, without taking it from Toledo, because Toledo has never visited it although ordered to do so, and is not to do so in future. Then, May 31, 1533, the Suprema says that Toledo can exercise jurisdiction there without giving Cuenca cause of complaint, and, in 1560, Sigüenza was restored to Toledo, yet in 1584 we find Cuenca exercising jurisdiction as far north as Soria. There would seem to have been some connection maintained between Murcia and Cuenca for, in 1746, the former, in enumerating its personnel, specifies nine calificadores in Murcia and four in Cuenca.[1304]

DAROCA. There would appear to have been for a time a tribunal in Daroca for, in the accounts of Juan Royz, receiver of Aragon, for 1498 there is an item of expenditure on the prison of the Inquisition there, which was duly passed.[1305]

DURANGO. See CALAHORRA. As defined by Ximenes, in 1509, Durango had jurisdiction over Biscay, Guipúzcoa, Alava and Calahorra, with some neighboring districts.[1306]

ESTELLA. See NAVARRE.

GALICIA, also known as SANTIAGO. The earliest allusion to this tribunal occurs in a commission issued at Coruña, May 20, 1520, to Doctor Gonzalo Maldonado as Inquisitor of Santiago. It was probably some time before the tribunal was in working order but in 1527 it had caused sufficient alarm for the Suprema to write to João III of Portugal asking for the arrest and surrender of those who had fled from it and, in the same year, a warrant for three hundred ducats was drawn to be distributed among the inquisitors and officials of the Inquisition of Galicia. This was followed by a similar payment in 1528, showing that the tribunal was not self-sustaining.[1307] Apparently the harvest was scanty and the tribunal was allowed to lapse, until the scare about Protestantism called attention to the ports of the North-west as affording ingress to heretics and their books, for we hear nothing more about it until 1562, when Philip II, in letters of June 2nd and 26th informs the governor and officials of Galicia that Valdés had despatched Dr. Quixano there as inquisitor; they are no longer to prosecute cases of heresy as they have been doing but are to lend him all aid and favor and are to allow him to dispose as he pleases of the seats in his public functions, without disputes as to precedence. In 1566 we hear of Bartolomé de Leon as receiver there, which would indicate that it was at work and was making collections.[1308] Still, it had a struggle for existence, for it was discontinued early in 1568, but it was re-established within a few years, if Llorente is correct in saying that its first auto de fe was celebrated in 1573. A letter of Dr. Alva, its inquisitor, October 31, 1577, speaks of having, in the previous year, sentenced Guillaume le Meunier, he being the only inquisitor, with the advice of a single consultor, showing that the tribunal was sparingly equipped.[1309] In later years it became one of the active tribunals of the kingdom. Its district comprised Coruña, Pontevedro, Orense and Lugo.

GRANADA. Granada, after its capture, was included in the inquisitorial district of Córdova until, in 1526, the tribunal of Jaen was transferred thither.[1310]

GUADALUPE. A temporary tribunal was organized here in 1485 which during its brief existence was exceedingly efficient (see p. 171).

HUESCA. See LÉRIDA.

JACA. A tribunal apparently existed here, which was annexed to Saragossa in 1521.[1311]

JAEN. A tribunal must have been established here about 1483, for two of its inquisitors took part in the assembly of Seville which framed the Instructions of 1484. It seems to have been discontinued, for September 2, 1501, Ferdinand ordered a certain Doña Beatrix of Jaen to abandon her house to the inquisitors sent thither, and to seek other quarters until they should finish the business that took them there. This indicates that only a temporary tribunal was intended but the situation was conveniently central and it was one of those retained by Ximenes in his reorganization of 1509, when he assigned to it the districts of Jaen and Guadix, with Alcaraz, Cazorla and Beas. It was still in existence in 1525, as shown by a royal letter of that date, but in 1526 it was suppressed and united with Córdova, the tribunal being transferred to Granada. In 1547, the official title of the tribunal was Córdoba y Jaen. Rodrigo tells us that it was re-established independently in 1545, but this is evidently an error and the name does not reappear in subsequent lists of tribunals.[1312]

LEON. In 1501 we hear of "inquisitors of the province of Leon," whose district cannot have been confined to that province, for Ferdinand, writing September 2nd to "Cousin Duke" tells him that they have occasion to go to his city of Coria (Extremadura) and asks that they may occupy his house while there. In 1514, also there is allusion to the receiver and alguazil of the Inquisition of Leon.[1313] Apparently the term is a synonym of the tribunal of Valladolid.

LÉRIDA. The provinces of Huesca in Aragon and Lérida and Urgel in Catalonia were united as an inquisitorial district at least as early as 1490, when we hear of "the inquisitors of Huesca and Lérida" taking testimony. In 1498, a letter of Ferdinand, October 8th, announces the transfer of Urgel to Barcelona. Allusions to the tribunal continue to occur in the correspondence of Ferdinand, who, in 1502, called away the inquisitor, as there was so little to do; Saragossa would attend to heresy and only the financial officials need be left. It was not discontinued however. In 1514, there was an attempt to murder the inquisitor, Canon Antist, but in 1519 he is still addressed as inquisitor of Lérida. In this same year, however, Charles V, in a letter of January 22nd, speaks of the tribunals of Huesca, Tarazona and Lérida having been united with that of Saragossa, and, when the people of Huesca complained, in the Córtes of Saragossa, of their citizens being carried away for trial, he ordered, under pain of a thousand florins, that no one should interfere with the jurisdiction of the Saragossa tribunal. October 9th an inspector reported that there was no need of a receiver or other officials there, whereupon they were all dismissed. In 1532, however, the inquisitors of Saragossa undertook to appoint a receiver for Lérida, but were told by the Suprema to cancel it as this was a function of the crown.[1314]

LOGROÑO. In 1570, as we have seen, the tribunal of Calahorra was shifted to Logroño, which, in 1690, defines its territory as the whole kingdom of Navarre, the bishopric of Calahorra and la Calzada, Biscay, Guipuzcoa, Burgos along the mountains of Oca and the sea-coast as far as San Vicente de la Barquera, thus comprising the modern provinces of Navarre, Guipuzcoa, Biscay, Santander, Alava, Logroño and a large part of Burgos.[1315]

LLERENA. Originally Extremadura and Leon were combined. In 1500, Enrique Paez is receiver for the sees of Plasencia, Coria and Badajoz and the Province of Leon. In 1509 Ximenes assigned to Llerena as its district, Plasencia, Coria, Badajoz and the lands of the military Orders, but as late as 1516 it is spoken of as the Inquisition of Leon, Plasencia, Coria and Badajoz. Its original seat was Llerena but, in 1516, it was transferred to Plasencia and the receiver was ordered to sell the houses purchased at Llerena for the prison because others will be wanted for the purpose at Plasencia. It was migratory, however and, in 1520, the people of Ciudad Rodrigo, Coria and Merida were notified that it was about to leave Plasencia and wherever it went accommodations must be provided for lodgement, audience chamber and prisons. Finally it settled permanently at Llerena and, towards the close of the sixteenth century, Zapata speaks of it as the first tribunal of the kingdom, with the widest jurisdiction.[1316]

MADRID. See CORTE.

MEDINA DEL CAMPO. The great importance of Medina del Campo as a centre of trade rendered inevitable its selection as the seat of a tribunal at an early period. In 1486 it was fully furnished with three inquisitors and an assessor, the Abbot of Medina serving as Ordinary. In 1516 we find it incorporated with Valladolid. When the court moved to Valladolid, the buildings of the Inquisition were wanted for its accommodation and the tribunal, in June 1601, was unceremoniously sent to Medina, where Dr. Martin de Bustos was turned out of his house to lodge it. Its stay was short, for in 1605, as we have seen, it was transferred to Burgos and there is no later trace of a tribunal at Medina.[1317]

MURCIA, also known as CARTAGENA. See also CUENCA. Murcia was a seat of one of the early tribunals, comprising the sees of Murcia and Cartagena. Cuenca, which was attached to it in the redistribution by Ximenes in 1509, was separated about 1520. Oran, some time after its conquest by Ximenes, was placed under the jurisdiction of Murcia. The see of Orihuela, although belonging to Valencia, on its suppression about 1510, was united to that of Cartagena and thus fell under the tribunal of Murcia, where it remained after the restoration to episcopal honors in 1564.[1318] The tribunal of Orihuela naturally followed the same course on its suppression.

NAVARRE. After the conquest of Navarre, in 1512, a tribunal was established in Pampeluna, where it did not long remain. Then, for a short period it was transferred to Estella. In 1515 we find it in Tudela, where Ferdinand orders the Archdeacon of Almazan to visit it as it is in much need of reform and, soon afterwards, he asks for a delegation of episcopal power, as Tudela was only a deanery. It was quartered in the convent of San Francisco, to relieve which, in 1518, the Suprema ordered appropriate buildings to be obtained. In 1521 and 1522 there was talk of removing it to Pampeluna; then it was extended over Calahorra; soon afterwards they were separated but finally, in 1540, they were united and so remained. Soon after the transfer to Logroño we find the tribunal describing itself as "en todo el Reyno de Navarra, Obispado de Calahorra y la Calzada y su distrito."[1319]

NAVY. See ARMY.

ORAN. Páramo tells us that when Ximenes conquered Oran he commissioned Fray Yedra as inquisitor there. Llorente places this in 1516 and calls the inquisitor Martin de Baydacar, Ximenes's provisor. At that time, however, there could have been no tribunal there for, July 9, 1516 the Governor Lope Hurtado de Mendoza was ordered to discover and punish those who were impeding the sale of property for the Inquisition, work which would have been entrusted to the tribunal had there been one. By this time it had probably been suppressed and placed under Murcia.[1320]

ORIHUELA. According to Llorente, Ferdinand, Aug. 7, 1507, united the tribunal of the bishopric of Orihuela to Valencia, which would infer its previous existence. It was reorganized in 1515, when Bishop Mercader appointed Pedro de los Rios as inquisitor and he was sent there with a staff of officials, and the magistrates were ordered to provide quarters for "el tiempo que fuere menester." This indicates that the tribunal was not expected to be permanent and it was probably not long afterwards that it was united with Murcia, q. v.[1321]

OSUNA. In 1488, among the presentations to prebends is one of Pedro Sánchez, qualified as Inquisitor of Osuna.[1322] Such tribunal can only have been short-lived and must speedily have been incorporated with that of Seville.

PAMPELUNA. See NAVARRE.

PERPIGNAN. August 9, 1495 an auto de fe was celebrated in Perpignan, but it was held by the inquisitors of Barcelona. In 1518 there was only a commissioner there but, in 1524, there was a tribunal, with Juan Navardu as inquisitor and Antonio Saliteda as secretary. It was not permanent however. In 1566, when de Soto Salazar was sent on his visitation to Barcelona he was instructed to ascertain and report promptly details for the benefit of the inquisitor about to be sent to Perpignan to reside for the future and what officials should be provided for him. It is doubtful whether this intention was carried out; in any event it was but transitory.[1323]

PLASENCIA. See LLERENA.

SANTIAGO. See GALICIA.

SARAGOSSA. Established in 1484, the tribunal gradually absorbed all the minor tribunals, but parted with Teruel to Valencia. See BARBASTRO, CALATAYUD, DAROCA, JACA, LÉRIDA, TARAZONA, TERUEL.

SEGOVIA. Segovia claimed the honor of being among the earliest cities, after Seville, to possess a tribunal, but there was no representative from there among the inquisitors assembled to frame the Instructions of 1484, owing doubtless to the resistance of the bishop Juan Arias Dávila.[1324] One must have been established soon afterwards for, in 1490, the prisoners accused of the murder of the Santo Niño de la Guardia were on trial there when Torquemada transferred them to Avila. (See AVILA.) In the redistribution by Ximenes, in 1509, Segovia was incorporated with Valladolid, but, in 1544 and again in 1599, the inquisitors of Toledo include it in their enumeration of their jurisdictions.[1325]

SIGÜENZA. A tribunal was early established in Sigüenza which must have been busy if we may believe the statement that at an auto de fe in 1494 it relaxed a hundred and forty-nine victims to the secular arm. In 1506, Deza dismissed the officials for the reason that it was about to be united with Toledo, a merger ratified by Ximines in 1509. Toledo neglected it and it was transferred to Cuenca, q. v. In the eighteenth century there would appear to be some kind of subordinate tribunal there, for about 1750, Saragossa, in a report of its personnel, states that one of its five inquisitors is assisting at Sigüenza.[1326]

TARAZONA. A tribunal established here in the early period was merged into that of Saragossa in 1519.[1327]

TARRAGONA. When, in 1643, the inquisitors of Barcelona were ejected, they were, after some delay, sent to open their tribunal at Tarragona, where they remained until the suppression of the Catalan rebellion in 1652.[1328]

TERUEL. In 1485 a tribunal was established in Teruel after some resistance. At what time it was transferred to Valencia does not appear, but a cédula of October 2, 1502 is addressed to the inquisitors of Valencia residing in Teruel and Albarracin, showing that it was then subordinate to Valencia. In 1518 it was discontinued and the district was subjected to the direct jurisdiction of the Valencian tribunal, but Cardinal Adrian, by a provision of Nov. 21st of the same year, transferred it to Saragossa and then, March 3, 1519 restored it to Valencia. This was felt by Aragon as a grievance and, at the Córtes of Monzon, in 1533 it asked that Teruel and Albarracin should be restored to the Saragossa tribunal, but the request was peremptorily refused and they remained subject to Valencia.[1329]

TOLEDO. In 1485 the tribunal of Ciudad Real was transferred to Toledo. At first the limits of its district seem not to be clearly defined for, in 1489 the inquisitors were told to go to Guadalajara and

Ferdinand ordered the local authorities to show them favor and allow them to make arrests. See CORTE, CUENCA, SEGOVIA, SIGÜENZA, VALLADOLID for sundry changes in its district. In 1565 the official designation is the city and archbishopric of Toledo, the city and bishopric of Sigüenza and the bishoprics of Avila and Segovia, which apparently remained permanent, except the detachment of Madrid.[1330]

TORTOSA. For some reason the bishopric of Tortosa, although part of Catalonia, was subject to the tribunal of Valencia. When, in 1697, Vendôme captured Barcelona, the tribunal emigrated to Tortosa and established itself in the Colegio Imperial. Although peace was declared soon afterwards it remained in Tortosa at least until 1700 and presumably stayed until the conclusion of the War of Succession, when it was reinstated in Barcelona in 1715.[1331]

TUDELA. See NAVARRE.

VALENCIA. The old Inquisition of Valencia was reorganized in 1484, and continued to the end. As seen above, it parted with Orihuela to Murcia, obtaining Teruel and Albarracin from Saragossa and Tortosa from Barcelona.

VALLADOLID. A tribunal was assigned to Valladolid in 1485, but did not get into working order until 1488. After this it was suspended to be revived in 1499, as appears from a letter of Isabella, Dec. 24, 1498. The northern provinces of Spain were comparatively free from heresy and Ximenes, in his reorganization of 1509, assigned to Valladolid the enormous district comprising the sees of Burgos, Osma, Palencia, Segovia, Avila, Salamanca, Zamora, Leon, Oviedo and Astorga and the abbeys of Valladolid, Medina del Campo and Sahagun. In 1516 the enumeration is the same except the omission of Zamora and the addition of Ciudad Rodrigo and Calahorra. Roughly speaking, it may be assumed to comprise the whole of the provinces of Old Castile, Leon and Asturias. Valdés, August 8, 1560, repeated April 12, 1562 made over the whole of this to Toledo, but the grant can only have been temporary for, in 1565 the Toledan inquisitors described themselves as of the city and archbishoprics of Toledo, the city and bishopric of Sigüenza, with the bishoprics of Avila and Segovia, and in 1579 we find the inquisitors of Valladolid styling themselves inquisitors of the kingdoms of Castile and Leon and the principality of Asturias. This enormous district it continued to retain, subject to the easternmost portion detached to Calahorra or Logroño and to its translation in 1601 to Medina del Campo and thence to Burgos, from which it returned to Valladolid, probably about 1630.[1332]

XERES. In 1495, Rodrigo Lucero is described as Inquisitor of Xeres. In 1499 the sovereigns appointed Alonso de Guevara Inquisitor of Cadiz and Xeres. The tribunal continued there for some time. In 1515 Ferdinand alludes to Luis de Riba Martin "our late receiver in the Inquisition of Xeres," who in dying had left to the treasury a legacy of 30,000 mrs. for the relief of his conscience.[1333] I have met no later reference to it and probably it was soon afterwards merged into the tribunal of Seville.

II. - LIST OF INQUISITORS-GENERAL

1483. Thomás de Torquemada. Appointed in 1483. Died Sept. 16, 1498.
1491. Miguel de Morillo is also inquisitor-general in 1491.

Additional Inquisitors-general, Appointed in 1494.
1494. Martin Ponce de Leon, Archbishop of Messina. Died in 1500.
Iñigo Manrique, Bishop of Córdova. Died March 4, 1496.
Francisco Sánchez de la Fuente, Bishop of Avila. Died Sept., 1498.
Alonso Suárez de Fuentelsaz, Bishop of Jaen. Resigned in 1504. Died Nov. 5, 1520.
1498. Diego Deza, Archbishop of Seville. Commissioned Nov. 24,
1498, for Castile, Leon and Granada, and Sept. 1, 1499, for all Spain. Resigned in 1507. Died July 9, 1523.

Separation of Inquisitions of Castile and Aragon.

Castile.
1507. Francisco Ximenes de Cisneros, Cardinal and Archbishop of Toledo. Commissioned June 5, 1507. Died Nov. 8, 1517.

Aragon.
1507. Juan Enguera, Bishop of Vich (of Lérida in 1511). Commissioned June 6, 1507. Died Feb. 14, 1513.
1513. Luis Mercader, Bishop of Tortosa. Commissioned July 15, 1513. Died June 1, 1516.
Fray Juan Pedro de Poul, Dominican Provincial of Aragon, also commissioned by Leo X. Died in 1516.

1516. Adrian of Utrecht, Cardinal and Bishop of Tortosa. Commissioned Nov. 14, 1516.

Reunion of Inquisitions of Castile and Aragon.
1518. Cardinal Adrian of Utrecht. Commissioned March 14, 1518. Elected to papacy Jan. 9, 1522. Continued to act until his departure for Rome from Tarragona Aug. 4, 1522.
1523. Alfonso Manrique, Cardinal and Archbishop of Seville. Commissioned Sept. 10, 1523. Died Sept. 28, 1538.
1539. Juan Pardo de Tavera, Cardinal and Archbishop of Toledo. Appointed June 10, 1539. Commissioned Nov. 7, 1539. Took possession Dec. 7, 1539. Died Aug. 1, 1545.
1546. Francisco García de Loaysa, Archbishop of Seville. Commissioned Feb. 18, 1546. Took possession March 29, 1546. Died April 22, 1546.
1547. Fernando Valdés, Archbishop of Seville. Commissioned Jan. 20,
1547. Took possession Feb. 19, 1547. Resigned in 1566. Died Dec. 9, 1568.
1566. Diego Espinosa, Cardinal and Bishop of Sigüenza. Commissioned Sept. 8, 1566. Took possession Dec. 4, 1566. Died Sept. 15, 1572.
1572. Pedro Ponce de Leon y Córdova, Bishop of Plasencia. Commissioned Dec. 7, 1572. Did not take possession; his brief arrived four hours after his death, Jan. 17, 1573.
1573. Gaspar de Quiroga, Cardinal and Archbishop of Toledo. Commissioned April 20, 1573. Took possession May 28, 1573. Died Nov. 12, 1594.
1595. Gerónimo Manrique de Lara, Bishop of Avila. Commissioned Aug. 1, 1595. Died Nov. 1, 1595.
1596. Pedro de Portocarrero, Bishop of Cuenca. Commissioned Jan. 1, 1596. Resigned in 1599. Died Sept. 20, 1600.
1599. Fernando Niño de Guevara, Cardinal and Archbishop of Seville. Commissioned Aug. 11, 1599. Took possession Dec. 23, 1599. Resigned in 1602. Died Jan. 1, 1609.
1602. Juan de Zuñiga, Bishop of Cartagena. Commissioned July 29, 1602. Died Dec. 20, 1602.
1603. Juan Bautista Acevedo, Royal Confessor and Patriarch of the Indies. Commissioned Jan. 20, 1603. Died July 8, 1608.
1608. Bernardo de Sandoval y Roxas, Cardinal and Archbishop of Toledo. Commissioned Sept. 12, 1608. Died Dec. 7, 1618.
1619. Luis de Aliaga, Royal Confessor. Commissioned Jan. 4, 1619. Resigned in 1621. Died Dec. 3, 1626.
1622. Andrés Pacheco, Bishop of Cuenca. Commissioned Feb. 12, 1622. Died April 7, 1626.
1627. Antonio de Zapata, Cardinal and Archbishop of Burgos, 1600-1605. Commissioned Jan. 30, 1627. Resigned in 1632. Died April 23, 1635.
1632. Antonio de Sotomayor, Royal Confessor and Archbishop of Damascus. Commissioned July 17, 1632. Resigned June 21, 1643. Died in 1648.
1643. Diego de Arce y Reynoso, Bishop of Plasencia. Commissioned Sept. 18, 1643. Took possession Nov. 14, 1643. Died June 20, 1665.
1665. Pascual de Aragon, Archbishop of Toledo. A document of Oct. 26, 1665, is drafted in his name. Resigned soon afterwards.
1666. Juan Everardo Nithardo, Royal Confessor and Cardinal. Commissioned Oct. 15, 1666. Banished Feb. 25, 1669, as ambassador to Rome. Died in 1681.
1669. Diego Sarmiento de Valladares, Bishop of Plasencia. Commissioned Sept. 15, 1669. Died Jan. 29, 1695.
1695. Juan Thomás de Rocaberti, Archbishop of Valencia. Commissioned Aug. 2, 1695. Died June 13, 1699.
1699. Alfonso Fernández de Córdova y Aguilar. Died Sept. 19, 1699, before the arrival of his brief.
1699. Balthasar de Mendoza y Sandoval, Bishop of Segovia. Commissioned Oct. 31, 1699. Resigned in 1705. Died Nov. 4, 1727.
1705. Vidal Marin, Bishop of Ceuta. Commissioned March 24, 1705. Died March 10, 1709.
1709. Antonio Ybañez de la Riva-Herrera, Archbishop of Saragossa. Commissioned April 5, 1709. Died Sept. 3, 1710.
1711. Francesco Giudice, Cardinal. Commissioned June 11, 1711. Resigned in 1716. Died Oct. 10, 1725.
1715. Felipe Antonio Gil de Taboada. Commissioned Feb. 28, 1715. Did not serve.
1717. Josef de Molines. Proclaimed Jan. 9, 1717, while in Rome. Detained in Milan by the Austrians and died there.
Juan de Arzamendi. Died without serving.
1720. Diego de Astorga y Cespedes, Bishop of Barcelona. Commissioned March 26, 1720. Resigned in 1720. Died Feb. 9, 1724.

1720. Juan de Camargo, Bishop of Pampeluna. Commissioned July 18, 1720. Died May 24, 1733.

1733. Andrés de Orbe y Larreategui, Archbishop of Valencia. Commissioned July 28, 1733. Died Aug. 4, 1740.

1742. Manuel Isidro Manrique de Lara, Archbishop of Santiago. Commissioned Jan. 1, 1742. Died Jan. 10, 1746.

1746. Francisco Pérez de Prado y Cuesta, Bishop of Teruel. Appointed July 26, 1746. Commissioned Aug. 22, 1746. Died in July, 1755.

1755. Manuel Quintano Bonifaz, Archbishop of Pharsalia. Commissioned Aug. 11, 1755. Resigned in 1774. Died Dec. 18, 1775.

1775. Felipe Beltran, Bishop of Salamanca. Appointed Dec. 27, 1774. Commissioned Feb. 27, 1775. Took possession May 5, 1775. Died Nov. 30, 1783.

1784. Agustin Rubin de Cevallos, Bishop of Jaen. Appointed Jan. 23, 1784. Commissioned Feb. 17, 1784. Took possession June 7, 1784. Died Feb. 8, 1793.

1793. Manuel Abad y la Sierra, Archbishop of Selimbria. Took possession May 11, 1793. Resigned in 1794. Died Jan. 12, 1806.

1794. Francisco Antonio de Lorenzana, Archbishop of Toledo. Took possession Sept. 12, 1794. Resigned in 1797. Died April 17, 1804.

1798. Ramon Josef de Arce y Reynoso, Archbishop of Saragossa. Resigned March 22, 1808. Died in Paris, Feb. 16, 1814.

1814. Xavier Mier y Campillo, Bishop of Almería. Took possession in August, 1814. In a series of documents he ceases to appear about June, 1818, and for some months the Suprema acts as in a vacancy.

1818. Gerónimo Castellon y Salas, Bishop of Tarazona. The earliest document in which I have met his signature is dated Oct. 21, 1818. He had no successor and died April 20, 1835.

III - SPANISH COINAGE

The question of values has significance in so many of the operations of the Inquisition that an outline of the successive mintages of Spain becomes almost a necessity. The subject is complicated, after the middle of the sixteenth century, by the progressive but fluctuating depreciation in the moneda de vellón, or base coinage, which became practically the standard of value in all transactions.

The monetary unit of Castile was the maravedí, anciently a gold coin of value but, in the fifteenth century, diminished to a fraction of its former estimation. A declaration of Ferdinand and Isabella in 1503 says that formerly the silver real was equal to 3 maravedís, but now it is worth 34.[1334]

The unit of weight was the marc, or half-pound, of 8 ounces or 4608 grains. The intermediate weights were the ochavo of 72 grains, the adarme of 36 and the tomin of 12. These were applicable to all the precious metals but, up to 1731, the marc of gold was reckoned to contain 50 castellanos of 8 tomines, making 4800 grains, whereby the grain was reduced 1/25.

The standard of fineness was fixed, by Ferdinand and Isabella, for gold at 23-3/4 carats, but was reduced by Charles V to 22 carats, at which it remained. For silver the standard maintained since the fourteenth century was known as once dineros cuatro granos (pure silver being doce dineros) equivalent to .925 fine. In 1709 Philip V reduced it to once dineros or .91667, and in some mintages even lower.

GOLD COINS. When Ferdinand and Isabella revised the coinage, in 1497, they ordered the marc to be worked into 65-1/3 excelentes de la granada. This coin was worth 374 maravedís and thus was practically the same as the ducat or escudo which was rated at 374. There were also the dobla alfonsi or castellano or peso de oro, equal to 485, the dobla de la banda to 365, the florin to 265. Thus the ducat, which was the coin most frequently quoted, was equivalent to 11 silver reales. The ratio between gold and silver fluctuated between 7 and 8 to 1.

In 1537 Charles V ordered coronas and escudos, 22 carats fine to be worked 68 to the marc and to be worth 330 maravedís, which he says was the weight and fineness of the best crowns of Italy and France. With the progressive depreciation in the value of silver, the coinage law of Philip II in 1566 raised the escudo from 330 mrs. to 400. The old ducats were to be current at 429 mrs., the castellanos at 544. The tendency of silver continued downward and in 1609 Philip III permitted the escudo to pass for 440 mrs., threatening three years' exile and a fine of 500 ducats for asking or receiving more. In 1612 he allowed the castellano in bullion to be sold for 576 mrs. under the same penalties for exceeding it. The escudo or crown remained the standard gold coin. In 1642 it was raised to 550 mrs.; in 1643 to 612 and then reduced to 510 owing to variations in the silver and vellón coinage. In 1651 it is rated at 16 silver reales, in 1652 at 14, in 1686 at 15, but with a new coinage of lighter weight silver it was raised to 19, and the doblon, or piece of 2 escudos, to 40 reales. For larger transactions multiples of the escudo were struck, known as doblones de a dos, de a cuatro and de a ocho, containing respectively 2, 4 and 8 escudos. The latter, which became popularly known as the Spanish doubloon, were rated in 1726 at 18 pesos or pieces of eight silver reales, in 1728 at 16, in 1737 at 15 and in 1779 at 16 again, the doubloon and the peso being virtually of the same weight, each a fraction under an ounce. In 1738, to supply the lack of silver money there were coined half-crowns of gold, worth in vellón 18 reales 28 mrs. This fraction was troublesome and, in 1742, the weight was changed to correspond with 20 reales, and the coins became known as veintenos or escuditos.

SILVER COINS. The silver unit was the real, which, under the coinage laws of Ferdinand and Isabella, was worked 67 to the silver marc, of 11 dineros 4 grains fine (.925), worth 34 maravedís. It long continued of this standard but, in the financial mismanagement under Philip IV, the weight was reduced by ordering the marc worked into 83 reales and 1 quartillo (83-1/4 reales), the old coinage in circulation being advanced 25 per cent. in value by making the peso equivalent to 10 reales instead of 8, but as this failed to afford the expected relief it was suspended in 1643, to be again tried in 1684 when the real was reduced to 84 to the marc, and the old coinage was rated at 10 to 8 of the new. In 1709 we first hear of the peseta, as a name applied to the French coin introduced by the War of Succession, rated at 2 reales, and subsequently used to denote the double real of Spanish mintage. At the same time the standard was reduced to 11 dineros or .91667 fine. During the subsequent years of the reign of Philip V the variations in the silver coinage were numerous and perplexing. The peso, escudo de plata, or piece of 8 reales, was the leading coin, and in 1726 it was ordered that it, whether minted in the Indies or in Spain, should be current for 9-1/2 reales, and, as this did not bring it to an equivalent with gold, in 1728 it was declared equal to 10 reales. This however was now confined to the mintage of the Indies, which came to be known as plata nacional; the small coinage of the Spanish mints was termed provincial and was allowed to remain current at a discount of 20 per cent. It was 77 reales to the marc and the fineness was only 10 dineros, reduced in 1728 to 9 dineros, 22 grains or .798 fine, rendering it in reality only about three-quarters the value of the standard. There were thus two entirely distinct silver currencies coexistent, and to these was added a third, popularly known as Marias--"plata nueva que vulgarmente se llaman Marías"--which was called in by decree of April 27, 1728, but which was still in circulation in 1736. Under these circumstances considerable circumlocution was necessary when quoting sums in silver to define the exact kind of coin meant as, for instance, in the coinage law of July 16, 1730, we are told that the allowance for expenses to the official known as the Fiel, was "un real de plata provincial, valor de 16 quartos de vellón." In fact, as we shall see, the debased coinage known as vellón had become the real standard of financial transactions.

In the later periods it will simplify the appreciation of amounts recorded to remind the reader that the peso, or piece of 8 reales, is the modern dollar, and the real, or one-eighth of this, is the coin familiarly known of old in various parts of the United States as the "bit," the "elevenpenny bit" shortened to "levy," the ninepence or the shilling. The maravedí was 1/34 of this, or about 3/8 of one cent.

In the colonies there is frequent allusion to the peso ensayado as distinguished from the peso de a ocho, which I gather to be a piece worth 400 maravedís, or nearly 11-3/4 reales--a little more than a ducat.

VELLON COINAGE. The debased coinage known as vellón was an alloy of silver and copper, which proved the source of unutterable confusion in Spanish finance. As we find it prescribed by Ferdinand and Isabella in 1497, it is merely a token coin convenient for small transactions, consisting of 7 grains of silver to the marc of copper, worked into 192 blancas, the blanca being one-half of the maravedí. Complaints were made that it was exported at a profit, so that it became scarce, and in 1552 Charles V, to remedy this, reduced the silver to 5 grains. The extravagant expenditures of Philip II rendered him eager to clutch at any expedient to relieve immediate necessities and, in 1566, he adopted the unfortunate device of issuing a moneda de vellón rica, with 2-1/2 dineros, 2 grains (98 grains) of silver to the marc of copper, to be worked into quartillos, 80 to the marc (worth 1/4 real or 8-1/2 maravedís), into quartos, 170 to the marc (worth 4 maravedís) and medios quartos, 340 to the marc (worth 2 maravedís). The blancas or half maravedís, were retained, but the silver in them was reduced to 4 grains to the marc, worked into 220 pieces. Although there do not appear ever to have been larger coins of vellón issued than those authorized by Philip II the flood of this inferior money supplanted the precious metals. It became the basis of all internal transactions and the precious metals were reduced virtually to the position of commodities. There was a restamping of this coinage in 1602, in which the silver was omitted, put into forced circulation at a value of 7 to 2. With all the power of Spain, backed by the treasures of the New World and wielded by an autocratic monarchy, it was impossible to maintain so vicious and artificial a currency at par, and there followed, during the seventeenth century, a series of the most desperate attempts to remedy the evils which were crippling the commerce and industry of the nation.[1335] In 1619 there was a solemn promise made that no more of the pernicious stuff should be issued for twenty years--a promise only made to be broken and renewed in 1632. In 1625, under the severest penalties, the premium on gold and silver was limited to 10 per cent., and in 1628 the nominal value was reduced one-half, but in 1636 the permissible premium on silver was recognized as 25 per cent., immediately after which the vellón coinage was restamped and trebled in value. In 1640 the premium was allowed to be 28 per cent. and in 1641 there was another restamping and the value was doubled, followed by recognizing the premium as 50 per cent. In some accounts before me of the salaries and expenses of the Supreme Council of the Inquisition, not dated, but evidently belonging to this period, the figures set down are increased when added, in one case by 28 per cent. and in another by 50, to adjust them to the currency in which they were expected to be paid. In other statements some items are specified as payable in vellón and others in plata. In the effort to bring the vellón to par in 1642, it was suddenly reduced to one-sixth of its current value and then, in 1643, it was raised four-fold. This resulted, in 1647, in a premium of 25 per cent., but when, in 1651, it was again restamped and restored to the value which it bore prior to 1642, the premium rose to 50 per cent. In June, 1652, another attempt was made to reduce it to one-fourth, but this seems to have been a failure and in November the edict was suspended. In 1660 its further issue was suspended and the experiment was again tried of an alloy containing 20 grains of silver to the marc, or about 1/230, which became known as moneda de molino de vellón ligado. This was so unsuccessful that, in 1664, its nominal value was reduced one-half and all other vellón currency was prohibited, while in February, 1680, a still further reduction of 75 per cent. in its value was ordered and in May its use was forbidden, it was declared to have no value as currency, and the premium of 50 per cent. was permitted as against other vellón coins, which had still continued in circulation. This lasted for four years, when in 1684 the moneda de molino was restored to circulation with a nominal value double that of the last reduction.[1336] With the eighteenth century the pretence of alloying copper with a fraction of silver was abandoned. In 1718 a pure copper coinage was issued and by this time the premium on specie recognized by law had advanced to nearly 100 per cent. In spite of the prohibitions to ask or receive more than this, people were forced to pay more. Traders kept the copper coinage tied up in bags representing the larger coins and refused to furnish the latter except at an advance.[1337] The premium gradually rose until, in 1737, the real de plata provincial was recognized legally as worth 2 reales de vellón and the real de plata nacional as worth 2-1/2. Although there were no coined reales de vellón, they were the standard money of account on which all transactions were based. In the laws regulating the mints the salaries of the officials are always stated in vellón. Thus, in 1718, the superintendent of the mint of Madrid has 24,000 reales de vellón, the treasurer 16,000, and so forth. In 1728 the superintendent is allowed 500 escudos de vellón, the contador 400, etc. In 1730 it is provided that the sum of 120,000 reales de vellón is to be placed in the hands of the treasurer for current expenses and he is to give security in 20,000 ducados de vellón on unencumbered real estate. From this it follows that, when the kind of coin is not specified, there may be some difficulty in estimating the value of a sum of money mentioned. The difference between silver and vellón went on increasing. In 1772, when a new coinage of gold and silver was issued, the gold escudo, worth 16 reales de plata, was declared to be worth 37-1/2 reales de vellón.

With the Revolution the old coinage passed away and was replaced by the decimal system, the peseta and céntimo being equivalent to the French franc and centime. Yet still prices continue to be quoted in reales, which are now rated at 25 céntimos, or about 5 cents of American money.

Nothing is more difficult than to ascertain accurately the variation in the purchasing power of money, but perhaps the price of labor affords the most trustworthy standard. In the fifteenth century this would seem to have been about 6 maravedís a day. In the eighteenth, common laborers employed in the mints received 3-1/2 reales de vellón per diem, while those in more confidential positions such as watchmen were paid 6.[1338]

***

As a matter of course the kingdoms of the Crown of Aragon had their independent systems of coinage, which were based on the old divisions of the marc, almost everywhere prevalent, of libras, sueldos and dineros, or pounds, shillings and pence, there being 20 sueldos to the libra and 12 dineros to the sueldo. In the documents of the early period there are frequent fluctuations in the relations between these coins and the Castilian system, but as a rule there were reckoned 20 Aragonese sueldos to the ducat, which therefore was equivalent to the libra. In Catalonia the sueldo barcelonense was 24 to the ducat, and there was also a coin known as morabatin, equal to 9 sueldos. Unification of currency throughout the monarchy was a desirable object, long frustrated by the stubborn particularism of the provinces. It was especially difficult to bring about in Catalonia, where the vellón coinage had been largely diluted by the allies during their long occupation of the principality in the War of Succession. An edict of 1733 informs us that there were 24 dineros to the Catalan real, but most of those in circulation of the coinage of 1653 had been restamped by the allies to double their nominal value. They had also coined dinerillos Catalanes with the same alloy of silver as the mintage of 1653, but with only half the weight, yet circulated at the full value. The edict denounces the dinerillos of both Aragon and Catalonia as an intolerable abuse and with superfluous emphasis orders their use to be abandoned, immediately in Aragon and in Catalonia as soon as sufficient money of vellón can be coined to take their place. The effort was futile for another edict of 1737 assimilates the dinerillo of Aragon and

Valencia to the Castilian ochavo, or piece of 2 maravedís, and the dinerillo of Catalonia to 1 maravedí. In 1743, in consequence of disputes arising between troops quartered in Catalonia and the peasants, it was ordered that the vellón money of Castile should circulate freely in Aragon, Catalonia and Majorca. As late as 1772 an edict calls in the local small coinage of Valencia and orders it replaced with Castilian money, but this was so unsuccessful that it was followed, in 1777, with one confining the use of these coins to Valencia and forbidding their circulation elsewhere. When the unification of the currency occurred does not clearly appear, but it probably was not until the revision of the monetary system in the present century.

    The old cruzado of Portugal, to which reference sometimes occurs, was virtually the same as the Spanish ducat.

DOCUMENTS

I - LETTER OF KING FERDINAND TO THE INQUISITOR-GENERAL TORQUEMADA, July 22, 1486.

(Archivo General de la Corona de Aragon, Registro 3684, fol. 102).
EL REY.

Devoto padre Prior. Vuestra carta vi e las otras de los otros inquisidores de Çaragoca y el memorial que vos embiaron. A la carta vuestra con otra de mi mano vos respondo e a las de los inquisidores e mandado responder e será la carta con la presente. E quanto a lo del memorial ó instruccion que escriben sobre lo que Don Juan de Ribera no faze la guerra fasta haber carta de mano mia e de la serenisima reina mi muy cara e muy amada mujer luego le ascribieramos salvo porque toda la gente suya havemos mandado venir para donde himos y sin gente ninguna cosa podria hazer. Plazera a nuestro senyor que con nuestra ida se remediará presto e volverse ha la gente a la frontera de Navarra e luego mandaremos a Don Juan que apriete a los de Tudela en guisa que fagan la razon. Quanto a lo que scriven en el tercero capitulo de la limosna que les parece se debe facer de sus bienes a los pobres penitenciados imponiendolos alguna pecuniaria sentencia, porque los conversos de aquella ciudad son muy conocidos y podria ser que allá les dieren a entender una cosa por otra me parece que les debeis escribir que envien relacion de quien son, specificando los nombres de cada uno e que bienes tienen e quantas sentencias e que penitencia les parece que se debe dar a todos e a cada uno dellos, porque, sabida la relacion de todo ello se podrá mejor determinar lo que en ello se debe facer. Quanto a la particion de los bienes dentre marido e muger quando el uno es sentenciado y el otro se falla inmune porque es cosa que esta en drecho y en fuero del reino me parece que lo debeis mandar veer a micer Ponce y otros letrados y que sea menester y mas convenga. Quanto al cinqueno capitulo que fabla de las carceles perpetuas es muy gran razon que se faga e yo enbio a mandar al receptor que las faga. Quanto al sexto capitulo en que dicen que se embie a mandar que se ha de dar a los encarcerados para su mantenemiento me parece escriban aca su parecer y entonce sobrello podremos determinar lo que paresca mas razonable. Quanto al seteno que dicen que han tomado un hombre para tormentar porque dicen que los nuncios no lo quieren facer ni fallan quien lo faga, me parece que por scusar tantos salarios devrian echar uno de los nuncios e que la persona que han tomado para tormentar sirviere de nuncio e se le diese el mismo salario e puesto que esto no se puede facer se debe limitar el salario, porque seiscientos sueldos es muy sobrado salario. Quanto al ocheno capitulo en que fabla del salario de Don Ramon de Mur es justa cosa que pues que bien sirve sea muy bien pagado, e se le den dos mil sueldos de salario. Quanto al noveno capitulo que fabla de los porteros estoy maravillado que pagando tan gran salario como se pagó al aguacil allende aquello se hayan de pagar porteros que acá como sabeis todo esta a cargo del aguacil. Debeis les mucho encargar a los inquisidores que lo miren porque se asi no lo fazen mas montarán los salarios que proceda de la inquisicion. Quanto al deceno capitulo que dice que han de facer e fazen un lugarteniente de aguacil para enviar de fuera, parece que se les debe escribir que en las cosas que buenamente escusar se pudieren lo deben escusar, faciendo ir a ello al alguacil principal, pero no pudiendo ir el fagase un lugarteniente como lo acostumbran de facer, pero sea el salario lo menos que ser pueda porque bien mirado son muy excesivos los salarios que se pagan a la inquisicion. En lo que dicen que tengo fecha merced de los bienes de Pedro de Urrea saben poco en la verdad porque es cierto que de aquellos ni de otros tengo fecha merced a nadie. Quanto al onceno capitulo en que demandan carta de marca e represalia para Tudela por el negocio de Martin de Santangel ha de preceder carta requisitoria la qual debeis mandar ordenar allá a micer Ponte y enviandola aca luego se despachará. En el dozeno esta ya respondido y quanto a lo que escriben en el treceno que no han egecutado los matadores de maestre Epila pluguierame mucho que vos escribieran las causas porque. Quanto al catorceno capitulo en que escriben que seria bueno que fuere maestro Crespo a entender en la inquisicion con el abad de Barbastro, buen hombre es sin duda e pareceme bien que vaya e asimismo me parece bien micer Tristan de la Porta para que vaya a fazer assesor como lo escriben en el quatorceno capitulo que buen letrado es e hombre de buena fama. En el dezeseyseno e ultimo demandan un escribano para los bienes que se han de litigar por justicia y lo han de determinar ellos como jueces. Verdaderamente demandan tantos oficiales y acrecentamiento de tantos salarios que es menester que se mire mucho en ello, mayormente que es cierto segun Camanyas me ha dicho que los escribanos de la inquisicion sienten a injuria que otro entiende en el dicho negocio sino ellos, mayormente que podrian poner en ello criado suyo de quien se confien. Si en todo lo sobredicho o en algo dello vos parece otra cosa vedlo alla y escrivitme vuestro parecer porque sobre todo se mire e se faga lo mejor.

Camanyas me dijo como vos habia fablado sobre los Judios de Teruel que les han mandado ir dentro de termino de tres meses e que dize se fizo con voluntad mia. Essa es la verdad que assi me plugo e me plaze dello e nunca será de otro parecer; verdad es que en lo del tiempo tienen razon porque creo que en tampoco tiempo no podrian pagar y cobrar deudas maiormente teniendo como tienen censales, ni podrian vender las casas y heredamientos que tienen e por esso sera bien si asi a vos paresciere que se les den otros seis meses de tiempo sobre los tres que los inquisidores han dado porque de aquellos segun dicen ha pasado ya buena parte. Vedlo vos e si os paresciere bien asi fagase. E por agora no ocurre otro que escrivir salvo que vos ruego mucho que de la salut de vuestra persona continuamente me fagais sabidor. Del Viso á XXII de julio de LXXXVI años. Yo el Rey. Por mandado del Rey. Camanyas.

II - EDICT OF MAY 30, 1492, REGULATING SETTLEMENTS WITH THE EXPELLED JEWS.

(Biblioteca Nacional de España, Seccion de MSS., Dd, 108, fol. 126).

Don Fernando et Doña Isabel, por la gracia de Dios Rey et Reyna de Castilla, etc.

Al Nuestro Justicia Maior et a los de nuestro Consejo et oydores de la nuestra Audiencia, Alcalles et otras Justicias de la nuestra Casa et Corte et Chancelleria e a los Corregidores e Assistentes, Alcalles, Merinos, Alguaciles et otras Justicias qualesquier de las Cibdades e Villas e Logares de los nuestros Reynos e Señorios et a cada uno et qualquier de vos a quien esta nuestra Carta fuere mostrada o su traslado signado de escrivano publico, Salud e gracia. Bien savedes et deveis saber como nos por algunas justas cabsas que a ello nos movieron complideras al servicio de Dios e nuestro e bien e pro comun de nuestros Reynos e nuestros subditos e naturales dellos, mandamos por nuestras cartas firmadas de nuestros nombres et selladas con nuestro sello, que todos los Judios et moradores y estantes en los dichos nuestros Reynos e Señorios salgan dellos de aqui ha en fin del mes de Jullio primero que viene deste presente año de la Data desta nuestra carta, so ciertas penas contenidas en las dichas nuestras Cartas. Agora por parte de algunas aljamas de los dichos Judios e personas particulares dellos nos es fecha relacion que ellos deven e son obligados a dar e pagar algunas contias de maravedises et otras cosas ha algunas personas Christianas e Moros nuestros subditos e naturales et ellos et otras personas les deven a ellos otras quantias de maravedises et otras cosas et que ellos no tienen con que pagar salbo con las dichas debdas et algunas bienes raices, et que si aquellos e las dichas debdas non les oviesen de recebir en pago por su justo precio et valor que recebirian agravio et daño, et nos fue suplicado que cerca de ello les mandasemos proveer de remedio como la nuestra merced fuese. Et porque nuestra merced e voluntad es que lo que asi mandamos cerca de salir de los dichos Judios se cumpla en el dicho termino et en ello non se ponga impedimento alguno, tovimoslo por bien. Por que vos mandamos a todos et a cada uno de vos en nuestros logares e jurisdicciones que luego que con esta nuestra carta o con el dicho su traslado signado como dicho es, fueredes requeridos, la qual mandamos que vos sea notificada dentro de veinte dias primeros siguientes de la data della fagais pregonar publicamente por ante escrivano publico por las Plazas e Mercados e otros logares acostumbrados que todos los Christianos e Moros a quien deven los dichos Judios qualesquier debdas, o Judios a quien devan Christianos o Moros otras debdas parescan et se presenten ante vos las dichas Justicias donde biben los deudores a pedir e liquidar et averiguar las debdas et otras abciones que los unos deban a los otros, las quales liquides e averigues et llamadas et oidas las partes, procediendo en la liquidacion simplemente et de plano sin estrepitu y figura de juicio, solamente sabida la verdad, por manera que todas las dichas debdas et abciones sean liquidadas et averiguadas e sentenciadas fasta mediado el dicho mes de Jullio primero que viene y las que hallardes que los plazos a que se han de pagar fueren llegados o llegaren al dicho termino, las hagais luego dar e pagar a las partes que lo ovieren de aver por las personas que las deven, et los Judios que non tovieren bienes muebles et semovientes para pagar lo que asi devieren castigades et apremiedes et costringades a los dichos Christianos e Moros a que tomen et resciban en pago de sus debdas otras debdas liquidadas con las partes que se deven a los Judios por Christianos o Moros, o en bienes rayces apreciados por su justo precio e valor por vos las dichas

Justicias con dos buenas personas que en ello entiendan et con tanto que los dichos Vienes rayces que asi se dieren en pago apreciados sean en lugares donde son vezinos et abitantes las personas a quien se deven las dichas debdas. Et en las debdas que se debieren por los dichos Judios que non llegaren los plazos durante el dicho termino de fasta mediado el dicho mes de Jullio, den seguridad dellas a vista de vos las dichas Justicias para las pagar a los plazos que las devieren et sinon dieren la dicha seguridad paguen luego las tales debdas, pues se han de ir et despues non avrian contra quien aver recurso. Et en quanto a las debdas que se deben a los dichos Judios por Christianos o Moros que non fueren llegados los plazos nin llegaren dentro del dicho termino, hazed que quede averiguado e liquidado segund dicho es para que puedan dexar los dichos Judios sus procuradores Christianos o Moros o persona en quien cedieren o traspasasen las tales debdas o otros sus bienes et abciones para que las cobren a los plazos et segund et en la manera que los debdores les estavan et fueron obligados para la qual todo que dicho es con todas sus incidencias et dependencias vos damos poder complido, lo qual todo haced et complid sin embargo de qualesquier leyes, fueros e derechos e ordenamientos que en contrario desto sean, con las quales et con cada una dellas dispensamos et las derogamos en quanto a esto atañe, quedando en su fuerza et vigor para delante. Et los unos nin los otros non fagades nin fagan endeal por alguna manera so pena de la nuestra merced et de diez mill maravedises para la nuestra camara al que lo contrario fisiese. Et demas mandamos al ome que les esta nuestra carta mostrare que los emplase que parescan ante nos en la nuestra Corte doquier que nos seamos del dia que los emplasasse fasta quince dias primeros siguientes so la dicha pena so la qual mandamos a qualquier escrivano publico que para esto fuere llamado que dende al que se la mostrare testimonio signado con su signo porque nos sepamos en como se cumple nuestro mandado. Dada en la Ciudad de Cordova a treinte dias del mes de Mayo, año del nascimiento de nuestro Salvador Jesu Christo de mill e quatrocientos e noventa e dos años.--Yo el Rey.--Yo la Reina.--Yo Ferrand Alvarez de Toledo, Secretario del Rey e de la Reyna nuestros señores la fize escrivir por su mandado.--En la forma acordada, Rodericus Dottor.--Registrada, Perez Francisco de Madrid, Chanciller.

(Hallase original en el Archivo de la Ciudad de Toledo).

III - TORQUEMADA'S INSTRUCTIONS TO INQUISITORS, Dec., 1484.[1339]

(Archivo General de Simancas, Consejo de la Inquisicion, Libro 933).

Otras Capitulaciones por el Reverendo Señor Padre Prior de Santa Cruz hechas por sus Altezas é confirmadas.

Por mandado de los serenisimos rey é reyna nuestros señores yo el prior de santa cruz, confesor de sus altezas, inquisidor general por la abtoridad apostolica en los reynos de Castilla é de Aragon, hordené los articulos siguientes cerca de algunas cosas tocantes á la sancta inquisicion é á sus ministros é oficiales los quales dichos capitulos mandan sus altezas que se guarden é cumplan é yo de parte de sus altezas é por la abtoridad susodicha asi lo mando é son las que se siguen.

1. Primeramente que en cada partido donde fuere necesario poner inquisicion é en los que agora la hay é se facen, aya dos inquisidores con un buen asesor los quales sean personas letrados de buena fama é conciencia los mas idoneos que se puedan haber é que se les dé alguacil é fiscal é notarios y los otros oficiales que son necesarios para la inquisicion los quales sean asi mesmo personas aviles é diligentes en su calidad é que á los dichos inquisidores é oficiales les den é sean situados sus salarios que deben haber, y es la merced de sus altezas é mandan que ninguno de los dichos oficiales lleve de su oficio derechos algunos por los abtos que hiciere en la dicha inquisicion ó en los negocios é cosas della dependientes so pena de perder el oficio, é mandan que ninguno de los inquisidores tengan oficial ninguno del dicho oficio por su familiar porque al bien del negocio é al servicio de sus altezas asi cumple.

2. Item plaze á sus altezas que en corte de Roma se ponga una buena persona que sea letrado é de buen celo para que procure los negocios tocantes á toda la inquisicion destos reinos é que sea pagado competentemente de los bienes confiscados por el delicto de la heregia é apostasia que pertinescen á sus altezas é que asi lo mandan á sus tesoreros.

3. Item por quanto en tiempo de Sixto papa quarto de buena memoria hemanaran de la corte Romana algunos rescriptos é bulas é confesionarios exorvitantes é contra derecho mucho en perjuicio de la inquisicion é ministros della, mandan sus altezas que se libren cartas é provisiones que juntas sean generates para todo el reino con las quales se impida é pueda impedir justamente la ejecucion de los tales rescriptos é bulas, si alguno los impetrare é quisiere usar dellos fasta que con el papa sea consultado é informado de la verdad por parte de sus altezas, por quanto no es de presumir que la intencion del santo padre sea dar impedimento en los negocios de la santa fe catolica, pero que las dichas provisiones de sus altezas no se publiquen fasta ver si el papa Inocencio octavo moderno

algunas bulas ó requisitos concede ó de lugar que se expidan en su corte en perjuicio de la sancta inquisicion.

4. Item es la merced de sus altezas porque los inquisidores é sus oficiales clerigos que trabajan en la dicha inquisicion sean aprovechados é honrados de mandar á sus embajadores que procuren en su nombre un indulto del papa para que sus altezas puedan nombrar á las dichas personas de la dicha inquisicion en ciertas iglesias de sus reinos en las primeras dignidades é beneficios que vacaren é que aquellos sean reservados para los nombrados de sus altezas.

5. Otrosi mandan sus altezas que por quanto tienen por bien de hacer merced de sus bienes á todos aquellos que como quier que fuesen culpados en el delicto de la heretica pravedat se reconciliaren bien é como deben en el tiempo de la gracia que los tales reconciliados puedan cobrar qualesquier debdas de qualesquier tiempo que les fuesen debidas para si é que su fisco no les embargue asi mesmo si algunos bienes muebles é raices hayan vendido, dado ó otorgado ó obligado antes de su reconciliacion que los dichos contractos queden firmos á las personas que administren los dichos bienes porque es la merced de sus altezas é mandan que los dichos reconciliados no puedan vender ni enagenar ni obligar dende en adelante los bienes raices que tovieren sin especial licentia de sus altezas porque quieren ser primero informados de como guardan la santa fe catolica é si son verdaderamente convertido á ella.

6. Item como quiera que sus altezas no tienen por bien de hacer gracia de los bienes á los hereges é apostatas que fueron reconciliados fuera del tiempo de la gracia para la reconciliacion y les pertinezcan todos los bienes de los hereges condempnados e reconciliados desde el dia que cometieron el dicho delicto de la heregia segun el derecho dispone y podria el fisco de sus altezas demandar los bienes que los tales ovieren vendido ó enagenado en qualquier manera é escusarse de pagar las debdas que los tales debiesen por qualquier obligaciones, salvo si en lugar de las tales ventas é enagenaciones paresciere y se hallare el prescio é otra cosa equivalente en los bienes de los tales hereges, pero por mas de clemencia é umagnidad con sus vasallos y porque si algunos con buena fe contrataron con los dichos hereges que no sean condempnados que sean reconciliados como dicho es hicieron antes que començase el año de setenta é nueve, valgan é sean firmes, con tanto que se prueben legitimamente por testigos dignos de fe ó por scripturas abtenticas que sean verdaderas é no simuladas en tal manera que si alguna persona hiciere alguna ynfinta ó simulacion en fraude del fisco cerca de qualquier contrato ó fuere participante en la dicha fraude ó colusion y fuere reconciliado le den cient azotes y le hierren con una señal de hierro en el rostro, y si fuere qualquier otro que no sea reconciliado aunque sea cristiano haya perdido todos sus bienes é el oficio é oficios que toviere é que su persona quede á su merced de sus altezas, é mandan que este capitulo sea pregonado publicamente en los lugares de la inquisicion porque ninguno pueda pretender ignorancia.

7. Otrosi que si algun caballero de los que han acogido ó acogieren en sus tierras los hereges que por temor de la inquisicion huyan y huyeron de las cibdades, villas é lugares realengos demandaren qualesquier debdas que digan serles debidas por qualesquier hereges que sean huydos á sus tierras que no el tesorero no les pague las debdas ya dichas ni el juez de los bienes confiscados se las mande pagar fasta que los dichos caballeros restituyan todo lo que los dichos confesos que cogieron en sus tierras llevaron consigo, pues es cierto que aquella pertenescia é pertenesce á sus altezas é que si sobre tales debdas fuere puesta demanda al procurador fiscal que el dicho procurador ponga por reconvencion é compensacion la cantidad en que poco mas ó menos le parescere que es obligado el caballero que pide su debda jurando que no lo alega maliciosamente.

8. Otrosi mandan sus altezas que ningun tesorero de los que son ó fueren puestos para recebir é recabdar los bienes confiscados por el dicho delicto no secresten ni occupen bienes de ningund herege ni apostata sin mandamiento especial de los dichos inquisidores é quando ellos dieren mandamiento para ello hagase la secrestacion por su alguacil é por ante notario de la inquisicion é por antel escribano del tesorero para que cada uno dellos haga registro del dicho secreto el qual mandan que se haga en personas llanas vecinos del lugar que tengan los dichos bienes é quel tesorero no toque en ellos fasta que la persona cuyos eran los dichos bienes sea condenada ó por reconciliacion declarada que fue herege é manda é mandan sus altezas que al tiempo de la secrestacion se oviere de hacer el tesorero sea requerido por el alguacil para que vaya á ver como se face.

9. Que si en los bienes asi secrestados como dicho es oviere é se fallaren algunas cosas que guardandolas se perderian asi como pan é vino é otras cosas semejantes que el tesorero procure con los inquisidores que las manden vender é al presente se vendan en publica almoneda é que el prescio de las tales cosas sea puesto en el dicho secreto en poder de los dichos secrestadores ó en un cambio como mejor los dichos inquisidores y el tesorero vieren, asi mismo si algunos bienes raices ovieren que se deban arrendar manden los dichos inquisidores al secrestador que juntamente con el dicho tesorero los arriende en publica almoneda.

10. Otrosi que el tesorero no venda bienes algunos ni reciba dineros ni qualesquier bienes algunos otros que sean confiscados é pertenescian al fisco de sus altezas sin que esten delante de dos notarios uno suyo del dicho tesorero é otro que sea puesto por magno de sus altezas para que cada uno dellos escriba sobre si los bienes é maravedises que el dicho tesorero rescibiere é haga registro é libro

ordenado de todo ello para que [de] los dichos libros é registros se tomen despues las cuentas al dicho recebdor.

11. Otrosi mandan sus altezas que cada uno de los recebtores que fueren puestos por su mandado recabten é resciban los bienes que fueren de los herejes vecinos é moradores en el partido donde son puestos é no se entremetan á ocupar ni tomar bienes de ningun hereje que pertenezcan á otra inquisicion mas que luego qualquier de los dichos tesoreros hobiere noticia de algunos bienes confiscados por el dicho delicto que pertenezcan á otro tesorero que lo hagan luego saber para que lo cobre é recabte so pena que el que lo encubriera pierde el oficio ó sea obligado al daño é menoscabo que por su negligencia se recresciere al patrimonio de sus altezas con el doblo.

12. Otrosi mandan sus altezas que a los inquisidores é oficiales que en este negocio de la inquisicion entienden el tesorero les pague los tercios de sus salarios adelantados en el principio de cada tercio porque tengan que comer é se les quite ocasion de recebir dadivas é que es comience el tiempo de su paga desde el dia que salieren de sus casas á entender en la dicha inquisicion, é que asi mesmo pague los mensageros que á sus altezas enviaren los dichos inquisidores é qualquier otras cosas que los inquisidores vieren que cumple al oficio asi como en carceles perpetuas ó mantenimientos de los presos ó otras qualesquier cosas é espensas.

13. Item que todos los mandamientos de qualquier calidad que sean que los inquisidores mandaren dar asi para su alguacil como para su tesorero ó para qualesquier otras personas cerca de los bienes ó prision de las personas de los herejes, los negocios de la inquisicion, sean tenidos de los asentar é asienten en sus registros é hagan libros dellos aparte, porque si alguna dubda se ofresciere se pueda saber la verdad de lo que paso.

14. Otrosi que las otras cosas que aqui no son declarados queden é se remitan á la buena discreccion de los inquisidores para que si se ofrescieren casos tales que á su parescer se puedan espedir sin consultar á sus altezas hagan segun Dios é derecho é sus buenas conciencias lo que les paresciere é en las cosas graves escriban luego con diligencia á sus altezas é á mi el dicho procurador para que sus altezas manden proveer en ello como cumpla al servicio de Dios nuestro señor é suyo, ensalzamiento de nuestra sancta fe catolica é á buena edificacion de la cristiandad. Dada en la ciudad de Sevilla, seis dias del mes de Deziembre, año del nascimiento de nuestro Salvador Jesucristo, de mil é quatrocientos é ochenta é quatro años.

IV - TORQUEMADA'S INSTRUCTIONS TO INQUISITORS, Jan., 1485.[1340]

(Archivo General de Simancas, Consejo de la Inquisicion, Libro 933).
La Forma que se debe tener en el proceder de los Inquisidores es la siguiente.

Primeramente que los inquisidores loego en legando en el lugar donde se ha de facer la inquisicion pongan sus cartas e edictos de treinta ó quarenta dias ó como mejor visto les fuese que todos los que en algun caso de heregia ó apostasia se fallaran culpados y en este dicho tiempo vernan con dolor sin fuerza ninguna á confesar sus errores y diran la verdad de todo lo que supiere no solamente de si mesmos mas de los otros que con ellos participaren en el dicho error, que estos tales sean recebidos con toda caridad, y abjurando sus errores en forma les sean dadas penitencias publicas ó secretas segun la infamia ó calidad del delito á alvedrio de los inquisidores y denseles algunas penitencias pecuniarias que paguen en cierto tiempo, y estos dineros sean puestos en mano de una persona fiable y den los inquisidores ó los escribanos la copia dellos al rey nuestro señor ó á mi como á inquisidor principal, para que se gasten en la guerra ó en otras obras pias y para que se paguen los salarios de los inquisidores y otros ministros que en la santa inquisicion entenderan, y seanles dexados todas los otros bienes que tuvieren asi mobles como raices, y cerca de los oficios publicos que tienen deben por ahora ser privados fasta que se vea su forma de vevir, y si fueren buenos cristianos y conocidamente se viere la enmienda en ellos pueden ser habilitados para que ayan los dichos oficios si fueren vacos ó otros semejables.

1. Otrosí si despues del tiempo del edicto algunos vinieren á se reconciliar, los quales non dejaron de venir por temor ni por menosprecio mas por enfermedad ó por otro justo impedimento, que con estos tales se use de misericordia como en el capitulo primero, pero si al tiempo que se vinieren á reconciliar fueron ya citados ó tienen contra si provantes, estos non gocen de la gracia de los bienes, pero los inquisidores se hayan con ellos misericordiosamente quanto de derecho y buena conciencia podieren facer segun la calidad del delito é infamia requiere é segund esto consultando con el rey nuestro señor se verá si se debierá fazer gracia de los bienes ó no.

2. Otrosí si á estos que asi bien se vinieren á reconciliar son debidas algunas deudas, que los deudores sean obligados sin embargo del fisco á ge les pagar, y si algunas ventas de sus bienes ovieren fechas que valgan y que por parte del fisco del rey nuestro señor no les sean impedidas, pero si estos tales tovieren esclavos cristianos que sean libres y forros, y si los hobieren vendido los que les

compraren non los puedan retener mas que luego los dejen forros y ellos recauden el precio de los vendidores.

3. Otrosí si algunos de los susodichos que se vinieren á reconciliar y no dizieren la verdad de sus errores é de los que fueron particioneros con ellos é despues se fallaren por las probanzas el contrario, estos tales sean havidos por contumaces é que vinieron fingidos á la confesion, no gocen de nada de lo susodicho mas antes se proceda contra ellos con todo rigor segun que el derecho en tal caso dispone.

4. Otrosí que ningun receptor debe sequestrar bienes de ningun herege nin apostata sin especial mandamiento en escrito de los inquisidores é que se pongan los tales bienes no en manos del receptor mas en manos de una persona fiable y que hagan el secuestro el receptor con el alguacil de la inquisicion y por delante de dos escribanos, uno del alguazil y otro del receptor, y estos escribanos cada una escriba por si todo lo que se sequestrare, y sean pagados los dichos escribanos de los bienes de los dichos hereges aunque despues se hayan de reconciliar, y el salario sea lo que los inquisidores mandaren.

5. Otrosí si algunos fueren absentados antes del tiempo del edicto y asi mesmo absentaren sus bienes y estos tales vinieren en el tiempo del dicho edicto confesando sus errores como arriba dicho es, gocen de la misma gracia de los bienes é fagase con ellos en la misma forma que en el capitulo primero está escrito, pero si en el tiempo del edicto non quisieren venir procedase contra ellos segun que en este caso el derecho dispone.

6. Otrosí que ni por los procesos de los vivos se deben de dejar de facer los de los muertos é los que se fallaren aver seydo é muerto como hereges ó judios los deben desenterrar para que se quemen y dar lugar al fisco para que occupe los bienes segun que de derecho se debe facer.

7. Otrosí que el receptor no venda bienes ningunos ni reciba sin que esten dos escribanos delante, los quales sean puestos ó por manos del rey nuestro señor ó de los inquisidores y cada uno dellos escriba el bienes que el receptor recibe y el precio por que los vende porque despues por aquellos libros se les tomarán las quentas.

8. Otrosí que á los inquisidores y oficiales que en este sancto negocio entienden les debe el receptor pagar sus tercios adelantados, porque tengan de comer y se les quiten la ocasion de recebir dadivas de ninguno y debe de comenzar el tiempo de su pago desdel dia que salieren de sus casas para entender en este sancto negocio.

9. Otrosí que continuamente los inquisidores fagan saber al rey nuestro señor é á mi todas las cosas que sucedieren en la dicha inquisicion é conoscieren que se deban escrevir, é que el receptor loego que por ellos le será mandado pague el trotero que ellos quieran enviar.

10. Otrosí que todos los mandamientos de qualquier calidad que sean que los inquisidores mandaren dar asi al alguazil como al receptor ó á otras qualesquier personas manden á los escribanos de la inquisicion los asienten en sus registros porque por allí se conozca la verdad de todo lo que pasare.

11. Otrosí que los inquisidores y el asesor esten juntos y muy conformes en la ejecucion de la justicia y buena administracion della é finalmente en todo quanto pertenece é se habrá de facer en la inquisicion, de manera que ni el inquisidor sin el asesor ni el asesor sin el inquisidor faga cosa alguna, é si lo ficieren que por el mismo caso sea ninguno.

12. Otrosí que esten los inquisidores é todos los oficiales de la inquisicion aposentados dentro de una casa, podiendose haber, porque esten juntamente é que quando ovieren de escrebir dichos negocios de la inquisicion é del estado della escriban los inquisidores y el asesor juntamente.

13. Otrosí que ningun oficial de la dicha inquisicion no tiene ningun derecho por cosa ninguna de su oficio pues que el rey nuestro señor les manda dar su mantenemiento razonable y les fara mercedes andando el tiempo é faciendo ellos lo que deben é que no recivan dadivas ni subornacoenes de ninguna persona y si se fallare que alguno el contrario ficiere por el mismo caso sea privado del oficio y mas este á la pena que los inquisidores darle quisieren, é á un cada vez que un tal caso conteciere informen á su alteza del rey nuestro señor porque se provea de otro oficial y entre tanto se ponga otro en lugar del tal delinquente aquel que los inquisidores acordaren fasta que el rey nuestro señor é yo proveamos.

14. Otrosí que en todas las otras cosas que á la santa inquisicion se requieren queda á juicio y buena discrecion de los inquisidores que ellos las fagan segun Dios é derecho é buenas conciencias se deben facer, y si algunas otras cosas vieren que el rey nuestro señor debe remediar las escriban y que se faran como cumple al servicio de Jesucristo nuestro señor y ensalzamiento de su santa fé y buena edificacion de la cristiandad.

FR. THOMAS, prior et inquisitor generalis.

V - INSTRUCTIONS OF SEVILLE, 1500.[1341]

(Archivo General de Simancas, Consejo de la Inquisicion, Libro 933).
Otras Instituciones.

Las capitulaciones infraescritas que ordinaron los muy reverendos señores inquisidores generales para instruccion de los inquisidores é prosecucion del oficio de la sancta inquisicion en la muy noble é muy leal cibdad de Sevilla á diez é siete dias del mes de Junio año de mil y quinientos.

1. Primeramente que los inquisidores de cada una inquísicion é partido salgan é vayan á todos los lugares é villas de sus diocesis é partidos donde nunca fueron personalmente é en cada una de las dichas villas é lugares hagan é resciban los testigos de la general inquisicion, é para que esto puedan mejor hacer é mas brevemente se espida, se aparten los inquisidores é vaya cada uno por su parte con un notario del secreto para rescebir la dicha pesquisa é informacion general, é despues de rescibida é hecha la dicha pesquisa general se tornen á juntar en la cibdad ó lugar donde tovieren su asiento para que alli vista por amos la testificacion que cada uno ha tomado puedan mandar prender á los que se hallaren culpados é testificados suficientemente para se poder prender segun se contiene en el capitulo de las instrucciones hechas en Toledo.

2. Item, que en las inquisiciones donde los inquisidores han andado é recebido la general testificacion que cada año el uno de los inquisidores salga por las villas y lugares á inquerir, poniendo sus edictos generales para los que algo saben tocante al crimen de la heregia que lo venga á decir, y el otro inquisidor quede á hacer los procesos que á la sazon oviere, é si no abra algunos salga cada uno por su parte segun arriba esta dicho.

3. Item, que los inquisidores de cada inquisicion pasen los libros ordinariamente por sus abecedarios dende el primero fasta el fin, para lo qual se ayuden del fiscal é notarios quando non andovieren por los lugares á tomar la testificacion como dicho es.

Sobre esto capitulo se ha de hacer principal relacion en la visitacion de manera que han de saber los inquisidores generales que es lo que han procedido de los dichos abecedarios.

4. Item, por quanto los inquisidores algunas veces proceden por cosas livianas non continentes herexia derechamente y por la palabras que mas son blasfemias que herejias, ó dichas con enojo ó yra, que de aqui adelante no se prenden ningunos desta calidad, é si dubda oviere que lo consulten con los inquisidores generales.

5. Item, quando prendieren alguno por el dicho crimen de herejia en poniendole la acusacion envien la copia della á los inquisidores generales y la probanza que tienen contra el verba ad verbum declarando los nombres de los testigos y las calidades de las personas y esto envien con el nuncio de la inquisicion á buen recabdo.

6. Item, que los inquisidores non consientan dilacion en los procesos é procedan sumariamente segun la forma del derecho que en este caso de la herejía habla.

7. Item, que los inquisidores de aqui adelante non dispensen con los que fueren condempnados a carcel perpetua ni les comuten la dicha carcel en otra penitencia é quando esta facultad de dispensar é comutar la dicha carcel los dichos inquisidores generales les reservan para si la dicha facultad é poder que ninguno otro pueda dispensar é comutar.

8. Item, que á los testigos conpurgadores no les sean leidos los dichos é dipusciones de los testigos del crimen que hay contra el acusado en la acusacion del fiscal, sino que guarde la forma del derecho que es que el acusado ha de jurar juxta formam juris que el [niega] el crimen de lo que esta asentado, ante los dichos testigos compurgadores, é que á ellos se les pregunte si creen que juro verdad ó no, sin hacerles otras preguntas.

9. Item, los inquisidores trabajen con los procesados que estaran bien testificados para poder ser condempnados como hagan conoscimiento de su culpa y la confiesen y tengan arrepentimiento, trayendoles persuasiones para ello é si fuere menester que trayan personas religiosas que los conviertan é con los que asi no estovieren testiguados tengan tiento que no les fagan confesar lo que no hicieren.

10. Item, que los inquisidores pregunten particularmente á los personas que dieren sus confesiones lo que saben de sus padres y hermanos y parientes é de otras personas qualesquiera por las particularidades que se requieren porque despues no se puedan escusar por ignorancia, é lo que asi digeren de otros se asiente en los libros é registros de oficio aparte de las dichas confesiones.

Henry Charles Lea

VI - EXTRACTS FROM THE REGISTER OF THE RECEIVER OF CONFISCATIONS AT VALENCIA, 1485-1486.

(Archivo General de la Corona de Aragon, Registro 3684, fol. 60).

A veynte y dos de julio el Rey nuestro senyor me mandó que asentase en el registro como su Alteza facia merced á su caballerizo Johan de Hoz e á Martin Navarro su repostero de plata de sendas escrivanias de aquellas tres que estan vacas en Toledo porque han sido privados dellas por el delito de la heregia Pero Gia de Alcuba e Alfonso Cota e Francisco Rodriguez escrivanos de numero reconciliados.

A diez y ocho de agosto de ochenta y cinco años plugo al Rey nuestro señor de librar á Johan de Tencino en los bienes de los hereges que á su Alteza pertenescan ó perteneceran de aqui en adelante en los reynos de Aragon aquellos diez mil sueldos de que le hizo merced en ayuda de su casamiento e aquellos seys mil seyscientos cincuenta y cinco sueldos ocho dineros que le son devidos de su quitacion con alvalaes de escribano de racion. Se mandó á mi que por memoria lo asentase en este registro.

A veynte de Agosto de LXXXV me mandó su Alteza que asentase en registro como faze merced á Pedro de Morales criado de Alfonso Carillo protonotario apostolico de una escrivania de las del numero que vacaran por el delicto de la heretica pravedad en Toledo.

A XXII de enero en la villa de Alcalá fizo merced al doctor micer Felix Ponte regente la cancelleria de una alqueria que Jaime Martinez de Santangel tenia en el termino de---- cabe la ciudad de Valencia e mandó á mi que le fiziere la provision della.

A XXIV de enero el Rey mi senyor fizo merced á Juan de Leca aposentador de su senyoria de uno de los primeros oficios que vacaran en Segovia por el reconciliacion ó en otra manera por el delicto de la heretica pravedad.

A XIV de febrero de LXXXVI en Alcalá de Henares el Rey nuestro senyor me mandó que assentasse en registro como faze merced á Martin de Tavara de la scrivania del numero que tiene Pero Alfonso Cota reconciliado.

VII - BRIEF OF JULIUS II RESPECTING THE TROUBLES IN CORDOVA.

(Bulario de la Orden de Santiago, Libro III, fol. 320).

/ Venerabilis frater salutem etc. Non sine summa animi molestia percipimus quosdam iniquitatis filios Catholicæ fidei rebelles, qui cum Christiani sint Judaicæ se perfidiæ participes præstant, officiales a te ad inquirenda hæreticæ pravitatis errata constitutos Cordubæ quorundam adminiculo complicum captivos fecisse et quod auditu quoque nefarium est mulctatos male et contumeliose habitos diu in vinculis detinuisse. Quæ res cum pessimi prorsus et perniciosissimi sit exempli, pro cura quæ Catholici gregis ab hæreticorum rabie defendendi una cum apostolatus officio nobis est demandata mature providendum duximus, ne lues tam pestifera serpat ulterius nec sua contagione rectos commaculat. Quam ob rem fraternitati tuæ cui jam pridie talia perquirendi facinora et reperta puniendi potestatem arbitriumque contulimus districte mandamus ut commissum sibi munus fervide et severe exerceat ac subnascentem in agro dominico zizaniam abolere et radicitus extirpare non cesset, fidelium defensioni ut par est die noctuque excubando. Præfatos vere qui tam abominandum scelus ausi sunt cum suis complicibus et quoscunque eis auxilium consilium favoremve ullum præstiterunt undique conquisitos ac debitis subjectis poenis exemplum cæteris statuet ne aliquando ad peccati similitudinem ex impunitate accendantur. Volumus autem hæc omni diligentia quamprimum a fraternitate tua curari et offici, nam exorientia tabiferæ pestis capita ne serpant in ipsis statim principiis sunt opprimenda, ad quod per ecclesiasticas censuras et universa juris remedia ut magis expedire videbitur, appellatione remota, procedes, in contrarium facientibus non obstantibus quibuscunque. Dat. Bononiæ.[1342]

VIII - PROPOSITION MADE IN OCTOBER, 1519, TO CHARLES V TO COMPOUND FOR THE CONFISCATIONS.

(Archivo General de Simancas. Patronato Real, Inquisicion, Legajo único, fol. 49).

Sy en las cosas de la inquisicion se pone orden de justicia por jueces no sospechosos que guarden el derecho e den cuenta de lo que hicieren, para que los buenos puedan bevir seguros y los que mal bivieren sean castigados como nuestro muy santo padre lo ordenare e mandare e las bulas e breves que sobre ello dieren sean obedecidas e cumplidas como de justicia e conciencia no se puede otra cosa hazer, avra personas que osaran servir al Rey nuestro señor en esta manera.

Habida consideracion que la codicia de los bienes es causa de todos los malos, e que es ley en los reynos de Castilla en las partidas que no sean confiscados los bienes de los que tovieren hijos catolicos e que a los principes queda muy poco provecho de la confiscacion porque todo se gasta en salarios, costa de jueces e recebtores que de ello enriquecen, puede su Mag^{d} justamente servirle por compusicion e venta que haga de todo el derecho que le pertinece a el e a sus descendientes para syempre jamas de la confiscation de los bienes de la dicha inquisicion en todos sus reynos e señorios abiendo para ello bula de nuestro muy santo padre en que asi mismo se mande y ordene que no pueda aber condenacion de bienes ni dineros por via de penitencia ni en otra manera. Por lo qual y por lo que se debe hasta agora de las confiscaciones e penas e compusiciones pasadas por qualesquier personas en qualquier manera-- dando para ello las provisiones e jueces que fueron menester--se dara por esto a su Magestad quatrocientos mill ducados; los cien mill ducados de ellos para el tiempo de su partida al ymperio, e los trecientos mill en tres años puestos en Flandes en las ferias de Emberes del mes de mayo de cada año cien mill ducados.

Y si paresciere algun inconveniente que esto se haga a perpetuo, aunque no le ay, abida consideracion a la dicha ley del reyno, y su Magestad fuere servido que sea por algun tiempo limitado, por el tiempo que fuere declarado por S. M. se daran doscientos mill ducados, los cinquenta mill para la partida e los ciento e cinquenta mill ducados en las dichas tres ferias de enberes.

E por que los jueces diputados para tan santo oficio estan mas libres para hacer justicia sin esperar de sostinerse de los bienes de los presos e su magestad no tenga que pagar salarios pues no ha de haber confiscacion demas de lo que asi se ha de dar por la dicha confiscacion se comprara la renta que fuere menester a vista e determinacion e moderacion de su magestad para pagar todos los salarios e cosas de la dicha inquisicion sobre lo que ya esta comprado e consynado para ello en algunas partes, comprandolo de la manera e segund que el rey catolico lo tenya mandado a çomençado a comprar.

E para la cobranza de lo susodicho se ha de dar otras tales cartas e provisiones como las que dio el rey catolico para cobrar las compusyciones del Andalucia e las que mas fuere menester, e para remediar qualquier agrabio que syntieren los que esto ovieren de pagar e proveer en ello e en la cobrança dello, lo que fuere necesario que se cometa al arzobispo de Toledo o a su gobernador para en los Reynos de la corona de Castilla, y el arzobispo de Çaragoça para los reynos de la corona de Aragon, para que ellos o las personas a quien le cometieren conozcan de ello e lo provean syn pleyto, e no otros jueces algunos, remota apelacion.

E abiendo efeto lo susodicho sy S. M. fuere servido de dar poderes e provisiones bastantes para cobrar e componer e ygualar todo lo que le es debido y pertenece en qualquier manera en los dichos sus reynos e señorios de qualquier otras confiscaciones e penas pertenecientes a la camera e fisco por las leyes e prematicas de los dichos reynos o en otra manera e qualesquier bienes que estan confiscados e adjudicados por delitos de que no este hecha merced e las tengan qualesquier personas de qualesquier tiempos pasados hasta en fin de este año, y le perteneciere de aqui adelante en estos quatro años venideros que se cumplan en fin del año de quinientos e veynte e tres, e que entre en esto lo que qualesquier personas de su voluntad vinieren, declarando que son en cargo, de que tengan finequito e no aya memoria ni recabdo por donde se le puede pedir quenta, e se puedan componer e cobrar lo que dieren, e por esto sanearan a S. M. cien mil ducados pagados en la dichas tres ferias de enberes, e sy mas valiere lo susodicho sea para S. M. quitando las costas e el salario que S. M. fuere serbido de dar por ello, e que si alguna merced o libranza se hiciere de bienes ó maravedises en lo susodicho durante este tiempo se reciba en cuenta.

E porque para el cumplimiento de todo lo susodicho se ha de dar seguridad bastante de personas que se obliguen a ello, se han de dar luego cedulas de S. M. libradas del Sr Cardenal por donde de licencia e facultad a las personas que en ello quisieren entender e obligarse e contribuir, que lo puedan hazer syn que por ello incurran ni se les pida pena ni achaque alguno de parte de la ynquisicion ni por otras justicias, las quales cedulas se han de dar en todo este mes de otubre, si los dineros han de estar prestos para la partida, porque de otra manera faltaria tiempo.

IX - MEMORIAL FROM GRANADA TO CHARLES V IN 1526.

(Archivo de Simancas, Patronato Real, Inquisicion, Legajo único, fol. 55).

Vuestra Magestad manda é á mandado poner la Sancta Inquisicion en esta Ciudad y Reyno de Granada, lo qual es muy loable y muy santo por que se vea de creer que la intencion y voluntad de Vuestra Magestad es que los malos christianos sean castigados y los bonos sean conocidos, y por que en la manera de proceder en el Sancto Officio pasan mas peligros los que buenos son que los que mal biben, asy de ser presos como condenados sin culpa segun que muchas veces a acaecido, todos los que bien biben y son catolicos christianos suplican a Vuestra Magestad mande enmendar la manera de proceder en que los testigos y carceles sean publicos como lo son en el pecado abominable y contra natura, que como en este son conocidos y castigados los malos asy lo seran en este otro, y los que son buenos y biben bien estaran seguros de ser acusados falsamente, y por que Vuestra Magestad use de tan justa peticion y misericordia con los que buenos son, de solo este pequeño Reyno de granada, serviran a Vuestra Magestad con cinquenta mill ducados para los gastos de este tan sancto viage sin lo que mas Vuestra Magestad podra aver de los otros sus Reynos y Señorios que sera en grandisima suma de dinero, y quitando este mucho secreto escusera Vuestra Magestad los incombenientes de pecados siguientes.

Lo primero que si los jueces son malos como puede acaecer por ser hombres humanos y no Santos como lo es el Officio, quando prenden doncellas y casadas de buenos justos y moças, ó quando las mandan venir secretamente ante sí como el Officio requiere en su mano sepan usar de ellos como cosa suya, lo qual ligeramente ya sentiran con el gran temor que lleban, y esto no habra lugar de se hacer en juicio publico.

Y la otra, que los escribanos de este secreto y los officiales que en este secreto tienen mano, seyendo mancebos, como en algunas partes lo son, tienen ó casi han de hacer lo misma con hijas ó mugeres ó parientas de presos, las quales ligeramente puedan alcanzar, y les sera concedido por saber algo de este secreto que les combenga, ó sí fuesen malas personas como entre los hombres se hallan, tambien tienen ocasion de bender por dineros este secreto, por que los que asy son malos con fin de ser aprovechados procuran estos officios, lo qual todo se quita con hacer la justicia publica.

En lo otro tienen a causa de este secreto que muchas animas que se han condenado al ynfierno e se pueden condenar por ser tan falsas, escusarseles a este camino, que por poder decir lo que dicen secreto muy ligeramente se condenan y dicen lo que no vieron por aver venganza de quien tienen mala voluntad como cada dia a sucedido, sy quando Dios le hace merced al falsamente acusado que se da por bueno sale destruydo demas de la infamia de su prision, lo qual se escusaria seyendo los testigos publicos.

E lo otro que para que el que falsamente se acusa no tenga remedio, puedense buscar los testigos por dineros, los quales por estos pecados se hallan oy con poco trabajo, y como el acusado no los conosca y lo que le acusan nunca hiso ni penso no puede caer en los acusadores, y aunque cayga en su enemigo contrario que lo hiso atestiguar, y como los jueces no sepan este secreto condenan justamente y el falsamente acusado muere sin culpa, y quedan sus hijos y debdos infamados para siempre jamas, lo qual no se podria hacer seyendo publicos los testigos.

E lo otro que como los que son malas personas y malos cristianos tengan y tienen odio y mala voluntad á los que son buenos porque no siguen sus malos costumbres y obras: diz que por sus delitos son presos y los confiesan; los primeros que acusan son los que saben que biben bien, por vengarse de ellos, y á estos les da lugar el secreto, que si publico lo obieren de decir no tendrian osadia de decir la mentira á la clara, por que se les probaria luego el contrario, y por este tienen menos seguridad los buenos que los malos, que como no hícieron ni pensaron lo que les acusan ni conoscan por platica ni conversacion á los acusadores ni por ventura saben sus nombres no pueden caer ni acertar en ellos, y desta manera son condenados justamente y mueren sin culpa por que no quieren conocer lo que no hicieron, y quedan destruydos sus hijos y debdos y disfamados, los quales seyendo los testigos publicos no se podria hacer.

E lo otro que á cabsa de este secreto mas facilmente se pueden librar los que han cometido el delicto de que son acusados, por que el que lo hizo bien sabe quando y como y ante quien, y luego pueden acertar en quien lo acusa, y tachándolo como se hace es dado por libre, y la sentencia es justa, y el culpado queda sin castigo. Lo qual es por el contrario a quel que falsamente se le acusa, que como no lo hizo ni sabe ni puede saber de donde le viene el daño, sino fuere por inspiracion divina, de la qual gracia no son dignas todas, pe ... y de esta manera pasan mucho mas riesgo y peligro ... que son buenos y catolicos cristianos que los que ... y biben mal, en lo qual de Vuestra Magestad ... poner este tan justo remedio que se le ... tiene puesto de su mano para la gobernacion ... y señorios, por que los buenos puedan biber ... ser malos sean conocidos y castigados.[1343]

X - BULL OF SIXTUS IV, APRIL 18 1482, TEMPORARILY REFORMING THE INQUISITION OF ARAGON.

(Archivio Vaticano, Sisto IV, Regesto 674, T. XV, fol. 366).

Sixtus Episcopus servus servorum Dei Ad perpetuam rei memoriam. Gregis Dominici nostræ custodiæ divina disponente clementia commissi vigilem et solicitam curam gerentes, Pastoris inhærendo vestigiis libenter juxta officii nostri debitum nostræ solicitudinis partes adhibemus ut errantes, relicto præcipiti tenebrarum devio, viam veritatis agnoscant, et per illam gradientes vitam consequantur æternam; perseverantes vero in eorum erroribus proditis contra eos a jure remediis compescantur, nec damnentur aliqui de quorum erroribus legitimis probationibus non constaret. Sane nuper nobis insinuatum extitit quod in Aragoniæ et Valentiæ ac Maioricarum Regnis, necnon Principatu Cataloniæ officium inquisicionis hæreticæ pravitatis non zelo fidei et salutis animarum sed lucri cupiditate ab aliquo tempore citra exercetur et quamplurimi veri et fideles Christiani illo mediante, admissis contra eos inimicorum, æmulorum, servorum aliarumque vilium et minus ydonearum personarum, probationibus nullis legitimis præcedentibus indiciis, carceribus etiam sæcularium judicum detrudentur, torquentur, hæretici etiam et relapsi declarantur, bonis et beneficiis spoliantur et traduntur curiæ sæculari et per illam ultimo supplicio afficiuntur in animarum periculum, perniciosum exemplum et scandalum plurimorum. Nos igitur multorum quærelis super hoc excitati, providere volentes ut tenemur quod officium ipsum debite peragatur et illo mediante nullus opprimatur indebite et injuste, Motu proprio, non ad alicujus nobis super hoc oblatæ petitionis instantiam, sed de nostra mera deliberatione et ex certa nostra scientia, auctoritate apostolica, præsentium tenore statuimus quod de cætero in Regnis et Principatu prædictis locorum Ordinarii seu eorum vicarii et officiales ac ejusdem hæreticæ pravitatis inquisitores in eorum civitatibus et dioecesibus deputati conjunctim dumtaxat juxta tenorem aliarum litterarum nostrarum contra Christianos Judaicæ superstitionis sectatores et ad illorum ritus transeuntes illosque Judaizando sectantes ac alios hæreticos quoscunque eorumque receptatores et fautores etiam super jam coeptis negotiis procedere et accusatorum et denuntiatorum et promoventium hujusmodi inquisitionis negotium, necnon testium quos desuper ad juramenta et dicta recipi continget, nomina et attestationes ac dicta totumque eorum processum personis ipsis ac earum procuratoribus et defensoribus publicare et aperire ac eis ad opponendum contra eosdem testes eorumque dicta et attestationes et processuum hujusmodi competentem dilationem inspectis testium numero et actorum qualitate moderandam assignare, et illis contra quos procedi continget eos quos petierint in advocatos et procuratores dare et per ipsas personas inquisitas ac eorum nomine comparentes oppositas in termino hujusmodi legitimas exceptiones et defensiones ac desuper legitimas probationes admittere. Ipsique insimul vel alter eorum ad minus per seipsos secundum juris dispositionem testes ad juramenta recipere et examinare debeant et aliter receptorum et examinatorum attestationes, nullum penitus etiam judicium vel adminiculum faciant in præmissis, nec detineantur personæ aliquæ occasione negotii inquisitionis hujusmodi in alio quam solito Ordinariorum locorum carcere, ad hoc etiam de jure deputato. Et si contingat a gravaminibus eis illatis ad Sedem Apostolicam appellari, Ordinarii, vicarii et officiales et inquisitores præfati appellationibus ipsis deferant venerenter dum tamen manifeste frivolæ non fuerint, et processus per eos habitos ad ejusdem Sedis examen remittere et in illis supersedere nullatenus differant, usquequo aliud ab eadem Sede habuerint in mandatis. Contrafacientes vero Ordinarii, vicarii et Officiales ac Inquisitores præfati et quicunque alii tam ecclesiastici quam sæculares cujuscunque status, gradus, ordinis et conditionis fuerint, quacunque ecclesiastica vel mundana dignitate præfulgentes et contrafieri procurantes consulentes vel suadentes, tacite vel expresse, directe vel indirecte, in præmissis per nos sicut præfertur provide statutis vel aliquo eorumdem, Episcopi et superiores interdicti ingressus ecclesiæ, reliqui vero excommunicationis sententiam eo ipso incurrant, a qua præterquam in mortis articulo constituti ab alio quam Romano Pontifice, etiam vigore cujuscunque facultatis de præsentibus mentionem non facientis, nequeant absolutionis beneficium obtinere. Et illius exemplo cujus vices gerimus in terris nolentes mortem peccantium sed cupientes potius conversionem eorum salutiferam, misereri potius quam ulcisci elegimus, præsertim ubi si alias procedatur exinde possint verisimiliter scandala exoriri, Ordinariis locorum et eorum vicariis et Officialibus generalibus ac Inquisitoribus præfatis et cuilibet eorum in omnibus Regnis, Principatu et dominiis supradictis ut quorumcunque Regnorum et Principatus prædictorum incolarum utriusque sexus ad aliquem ex eis recurrentium confessione diligenter audita pro quibuscunque excessibus criminibus et peccatis etiam quæ vitam et ritus ac mores Judaicos sectando aut alias a via veritatis et fide Catholica deviando, et in aliquem hæresim labendo usque in diem illam in qua confitebuntur commississe fatebuntur et censuras ecclesiasticas quas quomodolibet incurrissent auctoritate nostra in utroque foro poenitentiali et contentioso absque abjuratione de absolutionis beneficio eisdem recurrentibus providendi eisque poenitentiam salutarem et occultam injungendi motu, scientia et auctoritate prædictis facultatem et potestatem concedimus per præsentes. Ita quod in posterum prætextu criminis hæresis quam antea incurrisse dicerentur contra eos inquirere non possint nec eos nullatenus valeant molestari, dum tamen ad Inquisitionis processum super hujusmodi criminibus et inquisitorum personalem citationem executorii demandatam deventum non foret, ac Ordinariis, vicariis, Officialibus et Inquisitoribus prædictis ne contra illos quos eorumdem vel alicujus eorum assertione eis constiterit per aliquem ex eisdem vigore præsentium absolutos fuisse per ipsorum absolventium attestationem aut patentes literas, seu super eorum assertione confectum instrumentum, absque tamen ulla peccatorum quorum confessionem audivissent propalatione de commissis per eosdem confitentes criminibus hæresis cujuslibet, de novo procedere, aut confiteri modo prædicto volentes quominus id faciant impedire, nullatenus præsumant sub simili interdicti et excommunicationis sententia eo ipso ut præfertur incurrenda a qua pari modo nequeant ab alio quam Sede prædicta nisi in mortis articulo constituti absolutionis beneficium obtinere, eisdem motu scientia et auctoritate inhibemus. Eisdemque Ordinariis, Vicariis, Officialibus et Inquisitoribus sic absolventibus ac cuilibet eorum, motu, scientia et auctoritate prædictis, sub simili poena mandamus quatinus per se vel alium seu alios præsentes litteras ubi quando et quociens expedire cognoverint solemniter publicantes et illis quibus de absolutionis beneficio hujusmodi providerint ac alios quos contra præsentium tenorem gravari quomodolibet constiterit efficaci defensionis præsidio assistentes non permittant quempiam contra eorumdem præsentium literarum tenorem vexari seu quomodolibet molestari, et illos quos eis interdicti et excommunicationis sententiam hujusmodi incurrisse constiterit, illos irretitos esse publice nunciari faciantque ab aliis nunciari et ab omnibus arctius evitari ac, legitimis super hiis habendis servatis processibus, illos iteratis vicibus aggravare procurent. Et insuper, motu et scientia similibus, Ordinariis eorumque vicariis et Officialibus ac Inquisitoribus prædictis, sub censuris et poenis præfatis eo ipso incurrendis, mandamus quatinus incolas utriusque sexus Regnorum et Principatus prædictorum qui ad eos aut eorum quemlibet pro confessione et absolutione prædictis recurrerint absque aliqua dilatione seu mora eorum confessiones et cujuslibet eorum audiant et eis de absolutionis beneficio in utroque foro ut præfertur provideant, contradictores per censuram ecclesiasticam appellatione postposita compescendo, invocando ad hoc si opus fuerit auxilio brachii sæcularis, decernentes ex nunc omnes et singulos processus quos haberi et generaliter quicquid fieri vel attemptari contigerit contra præsentium tenorem quomodolibet nullius esse roboris vel momenti et haberi debere prorsus pro infectis. Non obstantibus apostolicis in provincialibus et sinodalibus conciliis editis constitutionibus et ordinationibus ac privilegiis et litteris dictæ Sedis, necnon ecclesiarum Regnorum et Principatus prædictorum ac curiarum eorumdem juramento confirmatione apostolica vel quavis alia firmitate roboratis, statutis et consuetudinibus ac stilo et observantiis quibus illa etiamsi de eis eorumque toto tenore seu quovis alio expressa habenda esset, præsentibus pro expressis habentes, illis alias in suo robore permansuris, quoad præmissa specialiter expresse derogamus contrariis quibuscunque. Seu si aliquibus communiter vel divisim a Sede præfata indultum existat aut interdici suspendi vel excommunicari non possint per litteras Apostolicas non facientes plenam et expressam ac de verbo ad verbum de indulto hujusmodi mentionem, et qualibet alia dictæ Sedis indulgentia generali vel speciali cujuscunque tenoris existat, per quam præsentibus non expressam vel totaliter non insertam effectus earum impediri valeat quomodolibet vel differri, et de qua cujusque toto tenore habenda sit in nostris litteris mentio specialis. Et quia difficile foret præsentes litteras ad singula loca deferri, volumus et apostolica auctoritate decernimus quod transumpto præsentium manu alicujus notarii publici subscripto et sigillo alicujus curiæ episcopalis munito ubique in judicio et extra tanta fides adhibeatur quanta ipsis originalibus litteris adhiberetur si illæ exhibitæ vel ostensæ forent. Nulli ergo etc. liceat hanc paginam nostrorum statuti, concessionis, inhibitionis, mandati, constitutionis, derogationis, decreti et voluntatis infringere vel ei ausu temerario contraire. Si quis autem etc. Datum Romæ apud Sanctum Petrum, Anno Incarnationis Dominicæ Millesimo Quadringesimo octuagesimo secundo, Quarto decimo Kal. Maii, Pontificatus Nostri Anno Undecimo.

    P. BERTRANDI.
    D. DE VITERBIO.
    Duplicata sub eadem data et scripta per eundem scriptorem et taxata ad xxx.

XI - KING FERDINAND TO POPE SIXTUS IV, MAY 13, 1482.

(Archivo General de la Corona de Aragon, Reg. 3684, fol. 7).

Sanctissime Pater: Ferdinandus etc. Aliqua fuerunt mihi relata, pater sancte, que si vera sunt maxima admiratione digna videntur: hec sunt quod sanctitas vestra concessit generalem remissionem neophytis de omnibus erroribus seu delictis per eos ante hac perpetratis provideritque ut nomina testium qui apud acta inquisitionum heretice pravitatis que nunc fiunt in provincia Aragonie testimonia perhibuerunt delatis revelentur et quod a sententia inquisitionis possit ad vestram sanctitatem appelari seu apostolicam sedem et etiam quod sanctitas vestra revocaverit ab ipsius inquisitionis officio scilicet Joanni Christoforo de Gualbis et fratrem Joannem Ort exaudiendo eorum neophitorum peticiones quibus etiam audientia deneganda est, postquam inquisitores ipsi modeste et decenter prosequuntur, aliter enim spectantes alios favorabiles et faciles sibi optinere inquisitores, et alia a S. V. impetrata indulta talem suscipiunt audaciam quod non timent in eorum erroribus persistere. Predicte autem relationi impendimus fidem nullam, quod talia visa sunt quod nullatenus concedenda erant per S. V. que hujusmodi sancte inquisitionis negotium dirigere debet. Et si per dictorum neophitorum importunas et astutas persuasiones ea concessa forsitan fuerint eis nunquam locum dare intendo. Caveat igitur S. V. contra dicti negotii prosequtionem quicquid impedimenta concedere et si quid concessum fuerit revocare et de nobis ipsius negotii cura confidere non dubitare. Sed postquam S. V. aperte novit quantum cedit imo preter astutisimas neophitorum circuitiones opus est in Dei servitium et cristiane fidei decus quod inquisitores heretice pravitatis secundum beneplacitum et voluntatem meam in his regnis et terris meis instituantur et regio meo favore freti onus inquisitionis exerceant et hoc quidem modo ea que agenda sint perfici possunt et aliter nihil bene ageretur circa ea quod facile quidem intellegi potest ex hoc quam superioribus temporibus dum de ejusmodi negotiis ego aut predecessores mei non nos intromittimus heretica pravitas in tantum succurruit et ejusmodi morbi contagio per cristianum gregem se extendit quod quamplurimi qui pro cristianis habebantur non modo non cristiane sed neque secundum legem aliquam vivere reperti sunt et multa que ab illis in Cristi neglectum et vilipendium fiebant aperta sunt et in dies efundentur in publicum que ita proh dolor eveniunt culpa atque nequitia inquisitorum preteritorum qui munibus et corruptelis ab inquisitionibus desistebant aut eas minus bene prosequebantur. Dignetur iccirco eadem S. V. hic mihi concedere circa inquisitiones predictas videlicet quod sanctitas vestra quamprimum confirmet predictos fratrem Joannem Cristoforum de Gualbes et fratrem Joannem Orts in dicto inquisitionis officio confirmetque eadem S. V. comisionem ad meam instantiam nuper factam per magistratus ordinis fratrum predicatorum fratri Gaspari Jutglar conventus illerdensis super instituendis et destituendis inquisitoribus in dicta provincia secundum beneplacitum et voluntatem meam. Aut si melius videbitur S. V. alicui alteri fratri similem comisionem faciat ut semper inquisitores nobis acceptos in dicta provincia habeamus, quoniam alios contra voluntatem nostram hujusmodi officium exercere nunquam permitere intendimus. Ita cum hec omnia fieri expedit pater sancte in obsequium Cristi et catholice fidei decus jubeat ergo Sanctitas vestra apostolicas provisiones et literas super predicta ilico expediri quod erit mihi vehementer gratum accipiamque singularis beneficii loco ab eadem Sanctitate vestra cujus almam personam Jesus optimus maximus feliciter et cum sacre Eclesie columna tueatur. Ex Corduba urbe XIII die maii a nativitate Domini MCCCCLXXXII. De vuestra santidad muy omil e devoto fijo que vuestros santos pies y manos besa el Rey de Castilla y de Aragon. Camanyus secretarius.

XII - MEMORIA DE DIVERSOS AUTOS DE INQUISICION CELEBRADOS EN ÇARAGOÇA DESDE EL ANO 1484 ASTA EL DE 1502 EN QUE SE REFIEREN LAS PERSONAS CASTIGADAS EN ELLOS.[1344]

Los serenisimos Reyes catholicos don Fernando y doña Isavel mandaron poner en Çaragoça el sacrosanto tribunal de la fe en el año de 1484. Lo mismo en Catalonia y Valencia.

Fue el primero Inquisidor Apostolico El Maestro Julian de la orden de Predicadores al qual se entiende que mataron los Judios atossigandole en unas rosquillas que le presentaron. El Glorioso Maestro Pedro Arbues de Epila llamado vulgarmente el Maestre Epila, fue muerto por los converses estando en los maytines de media noche en la seo de Çaragoça, de donde era canonigo a 17 de 7bre de 1485.

AUTOS DE FE DEL ANO 1484.
Auto primero. 1484.

A 10 de Mayo de 1484, domingo, se hizo auto de fe en la seo de Çaragoça. Predico el Inquisidor el Maestro Julian y fueron sacados en el los siguientes.

1. Primero, Leonora Eli por ceremonias Judaycas, y quando oya nombrar del SS.^{mo} nombre de Jesus respondia, called no le nombreys que es nombre de enforcado.
2. Felipe Salvador alias Santicos botiguero por ceremonias Judaycas, comer carne en viernes, y en la quaresma, este fue primo hermano de Pedro de la Cabra Judio.
3. Leonor Catorce Valenciana, muger del dicho Santicos, por ceremonias Judaycas, comer Amin[1345] y carne en viernes y savado y aver ayunado el ayuno de Quipur.
4. Isavel Muñoz Castellana, por los mismos delitos y que quando dezia el credo, y llegava à aquellas palabras et in Jesum Christum, dezia Aqui cayo el asno.

Todos estos fueron penitenciados por hereges y confiscadas sus haziendas.
Auto 2.

A 3 de Junio, en el patio de la casa del Arzobispo, predico el Santo martyr Pedro Arbues, fueron condenados a muerte,
1, 2. Dos hombres por hereges Judayzantes, el uno dellos fue aogado porque murio reducido.
3. Aldonza de Perpiñan, muger de Manuel de Almazan, por ceremonias de Judios, y aver bestido a doze pobres Judios en honor de las doze tribus de Israel, algunos años, Ayunar el Quipur y dar limosna a la cedaza, quemaronla en estatua por ser difunta. Auto 3. 1485.

A 20 de Diziembre, Biernes, A las espaldas del hospital de nuestra señora del Portillo. Predico el Prior de Predicadores, fueron quemados.
1. Alvaro de Segovia por ceremonias Judaycas, comer Amin y carnes degolladas en sus ritos, y en quaresma, Ayunar el Quipur, leer la Biblia en hebreo bajo de un pabellon, y despues la hazia adorar a sus hijos--quemado.
2. Joana Sinfa porque de Judia hecha Cristiana volvio a los ritos Judaycos y vivia como Judia,-- quemada. Auto 4. 1486.

A treze de febrero. En la seo. Predico el Maestro Crespo y sacaron en el tablado a
1. Jayme la Gasca con una bela ardiendo en las manos por ceremonias Judaycas. No le confiscaron los bienes por aver confessado dentro del tiempo.

Auto 5. 1486.

A 24 de febrero, Biernes, en nuestra señora del Portillo. Predico el Maestro Crespo, canonigo del Pilar. Sacaron en el a
1. Salvador Esperandeu el viejo zurrador, porque siendo Cristiano hizo ceremonias Judaycas, comio Amin, y Pan cotazo,[1346] y carne en la quaresma, guardava el savado, y travajava el domingo, ayunava el Quipur, y escarnecia al querpo de nuestro señor Jesu Cristo--fue quemado.
2. Gumien Berguero, siendo cristiano hizo todas las ceremonias de Judios y llevava abito de Rabi,

fue quemado.

    3. Ysavel de embon, muger de Gilabert Desplugas, siendo Cristiana dava azeyte a la sinagoga, y hazia ceremonias Judaycas--fue quemada.

    4. Dionis Ginot, notario, por casado dos veces viviendo la primera muger, y fugitivo--quemado en estatua.

    5. Pedro Navarro mercader, por ceremonias Judaycas y escarnecer el santisimo sacramento, y fugitivo--quemado en estatua.

    6. Maestro Martinez, jurista de Teruel por ceremonias Judaycas y aver quebrantado su carcel y huydose--quemado en estatua.

    Auto 6. 1486.

A 17 de Julio [Marzo] Biernes, en nuestra señora del Portillo, Predico el Maestro Crespo, y sacaron al tablada a

    1. Francisco Clemente notario por ceremonias Judaycas, quemado.

    2. A su muger por lo mismo, quemada.

    3. Miguel de Oliban çapatero por ceremonias y manjares Judaycos, y porque dezia que el buen Judio se podia salvar en su ley como el buen cristiano en la suya, y que la de Moysen era buena, y que nunca avia creydo en la S.^{ma} Trinidad ni en la Virgen nuestra señora Maria S.^{ma}, fue quemado.

    Auto 7. 1486.

Biernes a 28 de Abril, en el mismo lugar. Predico el Maestro Crespo. Fueron castigados los que se siguien.

    1. Pedro de Orrea, mercader, por ceremonias Judaycas, y averse hecho circuncidar y quando beja la cruz o el SS.^{mo} Sacr.^{to} se escondia por no benerarlos--fue quemado.

    2. Anton de Pomar Berguero, por ceremonias Judaycas, y siendo cristiano no savia el Paternoster ni el credo--fue quemado.

    3. Francisco Tornabal pelayre por Relapso, y casado con dos mugeres veladas--quemado.

    4. Maestro Puremiofer [Pedro Monfort], Vicario general de Çaragoça, por aver venido contra la Inquisicion en Mallorca y Çaragoça y dezir que el buen Judio se podia salbar como el buen cristiano, y entre los Judios jurava por la ley de Moysen y por los diez mandamientos, y dezirles que tenian buena y santa ley--quemado en estatua.

    5. Mossen Pedro Maños cavallero, que siendo cristiano se paso a las ceremonias Judaycas--quemado en estatua.

    6. Manuel de Almazan mercader, por ceremonias Judaycas, comer Amin y Arrequequer y dar limosna a la cedaza y pagar a un Rabi porque le fuesse a leer la ley de Moysen--fue quemado.

    Auto 8. 1486.

Domingo de la S^{ma} Trinidad a 21 de Mayo, dentro de la seo. Predico el Maestro Martin Garcia Inquisidor, sacaron a

    1. Joan Cid, sastre por ceremonias Judaycas, fue penitenciado y confiscados los bienes.

    2. Rodrigo Gris, carnicero, que siendo cristiano hazia ceremonias de Judios, y el Jueves S^{to} se harto de Gazapos.

    3. Jayme Redo, comia carnes en biernes S^{to}.

    4. Joan de Alcala, portero del Justicia de Aragon, por ceremonias Judaycas, y comer carne en quaresma, caso dos veces en vida de la primera muger.

    5. Gilabert Desplugas, por ceremonias Judaycas.

    6. Jayme de Caseda, corredor, por lo mismo.

    7. Anton Matheo, Botiguero, por comer carne en quaresma y gallinas en Viernes S^{to} y darles la bendicion a sus hijos passandoles la mano por la cara.

    Todos estos fueron penitenciados.

    Auto 9. 1486.

A 25 de Junio Biernes en la seo. Predico el Maestro Martin Garcia, fueron penitenciados por hereges los siguientes.

    1. Jayme Navarro mercader, por ayunos y ceremonias de Judios, yr a la sinagoga à orar, dezir que si Cristo n. S^{r}. fuera dios no temiera el morir.

    2. Felipe de Moros, mesonero de la Almunia, porque se caso con dos mugeres vivas, ceremonias de Judios, y aver llevado à ganar torpemente una muger cristiana.

    3. Clara Mateo, muger de Alvaro de Segovia, por ceremonias Judaycas y dezir que no estava nuestro Salvador en la ostia, y que no dezia verdad en la confession porque creya que todo era burla sino la leyde Moysen.

4. Leonor Romeo muger de Anton Mateo, ceremonias Judaycas.

5. Joan de Aragon, botiguero, en cuerpo y con bela en el tablado, por que tuvo conbiados a unos Judios, y dezia Cristianos de natura, Cristianos de mala ventura, y que mas valia dar à ganar al medico Judio que al Cristiano, y por sospechoso en la fe.

Auto 10. 1486.

A 30 de Junio, Biernes, en la puerta de la Seo, predico el Inquisidor Abad de Aguilar, fueron condenados a muerte

1. Joan de Pero Sanchez mercader, que dijo a Joan de la Badia que si matara al Inq^{r} Maestro Epila le daria 500 florines de oro, y mas dijo a Caspar de Santa Cruz y a Mateo Ram en casa de Juan de Esperandeu, y delante dellos encargo a Vidau frances que matasse al Inquisidor que el se lo pagaria muy bien, porque era tesorero del dinero que tenian para defenderse los Judios, y porque Judayzava y dezia que la mejor ley era la de Moysen, y que maldijo a su padre por averse tornado cristiano. Arastraron su estatua con una bolsa al cuello por Çaragoça y despues la quemaron en el mercado.

2. Joan de Esperandeu Zurrador por assesino de la misma muerte y porque un savado fue con Vidal frances y Mateo Ram a la Reja del estudio del Maestre Epila para arrancalla, y no lo executaron porque fueron descubiertos, y passados 4 o cinco meses fueron a la seo a Maytines tras del dicho Inquisidor y allandole arrodillado entre el altar mayor y el coro, esperandeo, durango frances, Ram y Abadia, dijo este al Vidau, dale que este es, y el Vidau le dio una cuchillada de rebes, que le abrio desde la cerviz asta la barba, y esperandeu le dio una estocada que le paso el brazo izquierdo, este era fino Judio y circuncidado, y lo arrastraron vivo y delante de la puerta mayor de la seo le cortaron los dos manos, y de alli le llebaron arrastrando al mercado y en la horca le cortaron la cabeza y le hizieron quartos y las manos las enclavaron en la puerta pequeña de la diputacion, y los quartos por los caminos.

3. Vidau durango frances zurrador, criado de Esperandeu confeso que avia ydo muchas vezes a casa de Gaspar de Santa Cruz y de Pero Sanchez y como ellos y Sancho de Paternoy trataban la muerte del Inquisidor, y como le allaron arrodillado los dichos Vidau y Mateo Ram, esperandeu y la badia y otros que el no conocio porque yvan con mascaras, y que el dicho Abadia llamo al dicho Vidau y le dijo aparte, cata que le des grande golpe en la cara, o, en el cuello, que de otra manera no lo mataras porque lleva cerbillera y Jaco de malla, y despues que el dicho la badia se lo mostro y certifico el que estava el Inquisidor el que estava arrodillado, le dio Vidau una cuchillada de rebes que le derrivo las varillas, y le corto la bena organical de la cerviz, y de este golpe murio, y poresto fue Vidau arrastrado por la ciudad y vuelto a la plaza de la seo le aogaron y cortaron las manos, y esto se hizo por no darle tanta pena como al otro, porque dijo toda la verdad, y despues de muerto lo arrastraron asta el mercado y le hizieron alli quartos que los pusieron por los caminos y las manos en la puerta de la diputacion. Auto 11. 1486.

A 28 de Julio, Biernes en la plaza de la seo, predico el Maestro Crespo, fueron condenados al fuego

1. Caspar de Santa Cruz porque siendo cristiano comia y ayunava y hazia ceremonias como Judio, y porque el y Joan de Perosanchez offrecieron a Juan de labadia 500 florines si matava al santo Inquisidor y que ellos le favorecerian, y como se allo en su muerte y en las Juntas donde le fraguaron, que fueron la primera en el temple, la 2da en Santa Engracia, la 3^{a} en el portillo, y por averse huydo a Tolosa de francia, donde murio, le quemaron en estatua, y a Geronimo de Santa Cruz su hijo que lo acompaño a Tolosa le dieron por penitencia que llevasse alla el processo o sentencia de su Padre y que hiziesse desenterrar los huesos y los quemasse y tragesse relacion dello de los Inquisidores de Tolosa, y assi lo execute.

2. Martin de Santangel, porque siendo cristiano hazia ceremonias de Judios, complice en la dicha muerte del santo Inquisidor, aver contribuydo en el dinero recogido para ella, traer en sus horas quatro oraciones en hebreo y aquellos rezava, quemaronle en estatua.

3. Violante Salvador, muger de Caspar de Santa Cruz, por ceremonias Judaycas, y no guardar el domingo. Por lo qual dezian sus criados que mas parecia su casa de Judios que de cristianos, y antes de yr a missa comia, y ponia tozino en la olla de los mozos y no en la suya porque guardava la ley de Moysen, quemaronla en estatua.

4. Garcia lopez, mercader, que siendo cristiano hizo ceremonias Judaycas y dava limosna a la cedaza, y tenia horas y Biblia en Hebreo, y nunca se confesso ni comulgo, y no creya que en la ostia consagrada estava dios, y tenia una mandragula en su cama y cada dia ponia en ella cinco sueldos y se yva a missa y quando querian alzar la ostia se salia de la yglesia, y entrava en su camara a ver la mandragula y allava diez sueldos en ella, y luego la adorava en el culo cada dia, quemaronle en estatua.

5. Pedro de Exea mercader, siendo cristiano hizo ceremonias Judaycas, comio Amin y Arruqueques y carne en dias prohibidos, yva a las cabañas de Judios y dava limosna por la ley de Moysen, y avia dado dineros a su muger para la bolsa contra la Inquisicion para efectuar la muerte del santo Inquisidor, de que tuvo mucho placer. quemaronle.

6. Violante Ruys muger de N. de Santa Maria siendo cristiana hizo ceremonias de Judios, comia

carne en dias prohibitos, nunca se santiguava ni arrodillava al alzar la ostia. quemaronla.
Auto 12. 1486.

A 6 de Agosto, domingo, predico el Maestro Garcia y salieron penitenciados por hereges
1. Joan de Santa Clara, por ceremonias y ayunos de Judios, volver los ojos por no ver alzar en missa, y quando contratava con cristiano de naturaleza lo procurava engañar, y se alegrava y dezia a otro confesso, Calle que estos cristianos de natura decaen poco a poco les daremos su ajo. Inviava a sus hijos à la Juderia para que les diessen la bendicion, y tenia una mandragula y la adorava en el culo, y dava limosna a la cedaza. fue penitenciado.
2. Diego de yta.
}
3. Clara Belenguer muger de }
Joan frances.
} Por ceremonias Judaycas y
4. Gracia Esplugas
} otros graves errores en la
5. Leonor salillas muger de } fe, y no creer en muchos
Pedro Santa Clara.
} misterios della.
Penitenciados.
}
Auto 13. 1486.

A 24 de setiembre domingo en la seo, predico el Maestro Martin Garcia, y salieron por hereges con corozas los siguientes.
1. Beatriz lobera por ceremonias Judaycas y dezir que los cristianos eran idolatras.
2. Violante Velviure, muger de Mr Gonzalo de Santa Maria, ceremonias Judaycas.
3. Isavel Cruyllas, muger de Pedro de Almazan, ceremonias Judaycas, y porque hizo enbendar a un hermano suyo difunto a lo Judayco, y a un hijo enfermo lo hizo passar tres vezes por bajo de la horca tapiada en fe de que sanaria, y dezir que los cristianos de natura eran cristianos de mala ventura, y aver comido huevos crudos el dia de la muerte de su hermano, ceremonia de Judios.
4. La muger de Redo, hazia parar una mesa con mantiles en la bodega, diziendo que vendria a comer en ella el diablo y que le daria muchos bienes de fortuna, y mandava a la criada que quando cubriesse la mesa no dizesse Jesus aunque viesse algo, y que la mataria si lo nombrava, y por ceremonias Judaycas.
5. Antona Rodriguez, por dichas ceremonias, y degollar las aves al modo Judayco, y echar sobre la sangre polbo, y hazer que le bendijesse un Judio los bestidos.
6. La muger del bermejo, no sabia el credo sino asta Patrem omnipotentem, y ceremonias Judaycas.
7. Joan de Pueyo, trasmudador por casado dos vezes.
8. Francisco del Royo, ceremonias Judaycas.
9. Miguel de Almazan, por no aver notificado que estava circuncidado estuvo con cirio al pie del altar. pareciasele la faba de la parte alta (?).
10. Maria de llano testifico que vivian como Judios luys y Joan de Joan Sanchez y su muger, y el luys sanchez tuvo noticia dello y offrecio a dicha Maria muchas vezes que si yva y dezia a los Inquisidores que lo que avia depuesto contra ellos era con malicia y le desdezia la casaria y le daria para un manto, y de lo mismo le ablo un dia m^{r} Alonso Sanchez en el carmen, y con esto la hizieron desdezir. Pero despues volvio a confessar la verdad, confirmando lo que avia testificado contra ellos primero. Por lo qual estuvo en la grada del tablado con un cirio.
Auto 14. 1486.

A 21 de Octubre savado en la plaza de la seo, predico el Maestro Martinez, fueron relajados al fuego los siguientes.
1. Bernad de Robas mercader, padre de Francisco de Robas, passo a las ceremonias de judios, y los Viernes Santos se ponia un capirote de Judio, y uno de estos Viernes el y otros confessos comieron gallinas y capones en cierta casa, y dezia, Pues estos cristianos de mala ventura hazen oy el llanto, hagamos nosotros el canto. quemaronle.
2. Galceran Belenguer velero, se passo a las ceremonias Judaycas, travajava los domingos, y decia que la ley de Moysen era mejor que la de Jesu cristo, y un dia passando unos frayles de la Compania de Santa Maria de Jesus, dijo como se hallaran burlados estos, pues no ay otro mundo sino este. quemaronle.
3 Gabriel de Aojales mercader, dezia ser mejor la ley de Moysen que la de los cristianos, y un dia

leyendo en presencia de otra persona la Biblia dijo, mirad si es mejor creer a todos estos profetas que no a lo que dizen aquellos doze borrachos, entendendolo por los doze Apostoles de Cristo n. s. passo a las ceremonias Judaycas y le quemaron.

4. Guillen de Bruysan mercader, hazia las mismas, y dezia que qualquier que viniesse contra la ley de Moysen haria mal fin, y que ella era mejor que la de los cristianos. quemaronle.

5. Gonzalo de Yta, por dichas ceremonias y comio en la Juderia y muchos vezes con su Padre que era Judio. quemaronle.

6. Rodrigo de Gris carnicero, Padre de mossen Gris, fue sacado primero en otro auto por herege, y aviendole penitenciado en darle por carcel una casa cave san Felipe, y con penas de Relapso se fue de la carcel y bolvio a cometer los mismos crimines, y en este auto le quemaron en estatua.

7. Maria Labadia muger de Martin Salvador panicero comia carne viernes y savados, y los viernes por la tarde ponia manteles limpios en la mesa, y dos lamparas encendidas colgadas en una querda a cada punta de la mesa, y los otros dias comia en mesa diferente, y dezia que no lo queria hazer delante de su yerno porque era cristiano de mala ventura, y que la ley de Moysen era mejor que la nuestra y que se avia allado y venido en la muerte del Inquisidor Me Epila, y por ceremonias Judaycas. La quemaron.

Auto 15. 1486.

A 29 de Noviembre domingo, en la plaza de la seo, predico el Me Martinez, y fueron condenados al fuego los siguientes.

1. Pedro de Moros, por ceremonias de Judios y dezir que la ley de Moysen era la mejor de todas, y que el Rey que hazia la guerra a los Moros venia contra el mandamiento de dios.

2. Alvaro de Sevilla carnicero, el dia que ayunava el ayuno de Quipur abrazava a otro confesso por ceremonia de Judios y dezia que la ley de Moysen era mejor que la de Cristo.

3. Cristoval de Gelba comia con los moros de sus manjares y conversava con ellos y dezia que era Moro y que le llamavan Alfans, y hazia oracion en la Mesquita como moro, y ceremonias Judaycas.

4. Joan de Vitoria por las mismas y por pedir por las Juderias para la cedaza, diziendo que era Judio.

5. Catalina Sanchez, Madre de Mossen Pedro Bagues por dichas ceremonias y hazer todas las cosas de los Judios y observar sus ritos.

6. Francisca Daniel muger de Jayme Daniel por dichas ceremonias y enbiar limosna para bendezir las fazes de sus hijos al Ravi de la Juderia y les hazia llevar antorchas delante de la Tora.

7. Blanquina Fernandez, muger de Pedro Fernandez corredor, por lo mismo que Francisca Daniel.

8. Blanca de Adam alias Leonor de Montesa, por lo mismo.

9. Maria Rodriguez passo a las ceremonias Judaycas, fue muger de Joan Rotoner tinturero, nunca supo el credo, hazia bendezir sus hijos al Ravi, no creya que en la ostia consagrada estuviesse dios, y quando massava hechava pedacillos de massa en el fuego, ceremonia Judayca.

10, 11. Pedro y Luys de Almazan, hijos de Manuel de Almazan porque estavan circuncidados los tenian por sospechosos en la fe, y assi les dieron por penitencia que mientras se dezia en la Yglesia el officio assistiessen con sendas belas, y los desterraron de Çaragoça por diez años.

Auto 16. En el portillo sacaron solamente a este reo. 1486.

Micer Francisco de Santa Fe complice en la muerte del Santo Me Epila estando preso en la Inquisicion viernes a 15 de Deziembre de este año 1486, entre ocho y nueve de la mañana se arrojo desde las almenas de la torre en donde estava su carcel, en camisa, y del golpe quedo muerto, y este dia lo llevaron junto al portillo, y alli le mandaron leer los Inquisidores su processo en donde se dijo como avia passado a las ceremonias Judaycas, y que en su casa enseñava a un Judio las oraciones dellas, y dezia que la ley de Moysen era mejor que la de cristo, y que qualquier buen Judio se podra salvar, era retajado, y leyda su sentencia le quemaron y pusieron los guesos en su camisa y en una cajuela lo hecharon por ebro abajo. Este auto lo quento por el 16, por averse hecho con toda esta solennidad.

Auto 17. 1486.

A 17 de Deziembre domingo en la seo predico el M^{o} Martin Garcia y fueron condenados por hereges los que se siguien.

1. Fernan lopez de Teruel porque siendo cristiano hazia ayunos y ceremonias de Judios, y dezia que la ley de Moysen era mejor que la de los cristianos, y quando se confessava nunca dezia verdad.

2. Bernad Sabadias por lo mismo y teniendo por mejor la ley de Moysen dezia que la de los cristianos toda era trancos barrancos (?).

3. Bartolome Sanchez por ayunos y manjares Judaycos, yr a la sinagoga con los Judios, y aver dicho a uno dellos, Cornelio bien te estas en la ley de Moysen que mejor es que la de los cristianos.

4. Gilabert de Almazan que siendo cristiano passo a los manjares y ceremonias Judaycas, dezir que tan bien se podra salvar el buen Judio como el cristiano y que no havia Infierno, y que el Parayso

era tener dinero, y que un dia que jurava por la ostia consagrada, sabiendo uno de los que le oyeron que mentia le dijo que porque jurava mentiendo, y le respondio que todo el juramento era burla, y quando alzavan en la missa se passeava sin arrodillaise jamas.

5. Beatriz Daniel, muger de caseda el calcetero, porque despues de vuelta cristiana siguio los ritos Judaycos.

6. Isavel Matheo, muger de Leonart Sanchez por lo mismo, y aver ydo a la fiesta de la circuncision de un Judio.

7. Isavel Belloc, muger de Leonart de Sabrelas, por ceremonias, manjares y ayunos Judaycos.

8. Salio tambien un cristiano por blasfemo de dios y de nuestra señora, atravesada la lengua por una caña el rato que duro el officio.

9. Un Judio por blasfemo, con freno en la boca, y espuerta de paja y coroza. estuvo assi quando duro el officio Auto 18. 1487.

A 21 de henero Jueves en la plaza del Portillo, predico el M^{o} Martinez, y salieron condenados al fuego

1. Joan de la badia difunto, sobre una cavalgadura, que el dia antes se desespero en la carcel comiendose una lampara de vidro a pedacitos, fue este malvado quien anduvo mas de año y medio por matar al Santo Inq^{r} Me Epila en compañia de Esperandeu, Mateo Ram, Vidau frances y otros Judios inducidores que yvan en su compañia con mascaras. este Juan de labadia fue quien dijo a Vidau frances dale que este es. Arrastraronle difunto, y le cortaron las manos, y lo hizieron quartos, que los pusieron por los caminos.

2. Pedro de Almazan mercader que despues de cristiano hizo ceremonias de Judios, inducidor y complice de dicha muerte, fue quemado in estatua.

3. Anton Perez, que vuelto cristiano hizo ceremonias Judaycas, y tratandose un dia en su presencia del S^{to} Inq^{dor} dizo que seria mejor matalle, y que se haria con 200 florines. fue quemado en estatua.

4. Joan Belenguer corredor, que despues de convertido a la fe volvio a los ritos de Judios y un Jueves santo lo hizieron azotador de Jesu cristo, y el se alababa dello, diziendo yo os juro a dios que yo me bengare y me tirare el deseo y le fustigare de azotes, yva con su muger a las cabañas de los Judios y dezia Yo Judio soy, y tengo placer de ser Judio. quemaronle en estatua.

5. Pedro de Vera notario, que vuelto cristiano volvio a los ritos y manjares Judaycos, ayunava el quipur, y era recogedor de la moneda y bolsa de los confesses, y encendia las lamparas de la sinagoga. quemaronle in estatua.
Auto 19. 1487.

A 15 de Febrero domingo, en la seo, Predico fray Pedro ferriz Prior de S. Augustin, salieron en el auto los siguientes.

1. Anton de ojos negros Çapatero, por ceremonias y ayunos de Judio y dezir que nuestra santa ley era burla y que no la creya.

2. Ramon Cruyllas, que siendo cristiano hazia ritos de Judio.

3. Jayme de Robas mercader, que vuelto cristiano passo a las ceremonias Judaycas y por consejo de Pedro de Urrea y de Alvaro de Segovia dava limosna a los Judios y dezia que el misterio de los santos corporales de daroca era cosa de burla y bellaqueria, y que no lo creya nada.

4. Joana de la Tiria, muger de diego de la Tiria sastre, vuelta cristiana uso de todas las ceremonias de Judios, no savia del credo sino asta creatorem celi et terræ, no creya que en la ostia consagrada estuviesse el cuerpo de Cristo dios y hombre, dezia que los Judios no le avian muerto y avia ayunado el quipur mas de 30 años.

5. Me Joan de lo poret bainero por casado dos vezes.

6. Leonor Calvo, segunda muger de loporet, en vida de su marido.
Auto 20. 1487.

A 15 de Marzo en la plaza de la seo Jueves. Predico el Maestro Miguel y fueron condenados al fuego

1. Joan Rodriguez, mercader, porque vuelto cristiano volvio a, las ceremonias y ritos de Judio, y dezia cristianos de natura cristianos de mala ventura, y quando alguno dezia Jesus respondia callad que es nombre de Penzat.

2. Pedro fernandez, corredor, despues de cristiano volvio a las ceremonias de Judio, y estando muy enfermo le dezia una hermana suya, hermano encomendaos al dios de Abraham, y el no le respondia.

3. Joan ortigas mayor, corredor, que vuelto cristiano Judayzo y comia carne en la quaresma, y dezia aquel refran de cristianos de natura &c., y porque sermonava en casa de un Judio la ley de Moysen donde azotavan la imagen de un crucefisso, y el era uno de los que azotavan, y despues lo hecharon en el fuego para que se quemasse. quemaronle en estatua a este impio.

4. Joan Ram, despues de hecho cristiano volvio a los ritos de Judio y llebaba una nomina escrita en hebreo, fue yerno de Joan de Perosanchez y factor y assessino del S^{to} Inq^{or} y daba dinero para hazerla.--quemaronle en estatua.

5. Mr Alonso Sanchez, por ceremonias y comidas de Judios, y porque bestido con roquete como Rabi leya à otros malos cristianos la ley de Moysen, y azotaban despues un crucifisso y lo arrojavan en el fuego. Ybase a la sinagoga a rezar con su capirote y tabardo de Judio y trabajo con todas sus fuerzas porque matassen al S^{to} Inq^{or}, y por ello prometio buena paga y lo trato con algunos diziendoles que sino querian matar al Inq^{or} Me Epila almenos matassen a Mr Martin de la Raga qui era Asessor de la enquesta. Arrastraron su estatua y despues la quemaron.

6. Garcia de Moros, notario, que vuelto cristiano volvio tan bien a las ceremonias Judaycas, y aver dicho dos dias antes que matassen al S^{to} Inq^{or} a un amigo suyo a quien el solicitava mucho para dicha muerte, haveys visto que caso ha sido matar a m^{r} Pertusa, pues antes de muchos domingos vereys otro caso mayor, y que despues de muerto el S^{to} Inq^{or} dijo a un otro amigo, que os pareze de esta muerte, quan bien hecha ha sido, y respondiendole el amigo que no dixesse tal, y reprehendendole dello, le bolbio a dezir, dejaos estar desso que todo se passara. Arrastraron y quemaron su estatua.

7. Leonor Perez, muger de Garci }
lopez.
} Todas tres por ceremonias
8. Angelina Sanchez, muger de
} ayunos y comeres
Guillen Buysan.
} Judaycos fueron quemadas
9. Gostanza de Segovia, muger de } en estatua.
luys de la cabra, argentero. }

10. Joan Frances, despues de cristiano hizo ceremonias de Judios y dezia el salmo de la maldicion porque dios matasse al Inq^{or} al Rey y a la Reyna, dezia que no avia otro parayso sino el dinero y que mas queria yr al Infierno con los ricos que al parayso, y quando yva a missa dezia por escarnio que yva a masar, fue sospechoso en la muerte del S^{to} Inq^{or}, quemaronle.

12 (11?). Mateo Ram, despues de hecho cristiano volvio a Judayzar y travajo mucho en procurar se effectuasse la muerte del S^{to} Inq^{or} y aunque esperandeu le hirio con una estocada en el brazo y Vidau con la cuchillada del cuello, este Mateo le dio una estocada que le passo el cuerpo. Arrastraronle y le cortaron las manos y las clabaron en la puerta de la diputacion, y despues le quemaron.

Auto 21. 1487.

El primero de Abril, domingo en el hospital, predico el M^{o} Martin Garcia, y pusieron en un cadalso a la puerta de la yglesia a un

1. Clerigo porque se avia fingido Inquisidor con una probision falsa en un lugar de Mossen Belenguer de Bardaxi, y avia hecho una prision a esse pueblo.

Auto 22. 1487.

A 6 de Mayo, domingo, en la seo predico el M^{o} Martin Garcia y estuvieron con cirios al pie del altar en todo el officio los siguientes.

1. Mossen Guillen Sanchez,
2. Joan de fatas, notario,
3. Pedro Augustin,
4. Bernardo Bernardi, florentin
5. Pedro Celdrion. Todos cinco porque fueron defensores de
6. Joan de Pero Sanchez, heretico, sacrilego, Matador del S^{to} Inq^{or} y invocador de Assessines y matadores. estando el dicho Joan de Perosanchez presso en la ciudad de Tolosa de Francia a instancia de un estudiante que se llamava Antonio Augustin, que despues fue--de Aragon, y de otros dos estudiantes que lo escrivieron luego con sus criados avisandolo a los Inq^{es} de Çaragoça como le avian hecho prender. Vinieron los criados con las cartas a la casa de los dichos Joan de fatas y Pedro Augustin su hermano, donde los detuvieron abriendo las cartas y las mostraron al dicho Mossen Guillen Sanchez hermano del dicho Joan de Perosanchez, y luego escrivieron todos los cinco a los estudiantes de Tolosa y a otros amigos para que alli renunciassen el reclamo de la prision y le hiziessen soltar, y assi se hizo, y despues de hecha esta diligencia con ellos dieron las cartas a los Inq^{res} y ellos despacharon a Tolosa para que lo tuviessen a buen recado, pero ya entonces estava libre de la carcel Joan de Perosanchez. For este delicto los hizieron abjurar a los cincos y que si tornavan a hazer tal o semejante delicto les darian la pena del derecho, y los condenaron a todos cinco en mil florines de oro y en las expensas hechas y por hazer, y los pribaron de sus officios quedando en arbitrio de los Inq^{res}

el priballos de officio y beneficio. Auto 23. 1487.

A 20 de Mayo, domingo en la seo, Predico el M^{o} Forcat, y huvo en el cadalso 6 mugeres y un hombre, y al pie del altar quatro hombres.
1. Leonor Castillo, muger de Alvaro de Sevilla, Judayzante.
2. Beatriz Coscolluela, muger de Pedro Pedraza, Judayzante.
3. Joana Trigo, muger de Joan de Altabas, Judayzante.
4. Isavel de Rueda, madre de Pedro Salvador, lo mismo.
5. Violante Mongua, muger de Jayme Santa Clara, lo mismo.
6. Maria del Rio, muger de Gonzalo Ruyz, Judayzante y comer carne en quaresma.
7. Joan de Altabas, pintor, por ceremonias de Judios.
8. Anton de Jassa, despues de cristiano por Judayzante comer arrecuques y Amin y carne en quaresma, y sospechoso de la muerte del S^{to} Inq^{or}.
9. Garcia de Moros el Joben estuvo con un cirio por sospechoso de la dicha muerte, y por yr a jugar a las canañuelas de los Judios.
10. Pedro Pinet, capellan de Alcañiz, que defendia cinco opiniones hereticas contra la s^{ma} trinidad.
11. Joan Traper por fautor y defensor de hereges, y aver querido matar a Anton Baptista por un testimonio signado que no se puede aver, y dezir yo tanto tengo de una missa como un asno de una albarda, y que queria hazer un hijo en savado para que fuesse Ravi y por sospechoso en la muerte del S^{to} Inq^{or}.
Auto 24. 1487.

A 18 de Agosto savado en la plaza de la seo, Predico el M^{o} Martin Garcia, fueron condenados a muerte y al fuego,
1. Diego de Gotor notario y procurador, que despues de convertido a la fe volvio a las ceremonias de Judio, y dijo que seria bien matar al S^{to} Inq^{or} porque no osasse venir otro, y que assi se desharia la enquesta.--quemaronle en estatua.
2. Pedro de Almazan menor, que convertido a la fe volvio a las ceremonias y manjares Judaycos, y dijo que seria bien matar al S^{to} Inq^{or} y dio dinero en la bolsa comun para dicha muerte, y averse allado con otros en azotar un crucifisso--quemaronle en estatua.
3. Pedro Salvador, hijo de martin Salvador, nieto de Joan de la badia porque cupo en la muerte del S^{to} Inq^{or}, y aver dado de puñaladas a la muger de Pedro el carnicero porque avia sido testigo en la enquesta contra su madre.--le quemaron en estatua.
4. N. muger de Pedro Navarro, botiguero que hecha cristiana volvio a los ritos, ayunos y ceremonias de Judios, y que al tiempo de alzar el SS^{mo} SS^{to} volvia los ojos por no verlo.--quemaronla.
5. La madre de Anton Romeo, que convertida a la fe volvio a los ritos de Judios.
6. Leonor de Bello, madre de Abadia, por Judayzante, quemada en estatua.
7. Valentina Tamarit, muger de luys de Joansanchez, lo mismo.
8. Mossen luys de Santangel, a quien el Rey don Jayme [Juan] armo caballero en la guerra de Cataluña, despues de convertido a la fe volvio a las ceremonias de Judio, y hazia oracion en hebreo, y tenia la Tora en un altar en la torre de la huerta, y teniendo enfermo a un hijo dijo que dios no le podra sanar, y a un capellan que le dezia unas missas, Mas creo y mas fe doy a un p^{r}. x^{r}. que dize mi hija casera suya que a quanto vos dezis. y a una ymagen de un crucifisso la azotava, y escupia en la cara, y le hazia muchos vituperios, y lo tenia embuelto en un trapello bien ligado con unas cabezadas de mula. y se avian ajuntado en su casa, que era la que agora es de Alonso Celdron Bayle, para tratar la muerte del S^{to} Inq^{or} los siguientes, Joan de Perosanchez, Gaspar Santa Cruz, Garcia de Moros, Mateo Ram, Micer Alonso Sanchez, Micer Montesa y otros. Y otra vez se juntaron en casa de dicho Montesa, otra en el Portillo, otra en Santa Engracia, otra en el Temple, y el dijo a los otros que matassen al Inq^{or} y a Mr Martin de la Raga, y a Mr Montes frances a todos tres y a alguno dellos, y como fue alli concertado tomo cargo dello el dicho Mossen luys Santangel porque era hombre de espada, y Joan de Perosanchez que era hombre dineroso, y ambos dieron la orden y recado para que se hiziesse la muerte. Micer Algar Reg^{te} le dio por sentencia que le fuesse cortada la cabeza en el mercado, y que le pusiesse en un palo, y que el cuerpo fuesse quemado fuera de la puerta quemada, y assi se execute.
Auto 25. 1487.

A 20 de Agosto lunes en la plaza de la seo, predico el M° Martinez, fueron condenados a muerte tres hombres y una estatua.
1. M Jayme Montesa Jurista, del qual dijo su processo que despues de convertido a la fe hazia ceremonias de Judio, y que un Viernes santo estando en Calatayud hizieron unas desponsalias de un

Judio con una Judia y dijo Mr Montesa a un escudero suyo que baylasse en ellas, y el le respondio que no baylaria en tal dia porque mas era dia de plorar, porque estando los cristianos en la yglesia en tales dias no era hora de reyr, y dijole Montesa que si facian el planto, que dios les diesse el crebanto, y esto otorgo muy largamente por escritura de su mano, y como se havia allado en el trato de la muerte del S^{to} Inq^{or} Me Epila, y como para ello se havian ajuntado en el temple dos meses antes que la executassen el y Mosen luys de santangel, Joan de Perosanchez, Gaspar de Santa Cruz, Garcia de Moros, Mr Alonso Sanchez, Martin de Santangel y otros que alli se hallaron, y que dieron poder a Joan Sanchez porque era dineroso, y a Mossen luys porque era de Espada, y a otros que no se nombran, que en ello diessen orden y recado para hazer esta muerte y la de M Martin de la Raga y de Mr Pedro Montes frances, y que los sobredichos se ajuntaron otra vez en el portillo y dijeron como que se tardava mucho, y que no se hazia nada, y respondieron los que lo tenian a su cargo como ya se travajava en ella y que tenian personas que la pondrian en execucion, y que havian estado dos noches en la seo en Maytines y no le havian podido allar y que no cuydassen dello que muy presto pondrian en effecto dicha muerte, y que al cavo de pocos dias se volvieron a juntar en Sta Engracia y les dijeron otra vez a los solicitadores de este caso que como se tardava tanto y respondieron que presto darian recado en dicha muerte, la qual perpetraron de alli a pocos dias. Mas dezian en su processo que habia el conbidado o allado a un hombre para si queria matar al Inq^{or} y que el hombre le respondio que no, y despues que fue muerto el Inq^{or} se topo con el dicho hombre y le dijo, Bueno fuera ganar 150 florines que ya es fecho aquello, a lo qual le respondio el hombre, Buen provecho os haga, que yo no me curo dello, Antes creo que todo este mal vendra sobre vosotros, a lo qual le respondio Mr Montesa lo fecho fecho es, que con el dinero lo faremos todo bueno con el Rey y con la Reyna, y todos los de la corte son nuestros, y los grandes de este reyno tan bien, que todo se passara. Y un dia despues del caso se hallaron dichos Mr Montesa y Gaspar de Santa Cruz y que le dijo 600 florines questa la muerte del Inq^{or}. fuele dada sentencia por Mr Algar Reg^{te} que le cortasen la cabeza en el mercado y la pusiessen en un palo, y le quemassen el cuerpo fuera de la puerta quemada.

    2. Leonor Montesa, hija de dicho Mr Jayme Montesa, muger de Joan de Santa fe de Tarazona, siendo Bautizada vivia como Judia y seguia sus ritos, y avia 50 años que ayunava el quipur y dava limosna a la cedaza y aceyte a las lamparas de la sinagoga. quemaronla.

    3. Violante de leon, Madre de Galceran de leon procurador por lo mismo que a la dicha leonor, y porque no creya que en la ostia consagrada estuviesse dios. quemaronla.

    4. Cristoval de Gelva, despues de convertido a la fe, Judayzo y passo a la ley de Mahoma, dieronle por carcel perpetua el hospital de nuestra S^{a}. de Gracia, como a Relapso, y quebranto la carzel, y le quemaron en estatua.

    Auto 26. 1487.

A 8 de Diz^{e} domingo en la seo, predico el Maestro Martinez, fueron sacados al cadaalso por hereges

    1. Doña Catalina de Cuenca que hecha cristiana volvio a las ceremonias de la ley de Moysen y tuvo algunos errores.

    2. Esperanza Quilloc.

    3. Clara Cerbellon, muger de Ginones verguero.

    4. Maria Rodriguez muger de Pedro Angel chapinero.

    5. Leonor Maza, muger de Jayme Garcia mercader.

    6. Isavel de Genua, muger de Bar^{o} de Soria potrero.

    7. Brianda de Gauna hija de Mossen Alvaro de Gauna.

    8. Gracia de Anguas Vivas, muger de Joan Ruyz calcetero y de Guillen Ruyz belero.

    9. Isavel de leon, muger de Joan de leon calcetero, fue a los desposorios de Jaque Judio hermano de su marido.

    Todos nueve por Judayzantes, ayunos y comeres de Judios.
    Auto 27. 1488.

A 10 de Febrero Domingo, en la seo, Predico el Maestro Alfonso forea, canonigo de nuestra Señora y salieron penitenciados en el

    1. Mossen Pedro Santangel Prior de daroca, dezia su processo que rogo y pago a Joan Gascon casero de la Torre de Mossen Luys porque digesse a los Inq^{es} que Mossen Luys era buen cristiano y que el lo havia visto disciplinarse delante de un crucifisso, y no era verdad. estas y otras cosas hizo por escapar a su hermano y por esse estuvo con un cirio en la mano delante del altar mayor, y no le privaron de nada.

    2. Joan Gascon porque testiguo en favor de Mossen Luys por rogarias del dicho Prior, dijo que havia dicho verdad en lo que avia testificado, le dieron la misma penitencia.

    3. Jayme diez de Almendarez señor de Cadreyta navarro porque tuvo en su casa y favorecio a Martin de Santangel a Garcia de Moros y a Gaspar de Santa Cruz y a su muger, y recivio dellos sesenta

florines que le dieron de oro. fue penitenciado como los precedentes.

   4. Manuel de Tudela pontero, por aver ydo a Villanueva muchas vezes a persuadir a una muger que se retratasse de lo que avia testificado contra Violante Ruiz Viuda de N. de Santa Maria, dieronle la misma penitencia.

   5. Elvira de Uncastillo por aver depuesto por rogarias del Prior de daroca en favor de su hermano el dicho Mossen luys de Santangel, y confesso que no era verdad lo que avia dicho contra el, la misma penitencia.

   6. Joan Julian corredor por aver solicitado por orden de Jayme trafer el qual le dio 20 florines de oro y casa franca de loguero a una muger para que se desdigesse. dieronle la misma penitencia.

   7. Nicolao suseda Borgoñon por casado doz vezes estuvo con coroza y fue condenado a carcel perpetua.

   8. Violante Ram, muger de N. Altabas por aver ayunado el quipur y ensenadolo a los muchachos que tenia, salio con coroza y carcel perpetua.

   9. Sancho de Peña panicero por casado dos vezes, coroza y carcel perpetua.

   10. Joan de Zamora porque estando en la ciudad de Medina ablando con unos hombres de la ostia consagrada que dichas aquellas palabras estava dios alli, respondio el andad alla que es burla que dios no baja a ella, que yo se como se hazen aquellas ostias con unos hierros, que todo es burla que alli no esta dios. diosele carcel perpetua.

   Auto 28. 1488.

   A 15 de Febrero Biernes sacaron muerto de la Aljaferia a

   1. Pedro Navarro chapinero que estava preso por herege y murio de enfermedad, sacaronle a quemar, y estava circuncidado, y circuncidava sus hijos, y vivia como Judio y ayunava el quipur.

   Auto 29. 1488.

   A 2 de Marzo, domingo en la seo, Predico el Maestro Martin Garcia y salieron a el las siguientes.

   1. Aldonza Ribas Altas que por estar enferma la llevaron en un escaño delante del altar mayor con coroza y manteta por Judayzante, esta era Madre de Maestre Ribas altas medico del Rey catolico don fernando el de la poma de oro que fue quemado vivo por traer en la poma un pergaminillo y en el pintado a cristo n. s^{r} crucificado y sobre el retratado el medico asentado de forma que parecia le besava la santa Imagen en el culo. dizen que viendo este pergamino el Principe don Joan que lo mostro al Rey catolico su padre y que de ay tuvo origen el mandar expeler los Judios de españa sino se convertian.

   2. Maria de Esplugas, hija de Gilaberte de Esplugas porque siendo cristiana usso de ceremonias y manjares de Judios, y por consilio de su madre ayunava el quipur, y despues que huvo visitado las yglesias un Juebes S^{to} fue a la Juderia à hacer colacion, y comio arecuques, no la privaron de bienes por averse ydo ella espontaneamente a delatar.

   3. Justina Macipe
   } Por comeres y ceremonias
   4. Pedro de Segovia
      } Judaycas.
   5. Joan de Prades, tegedor }
   6. Pedro fernandez, panicero } Por casados dos vezes.
   7. Pasqual de Reglas, labrador }
   8. Pedro Gomez, Alcayde } Ciudadanos de Tudela salieron delante
   9. Guillen de fatas
   } del altar mayor por solicitadores
   10. Martin de Aguas
   } de Joan de Perosanchez
   11. Pedro Manarriz
      } y de su muger, Martin de Sant
   12. Joan Bazquez
      } Angel, Gaspar de Santa Cruz y
   13. Joan de Aguas
      } su muger, Garcia de Moros,
   14. Joan de Magallon
   } Mossen Pedro Mañas y de los
   15. Joan de Carriazo
   } dos Pedro de Almazan mayor y
   16. Otro hombre
   } menor, todos hereges y factores
   } de la muerte del S^{to} Inq^{or}.

Auto 30. March 21, 1488, Eleven penanced.   Auto 31. May 4, 1488, Three penanced.   Auto 32. Aug. 10, 1488, Five penanced.   Auto 33. August 17, 1488, One penanced.   Auto 34. September 7, 1488, One penanced.   Auto 35. January 25, 1489, Fourteen penanced.   Auto 36. May 2, 1489, Two penanced and three burnt.   Auto 37. May 10, 1489, Thirty-eight penanced.   Auto 38. May 2, 1490, Twenty-nine penanced.   Auto 39. May 9, 1490, Twenty-seven penanced.   Auto 40. November 28, 1490, Seventeen penanced.   Auto 41. April 22, 1491, Eight penanced and one burnt.   Auto 42. May 15, 1491, Twenty-four penanced.   Auto 43. July 8, 1491, Ten burnt.   Auto 44. July 17, 1491, Six penanced.   Auto 45. March 28, 1492, Eleven penanced.   Auto 45 (sic). September 8, 1492, Twenty-one penanced.   Auto 46. September 28, 1492, Thirteen burnt.   Auto 47. November 11, 1492, Twelve penanced.   Auto 48. June 2, 1493, Nine penanced and thirteen burnt.   Auto 49. December 22, 1493, Seventeen penanced.   Auto 50. May 7, 1494, Six penanced.   Auto 51. January 9, 1495, Six burnt.   Auto 52. January 18, 1495, Seven penanced.   Auto 53. June 30, 1495, Six burnt.   Auto 54. July 2, 1495, Fourteen penanced.   Auto 55. October 7, 1496, Twenty-two penanced.   Auto 56. June 27, 1497, Ten penanced.   Auto 57. March 12, 1498, Seven penanced.   Auto 58. May 5, 1498, Three burnt.   Auto 59. February 22, 1499, Eleven burnt.   Auto 60. February (August?) 4, 1499, Seven penanced.   Auto 61. September 13, 1499, Four burnt.   Auto 62. September 15, 1499, Four penanced.   Auto 63. January 18, 1500, Six penanced.   Auto 64. May 31, 1501, Seventeen penanced.   Auto 65. March 15, 1502, Eleven burnt.

Resumen de los castigados en los Autos referidos.

Año 1484
7
1485
3
1486
80
1487
52
1488
45
1489
57
1490
73
1491
49
1492
58
1493
39
1494
6
1495
34
1496
22
1497
10
1498
10
1499
26
1500
6
1501
17
1502
11

602[1347]

XIII - LETTER OF CARLOS III TO THE POPE, DECEMBER 26, 1774, ASKING HIM TO CONCEDE THE FACULTIES OF INQUISITOR-GENERAL TO FELIPE BERTRAN, BISHOP OF SALAMANCA.

(Archivo General de Simancas, Secretaria de Gracia y Justicia, Legajo 629, fol. 15).

MUY SANTO PADRE. Por muerte del muy Reverendo en Christo Arzobispo, Don Manuel Quintano Bonifaz, ha vacado el cargo de Inquisidor General de todos mis Reynos, y descando que quien le huviere de succeder en este empleo sea el que mas convenga al servicio de Dios y de su Iglesia, conservacion y aumento de la fé catolica he nombrado al muy Reverendo in Christo Padre Don Bertran, Obispo de Salamanca por concurrir en su persona las calidades de virtud, sangre, autoridad y prendas que le hacen digno de ocuparle, y encargo á mi Ministro Plenipotentiario Conde de Floridablanca que en mi Real nombre suplique á Vuestra Santidad tenga por bien de mandar despachar á favor del referido Obispo de Salamanca Don Felipe Bertran el Breve que se acostumbra para exercer el expresado cargo, y pido á Vuestra Beatitud que dando entera fé y credito al Conde de Floridablanca en lo que á este intento representare en mi Real nombre se sirva Vuestra Santidad de acordar la gracia que solicito. Nuestro Señor guarde la muy Santa persona de Vuestra Beatitud al bueno y prospero Regimiento de su universal Iglesia. De Palacio á veinte y seis de Diciembre dí mil setecientos setenta y quarto.

D. V. Sant^{D.}

Muy humilde y devoto hijo Don Carlos, por la gracia de Dios Rey de las Españas, de las Dos Sicilias, de Jerusalem etc. que sus santos pies y manos besa.

EL REY.

MANUEL DE RODA.

FORMULA OF PAPAL APPOINTMENT (Ibidem, fol. 1).

Motu proprio et ex certa scientia ac matura deliberatione nostris, deque Apostolicæ potestatis plenitudine, te in prædicti Emmanuelis Archiepiscopi locum tenore præsentium Generalem Inquisitorem adversus hæreticam et apostaticam a Fide Christiana pravitatem in Castellæ et Legionis cæterisque Hispaniarum et ab eis dependentibus Regnis, Principatibus et dominiis eidem Carolo Regi mediate vel immediate subjectis ... Apostolica auctoritate tenore præsentium ad nostrum et Sedis Apostolicæ beneplacitum, creamus, facimus, constituimus et deputamus.

XIV - RESIGNATION OF INQUISITOR-GENERAL SOTOMAYOR.

(Archivo de Simancas, Consejo de Inquisition, Libro 176, fol. 1).
Letter to Philip IV.--

SEÑOR. Remito á V. M. esas papeles en razon de la renunciacion que V. M. me tiene mandado hazer de el oficio de Inquisidor general. Si en algo no fuesen á satisfacion de V. M. siempre me hallo con la misma obediencia á quanto V. M. fuese servido de mandarme, cuya Real persona guarde nuestro Señor como su Santa Iglesia lo a menester y como yo siempre se lo suplico. De Madrid en 21 de Junio, 1643.

Besa los Reales pies de V. M. su mas humilde criado
FR. ANTONIO.

***

A nuestro santisimo Padre Urbano 8, Sumo Pontifice de la Santa
Iglesia Romana que Dios guarde.--

B^{mo} P^{e}. Yo fray Antonio de Sotomayor, Arçobispo de Damasco, confesor de su Magestad Catholica del Rey mi señor Phelipe 4°, de su consejo de estado, comisario general de la santa Cruzada, Inquisidor general en sus Reynos y dominios; Hallandome muy cargado de años que son cerca de noventa, ó por lo menos ochenta y ocho y consiguientemente casi incapaz de poder condignamente satisfacer á oficios de tantas obligaciones me hallo obligado, postrado á sus santisimos pies, de suplicarle se digne de escusarme de obligaciones tan grandes á que con tanta dificultad podre satisfacer, nominando para dichos oficios las personas que el Rey mi señor tiene por bien de presentar á vuestra Santidad, que seran sin duda las que convengan á tan grande ministerio, y para suplir las muchas faltas que yo por mi insuficiencia uviere cometido en su administracion, para que, á la hora de la muerte que no se me puede dilatar, lleve este consuelo quando me uviere de presentar delante de la divina Magestad que sea siempre en favor de su santisima persona, favoreciendola con muchos favores como se lo suplico y suplicare siempre. De Madrid 24 de Junio, 1643.

Beatisimo Padre.
Besa el santisimo pie de vuestra Santidad su mas humilde siervo
FR. ANTONIO Inquisidor General.

XV - EXTRACTS FROM THE CONSULTA OF THE COUNCIL OF THE INQUISITION, MAY 5, 1646, ON THE INDEPENDENT SUPERIORITY OF INQUISITORIAL JURISDICTION OVER OFFICIALS.

(Archivo de la Corona de Aragon, Legajo 528).

Contra estas raçones suelen oponer los celadores de las regalias que la distribucion de los jurisdicciones es una dellas pegadas á los mismos guesos de los reyes, que con estos terminos significan su inseparabilidad real y de aqui infieren que en todo tiempo la pueden moderar y quitar sin que ninguna potestad se lo pueda impedir.

Señor, esta razon tiene el vicio de que prueba mucho y si no se limita y restringe á la intelligencia sana y catolica tira á destruir toda la jurisdiccion eclesiastica y para este efecto se valió de ella el Rey Jacobo de Inglaterra en el tratado que dedicó á todos los principes cristianos, provocandolos á todos á que se hiciese cada uno una cabeça de las Iglesias de sus reinos, como lo era de la anglicana, y la limitacion cierta y verdadera de la dicha razon es que la jurisdiccion civil y politica es inferior á la espiritual y eclesiastica y que para materias que le tocan por la potestad directa puede tomar y asumir por la potestad indirecta todo lo que ha menester para su conservacion y recta administracion sin que las puedan impedir ni disponer en ellas los principes seculares. Y que las mas propias regalias de la dignidad regia son de derecho humano positivo ó de derecho de las gentes, y la potestad suprema que ejerce la inquisicion por delegacion de la Sede apostolica en las causas de fee y concernientes á ella con todo lo demas de que necesita para su recto y libre ejercicio directa ó indirectamente pertenece al derecho divino, y como tal se sobrepone á todo derecho humano y de las gentes y no esta sugeto á fueros ni leyes humanas, y lo menos que se puede decir es que los principes seculares tienen obligacion de darsela como queda dicho, y aunque estos tengan derecho para que la que se tomare ó diere no sea mas que la que es menester, el juicio y arbitrio de la necesidad y de la extencion ó limitacion de aquella pertenece á aquel en quien reside la dicha potestad eclesiastica suprema, porque funda la que tiene en el derecho divino y no es posible que sallia la pureça de la fe y la obediencia y rendimiento que los principes deben á la Iglesia y á su cabeça sientan diferentemente de lo que aqui se dice, porque es el comun y verdadero sentir de los autores catolicos y lo que pide la subordinacion de los derechos humanos á los divinos y de los temporales á los espirituales de lo cual se infiere que el entendimiento verdadero del axioma ó modo de hablar referido se ha de restringir al uso de las jurisdicciones temporales que estan en una misma linea cuando no compiten lo divino con lo humano ni lo espiritual con lo temporal, porque estas y otras regalias temporales como ellas son tan inherentes á la potestad regia que no se puede desnudar dellas ni enagenarles enteramente.

Señor, todos estos principios son los solidos y seguros y hay en esta materia con que los señores reyes progenitores de V. M. se han conformado asi en el sentir como en el obrar y los autores regnicolas de la corona han sentido y escrito en la misma conformidad y todo lo que sale de estos terminos con las doctrinas nuevas que pretenden que V. M. es dueño absoluto de esta jurisdiccion con facultad plena de disponer en ella para quitarla es incierto, mal seguro para la conciencia, en nada conveniente para el Estado y muy peligroso el uso de ello no solo de caer en hierros gravisimos, que despues no tengan reparo sino de que Dios nuestro señor, cuia gloria es la mas interesada en el libre y recto ejercicio de la inquisicion, agraviado de lo que en esto se innovare, execute como suele castigos graves en los que pretenden estas mudanças que se apetecen con titulo de libertad á que aspiran siempre los reinos y son medio para perderlos, y quiera Dios que no sea una de las causas porque padece la Corona de Aragon tantos trabajos con la hostilidad de los que injustamente la pretenden usurpar, el no acabar de quietarse en las materias tocantes á la inquisicion, pretendiendo siempre introducir novedades en ella, conque no solo se desagrada á Dios nuestro Señor sino se ofende al Estado con las alteraciones que ocasionan los sospechosos en la fee que suele ser gente sediciosa de que el reino de Aragon tiene ejemplos presentes cuyos daños no se pudieran atajar sino es por medio de la Inquisicion....

(Siguen otras razones que aclaran lo que la inquisicion pretende demostrar, las cuales razones en sustancia son)

3ª Que la jurisdiccion de la inquisicion es espiritual y no pueden modificarla el rey y las cortes sin el consentimiento del Inquisidor General.

4ª Que por su condicion de espiritual la inquisicion esta sobre los fueros; los derechos con que la inquisicion usa de la dicha jurisdiccion son superiores á las fueros e independientes de ellos....

6ª Que si los brazos se obstinaban en no admitir las razones alegadas por la Inquisicion S. M. debia como el emperador Carlos V hizo en otras cortes el año 1516 (sic) acordarse de su alma y conciencia y preferir la perdida de parte de sus reinos á consentir en nada contra la honra de Dios y en diminucion y desautoridad del Santo Oficio que tanto los catolicos rey y reyna sus abuelos en sus testamentos y postrimeras voluntades lo dexaron caramente encomendado....

El obispo de Plasencia, inquisidor general y este Consejo suplicamos a V. M. se sirva mandar se haga assi como lo pedimos en las dichas consultas con ponderacion de tantas y tan solidas raçones como en ellas se proponen, excluyendo las pretensiones de los quatro braços y manteniendo á la Inquisicion en el derecho que tiene y en la posesion en que está de que toda su jurisdiccion sea tratada en aquel reino de Aragon como celesiastica y secular y la mas alta de todas como derivada del derecho divino en que la Iglesia funda la suya, para conocer de las causas de la fe, y para que no le falten los ministros necesarios con la independencia que ha menester para el recto y libre ejercicio de la dicha jurisdiccion, y aunque presumimos que los dichos brazos, vistas las dichas razones, mostraran su fidelidad á Dios y a V. M. para contentarse del acuerda que se tomare, si todavia persistieren en sus pretensiones negando los servicios que se les piden V. M. debe preferir el de Dios en que consiste el reinar y ordenara en todo lo que fuere del suyo. Madrid á 5 de Mayo de 1646.

XVI - DECREE OF PHILIP IV CONCERNING DISOBEDIENCE, MARCH 26, 1633.

(Archivo de Simancas, Inquisicion, Libro 32, fol. 56).

Uno de los mayores daños y de que han resultado mayores inconvenientes, en grave deservicio mio y de la quietud y conservacion de todos mis reinos, es el de la inobservancia y dilacion en la ejecucion de mis órdenes, pues importa poca resolverlas si no se envian y ejecutan a tiempo, pues pasada la sazon viene a ser infructuoso todo lo que se dispone, de que se han seguido daños tan irreparables que quizá son la parte principal del apretado estado en que nos hallamos; diversos recursos y advertencias he hecho a mis consejeros sobre esto y significado con vivo sentimiento el daño y encargado el reparo y aunque entiendo que en todos mis ministros debe ser igual a sus obligaciones la atencion y celo á mi servicio, la experiencia me ha mostrado que no ha bastado esto y que es necesario usar de medio mas eficaz y poderoso para que no se acabe de perder mi monarquia, pues me corre obligacion por el lugar en que Dios me ha puesto atajar su total ruina y entiendo ser la falta de obediencia y ejecucion lo que mas aprisa la puede causar.

Por este he resuelto dar forma y regla en ello, disponiendose por arancel como se han de ejecutar mis ordenes y penas en que se ha de incurrir por la inobservancia de ellas, segun la calidad de cada una, y asi se formara para ese Consejo el que la tocare bien ajustado, y se me enviará con distincion de las materias de oficio, hacienda y partes asi de gracia como de justicia, y de las penas en que han de incurrir todos y se han de executar por el mismo consejo correspondientes á la calidad de la inobservancia y omision en la ejecucion, previniendo bien todos los casos en que cada uno puede faltar y aquellos casos que pueden ofrecerse y se ofrecen, que no puedan ser comprendidos, tambien me los consultará el consejo, porque quiero saber los que son, y los aranceles se hagan en veinte dias y se me envien para que resuelva la forma en que han de quedar ajustados y se publiquen.

(RUBRICA DEL REY).

En San Lorenzo á 15 de Octubre de 1633. Al Arzobispo inquisidor general.

XVII - PROCLAMATION ON THE ARRIVAL OF AN INQUISITOR.

(Archivo de Simancas, Inquisicion, Libro 31, fol. 194).
PREGON.
Ahora oid que se os hace saber a todo hombre generalmente del parte del ilustrisimo y reverendisimo señor Don Antonio de Zuñiga, prior de Castilla del Orden de San Juan de Jerusalem, Capitan y lugarteniente general de la sacra cesarea magestad en el Principado de Cataluña y Condado de Rosellon y Cerdeña, que como á su ilustrisima y reverendisima señoria y Real Consejo se hayan presentado por el procurador fiscal del oficio de la sancta inquisicion unas letras o provisiones patentes de la prefata cesarea magestad y con su real sella sellada otorgadas al muy venerable religioso y amado del señor Rey Fray Juan Naverdu maestro en sacra teologia del orden de predicadores, inquisidor de la heretica y apostatica pravedad en el Principado de Cataluña y a los ministros del dicho sancto oficio en y con las quales entre las otras cosas por los respectos y causas en las dichas provisiones contenidas su Cesarea magestad manda con grandes penas al dicho señor lugarteniente general y otros oficiales de Cataluña asi mayores como menores que cada y quando que el dicho venerable inquisidor y los otros oficiales y ministros del dicho sancto oficio para exercer sus oficios demandaren ó alguno de ellos demandare auxilio lo haya de prestar y los dichos sus oficios permitan libremente exercitar sin impedimento alguno, y demandando el auxilio del brazo seglar incontienti lo hayan de dar, tomando y prendiendo qualesquier personas que por el dicho venerable inquisidor fueren nombradas y aquellas emprisionar y tener presas y haberlas de las jurisdicciones de qualesquier personas adonde el dicho inquisidor quisiere y mudar aquellas y castigar y punirlas con las debidas penas cada y quando por el dicho venerable inquisidor sera declarado y porque el dicho venerable inquisidor y otros oficiales y ministros del dicho sancto oficio mas libre y seguramente puedan ejercer los dichos sus oficios, su cesarea magestad al dicho venerable inquisidor sus compañeros, notario y alguazil y otros oficiales y ministros del dicho sancto oficio familiares y bienes de ellos y qualquier dellos pone y constituye debajo su especial guiaje, custodia, proteccion y encomienda real segun en dichas letras y provision real, la data de las quales fué en Valladolid á trece del mes de Febrero del año de la navidad de Dios nuestro señor mil quinientos y veinta y tres, aquestas y otras cosas mas largamente se contienen.
Por tanto queriendo su ilustrisima señoria que las cosas mandadas y proveidas por la sacra cesarea y real magestad sean á ejecucion devidas y á todo hombre manifiestas á su aplicacion del dicho procurador fiscal del dicho oficio de la sancta inquisicion por el tenor del presente publico pregon, notificando las dichas cosas á todo hombre generalmente dice y manda su ilustrisima y reverendisima señoria á todos y qualesquier oficiales ansi mayores como menores y á otras y singulares personas de qualquier estado dignadad o condicion que sean que la dicha y precalendada letra y provision real y todas y qualesquier cosas en ella contenidas y expresadas segun mejor y plenamente en ella se contiene del dicho sancto oficio de la sancta inquisicion tengan y guarden y hagan tener y guardar inviolablemente segun su narracion y tenor y contra aquella no hagan ni vengan, ni hacer ni venir permitan en manera alguna si desean no incurrir en las penas en dicha y precalendada real provision contenidas, y porque alguna no pueda de dichas cosas allegar ignorancia, manda su ilustrisima y reverendisima señoria el presente ser publicada por los lugares acostumbrados y guardase quien se ha de guardar.
EL PRIOR DE CASTILLA.
Vidit Joannes de Cardona, Cancellarius. Vidit Jacobus Ferrer, Registrator Thesaurarius. Gundisalbus de Cabra. Registrata in curia locumtenentis.
PUBLICACIONES DE LOS PREGONES.
Fué publicado el presente publico pregon por los lugares acostumbrados de Barcelona por mi Canals en lugar de Francisco de Sevia con son de quatro trompetas á veinte y tres de Diciembre de mil quinientos y veinte y tres. Canals.

XVIII - MEMORIA DE LA REFORMA DE MINISTROS DEL SANTO OFICIO QUE HIZO HACER EL REY EN 1646.

(Biblioteca Nacional de Madrid, Seccion de MSS. D 118, and S 294 fol. 122).

En las ultimas cortes que se celebraron en Aragon el año pasado de 1646, fue servido su Magestad (Dios le guarde) de aminorar el numero de familiares que conforme á fueros de aquel Reyno podia haver, extinguiendole á solo numero de 400, caviendo mas de 2000 en lo antiguo, y que se practicava como consta largamente por la concordia antigua entre el Reyno y la Inquisicion. Quitoles assimismo las exempciones de que gozaban dichos familiares en la forma que tanvien consta por los nuebos cabos donde se puede veer. Instaron sobre esto con apretadissimos esfuerzos los quatro brazos de dichas cortes y entre ellos algunos ministros de Inquisicion (que aun no vasto el serlo para que dejasen de manifestar el odio comun que contra ella y sus actiones tienen). Conociaselo su Magestad y antes de concederles cosa alguna que tocase á la Inquisicion (de quien dijo era las niñas de sus ojos) les mando ó pidió la dejasen en el estado que estava, y que como no le llegasen á ella concederia todo lo demas que pretendian, haciendo assimismo mercedes particulares á los Aragoneses, como con efecto les hiço mas de trecientas y sesenta que se publicaron en un dia, nombrandolas y las personas á quien las hacia. Nada de esto vasto para que dejasen de replicar con una y otra embaxada por parte de los brazos, deteniendo á su Magestad dos ó tres dias en el conbento de Santa Engracia de Zaragoza, estando el coche á la puerta para venirse á Madrid, hasta que viendo su pertinacia y que sin duda le detendrian mas sin concluir el solio en las Cortes que era lo que esperava, les concedió todo lo que en esta parte quisieron. Quedaron los Aragoneses muy contentos, pareciendoles haver vencido lo mas y que ya le faltava al Rey el unico recursso que tenia en aquel Reyno. Desde este dia fue postrandose la autoridad y mucha estimacion que la Inquisicion tenia en Aragon, excediendo en esta parte á otros, pues tal vez miraban á un Inquisidor con mas veneracion que al Arçobispo y Virrey y oy se vee lo contrario y aun se oye que algunos dicen ya se acabo la Inquisicion. Experimentase esto cada dia en los ministros de ella, pues, siendo conforme á las hordinaciones del Reyno que ningun vecino aloje en su casa mas que un soldado, no excediendo el numero de ellos al de los vecinos, no solo le hechan al familiar el que le podia tocar sino tuviese exempcion alguna, pero porque es familiar le hechan dos o tres. Muchos se an quejado de este agravio al Tribunal, y por escusar enpeños ó lo que podia resultar y se a tomado por expediente suabe escrivir al Comisario de la villa ó lugar donde se hace el agravio, hable con el Justicia ó Jurados de el, y que con buen modo les de á entender que no se deve hacer ni pasar por aquello, y aunque algunos an tenido atencion á ello á otros les a faltado, y tal vez ó los mas á sido necesario no darse el Tribunal por entendido ó tolerado, mirando al estado en que se alla, y tanvien á los ahogos que tiene el Reyno con los alojamientos. Hacen contribuyr á los familiares en los Vagajes y repartimientos concejiles y que no son concejiles, y ultimamente se vee y toca con las manos que en todo lo que no es negocio de fee tiene postradas las fuerzas antiguas el Tribunal de Aragon.

XIX - DECREE OF PHILIP III ON QUARRELS BETWEEN BISHOPS AND INQUISITORS.

(Archivo de Simancas, Inquisicion, Libro 29, fol. 177).

He mandado escribir estas cartas que aqui decis, pero, porque se ha visto y vee cada dia que las Inquisiciones particulares se meten en cossas que derechamente no tocan a la fe ni al Santo Oficio sino solo a estender y ampliar su jurisdiccion por fines particulares de que han resultado todas las dificultades y encuentros que las avido entre las Inquisiciones y los perlados y entretanto que esto no se remediare nunca dejara de averlas. Sera bien y assi os lo encargo que procureis componer esto de manera que los Inquisidores no se metan en mas de lo que les toca y que al mismo tiempo que yo mandare escribir a los obispos escribais vos a las Inquisiciones que por ningun casso se metan en cossa que derechamente no les toque, apercibiendoles que no solamente no lo consentireis pero que castigareis á los que hicieren lo contrario con demonstracion de rigor, y si excedieren no os contenteis con reprehenderlos blandamente sino que con efecto los castigueis, porque con esto se justificara lo que yo escribiere á los perlados y ellos se acomodaran á lo que fuere justo, y de otra manera tendran ocasion de acudir á mi por el remedio de sus agravios, lo cual es necesario que se escuse.

FOOTNOTES:

1. Romancero del Cid, pp. 12, 74, 77, 79, 87, 88, etc. (Frankofurto, 1828).--Crónica de Alfonso VII, 138-141 (Florez, España Sagrada, XXI, 403)--
"Castellæ vires per sæcula fucre rebelles: Inclyta Castella ciens sævissima bella Vix cuiquam regum voluit submittere collum: Indomite vixit, coeli lux quandiu luxit."
2. Fuero Viejo de Castiella, Lib. I, Tit. iii, § 3. Cf. Partidas, P. IV, Tit. xxv, ley 7.
3. See, for instance, the charter granted by Raymond Berenger IV of Barcelona, in 1108, to Olerdula, after a devastating Saracen inroad, and the charter of Lérida in 1148, after its capture from the Moors.--Marca Hispanica, pp. 1233, 1305. The same causes were operative in Castile.
4. The cities entitled to send procuradores to the Córtes were Burgos, Leon, Ávila, Segovia, Zamora, Toro, Salamanca, Soria, Murcia, Cuenca, Toledo, Seville, Córdova, Jaen, Valladolid, Madrid and Guadalajara.--Pulgar, Crónica, P. II, cap. xcv.
5. Marina, Teoria de las Córtes, P. I, cap. xvi, xx. (Madrid, 1820.)--Siete Partidas, P. II, Tit. xvi, ley 4.--Modesto de Lafuente, Hist. Gen. de España, IX, 34.--J. Bernays, Zur inneren Entwicklung Castiliens (Deutsche Zeitschrift für Geschichtswissenschaft, 1889, pp. 381 sqq.).
6. Crónica de Don Alfonso X, cap. clxxvi.--Barrantes, Ilustraciones de la Casa de Niebla, Lib. I, cap. xiv (Memorial histórico español, VIII).
7. Crónica de Don Alfonso XI, cap. lxxx.--Barrantes, op. cit. Lib. I, cap. xxvi, lxxx.
8. Ayala, Crónica de Pedro I, año XVII, cap. vii.
9. Córtes de los antiguos Reinos de Leon y de Castilla, II, 330 (Madrid, 1863).
10. Seguro de Tordesillas, Madrid, 1784.
11. Castillo, Crónica de Enrique IV, cap. lxxiv.--Valera, Memorial de diversas Hazañas, cap. xxviii.--Pulgar, Crónica, p. 3 (Ed. 1780).
12. Maldonado, Hechos de Don Alonso de Monrroy (Memorial histórico español, T. VI, p. 14).
13. Juan de Pineda, El Libro del Passo Honroso, Madrid, 1784.--Pulgar, Claros Varones, Tit. xiv.
14. Barrantes, Ilustraciones de la Casa de Niebla, Lib. VIII, cap. xxiv.
15. Valera, Memorial de diversas Hazañas, cap. xix., xl.--Amador de los Rios, Historia de los Judíos, III, 205.
16. Maldonado, Hechos de Don Alonso de Monrroy, pp. 17-19.
17. Maldonado, op. cit. pp. 65, 71, 72, 83.--Barrantes, Ilustraciones de la Casa de Niebla, Lib. VIII, cap. iii.--Hazañas valerosas de Pedro Manrique de Lara (Memorial histórico español, T. VI, pp. 123, 126).--Hernando del Pulgar, Crónica, P. I, cap. lxxxiii.
18. Maldonado, op. cit., pp. 23, 52, 71, 73.
19. Clemencin, Elógio de Doña Isabel, p. 127.
20. Castillo, Crónica de Enrique IV, cap. cliii.
21. Pulgar, Claros Varones de España (Elzevir, 1670, p. 6).--Castillo, op. cit. cap. cxliii.--Saez, Monedas de Enrique IV, pp. 3, 7, 23 (Madrid, 1805). At the Córtes of Segovia, in 1471, Henry ordered the destruction of all the private mints, but it is not likely that he was obeyed (Córtes de Leon y de Castilla, III, 830, Madrid, 1866). Garcia López de Salazar, a contemporary, tells us that the gold Enriques were originally 23-1/2 carats fine, but those struck in the royal mints gradually fell to seven carats, while the private mints made them what they pleased.--Saez, p. 418.
Spanish coinage is an intricate subject, and as some knowledge of it is necessary for the proper understanding of sums of money referred to hereafter, I have given a brief account of it in the Appendix.
22. Córtes de los antiguos Reinos de Leon y de Castilla, IV, 59-68.--Novisima Recopilacion, Lib. III, Tit. v, ley 10, 11.--Barrantes, Ilustraciones de la Casa de Niebla, Lib. VIII, cap. xxii.--Garibay, Compendio Historial, Lib. XVIII, cap. xvi.--Don Clemencin (op. cit. p. 146).
At the death of Henry IV, in 1474, the royal revenue had fallen to about ten million maravedís. By 1477 it increased to 27,415,626, by 1482 to 150,695,288, and in 1504, at the death of Isabella, it was 341,733,597.--Clemencin, p. 153.
23. Miscelánea de Zapata (Mem. hist. español, T. XI, p. 332).
24. L. Marinæus Siculus de Reb. Hispan. (R. Beli Rer. Hispan. Scriptt, p. 774).--Damiani a Goes Hispania (Ibid. p. 1237).
25. Pulgar, Claros Varones, Tit. xx; Letras No. iii.--Fléchier, Histoire du Cardinal Ximenes, II,

291 (Ed. 1693).

    The Córtes of Toledo, in 1462, among their grievances, include the factious turbulence of the clergy--"bien sabe vuestra alteza commo algunos obispos e abades e otras eclesiasticas personas se han fecho y de cada dia se fazen de vandos, e algunos dellos tanto e mas escandalizan vuestras cibdades e villas que los legos dellas."--Córtes de Leon y de Castilla, III, 711 (Madrid, 1866).

    26. Francisco de Medina, Vida del Cardenal Mendoza (Mem. hist. español, T. VI, pp. 156, 190, 193-4, 255, 293-4, 297, 304).

    27. Concil. Arandens. ann. 1473, cap. 3, 6, 9, 10, 11, 12, 13, 14, 15, 20, 25 (Aguirre, V, 344-50).

    28. L. Marinæi Siculi de Rebus Hispan. Lib. XIX.--Raynald. Annal. ann. 1483, n. 15; ann. 1485, n. 26.

    29. History of the Inquisition of the Middle Ages, Vol. II, pp. 180 sqq.

    30. Romancero del Cid, pp. 245, 269 (Francofurto, 1828).

    31. Ordenanzas Reales, Lib. VI, Tit. ix, ley 21.--Villanueva, Viage Literario, XVII, 256.

    32. Constitutions de Cathalunya, Lib. I, Tit. v, cap. 1 (Barcelona, 1588, p. 18). Similar laws adopted in 1534 and 1537 show that meanwhile it had been impossible to prevent papal encroachments.--Ib. cap. 3, 4.

    33. Ayala, Crónica de Don Juan I, año X, cap. vii.--Crónica de Don Enrique III, año III, cap. xvi.

    34. Alvar Gomez, De Rebus gestis a Francisco Ximenio, fol. 3 (Compluti, 1569).--Robles, Vida del Cardenal Ximenes, pp. 38-41.

    35. Castillo, Crónica de Enrique IV, cap. cv.

    36. Memorial histórico español, T. I, p. 236; II, 22, 25.--Gomez de Rebus gestis a Fran. Ximenio, fol. 9-11.

    37. Zurita, Añales de Aragon, Lib. XX, cap. xxii.--Mariana, Historia de España, Lib. XXIV, cap. xvi.

    38. Pulgar, Crónica de los Reyes Catolicos, Lib. II, cap. civ.

    The right as to bishoprics was finally conceded in 1523 to Charles V by Adrian VI (Mariana, Lib. XXVI, cap. 5).

    39. Francisco de Medina, Vida del Cardenal de Mendoza (Memorial histórico español, T. VI, p. 244).

    40. Boletin de la R. Acad. de la Historia, T. XXII, pp. 220, 227.

    41. Coleccion de Privilegios etc. T. VI, p. 117 (Madrid, 1833).

    42. Archivo de Sevilla, Seccion primera, Carpeta IV, fol. 85, § 3 (Sevilla, 1860).

    43. Ordenanzas Reales, Lib. III, Tit. i, leyes 3, 4, 5, 6, 8, 9, 10.--Novís. Recop. Lib. IV, Tit. i, leyes 3, 4, 5.

    44. Novísima Recop. Lib. XII, Tit. xxvi, leyes 3-5.

    45. Coleccion de Cédulas, III, 113 (Madrid, 1829)

    46. Coleccion de Cédulas, I, 246.

    47. Concil. Arandens. ann. 1473, cap. xxiv (Aguirre, V, 350).

    48. Córtes de Leon y de Castilla, II, 539; III, 33, 57, 122, 172, 192-6, 287, 328, 408.

    49. Pulgar, Crónica, III, lxvi.

    50. Coleccion de Cédulas, II, 49, 50 (Madrid, 1829).

    51. La Puente, Epit. de la Crónica de Juan II, Lib. V, cap. xxxiii.--L. Marinæi Siculi de Rebus Hispan. Lib. XIX.--Pulgar, Crónica, P. II, cap. li.--Bernaldez, Historia de los Reyes Católicos, cap. i (Sevilla, 1869).

    52. Galindez de Carvajal (Coleccion de Documentos para la Historia de España, XVIII, 254).

    53. Zurita, Añales de Aragon, Lib. XVIII, cap. 20, 21.--Castillo, Crónica de Enrique IV, cap. cxxiv.--Valera, Memorial de diversas Hazañas, cap. xx.--Pulgar, Crónica P. I, cap. ii; P. II, cap. xci.--Maldonado, Hechos de Don Alonso de Monrrey (Mem. hist. español, T. VI, p. 94).--Barrantes, Ilustraciones de la Casa de Niebla, Lib. VIII, cap. xxi.

    54. Castillo, Crónica de Enrique IV, cap. cxxxvii.--Clemencin, Elógio de la Reina Isabel, Append. I.

    55. Pulgar, Crónica, P. II, cap. ii; Letra xii.--L. Marinæi Siculi de Reb. Hisp. Lib. XIX.

    56. Machiavelli's judgement was as usual correct when he remarked (Il Principe, cap. xvi) "Il Re di Spagna presente se fusse tenuto liberale non avrebbe fatto nè vinto tante imprese."

    57. Archivo Gen. de Simancas, Consejo de la Inquisicion, Libro II, fol. 22

    58. "Con gran dificultad perdonava los yerros que se le hazian."--Barrantes, Ilustraciones etc., Lib. VIII, cap. xii.

    59. Palafox y Mendoza, Obras, T. VII, p. 333 (Madrid, 1762).--Ochoa, Epistolario Español, II, 14.

    60. Bergenroth, Calendar of Spanish State Papers, I, xxxiv-v. The value of the gold crown of the period was 4s. 6d. sterling (Ibid. p. 4) and 200,000 scudos was the marriage-portion of Katharine of Aragon when wedded to Prince Arthur of England (Ibid, p. lxiv), which is the equivalent of about £500,000 of modern money. For the oppression of the people see Gonzalo de Ayora (Boletin de la R.

Acad., XVII, 447-8). Cf. Clemencin, p. 185.

61. From the Notables of Cristóbal Núñez, printed by Padre Fidel Fita in the Boletin, XVI, 561.
62. L. Marinæi Siculi de Rebus Hisp. Lib. XXI.
63. Pet. Martyr. Angler. Lib. V, Epist. cxiv.
64. Colmeiro, Córtes de Leon y de Castilla, II, 43 sqq.
65. Pulgar, Crónica, P. II, cap. lxx.--Æl. Anton. Nebriss. Decad. I, Lib. vii, cap. 6.--Barrantes, Ilustraciones etc. Lib. VIII, cap. xv.--José Grestoso y Pérez, Los Reyes Católicos en Sevilla (Sevilla, 1891).--Zuñiga, Añales de Sevilla, ann. 1477, n. 5.
66. Pulgar, Crónica, P. II, cap. xcv.
67. Ferreiro, Fueros Municipales de Santiago, II, 65 (Santiago, 1896).
68. Ibidem, II, 314.
69. L. Marinæi Siculi Lib. XIX, XXI.--Pulgar, Crónica, P. II, cap. xxvii, lxxviii, xcvi, xcvii, xcviii; P. III, cap. xxxix, lxvi, c, cxxvii.--Capitulos hechos por el rey y la reyna en Sevilla a ix de Junio de M. y d. (sine nota).
70. Galindez de Carvajal (Coleccion de Documentos para la Historia de Españe, XVIII, 236).
71. Bernaldez, cap. xlii.
72. Pet. Martyr. Angler. Lib. V, Epist. cviii. As Cardinal Ximenes says in his letter of advice to Cardinal Adrian as to the conduct of Charles V in taking possession of his inheritance, "por lo qual fue ella tan poderosisima en su reyno, que todos del mayor á el menor temian virgam ferream de su justicia, y asi destruyó toda la tirannia." (Valladares, Semanario Erúdito, XX, 237).
73. Archivo Gen. de Simancas, Inquisicion Libros I, II.
74. The limitations on the royal jurisdiction are exemplified by the unseemly contest at Alcalá de Henares, in 1485-6, between Isabella and the Archbishop González de Mendoza, respecting her right to administer justice within his province. It lasted from December till the time for opening the campaign against Granada, when she removed to Córdova without having established her claim.--Francisco de Medina, Vida del Cardenal Mendoza (Mem. hist, español, VI, 264).

Yet her jurisdiction was one of the points on which Isabella wisely insisted with the utmost firmness. To quote Cardinal Ximenes again--"Ante todo la dicha Reyna cuidaba de defender su jurisdiccion Real, viendo que por ella los Reyes en Castilla se hacen mas poderosos y mas temidos de sus vasallos" (Valladares, Semanario Erúdito, XX, 238). When, in 1491, the royal court at Valladolid, presided over by Alonzo de Valdevielfo, Bishop of Leon, wrongfully allowed an appeal to Rome, she promptly dismissed the bishop and all the judges and replaced them with Juan Arias del Villar, Bishop of Oviedo, and other assessors.--Crónicon de Valladolid (Coleccion de Documentos para la Historia de España, XIII, 184-5).--Galindez de Carbajal (Ibid. XVIII, 278).

75. Memorial histórico español, T. II, pp. 68, 72, 86, 94, 102.
76. Benavides, Memorias de Fernando IV, Coleccion Diplomática, T. II, pp. 3, 7, 46, 75, 81, 178 (Madrid, 1860).--Vicente Santamaria de Paredes, Curso de Derecho Político, p. 509 (Madrid, 1883).--Córtes de los antiguos Reinos de Leon y Castilla, I, 247, 300 (Madrid, 1861).
77. Benavides, op. cit. II, 363.
78. Ferreiro, Fucros Municipales de Santiago, III, 44.
79. Coleccion de Privilegios, T. VI, p. 327 (Madrid, 1833).
80. Crónica de Don Juan II, año XXXVII, cap. i.
81. Córtes de Leon y de Castilla, III, 795.
82. Castillo, Crónica de Don Enrique IV, cap. lxxxvii, xc.--Barrantes, Ilustraciones etc. Lib. VII, cap. xxviii.--Garibay, Compendio Historial, Lib. XVII, cap. xxxi.--Coleccion de Cédulas, III, 103 (Madrid, 1829).--Bienvenido, Oliver y Esteller (Boletin, XIV, 382).
83. Pulgar, Crónica, P. II, cap. li.--L. Marinæi Siculi de Reb. Hisp. Lib. XIX.--Æl. Anton. Nebriss. Decad. I, Lib. VI, cap. 1-3.--Garibay, Comp. Historial, Lib. XVIII, cap. viii.
84. Zuñiga, Añales de Sevilla, ann. 1477, No. 1.
85. Zurita, Hist, del Rey Hernando, Lib. VIII, cap. V.--Galindez de Carvajal (Coleccion de Documentos para la Historia de España, XVIII, 319).
86. Barrantes, Ilustraciones etc. Lib. VIII, cap. xx.
87. Coleccion de Cédulas, I, 70, 124, 143, 183; III, 103.
88. Pulgar, Crónica, P. III, cap. xcv.--Palafox, Obras, VII, 338 (Madrid, 1762).--Fueros de Aragon, fol. 13 (Saragossa, 1624).
89. Coleccion de Cédulas, IV, 89.
90. Pulgar, Crónica, P. III, cap. xii.
91. Novís. Recop. Tit. xxv, Lib. XII.--Barrantes, Ilustraciones etc. Lib. VIII, cap xiii.--Coleccion de Cédulas, IV, 295.--See also the description of the perfected system which excited the admiration of the Venetian ambassador, Paolo Tiepolo, in 1563 (Relazioni, Serie I, T. V, p. 21).
92. Clemencin, p. 139.
93. Coleccion de Cédulas, IV, 136, 164, 173, 185, 336, 338; V, 669; VI, 425.--Novís Recop. Tit.

xxxv, Lib. XII, ley 18.

94. Córtes de los antiguos Reinos, IV, 356 (Madrid, 1882)--"E las leyes e costunbres son sujetas alos Reys, que las pueden hazer e quitar a su voluntad, e vuestra Alteza es ley viba e animada en las tierras."

95. Coleccion de Cédulas, IV, 333.

96. Mariana, Lib. XXVIII, cap. xi; Tom. IX, Append. p. xix.--Giustiniani, Historie degl'Ordini Militari, pp. 386, 425, 460 (Venezia, 1692).

97. Cartas de Ximenes de Cisneros, pp. 120, 131, 181 (Madrid, 1867).--Wadding, Annales Minorum, ann. 1516, n. 12.--Gachard, Correspondence entre Charles-Quint et Adrien VI, p. cxi (Bruxelles, 1859).

98. Thus Father Gams attributes the Spanish Inquisition to the national peculiarity of the Spaniard, who requires that the State should represent God on earth, and that Christianity should control all public life; he demands unity of faith and not freedom of faith. The Inquisition is an institution for which the Church has no responsibility.--P. Pius Gams, O. S. B., Die Kirchengeschichte von Spanien, III, II, 7, 8, 11, 12.

99. Septimi Decretal. Lib. V, Tit. i, cap. 5.

100. Paramo de Orig. Offic. S. Inquisitionis, p. 164.

101. Fortalicium Fidei, fol. 147^{b} (Ed. 1494).

102. Canon. Apostol. n. 69, 70.

103. Concil. Eliberitan. cap. 16, 49, 50, 78.

104. S. August, de Adult. Conjug. Lib. I, cap. xviii.

105. S. Ambros. Epist. XL, n. 26.

106. S. Joh. Chrysost. adv. Judæos Orat. I, n. 3, 4, 6. Chrysostom's indignation was especially aroused by the popular belief among Christians in the peculiar sanctity of the synagogues, which rendered oaths taken in them more binding than in a church.

107. Socrat. H. E. VII, xiii.

108. Lib. XVI, Cod. Theodos. Tit. viii, Ll. 6, 9, 12, 21, 22, 25, 26, 27; Tit. ix, Ll. 2, 3, 4, 5.

109. Novell. Theodos. II, Tit. iii.

110. Edict. Theoderici, cap. 143.--Cassiodori Variar. IV, 33, 43; v, 37. Cf. III, 45.

111. Concil. Agathens. ann. 506, cap. 40. This was embodied in the canon law (Gratian. Decr. Caus. XXVIII, Q. i, cap. 14). The apologetic tone in which Sidonius Apollinaris, Bishop of Clermont, speaks of Jews whom he likes and who "solent hujusmodi homines honestas habere causas" shows that the more enlightened churchmen felt that any favor shown to the proscribed race exposed them to animadversion (Epistt. Lib. III, Ep. 4; Lib. IV, Ep. 5).

112. Concil. Quinisext. cap. 11 (Decr. Caus. XXVIII, Q. i, cap. 13).

113. Gregor. PP. I. Epistt. XIII, 12 (Decreti Dist. XLV, cap. 3).

114. Ejusd. Epistt. I, 10, 35; II, 32; V, 8; VIII, 27; IX, 6; XIII, 12. It is true that Gregory strongly upheld the rule that Jews should hold no Christian slaves, but he permitted Christians to labor on their lands (Ibid, IV, 21).

115. Ibid, I, 47.--Venantii Fortunati Miscell. Lib. V, cap. 5.

116. Cassiodor. Variar. II, 27; X, 26.

117. Lex Roman. Visigoth. Lib. XVI, Tit. iii, iv; Novell. Theodos. II, Tit iii (Ed. Haenel, pp. 250, 256-8).

118. Concil. Toletan. III, ann. 589, cap. xiv.--Concil. Narbonn. ann. 589, cap. iv, ix.

119. Gotth. Heine, Biblioth. Vet. Monumentt. Ecclesiasticor. p. 118 (Lipsiæ, 1848).

120. S. Isidori Hispalens. de Fide Cathol. contra Judæos Lib. I, cap. 28; Lib. II, cap. 5, 9.

121. S. Isidori Chron. n. 120; De Regibus Gothorum, n. 60; Sententt. Lib. III, cap. 51, n. 4.

In the perfected doctrine of the Church it was simply a question of policy and possibility whether the faith is to be extended by force or not, for the pope is supreme and has the authority to punish all, whether Jew or Gentile, who do not conform to the gospel.--Eymerici Direct. Inquisitor, p. 353 (Ed. Venet. 1607).

122. Concil. Toletan. IV, ann. 633, cap. 57--adopted into the canon law (Decr. cap. 5, Dist. XLV)--as well as a decretal of Gregory IV--"Judæi non sunt cogendi ad fidem, quam tamen si invite susceperint, cogendi sunt retinere" (Ibid. cap. 4). See also Ll. Wisigoth. Lib. XII, Tit. ii, l. 4 (Recared I), continued in Fuero Juzgo, XII, ii, 4.

The Jew who had been baptized in infancy, or who accepted baptism as an alternative of death, and reverted to Judaism was to be prosecuted by the Inquisition as a heretic.--Nicholai, PP. IV. Bull. Turbato corde, 1288 (Bullar. Roman. I, 158, 179, 184, 263).--Cap. 13 in Sexto, Lib. V, Tit. ii.--Bernard. Guidon. Practica, P. v, § v, n. 1.--Pegnæ Comment. in Eymeric. Direct. Inquis., p. 349. For the established formula of interrogatory, of Jews see MSS. Bibl. National de France, Collect. Doat., T. XXXVII, fol. 258.

The forced conversion of Jews, so frequent throughout the Middle Ages, gave rise to many nice questions, exhaustively debated by the schoolmen. The subject is fully treated in a Tractatus de Judæorum et Christianorum communione, etc., printed in Strassburg about 1470 (Hain, 9465), in which, for convenient use and reference, is gathered together all the ecclesiastical legislation against the unfortunate race, forming a deplorable exhibition of human perversity.

123. Concil. Toletan. IV, ann. 633, cap. 58, 59, 60, 61, 62, 63, 64, 65, 66; Conc. VI, ann. 638, cap. 3; Conc. VIII, ann. 653, cap. 12; Conc. IX, ann. 655, cap. 17; Conc. X, ann. 656, cap. 7; Conc. XII, ann. 681, cap. 9; Conc. XIII, ann. 683, cap. 9; Conc. XVI, ann. 693, cap. 1.

Ll. Wisigoth. Lib. XII, Tit. ii, ll. 4-17; Tit. iii, ll. 1, 2, 10, 12, 16, 17, 19, 24 (Fuero Juzgo, ibidem.).

124. S. Juliani Toleti Vit. Wambæ, n. 5, 28 (Florez, España Sagrada, VI, 536, 556).

125. Concil. Toletan. XVII, ann. 694, cap. 8.

126. Roderic. Toletan. de Rebus Hispan. Lib. III, cap. xvi.--Morales, Corónica General, T. VI, p. 361. Isidor of Beja, however, is the best authority for the period, and he speaks of Witiza in terms of high praise (Isidor. Pacens. Chron. n. 29, 30). See also Dozy, Recherches sur l'Histoire et la Littérature de l'Espagne, I, 16-17 (3e Éd. Leipzig, 1881).

127. Rod. Toletan. op. cit. Lib. III, cap. xxii, xxiii.--Dozy, I, 49, 52.

128. Dozy, I, 17, 44, 53, 54, 56, 72, 74-5, 79, 350-1.

129. An interesting instance of Moslem toleration is seen in the Farfanes--Christians of Morocco who claimed to be the descendants of Goths deported at the conquest at the request of Count Julian. In 1386 they sent Sancho Rodríguez, one of their number, to Juan I to ask to be received back in Spain. Juan obtained from the King of Morocco permission for their departure, and promised to provide for them lands and support. In 1390 they came, numbering fifty cavaliers with their wives and children, and bringing a letter from the Moslem ruler speaking of them as nobles descended from the Goths and praising greatly their loyalty and valor. It was in riding out from Burgos to welcome them that Juan's horse fell and caused his death. In 1394 Henry III gave them a confirmation of their ancient nobility, and in 1430 and 1433 we still find them recognized in Seville as a distinct class.--Ayala, Crón. de Juan I, año X, cap. xx.--Zuñiga, Annales de Sevilla, Lib. VIII, año 1386, n. 2; año 1390, n. 3; Lib. IX, año 1394, n. 1.--Archivo de Sevilla, Seccion primera, Carpeta clxxiv, n. 4, 8.

130. Francisco Fernández y González, Estado de los Mudéjares de Castilla, pp. 14-18 (Madrid, 1866).--S. Eulogii Memorialis Sanctorum Lib. II, cap. xvi; Lib. III, cap. i (Migne's Patrologia, CXV, 787, 800).

131. Florez, España Sagrada, XI, 309 sqq.; V, Append. x.--Samsonis Abbatis Cordubensis Apolog. Lib. II (Ib. XI, 388 sqq.).--Alvari Cordubens. Epist. vii, viii (Ibid. XI, 147 sqq.).--Hostegesis was Bishop of Málaga, and the free exercise of discipline in the Mozárabic church is shown in the complaint of the cruelty with which he exacted the tercia or tribute due to him, causing delinquents to be paraded through the streets with soldiers scourging them and proclaiming that all defaulters should be similarly treated.--Florez, XII, 326.

132. S. Eulogii Epist. iii (Migne, CXV, 845-9).--Alvari Cordubens. Vit. S. Eulogii (Ibid. 712).--The description by Alvar of his education with S. Eulogio shows that the Christian schools of Córdova were flourishing and active (Ibid. cap. i, p. 708).

133. Alvari Cordubens. Vit. S. Eulogii, cap. iv, v.--Eulogii Memorialis Sanctorum Lib. II; Lib. III, cap. ii, iii, v, viii, xvii.--Ejusd. Vit. et Passio SS. Floræ et Mariæ.--Ejusd. Lib. Apologet. Martyrum.

134. Aimoini Translatio SS. Georgii, Aurelii et Nathaliæ, Lib. I; Lib. II, cap. xxviii.

135. Liutprandi Antopodosis, Lib. II, cap. i.

136. Dozy, Recherches, II, 178.

137. Fernández y González, p. 57.

138. Dozy, Recherches, I, 265, 269, 349, 352-61.--Orderici Vital. Hist. Eccles. P. III, Lib. xiii, cap. 2.

139. Crónica de Alfonso VII, cap. 46, 101 (España Sagrada, XXI, 360, 398).

140. Dozy, Recherches, I, 370-1.--Fernández y González, p. 19.--See also an essay on the Mozárabes of Valencia by Don Roque Chabás, in the Boletin de la Real Academia de la Historia, XVIII, 19.

141. Fernández y González, pp. 86-7, 93. The term Miramamolin, so often used by Christian writers as a personal name, is Amir-el-Momenin, or Prince of the Faithful, a title frequently assumed by Moorish rulers.

142. Fernández y González, pp. 92, 96.

143. Menéndez y Pelayo, Heterodoxos Españoles, I, 640-5.

144. Dozy, Recherches, I, 365-7, 372-9.

145. S. Eulogii Memorialis Sanctorum Lib. III, cap. iv.--Lindo's History of the Jews of Spain, p. 44 (London, 1848).

146. Lindo, p. 46.

147. Dozy, Recherches, I, 285-9.

148. Lindo, p. 62.
149. Lindo, pp. 156-7.
150. In the ballads the Moors are almost always represented as chivalric enemies. Even when celebrating their defeats, down to the capture of Granada, there is no contempt manifested and nowhere is to be seen a trace of religious acerbity. Many ballads have Moors as their heroes, as in those which celebrate the deeds of Bravonel and Reduan, and there is nothing to distinguish their treatment from that of Christians. Bravonel and Bernardo del Carpio are represented as companions in arms. When Bernardo is banished by his king he betakes himself forthwith to Granada to participate in a tournament, where

> Que hay unas Reales fiestas, Donde el premio será dado
> Al que mejor lo ficiere Sea Moro ó sea Cristiano;

and there he is warmly welcomed by Muza, the most gallant knight of the Saracens.--Romances Antiguos Españoles, I, 65 (Leipzig, 1844).

151. Villanueva, Viage Literario, XVI, 159.
152. Dozy, Recherches, II, 203, 233.
153. Dozy, II, 109, 111.--Edélestand du Meril, Poésies populaires Latines, pp. 312-13.
154. Chron. Sampiri Asturicens, n. 3, 22, 26 (España Sagrada, XIV, 439, 452, 455).
155. Chron. Pelagii Ovietens. (España Sagrada, XIV, 468, 472).
156. Fernández y González, pp. 34, 48, 114.
157. Crónica de Don Alfonso X, cap. xix-lviii.
158. Ibidem cap. lxxvi.--Barrantes, Ilustraciones, Lib. I, cap. vi, xi (Memorial hist. español, IX, 72-9, 92-8).
159. Crónica de Don Alfonso XI, cap. lvii, cxi, cxxv.
160. Ayala, Crónica de Don Pedro I, año XVII, cap. iv; año XIX, cap. iv, v; año XX, cap. vi.
161. Barrantes, Ilustraciones, Lib. VII, cap. xxii.
162. Memorial histórico español, I, 159.
163. Ibidem III, 151.
164. Coleccion de Documentos inéditos de la Corona de Aragon, I, 25.
165. Concil. Lateran. IV, ann. 1216 ad calcem (Harduin. VII, 75).--Cap. 6, 17, Extra, Lib. V, Tit. vi.--Concil. Lugdunens. I, ann. 1245, cap. xvii (Harduin. VIII, 394).--Concil. Ilerdens. ann. 1246 (Aguirre, VI, 318).--Concil. Vallisolet. ann. 1322, cap. xxii (Aguirre, V, 251).--Cap. 1 Extrav. Commun. Lib. V, Tit. ii.--Urbani PP. V, Bull. Apostolatus, 1364 (Bullar. Roman. Ed. Luxemburg. I, 261).--Nicholai PP. V, Bull. Olim, 1450 (Ibid. I, 361), and finally in the standard anathema of the bull in Coena Domini.

Considering the character of the Roman curia in the Middle Ages it would scarce be malicious to suggest that the chief object of these prohibitions was to create a market for licenses to violate them, and St. Antonino of Florence, about the middle of the fifteenth century, tells us that as a rule the Venetian merchants had them (S. Antonini Confessionale)

In spite of his laxity in practice, Alfonso X in the Partidas embodies the Lateran decree denouncing slavery for all who aid the Saracens in any manner (Partidas, P. IV, Tit. xxi, ley 4) and in 1253 he admitted papal control in such matters by obtaining in advance from Innocent IV ratification of certain treaties which he was negotiating with the princes of Africa (Fernández y González, p. 337).

166. Bullar. Roman. I, 263.--Eymerici Direct. Inquisit. p. 351(Ed. Venet. 1607).
167. Barrantes, Ilustraciones, etc., Lib. I, cap. iv, xiii, xiv, xx, xxi.--Ayala, Crónica de Don Pedro I, año III, cap. iii.
168. Chron. Sampiri Asturicens. n. 16, 24, 25 (España Sagrada, XIV, 447, 454, 455).--Marca Hispanica, p. 1232.
169. Partidas, P. IV, Tit. xxi, leyes 6, 8; Tit. xxii, ley 3. In the Fuero Real de España the only allusion to Moors is as slaves (Lib. IV, Tit. xi, ley 3; Tit. xiv, ley 1). It is virtually the same in the old Fuero of Madrid (Memorias de la R. Acad. de la Historia, VIII, 40).

The Church held that baptism manumitted the slave, even when the master was Christian, but when it sought to enforce the rule the masters resisted, either forbidding the baptism or demanding from the clergy the value of the slave and seizing pledges to ensure payment. Innocent III was much scandalized by this. In 1205 he complained to Alfonso IX that in place of requiring such converted slaves to be paid for at the price fixed by the canons he allowed the owner to determine the value, and thus the Bishop of Burgos had recently been forced to pay two hundred gold pieces for a girl not worth ten deniers (Innoc. PP. III, Regest. VIII, 50; IX, 150).

170. Partidas, P. IV, Tit. xxi, ley 7.
171. Fernández y González, pp. 21, 24-5.
172. Dozy, Recherches, I, 124-6.
173. Fernández y González, p. 28.
174. Ayala, Crónica de Don Pedro I, año II, cap. xvii.

175. Fernández y González, pp. 39, 45-6, 58.
176. Mondexar, Memorias de Alonso VIII, cap. cv, cviii.--Roderici Toletani de Rebus Hispan. Lib. VIII, cap. xii.
177. Villanueva, Viage Literario, XXI, 131.
178. Fernández y González, p. 97.
179. See the capitulation of Valencia in 1232 (Villanueva, XVII, 331); also the Constitutiones Pacis et Treugæ of Catalonia, in 1214, 1225, and 1228 (Marca Hispanica, pp. 1402, 1407, 1413), and also that of Rosellon, in 1217 (D'Achery, Spicileg. III, 587). In 1279 Pedro III of Aragon issues letters "to all his faithful Moors of the frontier of Castile and Viar," inviting them to come and populate Villareal, offering them the vacant lands there and pledging them security for all their goods (Coleccion de Documentos de la Corona de Aragon, VIII, 143).
180. Coleccion de Cédulas, V, 571, 573, 584, 600, 608, 622, 632; VI, 93, 106, 112, 220, 292, 308, 326, 385, 455. A charter of San Fernando III, in 1246, selling certain lands to the city of Toledo, says "vendo á vos, concejo de Toledo, á los caballeros é al pueblo, é á cristianos é á moros é á judios, á los que sodes é á los que han de ser adelant, todos aquellos terminos, etc."--Fernández y González, p. 319.
181. Fernández y González, pp. 117, 122, 123.--Memorial histórico español, I, 285.
182. Coleccion de Cédulas, V, 29.--Fernández y González, p. 294. In the charter of Hinestrosa (1287) the wergild for homicide is 500 sueldos. In that of Arganzon (1191) allusion is made to the wergild of 500 sueldos, but the special privilege is granted that the murderer shall pay only 250, the other 250 being remitted "for the sake of the king's soul." In the charter of Amaya (1285) the wergild is sixty maravedís.--(Coleccion de Cédulas, V, 222, 112, 205.)
183. Memorias de la Real Academia de la Historia, VIII, 39.
184. Leyes de Estilo, 83, 84.
185. Coleccion de Cédulas, V, 413.
186. Fernández y González, pp. 407, 409. By a confirmation of Pedro IV of Aragon, in 1372, to the aljama of Calatayud it appears that the Moors of the cities were accustomed to have special shambles where their meat was slaughtered and marked "secundum eorum ritum sive çunam."--Ibid. p. 384.
187. Coleccion de Documentos de la Corona de Aragon, IV, 130; VI, 145.--Fernández y González, pp. 286, 290, 386, 389.
188. Fernández y González, pp. 92, 94-5, 102.
189. Archivo de Sevilla, Seccion Primera, Carpeta I, n. 49.--Fernández y González, pp. 351, 353, 363.--Ordenanzas Reales, VIII, iii, 31.--Memorial histórico español, I, 81, 152.
190. Fernández y González, pp. 221, 286.--Coleccion de Documentos de la Corona de Aragon, VI, 157, 196.--Córtes de los antiguos Reinos, II, 309.
191. Aguirre, V, 225, 227; VI, 369.--Cap. 5 Extra v, vi.--Cap. 2 Extrav. Commun. v, ii.--Tratados de Legislacion Musulmana, p. 216 (Madrid, 1853).--Partidas, P. VII, Tit. xxv, leyes 2, 3.--Constitutions de Cathalunya, Lib. I, cap. 3, 4 (Barcelona, 1588).--Concil. Tarraconens. ann. 1245 (Aguirre, VI, 306).
192. Fernández y González, pp. 107-8, 120, 286, 359.--Memorial histórico español, I, 285.--For the manner in which the houses of conquered towns were distributed see the Repartimiento de Jerez de la Frontera by Alfonso X in this same year 1266, printed by Padre Fidel Fita (Boletin, Junio, 1887, pp. 465 sqq.).
193. Fernández y González, p. 346.
194. Coleccion de Documentos de la Corona de Aragon, VI, 255.--Partidas, P. VII, Tit. xxv, ley 10.
195. Tratados de Legislacion Musulmana, p. 7 (Madrid, 1853). In this collection the Leyes de los Moros probably date from about the year 1300. Ice Gebir's Suma de los principales Mandamientos was written in 1462. It would not be easy to find a more practical moral code than that presented in the short precepts assembled in Ice Gebir's first chapter (pp. 250 sqq.). It is somewhat surprising to learn that in the alchihéd, or holy war against Christians, it was forbidden to slay non-combatants--women, children, old men and even monks and friars unless they defended themselves by force (cap. xxxv, p. 333). Even harmless things, such as ants and frogs, are not to be deprived of life (cap. clvii, p. 400). The vital reproach to be brought against Islam is the position assigned to woman--her degradation in her relations to man, and her scant recognition as a human being. In a classification of society into twelve orders, the eleventh is that of baldios or robbers, sorcerers, pirates, drunkards, etc., and the twelfth and lowest is woman (Ib. cap. lx, pp. 412, 415).
196. The ballad chronicler relates how--
Et los moros é las moras Muy grandes juegos hacian, Los judíos con las toras Estos Reyes bien recibian. Fernández y González, p. 239.

197. Crónica de Juan II, año IV, cap. 26.
198. Coleccion de Documentos de la Corona de Aragon, VIII, 53.--Memorial histórico español, I,

239, 263; III, 439.

199. Fernández y González, p. 389.

200. Ibid. pp. 382, 386.

201. Janer, Condicion Social de los Moriscos de España, pp. 47-9, 161, 162 (Madrid, 1857).

Under the Saracen domination, Almería was the chief port of Spain, crowded with ships from Syria and Egypt, Pisa and Genoa. It boasted of a thousand inns for strangers and four thousand weaving shops, besides manufactures of copper, iron and glass (Dozy, Recherches, I, 244-5). For the wonderful wealth of the Moors under the caliphs of Córdova, showing the capacity of the race and of the land, see Conde's "Arabs in Spain," P. II, cap. 94. How unfitted was the Castilian chivalry to perpetuate this prosperity is seen in a letter of Alfonso X in 1258, reciting how he had peopled with Christians the flourishing city of Alicante, as it was a stronghold and one of the best seaports; how the allotment of lands had given dissatisfaction and on investigation he had found that the Christians could not live and prosper there, wherefore he now makes a new repartimiento (Memorial histórico español, I, 135).

202. Fernández y González, pp. 294, 321, 367. Cf. Concil. Vallisolet. ann. 1322, cap. xxii; C. Toletan. ann. 1324, cap. viii (Aguirre, V, 251, 259); Concil. Parisiensis, ann. 1212, Addend. cap. i (Martene Ampliss. Collect. VII, 1420).

203. Concil. Lateran. IV, ann. 1216, cap. lxviii (cap. 15, Extra, v, vi). This device originated among the Saracens of the East, who, in the eleventh century, required Jews and Christians to wear distinctive badges (Fernández y González, p. 16). The earliest trace of it in the West is found in the charter of Alais, in 1200, which prescribes distinctive vestments for Jews (Robert, Les Signes d'Infamie au Moyen Age, p. 7). In Italy, Frederic II obeyed the Lateran decree by ordering, in 1221, all Jews to wear distinguishing garments (Richardi de S. German. Chron. ap. Muratori, S. R. I., VII, 993), but he did not insert this in the Sicilian Constitutions or include his Saracen subjects. In 1254 the council of Albi prescribed for Jews a circle, a finger-breadth in width, to be worn upon the breast, and that of Ravenna, in 1311, a yellow circle (Harduin. VII, 458, 1370). In the fifteenth century, the Neapolitan Jews were required to wear as a sign the Hebrew letter Tau (Wadding, Annal. Minor. T. III, Regest. p. 392).

204. Raynald. Annal. ann. 1217, n. 84.--Amador de los Rios, Hist. de los Judíos de España, I, 361-2, 554.

205. Amador de los Rios, I, 362, 364.

206. Partidas, P. VII, Tit. xxiv, ley 11.

207. Córtes de los antiguos Reinos, I, 227.

208. Concil. Tarraconens. ann. 1238, cap. iv; ann. 1282, cap. v (Martene Ampliss. Collect. VIII, 132, 280).--Fernández y González, p. 369.--Constitutions de Cathalunya superfluas, Lib. I, Tit. v, cap. 12 (Barcelona, 1589, p. 8).

209. Ayala, Crónica de Enrique II, año VI, cap. vii.--Córtes de los antiguos Reinos, II, 281.

210. Ripoll Bullar. Ord. FF. Prædic. I, 479. It was apparently in return for a tithe of ecclesiastical revenues that Jaime pledged himself to the pope to expel the Moors, but he was too wise a statesman to do so, and as late as 1275 he invited additional settlers by the promise of a year's exemption from taxation. On his death-bed in 1276, however, partly, no doubt in consequence of a dangerous Moorish revolt, and partly owing to the awakened fears shown by his taking the Cistercian habit, he enjoined his son Pedro to fulfil the promise, and in a codicil to his will he emphatically repeated the request (Danvila y Collado, La Expulsion de los Moriscos, p. 24.--Swift, James the First of Aragon, pp. 140, 253, 290), but Pedro was obdurate.

211. Fernández y González, p. 109.

212. Constitt. Valentin. (Aguirre, V, 206).

213. Cap. 1 Clementin. Lib. V, Tit. ii.

214. Concil. Tarraconens. ann. 1329 (Aguirre, VI, 370).

215. Concil. Dertusan. ann. 1429, cap. xx (Aguirre, V, 340).--Raynald. Annal. ann. 1483, n. 45.

In 1370 the Carta Pueblo, granted by Buenaventura de Arborea to the Moors of Chelva specifically allowed their alfaquíes to cry Alá Zalá as was their wont in the time of Pedro, her late husband.--Fernández y González, p. 386.

216. Cap. 1 Clementin. Lib. II, Tit. viii; Lib. V, Tit. v.

217. Although the acts of the council of Zamora were fully confirmed by the Córtes of Palencia in 1313 (Córtes de los antiguos Reinos, I, 227, 240-1), it seemed impossible to enforce them. In 1331 the Córtes of Madrid ineffectually petitioned that Christians denying debts to Jews could offer another Christian as a witness and not be obliged to have a Jew. The Fuero Viejo de Castiella, as revised in 1356, however, grants the privilege (Lib. III, Tit. iv, ley 19). The editors of the Fuero, Asso and Manuel (Ed. 1847, p. 83) say that the practice varied, and that Henry III, in the Córtes of Madrid, in 1405, again granted the privilege. As early as 1263 Alfonso X had enacted that in mixed suits a Jew could not demand that his opponent should produce as witnesses a Christian and a Jew, but that the evidence of two good Christians should suffice.--Memorial histórico español, I, 207. The point has interest as an

evidence of the desire to protect Jews from imposition.
218. Amador de los Rios, II, 561-5.
219. Concil. Vallisolet. ann. 1322, cap. xxii (Aguirre, V, 250).
220. Innocent. PP. III, Regest. X, 69; XII, post Epist. 107.--Concil. Lateran. IV, cap. lxix (cap. 16, Extra, v, vi).
221. Fernández y González, p. 289.--Coleccion de Privilegios, VI, 97.--Partidas, P. VII, Tit. xxiv, ley 3.
222. Annal. Novesiens. ann. 846 (Martene Ampliss. Collect. IV, 538). Cf. Gest. Episc. Leodiens. Lib. II, cap. 41.--Hist. Treverens. (D'Achery Spicileg. II, 222).
223. Concil. Quinisext. cap. xi.--Gratian. cap. 13, Caus. xxviii, Q. I.
224. Cap. 13, Extra, V, xxxviii.
225. Concil. Salmanticens. ann. 1335, cap. xii (Aguirre, V, 269).
226. Ordenamiento de Doña Catalina, n. 10.
227. Fortalicium Fidei, fol. 147^{a} (Ed. 1494).
228. Mariana, Hist. de España, VIII, 69 (Ed. 1790).
229. Ordenanzas Reales, VIII, iii, 18.--Ripoll Bullar. Ord. FF. Prædic. IV, 44. As recently as 1580 Gregory XIII recited the prohibitions of employing Jewish physicians uttered by Paul IV and Pius V and deplored their inobservance which precipitated many souls to damnation, to prevent which he ordered their strict enforcement.--Septimi Decretal. Lib. III, Tit. vi, cap. 2.
230. Concil. Tarraconens. ann. 1329 (Aguirre, VI, 371).
231. Aguirre, V, 286-7. Pedro el Ceremonioso, the King of Aragon, was then only a boy of eighteen, who had ascended the throne in January, 1336.
232. Córtes de los antiguos Reinos, II, 311, 322-8.
233. Ordenanzas Reales, VIII, iii, 6.
234. Concil. Palentin. ann. 1388, cap. v, vi (Aguirre, V, 300).
235. Ordenamiento de Valladolid, i, xi (Fortalicium Fidei, fol. 176).--Fernández y González, pp. 400, 402.
236. Ordenanzas Reales, VIII, iii, 10, 19.
237. Padre Fidel Fita, Boletin, IX, 270-84, 289, 292.--It was not until 1555 that Paul IV adopted the same policy in Rome and established the Ghetto, or Jewish quarter.--Septimi Decretal. Lib. V, Tit. I, cap. 4
238. For a series of these capitulations see Coleccion de Documentos para la Historia de España, T. VIII, pp. 403 sqq.
239. S. Agobardi de Judaicis Superstitionibus; Ejusdem de cavenda. Societate Judaica.--Amulonis Episc. Lugdunens. Lib. contra Judæos ad Carolem Regem.
240. Stephani PP. VI, Epist. 2.
241. Cap. 7, 9, Extra, Lib. V, Tit. vi.
242. Concil. Paris, ann. 1212, P. V, cap. 2 (Martene Ampliss. Collect. VII, 102).
243. Innocent. PP. III, Regest. X, 190. Cf. Epistt. Select. Sæc. XIII, T. I, p. 414 (Pertz).
244. Cæsar. Heisterb. Dial. Mirac. Dist. II, cap. xxiv, xxv.--Bernaldez, Hist. de los Reyes Católicos, cap. xliii.--Vicente da Costa Mattos, Breve Discurso contra a heretica Perfidia do Judaismo, fol. 131, 132, 134 (Lisboa, 1623).--Bodleian Library, MSS. Arch. S. 130.
245. P. de Alliaco Canon. Reformat, cap. xliii (Von der Hardt, Concil. Constant. I, VIII, 430-1)
246. Chron. Turonens. ann. 1009.
247. Berthold. Constant, ann. 1096.--Otton. Frisingens. de Gest. Frid. I, Lib. I, cap. 37.--Vitoduran. Chron. ann. 1336.--Gesta Treviror. Archiepp. ann. 1337.
248. Rigord. de Gest. Phil. Aug. ann. 1182--Vaissette, Hist. Gen. de Languedoc, VIII, 1191-2 (Ed. Privat).--Nich. Trivetti Chron. ann. 1189.--Guill. Nangiac. Contin. ann. 1306.--Matt. Paris. Hist. Angl. ann. 1210.--Matt. Westmonast. ann. 1290.
249. Fuero Juzgo, Lib. XII, Tit. ii, ley 18.
250. Marca Hispanica, p. 1439.
251. Coleccion de Privilegios, VI, 96 (Madrid, 1833).--Memorial hist, español, I, 38, 124; II, 71.
252. Amador de los Rios, I, 185-6, 189.
253. Contin. Gerardi de Fracheto, ann. 1285 (Dom Bouquet, XXI, 7).
254. Amador de los Rios, II, 67.--Benavides, Memorias de Fernando IV, II, 331.
It indicates the independent position of Jews and Moors that they refused to pay tithes on lands acquired from Christians and their liability was enforced only after a vigorous and prolonged struggle.--See Cap. 18, Extra, Lib. v, Tit. xix (Concil. Lateran. IV).--Innocent. PP. III, Regest. VIII, 50; x, 61.--Concil Tarraconens. ann. 1291 (Aguirre, VI, 292).--Concil. Zamorens. ann. 1313, cap. x (Amador de los Rios, II, 564).--Memorial hist. español, I, 33, 160.--Fernández y González, pp. 348, 355, 380, 389.--Benavides, op. cit. II, 539, 541.
255. Concil. Roman. V, ann. 1078 (Migne's Patrologia, CXLVIII, 799).--Gregor. PP. VII, Regest.

IX, 2.
256. Amador de los Rios, I, 28-9.
257. Ibidem, II, 58.
258. Amador de los Rios, II, 74-5.
259. Leyes de Estilo, 89-90.
260. El Fuero Real, Lib. IV, Tit. iv, ley 7.--Partidas, VII, xxiv, 5. In 1322 Jaime II of Aragon forbids the molestation of Strogo Mercadell, a Jew, for taking a second wife.--Coleccion de Documentos de la Corona de Aragon, VI, 240.
261. El Fuero Real, Lib. IV, Tit. ii, leyes 1, 2, 3.
262. Lucæ Tudens. de altera Vita III, 3.
263. Alex. PP. II, Epist. 101 (Decreti Consid. XXIII, Q. viii, cap. 11).
264. Amador de los Rios, I, 189-90.
265. Roderici Toleti de Rebus Hispan. VIII, 2, 6.--Malo, Histoire des Juifs, p. 267 (Paris, 1826).
266. Villanueva, Viage Literario, XXII, 328, 329, 333.
267. Amador de los Rios, I. 370, 447-51.--Lindo's History of the Jews of Spain, P. 88.
268. Leyes nuevas, Núm. XII, XIII. Cf. Ley 7 (Alcubilla, Códigos antiguos, I, 182).
269. Partidas, P. VII, Tit. xxiv. The provision punishing with death male Jews for intercourse with Christian women only expressed existing legislation, even when the woman was a prostitute.--Benavides, Memorias de Fernando IV. II, 210.
270. Villanueva, Viage Literario, XIII, 332.--R. Nachmanidis Disputatio (Wagenseilii Tela Ignea Satanæ).--Coleccion de Documentos de la C. de Aragon, VI, 165.
271. Bulario de la Orden de Santiago, Lib. III, fol. 546 (Archivo hist, nacional de Madrid).
272. Coleccion de Documentos, VI, 167.--Villanueva, XIII, 336.--Ripoll Bullar Ord. Predic. I, 479.
273. Aguirre, VI, 369.
274. Coleccion de Documentos, VI, 170.
275. Amador de los Rios, I, 438.
276. Florez, España Sagrada, XLIV, 298.
277. Septimi Decretal. Lib. V, Tit. i, cap. 2.
278. Florez, op. cit., XLIV, 297-99.
279. Bernard d'Esclot, Cronica del Rey en Pere, cap. clii.
280. Coleccion de Documentos, VI, 194.
281. Villanueva, XXI, 165, 303.
282. Archivo gen. de la Corona de Aragon, Regist. 208, fol. 72; Regist. 229, fol. 239.
283. Amador de los Rios, II, 98-102.
284. Coleccion de Privilegios, VI, 129 (Madrid, 1833).--Benavides, Memorias de Fernando IV, II, 374.
285. Amador de los Rios, II, 90-4.
286. Córtes de los antiguos Reinos, I, 247.--Cap. 1, Clement. Lib. V, Tit. v.
287. Lindo's History of the Jews of Spain, p. 180.
288. Graetz, Geschichte der Juden, VIII, 327 (Ed. 1890).
289. Decreti P. II, Caus. xiv, Q. 3, 4, 5, 6.--Cap. 1, § 2 Clement. Lib. V, Tit. v.
290. Cap. 12, Extra, Lib. V, Tit. xix.--Concil. Lateran. IV, cap. 67.--Concil. Lugdunens. II, ann. 1274, cap. 26.--Cap. I Clement. Lib. V, Tit. v.--Concil. Pennafidelens. ann. 1302, cap. 9.
291. Marca Hispanica, pp. 1415, 1426, 1431.--Constitutions de Cathalunya superfluas, Lib. I, Tit. v, cap. 2.--Villanueva, Viage Literario, XXII, 301.--El Fuero Real, Lib. IV, Tit. ii, ley 6.
292. Marca Hispanica, pp. 1433, 1436.--Coleccion de Documentos de la C. de Aragon, VI, 170.--Córtes de los antiguos Reinos, I, 127, 227, 281.--Amador de los Rios, I, 393, 421, 587; II, 63, 69, 89, 121, 148.--Coleccion de Privilegios, VI, 111, 113.
293. Amador de los Rios, II, 139.
294. Córtes de los antiguos Reinos, II, 234.
295. Yanguas y Miranda, Diccionario de Antigüedades del Reino de Navarro, II, 93.
296. Ordenamiento de Alcalá, Tit. XXIII, ley 2. Cf. Ordenanzas Reales, Lib. VIII, Tit. ii, leyes 1-8.
297. Padre Fidel Fita, Boletin, XI, 404.
298. Amador de los Rios, I, 488.
299. Córtes de los antiguos Reinos, II, 325.--Amador de los Rios, II, 320.
300. Villanueva, XVII, 247.
301. Zurita, Añales de Aragon, Lib. VI, cap. lxxviii.--Amador de los Rios, II, 175-9, 284-5, 289-91.
302. Zurita, Lib. VIII, cap. xxvi, xxxiii.--Amador de los Rios, II, 260, 263, 299-300.
303. Raynald, Annal. ann. 1348, n. 83.

304. Guill. Nangiac. Contin. ann. 1366.--Quarta Vita Urbani V (Muratori, S. R. I., III, II, 641).
305. Ayala, Crónica de Pedro I, año VI, cap. vii.
306. Ibidem, año IX, cap. vii, viii.
307. Guill. Nangiac. Contin. ann. 1366.--Ayala, año XVII, cap. viii.
308. Amador de los Rios, II, 571-3.--Boletin, XXIX, 254.
309. Ayala, Crónica de Juan I, año I, cap. iii.
310. Zuñiga, Annales de Sevilla, año 1395, n. 2; año 1404, n. 4.
311. Amador de los Rios, II, 338-9, 579-89.--We have seen the prohibition, in the imperial jurisprudence, to erect new synagogues, and this was sedulously preserved in the canon law.--Cap. 3, 8, Extra, V, vi.

The twenty-three synagogues evidently refer to all in the diocese of Seville. At the time of the outbreak there were but three in the city.

312. Zuñiga, Annales de Sevilla, año 1379, n. 3; año 1388, n. 3.
313. Amador de los Rios, II, 592-4.
314. Acta capitular del Cabildo de Sevilla, 10-15 de Enero de 1391 (Bibl. nacional, MSS., Dd, 108, fol. 78).
315. Amador de los Rios, II, 613.
316. Acta capitular, ubi sup.
317. Zuñiga, Annales de Sevilla, año 1391, n. 1, 2, 3.--Ayala, Crónica de Enrique III, año I, cap. v, xx.--Barrantes, Ilustraciones de la Casa de Niebla, Lib. V, cap. xx.--Archivo de Sevilla, Seccion primera, Carpeta II, n. 53.
318. Ayala, Crónica de Enrique III, año 1391, cap. xx.--Mariana, Hist. de España, Lib. XVIII, cap. xv.--Colmenares, Hist. de Segovia, cap. xxvii, § 3.--Fidel Fita, Boletin, IX, 347.--Amador de los Rios, II, 360-3, 370-1, 382, 389, 391.--Zuñiga, Annales de Sevilla, año 1391, n. 2; año 1404, n. 4.--Archivo de Sevilla, Seccion primera, Carpeta CVII, n. 1.
319. Amador de los Rios, II, 595-601.
320. Amador de los Rios, II, 372-77, 398.--Bofarull y Broca, Hist. de Cataluña, V, 35.
321. História general de Mallorca, II, 319 (Ed. 1841).--Loeb, Revue des Études Juives, 1887, p. 172.--Villanueva, XXI, 224.
322. Revue des Études Juives, 1887, pp. 261-2.
323. Amador de los Rios, II, 392-4.--Coleccion de Doc. de la Corona de Aragon, VI, 430.
324. Coleccion de Documentos, VI, 436, 438, 441, 454.
325. José Fiter y Ingles, Expulsion de los Judíos de Barcelona, pp. 8-14 (Barcelona, 1876). This edict was renewed in 1479, 1480 and 1481 (Ibid. pp. 15-19).
326. Viage literario, XVIII, 20.
327. Amador de los Rios, II, 382-5.
328. Amador de los Rios, II, 400-2, 445, 599-604.--Zurita, Añales de Aragon, Lib. X, cap. xlvii.
329. Bernaldez, Hist. de los Reyes Católicos, cap. xliii.--The Jews likewise attributed their sufferings to this "Friar Vincent, from the city of Valencia, of the sect of Baal Dominic."--Chronicles of Rabbi Joseph ben Joshua ben Meir, I, 265-7.
330. Chron. Petri de Areniis, ann. 1408 (Denifle, Archiv für Litt. und Kirchengeschichte, 1887, p. 647).--Coleccion de Doc. de la Corona de Aragon, I, 118.--Chron. Magist. Ord. Prædic. cap. xii (Martene, Ampliss. Collect. VII, 387).--Salazar, Anamnesis Sanctt. Hispan. II, 513.--Tournon, Hommes Illustres de l'Ordre de S. Dominique, III, 37.--Mariana, Hist. de España, VI, 423 (Ed. 1790).--Alban Butler, Vies des Saints, 5 Avril.
331. Rabbi Sam. Marrochiani de Adventu Messiæ (Mag. Bib. Patrum, Ed. 1618, T. XI, p. 421).--Jo. Chr. Wolfii Biblioth. Hebrææ, I, 1099.--This tract was translated from Arabic to Latin in 1338 by the Dominican Alfonsus Bonihominis and was reprinted so recently as 1742, at Cassano by the Jesuits.
332. Mag. Bibl. Patrum, T. XII, P. II, p. 358. For the zeal of the convert to induce his brethren to follow him, see Hermanni Opusc. de Conversione sua, cap. xvi (Migne's Patrol. Lat. T. CLXX, p. 828).
333. D'Argentré, Collect. Judic. de novis Erroribus, I, I, 132.
334. Pugionis Fidei P. III, Dist. iii, cap. 21, 22.
335. Scrutinii Scripturarum P. II. See Graetz (VIII, 79) for a full account of Selemoh Ha-Levi and of the controversies to which his apostasy gave rise.
336. Amador de los Rios, II, 447; III, 108-9.--P. de la Caballería, Zelus Christí contra Judæos (Venetiis, 1592).--Libro Verde de Aragon (Revista de España, Tom. CV, p. 571).
337. Amador de los Rios, II, 413-16, 419-22.--Córtes de los antiguos Reinos, II, 544.
338. Fortalicium Fidei, fol. clxxii-iii.--Colmenares, Historia de Segovia, cap. xxviii.--Garibay, Compendio historial de España, Lib. XV, cap. 58.--Rodrigo, Historia verdadera de la Inquisicion, II, 44.--Padre Fidel Fita (Boletin, IX, 371).
339. Crónica de Juan II, año V, cap. xxii.
340. Fortalicium Fidei, fol. clxxvi-viii.--Amador de los Rios, II, 496-502.--Fernández y González,

Estado de los Mudéjares, pp. 400-5.

341. Amador de los Rios, II, 503, 515.--Villanueva, XXII, 258.

342. The Spanish historians claim that all the rabbis, except Joseph Albo and Vidal Ferrer, acknowledged the truth of Christianity and abjured the errors of Judaism (Amador de los Rios, II, 438-42; Zurita, Añales de Aragon, Lib. XII, cap. xlv), but Graetz (Geschichte der Juden, VIII, 120-1) states with greater probability, that the only concession made by the twelve was that the Haggadah passages of the Talmud are of no authority and even from this Ferrer and Albo dissented.

343. Zurita, Añales, Lib. XII, cap. xlv.

344. Amador de los Rios, II, 627-53; III, 38.

345. Concil. Basiliens. Sess. XIX, cap v, vi (Harduin. VIII, 1190-3).

346. Raynald. Annal, ann. 1442, n. 15.--Wadding, Annal. Minor, ann. 1447, n. 10.

347. Villanueva, XIV, 30.

348. Amador de los Rios, III, 12.

349. Libro Verde de Aragon (Revista de España, CVI, 257, 269).

350. Caballero, Noticias del Doctor Alonso Díaz de Montalvo, p. 251.

351. Pulgar, Claros Varones, Tit. XVIII.

352. Tristan. Caraccioli Epist. de Inquisit. (Muratori, S. R. I., XXII, 97).

353. Crónica de Juan II, año XIV, cap. ii.

354. Amador de los Rios, III, 583-9.

355. Raynald. Annal. ann. 1451, n. 5.

356. Amador de los Rios, III, 115-16.

357. Boletin, XXVI, 468-72.

358. Córtes de los antiguos Reinos, III, 717.

359. Colmenares, Hist. de Segovia, cap. XXXI, § 9.--Amador de los Rios, III, 164-7.--Fernández y González, p. 213.

360. Concil. Arandens. ann. 1473, cap. vii (Aguirre, V, 345).

361. Coleccion de Cédulas, I, 45.

362. Ordenanzas Reales, VIII, iii, 1-41.

363. Archivo general de la C. de Aragon, Regist. 3684, fol. 10, 33.

364. Padre Fidel Fita, Boletin, XV. 443.

365. Amador de los Rios, III, 288-90.--Coleccion de Cédulas, I, 134.

366. Amador de los Rios, III, 170-1.--Merchan, La Judería y la Inquisicion de Ciudad-Real, I, 647. Lindo (Hist. of the Jews of Spain, p. 244) estimates the Jews of Castile at this Period at between 200,000 and 300,000 over 16 years of age. Graetz assumes the total number as 150,000; Isidore Loeb at 50,000 or a little more.--Revue des Études Juives, 1887, p. 168.

367. Amador de los Rios, III, 88-9, 116-17, 206-10, 213-15, 217-18.

368. Amador de los Rios, III, 118-24.--Crónica de Juan II, año XLII, cap. ii, v.--Crónica de Alvaro de Luna, Tit. lxxxiii.

369. Merchan, La Judería y la Inquisicion de Ciudad-Real, I, 541-63.

370. Raynald. Annal. ann. 1449, n. 12.

371. Amador de los Rios, III, 125, 494.--Raynald. ann. 1451, n. 5.

372. Nic. Antonio, Bibl. vetus Hispan., II, n. 565.

373. In this I have chiefly followed a MS. account, evidently by a contemporary, preserved in the Bibl. nacional, MSS., G. 109. See also Amador de los Rios, III, 145-51; Valera, Memorial de diversos Hazañas, cap. xxxviii; Castillo, Crónica de Enrique IV, cap. xc, xci.

374. Merchan, op. cit., I, 641-3.

375. Castillo, op. cit., cap. cxlvi.--Mariana, Lib. XXIII, cap. xv.

376. Castillo, op. cit., cap. clx.--Valera, Memorial de diversas Hazañas, cap. clxxxiii.--Memorial hist. español, VIII, 507.

377. Valera, cap. lxxxiii-iv.--Castillo, cap. clx.--Memorial hist. español, VIII, 508.--Barrantes, Ilustraciones de la Casa de Niebla, Lib. VIII, cap. vi.--Amador de los Rios, III, 159-60.

378. Amador de los Rios, III, 234.

379. Pulgar, Crónica de los Reyes Católicos, II, lxxvii.

380. Padre Fidel Fita, Boletin, XV, 323-5, 327, 328, 330; XXIII, 431.

381. Historia de los Reyes Católicos, cap. cxi.

382. As this measure seems to have hitherto escaped attention, I give the text of the document--a passage in a letter from Ferdinand, May 12, 1486, to the inquisitors of Saragossa. "Devotos padres. Porque por esperiencia parece que todo el daño que en los cristianos se ha fallado del delicto de la heregia ha procedido de la conversacion y practica que con los judios han recebido las personas de su linage, ningun tan comodo remedio hay como apartarlo dentre ellos de la manera que se ha fecho en el arzobispo de Sevilla e obispados de Córdova e de Jaen, e pues en essa ciudad tanto e mas que en ninguna otra han dañado, es nuestra voluntad que los judios dessa ciudad luego sean desterrados dessa

dicha ciudad e de todo el arzobispado de Çaragoça e obispado de Santa María de Albarracin como por el devoto padre Prior de Santa Cruz vos sera escrito e mandado."--Archivo gén. de la C. de Aragon, Regist. 3684, fol. 96.

While this is apparently confined to the Saragossa Jews, a letter of Ferdinand to Torquemada, July 22, 1486, alludes to the Jews of Teruel having been ordered by the inquisitors to depart within three months. He deems them justified in complaining that the term is too short, seeing that they have to pay and collect their debts and sell their houses and lands and he therefore suggests an extension of six months additional.--See Appendix.

383. Zurita, Hist. del Rey Hernando, Lib. I, año 1492.--Mariana, Lib. XXIV, cap. xviii.--Páramo de Orig. Officii S. Inquisitionis, pp. 144, 156, 163 (Madriti, 1598).--Garibay, Comp. Hist. Lib. XIX, c. iv.

384. An account of the expulsion at the end of the Libro Verde de Aragon states this to be the cause (Revista de España, CVI, 567-8). Ribas Altas, however was burnt some years earlier, for in the Saragossa auto de fe of March 2, 1488, his mother Aldonça was burnt and the report alludes to his previous burning and relates the story.--Memoria de Diversos Autos, Auto 29 (see Appendix).

385. Barrantes, Aparato para la Historia de Extremadura, I, 458.

386. Revista de España, CVI, 568-70. This correspondence was long used as a weapon against the New Christians. See Vicente da Costa Mattos, Breve Discorso contra a heretica Perfidia do Judaismo, fol. 55-7, 166 (Lisboa, 1623). Rodrigo prints it (Historia verdadera de la Inquisicion, II, 47).

387. I have considered this notable case at some length in "Studies from the Religious History of Spain," pp. 437-68. It can be studied with accuracy in the records of the trial of one of the accused, Jucé Franco, printed by Padre Fidel Fita (Boletin, XI, 1887) with ample elucidations. The Catalan version of the sentence is in Coleccion de Documentos de la Corona de Aragon, XXVIII, 68. For the legend and cult of the Santo Niño see Martínez Moreno, Historia del Martirio del Santo Niño de la Guardia, Madrid, 1866.

388. Páramo (p. 144) seems to be the earliest authority for this story and, as he tells it, it seems rather applicable to an attempt of the Conversos to buy off the Inquisition, but modern writers attribute it to the Jewish expulsion. See Llorente, Hist. Crít. cap. VIII, Art. 1, n. 5; Hefele, Der Cardinal Ximenes, XVIII; Amador de los Rios, III, 272-3.

389. Manuel de novells Ardits vulgarment appellat Dietari del Antich Consell Barceloni, III, 94 (Barcelona, 1894).

390. Nueva Recopilacion Lib. VIII, Tit. ii, ley 2.--Novísima Recop., Lib. XII, Tit. i, ley 3.--Zurita, Hist. del Rey Hernando, Lib. I, año 1492.--Amador de los Rios, III, 603-9.--Boletin, XI, 425, 512.

391. Zurita, loc. cit.

392. See Appendix.

393. Páramo, p. 167.--Ilescas, Historia Pontifical, P. II, Lib. vi, cap. 20, § 2.

394. Amador de los Rios, III, 403.

395. Llorente, Hist. crít., Append, VI.--Archivo de Simancas, Inquisicion, Lib. 1; Lib. 3, fol. 87.

396. Bergenroth, Calendar of Spanish State Papers, I, 51.

397. Zurita, loc. cit.--Páramo, p. 166.

398. Graetz VIII, 348.--Bernaldez, cap. CXII.--The cruzado of Portugal was worth 365 maravedís, the same as la dobla de la banda. The ducat was worth 374.

399. Lindo, History of the Jews, p. 287.--Chronicle of Rabbi Joseph ben Joshua ben Meir, I, 327.

400. Graetz, VIII, 349.

401. Bernaldez, cap. CX.--Barrantes, Ilustraciones de la Casa de Niebla, P. IX, cap. 2.--Amador de los Rios, III, 311.--Lindo, p. 292.

402. Amador de los Rios, III, 312.--Boletin, IX, 267, 286; XI, 427, 586.

403. Graetz, VIII, 348.--Chrónicon de Valladolid (Coleccion de Documentos, XIII, 195).

404. Bernaldez, cap. CXII, CXIII.

405. Dami=a.o de Goes, Chronica do Rei D. Manoel, P. I, cap. cii, ciii.

406. Chronicles of Rabbi Joseph ben Joshua ben Meir, I, 328.--Amador de los Rios, III, 332-3.

407. Amador de los Rios, III, 320.--Zurita, loc. cit.

408. Archivo de Simancas, Inquisicion, Libro 927, fol. 124.--Isidore Loeb (Revue des Études Juives, 1887, p. 179).--Ilescas, Historia Pontifical, P. II, Lib. vi, cap. 20, § 2.--Kayserling, Biblioteca Española-Portugueza-Judaica, p. xi (Strasbourg, 1890).

409. Nueva Recopilacion, Lib. VIII, Tit. ii, ley 3.--Novís. Recop., Lib. XII, Tit. i, ley 4.--Archivo de Simancas, Inquisicion, Lib. 1.

410. Bernaldez, cap. CXI.

411. Arnaldin. Albertinus de Hæreticis, col. lix (Valentiæ, 1534).

412. Zurita, loc. cit.--Mariana, Tom. VIII, p. 336 (Ed. 1795).--Páramo, p. 167.

413. Revue des Études Juives, 1887, p. 182.

414. Chronicles of Rabbi Joseph ben Joshua ben Meir, I, 323-4.

415. Pet. Martyr. Angler. Lib. VIII, Epist. 157.
416. Joan. Pici Mirandulæ in Astrologiam, Lib. V, cap. xii.
417. Il Principe, cap. xxi.
418. Arnald. Albertinus de Hæreticis, col. lix.
419. Censura et Confutatio Libri Talmud (Boletin, XXIII, 371-4).

The Jews distinguished between unwilling converts, whom they termed Anusim and voluntary converts, or Meschudanim; the former they pitied and helped, the latter they abhorred. The Judaizing Christians were also sometimes called Alboraycos, from alborak (the lightning), the marvellous horse brought to Mahomet by the angel Gabriel, which was neither a horse nor a mule nor male nor female (Ibid. p. 379). A still more abusive popular appellation was Marrano, which means both hog and accursed. For the controverted derivation of the word see Graetz, Geschichte der Juden, VIII, 76 (Ed. 1890), who also (p. 284) admits the attachment of many of the Conversos to the old religion.

420. C. Dertusan. ann. 1429, c. ix (Aguirre, V, 337).
421. Ripoll Bullar. Ord. FF. Prædic. III, 347.
422. C. Basiliens. Sess. XIX, c. vi (Harduin. VIII, 1193).
423. Raynald. Annal. ann. 1451, n. 6.
424. Fortalicium Fidei, Prolog. (Ed. 1494, fol. ii^{a}). The date of the Fortalicium is commonly assigned to 1459, the year which it bears upon its rubric, but on fol. lxxvii^{b} the author speaks of 1460 years having elapsed since the birth of Christ and, as this is at nearly the first third of the book, it may not have been completed for a year or two later.
425. Nicol. Anton. Bibl. Vet. Hispan. Lib. X, cap. ix.
426. Amador de los Rios, III, 60, 136.--Valera, Memoria de diversas Hazañas, cap. iv.
427. Fortalicium Fidei, fol. cxlvi.
428. Colmenares, Hist. de Segovia, cap. xxxi, § 3.--Valera, loc. cit.
429. All recent Spanish authorities, I believe, assume that Fray Alonso was a Converso, but the learned Nicolás Antonio (loc. cit.) says nothing about it, and Jo. Chr. Wolff (Bibl. Hebrææ II, 1123) points out that he nowhere alludes to his own experience as he could scarce have failed to do when accusing the Jews of matters which they denied. He cites (fol. cxlix^{a}) Pablo de Santa María, Bishop of Burgos, for their prayers against Christians and another learned Converso as to a secret connected with the Hebrew letters (fol. xciv^{a}). His knowledge concerning the Jews was thus wholly at second hand and his assaults on the Judaizing of the Conversos have every appearance of emanating from an Old Christian.
430. The prayers attributed to the Jews were the subject of repeated repressive legislation. See Ordenanzas Reales, VIII, iii, 34.
431. Fortalicium Fidei, fol. cxlii-ix, clxxxi-iii.
432. Fuero Juzgo, XII, iii, 27.--Fuero Real, IV, i, 1.--Partidas, VII, xxiv, 7. In fact, these laws seem to have been a dead letter almost from the first. I have not met with an instance of their enforcement.
433. Fortalicium Fidei, fol. liii-liv, lxxv-vi, clxxviii-ix.
434. Bernaldez, Historia de los Reyes Católicos, cap. xliii. See also Páramo de Orig. Officii S. Inquisit., p. 134.

Bernaldez evidently derives his details from the inquisitorial sentences read at the autos de fe, in which these evidences of Judaism are recited in endless repetition.

435. Amador de los Rios, III, 142.
436. Castillo, Crónica de Enrique IV, cap. liii.--Mariana Historia de España, Lib. XXIII, cap. vi.
437. Modesto Lafuente, Hist. Gen. de España, IX, 227.
438. Boletin, XXIII, 300-1.
439. Vicente Barrantes, Aparato para la Historia de Extremadura, II, 362.
440. Córtes de los Antiguos Reinos de Leon y de Castilla, Madrid, 1861 sqq.
441. Archivio Vaticano. Sisto IV, Registro 679, Tom. I, fol. 52. I have printed this bull in the American Historical Review, I, 46.
442. It was during Isabella's stay in Seville that, on September 2d, she confirmed, followed by Ferdinand at Xeres, October 18, 1477, a forged decree, ascribed to Frederic II, granting certain privileges to the Inquisition of Sicily. This was done at the request of Filippo de'Barbarj, subsequently Inquisitor of Sicily, then at the court, whom both monarchs qualify as their confessor. He is said to have exercised considerable influence with them in overcoming the opposition to the establishment of the Inquisition in Castile. With regard to the forged decree of Frederic II, see the author's "History of the Inquisition of the Middle Ages," Vol. II, p. 288.
443. Zurita, Añales de Aragon, Lib. XX, cap. xlix.
444. Pulgar, Chronica, P. II, cap. lxxvii.--Bernaldez, cap. xliii.--Medina, Vida del Cardenal Mendoza (Memorial hist. español, VI, 235).
445. Páramo de Orig. Offic. S. Inquis. p. 134.

Padre Fidel Fita has pointed out the discrepancy in the dates.--Boletin, XVI, 559.

446. Bernaldez, Historia de los Reyes Católicos, cap. xliii.

447. Páramo, p. 135.--Medina, Vida del Cardenal Mendoza (Memorial histórico español, VI, 235).

448. Pulgar, Crónica, P. II, cap. clxxvii.--Pulgar (cap. iv) gives sole credit to Isabella for the extirpation of heresy.

449. The proceedings of this important assembly have been printed by Padre Fidel Fita (Boletin, XXII, 212-250).

450. Printed by Dom Clemencin, Elogio de Doña Isabel, pp. 595-7.

451. Fortalicium Fidei, Lib. II, consid. xi.--History of the Inquisition of the Middle Ages, I, 512-13.

452. This bull is embodied in the first proclamation of the inquisitors, Seville, January 2, 1481, printed by Padre Fita (Boletin, XV, 449-52). It had previously been looked upon as lost. Its main provisions, however, are embodied in the cédula of Dec. 27, 1480, printed in the notes to the Novísima Recopilacion, Ed. 1805, Tom. I, p. 260.

It is a little singular that the Inquisition possessed very few documents relating to its early history. In an elaborate consulta of July 18, 1703, presented to Philip V on the affair of Fray Froilan Diaz, the Suprema states that it had had all the records searched with little result; many important papers had been sent to Aragon and Catalonia and had never been returned; the rest were in a chest delivered to the Count of Villalonga, secretary of Philip III, to arrange and classify and on his arrest and the sequestration of his effects they disappeared.--Biblioteca Nacional, Seccion de MSS., G, 61, fol. 198.

It is quite possible that the contents of the chest form the "Bulario de la Inquisicion perteneciente á la Orden de Santiago," consisting of eight Libros, or folio volumes (five of originals and three of copies) now in the Archivo Histórico Nacional. It is from this collection that Padre Fita has printed the proclamation above alluded to and many other important documents, and it will be seen that I have made large use of it under the name of "Bulario de la Orden de Santiago." There are also vast stores of records in the Archivo Histórico Nacional of Madrid, in the archives of Simancas and Barcelona, and some in the Vatican Library. Llorente burnt many papers before leaving Madrid and carried others to Paris, some of which are in the Bibliothèque Nationale, fonds espagnol. The Biblioteca Nacional of Madrid also has a large number and others are dispersed through the various libraries of Europe or are in private hands.

453. See his brief of January 29, 1482, printed by Llorente, Historia Crítica, Append. n. 1.

454. History of the Inquisition of the Middle Ages, I, 331.

455. Archivo General de la Corona de Aragon, Reg. 3684, fol. 1. See Appendix.

456. Fidel Fita, Boletin, XVI, 452.--Llorente, Hist. Crít. cap. V, art. ii.--Relacion histórica de la Judería de Sevilla, p. 22 (Sevilla, 1849).

457. Boletin, XV, 453-7. This was fairly within the rules of the canon law but it did not put an end to the sheltering of fugitives from the Inquisition by nobles who doubtless found it profitable. In some instructions issued by Torquemada, December 6, 1484, there is one regulating the relations between such nobles and the receiver of confiscations.--Archivo de Simancas, Inquisicion, Libro 933.

458. Bernaldez, cap. xliv. The castle of Triana continued to be the seat of the Inquisition of Seville until 1626, when it was threatened with ruin by the inundations of the Guadalquivir, and the tribunal was removed to the palace of the Caballeros Tellos Taveros in the Colacion de San Marcos. In 1639 it returned to the castle, which had been repaired and it remained there until 1789, when the continual encroachment ofthe river caused its transfer to the Colegio known as las Becas.--Varflora, Compendio histórico-descriptivo de Sevilla, P. II, cap. 1 (Sevilla, 1789).--Zuñiga, Annales de Sevilla, año 1693, n. 1.

The Counts of San Lucar were hereditary alcaides of Triana; in return for surrendering the castle they received the office of alguazil mayor of the Inquisition, which continued to be held by their representatives the Marquises of Leganes--a bargain which was ratified by Philip IV, November 8, 1634. In 1707 the office was valued at 150,000 maravedís a year, out of which the holder provided a deputy.--Archivo de Simancas, Inquisicion, Legajo 1465, fol. 105.

459. Amador de los Rios, III, 247-8.--Bernaldez, cap. xliii.--Fidel Fita, Boletin, XVI, 450 sqq., 557 sqq.

As the parricide committed by the Fermosa Fembra entailed poverty and disgrace on her, through the confiscation of her father's property and the disabilities inflicted on his descendants, the Church interested itself in her fate. Rainaldo Romero, Bishop of Tiberias, secured for her entrance into a convent, but it can readily be understood that life there was not rendered pleasant to her and she quitted it, without taking the vows, to follow a career of shame. Her beauty disappeared and she died in want, leaving directions that her skull should be placed as a warning over the door of the house which had been the scene of her disorderly life. Her wishes were obeyed and it is still to be seen in the Calle del Artaud, near its entrance, hard by the Alcázar.--Amador de los Rios, III, 249.

460. Bernaldez, cap. xliv. Rodrigo tells us (Hist. verdadera de la Inquisicion, II, 74-6) that only

five were burnt who refused all offers of reconciliation and were impenitent to the last, but the contemporary Bernaldez says that Diego de Susan died as a good Christian in the second auto.

461. Bernaldez, cap. xliv.--Amador de los Rios, III, 250.--Field's Old Spain and New Spain, p. 279.

The remark of the good Cura de los Palacios in describing the quemadero is "en que los quemaban y fasta que haya heregía los quemarán." The cost of the four statues was defrayed by a gentleman named Mesa, whose zeal won for him the position of familiar of the Holy Office and receiver of confiscations. He was, however, discovered to be a Judaizer and was himself burnt on the quemadero which he had adorned.--Rodrigo, II, 79-80.

462. Bernaldez, cap. xliv.

463. Llorente, Añales de la Inquisicion, I, 44.

464. Amador de los Rios, III, 252. Rodrigo (Hist. Verdad. II, 76) states that the first act of the inquisitors was the issue of the proclamation of the Term of Grace on January 2d, but this is scarce consistent with the narrative of Bernaldez.

465. Bernaldez, cap. xliv.

466. Páramo, p. 136.--Boletin, XV, 462.

466a. It is very questionable whether a tribunal was established at Segovía thus early. Colmenares (Hist. de Segovia, cap. xxxiv, § 18) asserts it positively, but the only tribunals represented in the assembly of organization, held in November, 1484, were Seville, Córdova, Jaen and Ciudad-Real. There was at first some resistance at Segovia on the part of the bishop, Juan Arias Dávila, who was of Jewish descent.--Bergenroth, Calendar of Spanish State Papers, I, xlv.

In Ciudad-Real, the earliest inquisitors, in 1483, were the Licentiate Pedro Díaz de la Costana and the Doctor Francisco de la Fuente (Archivo hist. nacional, Inquisicion de Toledo, Legajo 154, n. 375). Neither of these was a Dominican and the latter subsequently became an inquisitor-general and bishop successively of Avila and of Córdova.

In Córdova the Inquisition was established in 1482, with four inquisitors--the Bachilleres Anton Rúiz de Morales and Alvar González de Capillas, Doctor Pedro Martínez de Barrio, and Fray Martin Cazo, Guardian of the Franciscan convent. The first auto de fe was celebrated in 1483, when one of the victims was the concubine of the treasurer of the cathedral, Pedro Fernández de Alcaudete, who himself was burnt on February 28, 1484. His servants resisted his arrest and in the fray the alguazil of the Inquisition was killed.--Matute y Luquin, Autos de Fe de Córdova, pp. 1-2 (Córdova, 1839).

467. "En publica forma e se avia fecho en esta dicha ciudad por el Doctor Thomás, juez delegado e inquisidor deputado por el reverendisimo señor Don Alfonso Carrillo, arzobispo que fué deste dicho arzobispado de Toledo."--Arch. hist. nacional, Inq. de Toledo, Legajos 139, n. 145; 143, n. 196.

468. Ibidem, Legajos 139, n. 145; 154, n. 356, 375.

469. Archivo hist. nacional, Inquisicion de Toledo, Legajo 262.

470. Páramo, p. 170.--Padre Fidel Fita has compiled a chronological list of the trials at Ciudad-Real preserved in the Archivo Hist. Nacional (Boletin, XI, 311 sqq.). These are included in the Catálogo de las Causas contra la Fe seguidas ante el Tribunal del Santo Oficio de Toledo, by D. Miguel Gómez del Campillo (Madrid, 1903).

471. Relacion de la Inquisicion Toledana (Boletin, XI, 293).

472. Relacion de la Inquisicion Toledana (Boletin, XI, 293-4).--Arch. Gen. de la Corona de Aragon, Reg. 3864, fol. 31.--Graetz, Geschichte der Juden, VIII, 323.--Pulgar, Crónica, P. III, cap. 100.

Legally, Jews were not allowed to testify against Christians and the prohibition to receive such evidence was emphatically included in the ferocious bull of Nicholas V, in 1447, but, as we shall see, in the Inquisition, all accusing witnesses, however infamous, were welcomed.

How distasteful Ferdinand knew would be the work prescribed to the Aragonese magistracy is seen by his imperious command that it must be done--"e por cosa del mundo no fagais lo contrario ni recusais de lo facer porque nos seria tan molesto que no lo podriamos con paciencia tolerar."

473. Relacion de la Inquisicion Toledana (Boletin, XI, 295-6).

In 1629 a well-informed writer tells us that many of those who came forward and thus accused themselves were in reality good Christians, who, in the time while Jews were yet tolerated, had associated with them in their synagogues and weddings and funerals and had bought meat of their butchers. Terrified at the proceedings of the Inquisition they came and confessed and were reconciled, thus casting an indelible stain on their posterity when the records of the tribunals were searched and their names were found.--Tratado de los Estatutos de Limpieza, cap. 10 (Bibl. Nac. Seccion de MSS. Q, 418).

474. Relacion (Ibid. pp. 292 sqq., 297, 299, 301-2, 303).

In the closing years of the fifteenth century and the opening ones of the sixteenth there seems to have been a special raid made on Guadalajara. In a list of cases of that period I find 965 credited to that place.--Arch. Hist. Nacional, Inq. de Toledo, Leg. 262, n. 1.

475. Páramo, pp. 138-9.--Fidel Fita in Boletin, XXIII, 284 sqq.--Archivo de Simancas,

Inquisicion, Libro 939, fol. 108.

476. Toledo, Cronicon de Valladolid (Coleccion de Documentos ineditos, XIII, 176, 179).--Pulgar, Chron. P. III, cap. 100.

477. Archivo de Simancas, Inquisicion, Libro I. Unfortunately my copy of this important volume and also of Libro 933 are not folioed. The dates of the documents however will sufficiently guide the investigator desirous of verifying the references.

478. A list of these, made in the last century, is printed by Padre Fidel Fita (Boletin, XV, 332). It is probably not wholly complete. Of later date than 1500 there are ten reconciliados--one each in 1509 and 1516 and eight in 1629--sent thither by the tribunals in which they were tried.

Further details as to the organization of the various tribunals will be found in the Appendix.

479. Colmenares, Hist. de Segovia, cap. xxxv, § 18.--Garibay, Compendio Historial, Lib. XVIII, cap. 16.

480. Páramo, p. 137.--Llorente, Añales, I, 73.--Zurita, Añales, Lib. XX, cap. xlix--Instruciones de Sevilla, 1484, Prólogo (Arguello, fol. 2).--Archivo de Alcalá, Estado, Legajo 2843.

In the conference of Seville in 1484, besides the inquisitors and the members of the Council there are mentioned as present Juan Gutiérrez de Lachaves, and Tristan de Medina, whom Llorente (Añales, I, 74) conjectures to have been assistants of Torquemada.

481. Folch de Cardona, in the Consulta of the Suprema to Philip V, July 18, 1703, states that the earliest bull in the archives was one of Sixtus IV in 1483 appointing Torquemada inquisitor-general with power to deputize inquisitors and to hear cases in the first instance. It was not till 1486 that Innocent VIII granted him appellate jurisdiction.--Bibl. Nacional, Seccion de MSS., G, 61, fol. 199.

The title of Inquisitor-general was not immediately invented. In a sentence pronounced at Ciudad-Real, March 15, 1485, Torquemada is styled simply "juez principal ynquisidor."--Arch. Hist. Nac. Inq. de Toledo, Legajo 165, n. 551.

482. Ripoll Bullar. Ord. FF. Prædic. III, 630; IV, 125. Yet modern apologists do not hesitate to argue that the papacy sought to mitigate the severity of the Spanish Inquisition (Gams, Zur Geschichte der spanischen Staatsinquisition, pp. 20-1; Hefele, Der Cardinal Ximenes, p. 269; Pastor, Geschichte der Päpste, II, 582), basing their assertions on the eagerness of the curia to entertain appeals, of which more hereafter.

483. Archivo de Simancas, Patronato Real, Inquisicion, Legajo único, fol. 28. anll, IV, 126.

486. Páramo, p. 156.

487. Arch. Gen. de la Corona de Aragon, Reg. 3486, fol. 45.--Páramo, p. 137.

488. Bulario de la Orden de Santiago, Lib. I de copias, fol. 6, 8.--"ad nostrum et dictæ sedis beneplacitum."

The original appointments of Miguel de Morillo and Juan de San Martin were similarly ad beneplacitum (Ibid. fol. 10), which may perhaps explain their assertion of independence of Torquemada.

489. Ibid. fol. 3, 11, 13, 15, 20; Lib. IV, fol. 91, 118, 137; Lib. V, fol. 117, 136, 138, 151, 199, 200, 251, 264, 295.--Archivo de Alcalá, Hacienda, Leg. 1049.

490. Instruciones de Sevilla (Arguello, Copilacion de las Instruciones, fol. 2, Madrid, 1630).

491. Páramo, p. 156.

492. Bulario de la Orden de Santiago, Lib. I de copias, fol. 8, 10.--Monteiro, Historia da Inquisiçaõ, II, 415.--Boletin, XV, 490.--Ripoll IV, 5, 6.

Somewhat similar was the question which arose, in 1507, on the retirement of Diego Deza and the appointment of Ximenes as inquisitor-general of Castile. His commission as usual contained the power of appointing and removing or punishing all subordinates, but those who derived their commissions from Deza seem to have claimed that they were not amenable to Ximenes and it required a special brief from Julius II, August 18, 1509, to establish his authority over them.--Bulario, Lib. III, fol. 68; Lib. I de copias, fol. 30.

493. Llorente, Añales, I, 214.--Francisco de la Fuente, as we have seen was inquisitor of Ciudad-Real as early as 1483. Alonso de Fuentelsaz in 1487 was one of the inquisitors of Toledo and was then merely a doctor.--Arch. hist. nacional, Inq. de Toledo, Leg. 176, n. 673.

494. Archivo de Simancas, Inquisicion, Libro 933.--"Inquisitores generales in omnibus regnis et dominiis serenissimorum regis et reginæ dominorum nostrorum subdelegati a reverendissimo patre nostro fratre Thoma de Torquemada ... inquisitore generali."

Yet we have the commission of Martin de Messina, in 1494, issued directly by the pope.--Bulario, Lib. I de copias, fol. 3.

495. Archivo de Simancas, Inquisicion, Lib. I.--Arguello, fol. 12.--Marieta, Hist. Ecles. Lib. XII, cap. xcii.

Torquemada was buried in a chapel of the church of his convent of Santo Tomás in Avila. In 1572 the body was removed to another chapel to make room for the interment of Francisco de Soto de Salazar, Bishop of Salamanca, when it gave forth a supernatural odor of delicious sweetness, greatly confusing to those engaged in the sacrilegious task. The Dominican provincial punished the authors of the translation and the historian Garibay petitioned the Inquisitor-general Quiroga to have the remains restored to their original resting-place, which was done in 1586.--Memorias de Garibay, Tit. X (Mem. hist. esp. VII, 393).

An anonymous biographer, writing in 1655, tells us that he retired to the convent of Avila two years before his death, Sept. 26, 1498 and that he has always there been reputed as a saint.--Biblioteca Nacional, Seccion de MSS., Ii, 16.

496. Arch. de Simancas, Patronato Real, Inquisicion, Legajo único, fol. 22.--Bulario de la Orden de Santiago, Lib. I, fol. 136.

497. Bulario de la Orden de Santiago, Lib. I de copias, fol. 11, 12.

498. Archivo de Simancas, Inquisicion, Lib. I.

499. Ibid. Lib. I; Lib. II, fol. 35.

500. Correspondence of Francisco de Rojas (Boletin, XXVIII, 462).

501. Bulario de la Orden de Santiago, Lib. I de copias, fol. 13, 15.

502. Ibid. fol. 20, 72.--Gachard, Correspondance de Charles-Quint et d'Adrien VI, p. 235.

503. Páramo, p. 137.

504. Pulgar, Crónica, P. III, cap. c.--Archivo General de Simancas, Inquisicion, Libro 933.

505. Inquisitor-general Manrique caused the Instruciones Antiguas to be printed collectively, with a supplement classifying the several articles under the head of the officials whose duties they defined. This was issued in Seville in 1537 and a copy is preserved in the Bodleian Library, Arch. Seld. A. Subt. 15. Another edition was issued in Madrid in 1576, a copy of which is in the Biblioteca Nacional of Madrid, Seccion de MSS. S, 299, fol. 1. It was reprinted again in Madrid, in 1627 and 1630, together with the Instruciones Nuevas, by Caspar Isidro de Arguello. It is to this last edition that my references will be made. All these texts vary in some particulars from the originals preserved in the Simancas Archives, Inquisicion, Libro 933. Where such deviations are of importance they will be noted hereafter. Professor Ernst Schäfer has performed the service of reprinting the Arguello edition, with a German translation, in the Archiv für Reformationsgeschichte,1904.

Llorente (Hist. Crít. cap. VI, art. 1) has given an abstract of the Instruciones Antiguas. Curiously enough, in none of the official collections are included the instructions issued by Torquemada in December, 1484, and January, 1485, except in a few extracts. As they have never been printed I give them in the Appendix, together with the 1500 Instructions of Seville, which are likewise for the most part inedited. What Llorente printed as Torquemada's additions (Añales, I, 388) are merely the extracts gathered from Arguello's compilation, where they are credited to El prior en Sevilla, 1485.

506. See the oath taken, July 20, 1487, by the officials of Catalonia and Barcelona to the inquisitor Alonso de Spina in Carbonell's De Gestis Hæreticorum (Coleccion de Documentos de la Corona de Aragon, XXVIII, 6).

The decretals in question were issued by Lucius III, Innocent III, Clement IV and Boniface VIII, and are embodied in the canon law as Cap. 9 and 13 Extra, Lib. V, Tit. vii and Cap. 11 and 18 in Sexto Lib. V, Tit. ii.

When, in 1510, the jurats of Palermo made difficulties in taking the canonical oath, Ferdinand indignantly wrote that he would take it himself if required.--Arch. de Simancas, Inquisicion, Lib. III, fol. 134.

507. Instruciones de Sevilla, § 1 (Arguello, fol. 3).

508. Páramo, p. 170.

509. Carbonell de Gestis Hæreticorum (Coleccion de Documentos de la Corona de Aragon, XXVIII, 12-17, 29, 40-49, 54-61). In these latter cases there is no distinction recorded between the fugitive and the dead, which would modify somewhat the proportions.

510. Manuel de Novells Ardits, vulgarment appelat Dietari del Antich Consell Barceloni, III, 58 (Barcelona, 1894).

511. Archivo de Simancas, Inquisicion, Libro 933.

512. Archivo de Simancas, Inquisicion, Libro 1. By a letter of February 22, 1501, Ferdinand and Isabella congratulate the inquisitors on their action in such cases; if other New Christians assert that they had been converted by force justice is to be executed on them.

In 1511 a ship belonging to Caspar de la Cavallería of Naples was seized in Barcelona. The master, Francisco de Santa Cruz, hurried to the court at Seville, where the inquisitor-general Enguera condemned the vessel and he gave security in its full value. Meanwhile the receiver of confiscations at Barcelona sold it without waiting for its condemnation, whereupon Ferdinand ordered the money returned and the vessel taken back.--Ibidem, Lib. III, fol. 139.

513. Ibidem, Lib. I.

514. Boletin, XV, 323.

515. Archivo de Simancas, Inquisicion, Libro 939, fol. 62, 146.

516. Ibidem, Libro I.

517. Ibidem, Lib. II, fol. 17.

518. Archivo de Simancas, Inquisicion, Lib. III, fol. 42. This letter is dated Dec. 22, 1509. It is duplicated January 19, 1510 (Ibid. fol. 48). Seven of the Duke's officials had been summoned to appear before the Suprema and had disregarded the order, which was repeated January 21st under pain of confiscation and punishment at the royal pleasure.--Ibid. fol. 57.
519. Ibidem, Libro 73, fol. 115.
520. Archivo de Simancas, Inquisicion, Libro I.
521. Archivo de Simancas, Inquisicion, Lib. I.
522. Ibidem, Lib. III, fol. 221.
523. Ibidem, Lib. III, fol. 22.
524. Ibidem, Lib. III, fol. 193, 214.
525. Archivo de Simancas, l'atronato real; Inquisicion, Legajo único, fol. 37.
526. Informe de Quesada (Biblioteca nacional, Section de MSS., T, 28).
527. Archivo de Simancas, Inquisicion, Libro I.
528. Archivo de Simancas, Inquisicion, Libro I.

The redistribution of offices may be reckoned among the influences which reconciled the Old Christians to the Inquisition. These had been largely in the hands of Conversos, causing so much jealousy that the prospect of acquiring them led numbers of aspirants to wish for the sharpest and speediest action. It was too slow for their eagerness and expectative grants were sought for and made in advance so as to profit by the next victim. The vacancies passed into the hands of the receivers and were distributed by the sovereigns as favor or policy might dictate. See Appendix for suggestive extracts from the register of the receiver of Valencia.

A significant case is that of Juan Cardona, public scrivener and notary of mortmains, who became disqualified by the condemnation of the memory of his father, Leonardo Cardona, whereupon Ferdinand treated his offices as confiscated and, by cédula of December 5, 1511, bestowed them on Juan Argent, notary of the tribunal which had rendered the sentence.--Archivo de Simancas, Inquisicion, Libro III, fol. 33, 161.

529. Archivo de Simancas, Inquisicion, Libro I.
530. Archivo de Simancas, Patronato Real, Inquisicion, Leg. único, fol. 46.--Juan Gomez Bravo, Catálogo de los Obispos de Córdova, I, 392.

In 1513 an attempt was made to review the trial of the parents and son, when Ferdinand summoned the Royal Council to sit with the Suprema in the case showing his determination that the sentence should not be set aside (Archivo de Simancas, Inq., Libro 9, fol. 146). The effort to obtain justice was unsuccessful for, in 1515, we happen to find Calcena in possession of a house renting at 9000 mrs. per annum which had formed part of the confiscation (Ibid., Libro 3, fol. 439).

531. Epistt. Pet. Mart. Anglerii, Epist. 374.--Zurita, Hist. del Rey Hernando, Lib. VII, cap. xxix.--Rodrigo, Hist. verdadera, II, 238. Cf. Lorenzo de Padilla, Crónica de Felipe I (Coleccion de Documentos, VIII, 153).
532. Archivo de Simancas, Patronato Real, Inquisicion, Leg. único, fol. 46.
533. Epistt. Pet. Mart., Epist. 385.
534. Archivo de la Catedral de Córdova, Cajon I, n. 300; Cajon J, n. 295, 296.
535. Boletin, XVII, 447-51.
536. Archivo de la Catedral de Córdova, Cajon I, n. 304.
537. Archivo de Simancas, Patronato Real, Inquisicion, Leg. único, fol. 46.--Zurita, Hist. del Rey Hernando, Lib. VII, cap. xxix.
538. Coleccion de Documentos, VIII, 336, 337.--Gachard, Voyages des Souverains, I, 519.
539. Archivo de Simancas, Gracia y Justicia, Inquisicion, Leg. 621, fol. 198.--Biblioteca nacional, Seccion de MSS., D, 118, n. 11, fol. 24.--Llorente, Añales, I, 328.--Gachard, Voyages des Souverains, I, 548.
540. Clemencin, Elogio de la Reina Isabel, pp. 144-5.--Pedraza, Hist. de Granada, P. IV, cap. xxxi (Granada, 1638).
541. Archivo de la Catedral de Córdova, Cajon J, n. 297.
542. Pet. Mart. Angler. Epist. 295.
543. Llorente, Hist. crít. Append. n. 9.--Correspondence of Rojas (Boletin, XXVIII, 448).
544. Dom Clemencin (Elogio, Illust. XVIII) prints a noble and touching letter of reproof from Talavera to Ferdinand. He had had the direction of royal consciences too long to feel awe of royal personages. Spiritually he felt himself the king's superior and his perfectly frank simplicity of character led him to manifest this without disguise.
545. Correspondence of Rojas (Boletin, XVIII, 444, 448).--Gachard, Voyages des Souverains, I, 534, 540.
546. Correspondence of Rojas (Boletin, XVIII, 452).

The story of Queen Juana la loca is one of the saddest in the annals of royalty and her treatment by her father, husband and son is a libel on human nature, but no one who has impartially examined all the evidence can doubt that she was incapable of governing.

547. Archivo de la Catedral de Córdova, Cajon A, n. 5.
548. Zurita, Hist. del Rey Hernando, Lib. VII, cap. vi.
549. Archivo de la Catedral de Córdova, Cajon I, n. 302.
550. Ibidem, n. 300.
551. Archivo de Simancas, Patronato Real, Inquisicion, Leg. único, fol. 46.
552. Archivo de la Catedral de Córdova, Cajon J, n. 295, 298.--Archivo de Simancas, Patronato Real, Inquisicion, Leg. único, fol. 46.
553. Archivo de la Catedral de Córdova, Cajon I, n. 301.
554. Lorenzo de Padilla, Crónica de Felipe I (Coleccion de Documentos, VIII, 153).--Archivo de Simancas, Patronato Real, Inquisicion, Leg. único, fol. 46.
555. Archivo de la Catedral de Córdova, Cajon I, n. 301.--Archivo de Simancas, loc. cit.
556. Archivo de la Catedral de Córdova, Cajon A, n. 5; Cajon I, n. 304.
557. Bulario de la Orden de Santiago, Lib. III, fol. 320.--See Appendix.
558. Pet. Mart. Epistt., 333, 334, 335.
559. Pedraza, Hist. eccles. de Granada, P. IV, cap. 31-34.
560. Pet. Mart. Epistt., 342, 344, 457.--Pedraza, loc. cit.

The Inquisition which had hunted him to the death could never forgive him for his escape. When, in 1559, Inquisitor-general Valdés compiled the first Index of prohibited books, a long-forgotten controversial tract against the Jews, printed by Talavera in 1480, was resuscitated and condemned in order to cast a slur upon his memory and this was carefully preserved through the long series of Spanish Indexes down to the last one in 1790.--Reusch, Die Indices Libror. Prohib., p. 232.--Indice Ultimo, p. 262.

561. Zurita, Hist. del Rey Hernando, Lib. VII, cap. xxix, xxxiv, xlii; Lib. VIII, cap. i, v.--Villa, La Reina Juana, pp. 462, 463.

Zurita, who, as an official of the Suprema, no doubt reflects the tradition of the Inquisition, says that many murmured at seeing Ferdinand, to win over Ximenes, sacrifice Deza, for the latter was a most notable prelate, a man of great learning and devoted to the king's service. He has claims too on our respect as the patron of Columbus, befriending and encouraging him when disheartened by the incredulity of the court.--Irving's Life and Voyages of Columbus, Book II, Chap. 3, 4; Book XVIII, Chap 3.

562. Correspondence of Rojas (Boletin, XXVIII, 440, 457).--Ciacconii et Oldoini Vit. Pontif. III, 261.
563. Gomesii de Rebus gestis Francisci Ximenii, fol. 77 (Compluti, 1569).
564. Pet. Mart. Epist., 339.
565. Archivo de la Catedral de Toledo, Cajon I, n. 303.
566. Biblioteca nacional, Seccion de MSS., G, 61, fol. 208.

The Licenciado Ortuño Ibañez de Aguirre was a layman whom Ferdinand forced into the Suprema against the earnest resistance of its members, probably with the view of screening Lucero. He was the âme damnée of Ferdinand who corresponded with him confidentially when he wanted anything done. His fidelity was stimulated with favors, as when in December, 1513, Ferdinand gave him an order on the receiver of Seville for 300,000 mrs. (Archivo de Simancas, Inquisicion, Lib. 9, fol. 145). Las Casas, however, expresses a favorable opinion of him and he was one of the executors of Isabella's testament.--Hist. de las Indias, Lib. III, cap. 138 (Coleccion de Documentos, LXVI, 81).

567. Pet. Mart. Epistt., 370, 382, 385.
568. In contrast with these spectacular proceedings was the removal, by the inquisitor-general in 1500, without even stating the reasons, of Diego Fernández de Bonilla, Inquisitor of Extremadura.--Llorente, Añales, I, 260.
569. Pet. Mart. Epist., 393.--Llorente, Memoria histórica, p. 145 (Madrid, 1812).--Llorente, Añales, I, 356.--Gomesii de Rebus F. Ximenii, fol. 77.--Lorenzo de Padilla (Coleccion de Documentos, VIII, 154).

Llorente's account of the proceedings at Valladolid is drawn from Bravo's "Catálogo de los Obispos de Córdova" (Córdova, 1778). It is perhaps worth remarking that, in my copy of that work, the sheet containing these passages is lacking--probably owing to inquisitorial censorship.

570. Archivo de Simancas, Inquisicion, Libro 3, fol. 12, 13, 21, 31, 32, 33, 41, 42, 43, 48, 58, 61, 62, 72, 80, 86, 130; Lib. 9, fol. 146; Patronato Real, Inquisicion, Leg. único, fol. 33.
571. Ibidem, Libro 3, fol. 23.
572. Archivo de Simancas, Inquisicion, Libro 3, fol. 84.
573. Ibidem, fol. 90, 106, 118, 119, 375.--Gomesii de Rebus Ximanii, fol. 77.
574. Archivo de Simancas, Inquisicion, Libro 9, fol. 26.
575. Archivo de Simancas, Patronato Real, Inquisicion, Leg. único, fol. 43.
576. Archivo de Simancas, Patronato Real, Inquisicion, Leg. único, fol. 43.

577. Ibidem, fol. 44, 45.
578. Archivo de Simancas, Inquisicion, Libro 3, fol. 47, 49, 63, 70, 329, 407.
579. Mariana, Hist. de España, T. IX, Append. p. lvi (Valencia, 1796).
580. Gomesii de Rebus Fr. Ximenii, fol. 173.--Cartas de Jimenez, p. 190 (Madrid, 1867).
581. Archivo de Simancas, Inquisicion, Libro 3, fol. 448; Libro 4, fol. 143, 152; Libro 9, passim; Libro 926, fol. 76, 166; Libro 940, fol. 59.
582. Bergenroth, Spanish State Papers, II, 281.--Cartas de los Secretarios de Cisneros, p. 209 (Madrid, 1876).
583. Archivo de Simancas, Inquisicion, Libro 13, fol. 68.
584. Ibidem, Libro 21, fol. 111.
585. Llorente, Añales, II, 94.--Cartas del Cardenal Jimenez, p. 115.--Gachard, Correspondance de Charles-Quint avec Adrian VI, p. 235 (Bruxelles 1859).
586. Archivo de Simancas, Inquisicion, Libro 921, fol. 38.
587. Ibidem, Libro 4, fol. 95; Libro 921, fol. 46.
588. Ibidem, Libro 5, fol. 17.
589. Ibidem, Libro 10, fol. 50.
590. Córtes de los antiguos Reinos de Leon y de Castilla, IV, 272.
591. Pet. Mart. Epistt., 620, 622.

Las Casas however gives to le Sauvage the highest character for intelligence and rectitude. He also speaks highly of Gattinara.--Hist. de las Indias, Lib. III, cap. 99, 103, 130 (Coleccion de Documentos, LXV, 366, 388; LXVI, 35).

592. Archivo de Simancas, Inquisicion, Libro 13, fol. 68-73.
593. C. v. Höfler, Papst Adrian VI, p. 144 (Wien, 1880).
594. This it rather assumed than expressed in Part. VII, Tit. xxvi, ley 3
595. Archivo de Simancas, Patronato Real, Inquisicion, Leg. único, fol. 49. See Appendix.
596. Colmeiro, Córtes de los antiguos Reinos de Leon y Castilla, II, 110 (Madrid, 1884).
597. Archivo de Simancas, Inquisicion, Libro 5, fol. 24.
598. From the Brussels Archives de l'État, Registre sur le faict des hérésies et inquisiteurs, fol. 652. Kindly communicated to me by Professor Paul Fredericq.
599. Archivo de Simancas, Patronato Real, Inquisicion, Leg. único, fol. 35.
600. Biblioteca pública de Toledo, Sala 5, Estante 11, Tabla 3.--See also Padre Fidel Fita in Boletin, XXXIII, 307.
601. Archivo de Simancas, Patronato Real, Inquisicion, Leg. único, fol. 55.--See Appendix.
602. Córtes de los antiguos Reinos de Leon y de Castilla, IV, 381, 415.
603. Mariana, Hist, de España, Lib. XXX, cap. xxiv.--Galindez Carvajal, Memorial, ann. 1515 (Col. de Doc. XVIII, 336)
604. Archivo de Simancas, Inquisicion, Libro 3, fol. 199, 200, 256, 259, 263, 267, 268, 271, 299, 311, 337, 339, 341, 344, 348, 352, 353, 354, 368, 392, 438, 449; Libro 72, P. 1, fol. 49, P. 2, fol. 47; Libro 73, fol. 193, 276; Libro 74, fol. 116; Libro 75, fol. 6.
605. Ibid. Libro 72, P. 2, fol. 116; Libro 73, fol. 142, 247-8; Libro 78, fol. 216, 226, 285; Libro 82, fol. 5.
606. Relazioni Venete, Serie I, T. V, p. 85.

This is virtually the same as the formula given by Antonio Pérez in his Relaciones, written in 1598: "Nos que valemos tanto como vos os hazemos nuestro Rey y Señor con tal que nos guardeys nuestros fueros y libertades y sino No!" (Obras, Ed. 1654, p. 163). The learned Javier de Quinto (Discursos políticos, Madrid, 1848) had not seen Soranzo's statement when he proved that this formula was invented by Hotman in his Franco Gallia, first printed in 1573. On the other hand there is nothing of the kind in the oath of allegiance taken to Charles V in 1518, though he was obliged first to swear to observe the fueros and privileges of the land.--Argensola, Añales de Aragon, Lib. 1, cap. lx.

A good account of the ancient constitution of Aragon will be found in Swift's "Life and Times of James the First, King of Aragon," London, 1894.

607. Monteiro, Historia da Santa Inquisiçaõ, II, 340.
608. Archivio Vaticano, Sisto IV, Registro 674, T. XV, fol. 13.

Even in the dormant condition of the Inquisition, there must have been some opportunities rendering the office of inquisitor desirable. A brief of Sixtus IV, Jan. 21, 1479 (Ripoll, III, 572), to the Dominican General, recites that his predecessor had appointed, some years previously, Jaime Borell as inquisitor of Valencia, who had recently been removed without cause by Miguel de Mariello, Provincial of Aragon, and replaced by Juan Marques. Sixtus now orders Marques ejected and Borell restored. Neither of these names appear in the documents of the period.

609. Archivo general de la Corona de Aragon, Registro 3684, fol. 7, 8.
610. Eymeric. Direct. Inquis. P. III, Q. cviii.
611. Arch. Gen. de la C. de A., Reg. 3684, fol. 9. This quaint document shows us the primitive

organization of a tribunal and the salaries regarded as ample. There are apparently two clerical errors which balance each other, in the salaries of the inquisitors and scrivener.

"La forma infra sequent es la voluntat nostra ques tenga en la solucio e paga dels salaris dels officials e treballants en la officio de la Inquisicio.

E primerament á cascu dels inquisidors que son dos, cent quaranta lliures cascun any que sumen CLXXX llrs. Item á un bon jurista que sia advocat dels inquisidors e advocat fiscal, cinquanta lliures lany L llrs. Item al procurador fiscal vint e cinch lliures lany XXV llrs. Item al scriva de la inquisicio doscentes lliures lany CC llrs. Item al alguacil et al sag cent e vint lliures CXX llrs. Item al porter que va citant vint lliures lany XX llrs. Item á Dominguez que reeb los actos de las confiscacions XXV llrs.

Que sumen tots los dits quantitats sex cent vint lliures moneda reals de Valencia, los quals e no mas es nostra voluntat que en la forma dessus dita se paguen á les sobredits persones. Dada en la vila de Medina del Campo á XVII dias de febrer del any de la nativitat de nostro senyor MCCCCLXXXII. Yo el Rey. Domínus Rex mandavit mihi Petro Camanyas."

612. Printed by Llorente, Hist. crít. Append. 1.
613. Arch. Gen. de la C. de A., Reg. 3684, fol. 3, 4.
614. Ibidem, fol. 1, 2, 4, 5.
615. Arch. Gen. de la C. de A., Reg. 3684, fol. 7, 8.
616. Archivio Vaticano: Sisto IV, Regestro 674, T. XV, fol. 366.

As Llorente states (Hist. crít. Append, n. 2) that the contents of this bull are unknown and as ignorance of its purport has wholly misled him, I give it in the Appendix.

617. Archivo Gen. de la C. de A., Reg. 3684, fol. 9.--It is significant that in the papal register there is a note appended to this bull "Duplicata sub eadem data et scripta per eundem scriptorem et taxata ad XXX" grossos?., showing that an authentic copy was obtained and paid for at the time by some one, doubtless to provide against accident or fraud.

618. Arch. Gen. de la C. de A., Reg. 3684, fol. 7. See Appendix. Bergenroth (Calendar of Spanish State Papers, I, xliv) gives an incorrect extract from it.

619. Arch. Gen. de la C. de A., Reg. 3684, fol. 8, 9.
620. Llorente, Hist. crít. Append. n. 2.--Fidel Fita (Boletin, XV, 467).
621. Ripoll, III, 622.--When Innocent VIII, by letters of February 11, 1486, confirmed or reappointed Torquemada, the qualification of his appointees was modified by requiring them to be fitting ecclesiastics, learned and God-fearing, provided that they were masters in theology or doctors or licentiates of laws or canons of cathedrals or holding other church dignities.--Páramo, p. 137.

Ferdinand, July 9, 1485, had requested that the condition of holding grades in the church should not be insisted upon for there were few of such who were fitted for the work.--Arch. Gen. de la C. de A., Reg. 3684, fol. 59.

622. Arch. Gen. de la C. de A., Reg. 3684, fol. 34.--Boletin, XV, 472.--Bulario de la Orden de Santiago, Lib. I, fol. 43.

Zurita (Añales, XX, xlix) is evidently in error in stating that Ferdinand, May 20, 1483, asked Sixtus to remove Gualbes and Orts.

623. Arch. Gen. de la C. de A., Reg. 3684, fol. 11.
624. Ripoll, III, 622.--Bulario de la Orden de Santiago, Lib. I, fol. 182.

When he had no further use for Gualbes Ferdinand also turned against him, for in March, 1486, on hearing that Gualbes proposed to visit a Dominican convent he wrote earnestly to the Governor and Inquisitor of Valencia to prevent it as it would be a scandal.--Arch. Gen. de la C. de A., Reg. 3684, fol. 90.

It is possible that there may have been some rancor on Ferdinand's part against Gualbes who, as an eloquent preacher and fervid popular orator, had done much, in 1461, to stimulate the resistance of the Catalans to Juan II, after the death of the heir-apparent, Carlos Prince of Viana, which was attributed to poison administered by Queen Juana Henríquez to open for her son Ferdinand the path to the throne (Zurita, Añales, Lib. XVII, cap. xxvi, xlii; Lib. XVIII, cap. xxxii). It is true that Zurita is not certain whether there may not have been two Cristóbal Gualbes (Lib. XX, cap. xlix) but Bofarull y Broca (Hist. de Cataluña, VI, 312) has no such doubts.

625. Zurita, Añales, Lib. XX, cap. lvi, lxv.
626. Arch. Gen. de la C. de A., Reg. 3684, fol. 11, 12.--Bulario de la Orden de Santiago, Lib. 1, fol. 51.
627. Arch. Gen. de la C. de A., Reg. 3684, fol. 19-22.
628. Ibidem, Reg. 3684, fol. 25, 26.
629. Zurita, Añales, Lib. XX, cap. lxv.--Páramo, p. 187.--Arch. Gen. de la C. de A., Reg. 3684, fol. 34.
630. Arch. Gen. de la C. de A., Reg. 3684, fol. 32, 34.
631. Bulario de la Orden de Santiago, Libro I, fol. 31.
632. Arch Gen. de la C. de A., Reg. 3684, fol. 61, 73, 86, 89, 90.

633. Archivo de Simancas, Inquisicion, Libro 688, fol. 504.
634. Portocarrero, Sobre la Competencia de Jurisdicion, fol. 64 (Madrid, 1624).
635. Archivo de Simancas, Inquisicion, Libro I.--Archivo hist. nacional, Inquisicion de Valencia, Leg. 309, Notarios, fol. 1.
636. Escolano, Hist. del Ciudad y Reyno de Valencia, II, 1442 (Valencia, 1611).
637. Archivo hist. nacional, Inquisicion de Valencia, Legajos 98, 374.
638. Arch. gén. de la de C. de A., Reg. 3684, fol. 16.

To Maestre Gaspar Juglar, inquisitor 3000 sueldos. " ---- ---- ----, inquisitor 3000 " " Maestre Pedro de Epila, inquisitor 1000 " " Micer Martin de la Raga, assessor 1000 " " Francisco de Santa Fe, notary 2000 " " Juan de Anchias, notary 1000 " " Ruy Sánchez de Suazo, promotor fiscal 2500 " " Don Ramon de Mur, advocate fiscal 1000 " " Diego López, alguazil 5000 " " Juan de Exea, receiver 1500 "

The blank for the second inquisitor is doubtless to be filled with the name of Maestre Martin García, who appears in a later portion of the document classed with Arbués (Pedro de Epila). The large salary of the alguazil arose from his bearing the charges of the prisons. The salaries of Arbués, Raga, Mur and Anchias were to begin with May 1st, showing that they alone were already at work. The rest were to commence on the day on which they would swear that they left their homes.

639. Memoria de diversos Autos (see Appendix).
640. Ibidem. In this MS. he is called Maestre Julian, presumably the error of a copyist. Lanuza (Hist. de Aragon, II, 168, 177) says that he died in January, 1485, in the monastery of Lérida; that some asserted that he was poisoned by the heretics and that the manner of his death was investigated by the chapter of his convent, but that no decision seems to have been reached. In 1646 a memorial from the authorities of Aragon to Philip IV classes Juglar with Arbués as a martyr to the faith.--Bibl. nacional, Seccion de MSS., Mm, 123.
641. Arch. gén. de la C. de A., Reg. 3684, fol. 12.
642. MS. Memoria (see Appendix).
643. Zurita, Añales, Lib. XX, cap. lxv.--Páramo, pp. 180-1.
644. Zurita, Añales, Lib. XX, cap. lxv.
645. Arch. gén. de la C. de A., Reg. 3684, fol. 28, 86.
646. Arch. gén. de la C. de A., Reg. 3684, fol. 29, 35.
647. Arch. gén. de la C. de A., Reg. 3684, fol. 12, 23, 27, 31, 35, 38, 39, 42, 47-9, 51-3, 55-8, 60, 63, 72, 98.

In 1502, with characteristic faithlessness, the inquisitors at Teruel proposed to collect all the debts due to the confiscated estates, but Ferdinand intervened and sternly forbade it.--Archivo de Simancas, Inquisicion, Libro 2, fol. 16.

648. Bibl. nacionale de France, fonds espagnol, 80, fol. 4.
649. Libro Verde de Aragon (MS., fol. 67).
650. Libro Verde (Revista de España, CVI, 281-2).
651. Zurita, Añales, Libro XX, cap. lxv.
652. Trasmiera, Epitome de la santa Vida y relacion de la gloriosa muerte del Venerable Pedro de Arbués, pp. 15, 32, 50 (Madrid, 1664).--Villanueva, Viage literario, XVIII, 50.
653. Arch. gén. de la C. de A., Reg. 3684, fol. 37, 38.
654. Memoria de diversos Autos (Appendix).--Libro Verde (Revista de España, CVI, 281-6, 288).--Raynald Annal. ann. 1485, n. 23, 24.--Zurita, Añales, Lib. XX, cap. lxv.--Juan Gines Sepúlveda, Descriptio Collegii Hespanorum Bononiensis.--Blancas, Aragon. Rerum Comment. p. 268.-- Bibliothèque nat. de France, fonds espagnol, 80, fol. 33.

In spite of these miracles and of innumerable others which manifested the sanctity of Arbués, the Holy See was distinctly averse to his canonization. A papal brief even ordered the removal from the cathedral of the sanbenitos of the assassins and strenuous efforts were required to procure its revocation.

Repeated investigations were made by successive popes without result--at the request of Charles V in 1537; of Philip III in 1604, 1615 and 1618; of Philip IV in 1622 and 1652, until at length in 1664 he was beatified (Trasmiera, pp. 98, 99, 133, 137, 139). The matter then rested for two centuries until, in 1864, it was taken up again and finally, June 29, 1867, he was canonized by Pius IX (Dom. Bartolini, Comment. Actor. Omnium Canonizationis, Romæ, 1868).

It is significant that the Inquisition did not await the tardy action of Rome. Instructions of the Suprema in 1603, 1623 and 1633 show that his feast was regularly celebrated with prescribed offices (MSS. of Royal Library of Copenhagen, 218^{b}, p. 257) and, during the 17th and 18th centuries, he is constantly spoken of, in the documents of the Inquisition relating to the feast, as San Pedro Arbués.

655. Memoria de diversos Autos, Auto 25 (Appendix).
656. Zurita, loc. cit.
657. Memoria, loc. cit.
658. Gams, Zur Geschichte der spanischen Staatsinquisition, p. 34.--Bibl. nationale de France, fonds espagnol, 81.

659. This brief is printed in the Boletin, XVI, 368 by Padre Fidel Fita, who is in error in assuming its obedience in France from the case of Juan de Pedro Sánchez, reported in an essay of mine on the Martyrdom of Arbués. This was merely an instance of friendly co-operation between the Inquisitions of Toulouse and Saragossa and occurred too early to be the result of the papal letters which were not received in Córdova until May 31, 1487.

We have seen (p. 191), by a case occurring in 1501, that Manoel of Portugal considered that there was no obligation to return fugitives from the Inquisition; it was a matter of comity to be decided on the merits of each case. There was a similar one in 1500, and when, in 1510 and 1514, fugitives were asked for, under plea that they were wanted as witnesses, Manoel refused to surrender them without absolute pledges that they should suffer no harm (Archivo de Simancas, Inquisicion, Libro 1; Libro 3, fol. 85, 107, 110).

When Portugal obtained an Inquisition, the two inquisitors-general, in 1544, came to an agreement, with the assent of the respective monarchs, which superseded extradition. The fugitive was to be tried in the country where he was captured and the Inquisition from which he had fled was to furnish the evidence.--Bibl. nacional, Seccion de MSS. X, 257, fol. 218.

660. Arch. gén. de la C. de A., Reg. 3684, fol. 75.--Amador de los Rios, III, 269.

661. Arch. gén. de la C. de A., Reg. 3684, fol. 103.

662. Ibidem, fol. 102 (see Appendix). It was Martin de Santangel, not Luis, who took refuge in Tudela. He was not caught, but was burnt in effigy, July 28, 1486.

663. Memoria de diversos Autos, Auto 29 (Appendix).

In after years, Ferdinand was less inclined to invade friendly territory. February 25, 1501, writing to the Archdeacon of Almazan, Inquisitor of Catalayud, about an inhabitant of Fitero, a town just beyond the border, he says that if the culprit can be arrested within his jurisdiction it can be done, but there must be no deceit and no scandal.--Archivo de Simancas, Inquisicion, Libro 1.

664. Zurita, Añales, Lib. XX, cap. lxv.--Llorente, Hist. crít. Cap. VI, Art. ii, n. 1.--Trasmiera, p. 101.

665. Arch. gén. de la C. de A., Reg. 3684, fol. 67, 68, 83, 86.

666. Memoria de diversos Autos, Auto 3 (see Appendix).

667. Zurita, loc. cit.--The order to receive the tribunal in the Aljafería bears date January 12, 1486 (Arch. gén. de la C. de A., Reg. 3684, fol. 83). Subsequently it was transferred to the archiepiscopal palace in order to let the Aljafería be occupied by a member of the royal family, but the inquisitors complained and were allowed to return in 1498. They encroached upon the royal apartments, much to Ferdinand's disgust, as expressed in a letter of September 30, 1511. In January, 1515, he ordered them to leave the palace and rent accommodations in the city, but finally they obtained permanent possession.-- Archivo de Simancas, Inquisicion, Libro 1; Libro 3, fol. 155, 321, 322.

668. Arch. gén. de la C. de A., Reg. 3684, fol. 76.

669. Memoria de diversos Autos, Auto 27, n. 3 (see Appendix).

670. Memoria de diversos Autos, Autos 10, 11, 14, 16, 18, 20, 22 (Appendix).

671. Bibl. nacionale de France, fonds espagnol, 81.--Memoria de diversos Autos, Auto 43, n. 6; Auto 45, n. 1.

672. Libro Verde (Revista de España, CVI, 287, 589.--Ibid. MS. fol. 65-74).

673. Memoria de diversos Autos, Auto 36, n. 1.--Bibl. nacionale de France, fonds espagnol, 80.

674. It is impossible to construct a full catalogue of the victims. Llorente undoubtedly exaggerates when he asserts (Hist. crít. Chap. VI, Art. v, n. 1) that the executions numbered more than 200 and so does Amador de los Rios (III, 266) in saying that the greater part of those who appeared in the Saragossa autos from 1486 to 1492 were accomplices in the murder. The sentences abstracted in the Memoria show that but few of them were concerned in it.

Anchias, the notary of the tribunal, in his account of the affair, only enumerates as put to death three treasurers of the fund, five assassins and four accomplices besides Sancho de Paternoy and Alonso de Alagon who escaped with imprisonment through friendly influences (Libro Verde, Revista, CVI, 287). The indications in the Memoria are incomplete as, after May, 1489, the crimes of the culprits are not stated but, so far as it goes and comparing it with the Libro Verde and other sources, I find nine executed in person, besides two suicides, thirteen burnt in effigy and four penanced for complicity. Besides these are two penanced for suborning false witness in favor of Luis de Santangel and seventeen for aiding or sheltering the guilty, and two for rejoicing at the crime. Altogether, fifty or sixty will probably cover the total of those who suffered in various ways.

The sanbenitos of the convicts, with inscriptions, were hung as customary in the cathedral and remain there to the present day (Amador de los Rios, III, 266). The swords of the murderers are still to be seen attached to the pillars near the entrance to the chancel (V. de la Fuente, in Oviedo's Quinquagenas, I, 73). One of the latter was removed in 1518, by order of Leo X, and when the commissioner who had performed the act died shortly afterward it was popularly regarded as a visitation of God (Archivo hist. nacional, Inquisicion de Toledo, Hacienda, Legajo 10).

675. Libro Verde (Revista, CVI, 250-1).--Archivo de Simancas, Inquisicion, Libro 1--Arch. gén. de la C. de A., Reg. 3684, fol. 100.--Garibay, Compendio história1, Lib. XIX, cap 1.--Amador de log Rios, III, 405.
676. Archivo de Simancas, Inquisicion, Libro 3, fol. 237; Libro 4, fol. 223.
677. Libro Verde (Revista, CV, 568).
678. Ibidem (Revista, CVI, 266, 269).
679. Libre dels quatre Senyals, cap. xiv (Barcelona, 1634, p. 34).
680. Zurita, Añales, Lib. XX, cap. lvi.
681. Arch. gén. de la C. de A., Reg. 3684, fol. 16.
682. Ibidem, fol. 24.
683. Arch. gén. de la C. de A., Reg. 3684, fol. 27. This request was repeated soon afterward.--Ibidem, fol. 45.
684. Ibidem, fol. 59.
685. Ibidem, fol. 72. It is probably to this attempt that may be attributed a tumult against the Inquisition at Lérida, alluded to by Llorente, Añales, I, 93.
686. Arch. gén. de la C. de A., Reg. 3684, fol. 86, 89.
687. Archivio Vaticano, Regest. 685 (Innoc. VIII), fol. 346. Cf. Bibl. nacional, Seccian de MSS., D, 118, p. 92.--Bulario de la Orden de Santiago, Lib. I, fol. 31.
688. Manuall de Novells Ardits, III, 58, 61 (Barcelona, 1894).
689. Ibidem, III, 66.
690. Carbonell de Gestis Hæreticorum (Coleccion de Doc. de la Corona de Aragon, XXVIII, 13, 16, 29).
691. Archivo de Simancas, Inquisicion de Barcelona, Córtes, Leg. 17, fol. 26.
692. Carbonell, pp. 36, 39, 40, 52, 83, 85, 137, 139, 140, 148, 149.--Archivo de Simancas, Inquisicion, Libro 1.
693. Archivo de Simancas, Inquisicion, Libro 927, fol. 303.
694. Ibidem, Libro 2, fol. 19.--MSS. of Bodleian Library, Arch. S, 130.
695. Archivo de Simancas, Inquisicion, Libro 2, fol. 5, 7, 10; Libro 13, fol. 385, 386.
696. Ordinacions del Regne de Mallorca, pp. 64, 85, 372-3 (Mallorca, 1663).
697. Historia general del Reyno de Mallorca, III, 362 (Palma, 1841).--Archivo de Simancas, Inquisicion, Libro 595.
698. Hist. gen. de Mallorca, III, 363.
699. Archivo de Simancas, ubi sup.
700. Archivo de Simancas, Inquisicion, Libro 1.
701. Archivo de Simancas, Inquisicion, Libro 72, P. II, fol. 6, 7, 121, 125; Libro 73, fol. 116-171; Libro 77, fol. 228; Libro 78, fol. 60.--Páramo, pp. 217-18.
702. Zurita, Hist. del Rey Hernando, Lib. IX, cap. xiv.
703. Llorente, Añales, II, 11.
704. Capitols concedits y decretats per lo Reverendissim don Juan Bisbe de Leyda e inquisidor general a supplicatio dels tres staments de Cathalunya convocats en los Corts de Montso ha 2 de Agost, 1512 (Pragmáticas y altres Drets de Cathalunya, Lib. I, Tit. viii, cap. 1; Lib. I, Tit. ix, cap. 3, § 6. Barcelona, 1589).
The articles agreed upon for Aragon are given by Llorente, Añales, II, 19.
705. Capitols y Actes de Cort, fol. xxviii (Barcelona, 1603).
706. Archivo de Simancas, Inquisicion, Libro 3, fol. 200.
707. Bulario de la Orden de Santiago, Libro I, fol. 137. Confirmed by a second and fuller one, September 2, 1513.--Archivo de Simancas, Inquisicion, Libro 921, fol. 21, 23.
708. Archivo de Simancas, Inquisicion, Libro 933; Libro 3, fol. 316.
709. Archivo de Simancas, Inquisicion, Libro 3, fol. 323, 456.--Parecer del Doctor Martin Real (MSS. of Bodleian Library, Arch. S, 130).
710. Archivo de Simancas, Inquisicion, Libro 3, fol. 337.
711. Ibidem, fol. 355.
712. Bulario de la Orden de Santiago, Libro I de copias, fol. 219.--Pragmáticas y altres Drets de Cathalunya, Lib. I, Tit. viii, cap. 2.
Ferdinand must have resolved on this policy about a year earlier, but delayed putting it into execution. In the Simancas archives, Patronato real, Inquisicion, Leg. único, fol. 6, there is a similar brief, but without the executive clauses, addressed to him and commencing Exponi nobis nuper fecisti. It bears date May 12, 1515, and was apparently held by him in reserve.
713. Archivo de Simancas, Inquisicion de Barcelona, Córtes, Leg. 17, fol. 2.
714. Llorente, Añales, II, 146-53.
715. Archivo de Simancas, Inquisicion, Libro 921, fol. 76.
716. Archivo de Simancas, Inquisicion, Libro 74, fol. 120.

717. Argensola, Añales de Aragon, Lib. I, cap. liv, lxxii (Zaragoza, 1630).--Llorente, Añales, II, 145-247.--Sayas, Añales de Aragon, cap. ii (Zaragoza, 1666).--Dormer, Añales de Aragon, Lib. I, cap. xxvi (Zaragoza, 1697).--Archivo hist. nacional, Inquisicion de Toledo, Hacienda, Leg. 10 (see also Padre Fidel Fita in Boletin, XXXIII, 330).--Bulario de la Orden de Santiago, Lib. I de copias, fol. 125.--Bergenroth, Calendar of Spanish State Papers, Suppl. p. 300.--P. Mart. Angler. Epistt. 631, 632, 634.--Bibl. nacional, Seccion de MSS., D, 118, fol. 8, 104.--Archivo de Simancas, Inquisicion, Libro 6, fol. 73, 76, 77, 78; Libro 9, fol. 25, 26; Libro 14, fol. 57, 61; Libro 72, P. II, fol. 207; Libro 73, fol. 32, 142, 143; Libro 74, fol. 170; Libro 921, fol. 72-6, 82, 84, 88, 90.

718. Archivo de Simancas, Inquisicion, Libro 73, fol. 144.

719. Constitucions fetes per la S. C. C. y R. Magestat de Don Carlos elet en Rey dels Romans ... en la primera Cort de Barcelona en lany MDxx. Capitols y modificacions y donacio dels bens de Conversos (Barcelona, 1520). Also in Pragmaticas y altres Drets de Cathalunya, Tit. viii, § 3.

720. Archivo de Simancas, Inquisicion de Barcelona, Córtes, Leg. 17, fol. 41, 66; Libro 4, fol. 123.

721. Archivo de Simancas, Libro 930, fol. 39.

722. Archivo de Simancas, Patronato Real, Inquisicion, Leg. único, fol. 38, 39. This paper is not dated but its character and the documents with which it is associated indicate that it belongs to this period.

723. Dormer, Añales, Lib. I, cap. xli.

724. Archivo de Simancas, Inquisicion de Barcelona, Córtes, Leg. 17, fol. 47, 48.

725. Ibidem, fol. 61, 64.

726. Arch. gén. de la C. de A., Fondos del antiguo Consejo de Aragon, Leg. 708.--Costitucions fetes ... en la tercera Cort de Cathalunya en lany 1534 (Barcelona, 1534).

727. Parecer del Doctor Martin Real (MSS. of Bodleian Library, Arch. S, 130).

728. Páramo, p. 138.

729. Archivo de Simancas, Inquisicion, Libro 1.

730. Ibidem, Libro 3, fol. 21, 27, 28, 353.

731. Archivo de Simancas, Inquisicion, Libro 1; Libro 933.

732. Ibidem, Libro 1; Libro 3, fol. 109.

733. See Appendix. All this of course is omitted from the later official compilations.

734. Archivo de Simancas, Libro 1; Libro 3, fol. 24, 441, 442.

735. Archivo de Simancas, Inquisicion, Libro 1; Libro 926, fol. 308.--Arch. gén. de la C. de Aragon, Reg. 3684, fol. 103.

736. Archivo de Simancas, Inquisicion, Libro 3, fol. 340, 402.

737. Archivo de Simancas, Inquisicion, Libro 3, fol. 346-81.

738. Ibidem, Libro 926, fol. 76

739. Archivo de Simancas, Inquisicion, Libro 3, fol. 423.

740. Ibidem, Libro 2, fol. 28, 29, 30.--Libro Verde de Aragon (Revista de España, CV, 573).

741. Raynald. Annal. ann. 1485, n. 81.--Llorente, Añales, I, 109-11.--Bulario de la Orden de Santiago, Lib. I, fol. 29, 33, 91, 101, 102.--Archivio Vaticano, Innoc. VIII, Regist. 682, fol. 263, 294.--Fidel Fita, Boletin, XV, 573-8, 587.

Pastor (Geschichte der Päpste, III, 249) erroneously regards this private and special reconciliation to be a general decree of Innocent VIII.

742. Carbonell, De Gest. Hæret. (Col. de Doc. de Aragon, XXVIII, 18, 29).

Their father, Pedro Badorch, was sentenced to perpetual prison in the auto of August 8, 1488, but was released March 26, 1490.

743. Archivo gén. de la C. de A., Regist. 3684, fol. 100.--Archivo de Simancas, Inquisicion, Lib. 1.

744. Archivo de Simancas, Inquisicion, Lib. 4, fol. 95.

745. Ibidem, Lib. 9, fol. 21, 63.

746. Gachard, Correspondence de Charles-Quint avec Adrian VI, p. 236.--Archivo de Simancas, Inquisicion, Lib. 73, fol. 105.

747. Archivo de Simancas, Inquisicion, Sala 40, Lib. 4, fol. 105, 114, 118, 128, 132, 138, 158, 177, 220, 223, 224.

748. MSS. of Library of University of Halle, Yc, Tom. 17.--Archivo de Simancas, Lib. 939, fol. 273.

749. Archivo de Simancas, Inquisicion, Libro 29, fol. 10.

750. Archivo de Alcalá, Estado, Legajo 3137.

751. MSS. of Library of Univ. of Halle, ubi sup.

752. Ibidem, Yc, 20, Tom. 9.

753. MSS. of Library of Univ. of Halle, Yc, Tom. 17.--Fueros en las Córtes de Barbastro y Calatayud de 1626, p. 16 (Zaragoza, 1627).

754. Archivo de Simancas, Inquisicion, Libro 55, fol. 217.

755. MSS. of Library of Univ. of Halle, Yc, T. 17.--Archivo de Simancas, Inquisicion, Libro 33, fol. 846-7, 851; Libro 35, fol. 509, 567.--Cartas de Jesuitas (Mem. hist. español, XVII, 35).

756. Archivo de Alcalá, Estado, Leg. 3137; Hacienda, Legajo 544^{2} (Libro 10).--Bibliotheca nacional, Seccion de MSS., G, 61, fol. 203.

757. Bulario de la Orden de Santiago, Libro V, fol. 137.

758. Archivo de Alcalá, Estado, Legajos 2843, 3137.--Archivo hist. nacional, Inquisicion de Valencia, Leg. 16, n. 6.

759. Archivo de Simancas, Gracia y Justicia, Leg. 629; Inquisicion, Libros 435, 559.--Archivo hist. nacional, Inquisicion de Valencia, Leg. 17, n. 4.

760. Gachard, Correspondence de Charles-Quint avec Adrian VI, pp. 38, 41, 54, 66, 75, 95, 193.

761. Bulario de la Orden de Santiago, Libro I de copias, fol. 35, 39, etc.

762. Archivo de Simancas, Gracia y Justicia, Legajo 629, fol. 1-14.--See Appendix.

The cost of the briefs to Bertran was 250 ducats for the commission and 50 for the dispensation. That to Bonifaz had been 245; there seems to have been a progressive advance for the briefs to Cevallos cost him 370.--Ibidem.

763. Llorente, Añales, II, 263.

764. Archivo de Simancas, Inquisicion, Sala 40, Libro 4, fol. 98.

765. Sandoval, Hist. de Carlos V, Lib. XVII, § 30.--Ciacconii Vitæ Pontiff. III, 519.--Zuñiga, Añales de Sevilla, Lib. XIV, años 1529, 1534.--Archivo de Simancas, Inquisicion, Libro 77, fol. 228; Libro 939, fol. 62, 115, 134; Patronato Real, Inquisicion, Leg. único, fol. 38, 39.

Llorente (Hist. crít., cap. XIV, art. ii, n. 5) attributes his second disgrace to Charles's anger at the prosecution of his favorite preacher Alonso Virués, which he assumed that Manrique ought to have prevented.

766. Ed. Böhmer, Francisca Hernández und Francisco Ortiz, pp. 140, 173.--Bulario de la Orden de Santiago, Libro III, fol. 133.

767. Cabrera, Relaciones, pp. 17, 33, 44, 579 (Madrid, 1857).--Hinojosa, Despachos de la Diplomacía Pontificia, I, 403 (Madrid, 1896).--Bibl. nacional, Seccion de MSS., Ii, 16.

768. Cabrera, Relaciones, pp. 50, 56, 67, 112, 129.--Bibl. nacional, ubi sup.--Bulario de la Orden de Santiago, Libro IV, fol. 137.

769. Bulario de la Orden de Santiago, loc. cit.--Cabrera, Relaciones, pp. 152, 154, 159, 162.

770. Cabrera, Relaciones, pp. 168, 310, 344, 573.--Bibl. nacional, Seccion de MSS., Ii, 16.

771. Cabrera, pp. 252-4.--Ticknor's Spanish Literature, II, 142.--Another Dominican, Fray Juan Blanco de Paz, is also credited with the paternity.

772. Archivo de Simancas, Gracia y Justicia, Legajo 621, fol. 11.--Archivo de Alcalá, Estado, Leg. 2843.--Cabrera, Relaciones, p. 588.--Cespedes y Meneses, Historia de Felipe Quarto, Lib. II, cap. 3.--Pellegrini, Relazioni di Ambasciatori Lucchesi, p. 62 (Lucca, 1903).--Llorente, Hist. crít. Cap. XXXVIII, Art. 1, n. 18.

773. Bibl. nacional, Seccion de MSS., Ii, 16.

774. Archivo de Simancas, Gracia y Justicia, Leg. 621, fol. 57. "Pareceme para este oficio mas á proposito el Cardenal Çapata, y asi le hago m^{d} de él, pero no se ha de publicar asta ser quien sera aproposito para el cargo del Gobernador del Arzobispado de Toledo, por que es mi voluntad que salgan con los officios en una dia."

775. Bibl. nacional, Seccion de MSS., X, 157.--Archivo de Simancas, Inquisicion, Libro 31, fol. 34, 637.

776. Cartas de Jesuitas (Mem. hist, español, T. XVII, pp. 110, 116, 122, 143, 172, 235, 255).--Pellicer, Avisos (Valladares, Semanario erúdito, XXXIII, 104).--Archivo de Simancas, Inquisicion, Libro 126, fol. 2. (See Appendix).

777. Cartas del Consejo, Tom. XIII (MSS. of American Philosophical Society).

778. Candamo, Controversias en la menor edad de Carlos II (Semanario erúdito, IV, 7).

779. There is a voluminous collection of documents on the subject in the Simancas archives, Inquisicion, Libro 33, fol. 963-1100.

780. Candamo, loc. cit., pp. 4-239.--Memorias históricas de la Monarquía de España (Semanario erúdito, XIV, 19).--MSS. of the Royal Library of Munich, Cod. Ital. 191, fol. 710.--Archivo de Simancas, Inquisicion, Leg. 1476, fol. 3.

781. Bulario de la Orden de Santiago, Libro V, fol. 118. This continued to be the practice, requiring a renewal of the brief every three years until 1774, when, as we have seen, Felipe Beltran obtained a dispensation good for his tenure of office, a favor repeated to his successors.

782. Proceso contra Fray Froilan Díaz, pp. 143-44.

783. Bulario de la Orden de Santiago, Libro V, fol. 136.

784. Printed by Llorente, Coleccion Diplomática, p. 27.

785. Belando, Historia civil de España desde 1700 hasta 1733, P. IV, cap. ix, xv (Madrid, 1744).

See also Macanaz's Commentary on Feyjoo's Teatro Crítico (Semanario erúdito, VIII, 27-9).

This volume of Belando's work was examined by the Council of Castile, before a license to print was issued, and was subjected to a second examination by order of Philip, before he would permit its dedication to himself and his queen. This, and the secret documents which it contains, show that its account of the Giudice affair may be regarded as authentic. This did not save the book from the Inquisition which condemned it in 1744 and, when the author asked to be heard in its defence and offered to make any changes required, he was thrown into prison and then relegated to a convent with orders to write no more books.--Llorente, Hist. crít., Cap. XXV, Art. i, n. 12.

The Marquis of San Felipe gives an account of the affair much less favorable to Macanaz and the royal prerogative.--Mémoires pour servir à l'Histoire d'Espagne sous le Regne de Philippe V, III, 120 sqq. (Amsterdam, 1756).

786. Puigblanch, La Inquisicion sin Mascara, pp. 412-15 (Cadiz, 1811).

Puigblanch says that he possessed a copy of this consulta signed by Macanaz at Montauban in 1720. So far as I am aware it has never been printed.

787. MSS. of Royal Library of Copenhagen, No. 210 fol.--I have printed this document in "Chapters from the Religious History of Spain," p. 483.

788. Archivo de Simancas, Inquisition, Sala 39, Leg. 4, fol. 57.

789. Alfonso Professione, Il Ministero in Spagna del Card. Giulio Alberoni, p. 244 (Torino, 1897).

790. Macanaz, Regalías de los Reyes de Aragon, Introd. pp. xix-xxv (Madrid, 1879).

791. Regalías de los Reyes de Aragon, Introd. p. xxviii.

792. Defensa crítica de la Inquisicion, I, 7-10, 18, 23.

The work was not printed in the lifetime of Macanaz but was issued by Valladares in 1788.

793. Valladares, Semanario erúdito, VIII, 221.

794. Ibidem, VII, 4, 127, 138; VIII, 168.--Regalías de los Reyes de Aragon, Introd. pp. xliii-iv.

795. Ferrer del Rio, Historia de Carlos III, I, 384 sqq.

796. Novísima Recop. II, iii, 9.

797. Llorente, Hist. crít. Cap. XLIV, Art. 1, n. 42, 43.--Modesto de Lafuente, Historia general de España, XXII, 97, 125.

798. Archivo de Simancas, Inquisicion, Libro 9, fol. 144, 192.

799. Ibidem, Sala 40, Lib. 4, fol. 153.

800. Relazioni Venete, Serie I, Tom. VI, p. 370.

801. Archivo de Alcalá, Estado, Leg. 3137.--Archivo de Simancas, Inquisicion, Libro 939, fol. 271.--Páramo, p. 150.

802. Bibl. nacional, Seccion de MSS., D, 118, fol. 183.--Cabrera, Relaciones, p. 560.

803. Archivo de Simancas, Registro de Genealogías, 916, fol. 66.

804. Discurso sobre el Origen, etc., de la Inquisicion, p. 70 (Valladolid, 1803).

805. Archivo de Alcalá, Estado, Leg. 3137.--Archivo de Simancas, Gracia y Justicia, Leg. 621, fol. 58-60.--Bibl. nacional, Seccion de MSS., G, 61, fol. 209-10; Pp, 28, § 13.--MSS. of Bodleian Library, Arch. S, 130.--Archivo de Simancas, Inquisicion, Libro 21, fol. 60.

806. Archivo de Simancas, Inquisicion, Libro 21, fol. 256.--Bibl. nacional, ubi sup.--Archivo de Alcalá, ubi sup.--Parets, Sucesos de Cataluña (Memorial hist. español, XXI, Append. p. 398).--Cartas de Jesuitas (Mem. hist. espan. XVI, 81, 205).

807. Archivo de Alcalá, ubi sup.--Archivo de Simancas, Inquisicion, Libro 33, fol. 846; Libro 35, fol. 509.--MSS. of Library of Univ. of Halle, Yc, T. 17.

808. Archivo de Alcalá, Hacienda, Legajo 544^{2} (Libro 10).--Bibl. nacional, Seccion de MSS. G, 61, fol. 22.--Proceso criminal contra Fray Froylan Díaz, p. 222.

809. Archivo de Simancas, Inquisicion, Libro 3, fol. 384.

810. Ibidem, Libro 939, fol. 136.

811. Ibidem, Libro 978, fol. 36.

812. Archivo de Simancas, Libro 29, fol. 59.

It is observable that the kings always addressed the Inquisition "por ruego y encargo" and never "por mandamiento."

813. Ibidem, Inquisicion de Barcelona, Córtes, Legajo 17, fol. 9.

814. Archivo de Simancas, Libro 20, fol. 340; Libro 26, fol. 37; Libro 43, fol. 297.

815. Ibidem, Libro 3, fol. 24, 397; Libro 5, fol. 8, 16, 21.

816. Archivo de Simancas, Inquisicion, Lib. 3, fol. 248, 250, 252.

817. Archivo de Simancas, Inquisicion, Lib. 76, fol. 227; Sala 40, Lib. 4, fol. 139.

818. Ibidem, Lib. 5, fol. 16.

819. Ibidem, Lib. 940, fol. 34.

820. Ibidem, Lib. 5, fol. 29; Lib. 73, fol. 106, 107, 301; Lib. 940, fol. 35, 36, 40, 41.

821. Ibidem, Lib. 78, fol. 162.

822. Archivo de Simancas, Inquisicion, Sala 40, Lib. 4, fol. 107, 110; Lib. 939, fol. 134; Lib. 940,

fol. 41, 42.

A pragmática of 1534, abandoning the royal claim on the confiscations under the crown of Aragon, can only have been of temporary effect.--Ibidem, Lib. 939, fol. 9.

823. Ibidem, Lib. 939, fol. 134; Sala 40, Lib. 4, fol. 164.
824. Archivo de Simancas, Lib. 80, fol. 2, p. 2; Sala 40, Lib. 4, fol. 252.
825. Bulario de la Orden de Santiago, Lib. I de copias, fol. 201, 203.--Bibl. nacional, Seccion de MSS., R, 90.--Páramo, p. 138.
826. Danvila y Collado, Expulsion de los Moriscos, pp. 184-6 (Madrid, 1889).
827. Archivo hist. nacional, Inquisicion de Valencia, Leg. 384.
828. Archivo hist. nacional, Inquisicion de Valencia, Leg. 5, n. 2, fol. 168, 169, 172.
829. Recop. de las Indias, Lib. I, Tit. xix, leyes 10, 11, 12, 30, § 1.--Solorzani de Indiar. Gubern. Lib. III, cap. xxiv, n. 11.--Archivo de Simancas, Inquisicion, Leg. 1465, fol, 78; Libro 40, fol. 44, 57, 74, 77, 85, 91, 103, 128, 139.
830. Archivo de Simancas, Libro 35, fol. 456.
831. Ibidem, fol. 281; Libro 21, fol. 224, 251.
832. Ibidem, Libro 40, fol. 218, 328; Libro 36, fol. 74.
833. Archivo de Simancas, Inquisicion, Libro 23, fol. 63.
834. Ibidem, Libro 38, fol. 281, 303, 398; Legajo 1465, fol. 36-8, 50.
835. Ibidem, Libro 40, fol. 85, 139.
836. MSS. of Bibl. nacional of Lima, Legajo 225, Expediente 5278.
837. Archivo de Simancas, Inquisicion, Libro 69, fol. 2, 69, 156, 563.
838. Bibl. nacional, Seccion de MSS Q, 4.
839. Archivo hist. nacional, Inquisicion de Valencia, Leg. 10, n. 2, fol. 157.--Archivo de Alcalá, Estado, Leg. 2843.--Archivo de Simancas, Inquisicion, Libro 559.

Jubilation, as we shall see hereafter, consisted in retirement on half-pay.

840. Archivo hist. nacional, Inquisition de Valencia, Leg. 13, n. 2, fol. 6, 13, 17; Leg. 14, n. 1, fol. 42.--Archivo de Simancas, Inquisicion, Libro 27, fol. 87; Libro 28, fol. 275.
841. Instruciones de 1484, §§ 3, 7 (Arguello, fol. 3, 4).--Archivo de Simancas, Inquisicion, Lib. 933. (See Appendix.)
842. Archivo gén. de la C. de A., Reg. 3684, fol. 83, 89, 102.
843. Boletin, XV, 594, 596.
844. Instruciones de 1498, § 5. (Arguello, fol. 12.)
845. Archivo de Simancas, Inquisicion, Libro 1; Libro 933.
846. Ibidem, Libro 1; Libro 2, fol. 9.
847. Archivo de Simancas, Inquisicion, Libro 3, fol. 135, 137, 169, 270; Libro 933, fol. 125; Libro 72, P. 1, fol. 72; P. 2, fol. 20. (Arguello, fol. 20, 25.)
848. MSS. of Royal Library of Copenhagen, 218^{b}, p. 236.
849. Simancæ de Cathol. Institt. Tit. xxiii.--Cf. R. Bellarmini de Potestate Papæ cap. 3.
850. Solorzano de Jure Indiarum, Tom. I, Lib. III, cap. i, n. 92.--In this Solorzano exaggerates cap. 3 of the Sixth Council of Toledo (Aguirre, III, 409).

All this is seriously brought forward by Antonio de Ayala, fiscal of Valencia, in an argument to prove the exemption from taxation of the Inquisition.--Arch. hist. nacional, Inquisicion de Valencia, Leg. 1, no. 1, fol. 11.

851. Córtes de Madrigal, 1476 (Córtes de los antiguos Reinos, IV, 74, 80).--Nueva Recop. Lib. II, Tit. v, leyes 36-39.--Salgado de Somoza, De Regia Protectione, P. I, cap. 1, 2
852. This cédula is not included in the Recopilaciones, but is printed by Salgado de Somoza, De Retentione Bullarum, P. II, cap. xxxiii, n. 13, and by Portocarrero, op. cit., § 74. There are also copies in Bibl. nacional, MSS., Cc, 58, fol. 5; Archivo de Simancas, Lib. 30, fol. 146; Lib. 939, fol. 300, and in MSS. of Library of Univ. of Halle, Yc, Tom. 17.
853. Archivo de Simancas, Libro 20, fol. 340.
854. MSS. of Bodleian Library, Arch. S, 130.
855. Bibl. nacional, Seccion de MSS., X, 157, fol. 244.
856. Archivo de Simancas, Inquisicion, Libro 13, fol. 16.--Llorente, Añales, I, 277.
857. Nueva Recop. Libro IV, Tit. 1, ley 18.--Consulta magna, 1696 (Bibl. nacional, Seccion de MSS., Q, 4).
858. Archivo de Simancas, Libro 927, fol. 323; Libro 21, fol. 84, 110; Libro 50, fol. 82.--Bibl. nacional, Seccion de MSS., X, 157, fol. 244.
859. Portocarrero, Sobre la Competencia, etc., § 52.
860. Archivo de Simancas, Inquisicion, Libro 940, fol. 196.
861. Llorente, Hist. crít. Cap. XXVI, Art. ii, n. 20-4.
862. Portocarrero, op. cit., § 73.
863. Por la Jurisdiction de la Inquisicion de la Ciudad y Reyno de Granada, Granada, 1642 (MSS.

of Bodleian Library, Arch. S., 130).

864. Bibl. nacional, Seccion de MSS., D, 118, fol. 151.

865. Archivo gén. de la Corona de Aragon, Legajo 528.--For some extracts from this paper see Appendix.

Various papers on both sides of these questions will be found in the Simancas archives, Libro 62, fol. 160, 312.

866. Archivo de Simancas, Inquisicion, Libro 32, fol. 56, 58. (See Appendix.)

867. Ibidem, Libro 25, fol. 58

868. Archivo de Simancas, Inquisicion, Legajo 1465, fol. 2-8.--MSS. of Library of Univ. of Halle, Yc, 20, Tom. 17.

869. Instrucciones de 1484, § 21. (Arguello, fol. 7.)

870. Archivo de Simancas, Inquisicion, Libro 31, fol. 193, 194. (See Appendix.)

871. Llorente, Hist. crít. Cap. XXVI, Art. 3. n. 11.

872. Pablo García, Orden de Procesar, fol. 73.--This is an official manual compiled by the Aragonese secretary of the Suprema. Originally issued about 1568 it was reprinted in 1592, 1607 and 1628. My references are to the last edition.

A somewhat different formula of this oath is given by Páramo, p. 573.

873. Archivo de Simancas, Inquisicion, Libro 688, fol. 514.--MSS. of Bodleian Library, Arch. S, 130.--Archivo hist. nacional, Inquisicion de Valencia, Legajo 1, Lib. 11, fol. 158.

874. Orden de Procesar, fol. 72.

875. Archivo de Simancas, Inquisicion, Libro 12, fol. 29.--Bibl. nacionale de France, fonds français, 2881, fol. 7

876. Archivo de Simancas, Inquisicion, Sala 39, Leg. 4, fol. 41.

877. Portocarrero, op. cit., § 1.--Solorzani de Indiar. Gubern., Lib. III, cap. xxiv, n. 16.--Archivo hist. nacional, Inquisicion de Valencia, Leg. 1, Lib. 3, fol. 49-69.

878. Archivo de Simancas, Libro 939, fol. 63.--Cf. Concil. Trident. Sess. XXV, De Reform. cap. 3.--Ferraris, Prompta Bibliotheca, s. v. Excom. Art. 5, n. 17.

879. C. Trident, ubi sup.

880. Bulario de la Orden de Santiago, Libro I de copias, fol. 10, 13, 15.--"Et quibuscunque judicibus et personis quibus tibi inhibendum videbitur etiam sub censuris et privationis et inhabilitatis poenis inhibendi."

881. Bulario de la Orden de Santiago, Libro IV, fol. 118, 137; Libro V, fol. 117, 136, 138, 151, 199, 200, 251, 264, 295.--Archivo de Simancas, Gracia y Justicia, Leg. 629.

This clause probably explains a peculiarity in the issue of Manrique de Lara's commission. After the death of Quiroga, Nov. 20, 1594, Clement VIII issued to Manrique, Feb. 10, 1595, a commission subrogating him to Quiroga, with the same powers, for six months until further letters could be made out. Then, August 1, 1595, the full elaborate commission is made out, containing this clause (Bulario, loc. cit., 118, 119). The new clause must have evoked prolonged debate, requiring five months for its settlement.

882. MSS. of Royal Library of Copenhagen, 218^{b}, p. 338.

883. Páramo, p. 537.--MSS. of Library of Univ. of Halle, Yc, Tom. 17.

884. Archivo de Simancas, Inquisicion, Libro 939, fol. 65; Libro 941, fol. 5; Libro 71, fol. 143.--MSS. of Royal Library of Copenhagen, 218^{b}, p. 300.--MSS of Bibl. nacional de Lima, Protocolo 223, Expediente 5270.

885. MSS. of Royal Library of Copenhagen, 318^{b}, p. 302.--Bibl. nacional, Seccion de MSS., D, 118, fol. 170.

886. Solorzano, De Gubernatione Indiarum, Lib III, Tit. xxiv, n. 53.--MSS. of Bibl. nacional de Lima, Protocolo 228, Expediente 5287.--Archivo de Simancas, Inquisicion, Legajo 1465, fol. 63.

887. Archivo gén. de la C. de Aragon, Leg. 528, n. 2.

888. MSS. of Bodleian Library, Arch. S, 130.--Cartas de Jesuitas (Memorial hist. español, XVII, 70-175).--Juan Gomez Bravo, Catálogo de los Obispos de Córdova, p. 643.

889. Ariño, Sucesos de Sevilla, pp. 103, 105; Appendix (Sevilla, 1873).--Archivo de Simancas, Inquisicion, Libro 937, fol. 220.

890. Archivo de Simancas, Inquisicion, Leg. 1465, fol. 46.--Archivo de Alcalá, Hacienda, Leg. 544^{2}, Libro 8.

891. Portocarrero, op. cit., § 57.

892. Cap. 9 in Sexto, Lib. V, Tit. ii.

893. Archivo hist. nacional, Inquisicion de Valencia, Leg. 4, n. 3, fol. 25.--Archivo de Simancas, Inquisicion, Libro 688, fol. 289.

894. MS. penes me.

895. Archivo gén. de la C. de Aragon. Leg. 528, n. 23.--Archivo de Simancas, Inquisicion, Libro 21, fol. 140.

896. Gratiani Decreti P. II, Caus. XVII, Q, IV, c. 29.

897. Bulario de la Orden de Santiago, Libro I de copias, fol. 139.--Archivo de Alcalá, Hacienda, Legajo 1049.

For some reason a similar brief was obtained from Paul V, November 29, 1606.--Archivo de Alcalá, loc. cit.

898. Bullar. Roman. II, 198.

This was by no means allowed to be a dead letter in Italy. In 1590 we chance to hear of the Inquisitor of Cremona relaxing to the secular arm three offenders under the bull. In some cases however of wounding or threatening witnesses, the galleys were substituted for capital punishment. There was, moreover, a spirit of conciliation in the Roman Inquisition offering a marked contrast to that of Spain. When, in 1635, at Macerata, some laymen were arrested for wounding certain officials of the tribunal and a question arose as to jurisdiction, the Congregation ordered the civil governor to try the cases as its delegate and not to apply the bull Si de protegendis, as the wounding had not arisen out of hostility to the Holy Office.--Decreta Sacr. Congr. S^{ti} Officii, pp. 34, 202 (R. Archivio di Stato in Roma, Fondo Camerale, Congr. del S. Offizio, Vol. 3).

899. Archivo de Simancas, Inquisicion, Libro 939, fol. 144.

900. Pegnæ Comment. lxi in Eymerici Direct. Inquis. P. III.

901. Archivo de Simancas, Inquisicion, Visitas de Barcelona, Leg. 15, fol. 20; Ibidem, Libro 940, fol. 45.--Bibl. nacional, Seccion de MSS., P V, 3, n. 69.

902. Archivo de Simancas, Inquisicion, Libro 925, fol. 681.

903. Archivo de Simancas, Inquisicion, Visitas de Barcelona, Leg. 15, fol. 9.

904. Archivo de Simancas, Inquisicion, Libro 940, fol. 190.

905. Franchina, Breve Rapporto della Inquisizione di Sicilia, pp. 72-5, 93 (Palermo, 1744).

906. Archivo gén. de la C. de Aragon, Leg. 528, n. 3.

907. Nic. Antonii Bibl. nova, II, 140.--Llorente., Hist. crít. Cap. XXIX, Art. 2, n. 10.--MSS. of Library of Univ. of Halle, Yc, 20, T. I.

908. Novis. Recop., Lib. I, Tit. v, leyes 14, 15.

909. Cap. 3 in Sexto, Lib. III, Tit. xxiii.--Cap. 1 Clementin., Lib. III, Tit. xvii.

910. Dormer, Añales de Aragon, pp. 132, 155.

911. For the numerous and extensive privileges of the hidalgo, see Benito de Peñalosa y Mondragon, Las Cinco Excelencias del Español, fol. 88 (Barcelona, 1629).

912. Archivo de Simancas, Inquisicion de Barcelona, Córtes, Leg. 17, fol. 52.--Ibidem, Libro 13, fol. 386.

913. Archivo de Simancas, Inquisicion, Leg. 1465, fol. 27; Libro 939, fol. 144.--Bibl. nacional, Seccion de MSS., D, 118, p. 102.--Modo de Proceder, fol. 45 (Bibl. nacional, D, 122).

914. Bibl. nacional, Seccion de MSS., S, 88, p. 102.

915. Archivo de Simancas, Libro 21, fol. 37; Leg. 1465, fol. 27

916. Archivo de Simancas, Inquisicion, Libro 40, fol. 168, 203, 212, 229, 294.--Modo de Proceder, fol. 9 (Bibl. nacional, Seccion de MSS., D, 122).--Archivo hist. nacional, Inquisicion de Valencia, Leg. 13, n. 2, fol. 42; Legajo 299.

917. Archivo hist. national, Inquisition de Valencia, Leg. 14, n. 2, fol. 28; Cartas del Consejo, Leg. 16, n. 9, fol. 7.

918. Archivo hist. nacional, Inquisicion de Valencia, Leg. 1, n. 1, fol. 11, 222.--Bibl. nacional, Seccion de MSS., D, 118, n. 2, fol. 17.

919. Modo de Proceder, fol. 44 (Bibl. nacional, D, 122).

920. Modo de Proceder, fol. 45 (loc. cit.).

921. Archivo de Simancas, Inquisicion, Libro 926, fol. 26.

922. Constitutions del Cort de 1599, n. 51 (Barcelona, 1603, fol. xvii).--Archivo de Simancas, Inquisicion de Barcelona, Córtes, Leg. 17, fol. 5.

923. Archivo de Simancas, Inquisicion, Libro 32, fol. 110.

924. Consulta magna (Bibl. nacional, Seccion de MSS., Q, 4).

925. Ant. Rodríguez Villa, La Corte y Monarquía de España, p. 16.

926. Consulta Magna of 1696 (Bibl. nacional, MSS., Q, 4).

927. Archivo hist. nacional, Inquisicion de Valencia, Leg. 9, n. 3, fol. 78.--MSS. of Royal Library of Copenhagen, 218^{b}, p. 222.--Bibl. nacional, MSS., D, 118, fol. 122.

928. Archivo hist. nacional, Inquisicion de Valencia, Leg. 3, fol, 71, 76, 101, 109, 111, 121, 123, 124, 125, 188, 213; Leg. 13, n. 2, fol. 71.

929. Ibidem, Leg. 14, n. 1, fol. 148.--Archivo de Simancas, Inquisicion, Libro 27, fol. 85.

930. Archivo hist. nacional, Inquisicion de Valencia, Leg. 16, n. 6, fol. 10, 19, 38; Leg. 4, n. 3, fol. 103, 115, 142, 166, 311.

931. Archivo de Simancas, Inquisicion, Libro 559.--Archivo de Sevilla, Seccion primera, Carpeta 58, n. 454 (Sevilla, 1860).

932. Archivo de Simancas, Inquisicion, Sala 40, Lib. 4, fol. 109.
933. Modo de Proceder, fol. 77 (Bibl. nacional, MSS., D, 122).--Archivo de Simancas, Inquisicion de Barcelona, Córtes, Legajo 17, fol. 20.
934. See the Libre dels quatre Senyals, Barcelona, 1634.
935. Portocarrero, op. cit., § 57.
936. Sayas, Añales de Aragon, cap. 85, p. 567.
937. Archivo hist. nacional, Inquisicion de Valencia, Leg. 5, n. 1, fol. 298,313, 339, 405.--Portocarrero, op. cit., § 58.
938. Archivo de Simancas, Inquisicion, Libro 688, fol. 66.--Archivo hist. nacional, Inquisicion de Valencia, Leg. 1, n. 6, fol. 634; Leg. 8, n. 2, fol. 73.
939. Gomesii de Rebus gestis a Fr. Ximenio, Lib. V, fol. 140.
940. Archivo de Simancas, Inquisicion, Libro 688, fol. 529.--Archivo hist. nacional, Inquisicion de Valencia, Leg. 2, n. 18.

There was a similar arrangement in Barcelona and, in 1532, the Suprema orders the inquisitors not to allow familiars to be compelled to pay this assessment.--Archivo de Simancas, Libro 77, fol. 44.

941. Archivo de Simancas, Inquisicion, Libro 19, fol. 289; Libro 688, fol. 66, 255.--Archivo hist. nacional, Inquisicion de Valencia, Leg. 1, n. 6, fol. 199.
942. Fueros y Actos de Corte in Barbastro y Calatayud, año de 1626 (Zaragoza, 1627, p. 20).--Archivo gén. de la C. de Aragon, Leg. 528, n. 3.
943. Archivo de Simancas, Inquisicion, Libro 20, fol. 54; Libro 62, fol. 457.
944. Archivo gén. de la C. de Aragon, Leg. 528, n. 3.
945. Archivo de Simancas, Inquisicion, Lib. 38, fol. 22; Libro 62, fol. 457, 526, 528, 544; Lib. 922, fol. 453.
946. Bibl. nacional, MSS., Mm, 464.--Archivo de Simancas, Gracia y Justicia, Leg. 621, fol. 45, 46.
947. Archivo de Simancas, Inquisicion de Barcelona, Córtes, Leg. 17, fol. 47, 48.
948. Archivo de Simancas, Inquisicion, Libro 939, fol. 63, 64.
949. Ibidem, Libro 940, fol. 220, 221. The excommunication latæ sententiæ worked of itself when the act was committed and did not require to be published. It was one of the worst ecclesiastical abuses and during the later middle ages was so lavishly employed that men scarce knew whether or not they were excommunicate under some mandate of which they had never heard.
950. This abuse existed in England under the name of Purveyance and Pre-emption, but there it was restricted to the royal household. It inevitably led to many abuses and was replaced, in 1660, with an excise on malt and spirituous liquors by 12 Carol. II, cap. 24, §§ 12-27.
951. Archivo hist. nacional, Inquisicion de Valencia, Libro 7 de Autos, Leg. fol. 391, 494; Leg. 2, n. 18; Leg. 13, n. 2, fol. 11.
952. Córtes de Leon y de Castilla, T. I, II (Madrid, 1861-3).--Colmeiro, Córtes de Leon y de Castilla, II, 122, 124, 136, 150, 162-3, 181, 193, 201, 277.
953. Fueros y Ordinacions del Reyno de Aragon, Lib. VII (Zaragoza, 1624, fol. 131.)
954. Arguello, fol. 22.
955. Archivo de Simancas, Inquisicion, Libro 1; Libro 939, fol. 144.
956. Archivo hist. nacional, Inquisicion de Valencia, Leg. 5, n. 2, fol. 304.
957. Parets, Sucesos de Catalonia (Mem. hist. Español, XX, 150-182; Appendix, pp. 219, 299, 301, 312).
958. Macanaz, Regalías de los Reyes de Aragon, p. 111 (Madrid, 1879).
959. Candamo, op. cit. (Valladares, Semanario erúd., IV, 13).
960. Archivo de Simancas, Inquisicion, Libro 939, fol. 144.
961. Fueros y Actos de Corte de Zaragoza, 1645-6 (Zaragoza, 1647, p. 10).
962. Archivo gén. de la C. de Aragon, Fondos del Concejo de Aragon, Leg. 708.
963. Archivo de Simancas, Inquisicion de Barcelona, Córtes, Leg. 17, fol. 20.--Actos de Corte del Reyno de Aragon, fol. 96 (Zaragoza, 1664).
964. Archivo de Simancas, Libro 23, fol. 42; Leg. 1157, fol. 23--Modo de Proceder, fol. 41-2 (Bibl. nacional, MSS., D, 122).
965. Archivo hist. nacional, Inquisicion de Valencia, Leg 2, n. 18.--Archivo de Simancas, Inquisicion, Libro 23, fol. 42.
966. Fueros y Actos de Corte, p. 12 (Zaragoza, 1647).--Bibl. nacional, MSS., D, 118, fol. 122.
967. Archivo de Simancas, Libro 26, fol. 69; Libro 66, fol. 78.--Archivo de la C. de Aragon, Fondos del Concejo de Aragon, Leg. 708.
968. Archivo hist. nacional, Inquisicion de Valencia, Leg. 2, n. 18.
969. Ibidem, Legajo 390.
970. Autos Acordados, Lib. VI, Tit. xiv, auto 4.
971. Archivo hist. nacional, Inquisicion de Valencia, Legajo 14, n. 2, fol. 9.

972. Ibidem, Legajo 299.
973. Autos Acordados, ubi sup.
974. Archivo hist. nacional, Inquisicion de Valencia, Leg. 4, n. 2, fol. 79; Leg. 16, n. 5, fol. 4.
975. Ibidem, Varios, Leg. 392; Leg. 492, n. 27.
976. Ibidem, Leg. 398; Cartas del Consejo, Leg. 17, n. 3, fol. 22.
977. See the Author's Inquisition of the Middle Ages, I, 382 sqq.
978. See for example the Vida de D. Diego, Duque de Estrada (Mem. hist, español, XII, 47).
979. Constitutions de Cathalunya, Lib. IX, Tit. xix, cap. 3, 4 (Barcelona, 1588, p. 495).--Novís. Recop., Lib. XII, Tit. xix, leyes 2, 8, 15.
980. Michael Albert, Repertorium de Pravitate Hæreticorum, s. v. Arma (Valentiæ, 1494).
981. Archivo gén. de la C. de Aragon, Regist. 3684, fol. 89.
982. Instrucciones de 1498, § 2 (Arguello, fol. 12).
983. Archivo de Simancas, Inquisicion, Libro 3, fol. 96, 125.--Bibl. national, MSS., D. 118, fol. 20.
984. Pragmáticas y altres Drets de Cathalunya, Lib. I, Tit. viii, cap. 1, § 16.
985. Archivo de Simancas, Inquisicion, Lib. 933.
986. Ibidem, Sala 40, Lib. 4, fol. 98.--Bibl. nacional, MSS., D, 118, fol. 20.
987. Archivo de Simancas, Inquisicion, Lib. 926, fol. 33.--Bibl. nacional, MSS., D, 118, fol. 20; D, 146.--MSS. of Bodleian Library, Arch. S, 130.

This article however was omitted from the Valencia Concordia of 1568.
988. Bibl. nacional, MSS., D, 118, fol. 20.--Portocarrero, § 57.
989. Bibl. nacional, MSS., D, 146.--Archivo hist. nacional, Inquisicion de Valencia, Cartas del Consejo, Leg. 5, n. 2, fol. 76.
990. Archivo de Simancas, Visitas de Barcelona, Legajo 15, fol. 20.
991. Archivo de Simancas, Inquisicion, Libro 19, fol. 161; Libro 927, fol. 329.
992. Archivo hist. nacional, Inquisicion de Valencia, Leg. 1, n. 6, fol. 48, 225.
993. Archivo gén. de la C. de Aragon, Leg. 528.--Actos de Corte del Reyno de Aragon, fol. 94 (Zaragoza, 1664).--Bibl. nacional, MSS., D, 146.
994. Archivo hist. nacional, Inquisicion de Valencia, Leg. 8, n. 2, fol. 405-7.
995. Ibidem, Leg. 1, n. 3, fol. 49.--Bibl. nacional, MSS., D, 118, fol. 20; fol. 54, n. 21; Ibidem, D, 146.

The commission as familiar issued March 7, 1642, by the tribunal of Toledo to Francisco de Gayeta of Madrid, says "y os damos licencia y facultad para que podais traer armas, asi ofensivas como defensivas, publica y secretamente, de dia y de noche, y mandamos en vertud de santa obediencia y so pena de excomunion mayor y de cincuenta mil mrs. para gastos desto Santo Oficio, á todas las dichas justicias y á sus alguaciles, executores y ministros no os toman las dichas armas ni os quebranten los dichos privilegios y exempciones de que los dichos familiares pueden y deben gozar, con sus personas y bienes, ni sobre ello os molesten ni ynquieten en manera alguna."

996. Archivo hist. nacional, Inquisicion de Valencia, Leg. 8, n. 2, fol. 407; Leg. 9, n. 1, fol. 436, 476, 499.
997. This was sound inquisitorial law, as the Suprema proved by citing the authorities. See, for instance, Pegnæ Comment. 105 in Eymerici Director. P. III and Bordoni Sacrum Tribunal, cap. 40, Q, 16, n. 24.
998. Archivo hist. nacional, Inquisicion de Valencia, Leg. 1, n. 3, fol. 49-69.
999. Ibidem.
1000. Bibl. nacional, MSS., R, 102, fol. 142.
1001. Archivo hist. nacional, Inquisicion de Valencia, Leg. 1, n. 3, fol. 49, 59, 64.
1002. Novís. Recop., Libro XII, Tit. xix, leyes 16-19.
1003. Archivo hist. nacional, Inquisicion de Valencia, Leg. 15, n. 11, fol. 45.
1004. Nueva Recop. Libro VI, Tit. iv, ley 7.
1005. Archivo de Simancas, Inquisicion, Libro 979, fol. 26.--Bibl. nacional, MSS., D, 118, fol. 20.
1006. Valencia Concordia of 1568, Art. 14 (MSS. of Bodleian Library, Arch. S, 130).
1007. Ordinacions y Sumari dels Privilegis etc. del Regne de Mallorca, p. 323 (Mallorca, 1663).
1008. Archivo de Simancas, Inquisicion, Libro 36, fol. 92, 98.
1009. Ibidem, Libro 49, fol. 240; Libro 23, fol. 42.
1010. Archivo de Simancas, Inquisicion, Libro 36, fol. 5, 92.--MSS. of Royal Library of Copenhagen, 218^{b}, p. 222.
1011. Ibidem, Libro 23, fol. 42; Libro 49, fol. 270.
1012. Archivo hist. nacional, Inquisicion de Toledo, Legajo 498.--MSS. of Royal Library of Copenhagen, 218^{b}, p. 182.
1013. Novís. Recop., Lib. VI, Tit. vi, ley 7, § 2; ley 14, cap. 35, §§ 4, 28, n. 7.
1014. Archivo de Simancas, Inquisicion, Libro 559.

1015. For the elaborate process of insaculacion in Catalonia, which amounted, in some degree, to a primary election, see Capitols de Cort de 1585, cap. 5, 6, 71, 72 (Barcelona, 1685, fol. 5-9, 46).

1016. Archivo de Simancas, Inquisicion, Libro 67, fol. 22; Libro 68, fol. 59.

1017. Portocarrero, op. cit., § 57.--Archivo de Simancas, Inquisicion, Libro 68, fol. 61; Libro 919, fol. 59; Inquisicion de Barcelona, Córtes, Legajo 17, fol. 60.

1018. Ibidem, Libro 919, fol. 58, 60, 65.

1019. Constitutions de Cathalunya, Lib. I, Tit. lvi, cap. 15.

1020. Archivo de Simancas, Inquisicion de Barcelona, Córtes, Leg. 17, fol. 20.

1021. Constitutions de Cathalunya, Lib. I, Tit. lvi, cap. 16.

1022. Archivo de Simancas, ubi sup., fol. 56.

1023. Ibidem, fol. 2, 28, 5.

1024. Archivo de Simancas, Inquisicion de Barcelona, Córtes, Leg. 17, fol. 87, 10, 92, 9.

1025. Archivo de Simancas, Inq. de Barcelona, Córtes, Leg. 17, fol. 2, 9, 14.

1026. Libro XIII de Cartas, fol. 215 (MSS. of American Philosophical Society).

1027. Ordinacions del Reyne de Mallorca, p. 297.--Archivo de Simancas, Inquisicion, Libro 68, fol. 98; Libro 69, fol. 97.

1028. Ibidem, Libro 68, fol. 32, 97, 224.

1029. Archivo de Simancas, Inquisicion de Barcelona, Córtes, Leg. 17, fol. 9.

1030. Modo de Proceder, fol. 40 (Bibl. nacional, MSS., D, 122).

1031. Llorente, Hist. crít. Cap. XXVI, Art. ii, n. 11.--Archivo de Simancas, Inquisicion, Libro 918, fol. 1053.

1032. Fueros y Actos de Corte en Zaragoza, 1645-6, pp. 11-12 (Zaragoza, 1647).

1033. Archivo hist. nacional, Inquisicion de Valencia, Leg. 299.

1034. Novís. Recop., Lib. I, Tit. iv, ley 4.

1035. Mendoza, Guerra de Granada, p. 71 (Ed. Ribadeneira).

1036. Fueros del Reyno de Aragon, Lib. I, Tit. De his qui ad ecclesias (Zaragoza, 1624).

1037. Archivo de Simancas, Inquisicion, Libro 13, fol. 120.

1038. Ibidem, Libro 926, fol. 33.

1039. MSS. of Bodleian Library, Arch. S, 130.

1040. Archivo de Simancas, Visitas de Barcelona, Leg. 15, fol. 20.

1041. MSS. of Bodleian Library, Arch. S, 130.

1042. Archivo de Simancas, Inquisicion de Barcelona, Córtes, Leg. 17, fol. 28.--Constitutions del Cort de 1599, Const. 50 (Barcelona, 1635, fol. xvii).

1043. Archivo de Simancas, Inquisicion, Libro 32, fol. 109.--Archivo hist. nacional, Inquisicion de Toledo, Leg. 498.

1044. Fueros y Actos de Corte, p. 11 (Zaragoza, 1647).

1045. Bibl. nacional, MSS., X, 157, fol. 244.

1046. Archivo hist. nacional, Inquisicion de Valencia, Leg. 1, n. 3, fol. 16, 406.--Bibl. nacional, MSS., R, 102, fol. 169.

1047. I have considered this subject in some detail in "Studies in Church History," pp. 177 sqq.

1048. Breve Memoria (Döllinger, Beiträge zur politischen, kirchlichen u. Cultur-Geschichte, III, 207).

1049. Le Plat, Monument. Concil. Trident., Tom. V, pp. 84, 565.

1050. Coleccion de Documentos, V, 83, 85.--See also Carranza, Comentarios sobre el Catechismo, fol. 230.

1051. Ordenamientos Reales, Lib. III, Tit. 1, leyes 4, 5 (Salmanticæ, 1560, pp. 790, 793).--Novís. Recop., Lib. II, Tit. i, leyes 6, 7, 8, 12; Lib. XII, Tit. xii, ley 6.

1052. Novís. Recop., Lib. II, Tit. ii, leyes 2, 3, 4, 6, 9, 10, 11, 18, 22, 23.

1053. Archivo de Simancas, Inquisicion, Libro 32, fol. 19.

1054. Instrucciones de 1498, § 2 (Arguello, fol. 12).--Archivo de Simancas, Inquisicion, Libro 939, fol. 144.

1055. Archivo de Simancas, Inquisicion, Libro 1.

1056. Ibidem, Libro 13, fol. 385, 386; Lib. 2, fol. 7, 10.

The tribunal of Murcia possessed a cédula of Ferdinand, February 28, 1505, ordering the payment of a debt to an official in which he used the expression that inquisitors are judges in all cases of officials and ministers. This seems to have been regarded as furnishing a foundation for the subsequent extension of jurisdiction, for the Suprema, November 22, 1635, ordered the original to be sent to it and a transcript was kept by the tribunal.--MSS. of Royal Library of Copenhagen, 218^{b}, p. 204.

1057. Archivo de Simancas, Inquisicion, Libro 3, fol. 104, 151, 242.

1058. Bulario de la Orden de Santiago, Lib. I de copias, fol. 219.--Pragmáticas y altres Drets de Cathalunya, Lib. I, Tit. viii, cap. 2.

1059. Archivo de Simancas, Inquisicion, Lib. 933.

1060. Archivo de Simancas, Inquisicion, Lib. 925, fol. 680.
1061. Ibidem, Lib. 3, fol. 452.
1062. Archivo de Simancas, Inquisicion, Lib. 9, fol. 1; Lib. 939, fol. 149.--MSS. of Bodleian Library, Arch. S, 130.
1063. Archivo de Simancas, Inquisicion, Lib. 939, fol. 147.
1064. Ibidem, fol. 144.
1065. Ibidem, Vistas de Barcelona, Leg. 15, fol. 20.--A summary of cases, apparently compiled about 1582, may be found in the Simancas Archives, Leg. 1465, fol. 79.
1066. Archivo de Simancas, Inquisicion, Lib. 7, fol. 6; Lib. 13, fol. 20, 370, 372; Lib. 688, fol. 18; Visitas de Barcelona, Leg. 15, fol. 20.--Archivo hist. nacional, Inquisicion de Valencia, Leg. 5, n. 1, fol. 200.--Bibl. nacional de Lima, Protocolo 223, Expediente, 5288.
1067. Archivo de Simancas, Sala 40, Lib. 4, fol. 206.
1068. Bibl. nacional, MSS., X, 157, fol. 244.
1069. Bibl. nacional, MSS., X, 157, fol. 244.--Archivo de Simancas, Inquisicion, Lib. 939, fol. 149.--All this shows how mistaken is the assertion of Llorente (Hist. crít. Cap. XLVII, Art. 1) repeated by Rodrigo (III, 365) and others, that Charles V, in 1535, suspended the royal jurisdiction (under which the Inquisition had cognizance of the affairs of its officials) and restored it in 1545. This action was confined to the tribunal of Sicily. The anonymous author of the Discurso historico-legal sobre el Origen etc. de la Inquisicion, p. 93 (Valladolid, 1803) seems to be the only one who has recognized this.
1070. Colmeiro, Córtes de Leon y de Castilla, II, 217.
1071. Bibl. nacional, MSS., X, 157, fol. 244.--MSS. of Bodleian Library, Arch. S, 130.--MSS. of Library of Univ. of Halle, Yc, 17.
1072. Nueva Recop., Lib. I, Tit. i, ley 18.--Novís. Recop., Lib. II, Tit. vii, ley 1.
It is not without interest to observe that the privileges of officials and familiars of the Roman Inquisition were much more limited than in Spain. Familiars had no exemption from public burdens or duties or military service and were subject to the secular courts in all criminal cases. When, in 1633, those of Jesi asked to have their civil suits tried by the Inquisition, the Congregation did not even answer them. The only officials entitled to the forum were those in continual active service, and there is nothing said about wives, children and servants sharing in the privilege. As in Spain, the number of familiars was excessive. Faenza was allowed 50, Ancona 40 and Rimini 30.--Decret. Sacr. Congr. S^{ti} Officii, pp. 197-8, 200 (R. Archivio di Stato in Roma, Fondo Camerale, Congr. del S. Offizio, vol. 3).
1073. The only allusion that I have met to this is its citation in the argument of the alcaldes del crimen of Granada in the case of Gerónimo Palomino. A copy is in Bodleian Library, Arch. S, 130.
1074. MSS. of the Royal Library of Copenhagen, 218^{b}, p. 202.
1075. Bibl. nacional, MSS., X, 157, fol. 144.--Novís. Recop., Lib. II, Tit. viii, ley 10.
1076. See the case of Montalvo and del Aguila, in 1642, when the arguments mainly turn on this point (MSS. of Bodleian Library, Arch. S, 130). Also that of Francisco Cases, about 1650, when both sides were able to cite precedents in their favor.--Arch. hist. nacional, Inquisicion de Valencia, Leg. 1, n. 1, fol. 638.
1077. MSS. of Royal Library of Copenhagen, 218^{b}, p. 125.
1078. Archivo de Simancas, Inquisicion, Lib. 38, fol. 264.--Nueva Recop., Lib. V, Tit. xxi, Declaraciones, ley 21, §§ 9, 10.--Autos Acordados, Lib. V, Tit. xxi, Autos 13, 16, 21, 22, 25.
1079. Autos Acordados, Lib. IX, Tit. viii, Auto 6.--Archivo hist. nacional, Inquisicion de Valencia, Leg. 10, n. 2, fol. 146.--MSS. of Royal Library of Copenhagen, 218^{b}, p. 265.
1080. Archivo de Simancas, Inquisicion, Libro 23, fol. 42.--Ibidem, Inquisicion de Barcelona, Córtes, Legajo 1, fol. 45.
1081. Ibidem, Sala 40, Lib. 4, fol. 107.
1082. Ibidem, Archivo de Simancas, Inquisicion, Lib. 922, fol. 17; Inquisicion de Barcelona, Córtes, Leg. 17, fol. 75.
1083. MSS. of Bodleian Library, Arch. S, 130.
1084. Archivo de Simancas, Inquisicion, Sala 40, Lib. 4, fol. 247.
1085. Relazioni Venete, Serie I, T. V, p. 86.
1086. Gachard, Don Carlos et Philippe II, T. I, pp. 100-2.
1087. Archivo de Simancas, Inquisicion, Libro 13, fol. 370-2.
1088. MSS. of Bodleian Library, Arch. S, 130.
1089. Archivo de Simancas, Inquisicion, Libro 688, fol. 59.
1090. Rojas de Hæreticis, P. I, n. 446.
1091. Archivo hist. nacional, Inquisicion de Valencia, Cartas del Consejo, Leg. 5, n. 1, fol. 150.
1092. Ibidem.
1093. Archivo hist. nacional, Inquisicion de Valencia, Leg. 1, n. 1, fol. 766; Leg. 8, n. 2, fol. 171, 172, 200, 219, 277, 322, 440, 442.--Archivo de Simancas, Inquisicion, Lib. 20, fol. 134-42.

1094. Archivo de Simancas, Inquisicion, Lib. 38, fol. 14.

1095. Archivo hist. nacional, Inquisicion de Valencia, Leg. 1, n. 3, fol. 26.

1096. Blancas, Aragonensium Rerum Commentarii, p. 26 (Cæsaraugustæ, 1598).--Julian Ribera, Orígines del Justicia de Aragon (Zaragoza, 1897).

1097. Fueros y Observancias del Reyno de Aragon, Lib. I, fol. 21-3; Lib. III, fol. 69-84 (Zaragoza, 1624).--Actos de Cortes del Reyno de Aragon, fol. 1 (Zaragoza, 1664).--Blancas, op. cit., p. 361.

1098. Ribera, op. cit., p. 182.--Blancas, op. cit., p. 499.--Argensola, Informacion de los Sucesos del Reino de Aragon, cap. xlv, lv (Madrid, 1808).

1099. Blasco de Lanuza, Historias de Aragon, II, 143 (Zaragoza, 1622).--Blancas, op. cit., Epist. prælim., p. 2.--Macanaz, Regalías de los Reyes de Aragon, pp. 85, 91.

1100. Fueros y Observancias del Reyno de Aragon, Lib. I, fol. 23.--Dormer, Añales de Aragon, Lib. II, cap. ix.--Blancas, op. cit., pp. 350-1.--Archivo de la Corona de Aragon, Leg. 528, n. 4.--Archivo de Simancas, Sala 40, Lib. 4, fol. 262.--Bibl. nacional, MSS., Mm, fol. 122.

1101. MS. penes me.

1102. Archivo de Simancas, Inquisicion, Libro 78, fol. 145, 192.

1103. Bulario de la Orden de Santiago, Lib. I de copias, fol. 219.--Archivo de Simancas, Inquisicion, Lib. 922, fol. 12.

1104. Actos de Corte del Reyno de Aragon, fol. 94-6 (Zaragoza, 1664).

1105. Bibl. nacional, MSS., D, 118, fol. 108, n. 38; Dd, 145, fol. 352.

1106. Archivo de Simancas, Inquisicion, Lib. 82, fol. 84.--Fueros de Aragon, fol. 222 (Zaragoza, 1624). Cf. Dormer, Añales de Aragon, Lib. II, cap. xxxviii.

1107. Bibl. nacional, MSS., Mm, 464.

1108. Archivo de Simancas, Inquisicion, Libro 30, fol. 474.

1109. Fueros y Actos de los Córtes de Barbastro y de Calatayud, pp. 20-22, 55-6 (Zaragoza, 1626).--Archivo de la Corona de Aragon, Leg. 528.--Archivo de Simancas, Inquisicion de Barcelona, Córtes, Leg. 1, fol. 12.

1110. Archivo de la Corona de Aragon, Leg. 528, n. 4.--Archivo de Simancas, Inquisicion, Sala 40, Lib. 4, fol. 127; Lib. 38, fol. 205, 209, 262, 280, 290.

1111. Archivo de Simancas, Inq., Gracia y Justicia, Leg. 621, fol. 90.

1112. Archivo gén. de la C. de Aragon, Leg. 528.

1113. Archivo gén. de la C. de Aragon, Leg. 528.

1114. Bibl. nacional, MSS., Mm, 122.

1115. Fueros y Actos de Corte en 1645 y 1646, pp. 1-2, 11-12 (Zaragoza, 1647).

1116. Bibl. nacional, MSS., D, 118, fol. 122 (see Appendix).--Joaquin Sánchez de Toca, Felipe IV y Sor María de Agreda, p. 282 (Madrid, 1887).

1117. Archivo gén. de la C. de Aragon, Leg. 528.--Llorente tells us (Hist, crít., Cap. xxxviii, Art. 1, n. 27) that Choved (or Gobea) was caught and tried but escaped the gallows by steadfast denial under repeated torture.

1118. Archivo de Simancas, Inquisicion, Libro 37, fol. 379.

1119. Archivo de Simancas, Inquisicion, Lib. 38, fol. 22.

1120. Archivo gén. de la C. de Aragon, Legajo 528.

1121. Archivo de Simancas, Inquisicion, Lib. 27, fol. 242.

1122. Ibidem, Inquisicion de Barcelona, Córtes, Leg. 17, fol. 15.--Archivo gén. de la C. de Aragon, Leg. 708.

1123. Archivo de Simancas, Inquisicion, Libro 933.

1124. Ibidem, Lib. 3, fol. 308, 309; Lib. 72, fol. 2.

1125. Pragmáticas y altres Drets de Cathalunya, Lib. II, Tit. viii, § 3.--Archivo de Simaricas, Inquisicion de Barcelona, Córtes, Leg. 17, fol. 39, 41.

1126. Archivo de Simancas, Inquisicion de Barcelona, Córtes, Leg. 17, fol. 5.

1127. Constitutions de Cathalunya superfluas, Lib. I, Tit. iv (Barcelona, 1589).

1128. Archivo de Simancas, Inquisicion, Lib. 930, fol. 49.--Portocarrero, § 78.

1129. Archivo de Simancas, Inquisicion, Visitas de Barcelona, Leg. 15, fol. 2.

1130. Ibidem, Inquisicion de Barcelona, Córtes, Leg. 17, fol. 9.

1131. Archivo de Simancas, Visitas de Barcelona, Leg. 15, fol. 20.

1132. Ibidem, Inquisicion de Barcelona, Córtes, Leg. 17, fol. 74.

1133. Ibidem, fol. 20, 81.

1134. Archivo de Simancas, Inquisicion, Lib. 65, fol. 184.

1135. Valladares, Semanario erúdito, XXVIII, 219.--Salgado de Somoza, de Retentione Bullarum, P. II, cap. xxxiii, n. 137-8.--Relazioni Venete, Serie I, T. VI, p. 367.

1136. Archivo de Simancas, Inquisicion, Lib. 82, fol. 52; Lib. 65, fol. 184.

1137. Cabrera, Relaciones, p. 31.

1138. Constitutions fets en la primera Cort celebra als Cathalans en lo any de 1599 (Barcelona,

1603).--Archivo de Simancas, Inquisicion de Barcelona, Córtes, Leg. 17, fol. 2, 5, 28.

1139. Archivo de Simancas, loc. cit., pp. 2, 5, 44.

1140. Bofarull y Broca, Historia de Cataluña, VII, 282-3.

1141. Archivo de Simancas, Inquisicion de Barcelona, Córtes, Leg. 17, fol. 9, 67.

1142. Archivo de Simancas, Inquisicion, Libro 30, fol. 474; Inquisition de Barcelona, Córtes, Leg. 17, fol. 18, 67, 87.

1143. Archivo de la Corona de Aragon, Fondos del Consejo de Aragon, Leg. 708.--Archivo de Simancas, Inquisicion, Lib. 21, fol. 84.--MSS. of Library of Univ. of Halle, Yc, 17.

1144. Parets, Sucesos de Cataluña (Mem. hist. español, XX, 91).--Archivo de Simancas, Inquisicion de Barcelona, Córtes, Leg. 17, fol. 15, 18, 19.

1145. Archivo de Simancas, Inquisicion, Lib. 21, fol. 83.

1146. Archivo hist. nacional, Inquisicion de Valencia, Leg. 9, n. 1, fol. 561, 572, 573, 575.

1147. Parets, Sucesos de Cataluña (Mem. hist. español, Tom. XX, 164-82; Append. 299, 301, 318, 426; Tom. XXI, Append. 158, 193, 409; Tom. XXII, 10, 27; Tom. XXV, Append. 290.)

1148. Parets, Tom. XXII, p. 30; Append. p. 243.--Archivo de Simancas, Inquisicion, Lib. 33, fol. 675.

1149. Parets, T. XXII, Append. pp. 308, 330; XXV, Append. pp. 391, 403.

1150. Archivo de Simancas, Inquisicion, Lib. 33, fol. 175, 830; Lib. 21, fol. 309.

1151. Parets, Tom. XXIV, p. 316.--Archivo de Simancas, Lib. 65, fol. 41.

1152. Archivo de Simancas, Inquisicion, Lib. 65, fol. 41, 48; Lib. 22, fol. 83.

1153. Ibidem, Lib. 65, fol. 31, 50; Lib. 36, fol. 74.--Archivo hist. nacional, Inquisicion de Valencia, Leg. 9, n. 2, fol. 323.

1154. Parets, T. XXIV, pp. 137, 147, 296.--Proceso contra Anthoni Morell (MSS. of Am. Philos. Society).

1155. Parets, T. XXV, p. 142.

1156. Archivo de Simancas, Inquisicion, Lib. 38, fol. 390.

1157. Archivo de Simancas, Inquisicion, Lib. 65, fol. 81.

1158. Parets, T. XXV, p. 171.--MSS. of Am. Philos. Society.

1159. MSS. of Library of Univ. of Halle, Yc, 17.

1160. Archivo gén. de la C. de Aragon, Fondos del Consejo, Leg. 708.--Libro XIII de Cartas (MSS. of Am. Philos. Society).

1161. Libro XIII de Cartas, p. 240.

1162. Bibl. nacional, MSS., PV, 3, n. 69.--Libro XIII de Cartas (ubi sup.).

1163. Archivo gén. de la C. de Aragon, Leg. 528. (The alguazil mayor was usually a man of rank.)

1164. Archivo gén. de la C. de Aragon, Leg. 708.--Archivo de Simancas, Inquisicion, Libro 66, fol. 179, 189, 228, 252, 283.--Bofarull y Broca, Hist. de Cataluña, VIII, 385.

1165. MSS. of Library of Univ. of Halle, Yc, 17.

1166. Archivo de Simancas, Inquisicion, Lib. 66, fol. 460.

1167. Capitols de Cort en lo any 1706, cap. 34 (Barcelona, 1706, p. 70).

1168. Archivo hist. nacional, Inquisicion de Valencia, Seccion Varios, Leg. 390.

1169. Ibid., Legajo 13.--Archivo de Simancas, Inquisicion, Sala 39, Leg. 4, fol. 23.

1170. Portocarrero, §§ 21, 22.

1171. Portocarrero §§ 51, 54, 58, 60, 61, 65, 96, 97.

1172. Lafuente, Hist. gén. de España, XIV, 417, 432.

1173. This account is derived from the printed argument of the alcaldes, a very temperate and manly document, of which a copy is in the Bodleian Library, Arch. S, 130.

1174. Archivo de Simancas, Gracia y Justicia, Leg. 621, fol. 5.

1175. Archivo de Simancas, Gracia y Justicia, Leg. 621, fol. 45, 47.

1176. MSS. of Royal Library of Copenhagen, 218^{b}, p. 349.

1177. Archivo de Simancas, Gracia y Justicia, Leg. 621, fol. 30-45.

1178. The three passages cited were Simancas, de Cathol. Institt. Tit. xxxiv, n. 6; Sousa, Aphorismi Inquisit. Lib. I, cap. 1, n. 16, and Peña in Eymerici Directorium, P. III, Comment. 61. Of the three Sousa comes nearest to supplying what was wanted in saying that the officials of the Inquisition are punishable, for official delinquencies, by those who appoint them.

1179. Bibl. nacional, MSS., X, 157, fol. 244; D, 118, fol. 151, 188.

1180. Consulta Magna (Bibl. nacional, MSS., Q, 4).

1181. Archivo de Simancas, Inquisicion, Libro 20, fol. 138.

1182. Ricci, Synopsis Decretorum S. Congr. Immunitatis s. v. Testis, n. 1.

1183. Archivo hist. nacional, Inquisicion de Valencia, Leg. 1, n. 1, fol. 157.

1184. Ibidem, Leg. 1, n. 3, fol. 3, 11, 25.

1185. Archivo de Simancas, Inquisicion, Lib. 13, fol. 145.

1186. Modo de Proceder, fol. 27-9 (Bibl. nacional, MSS., D, 122). The date of this is 1645.

1187. Actos de Corte del Reyno de Aragon, fol. 96 (Zaragoza, 1664).
1188. Archivo de Simancas, Inquisicion, Lib. 926, fol. 27.
1189. These details are furnished by a memorial to the king, a copy of which is in the Bodleian Library, Arch. S, 130.
1190. Bravo, Catálogo de los Obispos de Córdova, p. 580.
1191. Archivo de Simancas, Inquisicion, Lib. 29, fol. 177; Lib. 30, fol. 1 (see Appendix).
1192. Ibidem, Lib. 30, fol. 108.--MSS. of Royal Library of Copenhagen, 218^{b}, p. 348.
1193. Archivo de Simancas, Inquisicion, Lib. 52, fol. 34.
1194. Archivo de Simancas, Inquisicion, Lib. 21, fol. 346; Lib. 52, fol. 26, 37; Lib. 54, fol. 64.--Bullar. Roman., V, 367.
1195. Archivo de Simancas, Inquisicion, Lib. 52, fol. 86.
1196. Archivo de Simancas, Inquisicion, Lib. 25, fol. 23, 54, 86-105; Lib. 52, fol. 53, 86, 92, 100, 125, 335.
1197. Ibidem, Lib. 52, fol. 335.
1198. Archivo de Simancas, Inquisition, Lib. 52, fol. 292, 312, 335.
1199. Archivo de Simancas, Inquisicion, Lib. 940, fol. 161; Lib. 21, fol. 300.
1200. Ibidem, Legajo 1473.
1201. Ibidem, Lib. 3, fol. 425.
1202. Archivo de Simancas, Inquisicion, Lib. 927, fol. 323.
1203. Ibidem, Lib. 940, fol. 161.
1204. Ibidem, Lib. 52, fol. 222.
1205. Cabrera, Felipe Segundo, Lib. X, cap. xviii.
1206. Archivo de Simancas, Visitas de Barcelona, Leg. 15, fol. 1, 20.
1207. Archivo de Simancas, Inquisicion, Lib. 926, fol. 19.--Archivo hist. nacional, Inquisicion de Valencia, Leg. 1, n. 1.
1208. Modo de Proceder, fol. 31-9, 86-97 (Bibl. nacional, MSS., D, 122).--Archivo hist. nacional, Inquisicion de Valencia, Leg. 365, n. 45.--Archivo de Simancas, Inquisicion, Lib. 926, fol. 23.--Rojas de Hæret. P. I, n. 442.
1209. Llorente, Hist. crít. Cap. XXVII, Art. 1, n. 3, 4.
1210. Consulta Magna (Bibl. nacional, MSS., Q, 4).
1211. Bibl. nacional, MSS., D, 118, fol. 188.
1212. Autos Acordados, Lib. IV, Tit. 1, Auto 4, cap. 13, 14, 18.--Novís Recop. Lib. II, Tit. vii, ley 5.--Archivo de Simancas, Inquisicion, Leg. 1465, fol. 99.
1213. I am not aware that this interesting document has been printed. There are copies of it in the Bibl. nacional, MSS., Q, 4, and G, 344, and in the Library of the University of Halle, Yc, 17.
1214. Llorente, Hist. crít. Cap. XXVI, Art. ii, n. 35; Cap. XXXIX, Art. ii, n. 17.
1215. Riol, Informe (Semanario erúdito, III, 157).
1216. Archivo hist. nacional, Inquisicion de Valencia, Leg. 1, n. 3, fol. 16.
1217. Archivo hist. nacional, Inquisicion de Valencia, Leg. 10, n. 2, fol. 178.
1218. Bibl. nacional, MSS., R, 102, fol. 147-60.
1219. Autos Acordados, Lib. IV, Tit. i, Gloss 1.
1220. Archivo de Alcalá, Hacienda, Leg. 544^{1} (Libro 10).
1221. Ibidem, Estado, Leg. 2843.
1222. Archivo hist. nacional, Inquisicion de Valencia, Leg. 14, n. 3, fol. 132.
1223. Ibidem, Leg. 1, n. 3, fol. 3, 16.
1224. Novís. Recop., Lib. II, Tit. vii, leyes 9, 10.
1225. Archivo hist. national, Inquisicion de Valencia, Leg. 15, n. 11, fol. 45.
1226. Archivo de Simancas, Inquisicion, Lib. 13, fol. 16.--Proceso contra Joaquin de Tunes (MSS. of Am. Philos. Society).
1227. Actos de Corte del Reyno de Aragon, fol. 96 (Zaragoza, 1664).
1228. Archivo de Simancas, Inquisicion, Lib. 942, fol. 22.
1229. Ibidem, Visitas de Barcelona, Leg. 17, fol. 20.
1230. Modo de Proceder, fol. 21-29 (Bibl. nacional, MSS., D, 122).--Archivo hist. nacional, Inquisicion de Toledo, Leg. 498.
1231. Portocarrero, op. cit., fol. 47, 48.
1232. Archivo hist. nacional, Inquisicion de Valencia, Leg. 16, n. 5, fol. 25, 27, 39, 52, 72.
1233. Ibidem, Leg. 17, n. 3, fol. 10.
1234. Archivo de Simancas, Inquisicion, Lib. 559.
1235. Ibidem, Lib. 890.
1236. Ibidem, Lib. 890; Lib. 435^{2}.
1237. Ibidem, Lib. 890.
1238. Portocarrero, op. cit., fol. 52.

1239. Archivo hist. nacional, Inquisicion de Valencia, Leg. 1, n. 3, fol. 49; Leg. 8, n. 1, fol. 422, 423; Libro 7 de Autos, Leg. 2, fol. 178.
1240. Archivo de Simancas, Inquisicion, Leg. 1465, fol. 79.--MSS. of Royal Library of Copenhagen, 218^{b}, p. 351.
1241. Autos Acordados, Lib. IV, Tit. 1, Auto 3 (Nueva Recop., Lib. II, Tit. vii, ley 3).
1242. Archivo de Simancas, Inquisicion, Leg. 1465, fol. 42.
1243. Archivo de Simancas, Inquisicion, Leg. 1465, fol. 47; Lib. 918, fol. 830.--Bibl. nacional, MSS., R, 102, fol. 157-8.--Autos Acordados, Lib. IV, Tit. 1, Auto 5.
1244. Novís. Recop., Lib. II, Tit. vii, ley 5.
1245. Autos Acordados, Lib. IV, Tit. 1, Gloss 1.
1246. Novís. Recop., Lib. IV, Tit. 1, ley 18.
1247. Archivo de Simancas, Gracia y Justicia, Leg. 621, fol. 82; Inquisicion, Leg. 1465, fol. 50.--Llorente, Hist. crít., Cap. XXVI, Art. ii, n. 3.
1248. Archivo de Simancas, Inquisicion, Lib. 21, fol. 127.
1249. Autos Acordados, Lib. IV, Tit. 1, Auto 10.--Archivo de Simancas, Inquisicion, Leg. 1465, fol. 41.
1250. Floridablanca, Memorial á Carlos III (MS. penes me).
1251. Archivo de Simancas, Libro 939, fol. 64.
1252. Archivo de Simancas, Patronato Real, Inquisicion, Leg. único, fol. 44.
1253. Cartas de Jesuitas (Mem. hist. español, XVI, 366).
1254. Archivo de Simancas, Inquisicion, Sala 40, Lib. 4, fol. 141-7.
1255. Ibidem, fol. 179, 182, 195-6, 199, 201, 205, 212, 217.
1256. Ibidem, fol. 255-61; Visitas de Barcelona, Leg. 15, fol. 2.
1257. Archivo de Simancas, Inquisicion, Visitas de Barcelona, Leg. 15, fol. 20.
1258. MSS. of Royal Library of Copenhagen, 218^{b}, p. 125.--Archivo de Simancas, Inquisicion, Lib. 32, fol. 109, 117.
1259. Archivo de Simancas, Inquisicion de Logroño, Leg. 1, n. 21, 22; Inquisicion, Leg. 1157, fol. 90.
1260. Modo de Proceder, fol. 43 (Bibl. national, MSS., D, 122).
1261. Discurso en razon del acuerdo que se puede tomar entre las jurisdicciones (MSS. of Bodleian Library, Arch. Seld. A. Subt. 13; Arch. S, 130).
1262. MSS. of Royal Library of Copenhagen, 218^{b}, p. 201.
1263. Archivo de Sevilla, Seccíon primera, Carpeta X, n. 213 (Sevilla, 1860).
1264. Arguello, fol. 23.--MSS. of Royal Library of Copenhagen, 218^{b}, p. 221.
1265. Archivo de Simancas, Inquisicion, Libro 27, fol. 88.
1266. Archivo hist. nacional, Inquisicion de Valencia, Leg. 1, n. 3. fol. 16.
1267. Ibidem, Leg. 5, n. 2, fol. 157, 158.--Archivo de Simancas, Inquisicion, Lib. 940, fol. 172.
1268. Archivo hist. nacional, Inquisicion de Toledo, Leg. 498.
1269. Archivo de Simancas, Inquisicion, Lib. 926, fol. 15-26.
1270. Archivo hist. national, Inquisicion de Valencia, Leg. 10, n. 2, fol. 178.
1271. Archivo de Simancas, Inquisicion, Sala 40, Lib. 4, fol. 215.
1272. Ibidem, fol. 180.
1273. Proceso contra Juan Requesens (MSS. of Am. Philos. Society).
1274. Bibl. nacional, MSS., Mm, 464.--Archivo gén. de la C. de Aragon, Leg. 528.--Archivo de Simancas, Lib. 27, fol. 88.
1275. Archivo de Simancas, Inquisicion, Leg. 1157, fol. 90.
1276. Dépêches de M. de Fourquevaux, I, 166 (Paris, 1896).
1277. Modo de Proceder, fol. 41-2 (Bibl. nacional, MSS., D, 122).--Archivo de Simancas, Inquisicion, Lib. 23, fol. 45, 57.
1278. Discurso historico-legal sobre el Origen, Progresos y Utilidad del Santo Oficio, Introd. pp. i-iv, p. 139 (Valladolid, 1803).
1279. Bibl. nacional, MSS., Tj, 28.--Llorente, Añales, I, 252.
1280. Archivo de Alcalá, Hacienda, Leg. 1049.
1281. Archivo de Simancas, Inquisicion, Lib. 940, fol. 58.
1282. Páramo, pp. 224-6.
1283. Franchina, Breve Rapporto della Inquisizione di Sicilia, p. 98.--Juan Gómez de Mora, Relacion del Auto de Fe celebrado en Madrid, este año de 1632 (Madrid, 1632).
1284. Archivo hist. nacional, Inquisicion de Valencia, Leg. 4, n. 3, fol 70; Leg. 17, n. 3, fol. 5.
1285. Boletin, XV, 333-45; XXIII, 415-16.--Llorente, Añales, I, 253.
1286. Carbonell de Gestis Hæreticor. (Coll. de Doc. de la C. de Aragon, XXVIII, 137, 139).--Archivo de Simancas, Inquisicion, Lib. 72, P. I, fol. 61; P. II, fol. 72, 110.
1287. Bibl. nacionale de France, fonds español, 80, fol. 44.--Llorente, Añales, II, 242.

1288. Archivo de Simancas, Inquisicion, Visitas de Barcelona, Leg. 15, fol. 4.--Proceso contra Estevan Ramoneda, fol. 72 (MSS. of Am. Philos. Society).

1289. Archivo de Simancas, Inquicicion, Lib. 1; Leg. 1465, fol. 32; Lib. 56, fol. 605, Llorente, Añales, II, 5.

1290. Llorente, Añales, I, 213, 252; II, 3.--Archivo de Simancas, Inquisicion, Lib. 4, fol. 1, 7, 104, 159, 162; Lib. 5, fol. 24; Lib. 73, fol. 211; Lib. 76, fol. 51, 53; Lib. 78, fol. 216, 258; Lib. 79, fol. 17, 226; Lib. 80, fol. 1.

1291. Archivo de Simancas, Inquisicion, Lib. 2, fol. 8; Lib. 74, fol. 120.--Informe de Quesada (Bibl. nacional, MSS., Tj, 28).

1292. W. de Gray Birch, Catalogue of MSS. of the Inquisition in the Canary Islands, I, xvi, 5, 6 (London, 1903).

1293. Archivo de Simancas, Inquisition, Lib. 939, fol. 62.

1294. Matute y Luquin, Autos de Fe de Córdova, pp. 1, 75.

1295. MSS. of Library of Univ. of Halle, Yc, 20, Tom. III.--Archivo hist. nacional, Inquisicion de Toledo, Leg. 113, n. 6.

1296. MSS. of Royal Library of Copenhagen, 218^{b}, p. 206.--MSS. of Library of Univ. of Halle, Yc, 20, T. VII.

1297. MSS. of Library of Univ. of Halle, Yc, 20, Tom. VI, X.

1298. Rodríguez de Villa, La Corte y Monarquia de España, p. 47.--Cartas de Jesuitas (Mem. hist. español, XIV, 6).

1299. MSS. of Library of Univ. of Halle, Yc, 20, Tom. IX, VI.

1300. Bibl. nacional, MSS., D, 118, fol. 146, n. 49.

1301. Archivo de Simancas, Inquisicion, Lib. 1024, fol. 28.

1302. Archivo de Simancas, Inquisicion, Leg. 1474, fol. 67.--Archivo hist. nacional, Inquisicion de Toledo, Leg. 1.

1303. Archivo de Alcalá, Estado, Leg. 2843.--Archivo de Simancas, Inquisicion, Leg. 1474, fol. 15.

1304. Archivo de Simancas, Inquisicion, Lib. 3, fol. 84, 440, 445, 454; Lib. 4, fol. 9; Lib. 933; Lib. 939, fol. 63, 139; Lib. 9, fol. 29; Leg. 1157, fol. 144; Inquisicion de Corte, Leg. 359, fol. 3.--Llorente, Añales, II, 3.

1305. Archivo de Simancas, Inquisicion, Lib. 1.

1306. Llorente, Añales, II, 4.

1307. Archivo de Simancas, Inquisicion, Lib. 940, fol. 38, 39, 53; Lib. 76, fol. 74.

1308. Archivo de Simancas, Inquisicion, Lib. 930, fol. 127; Lib. 926, fol. 141; Lib. 940, fol. 101.--Cf. Novís. Recop. Lib. II, Tit. vii, ley 1, nota 9.

1309. Schäfer, Beiträge, II, 76, 77.--Llorente, Hist. crít. Cap. XLVI, Art. i, n. 11.

1310. Archivo de Simancas, Inquisicion, Lib. 926, fol. 80.

1311. Llorente, Añales, II, 242.

1312. Arguello, fol. 1.--Archivo de Simancas, Inquisicion, Lib. 1; Lib. 929, fol. 297; Sala 40, Lib. 4, fol, 164.--Llorente, Añales, II, 2.--Rodrigo, Hist, verdadera, II, 261.--Juan Gómez de Mora, Relacion del Auto de la Fe de 1632.

1313. Archivo de Simancas, Inquisicion, Lib. 1; Lib. 3, fol. 381.

1314. Bibl. nationale de France, fonds espagnol, 80, fol. 24, 26.--Archivo de Simancas, Inquisition, Lib. 1; Lib. 72, P. I, fol. 2, 177, 198; Lib. 9, fol. 24, 68; Lib. 77, fol. 53.

1315. Archivo de Alcalá, Hacienda, Leg. 498.

1316. Archivo de Simancas, Inquisicion, Lib. 1; Lib. 3, fol. 447; Lib. 5, fol. 9, 27.--Llorente, Añales, II, 3.--Miscelanea de Zapata (Mem. hist. español, XI, 59).

1317. Archivo de Simancas, Patronato Real, Inquisicion, Leg. único, fol. 28.--Archivo gén. de la C. de Aragon, Regist. 3684, fol. 94.--Archivo de Simancas, Inquisicion, Lib. 4, fol. 1; Legajo 1465, fol. 31, 32.--Cabrera, Relaciones, p. 107.

1318. Archivo de Simancas, Inquisicion, Lib, 4, fol. 95, 96; Lib. 3, fol. 453.--Archivo hist. nacional, Inquisicion de Valencia, Leg. 61.--Gams, Series Episcoporum, p. 55.

1319. Archivo de Simancas, Inquisicion, Lib. 3, fol. 316, 366; Lib. 72, P. I, fol. 116; Lib. 73, fol. 142, 247, 248.--Archivo hist. nacional, Inquisicion de Toledo, Leg. 498.

1320. Páramo, p. 159.--Llorente, Añales, II, 91.--Archivo de Simancas, Inquisition, Lib. 3, fol. 453.

1321. Llorente, Añales, II, 5.--Archivo de Simancas, Inquisicion, Lib. 3, fol. 332, 333.

1322. Informe de Quesada (Bibl. nacional, MSS., Tj, 28).

1323. Carbonell de Gestis Hæret. (op. cit. XXVIII, 83).--Archivo de Simancas, Inquisicion, Lib. 72, P. II, fol. 57, 59; Lib. 930, fol. 40; Lib. 13, fol. 372.

1324. Bergenroth, Calendar of Spanish State Papers, I, xlv (London, 1862).

1325. Colmenares, Historia de Segovia, Cap. xxxiv, § 18.--Padre Fidel Fita (Boletin, XXIII, 415).-

-Llorente, Añales, II, 3.--Proceso contra Mari Naranja; Proceso contra Catalina Machado (MSS. penes me).

1326. Llorente, Añales, I, 217, 317, II, 3.--Archivo de Simancas, Inquisicion de Corte, Leg. 359, fol. 1.

1327. Archivo de Simancas, Inquisicion, Lib. 9, fol. 24; Lib. 926, fol. 141.

1328. Archivo de Simancas, Inquisicion, Lib. 65, fol. 31, 50; Lib. 36, fol. 74.--Archivo hist. nacional, Inquisicion de Valencia, Leg. 9, n. 2, fol. 323.

1329. Archivo gén. de la C. de Aragon, Regist. 3684.--Archivo de Simancas, Inquisicion, Lib. 2, fol. 16; Lib. 72, P. II, fol. 40, 169; Lib. 74, fol. 133; Inquisicion de Barcelona, Cortes, Leg. 17, fol. 47, 48.

1330. Archivo de Simancas, Inquisicion, Lib. 939, fol. 62.--MSS. of Library of Univ. of Halle, Yc, 20, Tom. VIII.

1331. Proceso contra Ignacia----; contra Estevanillo F. (MSS. of Am. Philos. Society).--Archivo hist. nacional, Inquisicion de Valencia, Seccion Varios, Leg. 13.--Archivo de Simancas, Inquisicion, Sala 39, Leg. 4, fol. 23.

1332. Archivo de Simancas, Inquisicion, Lib. 1; Lib. 4, fol. 1; Lib. 929, fol. 63.--MSS. of Library of Univ. of Halle, Yc, 20, T. VIII.--Llorente, Añales, II, 3.--Bibl. nationale de France, fonds espagnol, 354, fol. 242.

1333. Informe de Quesada (Bibl. nacional, MSS., Tj., 28).--Llorente, Añales, I, 252.--Archivo de Simancas, Inquisicion, Lib. 3, fol. 423.

1334. Coleccion de Cédulas, IV, 388, 400 (Madrid, 1829).

1335. As an incident to this fictitious valuation of the vellón coinage, counterfeiting flourished to an enormous extent, unrepressed by the severest penalties. The importation of coins manufactured abroad added to the confusion, for it was too lucrative to be prevented by even the most rigorous measures. In 1614 a chronicler states that since the recent doubling of the nominal value of the cuartos five or six millions in vellón money had been brought from England and Holland, stowed in vessels under wheat. It was exchanged for silver at 30 per cent. discount and the silver exported. The remedy devised was to bring inland twenty leagues from the coast the foreign traders engaged in the business, but this remedy was found to be worse than the disease and was abandoned (Cabrera, Relaciones, pp. 551, 553). We shall see hereafter that the Inquisition was invoked to put an end to this traffic.

1336. Under these perpetual changes it will be readily understood how difficult it is to estimate values at any special period. In a document of 1670 I find the doblon converted into reales de vellón at the rate of 1 to 81, although in this case the doblon was of 4 pesos or 32 reales de plata. Similar to this is the conversion in another item of 162 reales de plata into 405 reales de vellón, showing that vellón was at a discount of 60 per cent. or specie at a premium of 150.--Arch. de Simancas, Inquisicion, Leg. 1476, fol. 2, 61.

The unutterable confusion produced by these sudden and arbitrary changes in the legal value of the coinage is illustrated by a contention, in 1683, between the auditor-general and the receiver-general of the Suprema, respecting the accountability of the latter for funds on hand and receipts and payments at the time when the pragmática of February 10, 1680, went into effect, involving points of which the equities were not easy to determine.--Ibid., Leg. 1480, fol. 129.

1337. It was probably from this that the custom arose in giving receipts for money to reserve or to renounce, as the case might be, "las leyes y excepciones de la non numerata pecunia."

1338. Full information as to the coinage of the fifteenth century will be found in Saez, Demostracion del Valor de las Monedas que corrian durante el Reinado de Don Enrique IV (Madrid, 1805).

For the subsequent period reference is made to the very voluminous series of laws and decrees preserved in the Nueva Recopilacion, Lib. V, Tit. xxi; the Autos Acordados, Lib. V, Tit. xxi and xxii, and the Novisima Recopilacion, Lib. IX, Tit. xvii.

1339. These instructions are supplementary to those issued by the assembly of Inquisitors in Seville, Nov. 29, 1484. Some of them are printed by Arguello, but they are not in the Granada edition of 1537 of the Instructions.

1340. These instructions partly repeat and partly supplement those of December, 1484. So far as I am aware they are inedited. They are not in the Granada edition of the Instructions, nor do they correspond with the fragments printed by Arguello (Instrucciones del Santo Oficio, Madrid, 1630, fol. 16-23) as the Instructions of January, 1485, and by Llorente, Añales, I, 96-99, 388-94.

1341. Both the Granada edition of 1537 and Arguello print only the first four articles of these Instructions. Llorente describes them (Añales, I, 261) as being in seven articles of which the last two are not in this original document.

1342. The date of Bologna fixes the time of this brief between Nov. 10, 1506, when Julius II entered that city, and Feb. 22, 1507, when he left it.--Raynald. Annal. ann. 1506, n. 30; 1507, n. 2.

1343. The end of the document is torn.

1344. This MS. I procured from a bookseller in Madrid, and I know nothing of its provenance. It is in small quarto, with 62 unnumbered pages of a handwriting which I should attribute to the seventeenth or early eighteenth century; about three pages towards the middle are in a different hand, with some blanks filled in by the scribe of the rest of the MS., as though the copying had been entrusted to a second writer who had proved unable to decypher the original. The record bears on its face every mark of authenticity. There are occasional discrepancies in names and dates between it and the list at the end of the Libro Verde, but in general they correspond, as it also does with such trials of the period as I have examined from the Llorente MSS. in the Bibliothèque Nationale. It supplies much that is lacking, and the abstracts of the sentences of the murderers of San Pedro Arbués are sufficient to render it a document of interest, besides the light which the sentences in general throw upon the business of the Inquisition. I transcribe in full the earlier portion, with the final "Resumen." Of the remainder, which consists of little more than lists of names of convicts and penitents, I only give a summary.

The MS. has much in common with the anonymous Orígen de la Inquisicion cited by Llorente (Añales, I, 76, 94, 114, etc.) which he says is in the Academia de la Historia and was written in 1652.

1345. Amin was a kind of Jewish broth. In the trial of Juan de la Caballeria, in 1488, there is an allusion to "hamin y otras potages de Judios."--MSS. Bib. Nat. de Paris, fonds espagnol, 81.

1346. Unleavened bread--"panem azmum sive cotaco comedendo"--Trial of Beatrix de la Cavallería, MSS. Bib. Nat. de France, fonds espagnol, 80, fol. 175.

1347. The total number is 614. There is a mistake of 3 in the addition, and errors in several years.

*
*
*
*
*

Typographical errors corrected by the etext transcriber:
repress the the robberies=> repress the robberies {pg 29}
Many chiefs of the synogogue=> Many chiefs of the synagogue {pg 113}
Cordinal González de Mendoza=> Cardinal González de Mendoza {pg 138}
fifty horesemen=> fifty horsemen {pg 175}
in the war with Naples=> in the war wtih Naples {pg 184}
in a letter, Janary 12, 1501=> in a letter, January 12, 1501 {pg 186}
with the Inquisiton=> with the Inquisition {pg 277}
from Igualada, Februrary=> from Igualada, February {pg 277}
to exprees her satisfaction=> to express her satisfaction {pg 312}
to emancipate itsef from all control=> to emancipate itself from all control {pg 343}
kept in the royal chancillery=> kept in the royal chancellery {pg 354}
was carried up to to the king=> was carried up to the king {pg 360}
occupied by the trbunal=> occupied by the tribunal {pg 389}
The Inquisiton, as usual=> The Inquisition, as usual {pg 475}
This account it derived from=> This account is derived from {pg 487 n.}
protect its familars=> protect its familiars {pg 511}
which he addresed=> which he addressed {pg 511}
the jurisdiction of the Inquisiton=> the jurisdiction of the Inquisition {pg 521}
Archivio General de Simancas=> Archivo General de Simancas {pg 576}

www.ingramcontent.com/pod-product-compliance
Lightning Source LLC
Chambersburg PA
CBHW020745160426
43192CB00006B/251